the Theatre
an introduction

NEW YORK • CHICAGO • SAN FRANCISCO • TORONTO • LONDON

the 🏛 Theatre
an introduction

Oscar G. Brockett

Indiana University

Holt, Rinehart and Winston

 **PREFACE**

This book is an introduction to study of the theatre. It aims to arouse the wide range of interests—critical, historical, esthetic, practical—necessary to a well-rounded view. Of course, no single volume can cover exhaustively every one of these areas. It is intended primarily as a text for courses variously titled "Introduction to the Theatre," "Survey of the Theatre," "Introduction to Theatrical Practice," and the like. The approaches and contents of such courses differ considerably. Some concentrate upon dramatic forms and styles; others emphasize the historical development of the theatre; others are restricted to contemporary theatrical practice; while still others combine elements from each of these approaches.

This volume is designed to be useful for any of these emphases. Part One treats the theatre as an art form, discusses critical methods and outlines the elements of dramatic construction, forms, and styles. Thus, it serves as an introduction to the other parts of the book. Part Two surveys developments from early Greek drama to the beginning of the modern theatre around 1875. Representative dramatists, forms, styles, and practices are discussed and their significance explored. Part Three is devoted to a consideration of the major movements in theatre and drama since 1875. Part Four outlines contemporary American theatrical practice from the writing of the play through performance. Its emphasis is upon principles and techniques rather than upon "how to do it" details. The final chapter discusses professional opportunities in the theatre today.

The book has been organized so that an instructor may select those portions which are most useful for his particular needs. Each section is an integral part of a whole, but each may be used separately or combined in various ways with portions of other sections. For example, a course which concentrates upon contemporary theatrical practice might use Parts One and Four, while a course which emphasizes historical developments might use Parts One, Two, and Three. Instructors of courses which deal with forms and styles will find that these are treated at some length in Parts One, Two, and Three.

A word about the discussion of plays in the text is necessary. With the exception of Chapter 8, each chapter from 4 through 14 contains a detailed examination of one or more representative plays. There is no intention of restricting the examination of plays to those discussed in the text.

Rather, the discussions illustrate a method of play analysis and emphasize the special considerations which are important for plays of each type or period. It has seemed best to use a few plays as examples rather than to refer to numerous works unfamiliar to students. The author assumes that an instructor will choose to have his students read some of the plays discussed at length, and that he will select others as well.

The range of this book does not allow the inclusion of every playwright, actor, director, or other theatrical artist of importance. The intention has been to lay a foundation upon which to build in the future, rather than to attempt an extensive treatment of each topic.

No book of this scope could be written without the aid of numerous scholars who have studied each of the areas in detail. I have made use of their knowledge on every page and it is impossible to acknowledge my indebtedness to each one. The bibliography lists the most important or useful works in connection with each chapter. Student and instructor are referred there for authoritative additional reading.

I acknowledge gratefully the assistance of a number of persons in the preparation of this book. My greatest debt is due H. Clay Harshbarger, Chairman of the Department of Speech and Dramatic Art at the University of Iowa, who supplied me with research assistants and secretarial help, and whose support over a number of years has made this textbook possible. I would also like to acknowledge the help of my colleagues at the University of Iowa Theatre, whose work is represented liberally in the illustrations throughout. The University of Iowa Libraries and Photographic Service have been of special help in gathering and reproducing the pictorial material, and Mrs. Nancy Cole has spent countless hours verifying facts, resolving contradictions, and locating suitable illustrations.

The following organizations and persons have permitted me to use illustrations: The Metropolitan Museum of Art; the Victoria and Albert Museum; the Bibliothèque Nationale; Verlag W. Kohlhammer; the Stratford (Canada) Shakespearean Festival; the Oregon Shakespeare Festival; the Greek National Theatre; the Smithsonian Institution; the Columbia University Press and Glynne Wickham; the Mermaid Theatre, London; Alois M. Nagler; Ernest Benn, Ltd.; the Old Vic Company and Angus McBean; Northwestern University Theatre and Lee Mitchell; the Yale University Library; Yale University School of Drama; the Bibliothèque de l'Arsenale; the Hoblitzelle Theatre Arts Library and the Stark Collection of the University of Texas Libraries; the Department of Drama, University of Texas and Paul Reinhardt; the Fondation Adolphe Appia, Berne; Carl Hensler, Brussels; Cornell University Theatre and Darkes Albright; Stanford Players and Wendell Cole; Friedman-Ables; Graphic House; Century Lighting, Inc.; Kleigl Brothers; the Theatre of Western Springs and James Hull Miller; Alex Wallace; Charles Watson; the Metropolitan Opera; the New York City Ballet and Martha Swope.

 CONTENTS

the Theatre
an introduction

PART ONE

BASIC PROBLEMS

Pantalone (1550). Illustration by Maurice Sand—son of Casimir Dudevant and novelist George Sand, Baroness Dudevant —for his work on actors and types of Italian comedy, *Masques et bouffons*, 1859.

Chapter 1

THE THEATRE AS AN ART FORM

It has been said that the theatre dies every night, only to be reborn each day, for it exists whenever actors perform before an audience. The ephemeral nature of the theatre makes it difficult to recapture a performance after it has ended. Unlike a novel, a painting, or a statue, each of which remains relatively unchanged, the theatre exists only in those moments when a performance is seen—then it is gone and lives only in the play script, in the programs, the pictures, the reviews, and the memories of those who were present.

Although the theatre is the most ephemeral of the arts—except music—it is one of the most powerful in its effect, for while an audience watches, living human beings perform scenes which interpret man's experience as though it were happening at that very instant. By this means the theatre approximates life as it is lived and felt moment by moment. Like life, each episode is experienced and then immediately becomes part of the past.

The theatre is also the most objective of the arts, since characteristically it presents both outer and inner experience through speech and action. As in life, it is through listening and watching that we come to know individuals both externally and internally. What we know of their minds, their personalities, their motivations comes to us through what they say, what they do, and through what others tell us about them. The novel may deal at length with the unspoken thoughts and feelings of its charac-

Terracota figure of an actor found in an Athenian grave; probably fourth century B.C. Courtesy of the Metropolitan Museum of Art, Rogers Fund, 1913.

ters, but the dramatist can indicate these inner stirrings only through their external signs. This limitation, however, serves to give the theatre a life-likeness which other arts cannot match.

The theatre is also the most complex of the arts, since it requires many artists for its creation—the actor, the playwright, the director, the scene designer, the costumer, the light designer, the choreographer, the musician. This complexity has led many to call it a mixed art since it combines the written word of the literary artist, the scenic background of the architect and painter, the speech and movement of the actor, the music of the composer, and the dance patterns of the choreographer. Others have called it an impure art because it is not the product of a single mind. These labels imply that several artists cannot achieve a unified result and that the theatre is therefore imperfect and inferior. Certainly the theatre can rarely achieve the absolute purity of form possible in a novel, a poem, or a painting, but it has its own kind of unity.

In its very complexity lies much of the theatre's strength, for its varied appeals—action, speech, music, dance, painting—combine in one art product the charms of all the other arts, though in a new and distinctive form. Because it requires many artists for the production of a single work, during different periods and in varying types of theatrical entertainment one or another of the theatre arts has become dominant—at times acting, at others playwriting, scenic and costume design, or directing. But, characteristically, all artists work together for the creation of a single product.

In the earliest theatrical performances all artistic functions were served by one person; gradually, specialists emerged and the various theatre arts became separated. Historically speaking, the actor and the playwright attained recognition first, undoubtedly because their functions are basic and closely related. Drama tells its story and presents its conflicts entirely through the speeches and actions of characters, who are themselves subject to the drama and participants in its action. It, therefore, assumes the existence of the actor who will lend his body, his voice, his action, his very existence for the time needed to play out the drama.

The actor and the playwright are by necessity complementary, since each ultimately needs the other for the completion of his art. The actor may practice his profession without the aid of the playwright as such, for he may improvise his speech and action—that is, he may become his own dramatist—but unless his improvisation achieves a high degree of excellence, it will not command attention for any length of time. To hold attention, a performance must, as a rule, be organized so as to tell a story, to reveal a character, or to illustrate an idea. As the length of the performance increases, there is a corresponding need for greater ability to interweave story, character, and ideas. As these demands are met successfully, the actor approaches more and more the function of the playwright.

A scene from a *commedia dell'arte* performance. From G. Lambranzi's *Nuova e Curiosa Scuola de Balli Theatrali.* Nuremburg, 1716.

On the other hand, the person best able to construct an interesting series of events is not necessarily the one best able to enact these events for an audience. Thus, the specialized demands made upon the actor and the playwright have led to separate, though closely related, professions.

The history of the theatre has often been treated as though it were synonymous with the history of drama. Although it may distort the truth, there are very good reasons for such an approach. It is through the written drama that we get our clearest impressions of the theatre of the past; it is the element from which the other theatre arts take their cues. They fill out and bring to life the outline which the drama presents. The play is the goal toward which the other theatre arts are directed. Furthermore, it is only the play script which has come down to us in a more or less unchanged form; we know the other theatre arts only through second-hand accounts such as descriptions of the acting or pictorial representations of single scenes.

The history of the theatre is usually constructed around drama for still another important reason: the play script forms a bridge between our own values and those of the past. We are able to appreciate and understand other eras only when we can find in them ideas and attitudes which have meaning today, for we remain untouched by that which has no relevance to ourselves. The theatre arts of the past, when viewed in isolation from drama, may seem totally disconnected from the present, but the great plays of other times offer a means by which we can come into contact with the feelings, the thought, the life of these periods. This contact can then serve as a bridge to aid our understanding of the theatre's contributing arts.

But while the play may be the key to understanding of the composite theatre, it is not synonymous with theatre, for a script offers only a suggestion of what should or did happen in its presentation. Plays are written to be performed and are not complete until they are filled out by actors, costumes, and scenic background.

The interdependence of the playwright and the actor is clear, but these artists also need the help of a director, designers, musicians, and dancers. The need for the director arises as soon as more than one actor is involved, for someone must mediate the differences of opinion which arise as to positions on stage, correct line readings, or interpretations of meaning. But the director is more than a mediator; for it is his responsibility to design, to edit, and to coordinate stage action with visual background, costumes, lights, music and all other elements. Either the playwright or the actor may serve this function, but insofar as either one does he is serving as a director.

The various elements which the director coordinates are the products of separate artists. The visual background, for example, is the work of the set, lighting, and costume designers, who seek to interpret the qualities found in the script through visual means. The scenic designer not only indicates place and historical period, he also finds the architectural forms, the light and shadow, the colors, the line, and the composition which create a visual equivalent of the action. In like manner, the costumer, the lighting designer, and the choreographer seek to embody the mood and spirit of a play through visual means.

It is the mutual and interdependent workings of the various arts comprising that complex product, the theatre, which will be pursued in this book.

WHAT IS ART?

In the preceding discussion the theatre has been referred to repeatedly as an art form. But what is art? Probably no term has been so widely discussed with so little clear definition.

Until the eighteenth century the term *art* was used almost exclusively to mean the systematic application of knowledge or skill to achieve a desired result. The word is still used in this sense, as when one speaks of the art (or craft) of medicine. In the eighteenth century it became customary to group certain arts under the heading of the Fine or Beautiful Arts. Around the same time the idea arose that these fine arts are the product of genius, whose methods cannot be reduced to any known rules or principles, as the older meaning had implied. This idea was developed until art was thought to defy any systematic approach to its creation, and the term began to be used in a sense almost opposite in meaning to the

Teatro Olimpico, Vicenza. Built between 1580 and 1584 by Italian architect Vincenzo Scamozzi from the basic design by Andrea Palladio. (Inigo Jones later imported Palladio's classical style into England where *Palladian* motifs became popular.) Photograph—O. G. Brockett.

older definition. As a result, since the beginning of the nineteenth century, art has been spoken of frequently as though it were too lofty and esoteric to be fully comprehended and too much of a will-o'-the-wisp for close examination.

Although it is perhaps true that no universally accepted explanation of art exists, its nature can be revealed by examining its relationship to other human activities. First of all, and most broadly, art is an aid in understanding the world. As such, it may be compared to history, philosophy, or science, which attempt to formalize or discover and record patterns in man's experience. Art may deal with the same subject matter as these other approaches, may even use some of the same methods. For example, history seeks to record the facts of man's past, but since it cannot report everything about man's living from day to day, it tends to select those facts which seem significant and which appear to compose a pattern of cause and effect. Thus, history, like art, selects, arranges, and gives emphasis to its materials.

Philosophy seeks to find the truths and principles underlying all being and to relate them to human existence. A play also may seek to suggest answers to such a quest. Such branches of science as psychology and sociology seek to determine the causes and probabilities of certain kinds of behavior; a play, too—especially a modern one—is bound to have some of these concerns. Each approach to man's experience attempts to discover and to put into a communicable form conclusions about man and the world in which he lives.

There are, however, significant differences in the methods used by the various approaches. History, philosophy, and science attempt to set their conclusions down in logical expository prose; a point of view is expressed, and proof is marshaled to support that view and to gain its acceptance. These methods are directed principally to the intellect.

Art, on the other hand, attempts to work primarily through direct involvement of its audience's emotions, imagination, and intellect, and by presenting experience directly. A play, consequently, shows events as though occurring at this moment before our eyes; we absorb these events in the way we absorb life itself—through their direct operation upon our senses. Art differs from life by stripping away all irrelevant details and organizing events so that they compose a significant, connected pattern. Thus a play illuminates and comments on human experience at the same time that it appears to create human experience.

Another distinguishing characteristic of art is its manipulation of imagination. Although it may present human experience, an art experience is clearly not the same as a life experience. Even an historical drama is an imaginative recreation of events; the characters' motivations and dialogue as a rule must be invented, and certainly the audience knows that what it is seeing is not the historical event itself but a fictional version of the original. However, just as we do not mistake a statue for a real person, so, actually, we do not mistake stage action for life action. Rather, we usually view a play with what Coleridge called a "willing suspension of disbelief." By this he meant that, while we know that the events of a play are not real, we agree for the moment not to disbelieve their reality. One important qualification must be added, however: we are not moved to action by what we see on the stage as we would be by a life action. We sit absorbed in watching one man kill another, but we make no attempt to rescue the victim or to call the police. This is a vicarious experience, one we can enter into without the demand for either decision or action. We watch in a kind of suspended animation, a quality sometimes called "esthetic distance," since we seem to be far enough away from the event to enter a state of

A sketch by Philippe Jacques de Loutherbourg for the battle scenes in Shakespeare's *Richard III*. This sketch was made about 1775 when the noted landscape, marine, and battle painter was engaged by David Garrick to superintend scene painting at the Drury Lane Theatre.

detached contemplation, which removes us from the events.

At the same time, however, the distance must not be so great as to induce indifference. Therefore, while a degree of detachment is necessary, a feeling of involvement with the characters and the situation is of equal importance. This feeling of kinship and involvement is sometimes called *empathy*. Thus we watch a play with a double sense of involvement and detachment, of entering into the experience but without any need for action on our part. It is both a removed and an intensified reaction of a kind seldom possible outside an esthetic experience.

Thus far we have been concerned with art principally as it is seen in drama. Along with other types of literature, however, drama is the art form most apt to have an intellectual content which relates it to areas of knowledge such as history, philosophy, and science. But what of other art forms in which the content is more abstract?

Each art form uses a different group of techniques and, therefore, is best equipped to deal with a particular aspect of human experience. Music, for example, uses rhythm, melody, and harmony to create and express states of feeling. We value music not so much for what it "says" as for what it does to us. It may calm or excite. Whenever it engages our attention, we are bound up in it and respond to its rhythmic patterns consciously or unconsciously. The more completely our attention is engaged the less we are conscious of other factors outside of the musical experience. At such times we may work or dance without being aware of effort; our energies seem released and we have a sense of freedom and power—of inner harmony. It is only after the music has stopped that we become aware of fatigue and frustration, for during the musical experience, states of feeling, expressed in terms of time and sound, have become the center of our existence.

The universal appeal of music is partially explained by its rhythmic qualities. Aristotle said that a sense of rhythm is natural to man; other writers have related all art to the rhythmic patterns of life itself: birth, growth, maturity, decline, and death; the cycle of the year; and the heartbeat. The rhythmic element in music is related to the basic feeling states of man, to the most fundamental facts of his existence, and the sense of order and harmony which it produces is the result of its fulfillment of unconscious needs.

The structure of music is a marked source of satisfaction. Both melody and rhythm have patterns. Some sound combinations are harmonious while others are inharmonious or dissonant; we are pained when unpleasant combinations strike our ears. Each composition has its own patterns—the longer we listen the clearer the patterns become and the more definite grow our expectations. If a musical phrase is broken off in the middle, we desire to have it completed and sense satisfaction when it is. Thus, structural patterns—which create expectations, lead to frustrations or postponements, and ultimately to completion and satisfaction—are an important part of music's effect.

Music, then, as an art form, makes its appeal through the ear. It organizes sound and time into feeling states which relate to our basic patterns of sensation.

Painting makes its appeal through the eye, formalizing man's relationship to space. It uses line, mass, and color to create pleasing compositions which are expressive both of order and harmony, of emotions and perceptions. Its content may be representative of real-life objects or it may be totally abstract. Though recognizable subject matter may add another source of pleasure, the appeal of painting does not lie in its ability to produce exact likeness. Rather, it allows man to experience and understand spatial relationships esthetically.

Each art makes its own distinctive appeal to different senses and through differing means. All art expresses and organizes our perceptions about feeling, emotion, growth, and movement—about life itself. Each art form selects, arranges, and gives emphasis to its elements—out of this organization, this form, significance emerges.

Significance is a many-faceted concept, however, for it comprises all of the things communicated or expressed by an art work. Some of these might be called intellectual significances; others are closely involved with feelings and emotions.

Intellectual significance may be illustrated by turning once more to drama. In *King Lear*, for example, Lear divides his kingdom between two of his three daughters and gives up all power as ruler. The two daughters cast him out; eventually the formerly great king becomes virtually a beggar and a madman. Further events bring about his death. From this series of occurrences we may reach certain conclusions about the relationship of parents to children, about ingratitude, emotional blindness and so on. Such conclusions are largely intellectual, for they are based upon our perception of the logical connection between a series of events.

The same sequence, however, has emotional significance of considerable complexity. As the events transpire, expectations, hopes, fears, indignation, and other emotions are aroused; these are thwarted, satisfied, or transformed. With the end of the play comes a feeling of completion, of catharsis, a sense of moral fulfillment. This kind of significance is dependent in large part upon the subject matter, but it is also partially a result of the tempo, rhythm, and structure of the play.

The total significance of any work of art is difficult to evaluate. It appeals in varying degrees to different persons, and what the spectator gleans from a work of art depends in part upon his own background and his own sensitivity to emotions and ideas.

Art, then, is one way of ordering, clarifying, and understanding experience. Each art form uses its own special techniques, but each manages to express itself in ways which offer both significance and pleasure at the same time. Of all the arts, the theatre is probably the one most closely related to the patterns of life and normal experience. It is the art form that most nearly encompasses all of the other arts.

THE PROBLEM OF VALUE IN ART

Art may not appear to be useful. It does not produce the obvious benefits offered by medicine or engineering; it does not promise any advances for civilization; it may seem impractical when compared with business. Its purpose, thus, remains vague to most persons; many think of it as play and therefore not fundamentally important. The financially successful artist frequently is honored not because he is a good artist but because he has become successful in a business sense.

And, since people cannot agree upon the worth of individual works of art, many question the value of art itself. Even those who profess to love art frequently cast doubt upon its worth; those of conservative taste accuse "modern" art of being an elaborate hoax, while the admirers of modern art reply that conventional forms are shallow and outmoded. Under such a cross fire of argument it is hardly surprising that the public may develop doubts about art in general.

Too, many persons distrust anything which appeals openly to the emotions. Americans in particular have long been suspicious of their emotional reactions, while the appeal to logic and intelligence has been stressed. Activities which emphasize the latter have been valued, therefore, over those elevating the former. To many, the display of feelings and emotions suggests a lack of control.

There are many other reasons why art has been disdained, but these are among the most frequently expressed. Those who advance these objections fail to recognize that art deals with the basic aspects of man's existence which we are constantly trying to understand, and that art, although on the surface seeming to be without purpose, aids us to relax, to find harmony within ourselves, and to understand both ourselves and our world. For these reasons, art has played an important part in all periods of history; and because it fills such basic needs, it will always be a part of men's lives, even the lives of those who do not understand it or say they have no interest in it.

Of course, not all art is good. As with all human activities, it has a range of quality from excellent to unsatisfactory, and we are constantly faced with the problem of distinguishing its worth and the relative value of different works. (Is *Hamlet* a good play? Is it better than *Death of a Salesman*? These questions illustrate the problem.) Many avoid such issues by refusing to call works they do not like "art."

Art often is used as a term of praise rather than as a category for classifying the products of man's mind and imagination. Thus we hear people say about a play, "It may be good theatre, but it isn't art." Others set up the categories *art* and *show business* and divide plays according to whether they are of "great importance" or "mere entertainment." Such divisions have doubtful value since they fail to clarify adequately how the preferred plays differ from those excluded. Were *art* defined more broadly and basically, such misuses and abuses might be avoided and we would be forced into a closer examination of the bases of judgment.

Art is an approach to human experience, and those products which are created from the viewpoint of art must be dealt with as attempts at art— even if they are not successful. The problem is to discover how and why some have failed and others have succeeded.

No one can lay down a full set of rules for judging art, but methods of approach can be suggested and demonstrated. Skill in judgment, however, demands experience with or knowledge of the art form being evaluated. The material which follows is aimed at helping to give a key to that knowledge and experience and to lay the foundations for formulating intelligent and sensitive reactions to the theatre as one form of art.

A Greek vase painting depicting satyrs. From Furtwängler-Reichold, *Griechische Vasenmalerei*, 1904.

Chapter 2

THE AUDIENCE AND THE CRITIC

In the preceding discussion of the theatre as an art form, one important ingredient, the audience, was ignored. For all arts the existence of an audience is imperative. For most, the audience may be thought of as separate individuals—the reader of a novel or a poem, the viewer of a painting or a piece of sculpture—each of whom may experience the art work in isolation. But for the performing arts—theatre, music, and dance—a group audience must be assembled at a given time and place for the purpose of experiencing together an artistic performance.

The audience is a powerful influence in the theatre. Its effects should be considered from a number of viewpoints: Why does an audience attend the theatre? How does an audience's financial support affect theatrical offerings? What effect does an audience's expectations and demands have on theatrical productions?

WHY DOES AN AUDIENCE ATTEND THE THEATRE?

One of the most powerful motives for attendance at a theatre is the desire for *recreation* or *relaxation*. Almost everyone at a performance expects to be entertained; this implies a suspension of personal cares, a relaxation

William Hogarth's "The Laughing Pit" showing spectators in the pit, beaux and orange girls in the boxes, musicians in the orchestra pit. Note the spikes to prevent spectators from climbing onto the stage, and the candles on the front of boxes. From an eighteenth-century engraving, courtesy of the University of Iowa Library.

of tensions, and a resultant feeling of well-being, satisfaction, and renewal.

Almost everyone agrees that the theatre should be entertaining, but not all agree on what constitutes entertainment. Many would exclude any treatment of controversial subject matter or social problems on the grounds that an audience goes to the theatre to escape from cares and not to be confronted with problems. This attitude is frequently labeled the "tired businessman's" approach, and it is sometimes charged that the American professional theatre has become merely a place to relax after a hard day's work, or a spot to take prospective clients to put them in the proper frame of mind for business dealings.

There is a smaller audience which looks to theatre for *intellectual stimulation*. It too desires to be entertained, but it argues that the theatre, in addition, should be seriously concerned with important human problems, with new insights and provocative perceptions. This audience is inclined to view "theatre-as-recreaton" as a debasement of art. Both of these points of view are valid in part but neither should gain complete acceptance. The whole range of drama should be available to audiences, for the health of the theatre depends upon the breadth of its appeal.

In America today the success of a play is frequently judged by its ability to attract large audiences over a considerable period of time. But is a play to be considered a failure if it does not achieve financial success on Broadway? Not necessarily. A dramatist has a right to select his audience just as much as an audience selects a play. And, actually, he does so when he chooses his subject matter, themes, characters, and language; consciously or unconsciously, he has an ideal spectator in mind. Although he may hope for universal acceptance, he desires the favorable response of one particular segment of the population. This restricted group is his primary audience, and a play should be deemed successful if it achieves the desired response from the audience for which it was intended. Most American theatres, unfortunately, are operated on the principle that public taste is uniform, or that the only valid taste is that of the majority. Little is done to meet the requirements of minority audiences.

FINANCIAL SUPPORT AND THEATRICAL PROGRAMMING

If a theatre is to stay in operation it must be concerned with its ticket sales unless financial support is available from other sources. In America there is an almost superstitious belief in the box office as the only acceptable means of support. Advocates of this point of view argue that if money is accepted from any other source, freedom is sure to be lost, since support often leads to control. They admit that the theatre may be at the mercy of public whim, but they either see this as a healthy state or as the best available choice.

Advocates of a more diversified theatre than that to be found in America usually point to Europe, where many governments—both national and local—appropriate money each year to subsidize selected theatres. These subsidies have not led to undue interference with the affairs of the theatres (though this is no valid argument that it could not do so in America).

The purposes of a subsidy may be several. First, it permits a theatre to present programs without the necessity of commercial success. Second, it enables a theatre to sell tickets at a lower cost and to make productions more available to many financial brackets of the population. Third, a subsidy can be used to support a repertory company. (A repertory company usually hires a group of actors for an entire season and produces a number of plays performed in rotation. This arrangement allows the company to provide a cross section of drama that appeals to a wide range of tastes.)

One should be wary of the temptation to apply European solutions to American problems, however. First of all, the society of Europe tends to be more clearly stratified than that of America, for there are more distinct divisions into social classes, wider ranges in the amount of education, and other factors which create marked and clearly defined levels of taste. Furthermore, many persons believe that government support might have adverse effects on the theatre in America. They argue that fear of governmental investigations would lead to an overly cautious approach and that a theatre which offends no one is a sterile and dull institution.

But, although American theatres do not have the kind of subsidies that many of those in Europe enjoy, by far the majority do receive some form of subsidy. Almost all educational theatres in America operate in buildings supplied free of cost and with staffs paid from funds other than ticket sales. It is these theatres which offer the most diversified theatre programs. Community theatres also are subsidized by the voluntary labor of members, and some receive financial help from a local government as well. Many professional theatres outside of New York receive aid from philanthropic foundations. Only the commercial professional theatre of New York depends—almost exclusively—upon box office receipts for its survival, but its prestige makes its welfare of crucial importance to the theatre throughout the United States. Regardless of source, financial support is necessary, and audiences affect the kinds of plays presented in proportion to a theatre's dependence upon their patronage for its income.

THE AUDIENCE'S EXPECTATIONS AND THEATRICAL OFFERINGS

Audiences also affect the theatre through their expectations. They become accustomed to certain techniques and subject matter and quite frequently they resist change. Audiences are not resistant to all changes, however, for they have flocked to new modes of musical comedy, new styles of production, and have welcomed other innovations.

Audiences usually resist what they do not understand. In the late nineteenth century, Ibsen (now usually designated the founder of modern drama) was denounced by many audiences, and his plays were forbidden production in many countries. To audiences of the time, Ibsen's plays seemed to advocate immoral actions and to deal with subjects unsuitable for public discussion. It is difficult today to understand the uproar, since these very works which were greeted originally with such righteous indignation may now be seen in the most conservative theatres. Yet audience response does make it difficult for playwrights with new ideas and techniques to find a place in the theatre, and it discourages rebellion against accepted conventions.

On the other side, some innovations become popular immediately. For example, melodrama gained almost instant acceptance in the nineteenth century and virtually drove every other play form from the stage.

Audiences probably wish to encounter novel experiences, but as a rule they want the new to be presented in clear and recognizable terms. If not readily understood, the new is likely to be rejected. Clearly, audience response plays an important role in determining theatrical offerings, for producers cater to audience taste whenever their livelihood depends on box-office receipts.

WISE USE OF AUDIENCE INFLUENCE

The average audience member, however, is not aware of exerting any pressure on the fate of the theatre. He is like the voter in a democracy who finds it hard to believe that his vote makes any difference, or that his actions can in any way influence governmental policy. But the answer to the person who cares about the theatre must be much the same as the answer to one who cares about his country: he does have power and he should learn how to use it.

If any audience member is to use his power wisely, he must first try *to understand* the theatre and how it works. Second, he should acquire the ability *to judge* the relative merits of plays and theatrical performances. Finally, confident in his understanding and judgment, he should *work for that which seems of value* to him. If all those who like the theatre were to exert themselves in its behalf, a diversified theatre capable of appealing to all levels of taste—a truly healthy theatre—would result. But before anyone can work intelligently toward the future, he must acquire understanding and judgment—he must *seek to become a critic of the theatre.*

THE CRITIC

In a sense everyone who witnesses a play is a critic since he passes some kind of judgment, however fleeting, upon what he sees. The title of critic is usually reserved, however, for those persons who formulate their judgments for publication. Professionally, the critic is an experienced and sometimes trained audience member who understands plays and the theatre well enough to assess the effectiveness of its composite work, and he is one who understands the audience well enough to express his evaluations in terms comprehensible to it.

Criticism should be illuminating to both the creators and the audience of a theatre piece. In making explanations or in passing judgments, most critics refer to specific passages in a play, to characterization, structure, to acting, or to other aspects of staging. In this process, they are of service to the theatre worker as well as to the public, for they are seeking to point out the reasons for success or failure.

But a single piece of criticism will not serve the needs of all persons, for, just as a playwright selects an audience for his work, so too the critic has an audience or type of reader in mind. The reviews of plays published in the New York daily newspapers are addressed to a general public, and almost no background or knowledge is taken for granted. On the other hand, the criticism written for literary quarterlies is addressed to a more sophisticated and selected audience. Therefore, not all criticism can be read in the same way.

Even when the critic's assumptions are clear, however, there is often a wide range of response to his work. One reader will find a given piece of criticism illuminating, while another will find nothing of value in it. Just as one is drawn to certain kinds of plays, he is also drawn to certain types of criticism. The critic who can retain the attention and respect of his particular audience is a successful critic. But, just as certain plays may continue to be acted for generations, so criticism may also remain illuminating to many readers in widely separated times. Most popularly read criticism, like most drama, however, speaks for the moment, serves its purpose, and is then forgotten.

Not everyone need aspire to be a practicing critic (in the sense of writing and publishing his judgments), but everyone interested in the theatre can become a better judge by acquiring the background necessary for an adequate understanding of plays and theatrical performances.

THE MEANING AND PURPOSES OF CRITICISM

Criticism, to many, implies the making of adverse comments, but its true meaning is "the act of making judgments." This judgment should consider

The battle at the Comédie Française between Classicists and Romanticists on the opening night of Victor Hugo's *Hernani* (1830). The play's triumph signaled French acceptance of romanticism. From Frederic Loliee's *La Comédie Française*. Paris, 1907.

both the excellent and the poor—the effective and the ineffective—in a play and its production. Criticism has three main purposes: exposition, appreciation, and evaluation. A piece of criticism is seldom devoted solely to one of these purposes; usually all are found in conjunction.

The purpose of expository criticism is to explain a play or factors which affect it. The critic may study the author, the time in which the play was written, the source of the ideas expressed, and similar factors. In this approach, no judgment of worth need ever be made. For example, a critic might study Shakespeare's *Richard III* and then explain to his readers how the play is constructed, and, although his examination should lead to a better understanding of the play, it need not necessarily judge its effectiveness.

Appreciative criticism, on the other hand, is usually written by a critic who has already decided that a work is good. His principal motive then is to make others feel the power of the play. He may proceed by describing his own responses to the work and then attempt to evoke similar feelings in the reader. He may also by analysis show the playwright's superiority in play structure, characterization, creation of mood, and other areas.

The evaluative critic may employ exposition, appreciation, or even condemnation. His principal aim is to arrive at a judgment on the effectiveness of a play. As a rule, he begins by analyzing the structure, characterization, themes, language, and use of visual elements. Upon this evidence, coupled frequently with information drawn from other sources, he builds his evaluation. A critic writing for a daily newspaper may offer little evidence for his judgment. His aim is to assess a play's merits for the prospective theatregoer.

THE BASIC PROBLEMS IN CRITICISM

In pursuing his work, the serious critic is concerned with three basic problems: understanding the play; assessing its effectiveness in terms of its aims; and judging its ultimate worth as a work of art.

In attempting to understand a play, the critic must make sure that all of the important keys to its meaning have been explored. First, he must analyze the play, preferably through a study of the manuscript. But before he can fully understand the script, other explorations may be necessary. Sometimes a study of the author and his background is essential. If the play is a work from the past, it may be necessary to examine the dominant religious or psychological beliefs of that period, or to determine the stage conventions for which the play was written. The critic should be content only when he has undertaken all of the necessary steps for understanding.

While these methods are those used by the literary critic, they are also employed by theatre workers in their study of a script prior to its production. Unless the director, the actors and the other artists involved understand a drama, it will be difficult for them to produce it satisfactorily. Although the literary critic and the theatre worker may arrive at the same conclusions in their studies, the theatre worker usually finds that his understanding of the play is modified during the rehearsal period. As the play takes shape on stage, he discovers qualities of which he was previously unaware, for plays do not reveal all of their potentialities on the printed page. Conversely, however, not all of the implications found in a script can be projected to an audience. Whenever possible a play should be studied both on the printed page and in performance.

Many critics, however, write about plays which they have not read and which they know only from having seen once. Obviously, understanding may be severely limited under such circumstances, and most frequently the critic restricts himself to reporting impressions without pretending to provide an analysis of the play. In this case the critic's comprehension of the play will depend in large measure upon the quality of the performance he has seen.

After a play is understood, it may be judged in terms of how well it fulfills its intentions. Rarely is the intention of a play openly stated. Rather, it must be determined in the process of probing analysis to gain understanding of the work. Intention is indicated through such elements as the tone (a play may be humorous, satirical, serious, whimsical and so on), the ideas and their treatment, the kind of dialogue used, the characters and the conflicts in which they take part. The critic comes to recognize whether the author is attempting to arouse indignation at some social injustice, is deriding a political position, or is merely trying to offer an evening of entertainment. Having decided upon the play's purpose, he can then assess how completely this purpose has been realized.

This assessment can be based entirely upon a study of the script, but it is frequently helpful and always wise to note the response of an audience during performance. An audience, however, is not always to be trusted. For example, the play may not have been satisfactorily performed, and, while the response may be an accurate measure of the audience's degree of enjoyment, it will not give a true indication of the play's potential power. Other factors—such as unfamiliar dramatic techniques or complex ideas—may be responsible for an audience's failure in comprehension. In such cases, the fault does not necessarily lie with the play, but may indicate shortcomings in the audience. But if the play has been adequately performed and understood, then audience response is of great importance in determining whether the intention of the playwright has been effectively achieved.

It is possible, however, to understand a play and to judge it successful in carrying out its intention and, at the same time, to find it inadequate in the ultimate sense of artistic fulfillment. Before passing final judgment, the critic must ask whether the play's accomplishments are important enough to merit commendation.

It is here that the critic faces his greatest problem, for there are few universally accepted standards of worth. Since he cannot take for granted that his readers will share his system of value, the critic should indicate by what yardstick he is measuring worth. He may set up purely artistic standards; he may use certain moral or religious criteria; he may judge a play in relation to other works of the same type; or he may use still other yardsticks. The criteria of judgment used by contemporary critics vary widely. For example, some critics believe that any worthy play should be seriously concerned with social, political, or economic problems, while others believe that such concerns lead inevitably to propagandistic and dull drama; some critics believe that tragedy is always better than farce, while others believe that the play's type is unimportant. The critic's own values inevitably enter into his judgment at this level of criticism. The best critic will recognize that his preferences play a large part in his critical judgment and will make these clear to his readers either through direct statement or by implication.

Frequently, critics take the worth of certain plays for granted and restrict themselves to exposition or appreciation. For example, in dealing with a play by Shakespeare, the critic usually assumes that his readers are convinced of the work's greatness and he proceeds to explore some facet, such as characterization, as a means of improving the reader's perception of subtle nuances in the work. Most criticism, however, deals directly or by implication with all three of the main problems of criticism.

Because the theatre itself is a vast composite and because each of us is subject to many influences, it is difficult to become a good theatre critic. The qualities for which the would-be critic must strive, however, are these: he must be sensitive to feelings and ideas; he must become as well acquainted as possible with the theatre of all periods and of all types; he must be willing to explore plays until he understands them thoroughly; he must be aware of his own prejudices and values; he must be articulate and clear in expressing his judgments and their bases. Perhaps most important of all, he must be willing to alter his opinion when new experiences and evidence reveal inadequacies in his earlier judgment, for criticism is a continuing process and not a dogmatic position to be defended.

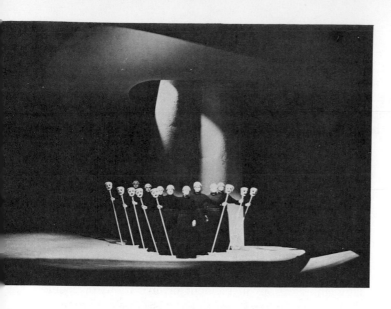

Chapter 3

DRAMATIC STRUCTURE, FORM, AND STYLE

All play production revolves around the script. It is necessary, therefore, to explore the structure of drama as a key to the analysis of individual plays.

DRAMATIC ACTION AND ITS CHARACTERISTICS

Broadly speaking, a play is the representation of man in action. But the action of a play is not composed merely of physical movement, for it depicts, as well, those mental and psychological activities which motivate external behavior. "Man in action," therefore, includes the total range of feelings, thoughts, and deeds.

A single play of necessity depicts only that limited part of human behavior which the playwright chooses to present. Thus, the action of each drama is unique in its details. Nevertheless, all effective plays share a number of common qualities from which we may deduce the desirable characteristics of dramatic action.

Aristotle declared that a play should have a beginning, a middle and an end. On the surface, this statement seems obvious and overly simple, but it represents a vital truth. Basically, it implies that a play must be *complete and self-contained*, that everything necessary for its understanding must be included in the play itself. The beginning is the point

Scene from a performance of Sophocles' *Oedipus Rex*. From *The New Theatre in Germany*. Photograph—Pit Ludwig. Courtesy of the Exhibition circulated by the Smithsonian Institution.

in the total plot at which the playwright chooses to start the action, and is itself the foundation upon which the succeeding action is built. The middle develops the potentialities found in the beginning, and the end resolves and completes the action.

Dramatic action should be *purposeful*. It should be organized so as to arouse a specific response, such as pity and fear, joy and ridicule, indignation, thoughtful contemplation, laughter or tears. The purpose may be simple or complex, but the events, the characters, the mood, and all other elements should be shaped with a dominant purpose in mind.

Dramatic action should be *unified*. All elements should be related to its central purpose. Everything should contribute to that purpose and nothing should be irrelevant or expendable.

Dramatic action should be *varied and complex*. Although the action must be unified, many complications in incident or revelations of character should occur if suspense and interest are to be maintained. The means used for achieving unity, therefore, must be imaginative and varied so that monotony and predictability are avoided.

Dramatic action should *engage and maintain interest*. The characters must seem worthy of audience involvement, or the situation must be novel enough to arouse interest in its outcome, or the issues must seem vital enough to warrant individual concern.

Dramatic action should be *probable* (that is, all of its elements should be logically consistent). Probability is the quality which most persons have in mind when they speak of a play's believability. But probability, or believability, does not depend upon a similarity to real life, for a play which deals with impossible events may be called believable if the incidents occur logically within the framework created by the playwright. This point can be better understood through an example drawn from a non-realistic drama. In *The Bald Soprano* a clock strikes seventeen times as the curtain rises; Mrs. Smith promptly announces that it is nine o'clock and launches into a bizarre speech on virtues of English middle-class life. This opening informs an audience that the play is abandoning everyday logic. As the drama progresses, the rules of the game are unveiled, according to which events occur. The audience expects a playwright to observe his own established rules with consistency; anything which violates the peculiar logic set up will seem out of place, and, therefore, unbelievable.

METHODS OF ORGANIZING DRAMATIC ACTION

A dramatic action is composed of a sequence of occurrences which must be organized in terms of the play's purpose. Organization is ultimately a matter of directing attention to relationships which make up a congruent pattern and which show the connection between scenes. The most common sources of unity are themes and ideas, character, and the cause-and-effect relationship of events.

The dominant organizational principle has always been the *cause-and-effect* arrangement of incidents. Using this method, the playwright sets up in the opening scenes all of the necessary conditions—the situation, and the desires and motivations of the characters—out of which the later events develop. The desires of one character come into conflict with those of another, or two conflicting desires within the same character may lead to a crisis. The attempts to surmount the obstacles created make up the substance of the play, each scene growing logically out of each one preceding it.

Less often a dramatist uses a *character* as the principal source of unity. In this case, the incidents are held together because they all revolve around the same person. Such a play may dramatize the life of a historical personage, or it may show a character's responses to a series of experiences. This kind of organization may be seen in much of the work of Christopher Marlowe.

A playwright may organize his material around *a basic idea,* each scene closely linked because each illustrates an aspect of a larger theme or argument. This device can be clearly seen in Bertolt Brecht's *The Private Life of the Master Race,* which treats the rise of the Nazi party in Germany in a series of scenes held together only by the fact that each illustrates the inhumanity of the Nazi ideology. The order of the scenes is arbitrary, except that they build in emotional intensity.

All three methods of organizing action may be used in the same play, although one will usually be dominant. But, regardless of its source of unity, a play normally relies upon *conflict* to arouse and maintain interest and suspense. In fact, the most commonly held idea about drama is that it always involves conflict—of one character with another, of desires within the same character, of a character with his environment, of one ideology with another.

Although conflict plays a major role in most plays, there are dramas in which it is of little significance. *Our Town,* for example, makes relatively little use of conflict. Instead, a narrator (the Stage Manager) begins scenes at important moments and interrupts them when his point is made. He shows a typical day in the life of a village, Grovers Corners, and suggests that morning, midday, and evening are related to childhood, maturity, and death. Through the play, the audience relives the basic events of life. Although momentary conflicts occur within individual scenes, there is no major conflict.

Whether or not conflict is involved, the action of drama must be *organized in a climactic order*—the scenes must increase rather than decrease in interest. This effect is achieved through the revelation of new aspects of character, by increasing suspense (the decisive moment is felt to be moving nearer and nearer), or by increasing emotional intensity. Although the arrangement is from the lesser to the greater, within this over-all movement there are moments of contrast or repose (such as the comic scenes in Shakespeare's tragedies) which afford a temporary change from the dominant pattern.

Organization may also be approached through examination of the parts of drama. Aristotle has listed these parts as plot, character, thought, diction, music, and spectacle. Although music is no longer an invariable part of drama and will not be treated in this chapter, Aristotle's division is still very useful.

PLOT

Plot is the over-all structure of a play, and may be examined in terms of its beginning, middle, and end. Let us examine some typical structural patterns.

THE BEGINNING. The beginning of a play establishes the place, the occasion, the characters, the mood, and the level of reality or probability. It brings the plot to the point where the conflict or issues become clear.

A play is like coming upon previously unknown places and persons. Initially, the novelty may attract attention, but, as the facts about the people and the place are established, interest either wanes or increases. The playwright is faced, therefore, with a double problem: he must give essential information, but at the same time create expectations sufficient to make the audience desire to stay and see more.

The beginning of a play involves *exposition,* or the setting forth of the necessary background information—about prior events, the identity of the characters, and the present situation. While exposition is necessary in the opening scene of every play, it is not confined to the beginning, for in most plays the background is only gradually revealed.

The amount of exposition necessary is partially determined by the *point of attack,* or the moment at which the story starts. Shakespeare uses an early point of attack (that is, he begins his stories at their inception and tells them in a chronological sequence). Greek tragedies, on the other hand, have late points of attack, and prior events must be narrated rather than shown.

A playwright motivates the presentation of expository material through any of a number of devices. For example, Ibsen frequently introduces a character who has returned after having been away for some time.

Answers to his questions about happenings during his absence supply an audience with the necessary background information.

Although a play opens with expository material, attention is usually focused early on a question or a potential conflict. The beginning of a play, therefore, normally includes what may be called an *inciting incident*, or an occurrence which sets the main action in motion. In Sophocles' *Oedipus Rex* (or *Oedipus the King*), a plague is ravishing Thebes, and Oedipus has sent to the oracle at Delphi for guidance. The oracle declares that the murderer of Laius must be found and punished before the plague will end. This is the event (introduced in the Prologue) which sets the action in motion.

The inciting incident usually leads directly to the *major dramatic question* around which the entire play is organized—the thread or spine which holds events together. This question may undergo a number of changes as the play progresses. For example, the question first raised in *Oedipus the King* is: Will the murderer of Laius be found and the city saved? Later this question is modified, however, as interest shifts to Oedipus' own involvement in guilt. Although the major dramatic question in some plays may be obscure, the attempt to define the focal point of action is always useful. When the major dramatic question (or principal issue) becomes clear to an audience, the play's beginning is over.

THE MIDDLE. The middle of a play is composed of a series of complications. A *complication* is any element introduced into a play which serves to alter the direction of the action. Complications may arise from the discovery of new information, the unexpected opposition of certain characters, the unexpected necessity of choosing between courses of action, or from other sources.

Complications serve to narrow the possibilities of action and to create suspense. At the opening of a play the potentialities are almost infinite, since the story might develop in a number of directions. As complications arise, however, the choices required of the characters reduce the alternatives. As a result, the audience comes to sense the direction of the action, and, as the possibilities become more limited, a feeling of approaching crisis develops. Finally, there comes a moment when the alternatives have been so reduced that the next discovery will answer the major dramatic question. This is the climax, the moment of crisis or the peak, toward which the play builds, after which there is gradual release in emotional tension leading to resolution and the play's end.

The substance of most complications is *discovery*. In one sense everything presented in a play is discovery if by that term is meant the revelation of things not previously known. The term is normally reserved, however, for occurrences of sufficient importance to alter the direction of action.

Discoveries may involve objects (a wife discovers in her husband's pocket a weapon of the kind used in a murder), persons (a young man discovers that his rival in love is his brother), facts (a young man about to leave home discovers that his mother has cancer), values (a woman discovers that love is more important than a career), or self (a man discovers that he has been acting from purely selfish motives when he thought he was acting out of love for his children). Self-discovery is often the most powerful.

A complication is usually introduced by one discovery and concluded by another. A complication is set in motion by the appearance of some new element which requires a new line of action. But the steps taken to meet the new demands also give rise to tensions and conflicts which build to a climax, or peak of intensity. The climax is accompanied, or brought about, by still another discovery, which serves to resolve the existing complication but which precipitates another. Each complication, thus, has a beginning, middle, and end—its own development, crisis, and resolution—just as does the play as a whole.

The implications of each discovery are not always followed up immediately. Frequently a playwright is dealing with a number of characters and not every revelation involves all of them. Several complications, therefore, may intervene between the introduction of a discovery and its development. In such cases, the play pursues first one line of action and then another in an alternating or overlapping pattern of complications.

Means other than discoveries may be used to precipitate complications. Natural disasters (such as earthquakes, storms, shipwrecks, and automobile accidents) are used. These are apt to seem especially contrived, however, if they resolve the problem (for example, if the villain is killed in an automobile accident and the struggle is automatically terminated). Sometimes complications are initiated by quite innocent action on the part of a character. For example, a father arranges a trip for his daughter without realizing that she has fallen in love and wants to stay at home.

In most complications, the event is not as important as its effect upon the characters involved. The attempts of each to meet the situation give rise to the succeeding action and lead to new complications.

The series of complications culminates in the *crisis,* or turning point of the action, which opens the way for the resolution. For example, in *Oedipus the King,* Oedipus sets out to discover the murderer of Laius; the crisis is the moment when Oedipus realizes that he himself is the guilty person. The crisis usually comes near the end of the play, but it sometimes occurs considerably earlier. Regardless of its position, the middle of the play is over when the crisis, or climax, is reached.

THE END. The final portion of a play, called the *resolution* or *dénouement*, extends from the climax to the final curtain. Although it is usually brief, it may be of considerable length. It serves to tie off the various strands of action and to answer the questions raised earlier. It brings the situation back to an equilibrium and satisfies audience expectations.

The climax normally leads to the *obligatory scene* (that is, the one scene which the dramatist must show if the play is to be satisfying to an audience). During much of a play's action, important facts are hidden or ignored by the characters. The audience senses, however (either consciously or unconsciously), that eventually these facts will be revealed, since the entire action points in that direction. The obligatory scene, then, answers the question: What will happen when all of the facts are revealed? It shows the opposing forces, each with full knowledge, meeting face to face. Since the final piece of vital information is usually withheld until the moment of crisis, the obligatory scene is normally a part of the play's resolution.

The functions of the obligatory scene may be divided among a series of complications. For example, a number of scenes may show how the tables are turned on a man who has been deceiving everyone. In such cases, the resolution may be as absorbing as the complications preceding the climax.

The resolution should create a sense of completion and fulfillment. The audience should be able to see clearly how the ending came about, even though it could not have predicted the outcome in advance. Everything that precedes the final curtain should contribute to the probability of the resolution, for a play ought to be a self-contained unit, complete in itself, with clear development through beginning, middle, and end.

CHARACTER AND CHARACTERIZATION

Character is the principal source for plot, for incidents can be developed mainly through the speech and behavior of dramatic personages. Furthermore, action usually arises out of the conflicting desires of these characters.

Characterization is the means of differentiating one dramatic personage from another. Since a dramatist may endow his agents with few or many traits, characterization varies markedly in complexity. In analyzing the characters of a play, it is helpful to look at four levels of characterization. (This approach is adapted from the writings of Hubert Heffner.)

The first level of characterization is *physical*—supplying such basic facts as sex, age, size, and coloration. It is true, of course, that a dramatist may not supply all of this information; it must then be decided upon by the director during production. The physical is the simplest level of characterization, however, since it reveals external traits only.

A second level is *social*. It includes economic status, profession or trade, religion, family relationships—all those factors which place a character in his environment.

The third level is the *psychological*. It reveals habitual responses, attitudes, desires, motivations, likes and dislikes—the inner workings of the mind, both emotional and intellectual, which lead to action. Since habits of feeling, thought, and behavior define character more fully than do physical and social traits, and since drama usually arises from desires in conflict, the psychological is the most essential level of characterization.

The fourth level is *moral*. Although implied in all plays, it is not always shown. It is most apt to be clearly represented in serious plays, especially tragedies. Almost all human action suggests some ethical standard. In many plays, however, the moral implications are ignored and decisions are made in terms of expediency. This practice is typical of comedies, since moral deliberations are apt to turn any action into a serious one.

Moral decisions more clearly differentiate persons than any other kind. The choices made by a character when he is faced with a moral crisis show whether he is selfish, a hypocrite, or one who always acts according to his beliefs. A moral decision usually causes a character to examine his own motives and values, and in the process his true nature is revealed both to himself and to the audience.

A playwright may emphasize one or more of these levels. Some writers pay little attention to the physical appearance of their characters and concentrate upon psychological and moral traits; other dramatists may describe appearance and social status in detail. In assessing the completeness of a characterization, however, it is not enough merely to make a list of the traits assigned and the levels of characterization used. It is also necessary to ask *how the character functions in the play*. For example, the audience needs to know little about the maid who only appears to announce dinner; any detailed characterization would be superfluous and would call attention to an extremely minor role. On the other hand, the principal character needs to be drawn in detail. The appropriateness and completeness of each characterization, therefore, may be judged only after an analysis is made of its function in each scene and in the play as a whole.

A character is revealed through a number of devices: through descriptions in *stage directions, prefaces, or other explanatory material* not part of the dialogue or action; through *what he himself says*; through *what others say about him*; and, perhaps most important, through *what he does*. It is not enough, however, for a dramatist to assign characteristics to his personages; some action must be motivated or explained by each quality if it is not to be irrelevant or even misleading. The relative importance of each trait, therefore, must be assessed in terms of its necessity to the play's action.

It is not always easy to perceive a character's actual nature, since information about him is usually given in fragments scattered throughout the play. Furthermore, many different or even contradictory images may be presented. For example, a character may see himself as a certain kind of person; for one reason or another, however, he may try to project a different image to others; in turn, each of the other characters will see him from a different angle. Because the dramatist builds character through this composite approach, the audience must always watch for clues that indicate which statements and actions are to be accepted as accurate revelations of character.

Characters are defined in much the same way as words: first they are placed in a broad category (typified), and then differentiated (individualized) from other examples of the same type.

Typification is necessary for placing characters in the broad context of human experience. If a character were totally unlike any person the spectators had ever known, they would be unable to relate themselves to him. Most characters, however, may be placed in a category, such as the doting mother, the bashful young man, or the dumb blonde.

If the playwright has gone no further, the audience may find the personages oversimplified and may speak of them as "type" characters. Most dramatists, however, assign additional traits which serve as *individualization* of characters within broad categories. Thus, typifying qualities keep a character within the realm of the familiar, while individualizing traits make him strange and different.

A playwright is also concerned with making his characters *sympathetic* or *unsympathetic*. Most frequently authors create sympathetic characters by taking traits admired in real life and assigning them to personages in the play. On the other hand, many modern playwrights have created sympathy for abnormal characters by exploring the reasons behind their behavior; such persons are usually shown to be victims of circumstances and as objects more worthy of compassion than vilification. Normally, however, sympathetic characters are given major virtues and lesser foibles, while the reverse procedure is used for unsympathetic characters. The more a character is made either completely good or bad, the more he is apt to become unacceptable as a truthful reflection of human behavior.

Acceptability, however, is in part related to the type of play in which the characters appear. Melodrama, for example, oversimplifies human psychology and clearly divides characters and actions into good and bad. Tragedy, on the other hand, is normally concerned with complex forces at work both within and without man. It therefore requires more complete characters than melodrama, which may function very well with type characters. The audience usually demands only that characterization be sufficient for the play's purpose.

THEMES AND IDEAS

The third basic element of a play is *thought*. It includes the ideas, the arguments, the over-all meaning and significance of the action. It is present in all plays, even those which seem to be without purpose, for a playwright cannot avoid expressing ideas, and his combination of character and events always projects a view of human behavior.

The subject of a play is both general and specific. For example, *King Lear* embodies the general topic of child–parent relationships in a complex and specific story. Thus, the general topic, or theme, serves as a point of focus around which specific events are organized. Although a play may have a number of themes, one is usually dominant. One way of studying a play, therefore, is to identify its themes and to examine the ways in which they have been embodied. This procedure helps to define the author's over-all purpose and his methods of writing.

The general and specific subjects of a play are related to the concepts of *universality* and *individuality*. Universality is that quality which enables a play to communicate with sizable audiences, often even after centuries have passed. To say that *Hamlet* has universal significance does not mean, however, that we should be able to put ourselves in Hamlet's position as a prince or as the avenger of his father's death. The universal elements are rather to be found in the conflict between a son's duty to his father and his feelings for his mother, between personal integrity and religious faith, between justice and corrupt political power, and in the spectacle of the "underdog" pitted against overwhelming forces. These are situations which might confront human beings of any social class in any period. They provide a common point of contact between Hamlet and the audience.

On the other hand, every story must be individualized if it is to be believable and interesting. *Hamlet*, therefore, has many elements which depart markedly from normal experience and keep the story from being hackneyed and overly familiar. It is such skillful combinations of the universal and the individual which make significant and affecting drama.

The significance or ultimate meaning of a play's action is normally implied rather than directly stated. It is to be discovered in the relationships between characters, the ideas associated with sympathetic and unsympathetic characters, and conflicts and their resolutions.

Occasionally, on the other hand, a play's meaning is clearly stated in the script. The characters may advocate a certain line of action, point of view, or social reform. Sometimes dramas using such methods are classified as *propaganda* or *social problem* plays, since they aim to persuade an audience to act or think in a particular way.

An author who wishes to persuade an audience has two paths open to him. He may subordinate his message to the story, and depend upon the latter's implications to be sufficiently persuasive. In this case, he risks being misunderstood. Or, he may make his position quite clear (usually through a direct statement by an admirable character). In this case, while the dramatist leaves no doubt as to his purpose, he may alienate his audience, who may conclude that the play has been an excuse for delivering a sermon. In the hands of the unskillful dramatist this is frequently the result, for the characters seem lifeless mouthpieces for the author. On the other hand, expert dramatists, such as Ibsen, Shaw, and Arthur Miller, have made themselves quite clear while creating compelling and vital plays.

The dramatist who is too intent upon achieving complete clarity, however, may bore his audience. To be explicit, the possible meanings of words and actions must be restricted. These restrictions may eliminate those connotations and implications which let an audience supply meanings as well as find them. Ambiguity is basic to human experience: we think we see the meaning of actions, but another interpretation is always possible. Life does not come equipped with meanings which are unmistakable; we ponder over our experience and try to find significance in it, but we can never be certain that we have solved the riddles. Since human experience is the raw material of drama, the playwright who sees no ambiguities in life may well create a world on the stage which is too orderly for an audience to accept. On the other hand, everyone simplifies experience in the process of generalizing about it. The dramatist does this also in his attempt to create the semblance of life, but his selection must be such that it commands belief.

Dramatists in different periods have used various devices to project themes and ideas. Greek playwrights made extensive use of the *chorus*, just as those of later periods employed such devices as *soliloquies, asides*, and other forms of *direct statement*. In every period, however, dramatists have relied principally upon *implication*.

Still other tools for projecting meaning are *allegory* and *symbol*. In allegory, characters and events represent ideas or qualities; characters become personifications (good deeds, mercy, greed, and so on), and the over-all significance of an allegory can usually be reduced to a clear moral statement. Its most famous examples are the Medieval morality plays, such as *Everyman*.

A symbol is a concrete object or event which, while having meaning and interest in itself, also suggests a concept or set of relationships. For example, the orchard in Chekhov's *The Cherry Orchard* is both a real object and a symbol. As an object, once useful, then admired merely for its beauty, it is finally cut down to make way for homes to be occupied by merchants. As a symbol, it represents Russian aristocracy which having lost its usefulness must make way for the more vigorous middle class. The orchard takes on a double meaning—literal and symbolic—enabling it to act as a comment not only on the characters in the play but on Russian society in general. The symbol is a favorite device with modern writers, for it allows them to maintain a realistic framework and at the same time to suggest deeper meanings.

While some plays, such as farces, may not explore ideas of great significance, all plays comment upon human life in some way.

DIALOGUE

Dialogue is the playwright's principal means of expression. When a play is presented in the theatre, actors, scenery, lighting and other elements are added, but to convey his basic conception, the dramatist must depend upon his skill in writing dialogue.

Dialogue must serve many functions. First, it must *impart information*. It has to set forth the necessary exposition and convey the important facts, ideas, and emotions in each scene. Second, dialogue must *reveal character*. The speeches of each personage reveal both his emotional and rational responses to each situation.

Third, dialogue must *direct attention* to important plot elements. Significant information and responses require emphasis. Dialogue points up conflicts and complications, and it prepares for future happenings. It builds suspense by making the audience aware of future possibilities, for while scenes always occur in the present, they are constantly directing attention toward possible future results. This creates a sense of forward movement and expectancy.

Fourth, dialogue must *reveal the themes and ideas* of a play. It has to provide clues to significant meanings while it is revealing character and developing action. Fifth, dialogue must help to *establish the tone and level of probability*. It can indicate whether the play is comic or serious, farcical or tragic. It also can suggest the degree of abstraction from reality. Sometimes the use of poetry indicates that the play will not follow everyday reality. The choice of words, the type of colloquialisms, the length of speeches, the use of broken phrases and interrupted sentences, and other linguistic devices are clues to the level of probability within which the play is operating.

Sixth, dialogue must help to *establish tempo and rhythm*. Tempo is the pace at which a scene is played. The tempo of a love scene is apt to be much more leisurely than that of a duelling scene, for example, and the dialogue must be written to reflect and provide the proper tempo. Rhythm is the recurring pattern which results from the flow of speeches. Halting speech creates one rhythmical pattern while animated, excited speech creates another. Tempo and rhythm together help to create a sense of forward movement or of retarding action. When the rhythm of each scene is built to an internal climax (like the pattern of an individual movement within a symphony), it holds an audience unconsciously in alert attention.

The dialogue of every play, no matter how realistic, is more abstract and formalized than everyday speech. A dramatist always selects, arranges, and heightens language more than anyone ever does in normal conversation. Consequently, in a realistic play, although the dialogue is modeled after everyday usage, the characters are more articulate and state their ideas and feelings more precisely than would their real-life counterparts. On the other hand, realistic dialogue retains the rhythms, tempos, and basically the vocabulary of everyday or colloquial speech.

The dialogue of nonrealistic plays may deviate markedly from normal speech. It frequently employs a larger vocabulary, abandons the rhythms of everyday speech, and makes considerable use of imagery and metrical lines. This less restricted vocabulary allows a more precise choice of words, avoids the frequent repetitions of colloquial speech, and permits a more forceful expression of emotions when characters must transcend the ordinary.

Imagery is always found in poetic drama, but it may appear in realistic plays written in prose. The simile is widely used even in real-life speech ("He was as mad as a hornet," or "She's as nervous as a cat on a hot tin roof"). A simile makes a direct comparison between two qualities or things, and helps to point up likenesses which reveal character, situation, or meaning. A metaphor makes an indirect comparison between dissimilarities ("God is my fortress"). There are other kinds of imagery, but all serve to set up comparisons, connotations, or suggestions which enlarge the literal meaning expressed in speech.

Furthermore, the use of a large number of similar images affects the tone of a play. The dark, somber quality of *Hamlet*, for example, is partially explained by the overwhelming number of images concerned with death and decay. An audience may not be aware of this imagery, but its frequent repetition unconsciously influences audience reaction.

Dialogue, like the other elements of a play, must use both the familiar and the unfamiliar (the typical and the individual). Aristotle said that good dialogue should be both *clear* and *distinctive*. Clarity results from the use of ordinary words, but familiar words when used alone may lead to dullness. "Diction becomes distinguished and nonprosaic by the use of unfamiliar terms, i.e., strange words, metaphors, lengthened forms, and everything that deviates from the ordinary modes of speech. But a whole statement in such terms will be either a riddle or a barbarism," added Aristotle. Good dialogue, then, should strike a middle ground between overly familiar and strange language. The familiar gives clarity, the strange adds variety.

Dialogue should also be *adapted to the stage*. Sometimes a dramatist writes speeches which sound stilted and unnatural when spoken because he has failed to take into account both the limitations and the possibilities of the voice and ear. The good playwright is always concerned with how dialogue will sound, and how the human voice will affect the written language.

The basic criterion for judging dialogue, however, is its *appropriateness* to the characters, the situation, the level of probability, and the type of play. Almost any type of dialogue will be acceptable to an audience if it is in keeping with the other elements in the script.

SPECTACLE, SETTING, AND COSTUMES

After dialogue, the visual elements of a play are the playwright's principal means of expression. The reader must fill in those elements which are provided by a stage production. Unless he can envision the action, the characters, the lighting, the setting, the costumes, the properties, and the spatial relationships, he may fail to grasp the power of the material.

Many older plays contain almost no stage directions to describe the setting or the movement and physical appearance of the characters. The dialogue, therefore, must be analyzed carefully for information about these elements. As the visual background became increasingly important in the nineteenth century, stage directions became detailed correspondingly and have continued to give the reader considerable help in visualization.

The functions of settings and costumes are several. First, they *give information*. They help to establish where and when the action occurs (a living room, a castle, a prison; the historical period, the time of day, and the season of the year). Second, they *aid in characterization*. They help to establish such social factors as the economic level, the class, and the profession to which the characters belong. They aid in projecting the psychological aspects of character through demonstrating tastes (in the clothes worn, the rooms in which the characters live, and the like). Psychological factors are also revealed through the spatial relationships among characters.

Charles Kean's production of Shakespeare's *Henry VIII* in 1859. The scenery and costumes used typify the antiquarian approach in vogue at that time. Courtesy of the Victoria & Albert Museum. Crown Copyright.

Settings help to *establish the level of probability*. An abstract setting suggests one level of probability to an audience, while a completely realistic setting indicates another. Costumes, lighting, the actors' gestures and movement all establish the play's level of reality. The setting establishes *mood and atmosphere* by giving clues about the relative seriousness of the action, and by providing the proper environment for tragedy or comedy, fantasy or realism.

Settings, like the other elements of a play, must be *appropriate* and *expressive of the play's values*; they should have both *clarity* and *distinction*; and should be *practicable*. (The physical problems of transferring the written script to the stage will be considered at length in Part Four of this book.)

FORM IN DRAMA

The parts of drama may be combined in a number of ways, and certain recurring combinations have led to the division of plays according to their dramatic form. Because it has been used to designate a variety of concepts, *form* is difficult to define. A basic meaning is the arrangement or shaping of a work of art.

Ultimately, there are three determinants of form. First, form is affected by the material being shaped. In actuality, it is difficult, if not impossible, to separate form and matter, since no one can comprehend a formless object. Nevertheless, the matter (the action, the characters, the ideas) of comedy differs sufficiently from that of tragedy to indicate that one has been shaped to arouse laughter or ridicule while the other is designed to instigate pity or fright.

Second, the writer (or the maker of an object) is a determinant of form. Each man's view of life and drama differs somewhat from that of others, and his own peculiar talents and intentions show in his work. Thus, while both Sophocles and Euripides wrote tragedies, the forms of their plays show certain differences. Third, the intended purpose of an object helps to determine its form. Tragedy must have a design quite different from comedy.

Since no two plays ever have the same material, author, and purpose, each play is unique. On the other hand, all plays share certain qualities. Because each play is both unique and similar to other works, two major concepts of form have developed: form as *fixed* and as *organic*. The doctrine of fixed forms suggests that the characteristics of dramatic types can be clearly isolated and defined, and that plays may be judged according to how well they adhere to the requirements of a particular type. Organic form, on the other hand, suggests that a play takes shape and grows as a plant does, and that each play must be free to follow its own needs, its own laws, without reference to any previous ideas of form.

Each of these two views is partially right. Most plays can be classified according to type, and the major characteristics of each type can be listed. Furthermore, in criticizing a play, it is usually helpful to compare it with other works of the same type, and references to categories may save much time (for example, a term such as *comedy of manners* summarizes many qualities and communicates quickly, provided that all readers understand the meaning of the designation).

On the other hand, each play is unique in some respects and should be appreciated for its individuality. Sometimes it is difficult to classify a play according to form, and the attempt to label it often assumes more importance than understanding it. For example, arguments as to whether *Death of a Salesman* can rightfully be called a tragedy have frequently consumed undue attention in analysis. One form is not necessarily better than another, for there are both excellent and poor examples of each. Thus, while the classification of plays according to form is often helpful, it should not be overemphasized.

An almost endless number of forms and subforms have been

suggested by critics. Ultimately, all are derived from three basic qualities: the serious, the comic, and the seriocomic. In turn, these three divisions are epitomized in the three primary forms: tragedy, comedy, and melodrama.

TRAGEDY. A tragedy presents a genuinely serious action, and a mood which underscores the play's serious intention is maintained throughout (although there may be moments of comic relief). A tragedy raises important questions about the meaning of man's existence, his moral nature, and his social and psychological relationships.

Most of the tragedies written prior to the eighteenth century show an interaction between cosmic and human forces: a god, providence, or some moral power independent of man usually affects the outcome of the action as much as do the human factors. Many plays imply that the protagonist has violated a moral order which must be vindicated and re-established. Since superhuman forces are at work, the outcome often seems inevitable and predetermined by fate.

Beginning in the eighteenth century, the supernatural element gradually disappeared leaving only social and psychological forces. Consequently, the conflicts were reduced to those of the strictly human realm. The action no longer involves the will in conflict with divine laws, but rather is restricted to the will in conflict with human laws, institutions, and psychological forces. Since man-made problems may be understood and solved, happy resolutions are more easily justified. Because this later drama has been concerned primarily with everyday problems, many have refused to call it tragedy and have substituted instead the term *drama* or *drame*.

The protagonist of tragedy is a person whom we can understand and who arouses our sympathy and admiration. In some cases, however, our admiration and sympathy may be limited. Macbeth, Richard III, and Medea are examples of tragic protagonists who have noble qualities and whose indomitable wills we can admire, but of whose actions we cannot approve. Normally, the protagonist is ethically superior but not perfect: he is sufficiently above the average to inspire approval, but he has certain imperfections which make him enough like ourselves to be understandable and human.

Most often the tragic protagonist encounters disaster through his pursuit of a worthy aim; in following one ideal he violates some other moral or social law which overpowers him. A recurring motif of serious drama is the imposition of a duty, the performance of which will inevitably lead to loss of life, love, reputation, or peace of mind. The protagonist thus is faced with choosing between two lines of action, each of which under other circumstances would be good, but which have been placed in seemingly irreconcilable opposition.

In most tragedies written prior to the eighteenth century the protagonists are members of the ruling class, but in succeeding periods they have been drawn increasingly from the middle and lower classes. Many critics have questioned whether the average man can acquire the stature necessary to become a tragic hero. There seems little basis, however, for the assumption that social class has any connection with nobility of character and action. Although most modern serious drama is less powerful than the best tragedies of the Greeks and of Shakespeare, the difference is one of degree. (The reverence accorded to tragedy seldom extends to other forms; for example, few critics have ever implied that a play should not be called a comedy merely because it is less powerful than certain other comedies or because it differs from the work of other periods.)

The emotional effect of tragedy is usually described as the "arousal of pity and fear," but these basic emotions include a wide range of other responses: understanding, compassion, admiration, apprehension, foreboding, dread, awe, and terror. Pity and fear are rooted in two instinctive human reactions: the desire for self-preservation and concern for the welfare of others. Aristotle, in the *Poetics*, says pity is aroused by the apprehension of some pain or harm about to befall someone like ourselves; that were we in the position of the endangered person we would feel fear. Thus, pity and fear are complementary emotions. To feel pity, we must perceive some likeness between ourselves and the tragic character, and we must be able to imagine ourselves in his situation.

Aristotle further argues that if we fear too much for ourselves we cannot pity others, for panic drives out altruistic concerns. Fear, then, is an emotion which stems from the instinct for self-preservation, while pity transcends self-concern. Fear enables us to identify with the struggling protagonist, while pity carries us outside of ourselves and unites us with all that we admire in humanity. The degree to which these responses are aroused by a particular play depends upon the nature of the protagonist and the action in which he is involved.

COMEDY.   The action of comedy is based on some deviation from normality in incident, character, or thought. The deviation, however, must not pose a serious threat to the well-being of normal persons, and a comic (or "in fun") mood must be maintained. There is no subject, regardless of how trivial or important, which cannot be treated in comedy, provided that it is placed in a framework which exploits its incongruities.

Comedy also demands a treatment which will allow the audience to view the situation, characters, or ideas objectively. Henri Bergson, in *Laughter*, has stated that comedy requires an anesthesia of the heart, for it is difficult to laugh at anything with which we are too closely allied either through sympathy or hatred. For example, we might find the sight of a man slipping on a banana peel ludicrous, but if we discover that he has recently undergone a serious operation, our concern will destroy the laughter. Likewise, we may dislike some things so intensely that we cannot see their ridiculous qualities. On the other hand, an audience cannot be objective about all elements of a comedy, for sympathy must be aroused for the normal. Part of comic pleasure comes from witnessing the eventual triumph of the normal over a threat from the abnormal.

The variety found in the comic form may be attributed to three factors: the relative emphasis placed on situation, character, or idea; the degree of objectivity with which the protagonist is treated; and the nature and implications of the conflict. Because of its wide range, comedy is frequently divided into a number of subcategories. The most common of these may be of some help in understanding the limits of the comic form.

A *comedy of situation* shows the ludicrous results of placing characters in unusual circumstances. For example, a number of persons are planning to attend a masked ball, but each, for his own reasons, tries to conceal his intentions. The devices for getting rid of each other, the attempts to elude discovery when all appear at the same ball, the reactions upon being recognized, and the eventual reconciliation of the characters make up the comic action. In such a play, character and idea are of minor importance.

A *comedy of character* grows out of the eccentricities of the comic protagonist. For example, some of Molière's best plays show the ridiculous results of hypochondria, miserliness, and hypocrisy.

A *comedy of ideas* develops a conflict over a concept or a way of thought. This type is probably best exemplified in the work of George Bernard Shaw.

A *comedy of manners* combines attributes of comedies of situation, character, and idea. It is based upon incongruities which arise from the adherence to an accepted code of behavior at the expense of normal desires and responses. "Comedy of manners" is usually applied only to plays about aristocratic and sophisticated characters who converse in sparkling and witty dialogue. The latter characteristic has also given rise to another label for these plays, *comedy of wit.*

Social comedy is related to both the "comedy of manners" and the "comedy of ideas," for it treats social values, standards of behavior, or accepted ways of thought. It is more inclusive than either of the other categories, since it need not be restricted to fashionable society, and in it *ideas* may be defined more broadly. If the comedy aims at remedying society or behavior, it is sometimes called "corrective comedy."

A *romantic comedy* treats the struggles, often those connected with a love affair, of characters who are basically admirable. It is best illustrated by Shakespeare's *Twelfth Night* and *As You Like It*, in which the main characters are lovers pursuing normal and sympathetic goals. These characters arouse a comic response only because of the devices they use in seeking happiness and the misunderstandings which result. The more boisterous action is relegated to subplots and minor characters. Thus, romantic comedy reverses the usual comic pattern, in which the sympathetic characters play minor roles while the major emphasis is placed on the ridiculous characters.

Many critics treat *farce* as a separate form, although there is little to distinguish it from a comedy of situation. Nevertheless, farce is often used as a classification for those plays, or portions of plays, which rely principally upon buffoonery or accidental occurrences. Pies in the face, falls, beatings, the naïve or mistaken views of simple characters, the ludicrous situation arising from coincidences or circumstantial evidence exemplify the devices of farce. Farce is generally thought to have no purpose beyond entertainment. While it is true that some farcical plays seem to be without serious purpose, farce is an important element in many of the most famous comedies, particularly those of Aristophanes and Molière.

Although these subcategories are the most usual ones, many others exist. Most comedies can be placed in one of the divisions discussed above, but almost all will have some elements which relate them to other types. A comedy of character, for instance, may contain elements normally associated with farce, a comedy of manners, or a comedy of ideas. Labels, therefore, need to be used with some flexibility if they are to be helpful.

All comedy seeks to arouse emotions which lie in a range between joy and scorn. At one extreme, Shakespeare's "romantic comedies" elicit a response which can best be described as a feeling of well-being. They may bring forth smiles or quiet laughter, but seldom boisterous laughter. On the other hand, Ben Jonson's *Volpone* at times becomes almost too painful for laughter. These extremes of the gentlest and the bitterest ridicule mark the limits of comic response.

Comedy seldom raises great moral and philosophical questions as tragedy does. Rather, it concentrates upon man in his social relationships. It reaffirms the need for a society which allows normal human impulses adequate scope while putting a check on deviations which threaten to destroy what is good in it.

MELODRAMA. Although the term *melodrama* was not widely used prior to the nineteenth century, the form has existed since the fifth century B.C. In some periods it has been called *tragi-comedy*, and today

Many variations on melodrama were exploited in the nineteenth century. Among the most popular were the equestrian dramas, which combined daring horsemanship with melodramatic plots. The illustration above depicts a performance at Astley's Amphitheatre in London in 1815. From *Londina Illustrata*.

melodramas are often labeled *dramas* because the term *melodrama* is in disrepute.

A melodrama deals with a serious action. Its seriousness, however, is only temporary and is usually attributable to the malicious designs of an unsympathetic character. A happy resolution is achieved, therefore, by neutralizing or destroying the power of the villain.

Melodrama depicts a world in which good and evil are clearly separated, and the conflict almost always involves a sharply defined moral issue. There is seldom any question as to where the audience's sympathy should lie.

The characters in melodrama are divided normally into those who are completely sympathetic and those who are completely antipathetic. For the sake of variety, there may also be one or more simple-minded or uninhibited characters who provide comic relief. The unsympathetic characters usually initiate (or set in motion) all of the complications, while the sympathetic characters seek only to free themselves from danger. Thus, the characters do not grow and change, as in tragedy, for each has made his choice before the play begins and remains consistent throughout.

The action of melodrama develops a powerful threat against the well-being of a wholly admirable and innocent protagonist. It shows his entanglement in a web of circumstances and his eventual rescue from death or ruin, usually at the last possible moment.

The appeals, therefore, are strong and basic, for the incidents, which seek to build the most powerful suspense possible, create a desire to see wronged innocence vindicated and unchecked evil chastised. The emotions aroused by melodrama range from dread and concern for the protagonist to hatred for the antagonist.

Melodrama has a double ending in which the good characters are rescued and rewarded and the evil are detected and punished. Thus, this form is related to tragedy through the seriousness of its action, and to comedy through its happy conclusion. It has been a popular form throughout history, for it assures audiences that good always triumphs over evil.

STYLE

Although the basic characteristics of a dramatic form remain unchanged, plays of the same type vary considerably from period to period and from author to author. One of the factors which accounts for this variety is style. Like form, *style* is difficult to define because it has been used to designate many concepts. Basically, however, style is a quality which results from a characteristic mode of expression or method of presentation. It may be applied to the dramatic expression of a period, a nation, a movement, or an author.

In most periods the dramas of many nations have shared common qualities which stem from contemporary religious, philosophical, and psychological beliefs, and from current dramatic and theatrical conventions. As a result, we may speak of an eighteenth-century style. Within a period, however, there are differences which are attributable to nationality, and we may distinguish a French from an English style. The dramas written by the adherents of romanticism, expressionism, and other movements also show typical qualities which permit us to identify the stylistic features of these movements. Finally, the plays of each individual author have distinctive qualities which set them off from the work of all other writers. Thus, we may speak of Shakespeare's or Sophocles' style.

Most contemporary discussions of theatre and drama treat style primarily in terms of period and movement. These aspects will be explored

A scene from Giraudoux's *Ondine* showing the use of movement to establish style and mood. Directed by Willard Welsh.

in some detail in the chapters which follow. Style is usually divided into a number of categories: classicism, neoclassicism, romanticism, realism, naturalism, expressionism, and symbolism. Since each of these is associated with a specific period, or periods, their treatment also includes a consideration of style as it relates to an age.

Style in the theatre is the result of three basic influences. First, it is grounded in a fundamental conception of truth and reality. Dramatists belonging to different movements or living in different periods have found varying answers to the questions: What constitutes ultimate truth? To what sources shall we look in our search for reality? At times it has been argued that surface appearances mask the true reality found in the inner workings of the mind or in the spiritual realm. At others, it has been maintained that truth is restricted to that which can be studied objectively, and, therefore, is to be found only in those things which can be felt, tasted, seen, heard, or smelled. To advocates of the latter view, the details of daily existence hold the key to truth, while to the former the same details only hide the truth. Playwrights in all ages have attempted to depict the truth as they have seen it. But each playwright's conception of truth is determined by his basic temperament and talents, and the religious, philosophical, social, and psychological influences on him. Because each age and movement has many homogenous features, we may generalize about the conceptions of truth which underlie its artistic products; within this broad framework we may then isolate the views of a particular author. In such definitions will be found the raw material of drama and one of the basic determinants of style.

Second, style results from the manner in which the playwright employs his means of expression. Given his particular view of reality, the dramatist must search for an adequate mode to communicate it. His perceptions will be reflected in the kinds of situations, characters, and ideas he invents, in his manipulation of language, and in his suggestions for the use of setting and costumes. Thus, the playwright who believes that truth is embodied in the details of daily existence will probably invent incidents and characters modeled closely upon contemporary life, and his dialogue, settings, and costumes will mirror faithfully the speech, places, clothing, and behavior of daily existence. On the other hand, the playwright who believes that truth must be sought in some psychological or spiritual realm will depart from the standards of observable reality and may deliberately distort or eliminate details in order to force the audience to look behind the surface. Thus, the playwright, through his handling of the parts of drama, expresses his particular vision of human conduct.

Third, style results from the manner in which the play is presented in the theatre. The directing, acting, scenery, costumes, lighting, and sound used to translate the play from the written word to the stage all affect its stylistic attributes. Normally the producer of a play attempts to find a theatrical style which is as close a counterpart of the written style as possible. On the other hand, plays are sometimes presented in a manner which is at variance with that of the script. Such departures, however, are usually made deliberately and for the sake of some effect greater than that which could be achieved by the typical approach.

Ultimately, then, style in drama and production results from the manner in which means have been adapted to ends. It does much to create that sense of unity and wholeness which is aroused by all effective drama.

In many contemporary discussions of the theatre, the term *stylization* is often used to indicate any deviation from realism. This terminology may be helpful but it is very imprecise, since realism is itself a style and since the departure from realism might be in any number of directions.

A discussion of structure, form, and style must remain abstract, however, until applied to specific examples. The chapters which follow show how these principles have been put into practice. Each chapter in

Parts Two and Three summarizes briefly the development of theatre and drama in a particular era, exploring the artistic and intellectual background and the theatrical conventions needed for understanding the plays of that period. One or more representative plays are analyzed and treated both as documents tied to a specific time and place and as artistic products which transcend their age. Pertinent points about structure, form, and style are considered and a critical method is shown in practice.

A chronological order has been followed because each period is in part an outgrowth of what has gone before. After following the theatre through history, Part Four examines in detail the principles and working procedures of the contemporary American theatre. Thus, the historical material will provide a perspective from which to view our present situation.

PART TWO

THE THEATRE OF THE PAST

Chapter 4

THE THEATRE OF ANCIENT GREECE

THE ORIGINS OF THEATRE

No one really knows how the theatre began, but there are many theories about its inception in Greece. The theory most widely accepted today is based upon a supposed relationship between theatre and ritual. The argument is developed as follows:

In the beginning, man viewed the natural forces of the world, even the seasonal changes, as unpredictable, and he offered sacrifices in an attempt to influence the unknown and feared powers. Gradually the means used in making these appeals were formalized and became rituals; those persons who were especially effective at performing the rites took on these duties for the entire tribe and became priests. Ritual contains many of the seeds of drama, for the early priest could wear a mask and assume the appearance of another—a supernatural being, a man, or even an animal.

Facing Part Two: An ivory statuette of a tragic actor; probably Roman although the Greek tragic actor of the Hellenistic period undoubtedly wore similar costumes and masks. Note the high headdress, distorted features of the mask, and thick-soled boots concealed beneath robe. Statuette stands on two pegs used for attachment to a base. Reprinted from *Monumenti Inediti*, Volume XI, 1879: Instituto di Corrisp. Archeol.

Above. The theatre at Epidaurus during a recent production. Note the modern stage house erected over the ruins of the ancient *skene*.

He might act out certain activities—such as hunting—in order to insure a favorable outcome. The priest, consequently, had to have certain attributes of the actor as well as the priest.

Stories which explained fancifully the origins, or veiled the secrets, of particular rituals gradually appeared. As man progressed in his understanding of the world, certain rites, such as those involving human sacrifice, were abandoned, but the stories which grew up around them remained and came to be called myths. Eventually the origins of the myths were forgotten, but the myths persisted as valued stories. These formed the material for drama. As religion and drama gradually separated, so too did the functions of the actor and the priest.

This theory has much to recommend it, since it is probably true that primitive people do not distinguish among the various aspects of their lives (work, religion, theatre) as clearly as more advanced societies do; the transition to specialized and separate activities comes about only gradually. The weakness of the theory lies in the fact that all of man's attempts to deal with his world (science, philosophy, art) were in the beginning part of ritual just as much as the theatre was. It does not explain why the theatre continued to grow in importance after it was divorced from ritual.

A clue to the origin of theatre in the nature of man is found in the writings of Aristotle, a Greek philosopher of the fourth century B.C., who stated that there is an instinct for imitation in human beings—that man both enjoys imitating others and seeing such imitations. Furthermore, he added, imitation is one of man's chief methods of learning about his world. Children learn speech and the accepted modes of behavior from others. Most persons also have a desire to know how it would feel to be someone else, or why others act as they do. Imitation, therefore, is a source of understanding, knowledge, and pleasure.

The storytelling instinct is also basic in man, and this impulse, in part, gave rise to drama. Aristotle recorded that Greek drama originated in the dithyrambs, or hymns, in honor of the god Dionysus. These hymns related the story of Dionysus; gradually episodes were acted out and drama emerged. There are numerous other theories about the origins of drama, but by the time our records begin, the theatre was already a powerful force in the life of Greece.

THE BEGINNINGS OF DRAMA IN GREECE

Although there is some indication that drama appeared in Egypt as early as 4000 B.C., the existing references are scarce and unclear. It is to Greece that we must turn for the first definite information about the theatre and for the first great drama of the world.

For several centuries Greek drama was presented only in connection with the festivals honoring Dionysus, the god of wine and fertility. Supposedly the son of Zeus (the greatest of Greek gods) and Semele (a mortal), Dionysus was killed and dismembered, and then resurrected by Zeus. The myths which grew up around him were closely related to the life cycle and to seasonal changes: birth, growth, decay, death, and rebirth; spring, summer, fall, and winter. His worship was designed to ensure the return of spring. As the god of wine and fertility, he also represented many of the world's irrational forces, and his worship was a recognition of man's elemental passions. In the early centuries of Dionysian worship, sexual orgies and drunkenness were accepted parts of the religious impulse, but as time went by these were gradually sublimated, though the basic purpose of Dionysian worship—the inducement of fertility—remained unchanged.

The inclusion of such irrational forces within the sphere of religion illustrates well the Greek belief that the failure to give due honor to any part of nature might lead to destruction. The Greeks constantly sought to achieve harmony among all of the conflicting forces within and around themselves.

The worship of Dionysus was introduced into Greece from Asia Minor around the thirteenth century B.C. By the seventh or eighth centuries, contests were already being held for choral dances at the festivals in honor of Dionysus. These dances were accompanied by dithyrambs, or ecstatic hymns, in honor of the god. It is out of these hymns and dances that Aristotle says drama developed.

The Greeks did not have a holy day comparable to our sabbath. Rather they had a series of religious festivals throughout the year honoring various gods. By the sixth century B.C. there were four festivals each year in honor of Dionysus alone: the Rural Dionysia (in December); the Lenaia (in January); the Anthesteria (around the end of February); and the City or Great Dionysia (around the end of March). Plays came to be performed at all of these, with the exception of the Anthesteria, but no plays were given at the festivals in honor of any of the other gods.

The first definite record of drama in Greece is found in 534 B.C. In that year the City Dionysia was reorganized and a contest for tragedy was instituted. It is assumed that drama existed prior to that time, for otherwise a contest would be difficult to explain. The only recorded dramatist of this period was Thespis; it was he who won the first contest. Since he acted in his own plays, he is also the first known actor, hence the practice of calling actors *Thespians.*

The drama of Thespis was relatively simple, since it involved only one actor and a chorus. This does not mean that there was only one speaking character in each play, but rather that all characters were played by the same actor. This single actor used masks in shifting his identity;

when he left the stage to change roles, the chorus filled the intervals with singing and dancing. The chorus, therefore, was the principal unifying force in this early drama. Face-to-face conflict between opposing characters, which most later periods have considered a necessary feature of drama, was impossible so long as there was only one actor. It was not until a second actor was introduced at the beginning of the fifth century that drama as we know it became possible.

THE FIFTH CENTURY

Although drama was written and performed in Greece for many centuries, plays by only five writers—Aeschylus, Sophocles, Euripides, Aristophanes, and Menander—now exist. Out of the vast number of plays written, only forty-six survive—thirty-two tragedies, twelve comedies, and two satyr plays. All but four of these plays were written during the fifth century.

Aeschylus (525–456) is the earliest dramatist whose plays have survived. He began competing in the tragic contests around 499 B.C., but he did not win a victory until 484; after that time he won thirteen contests. The titles of seventy-nine of his plays have come down to us but only seven works remain: *The Persians* (472), *Seven Against Thebes* (467), the trilogy of plays made up of *Agamemnon*, *Choephoroe*, and *Eumenides* (458), *The Suppliants*, and *Prometheus Bound* (exact dates unknown). *The Persians* is unique among surviving Greek dramas in having been based on an historical event (the Persian war) rather than on mythology, although other plays on historical subjects were written.

Aeschylus' major innovation in drama was the introduction of the second actor, which allowed face-to-face conflict for the first time. The increased emphasis upon the actor reduced the importance of the chorus, though it remained a dominant force.

The power of Aeschylus' drama can best be appreciated through his trilogy, usually called the *Oresteia*, one of the great monuments of dramatic literature. Aeschylus was almost always concerned with man's relationship to the gods and the universe. The *Oresteia* demonstrates his interests well, for here he deals with growth in the concept of justice. In the first two plays the characters conceive of justice as personal revenge, but in the final play, private justice is replaced by the impersonal power of the state. This evolutionary process is demonstrated through a powerful story of murder, revenge, and remorse.

Sophocles (496–406) is frequently called the greatest of the Greek dramatists. He is credited with over a hundred plays, of which only seven now exist: *Ajax* (dated variously from 450 to 440), *Antigone* (around 440), *Oedipus the King* (approximately 430 to 425), *Philoctetes* (409),

Electra and *Trachiniae* (dates unknown, though considered to be late plays), and *Oedipus at Colonus* (written shortly before Sophocles' death). In addition a substantial part of *The Trackers*, a satyr play, is extant. He won eighteen contests, the first in 468 when he defeated Aeschylus. Sophocles introduced a third actor and thus allowed for still greater dramatic complexity than had been possible with two actors. He was much more concerned with human relationships than with the religious and philosophical issues which had interested Aeschylus. His dramas also place more emphasis upon building skillful climaxes and well-developed episodes than did those of Aeschylus, which were sometimes crude in their structure. The qualities of Sophocles' drama will be explored at greater length in the detailed examination of *Oedipus the King*.

Euripides (484–406) was the last of the great Greek tragedians. He is said to have written ninety-two plays, of which seventeen tragedies have survived. Among these the most famous are: *Alcestis* (438), *Medea* (431), *Hippolytus* (428), *Ion*, and *Electra* (dates unknown), *The Trojan Women* (415), and *The Bacchae* (produced after his death). In addition, *The Cyclops* is the only complete satyr play which now exists. Although Euripides achieved great popularity in later times, he was not widely appreciated in his own day, winning only five victories in the tragic contests.

Euripides reduced the role of the chorus even further than his predecessors had, and in his works its connection with the rest of the play was often vague. His interests were principally philosophical and psychological. He was a skeptic who questioned many Athenian ideals; even the Gods did not escape his probing and were frequently made to appear petty and ineffectual; he examined the motives of his characters and found little to admire. But he also turned toward melodrama in his plots and frequently resorted to contrived endings. Thus he has been admired for his ideas and his psychological realism, but has been criticized for faulty dramatic structure. With his death, the great era of Greek tragedy came to an end.

The characteristics of Greek tragedy can best be appreciated through a detailed examination of a representative example. Here, *Oedipus the King* will be used. First, however, it is necessary to study the theatrical conditions which prevailed about 430 B.C., the approximate date of its first production.

PLAY PRODUCTION IN GREECE

The City Dionysia was one of the great religious and civic occasions of the year, and it was at this festival that *Oedipus the King* was presented. If a tragic dramatist wished to enter plays at the City Dionysia, he applied for a chorus to the principal civic magistrate (the *archon eponymous*). It is not known how this official decided among the applicants, but three tragic writers were granted choruses for each City Dionysia.

The magistrate also appointed the *choregoi,* or wealthy citizens who bore the expense of the choruses. One *choregus* was appointed for each dramatist and the *choregoi* and playwrights were matched by lot. *Choregoi* for the next City Dionysia were appointed approximately one month after the conclusion of the preceding City Dionysia. This allowed almost a year for planning and rehearsal.

The *choregus* paid for the training of the chorus and their costumes, the musicians, the supernumerary actors and their costumes, and perhaps for the scenery. In other words, he was responsible for everything except the speaking actors. Since he might be either generous or miserly, the *choregus* could seriously affect the playwright's chances of mounting his play satisfactorily. Usually, however, the *choregus* looked upon the proper outfitting of his plays as a civic duty and as a matter of personal pride.

If a playwright were granted a chorus, he supplied three tragedies and a satyr play, as well as any music which might accompany them. With rare exceptions, the playwright also directed his own works and was in charge of the production as a whole. Until the time of Sophocles the playwright acted in his own plays, and many did after that time as well. For his efforts, the playwright was no doubt given some financial remuneration by the state and there was a prize for the winner of the contest, but the amount of money which a playwright might receive for his work is unknown. It is extremely doubtful, however, that any of the Greek dramatists of the fifth century earned a living from work as a writer.

The state paid the actors and supplied their costumes; it also furnished the theatre in which the plays were performed. Dramatic production in the fifth century, thus, was financed either by wealthy citizens or by the state, and it was looked upon as a religious and civic function of major importance.

The City Dionysia, at which the plays were produced, was considered so important that no legal proceedings were allowed and prisoners were released during the festival. It opened with a procession in which the statue of the god Dionysus was taken from his temple at the foot of the Acropolis and carried outside the city. His entry into Athens was then re-enacted to the accompaniment of much revelry. The ceremony concluded with a sacrifice to the god.

The next principal feature of the festival was the performance of dithyrambs (hymns to Dionysus sung and danced by choruses of fifty). There were ten choruses each year, five for men and five for boys. Next came the contest for comedies, five being given on a single day; this was followed by three days devoted to the tragedies. On each of these days, three tragedies and a satyr play were performed. After the festival ended, there was a day devoted to awarding prizes and to considering complaints of misbehavior during the festival.

At this civic and religious celebration everyone was welcome. Admission was probably free originally, but was later set at the small sum of two obols. A public fund was established, however, to provide tickets for those who could not afford the price of admission. The theatre was, therefore, considered to be the right of everyone rather than a function for the few.

The audiences took a keen interest in the contests. At each City Dionysia prizes were awarded to the best plays (there was a prize for the best comedy and for the best group of tragedies, the honor being shared by the playwright and the choregus), to the best tragic actor, and to the best dithyrambic choruses. The state supervised the judging, and elaborate precautions were taken to insure that voting would be secret.

THE THEATRE OF DIONYSUS

The plays were presented in the Theatre of Dionysus situated on the slope of the Acropolis above the Temple of Dionysus. This theatre underwent

Below. The ruins of the Theatre of Dionysos at Athens today. Evidences of the remodeling of *c.* 270 A.D. remain. From Ernst Fiechter, *Antike Griechische Theaterbauten*, courtesy Verlag W. Kohlhammer GmbH. *Right*. Ground plan of the Precinct of Dionysos at Athens showing the Theatre and the Temple of Dionysos. From Dorpfeld-Reisch, *Das Griechische Theater*, 1896.

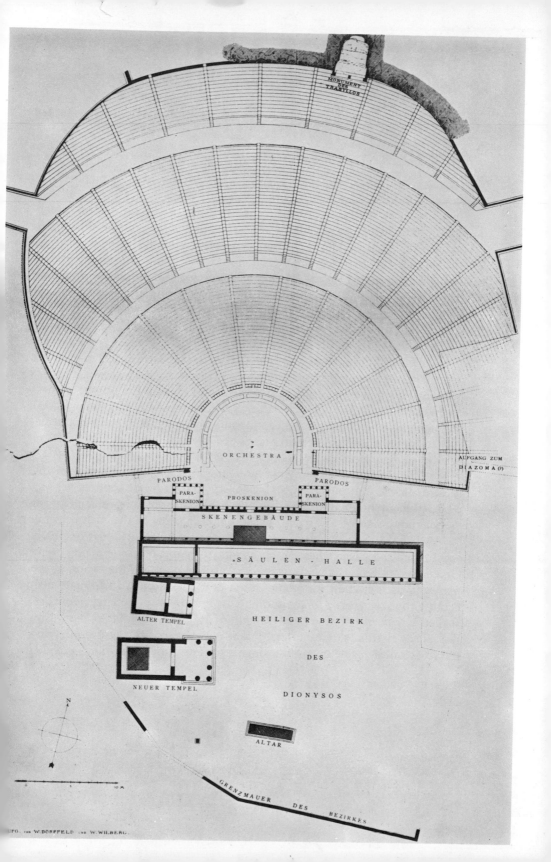

MONUMENT
DES
THRASYLLOS

ORCHESTRA

AUFGANG ZUM
DIAZOMA (?)

PARODOS   PARODOS

PARA-   PARA-
SKENION   PROSKENION   SKENION

SKENENGEBÄUDE

»SÄULEN-HALLE«

ALTER TEMPEL

HEILIGER BEZIRK

NEUER TEMPEL

DES

DIONYSOS

N

ALTAR

GRENZMAUER DES BEZIRKES

0   10 M.

AUFG. von W.DÖRPFELD und W.WILBERG.

Drawings on both pages by Ernst Fiechter of varying conceptions of the stage house for the Theatre of Dionysos in the fifth century B.C. From Fiechter, *Antike Griechische Theaterbauten*, courtesy Verlag W. Kohlhammer GmbH, Stuttgart.

many changes. In the sixth century it consisted of the hillside on which the spectators stood or sat, and a flat terrace at the foot of the hill for the performers. In the middle of this terrace or *orchestra* (the "dancing place") was an altar (or *thymele*). There was no stage or scenic background. Seats were gradually added for the spectators, forming an auditorium or *theatron* (the "seeing place"). During the fifth century this basic structure was gradually elaborated; a scene house was added, and the whole theatre was finally reconstructed in stone, though this reconstruction was not completed until well into the fourth century.

The auditorium was the first part of the theatre to assume a permanent form. Stadiumlike seating was provided by setting stones into the hillside. This auditorium was semicircular and curved around the orchestra (which was circular). The theatre was very large—it seated about 14,000 persons—and the orchestra was approximately sixty-five feet in diameter. The auditorium and the orchestra remained relatively unchanged, and there is little disagreement today about their features.

The stage house (or *skene*) was late in developing as a part of the theatre. It was the last part to be constructed in stone, and it was remodeled many times after that. For all of these reasons, it is difficult to get a clear impression of the scenic background of plays in the fifth century.

The skene (which was unknown in the sixth century) was originally constructed as a place where actors might dress and retire to change roles. Gradually this house came to be used as a background for the action of the play, and its usefulness for scenic purposes was exploited. In the late fifth century the skene was a long building which, with its projecting side wings (called *paraskena*), formed a rectangular background for the orchestra on the side away from the spectators. It was not joined to the auditorium, and the space on each side between the paraskena and the auditorium provided

entrances into the orchestra. These entrances are called *paradoi*. For a plan of the theatre as a whole see the illustration on page 57.

The appearance of the skene is much debated. Most of the plays are set before temples or palaces, but some take place outside of caves or tents, or in wooded landscapes. There is much controversy over the extent to which the stage may have been altered to meet these differing demands.

Since it was not entirely permanent, the appearance of the skene could have been changed from year to year, or from play to play. A series of holes has been discovered just forward of the skene's foundations, and it has been suggested that upright timbers, to which scenery was attached, were set in these holes. Such a device would permit rapid alterations in the scenic background. It is impossible to know the truth, but, considering the lack of realistic detail in the plays, it seems unlikely that the Greeks ever attempted to create the illusion of a real place in their theatre. Some indication of a play's setting may well have been given, however, through scenic devices.

It is generally agreed today that there was no raised stage in the theatre of the fifth century. Again, there is not enough evidence to settle the question definitely. Since the plays seem to require that the actors and the chorus mingle freely, if a platform were used it was probably low enough to allow free access between stage and orchestra. If there were no stage, both the chorus and actors would have used the acting area composed of the orchestra and the rectangular space formed by the scene house. The roof of the stage house also could be used when needed.

The actors most frequently entered from the stage house, while the chorus used the paradoi. There are examples, however, of the chorus entering from the stage house, and of actors using the paradoi. The number of openings required for entrances and exits varies from play to play, and this has led to some difference of opinion about the number of doorways in the stage house. It is customary to show three doors in the skene and one in each of the paraskena, but the number is far from certain.

When the available information about the Greek theatre structure is assembled, a fairly clear picture of its basic outlines emerges, but the

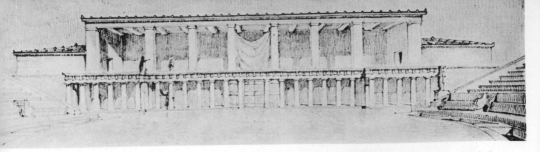

A conjectural reconstruction of the stage of the Theatre of Dionysos remodeled to conform to the Hellenistic ideal about 150 B.C. From Fiechter.

details of the scenic background remain uncertain. Some of the many possibilities may be seen in the preceding drawings.

While most of the action of Greek plays takes place out of doors, occasionally interiors must be shown. For example, most deaths occur off stage, but the bodies are frequently displayed afterward. For this purpose the large central doorway seems to have been opened and a wheeled platform moved forward. This device is called an *eccyclema* or *exaustra*.

Another effect frequently demanded in Greek plays is the appearance of gods. These characters may descend to the orchestra level or be lifted up from the orchestra to the roof of the stage house. For this purpose, a cranelike device called the *machina* was used. The overuse of gods to resolve difficult dramatic situations led to the expression *deus ex machina* to describe any contrived ending. The eccyclema and the machina are the only two machines which can definitely be ascribed to the fifth century, and these were not used extensively.

It is possible, however, that *periaktoi* were also in use, although these probably belong to a later period. Periaktoi are constructed of three flats put together to form a triangle; the triangle is then mounted on a central pivot. Since each surface can be exposed or concealed as desired, it may be used for sudden revelations or for suggesting changes of scene.

THE ACTOR

The number of speaking actors in Greek tragedy was restricted to three. There might be "extras" but these were not considered to be actors. In the second half of the fifth century the state supplied three speaking actors for each tragic playwright competing in the contests. One principal actor was assigned to each playwright by lot. The playwright and his principal actor then chose the other two actors. All were male and all acted in each of the four plays presented by the same dramatist. Since there were only three actors, each was expected to play a variety of roles.

The style of acting cannot be determined with any certainty. The plays themselves call for simple realistic actions (such as weeping, running, and falling on the ground). On the other hand, many elements argue against any marked realism. The fact that the same actor played many roles and that men assumed women's parts suggests that performances could never have been very close to real life. Furthermore, some plays could be performed by three actors only if the same role were played by a different actor in different scenes of the play. The large musical element, the use of dance, and the rather abstract treatment of the story also argue against a realistic style of acting.

The acting style, nevertheless, should not be thought of as devoid of clearly identifiable human actions. The details of daily life were stripped away, but the audience was still able to identify with the characters. The acting style suggested by the scripts may be characterized as simple, expressive, and idealized.

COSTUME

A precautionary note seems necessary at this point. Many theatre historians have failed to distinguish between the practices of the fifth century and those of later Greek times. Nowhere is the failure more misleading than in the treatment of costumes. Frequently the tragic actor is depicted as wearing a high headdress, a mask with distorted features, thick-soled boots, and padded clothing. This costume may have been typical of later periods, but has little to do with the practices of the fifth century, the more typical features of which are outlined below and shown in the accompanying illustrations.

All the actors in Greek tragedy wore masks constructed of lightweight linen, cork, or wood. There were several reasons for this practice: each actor played a number of roles; all the actors were male though many of the characters were female; the range of age and character types played by a single actor was great. (There is little evidence to support the argument that the mask acted as a megaphone for the voice.) Although the mouths were open, the features were not exaggerated to any marked de-

The Greek comic actor and his costume. Terracotta statuette from an Athenian grave *c.* fourth century B.C. Courtesy of the Metropolitan Museum of Art, Rogers Fund, 1913.

A redrawing from a vase painting of a type of costume probably used for tragedy in the fifth century B.C.

gree. Headdresses seem to have followed relatively closely those normally worn during the period.

A variety of clothing was used for stage purposes. A long-sleeved, ankle-length, heavily embroidered tunic, or *chiton*, was probably worn by supernatural beings and by non-Greek characters. This garment was not worn in Greek daily life. An ankle-length, sleeved, undecorated chiton, and a knee-length, sleeveless, undecorated chiton (both of which were worn in daily life) were used for the Greek characters. The selection of the costume was determined by its appropriateness to the role. The tragic actor usually wore a high-topped boot, called a *cothurnus*. This was a soft, flexible footcovering in common use at the time.

While the actor's appearance was somewhat changed from the normal by his costume (largely because of the mask or the embroidered garment), he remained relatively undistorted. His costume allowed for freedom of movement and speech and for the rapid changes of roles.

THE CHORUS, MUSIC, AND DANCE

Although the chorus had been composed of twelve members in the first part of the fifth century, its number was increased to fifteen by Sophocles. Usually the chorus performed in unison, but at times it was divided into two semichoruses of seven members, which might perform in turn or which might exchange or divide speeches. The chorus leader sometimes had solo lines, but the chorus spoke and sang as a group (though some modern editions of the plays divide the speeches and assign them to individual chorus members).

The chorus usually makes its entrance after the prologue (or opening scene) and remains until the end of the play. It serves many functions. First, it is an actor in the drama. It expresses opinions, gives advice, sometimes threatens to interfere in the events of the play. As a rule, it is sympathetically allied with the protagonist.

Second, the chorus often establishes the ethical framework of the play. It may express the author's views and set up a standard against which the actions of the characters can be judged. Third, the chorus is frequently the ideal spectator. It reacts to the events and characters as the author would like his audience to respond.

Fourth, the chorus helps to set the mood of the play and to heighten its dramatic effects. For example, a mood of foreboding may be created through the chorus' expression of doubts about what is to come; or the chorus may help to achieve more powerful reversals, as when its expression of elation is followed immediately by disastrous events.

Fifth, the chorus adds color, movement, and spectacle. Originally, all the choral interludes were accompanied by music and were both sung and danced. Thus, it offered powerful auditory and visual appeals.

Sixth, the chorus serves an important rhythmical function. This may best be explained through an analogy. A typical Greek temple has columns all around the exterior, without which there would be an uninteresting continuous blank wall. The columns serve to make the eye pause but do not prevent it from moving on. Greek drama without its choral passages would have a similar effect, for the action would move too fast. These retardations—these pauses in which to look backward and forward—contribute enormously to the over-all emotional effect; they are part of the design without which the whole would be incomplete and unsatisfying.

The exact nature of Greek music and dance is unknown. No Greek

Other possible costumes for tragedy. From Furtwängler-Reichold, *Griechische Vasenmalerei.* Series I, 1904.

Sophocles' *Electra*. Directed by George Kernodle.

music has come down to us, but we do know that the Greeks believed that both music and dance had ethical content—that some types were moral and others were immoral. Since tragedy displays a strong ethical bias, it is reasonable to assume that in most plays the music and dance displayed the qualities which the Greeks associated with stateliness and moral uprightness.

OEDIPUS THE KING

With this background in mind, Sophocles' *Oedipus the King* will now be examined as an example of Greek tragedy.

THEMES AND IDEAS. As in all great plays, there are a number of important themes. One is stated in the final lines of the play:

> Count no mortal happy till
> he has passed the final limit of his life secure from
> pain.

The whole play shows the fall of Oedipus from the place of highest honor to that of an outcast and demonstrates the uncertainty of human destiny. A second theme is man's limitation in controlling his fate. Oedipus is a man who attempts to do his best at all times. He wants to help his people. He has taken what he considers the necessary steps to avoid the terrible fate predicted by the oracle (that he will kill his father and marry his mother). But man is limited in his vision, no matter how he may attempt to avoid mistakes. The contrast, then, between man seeking to control his destiny and a relentless fate which determines destiny is clearly depicted. But while fate (or the will of the gods) is always the superior force in the play, it works through man. It is Jocasta's attempt to destroy the infant Oedipus, Oedipus' attempt to avoid his parents, and Oedipus' attempt to discover the murderer which lead inevitably to the outcome. And at the end, while Oedipus accepts his fate, as he must, he still does not see himself entirely as the instrument of the gods:

It was Apollo, friends, Apollo,
that brought this bitter bitterness, my sorrows to
completion.
But the hand that struck me
was none but my own.

It is significant that no attempt is made to explain why destruction comes to Oedipus. It is implied that man must submit to fate and that in struggling to avoid it he only becomes more entangled. There is then an irrational, or at least an unknowable, force at work. This idea is emphasized through the various attempts to communicate with the gods (through oracles) and to propitiate them. The plague is viewed as a punishment from the gods, the exiling of Oedipus is an attempt to placate them, but no one asks why the gods have decreed Oedipus' fate. The truth of the oracles is established, but the purpose is unclear. The Greek concept of the gods, however, did not demand that all the gods be benevolent, since all forces were deified whether good or evil. Therefore, a god might visit evil upon man, and man had to be constantly on guard not to offend any of the many gods.

Another theme, which may not have been a conscious one with Sophocles, is that of Oedipus as a scapegoat. The city of Thebes will be saved if the one guilty man can be found and punished. Oedipus, in a sense then, takes the sins of the city upon himself, and in his punishment lies the salvation of others. Thus, Oedipus becomes a sacrificial offering to the gods. There is a distant parallel here with the crucifixion of Christ, the sacrificial lamb offered up for the sins of all those who believe in Him.

A performance of *Oedipus the King* by the Greek National Theatre at Epidaurus. Directed by Alexis Minotis. Photograph courtesy of the Greek National Theatre.

This parallel cannot be extended very far, however, since there are more points of difference than of similarity in the two figures.

Another motif—blindness versus sight—is emphasized in poetic images and in various overt comparisons. A contrast is repeatedly drawn between the physical power of sight and the inner sight of understanding. For example, Tiresias, though blind, can see the truth which escapes Oedipus, while Oedipus, who has penetrated the riddle of the Sphinx, cannot solve the puzzle of his own life. When it is revealed to him, he blinds himself in an act of retribution.

These themes indicate that *Oedipus the King* is a comment in part on man's relationship to the gods and on man's attempt to control his own destiny. While the Greek views of these problems may not be ours, the problems and many of the implications are still vital and meaningful.

PLOT AND STRUCTURE. The skill with which *Oedipus the King* is constructed can be appreciated if we look at the complexity of the story (which actually begins with a prophecy prior to the birth of Oedipus) and compare this with the events which occur in the very limited time span of the play. There is a simultaneous movement backward and forward in time as the revelation of the past moves Oedipus ever nearer to his doom in the present.

The division of the play into a prologue and five episodes separated by choral passages is typical of Greek tragedy. The prologue is devoted principally to exposition: a plague is destroying the city of Thebes; Oedipus promises to help and explains the action already taken; Creon returns from Delphi with a command from the Oracle to find and punish the murderer of Laius; Oedipus promises to obey the command. Thus, all of the necessary information is given in a very brief scene, and the first important question (who is the murderer of Laius?) is raised. The prologue is followed by the *parados,* or entry of the chorus, and the first choral song, which recapitulates the plight of Thebes and offers prayers to the gods for deliverance.

The first episode begins with Oedipus' proclamation and curse upon the murderer. This proclamation has great dramatic power because Oedipus is unknowingly pronouncing a curse upon himself. Then Tiresias, the seer, enters. It is important to remember that Oedipus has sent for Tiresias on the advice of Creon, since otherwise Oedipus' suspicion of conspiracy between Creon and Tiresias is not understandable. Tiresias' refusal to answer questions provokes Oedipus' anger, the first display of a response which is developed forcefully throughout the first four episodes. It is his quick temper, we later discover, that caused Oedipus to kill Laius. By the time Tiresias has been driven to answer, Oedipus suspects some trickery. This complication is necessary, for had Oedipus called in Tiresias, heard his story and believed him, the play would be over. Sophocles, however,

Oedipus the King directed by Tyrone Guthrie, 1955. Center: Douglas Campbell as Oedipus. Rear: Eleanor Stuart as Jocasta, Robert Goodier as Creon. Production photograph by Donald McKague, courtesy of the Stratford Shakespearean Festival Foundation of Canada.

has boldly brought out the truth but has cast doubt upon it, for, as Oedipus points out, if Tiresias knew the truth why did he not speak out at the time of Laius' murder? The scene ends in a stalemate of accusations.

It is interesting to note that while all of the first four episodes move forward in the present, they go successively further backward in time. This first episode reveals only that part of the past immediately preceding Oedipus' arrival at Thebes.

The choral passage which follows the first episode reflects upon the previous scene, stating the confusion which Sophocles would wish the audience to feel. The chorus ends by declaring that since Oedipus has saved the city in the past it will continue to have faith in him until he is proven wrong.

The second episode builds logically upon the first. Creon comes to defend himself from the accusations of conspiracy with Tiresias. Oedipus, however, is not open to reason. Jocasta is drawn to the scene by the quarrel and she and the chorus persuade Oedipus to abate his anger. This quarrel illustrates Oedipus' complete faith in his own righteousness. In spite of Tiresias' accusation, no suspicion of his own guilt has entered his mind. Ironically, it is Jocasta's attempt to placate Oedipus which leads to his first suspicion about himself. She tells him that oracles are not to be believed and as evidence points to Laius' death, which did not come in the manner prophesied. But her description recalls to Oedipus the circumstances under which he has killed a man. He insists that Jocasta send for the one survivor of Laius' party. Thus, a considerable change occurs within this scene—the self-righteousness of Oedipus is shaken, and the possibility of his involvement creates additional suspense. The scene also continues the backward exploration of the past, for Oedipus tells of his life in Corinth, his visit to the Oracle of Delphi, and the murder of the man who is later discovered to have been Laius.

The choral song which follows is concerned with the questions Jocasta has raised about oracles. The chorus concludes that if oracles are proven untrue then the gods themselves are to be doubted. The song, while reflecting upon the scene immediately past, looks forward to a solution of the question.

Though Jocasta has called oracles into question, she obviously does not disbelieve in the gods themselves, for at the beginning of the third episode she makes offerings to them. She is interrupted, however, by the entrance of the Messenger from Corinth, who brings news of the death of Oedipus' supposed father, Polybus. But this news, rather than arousing grief, as one would expect, is greeted with rejoicing, for it seems to disprove the oracle which had predicted that Oedipus would kill his father. This seeming reversal only serves to heighten the effect of the following events. Oedipus still fears returning to Corinth because the oracle also has prophesied that he will marry his own mother. Thinking that he will set Oedipus' mind at ease, the Messenger reveals that he himself brought Oedipus as an infant to Polybus. The circumstances under which the Messenger acquired the child bring home the truth to Jocasta. This discovery leads to a complete reversal for Jocasta, for the oracles she has cast doubt upon in the preceding scene have suddenly been vindicated. She strives to stop Oedipus from making further inquiries, but he interprets her entreaties as fear that he may be of humble birth. Jocasta goes into the palace; it is the last we see of her, though her actions are later revealed.

This scene not only has revealed the truth to Jocasta, it has diverted attention from the murder of Laius to the birth of Oedipus. It goes backward in time to the infancy of Oedipus. Only one more step remains.

The choral song which follows is filled with romantic hopes, as the chorus speculates on Oedipus' parentage and suggests such possibilities as Apollo and the nymphs. The truth is deliberately kept at a distance here in order to make the following scene more powerful. These speculations, however, do serve to concentrate attention on the question while diverting it from the right solution.

This extremely brief choral song is followed by the entry of the

Herdsman (the sole survivor of Laius' party at the time of the murder and the person from whom the Corinthian Messenger had acquired the infant Oedipus). The Herdsman does not wish to speak, but he is tortured by Oedipus' servants into doing so. In this very rapid scene everything that has gone before is brought to a climax. We are taken back to the beginning of the story (Oedipus' birth), we learn the secret of his parentage, we see the truth of the oracle, we find out who murdered Laius, we discover that Oedipus is married to his mother. The climax is reached in Oedipus' cry of despair and disgust as he rushes into the palace. The brief choral song which follows comments upon the fickleness of fate and points to Oedipus' life as an example.

The final episode is divided into two parts. A Messenger enters and describes what has happened offstage. The "messenger scene" is a standard part of Greek drama, since Greek sensibilities dictated that scenes of extreme violence take place offstage, though the results of the violence (the bodies of the dead, or in this case Oedipus' blindness) might be shown on stage. It is doubtful, however, that spectators of any age could witness without revulsion the sight of Oedipus jabbing pins into his eyes. Following the messenger scene Oedipus returns to the stage and seeks to prepare himself for the future.

Oedipus the King is structurally unusual: the resolution scene is the longest in the play. Obviously, Sophocles was not primarily concerned with discovering the murderer of Laius, for the interest in this lengthy final scene is shifted to the question: What will Oedipus do now that he knows the truth?

Up to this scene the play has concentrated upon Oedipus as the ruler of Thebes, but in the resolution Oedipus as a man and a father becomes the center of interest. By this point he has ceased to be the ruler of Thebes and has become the lowest of its citizens, and much of the intense pathos is due to this change. An audience may feel for Oedipus the outcast as it never could feel for the self-righteous ruler shown in the prologue.

Oedipus' act of blinding himself grows believably out of his character, for it is his very uprightness and deep sense of moral outrage which causes him to punish himself so terribly. Although he is entirely innocent of intentional sin, he considers the deeds themselves (murder of a blood relative and incest) to be so horrible that ignorance cannot wipe away the moral stigma. Part of the play's power resides in the revulsion with which people in all ages have viewed patricide and incest. That they are committed by an essentially good man only make them more terrible.

Oedipus the King maintains completely the unities of action, time, and place. There is nothing in the play which is not immediately relevant to the story being told. There are no subplots, and even the main plot is treated as simply as its events will allow. The time which elapses in the play coincides with the amount of time it would take in performance, and all of the events occur in the same place. The play, thus, has a late point of attack and shows only the final stages of the story. Out of very simple means, the playwright has created a drama of concentrated and powerful effect.

CHARACTERS AND ACTING.   Sophocles pays little attention to physiological levels of characterization. The principal characters—Oedipus, Creon, and Jocasta—are mature persons, but Sophocles has said almost nothing about their ages or appearance. One factor which is apt to distract modern readers—the relative ages of Jocasta and Oedipus—is not even mentioned by Sophocles, for it is basically unimportant. According to legend, Jocasta was queen of Thebes when Oedipus answered the riddle of the Sphinx. His reward, being made king, carried with it the stipulation that he marry Jocasta. Sophocles, it should be noted, never questions the suitability of the marriage on the grounds of a disparity in age.

Although Sophocles does not dwell on the physical attributes of his major characters, he does give brief indications of age for other roles. The Priest in the Prologue is spoken of as being old; the Chorus is made up of Theban Elders; Tiresias is old and blind; the Herdsman is an old man. In almost every case, age is associated with wisdom and experience. On the other hand, there are a number of young characters, none of whom speak: the band of suppliants in the Prologue includes children, and Antigone and Ismene are very young. Here the innocence of childhood is used to arouse pity.

On the sociological level of characterization, Sophocles again indicates little. Oedipus, Creon, and Jocasta hold joint authority in Thebes, although the power has been delegated to Oedipus. Vocational designations —a priest, a seer, a herdsman, servants—are used for some of the characters.

Sophocles is principally concerned with psychological and ethical characteristics. For example, we never know how old Oedipus is, but we learn about his moral uprightness, his reputation for wisdom, his quick temper, his insistence on discovering truth, his suspicion, his love for his children, his strength in the face of disaster. It is these qualities which make us understand Oedipus. But even here, a very limited number of traits, only those which are necessary to the story, are shown.

Creon is given even fewer characteristics. He has been Oedipus' trusted friend, his brother-in-law, and is one of the rulers of Thebes. He is quick to defend his honor, and is a man of common sense and uprightness who acts as honorably and compassionately as he can when the truth is discovered. Jocasta is similarly restricted. She strives to make life run smoothly for Oedipus, she tries to comfort him, to mediate between him and Creon, to stop Oedipus in his quest; she commits suicide when the truth becomes clear. We know nothing of her as a mother, and the very existence of the children is not mentioned until after her death.

This treatment of character—the use of few but essential traits—is another sign of Sophocles' economy in writing. To understand his methods, it may help to compare them with those of most modern playwrights who tend to build up characters from a large number of small details.

In the first production of *Oedipus the King,* all of the speaking roles would have been taken by three actors. The most likely casting would be as follows: the first actor would play Oedipus throughout, since he is present in every scene; the second actor would play Creon and the Messenger from Corinth; the third actor would play the Priest, Tiresias, Jocasta, the Herdsman, and the second Messenger. The greatest range is required of the third actor, while the greatest individual power is required of the first. The demands made on the third actor raises questions about the degree to which he differentiated between characters and the importance masks and costumes played in keeping characters separated for the audience. One should remember, however, that no two of the roles played by the third actor closely resemble each other and that the separation in terms of type might make his task simpler than it appears.

In addition to the three speaking actors, a large number of supernumeraries is required, many of whom no doubt appeared in more than one scene. For example, the band of suppliants in the Prologue includes children, two of whom could later appear as Antigone and Ismene. Some who portrayed suppliants probably also later appeared as servants and attendants. To the actors must be added the chorus of fifteen members. The total number in the cast, therefore, was probably not less than thirty-five.

Just as the details of characterization are few, so too the kinds of actions required of the actors are restricted. The physical action specifically demanded by the script is slight: entering, exiting, kneeling, pouring of sacrificial offerings, torturing of the Herdsman, and displays of anger. The use of masks, the doubling of roles, the fact that Jocasta was played by a man, the relatively small range of action—all these factors suggest that, while the aim was to create moving representations of human actions, the over-all effect would be considerably more abstract than the acting normally seen in the modern theatre.

SETTING, SPECTACLE, MUSIC, AND DANCE. The reader used to all the stage directions given in modern scripts may find a Greek tragedy lacking in spectacle upon first reading. If he tries to envision the action as it unfolds moment by moment, however, quite a different impression results.

First of all, the Greek theatre had no curtain. The play begins, therefore, with the procession of the Suppliants through one of the *paradoi*. Oedipus arrives to hear their pleas; then Creon enters. Later the Suppliants leave, and immediately the Chorus enters with a song which is accompanied by music and dance. This simple outline of the Prologue and parados is indicative of the complexity and variety found throughout the play.

The setting of *Oedipus the King* is simple. The stage house represents a palace; no changes are made and no machinery is needed. Relatively few of the characters enter from the palace: Oedipus, Jocasta, the second Messenger, Antigone, and Ismene, and sometimes Creon. Most of the characters, however, enter either through the paradoi or from the paraskene. The Chorus and the Suppliants would also enter through the paradoi and would perform in the orchestra.

There would be an altar in the middle of the orchestra, but there would also be altars near the stage house upon which Jocasta could place her offerings. Since the play was performed out of doors in daylight, no artificial illumination was necessary.

Costumes also would add to both setting and spectacle. Since most of the characters, including the Chorus, are dignified Greek citizens, they probably would wear long chitons. But there would also be many distinctions among the characters. Suppliants would carry branches as symbols; the Priest, Tiresias, and the Herdsman would each wear a garment distinctive of his occupation. The rich costumes of Oedipus, Jocasta, and Creon would contrast effectively with the simpler garments of the servants. Each character also would wear a mask indicative of his age and character.

Choral dancing is an important element of spectacle. Since dance had ethical connotations for the Greeks, it was in keeping with the moral position represented by the chorus of the play. The Chorus in *Oedipus the King* is made up of elderly and wise men. Thus, whatever dance they performed must have been dignified and stately, and probably appealed as much through shifting patterns as through dance steps.

The aural appeals were several: instrumental music, singing, and the speech of actors. The Greeks placed great emphasis on oral reading. The actors' voices must therefore have been trained, and their vocal techniques probably created considerable aural beauty. Plays were performed with musical accompaniment. Occasionally music was used during the episodes, but normally it was reserved for choral passages, all of which were sung and danced to flute music. Not only does music offer an appeal in its own right, it is also helpful in staging choral interludes, for it makes singing and dancing in unison much easier. Furthermore, music, through volume and tempo, aids in building choral passages to a climax. Movement, music, and song were combined to make the choral interludes among the most striking and effective features of Greek tragedy.

Oedipus the King during the 1960 presentation at Epidaurus. Photograph courtesy of the Greek National Theatre.

When the dramatic, visual, and musical appeals of Greek drama are considered, it becomes easier to understand why these plays, even after the passage of 2500 years, are still powerful and meaningful works of art.

GREEK COMEDY

Greek comedy developed later than tragedy. It was not officially recognized as a part of the festivals—that is, it was not granted a chorus—until about 487 B.C. when it became a regular part of the City Dionysia. After 487, one day of each festival was devoted to the presentation of five comedies. At the City Dionysia, however, comedy was always thought of as inferior to tragedy; it was to find its true home at the Lenaia—another of the Dionysian festivals—at which it was given official state support beginning around 442 B.C. At the same time contests for both comic poets and comic actors were inaugurated. The festival arrangement and the production procedures were similar to those for the City Dionysia, though the Lenaia festival was less elaborate. Five comic poets competed at the Lenaia, as at the City Dionysia.

Comedy used a chorus of twenty-four members. Like the tragic chorus it might be divided into two semichoruses, and it also sang and danced and served the same functions as the tragic chorus. But its music and dance were directed toward creating comic effects as a rule, although Aristophanes frequently inserted beautiful lyrical choruses into his comedies.

There were no restrictions on the number of actors in comedy; its acting style was an exaggeration of everyday behavior for purposes of comic effect.

The costume was usually a very tight, too-short chiton worn over flesh-colored tights. It created a ludicrous effect of partial nakedness. This effect was further emphasized by the phallus, which was almost always attached to the costumes of male characters. The phallus was both a source of ribald humor and a constant reminder of the Dionysian purpose of the festival. Masks also served to emphasize the ridiculous appearance of the characters. (See the illustrations on pages 3, 61, 77, and 87.)

Masks and costumes might also be more specialized in their function. Sometimes portrait masks—that is, masks which resembled actual persons—were used. For example, when *The Clouds* was first produced Socrates is said to have stood up in the theatre so the audience might compare the actor's mask with his own facial features. Many of the plays have nonhuman choruses—of birds, frogs, clouds, or wasps—and masks and costumes were used to create the appropriate distinctions.

Principally, however, comedy differed from tragedy in its subject matter. Most typically it was concerned with contemporary matters of politics or art, with questions of peace or war, with persons or practices disliked by the comic writer. Occasionally the playwright used mythological material as a framework for his satire, but usually the comic writer invented his own plots. The comic playwright also employed many references to contemporary persons or situations. These were no doubt a source of considerable pleasure to the audiences of the day, but of course are often obscure to a modern reader.

Numerous authors wrote Old Comedy, as the plays prior to 380 B.C. are called, but only the work of Aristophanes (*c.* 448–*c.* 380) still exists. He wrote about forty plays of which eleven have survived: *The Acharnians* (425), *The Knights* (424), *The Clouds* (423), *The Wasps* (422), *Peace* (421), *The Birds* (414), *Lysistrata* (411), *Thesmophoriazusae* (411), *The Frogs* (405), *Ecclesiazusae* (392 or 391), and *Plutus* (388). Aristophanes began competing in the contests in 427, and though he may have acted in a few of his plays, he usually depended on others to produce his works.

His comedies mingle farce, personal abuse, fantasy, beautiful lyric poetry, literary and musical parody, and serious commentary on contemporary affairs. *The Clouds* will be examined in some detail as an example of Aristophanes' work. It was produced at the City Dionysia in 423 B.C. and was awarded the third prize.

THE CLOUDS

THEME AND IDEAS. The basic theme of *The Clouds* is the corrupting influence of the Sophists, in whose teachings Aristophanes saw a danger to the very basis of Athenian life. The Sophists were interested in rhetoric and argumentation, but, because they were skeptical of absolute values, to Aristophanes they appeared more anxious to win contests than to defend valid positions.

While Socrates was not actually a Sophist, he was probably the most colorful figure among the current teachers. Aristophanes did not pretend to present Socrates' ideas accurately, but used him to epitomize

Production photograph of *The Clouds* as presented in 1951 by the Greek National Theatre. Reproduced by permission.

the Sophistic teacher. Nor are the ideas of the Sophists truthfully represented; they too are altered for comic purposes.

The satire is directed at two aspects of the movement: its ideas and methods, and its effects. The scenes in the school are concerned with the first of these, while Phidippides' treatment of his father is designed to show the latter.

PLOT AND STRUCTURE. The plot of Old Comedy consists of a "happy idea" and the results of putting it into practice. In *The Clouds* the idea is conceived that payment of debts can be avoided by using the "wrong logic" of Sophistic learning. After much ridicule of its methods, the new learning is put into practice with the anticipated results. But while it is effective in ridding Strepsiades of his debtors, it has also taught his son, Phidippides, to beat and abuse him.

The typical structure of Old Comedy is: a *prologue*, during which the happy idea is conceived; the *parados*, or entry of the chorus; the *agon*, or debate over the merits of the idea, ending with a decision to adopt it; the *parabasis*, a choral passage addressed to the audience and most frequently filled with advice on civic or other contemporary affairs; a *series of episodes* showing the happy idea in practice; and the *komos*, or exit to feasting and general revelry. Although all of the usual structural features are present in *The Clouds*, they have been rearranged. The deviations will be noted in the discussion which follows.

In the prologue, Strepsiades sets forth his predicament in a straightforward monologue which gives all of the necessary exposition. He is heavily in debt because of the extravagances of his son, Phidippides. He concludes that the only solution is to send his son to Socrates' school to learn how to avoid paying the debts. When Phidippides refuses to attend school, Strepsiades decides to go himself. The scene shifts instantly from Strepsiades' house to Socrates' school. A number of satirical and farcical jokes about the school and its students concludes the prologue.

The parados follows. Like many Greek comedies, *The Clouds* takes its title from the chorus, which frequently, as it does here, points up the element of fantasy. The clouds represent the spirit of the new learning which leads men on and then punishes them. The opening song also illustrates the element of lyrical poetry for which Aristophanes is noted.

Usually the agon follows the parados, but in *The Clouds* an episode is introduced to ridicule additional aspects of the new learning. This episode is followed by the parabasis, which denounces the audience for not properly appreciating Aristophanes' merits. He unashamedly praises himself and ridicules his opponents.

The parabasis is followed by still another episode showing Strepsiades' inability to absorb the new learning. It is implied that a man brought up in the old straight-laced ways of Athens cannot really understand the subtleties of the new way. After a choral ode, Strepsiades finally forces Phidippides to attend Socrates' school.

At this point, the long-delayed agon, or debate, occurs. The participants are personifications of Right Logic and Wrong Logic, another illustration of the fantastic nature of Old Comedy. As is usual, at the end of the agon all of the characters agree upon a line of action; here it is decided that Phidippides will be educated in the tradition of Wrong Logic.

This decision is followed by a short second parabasis, directed to the judges of the contest, suggesting that Aristophanes should win the prize. Time passes very rapidly in the next thirty-five lines, for at that point Phidippides re-enters having already completed his training.

A series of episodes showing the results of Strepsiades' plan follows: the creditors appear one by one and are effectively silenced. Strepsiades is overjoyed with his success and leads Phidippides away for feasting and revelry. This exit constitutes the komos and would normally conclude the play.

The joy is short-lived, however, for after a brief choral ode Strepsiades reappears, having been beaten by Phidippides, who then proves by his new learning that it is his duty to beat his father. The play ends as Strepsiades, in a fit of rage and frustration, attempts to burn Socrates' school. Such an ending is atypical of Old Comedy, for as a rule joy and harmony prevail.

The unity of Old Comedy is to be found in its ruling idea rather than in a sequence of causally related events. Its structure, therefore, often seems haphazard. The episodes which show the idea being put into practice are especially apt to seem disconnected. The order could be re-

Bird costumes probably used in Old Comedy. From Dieterich, *Pucinella*, 1897.

arranged and the number of episodes could be increased or reduced without seriously altering the story. They do build in comic intensity, however, and they carry out the author's purpose effectively.

The treatment of time and place in *The Clouds* is dictated by dramatic needs, without any attempt at creating an illusion of reality. Sometimes hours or days are assumed to have passed during one or two speeches, and the place changes at will. Stage illusion is broken frequently: the characters make comments about the audience, and the chorus addresses the spectators directly in the parabasis.

The element of fantasy can be seen in both the personification of the clouds and in the exaggeration of ideas and situations. Thus, while the incidents are related to contemporary affairs, they are treated through the techniques of the "tall story."

CHARACTERS AND ACTING. Aristophanes' plays seem to indicate that all men are governed by physical instincts and are in part corrupt and selfish. That Aristophanes held this opinion of his audience as well is suggested by his frequent practice of implying that the adoption of his point of view will bring monetary and sexual rewards.

Old Comedy puts much more emphasis on the physical aspects of character than does tragedy. Aristophanes' major characters are usually drawn from the well-to-do landowners (comparable to the middle class today), while the minor characters are either members of the same class or slaves. Occasionally heroes or gods appear, but they are always brought down to the level of ordinary humanity by emphasizing their physical instincts.

The main character in a play by Aristophanes is the common man, but one who is worse than the average audience member considers himself to be. Although any comedy may arouse a feeling of superiority, Aristophanes puts this response to special use. Because he wants reform, he makes it seem possible by making the audience feel that it is wiser than the characters in the play.

Aristophanes' characters are never villainous, merely ridiculous. Rather than focusing attention upon the moral nature of the "idea," he emphasizes the ludicrous or happy results of adopting it. Thus, the characters are usually concerned with expediency—how well a plan can serve their own selfish purposes—rather than with rightness. Strepsiades, for example, never considers the moral implications of cheating his creditors, only the means by which it can be done. But, although the moral issues are never allowed to become the center of his plays, Aristophanes never lets

A reconstruction of the Hellenistic theatre at Oropos. Painted panels could be set between the columns below, while some scenic representation may have been used in the alcoves at the rear of the raised stage. From Ernst Fiechter, *Antike Griechische Theaterbauten*, courtesy Verlag W. Kohlhammer GmbH.

the audience forget that the situations have wider and more important applications. Again, he achieves his purpose in part by allowing his audience to feel morally superior to the characters.

The acting style emphasizes the physical, ridiculous, and ordinary details of everyday life. For example, at the opening of *The Clouds*, Strepsiades and Phidippides, wrapped in blankets, are snoring; Strepsiades awakens and sends for a lamp and his account books. Later the characters catch bedbugs, beat each other, and climb onto the roof.

Old Comedy is as far removed from tragedy as possible; it highlights one aspect of man's life, while tragedy pinpoints another. Thus, comic acting was probably no more realistic than that in tragedy; its deviation from normal behavior, however, was in a completely different direction, for it ridiculed humanity just as tragic acting dignified it.

SETTING, SPECTACLE, DANCE, AND MUSIC. *The Clouds* demands a more complex setting and shows more clearly the facilities of the Greek theatre than does *Oedipus the King*. One interior and two exterior scenes are indicated. The interior was probably suggested by the *eccyclema*, while the two exteriors could be distinguished by the widely separated doors of the *skene*. The *machina* and the roof of the scene house were also used.

Many of the jokes in *The Clouds* are "sight gags." For example, Socrates is suspended in the machine (usually reserved for the gods) to indicate the pretentiousness and essential impracticability of the new learning. Other elements of note include the cloud costumes of the chorus, the grotesque and ludicrously obscene appearance of other characters, and the lively music and dance.

Thus, Old Comedy is a theatrical form of varied appeal. It is a strange mixture of fantasy, farce, and poetry which celebrates man's instincts while demanding that he act rationally. It is the reverse side of the

Scene from Greek New Comedy. Drawing of a bas relief; from Pougin, *Dictionnaire*, 1885.

Greek theatres built after about 325 B.C. are usually called Hellenistic. The ruins of Epidaurus are shown here. It is the best preserved of all the ancient Greek theatres and is frequently used for current productions as may be seen in previous illustrations. Photograph—O. G. Brockett.

coin of which tragedy is the face. Together they indicate the range of the Greek view of man.

THE SATYR PLAY

During the fifth century B.C., each writer of tragedy was required to present a satyr play, along with three tragedies, whenever he competed in the festivals. A satyr play was comic in tone, usually burlesqued a Greek myth, and used a chorus of satyrs. Following the three tragedies, it formed a kind of afterpiece, since it was short and sent the audience home in a happy frame of mind.

Only one complete satyr play—the *Cyclops* by Euripides—still exists. It is divided into five sections by four choral odes after the manner of tragedy and is a parody of the rather serious story—found in the *Odyssey*—of Odysseus' encounter with the Cyclops. A substantial part of one other satyr play—*The Trackers* by Sophocles—is also extant. It deals with Apollo's attempts to recover a herd of cattle stolen from him by Hermes and has the same structural features as the *Cyclops*. Although the satyr play was a regular feature of the Athenian theatre of the fifth century, it has had little subsequent influence and ceased to exist as a form when Greek drama declined.

LATE GREEK DRAMA

The great writers of Greek tragedy were no longer alive when Aristophanes died in approximately 380 B.C. Consequently, the fourth century saw the decline of Greek drama, though no lessening in the popularity of the theatre.

In the fourth century the Macedonians overran Greece and their leader, Alexander the Great, conquered all of Asia Minor and the northern part of Africa. The Greeks had already established colonies in southern Italy and Sicily, and by the end of the fourth century almost all of the known world was rapidly being Hellenized. The center of learning shifted from Athens to Pergamum (in Asia Minor) and Alexandria (in Egypt), and theatres were built wherever Greek influence was felt.

While the taste for tragedy continued, comedy was the preferred form. But the comedy which satisfied this taste was not that of Aristophanes, for citizens were no longer free to ridicule their rulers or to demand reforms. Athens and all other Greek territories were now ruled by an emperor. The New Comedy (as it has been called) which amused these people is most intimately associated with Menander (*c.* 342–292 B.C.), a native of Athens. He is said to have written over one hundred comedies of which only one, *Dyskolos,* remains in its entirety (rediscovered in 1957). Substantial portions of a few other plays by him also exist.

New Comedy was divided into five parts by four choral interludes. By this time, however, the chorus was of little importance and served merely to break the play into scenes. The major change came in subject matter, which was now drawn from the everyday life of middle-class Athenians. The plays are light in tone and typically show a son's attempt to marry in spite of his father's opposition. The son is usually aided by a clever slave, who is the major source of humor. Eventually the father is reconciled to the son's choice, frequently because the girl is discovered to be the long lost child of a friend.

New Comedy used costumes which were reasonably close copies of everyday garments, and masks which depicted basic character types of the period. Altogether, it marked a movement toward realism in staging, and toward conventionalization in depicting human behavior.

At the same time, the staging of tragedy moved further away from realism. It is to this period (usually called the Hellenistic age) that the distorted masks, high headdresses, thick-soled boots, and padded bodies of tragic actors belong. New theatres were built with stages raised from nine to twelve feet above the level of the orchestra. Naturally, the actor became increasingly the center of interest as he performed on this new stage high above the chorus. Plays now ceased to be performed exclusively for the Dionysian festivals and were given on many other civic or religious occasions.

As the fondness for theatrical performances grew, the demand for trained personnel became so great throughout the world of that day that performers organized the Artists of Dionysus. This organization furnished actors, trainers for choruses, musicians, and other personnel needed for the production of plays. It set fees for services, and its rights were recognized by international agreement. Many of its members were exempt from military service, had freedom of travel, and frequently served as ambassadors between states.

In the third century B.C. Rome began to expand as a power and came into contact with the theatre for the first time. As it absorbed the Hellenic world it took over the theatre and transformed it in accordance with its own needs. The distinctively Greek theatre had almost disappeared by the second century B.C. and from then until the sixth century A.D. the theatre was principally a Roman institution.

Chapter 5

ROMAN THEATRE AND DRAMA

Tradition has it that Rome was founded in the eighth century B.C. For several centuries it remained a small town of little consequence and did not begin to assume prominence until the third century B.C. But by the beginning of the Christian era it had extended its power over most of the known world.

The Romans were remarkable for their ability to adapt to their own needs whatever attracted them elsewhere. Thus, when they found drama interesting (first in the colonies in Sicily and southern Italy), they imported it to Rome.

Although performances of a theatrical nature may have been given in Rome at an earlier date, the first regular drama was performed in 240 B.C. The play was the work of Livius Andronicus, a Greek, and from this time on drama was a regular part of Roman life. Almost every element of Roman theatre and drama was an alteration of some Greek practice. This does not mean, however, that the Romans made no contributions, for their tastes led them to much that was fresh and original.

Unfortunately out of the vast number of Roman plays the works of only three dramatists survive: twenty comedies by Plautus, six comedies by Terence, and nine tragedies by Seneca. The comedies of Plautus and Terence date from about 205 to 160 B.C., the tragedies of Seneca from the first century A.D.

A somewhat fanciful reconstruction of a *naumachia*. From Laumann, *La Machinerie au Théâtre*, 1897. See page 92.

ROMAN FESTIVALS

The *ludi* or festivals in Rome at which plays were performed were not associated with the worship of Dionysus, but were of various types. Most were official religious celebrations, but some were financed by wealthy citizens for special occasions, such as the funeral of a distinguished figure or the triumphal entry of a victorious army. Originally (in 240 B.C.), drama was given only at the *ludi Romani,* or Roman Games, and probably only for a single performance. But the popularity of dramatic entertainments insured their gradual expansion, and as the number of Roman festivals was increased so were the occasions for presenting plays. By 78 B.C. public religious festivals devoted 48 days each year to dramatic entertainments. By A.D. 354 there were 175 public festival days of which 101 were devoted to theatrical spectacles.

In the time of Plautus and Terence (the second century B.C.) plays were given principally at four festivals: the *ludi Romani* held in September devoted at least four days to drama; the *ludi Plebeii,* established in 220 B.C. and held in November, gave over at least three days to plays; the *ludi Apollinares,* begun in 212 B.C. and held in July, devoted approximately two days to drama; and the *ludi Megalenses,* started in 204 B.C. and held in April, had six days of theatrical entertainments.

All public festivals were religious celebrations in honor of the gods, but the Romans were more concerned with the letter than the spirit of the celebration. They believed that each festival, in order to be effective, must be carried through strictly according to prescribed rules and that any mistake necessitated repeating the entire festival, including the plays. Since such repetitions were frequently necessary, many more days were devoted to drama than might be supposed.

PRODUCTION ARRANGEMENTS

Theatrical-production expenses, as in Greece, were undertaken by the state or by wealthy citizens. The Senate made an appropriation for each festival as a whole, and frequently the officials in charge contributed additional funds. These officials normally contracted for productions with the manager of a theatrical company, who from this point on was responsible for all details of production: finding a script, providing the actors, musicians, costumes, and so on. Furthermore, although each manager was assured of a certain sum of money, special incentives were provided in the form of prizes for the most successful troupes.

The manager probably bought the play script outright from the author; it then remained the manager's property and might be played as often as he wished or as audiences demanded.

A reconstruction of the theatre at Ostia. It is one of the oldest permanent Roman theatres, having been built between 30 and 12 B.C. From D'Espouy, *Fragments d'Architecture Antique*. Volume I, 1901.

Admission was free to everyone, seats were not reserved, and audiences were unruly. The programs were lengthy, being composed of a series of plays. No refreshments were available in the auditorium and, since the plays often had to compete with such rival attractions as chariot races, the troupes were forced to provide a kind of entertainment that would satisfy the tastes of a mass audience.

THE THEATRE AND STAGE IN THE TIME OF PLAUTUS AND TERENCE

Besides paying basic production expenses, the state supplied the theatre in which plays were presented. In the time of Plautus and Terence, it was a temporary one, for no permanent theatre was built in Rome until 55 B.C. Since plays were given in connection with religious festivals each of which honored a specific god, and since each god had his own precinct and temple, it is likely that at each festival a theatre was set up near the temple of the god being honored.

Current ideas of the features of this theatre are derived largely from those of the stone structures still in existence. Most of the surviving theatres, however, date from the first century A.D. or later, and do not necessarily provide an accurate picture of the earlier temporary structures.

The theatre of Plautus and Terence probably included: temporary scaffolds (outlining a semicircular orchestra) which provided seating for the spectators, and a long narrow stage rising about five feet above the orchestra level (the existing stages are over one hundred feet long), which was bounded by the stage house at the back and ends.

The appearance of the stage background, called the *scaenae frons*, is disputed. Some think it was a flat wall upon which columns, statues, or other details were painted. Others believe that there were three-dimensional niches and porticoes and, as evidence, point to the many scenes in Roman comedy which require one character to remain unseen by others, even though all are on stage at the same time. The back wall of the stage probably contained three openings, each of which was treated in comedy as the entrance to a house. The stage then became a street, and the entrances at either end of the stage were assumed to be continuations of that street. Windows and a second story were also required by some plays and the background must have provided for these as well.

COSTUMES AND MASKS

Costumes in the Roman theatre varied with the type of play. The works of Plautus and Terence were adapted from New Comedy and retained the Greek setting and garments. Other playwrights, however, often wrote of Roman characters and the costumes varied accordingly. In either case, the costumes were similar to those of daily life, though those of the more ludicrous comic characters were perhaps exaggerated.

Since most of the characters in Roman comedy were "types," the costumes also became standardized. There is evidence to suggest that certain colors were associated with particular occupations, such as yellow for courtesans and red for slaves. This conventional use of color extended to wigs also. All of the actors wore masks, which made the doubling of parts much easier and simplified the casting of such roles as the identical twins in *The Menaechmi*. Each actor in comedy also wore a thin sandal or slipper, called a *soccus*.

COMIC PLAYWRIGHTS

Although there were numerous comic writers in Rome, the work of only two—Plautus and Terence—has survived. Titus Maccius Plautus (*c.* 254–184 B.C.) is the earliest Roman playwright whose works still exist. Innumerable plays have been attributed to him, but the titles of only twenty-one have been agreed upon; of these twenty survive. The oldest dates from about 205 and the last from about the time of his death. Some of his most famous works are: *Amphitryon, The Pot of Gold, The Captives, The Braggart Warrior* and *The Twin Menaechmi*.

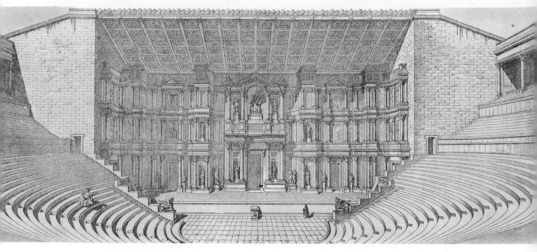

The Roman theatre at Orange is the best preserved in France and is now being used once more for theatrical performances. It was built in the first or second century A.D. Its *scaenae frons* measures approximately 118 feet high and 338 feet long. The illustration above is a reconstruction of the original theatre. The photograph below shows the same theatre in modern times. From Durm, *Die Baustile*. Volume II, 1905.

Publius Terentius Afer, commonly called Terence, was born in 195 (some accounts say 185) and died in 159 B.C. A native of North Africa, he was brought to Rome as a slave and later freed. He became the friend of many of the great men of his day. It is believed that he wrote only six plays—all of which still exist: *The Woman of Andros, The Self-Tormenter, The Eunuch, Phormio, The Mother-in-Law,* and *The Brothers*.

THE CONVENTIONS OF ROMAN COMEDY

All existing Roman comedy is based on Greek New Comedy, although significant changes have been made in the process of adaptation. First, the chorus has been abandoned, doing away with the division into acts or scenes. (The divisions found in most modern editions were made in later times.) Second, the musical elements formerly associated with the chorus are scattered throughout the plays. In some respects a Roman comedy resembles a modern musical, for certain scenes are spoken, others recited to musical accompaniment, and there may be a number of songs. In Plautus' plays about two-thirds of the lines are accompanied by music, and the average number of songs is three. Although Terence does not use songs, music accompanies approximately half of his dialogue.

Roman comedy, like Greek New Comedy, does not concern itself with political and civic questions, but rather with everyday domestic affairs. Almost invariably the plots turn on misunderstandings of one sort or another: mistaken identity (frequently involving long lost children), misunderstanding of motives, or deliberate deception. Sometimes the misunderstanding leads to rather pure farce, as in many of Plautus' plays, but it is also used for sentimental effects by Terence, who emphasizes the problems of lovers or parental relationships.

Plautus' plays usually have a single plot with rather complicated intrigue. In an expository prologue he explains the dramatic situation, and the episodes then develop its farcical possibilities.

Terence, on the other hand, uses a double plot, dispenses with the expository prologue, and treats his characters with sympathy and delicacy. His plays may be classified as romantic comedies, whereas those of Plautus are comedies of situation.

Roman comedy deals with the affairs of the well-to-do middle class, and the characters fall into clearly defined types: the old man who is concerned about his wealth or children, the young man who rebels against authority, the slaves, the parasite, the courtesan, the slave dealer, and the cowardly soldier. A number of other types appear with less frequency. Of all the characters, the most famous is perhaps the slave who, to help his master, devises all sorts of schemes, most of which go awry and lead to further complications. Very few respectable women appear in Roman comedy, and though love affairs may be the source of a play's misunderstandings, the women involved are often kept off stage. The number of characters varies from seven to fourteen, although the average is from ten to twelve.

All action takes place in the street. This often leads to the necessity of staging scenes out of doors that would more logically occur inside, and characters must frequently explain what has happened indoors. Occasion-

The *fabula Atellana* and mime were influenced by the *phlyakes* comedy of Sicily and southern Italy. *Phlyakes* comedy dealt primarily with mythological travesty and farcical situations; it flourished *c.* 400–200 B.C. As this vase painting shows, the costumes were similar to those of Greek Old Comedy. From Dorpfeld-Reisch, *Das Griechische Theater,* 1896.

ally the conventions of Roman comedy strain the modern reader's belief, but they were apparently accepted without question by Roman audiences.

The Menaechmi, probably the most popular of Plautus' plays, will be examined as an example of Roman comedy. In it, the comic possibilities of mistaken identity involving identical twins are handled with especial effectiveness.

THE MENAECHMI

PLOT AND STRUCTURE. As in most of Plautus' plays, *The Menaechmi* begins with a prologue which clarifies the backgrounds of the dramatic action. All important information is repeated more than once. At the same time, Plautus works in several jokes about the theatre, and tries to put the audience in a comic frame of mind.

Following the prologue, the introductory scenes of the play establish the present conditions out of which the comedy will grow: the dispute between Menaechmus I and his wife; the visit of Menaechmus I to the courtesan, Erotium, his gift to her of a dress stolen from his wife, their plans for a banquet later in the day, and the departure of Menaechmus I to the Forum; the entrance of Menaechmus II and his slave, Messenio. The remainder of the play presents a series of scenes in which the two Menaechmi are in turn mistaken for each other and accused of acts about which they know nothing. Eventually they meet, and the complications are resolved.

Menaechmus II's failure to guess the cause of his difficulties, inasmuch as he has come to Epidamnus to look for his identical twin, is sometimes said to be a weakness in the play. Indeed, even when he is brought face to face with his brother, he is unable to recognize the truth until it is pointed out by his slave. Plautus has overcome this objection in part, however, by having Messenio warn Menaechmus II that Epidamnus is famous for its swindlers. Messenio even suggests that Erotium, who greets Menaechmus by name, has sent a servant to the docks to seek out information about new arrivals.

Plautus has been less successful in making Menaechmus II's search for his brother believable. Both twins are depicted as completely selfish men, and consequently it seems unlikely that Menaechmus II would devote years to seeking a brother he has not seen since early childhood. But such objections are quibbles in the light of Plautus' main intention—to entertain his audience. In performance the inconsistencies go unnoticed, and it is only on reflection that they become obvious.

Plautus subordinates everything to his main purpose. He brings characters on stage when he needs them and sends them away when the need is gone. Although this is not unusual in drama, Plautus does not always try to hide his contrivances. For example, the wife of Menaechmus I sends for her father, and he appears four lines later though he lives some distance away; in other cases, he allows characters to see each other only when it suits his dramatic purposes. He also uses eavesdropping as a motivation for a number of complications.

Nevertheless, Plautus has developed his material with great economy. Not only has he eliminated everything that does not contribute to his principal aim, but he has made effective use of such devices as the stolen dress. This garment is a source of unity since it passes through the hands of practically all the characters and is used as evidence to support almost all the charges brought against the two Menaechmi.

Although Plautus' comic sense is everywhere evident, it may be seen at work especially in the reunion, which might have concluded the play on a sentimental note. Instead, the final lines give the story a twist in keeping with the sophisticated tone of earlier scenes: Menaechmus I offers all of his goods for sale—including his wife if anyone is foolish enough to buy her.

CHARACTERS AND ACTING.   The characters of *The Menaechmi* bear a close resemblance to those found in the plays of Aristophanes, for they too are motivated principally by selfish and material interests. With the possible exceptions of Messenio and the father, none of the characters may be considered admirable. Unlike Aristophanes, however, Plautus has little interest in social satire. He concentrates on the ridiculous situation and the characters without exploring the significance of either to society. Consequently, when his characters indulge in adultery, stealing, or deception, they merely contribute to the over-all tone of good-humored cynicism.

As in all Roman comedy, the characters in *The Menaechmi* are types rather than individuals. Some roles are summed up in their names: Peniculus (or "Brush") suggests the parasite's ability to sweep the table clean; the cook is called Cylindrus (or "Roller"), and the courtesan is named Erotium (or "Lovey"). Each character has a restricted number of motivations: the twins wish to satisfy their physical desires; the wife wants to reform her husband; the father desires to keep peace in the family; and the quack doctor is seeking a patient upon whom he can

Production photograph of Plautus' *The Menaechmi*. Directed by Harrold Shiffler; scenery by Richard Baschky.

practice a lengthy and costly treatment. In spite of the restricted number of traits, however, each character is sufficiently delineated for its purpose in the play.

The ten speaking roles of *The Menaechmi* could easily be performed by a company of six actors. In the Roman theatre, all parts were played by men; extras (used in nonspeaking roles) were employed as needed. The play does not require actors who are skilled in the subtle portrayal of a wide range of emotions. Rather, they must have that highly developed comic technique which produces precision in the timing of business and dialogue. The scenes of quarreling, drunkenness, and madness indicate that physical nimbleness is essential.

SCENERY AND MUSIC. Since *The Menaechmi* is set in a street before two houses, the stage and its architectural background would be sufficient to meet the scenic demands. The frequent eavesdropping and the failure of characters to see each other suggests that there probably were alcoves or projections in which the actors could conceal themselves.

The costumes were based on those of everyday Greek life, but were conventionalized according to social class, occupation, age, and sex. Each of the characters also wore a mask and wig. Since the performances took place out of doors and during the day, no artificial illumination was required.

Because the music is now lost, it is sometimes difficult for the modern reader to remember that music played an important role in the original production of *The Menaechmi*. Well over half of the dialogue was accompanied by the flute, and a number of the characters had "entering" songs on their first appearance. (These songs are now printed as dialogue and are not labeled as songs in most editions of the play.) The total effect must have been comparable to that of present-day musical comedy.

Thus, *The Menaechmi* is a farcical comedy designed primarily to divert an audience. It is very successful in fulfilling this aim, and the play's worth is clearly demonstrated by the fact that it has continued to entertain audiences throughout the more than two thousand years which have passed since its first presentation.

OTHER ROMAN DRAMA

The Roman comedy which has survived is of the type called *fabula palliata* (*fabula* means play, and *palliata* designates a Greek garment worn by the characters). There were, however, several other kinds of Roman drama. The *fabula togata*, or comedy on Roman themes, while modeling its form and techniques on Greek New Comedy, drew its material from life in the country towns of Italy.

Tragedy also played an important role in the Roman theatre. As with comedy, Greece provided the models upon which the Roman playwrights built. Also like comedy, tragedy is usually divided into two types, depending upon whether it used Greek or Roman themes. The former is called *fabula crepidata*, and the latter *fabula praetexta*. Both types feature horrifying plots, totally good or totally depraved characters, melodramatic effects, and bombastic speeches.

The only Roman tragedies which now exist are based on Greek themes and all are the work of Seneca. Lucius Anneus Seneca (4 B.C.– A.D. 65) was a philosopher and satirist, and one of Nero's principal advisers. Nine of his tragedies are extant, of which five are modeled directly upon plays by Euripides. A tenth is sometimes attributed to Seneca, but is undoubtedly the work of a later author.

Seneca was not a professional dramatist and his plays probably were not staged. Nevertheless, he was a major influence on Renaissance tragedy, and it is important, therefore, to understand the characteristics of his work.

First, Seneca's plays are divided into five acts by choral interludes. These interludes, however, are almost entirely irrelevant and can be eliminated without serious loss. Although the Renaissance dramatist seldom used a chorus, he was influenced by Seneca's five-act structure.

Second, Seneca wrote elaborately constructed speeches which often resemble forensic addresses, and his work as a whole tends to emphasize

Scene from a Roman comedy. After a wall painting in Pompeii. From Navarre, *Dionysos*, 1895.

rhetorical display. The presence of similar qualities in Elizabethan drama may be attributed in part to his influence.

Third, Seneca was a moral philosopher, and his plays are filled with *sententiae* (brief moral statements, resembling proverbs, about human behavior). The plays abound with sensational deeds, which are used to illustrate the evils of unrestrained emotion. The characters often lack self-control and set out to perform evil acts from which they cannot be dissuaded. Thus, moral lessons are taught through horrifying examples and sententiae, a practice followed by many Renaissance dramatists.

Fourth, Seneca's plays show many violent actions. In *Oedipus*, Jocasta kills herself on stage by ripping open her abdomen; in another play, a dismembered body is reassembled; and in *Thyestes* the bodies of children are served at a banquet. Such deeds of horror are found also in many plays of the Renaissance.

Fifth, Seneca is preoccupied with magic and death, as may be seen from his frequent use of ghosts and magical rites. This emphasis on the close connection between the human and supernatural worlds may be found in Renaissance drama.

Sixth, each of Seneca's main characters is dominated by a single motive which drives him to his doom. Most frequently the motivations, such as revenge, are either evil or obsessive. Again, this practice was to be taken up by writers in the Renaissance.

Seventh, many of Seneca's technical devices were to influence later dramatists. Soliloquies and asides occur frequently, and most of the plays include a *confidant* (a character whose main function is to listen to and advise the principal character).

Today Seneca's plays are almost universally damned but, since they are the only surviving Roman tragedies, they cannot be ignored. Furthermore, when Renaissance writers turned to the past, they were attracted by his work rather than by that of the Greek tragedians.

In addition to comedy and tragedy, a number of minor dramatic types were performed in the Roman theatre. It is interesting to note that after the first century B.C. there is no record of an author making a living from regular comedy or tragedy. Rather, the stage was taken over by minor dramatic forms—the *fabula Atellana*, the mime, and the pantomime.

The *fabula Atellana*, a short farce, was one of the oldest of Roman theatrical forms, having been imported from Atella, an area near Naples.

It always used the same characters, the most important of which were: Maccus, a fool or stupid clown; Bucco, a glutton or braggart; Pappus, a foolish old man who was easily deceived; and Dossenus, a cunning swindler and glutton, who was probably hunchbacked. In its early performances, the dialogue was probably improvised, and the plays were used as after-pieces at festivals. The plots involved various forms of trickery, cheating, and general buffoonery in a rural setting. Music and dance also played an important part. The *fabula Atellana* was converted into a literary form in the first century B.C., and after this time the short farce became the most popular dramatic type.

The mime may be traced back to the fifth century B.C. in Greece, but the earliest record of its appearance in Rome is 212 B.C. The mime troupes were "strolling players" and probably appeared in most parts of the world on makeshift stages. Their plays were short, topical, farcical, and, in the beginning, improvised. While the mime had certain features in common with the *fabula Atellana*, there were also important differences: the female roles were played by women (the earliest record of actresses), no masks were worn, and the subject matter was primarily urban.

Like the Atellan farce, the mime became a literary form in the first century B.C. The subjects of the later mime were principally adultery and unnatural vices, and the language was frequently indecent. These characteristics set the rising Christian religion against the mime troupes, who retaliated by ridiculing the sacraments and beliefs of the church. Thus, the mime was more responsible than any other factor for the church's opposition to the theatre.

One other dramatic type, the pantomime, was popular in late Rome. This silent interpretative dance was performed by a single actor who played many roles, each of which was indicated by a mask with a closed mouth. A chorus narrated the story, which was serious and drawn from mythology, and the entire action was accompanied by music. Pantomime largely replaced tragedy, and was very popular with the ruling classes.

The degeneration of the theatre under the Roman Empire—which superseded the Republic in 31 B.C.—is further illustrated by the fact that gladiatorial contests were held in the orchestras and on the stages of theatres. Furthermore, in many theatres the orchestras could be flooded for the presentation of sea battles—called *naumachia*. Spectacular, sensational, indecent, and exotic elements were increasingly emphasized. The plays of Plautus and Terence were occasionally staged, but during the Empire the usual fare was mime, pantomime, and nondramatic spectacle.

THE THEATRE BUILDING OF THE ROMAN EMPIRE

The permanent theatres of both Greece and Rome were constructed after their great dramas had been written. The first permanent theatre on the

Roman plan was built at Pompeii about 75 B.C., for Rome itself did not have a permanent theatre until 55 B.C. New theatres were built wherever Rome's dominance extended and most of the existing Greek theatres were remodeled along Roman lines. The latter structures are often called Greco-Roman theatres, since they display characteristics of both types.

The typical Roman theatre was constructed on level ground— unlike the Greek, which used a hillside to support its seats. The stage house and the auditorium were of the same height and formed a single architectural unit. (In a Greek theatre, the scene building and the auditorium were not joined and were, in effect, two separate structures.) The orchestra of a Roman theatre was a half-circle with the front of the stage set on its diameter, and the seats of the auditorium following the lines of its circumference. The auditorium typically seated between 10,000 and 15,000 spectators, and was sometimes covered with an awning.

The stage itself was raised about five feet above the level of the orchestra, and, on the average, measured 120 feet in length and 20 feet in depth. It had a permanent architectural background (called the *scaenae frons*) with a minimum of three doors in the rear wall (though frequently there were more), and at least one at either end of the stage. The *scaenae frons* was about three stories high, was decorated with columns, niches, statues, and porticoes, and, in some cases, was gilded or painted.

Two other features distinguish the Roman from the Greek stage. First, beginning around 133 B.C., a curtain was used in the Roman theatre. It was dropped into a slot at the front of the stage at the beginning of a performance and was raised at the end. Second, the Roman stage had a roof, which served at least two functions: it protected the elaborate *scaenae frons* from the weather, and it supported the curtain.

THE END OF DRAMA IN ROME

The immorality and decadence of the Roman theatre alienated the early Christians of Rome. Then Christianity, at first of little importance, was recognized as the semiofficial religion of Rome by the Emperor Constantine, who ruled from A.D. 312 to 337. Thereafter, the theatre encountered increasing difficulties. In the fifth century mime performers were excommunicated, and in the sixth century the theatres were closed by Justinian. The last recorded theatrical performance in ancient Rome occurred in A.D. 533.

The accomplishment of the Roman theatre is not great when compared with the Greek, but it did produce three playwrights of importance— Plautus, Terence, and Seneca. Furthermore, its drama and theatre were major influences on Renaissance writers and theatre artists, and consequently helped to shape the modern theatre.

Chapter 6

MEDIEVAL THEATRE AND DRAMA

Although it is sometimes stated that theatrical activities were completely suppressed throughout the Dark Ages, numerous contemporary documents attest to the continued presence of *mimes, histriones,* and *ioculatores* (Latin terms for actors). Little is known about these performers, however, for the opposition of the all-powerful church made it impossible for them to present plays openly. Actors were forbidden the sacraments of the church, and, between the sixth and tenth centuries, religious authorities issued frequent injunctions against both presenting and attending theatrical performances.

In addition to these surreptitious theatrical activities, many pagan rites and festivals containing dramatic elements also persisted despite Christian opposition. For example, the dance around the Maypole, originally a fertility rite, continued to be performed in many parts of Europe.

The theatre could not develop openly again, however, until the church began to make use of dramatic interludes in its services. This introduction, begun in the tenth century, was the first step in restoring the theatre to a respected place in society, though this was not the church's intention.

DRAMA IN THE CHURCH

It is not clear why the church began to use dramatic elements, but the

A booth stage such as might have been used by traveling players during the Middle Ages and Renaissance. After a colored design in a fifteenth-century manuscript. From *L'Ancienne France: Le Théâtre* . . . , 1887.

most likely answer is that it wished to make its lessons more graphic. Furthermore, since the majority of persons could not understand Latin (the language of the church), spectacle had already become an important means of vivifying church doctrine, and dramatic interludes were merely a further development of this tendency.

Another factor which encouraged the introduction of dramatic incidents was the organization of the church year around the principal events of the Old and New Testaments. The calendar begins in November with Advent, a period of preparation for the birth and second coming of Christ; next comes Christmas and Epiphany (the revelation of Christ to the Gentiles). The forty days of Lent, which commemorate the wanderings of both the Israelites and Christ in the wilderness, is followed by the events connected with the death and resurrection of Christ, culminating in Easter. After Easter comes Ascension and Pentecost, or Whitsunday, the traditional time for baptisms. Thus, the church calendar itself suggested the dramatization of the incidents appropriate to each season. Easter was the first of these to receive dramatic treatment in church services. Later other events were dramatized, but the chief productions were devoted to Christmas and Easter.

In the Middle Ages there were two kinds of services: mass, and the office of the hours. Mass, which includes the sacrament of bread and wine, was performed each day in a pattern that permitted little variation. On the other hand, the hours services (eight each day) were relatively simple and flexible. It was in the latter that drama developed.

The oldest existing church drama is the *Quem Quaeritis* trope, reproduced here in its entirety. (A trope means any interpolation into the services.) As the three Marys approach the tomb of Christ, Angels say:

	Whom seek ye in the tomb, O Christians?
Maries:	Jesus of Nazareth, the crucified, O Heavenly Beings.
Angels:	He is not here; he is risen as he foretold.
	Go and announce that he is risen from the tomb.

This simple beginning gradually grew more elaborate as both prior and succeeding incidents were added. For example, on the way to the tomb the women stop at a perfume-seller's stall to buy oils to anoint the body of Christ. After meeting the Angels, they rush away to tell the Disciples.

Drama was not produced in all churches of the period, but was found, as a rule, only in cathedrals and monasteries—in other words, in those churches which had enough clergy to present plays. The actors, and sometimes the audiences, were priests.

Between approximately A.D. 900 and 1250, drama was staged indoors, but in the thirteenth century it began to be moved outside. By that time,

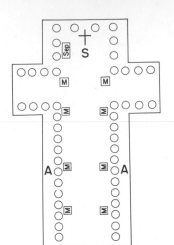

A ground plan of a Medieval cathedral. A—aisles.
M—mansions. S—sanctuary. Sep—sepulchre.

staging conventions which were to be used until the sixteenth century
had crystallized.

Stage space was divided into two parts: the *mansions*, and the
platea. The mansions (also called stations, seats, or *sedes*) were simple
scenic devices for indicating the location of incidents. For example, a
throne might be used to suggest the residence of Pilate. Each place was
represented by a different mansion, and they all remained in view throughout the play.

Since the action could not be performed in the limited space provided by the typical mansion, the actors used as much of the adjacent
floor area as they needed. Often the same space was used in many different
scenes. This generalized acting area was called the *platea* (place, or
playne). Thus a series of mansions was arranged around a neutral playing
space, and the performers moved from one mansion to another as the
action demanded. (See the accompanying illustrations.)

A page from the manuscript of the Valenciennes Passion Play, with the simultaneous
depiction of several scenes. Courtesy of the Bibliothèque Nationale.

The stage for the Passion Play produced at Valenciennes, France, in 1547. From the left the various mansions represent: Paradise, Nazareth, the Temple, Jerusalem, a palace, the Golden door, the sea, and Hell's mouth. From a manuscript in the Bibliothèque Nationale; reproduced through their courtesy.

The Fool and the Devil. From a woodcut in Sebastian Brant's *Ship of Fools*, published in 1497.

THE REMOVAL OF DRAMA FROM THE CHURCH

Why drama was moved out of doors is not clear. The most likely answers are that plays had begun to interfere with church services, and had become too elaborate for proper indoor staging. Although drama continued to be presented in some churches until the seventeenth century, in the majority the shift to outdoor performance came during the thirteenth century.

After drama was moved outside, secular organizations began to assist in its production, and by the late fifteenth century they had assumed the primary responsibility. The principal groups active in play production were the powerful Medieval trade guilds, but in some instances special societies were formed for the purpose of presenting religious plays.

Most scholars have argued that the church abandoned the drama when it was moved outdoors. Recent studies, however, have questioned the correctness of this older view, for while the church participated less and less in the actual process of production, its approval continued to be necessary. Plays dealt with religious matters, and the church could not afford to ignore such powerful teaching instruments. Furthermore, each trade guild had its own priest, patron saint, and chapel, and was not entirely a secular organization. Thus, it is likely that the production of plays continued to be a cooperative venture, in which the church supplied approval and encouragement while secular groups provided the money and personnel.

Few changes were made in drama during the first century after it was moved out of doors. The plays were still, as a rule, performed in Latin and primarily by the clergy. But in the fourteenth and fifteenth centuries many changes occurred as secular influence increased.

After this time plays were presented in the vernacular, or local languages, rather than in Latin. The introduction of nonclerical actors enlarged the supply of performers, and secular organizations began to provide considerable sums of money for the production of plays. All of these factors help to explain why the scripts written between the fourteenth and sixteenth centuries made increasingly greater demands for large casts and spectacular special effects. This elaboration reached its culmination in a French play which attempted to dramatize the events of the Bible from the Creation to the Last Judgment; it required forty days for performance.

STAGING TECHNIQUES

When drama was moved outside, it was staged at first before the great west door of the church. This door usually opened onto a raised porch from which steps led down to the town square. The platform became a stage and the town square provided space for the audience. Later the stage was moved to other locations, but the long rectangular platform against a building remained the typical arrangement in Medieval staging. Many variations, however, were used. In some places the mansions were set up around the town square, and elsewhere the old Roman amphitheatres were used. Perhaps the most drastic departure was the practice of erecting mansions on wagons and drawing them from one place to another.

All of these diverse arrangements, however, shared a number of characteristics. First, all used the staging conventions inherited from the church—a series of mansions and a generalized acting area. Second, the performances were made up of a series of short plays, each of which was more or less complete in itself. The order of the plays was determined by the Bible rather than by any causal relationship among them. Third, every series involved three planes of action, Heaven, Earth, and Hell, which might be arranged either horizontally or vertically. The typical platform stage used a horizontal placement, with Heaven always on the right and Hell on the left (as one faced the audience). The earthly scenes were staged between these two points. The wagons used a vertical arrangement, although a single wagon seldom depicted all three levels.

Fourth, the greatest attention was devoted to making special effects convincingly realistic. Although such efforts may be explained in part by a love of spectacle, an equally important factor was the fear of raising doubts about the miraculous events described in the Bible. Regardless of their motives, Medieval producers welcomed the challenge posed by such episodes as Christ walking on the water and being lifted up to the top of a temple. Special pains were also taken in the depiction of Hell and its horrors. The entrance to Hell was often represented as the mouth of a fire-breathing monster (hence the name "hell mouth"), and fire, smoke, and the cries of the damned issued from within.

To achieve these special effects, a considerable amount of stage machinery (called "secrets") was invented. Much of it was operated from under the stage; numerous trap doors also permitted the appearance and disappearance of persons and objects. For the scenes which required "flying," pulleys and lines were attached to adjoining buildings. The overhead machinery might be hidden by cloths painted to represent clouds or the sky.

Such machinery was not the work of amateurs. As effects became more and more elaborate, professional machinists and stage managers emerged. For a play staged at Mons in 1501, technicians were hired to construct the "secrets," and seventeen people were needed to operate the hell machinery alone; five men were paid to paint the scenery, and four actor–prompters were employed both to act and to help with the staging. Thus, while the majority of persons connected with a production were amateurs, professional theatre workers gradually came into existence as productions grew in complexity.

Obviously special effects could be more extensive on a fixed stage than on a wagon. It is not surprising, therefore, that the continental theatre with its stationary platforms developed more elaborate stage machinery than did the English theatre with its wagon stages.

It was not the sole aim of the Medieval stage to produce convincing special effects, however, for these realistic features were coupled with fragmentary scenery and symbolic devices. No place was depicted in its entirety: a small building might represent Jerusalem; a chair under a portico might become the palace of Herod. Moreover, all of the places needed for the play were present simultaneously, thus further preventing the illusion of a real place. Typically, even the wagon stages carried more than one mansion.

Just as the stage usually included mansions representative of Heaven, Earth and Hell, so too the costumes had to distinguish between the inhabitants of the three realms. God, the angels, the saints and certain Biblical characters wore church garments, often with added accessories. For example, angels wore church robes with wings attached, while God was dressed merely as a high church official. Each of the saints and important Biblical personages was also associated with a specific symbol. For example, St. Peter was identified by his keys to the Kingdom of Heaven. Since the audience was familiar with such visual symbolism, the mere display of an emblem served to identify the character.

Secular, earthly characters wore the contemporary Medieval garments appropriate to their ranks. The greatest imagination went into costuming the devils, who were usually fancifully conceived with wings, animal claws, and beaks, or horns and tails. While Heaven and its representatives were intended to inspire awe and reverence, Hell and its inhabitants were expected to arouse fear and scorn. The human beings who dwelt between were representative of the common man caught between the forces of good and evil.

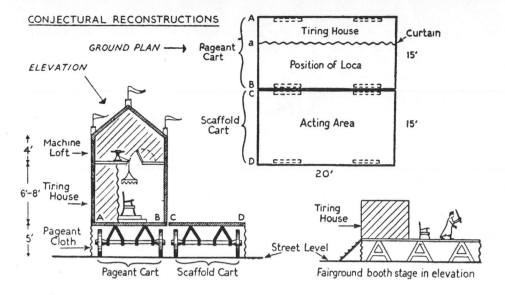

A conjectural reconstruction of an English pageant wagon and stage. From Glynne Wickham's *Early English Stages*, Volume I, 1959. Courtesy of Columbia University Press and Mr. Wickham.

CONVENTIONS OF THOUGHT AFFECTING MEDIEVAL DRAMA

Since we no longer think in Medieval terms, some attempt to recapture the concepts of the Middle Ages is essential; otherwise the drama of the period is apt to seem childish and naïve. Two kinds of time, eternal and temporal, were posited. In the Medieval view, God and the Devil exist in eternity, as does man's immortal soul. Eternity has neither a beginning nor an end, but man, as a physical being, does. If man considers only his earthly life, therefore, time may appear to be limited, but if he relates himself to God, he sees that life is merely a preparation for eternity, in which his immortal soul participates. When he leaves his earthly existence he enters upon eternal salvation or damnation. Thus temporal existence is a short interlude, a preface to the ultimate reality, which is eternal. The central part of the stage, then—the earthly and temporal realm—was framed by Heaven and Hell, the eternal realms. Man must choose one way or the other.

For the Medieval mind, earthly time and place were relatively unimportant. The historical period or geographical location of an event were of little importance when set against the framework of eternity. Consequently, no sense of history is found in Medieval plays. Audiences were not offended when ancient Israelites or Roman soldiers were dressed in Medieval garments, or when Old Testament characters referred to Christian saints.

The attitude toward time is partially reflected in the structure of

A scene from *The Miracle of Notre Dame*, a French miracle play of the fourteenth century. The episode depicted is about Robert le Diable. From Pougin, *Dictionnaire Historique et Pittoresque du Théâtre . . .*, 1885.

Medieval cycles, in which a series of short plays dramatized Biblical material beginning with Creation and concluding with the Last Judgment. Although not all cycles were so ambitious, most of them encompassed lengthy segments of time and a variety of events. There was seldom any causal relationship among plays and often not even among the incidents of a single play. Again, however, such techniques are not necessarily signs of poor playwriting. For the Medieval mind, Providence played a large part in human affairs, and events were thought to happen simply because God willed them. Since an audience brought this frame of reference to the theatre, it did not demand to see these concepts overtly dramatized in plays.

Another factor which sometimes puzzles the modern reader is the presence of comic elements in religious plays. Our austere view of religion, however, dates only from the sixteenth century, when the church was reformed. Prior to that time, the church permitted many satirical elements in its festivals. The Feast of Fools, for example, was a kind of New Year's rite during which the minor clergy were allowed to ridicule the mass and the church officials. It is not surprising, then, that comic elements were included in these plays. Usually, however, comedy was associated only with the devils and evil persons, or with the non-Biblical, lower-class characters.

THE MYSTERY PLAY

The Mystery play, which drew its subjects from scripture, was the major form of Medieval drama, being produced throughout western Europe. Its name is probably derived from *mystère*, the French word used in the Middle Ages to designate any trade or craft. Thus, "mystery" came to mean those plays produced by the trade guilds. Other names were used elsewhere. In Italy, *sacre representazzione* and in Spain, *auto sacramentale* were common designations.

The dramas most readily available for study are those written in English. Although cycles of mystery plays were produced in over one

Detail from Denis von Alsloot's "The Triumph of Isabella," 1615. Although these wagons were not used for play production, they suggest those employed in staging the English cycle plays. Courtesy of the Victoria and Albert Museum. Crown copyright.

hundred English towns during the Middle Ages, most of the plays extant come from four cycles: the York, containing forty-eight plays; the Chester, containing twenty-four; the Townley manuscript plays or Wakefield cycle, containing thirty-two plays; and the Coventry or N——Town cycle (the place is disputed), containing forty-two plays.

STAGING OF CYCLE PLAYS IN ENGLAND DURING THE FIFTEENTH CENTURY

English plays were usually staged as a part of the Corpus Christi festival (honoring the sacraments of bread and wine, or the *host*), which typically comes in early June. The essential feature of the Corpus Christi celebration was a procession of the Host through the town. It may be for this reason that the English adopted the processional form of staging–that is, the mounting of plays on wagons, and the movement of these wagons to a series of places throughout a town.

Although plays were not given each year, they were presented at reasonably regular intervals, and on those occasions the Corpus Christi festival was extended, since an average of four or five days was needed to perform the cycles. The town council decided whether the plays were to be included, and the guilds assumed primary responsibility for production.

Each trade guild was assigned one play, or, in the case of small guilds, two or more might produce a play together. The master copy of the cycle, which had the approval of the church, was retained by the town council, and each guild was cautioned to stage its play with care and to remain faithful to the text. A fine was imposed if a guild was proven negligent.

No adequate description of the pageant wagons has been preserved. They were probably as large as the narrow city streets would permit and were designed to meet the requirements of specific plays (each guild always presented the same play). A wagon almost always had to carry two or more mansions, and might need machinery for special effects as well. In some plays, places or characters were "discovered" during the action; in others, persons or objects ascended or descended either from above or beneath the stage. The account books of the guilds show sizable expenditures for painted drops, curtains, properties, special effects, and for the pageant wagon itself.

There is much disagreement as to where the acting took place. Some argue that it occurred only on the wagon; others believe that the actors used both the wagon and the street; and still others state that the wagons were pulled up alongside a platform, which served as the acting area, or *platea*, while the wagon provided the mansions. The last-mentioned argument is a persuasive one, since the action of many plays is too complex to be staged on a wagon which also carried scenery. Furthermore, it appears unlikely that very many scenes were played in the street itself, for the standing spectators would have obstructed the view of much of the audience. On the other hand, the actors did make occasional use of the street, and it is possible that the wagon, a platform, and the street were all used as acting areas.

The actors were primarily amateurs, though they might have received some pay for their services, and account books indicate that they were provided with considerable quantities of food and drink during the rehearsal period. A few actors were paid large sums, however, and it is likely that these were professional performers who played the leading roles, helped with the staging, and coached the amateurs.

Most characters could be costumed from either the ecclesiastical or the ordinary garments of the day, but occasionally special costumes were required for the devils or other exotic figures. Music figured prominently in some plays and was often used to fill the interval between plays. For the latter purpose, professional musicians were sometimes hired.

An episode from "The Creation of Noah's Ark" *The Wakefield Mystery Plays*. Production photograph courtesy of the Mermaid Theatre at Puddle Dock, London.

Each guild presented its play at several places, the first of which was always the church or monastery. The other locations were chosen by the town council. Thus, audiences gathered at a number of points and the plays were brought to them in a manner which combined a parade and dramatic entertainment.

THE SECOND SHEPHERDS PLAY

The Second Shepherds Play is probably the best known of the English cycle plays. It is the thirteenth part of the Wakefield cycle, from which thirty-two plays—on the usual subjects ranging from Creation to the Last Judgment—have survived.

PLOT AND STRUCTURE. The majority of *The Second Shepherds Play* is an elaboration of a single sentence from the *New Testament* (Luke 2:8): "And there were in the same country shepherds abiding in the field, keeping watch over their flock by night." This hint was transformed into a Medieval story rich in contemporary details and farcical humor. The number of shepherds is not specified in the *Bible*, but three are used in the play, probably to suggest a parallel with the three wise men.

Like most Medieval dramas, *The Second Shepherds Play* has an early point of attack. It introduces in leisurely fashion the characters and situation as each shepherd in turn complains about a different problem: general social conditions, marriage, insufficient food and drink. The opening is made even more casual by the inclusion of a song.

Yet this simple beginning serves several purposes which may not be readily apparent. First, through the various complaints, it depicts a world that needs some correction—one that stands in need of Christ's coming. Second, it relates the Biblical story to the contemporary scene and thereby to the audience. Thus, the coming of Christ is placed in the atmosphere of the Middle Ages. Third, the introduction prepares for an unusual occurrence by the third Shepherd's recital of abnormal conditions, concluding with:

> We that walk on the nights our cattle to keep,
> We see sudden sights when other men sleep.

There is little forward movement in the story, however, until Mak appears.

Mak's reputation as a trickster is established immediately by the Shepherds' concern for their sheep. Soon, however, they all lie down for the night. When the Shepherds are safely asleep, Mak steals a sheep and carries it home to his wife, Gill. As a precaution against discovery, she suggests that they place the sheep in a cradle and pretend that it is a newborn baby. Mak then goes back to the fields and lies down as before.

The Shepherds awake and, with difficulty, arouse Mak, who has been feigning sleep. After Mak takes his leave, the Shepherds discover that a sheep is missing and they immediately suspect Mak. While the Shepherds search the house, Mak protests his innocence and Gill counterfeits childbirth pains. As they are leaving, one of the Shepherds remembers the child and insists upon presenting a gift to it; the sheep is discovered and Mak is tossed in a blanket as punishment. This portion of the play is closely related to the Medieval farce (to be discussed later) in the characterizations of Mak and Gill, in the comic inventiveness of the plot, and in its resolution. It also shows much greater skill in writing than other parts of the play.

After recovering their sheep, the Shepherds return to the field. A marked change now takes place as the tone of the play becomes serious and devotional. An Angel appears and announces the birth of Christ; the Shepherds go to Bethlehem, worship the child and present their gifts. Christ has appeared within a familiar scene; his promise is not to some forgotten past, but to the immediate present.

THEMES AND IDEAS. *The Second Shepherds Play* has frequently been viewed as a work composed of two unrelated stories of sharply contrasting tone. A close examination of the work, however, reveals that it is unified through its themes and ideas. The most important of these are man's depravity and the promise of salvation. They are placed side by side in the form of a demonstration.

The Shepherds symbolize the common man; they are involved first with Mak (the godless man) and then with the Christ child (God incarnate). The many parallels between the two stories suggests that this juxtaposition is intentional. In both there is a father, mother and child; the child is in a cradle; one "child" is a lamb, and the other is Christ, the

"Lamb of God"; the Shepherds present gifts to both. The difference between the two stories is to be found in the significance of the events: one shows a world in need of Christ, and the other portrays his arrival. Succeeding plays in the cycle dramatized both the life and the teachings of Christ.

A production photograph of a scene from *The Second Shepherd's Play* at the Mermaid Theatre, London. Courtesy of the Mermaid Theatre.

CHARACTERIZATION AND ACTING.   There are seven roles—not counting the infant—in *The Second Shepherds Play*. All parts were played by men, and the same actor could have played both Gill and Mary.

Little is indicated about the physical appearance of the characters. All are adults of unspecified age except the third Shepherd—a boy—and the Christ child—probably represented by a doll. The sociological traits are also limited. The Shepherds, Mak and Gill, are peasants; it is implied that Mak lives by stealing.

Psychological characterization is slight, but effectively drawn. The three Shepherds are differentiated primarily through their opening monologues, in which each is concerned with a different problem. All are generous as may be seen from their reactions to the supposed child of Gill and to the Christ child, and from their decision not to prosecute Mak. (In Medieval times, stealing was a capital offense.) A good impulse, the desire to give the "child" a gift, leads to the uncovering of Mak's guilt. Mak is a clever knave, who is somewhat henpecked and cowardly. Gill is shrewish and clever; it is her idea to put the lamb in the cradle and pass it off as a child. Because they each have only one speech, Mary and the Angel are characterized least and seem especially stiff and stereotyped when compared with the other characters.

The role of Mak requires more acting skill than any other. The comic plot progresses principally through him, and he must convey a rather wide range of responses, many of which are supposed to communicate one impression to the Shepherds and another to the audience. Since the sheep–stealing scenes are meant to be comic, both Mak and Gill must be able to convey the ludicrous aspects of the situation.

The Shepherds' roles, while longer than those of Mak and Gill, are more nearly serious and demand little exaggeration. They must project the humorous points in the opening speeches and be able to pass from the bantering tone of the first part to the devout tone of the final scene. There is a considerable amount of physical action in the play and, with the exception of the Angel's appearance, all of it is reasonably realistic. Transitional action, however, is indicated only sketchily. For example, the Shepherds lie down and appear to fall asleep instantly. The actors, therefore, must supply many details or the action will seem abrupt.

Most of the actors must sing. The Shepherds have a song in the introductory scene and another at the end of the play. Mak sings a lullaby to his stolen sheep, and the Angel sings *Gloria in excelsis*.

SPECTACLE AND MUSIC. *The Second Shepherds Play* calls for three scenes—the fields, Mak's house, and the stable at Bethlehem. One mansion might be sufficient, however, since the fields really require no background, and the other two are so similar in scenic demands that the same mansion could be used for both.

No doubt the mansion used for Mak's house and the stable was equipped with a curtain which could be drawn to reveal the interior. Neither Gill nor Mary is visible throughout the play; rather each is "revealed" at the right moment. Mak's house must have a door (at which he knocks), a cradle, and a bed. All of these would be appropriate items for the stable (the bed for Mak's house need only be made of straw).

It is difficult to imagine this play being performed on a wagon which would, at the very least, have to be divided into two parts. It is more logical to suppose that the wagon carried only the necessary scenic background and could be pulled up alongside another platform which would serve as the platea, or generalized acting area. Such an arrangement would effectively solve most of the difficulties of staging.

The costume demands for the play are simple: for the Shepherds, Mak and Gill, the everyday contemporary dress of the lower classes; for the Angel, an ecclesiastical garment with wings added; for Mary, an upper-class Medieval garment, to which would be added the symbols associated with her.

The musical requirements are also relatively simple. The Shepherds' first song and Mak's lullaby would have been contemporary popular songs. The *Gloria*, sung by the Angel, and the Shepherds' final song would have been taken from contemporary church music.

Although the staging demands are simple, *The Second Shepherds Play* has a considerable range of visual and aural appeals. Its variety makes it an excellent example of that combination of teaching and entertainment which was the essence of Medieval drama.

COMPARISON WITH GREEK AND ELIZABETHAN THEATRE

Although there are few similarities between Medieval and Greek plays, there are striking parallels in the conditions of theatrical representation. In the beginning both were intimately connected with religious observances and gradually became secularized. In both, the theatre was supported by wealthy citizens or organizations and was a combined civic and religious function open to all classes. Although the plays were presented at religious festivals, secular and comic elements were prominent in both.

On the other hand, Medieval plays have much in common with Elizabethan drama, although there are few parallels in theatrical organization. By the end of the sixteenth century, the theatre had become a business enterprise and had almost totally ceased to perform religious or civic functions. The physical arrangement of the Medieval stage continued to be influential in England, however, and many characteristics of Elizabethan drama are probably derived from the Medieval play. These traits include: an early point of attack; a loosely organized plot which encompasses long periods of time and many places; a mixture of the serious and comic in a single play; and an interest in moral instruction.

OTHER RELIGIOUS DRAMATIC FORMS

Thus far, only church drama (often called *liturgical* drama) and cycle (or *mystery*) plays have been discussed. Actually, however, there are many kinds of Medieval drama.

Miracle plays dramatize incidents from the lives and works of the saints and martyrs. Although many of the deeds shown in the plays are fictional, all demonstrate miraculous powers at work or divine intercession in human affairs. This type of play was staged in connection with the feast day of a particular saint by groups especially associated with him. Although it was less extensively developed than the mystery play, it was an important part of Medieval theatre.

Morality plays flourished between 1400 and 1550. They were a significant development since they dramatize the spiritual trials of the average man, whereas mystery and miracle plays treat Biblical or saintly characters. Some examples of the morality play are: *Pride of Life* (*c.* 1410), *The Castle of Perseverance* (*c.* 1425), *Mankind* (*c.* 1475), and *Everyman* (*c.* 1500).

The plays are allegories about the moral temptations which beset all men. The protagonist (usually called Mankind or Everyman) is advised and cajoled by personifications of good and evil (such as good and bad angels, the seven virtues, and the seven deadly sins), and is surrounded by such characters as Mercy, Good Deeds, Knowledge, Mischief, and Death.

The purpose of the morality play is clarified if the place of the action is considered to be man's soul, for it is the struggle to possess this battlefield which constitutes the drama. In the conflict, man seems to play little active part, because so many of the personifications are human drives and motivations. When these psychological forces are externalized, the protagonist is left with few traits. As a result, he is more apt to resemble a puppet than a human being. The other characters are also one-dimensional, since each personification represents only the essence of a quality, such as pride or wealth. The exception is Vice, a misguided, mischievous, and frequently humorous character sometimes used to satirize contemporary manners.

The most famous morality play is *Everyman*. It is atypical, however, because it is restricted in scope. Whereas most morality plays cover man's entire life, *Everyman* deals only with his preparation for death. Everyman searches to find one among his former companions (Kindred, Goods, Beauty, Strength, Discretion, Five Wits) who will accompany him to the grave; eventually only Good Deeds goes with him. In his search, Everyman comes to understand his past life and its relation to his salvation. *Everyman* is a moving drama which has universal appeal, since all men must face death and must do so alone.

During the sixteenth century the morality play was gradually secularized, and its typical subjects were replaced by such new ones as the proper training of rulers and the content of good education. Then, at the time of the religious reformation in England, it became a vehicle for controversy. For example, John Bale (1495–1563) mixed its abstract figures with historical personages in his *King John*, which denounced the papacy. Such changes moved the morality play increasingly toward a drama with completely secular subject matter and human characters.

Since morality plays were performed by small professional troupes, they are more closely connected with the development of professionalism than are cycle plays. Thus, both in content and presentation, the morality play pointed toward the establishment of a secular and professional stage.

SECULAR DRAMATIC FORMS

In addition to religious and didactic plays, there were a number of secular dramatic forms in the Middle Ages. The first, and probably least important, is the *folk play*, which depicts the adventures of such popular heroes as Robin Hood or St. George. The folk play is noteworthy principally, however, for such elements as sword fights, dances, deaths and resurrections, which are derived from pagan fertility rites. Folk plays were performed by amateurs, who went from house to house, usually at the Christmas season. This type of play, however, had little influence on later drama.

The *farce* is probably the most interesting and important of secular forms. It was especially well developed in France, although it also had important exponents in England, the best known of whom is John Heywood (*c*. 1497–1580). The farce is lacking in religious or didactic elements, and shows, rather, the ridiculous depravity of man.

Probably the best example of Medieval farce is *Pierre Patelin*, an anonymous French play of the fifteenth century. Patelin, a lawyer, is near financial ruin. He, nevertheless, persuades a merchant to let him have a

A scene from *The Salzburg Everyman*, a modern adaptation of *Everyman* by Hugo von Hofmannsthal, at the Goodman Memorial Theatre. Translated and directed by John Reich; setting—William Ryan; costumes—Sylvia Wintle; lighting—G. E. Naselius. Starring Donald Buka (clasped by **Death**). Courtesy of the Art Institute of Chicago.

fine piece of cloth. The merchant agrees to come to Patelin's house to collect his money and to have dinner. When the merchant arrives, Patelin is in bed, and his wife swears that he has not been out of the house. Patelin pretends madness, beats the merchant and drives him away. This part of the plot is rather loosely joined to a second one. Patelin meets a shepherd and agrees to defend him in court against a charge of sheep-stealing. He cautions the shepherd to answer only with a "baa" no matter what anyone says to him. In court, the accuser turns out to be the cloth merchant, who creates such bewilderment with his alternating charges against Patelin and the shepherd that the judge (in view of the confusion and the shepherd's seeming feeble-mindedness) dismisses the case. When Patelin tries to collect his fee, however, the shepherd runs away, calling "baa." The story shows a series of clever knaves outwitting each other. The final comic twist comes when the master knave is outwitted by an apparent simpleton. *Pierre Patelin* is filled with high spirits and cynicism; it has remained popular with audiences for centuries.

A final dramatic form is the *secular interlude*, a nonreligious serious or comic play. It began to appear near the end of the fifteenth century, and was performed by traveling players or by troupes employed by noblemen. Such plays were probably called "interludes" because they were performed between the parts of a celebration (for example, the courses of a banquet). In the sixteenth century, the secular interlude was not always distinguishable from the morality play or the farce. All eventually came closer together and finally merged in Elizabethan drama.

DECLINE AND TRANSITION

Many factors account for the decline of Medieval drama. First, the increasing interest in classical learning (to be discussed in a later chapter)

Scene from *Pierre Patelin*. After a woodcut illustration in the first edition of the play printed in 1490. From *L'Ancienne France: Le Théâtre . . . et La Musique . . .*, 1887.

A banquet with interlude entertainment. A nineteenth-century reconstruction from Pougin's *Dictionnaire Historique et Pittoresque du Théâtre* . . . , 1885.

introduced many new concepts which affected the writing and staging of plays. Second, changes in the social structure gradually destroyed the feudal and corporate life which had encouraged such community projects as the presentation of cycle plays. Third, and perhaps most decisive, dissension within the church led to the prohibition of religious plays. After the Church of England was officially established in 1536, cycle plays were altered so as to delete any reminders of Rome. Continuing strife, however, caused Elizabeth I to forbid religious plays when she came to the throne in 1558. Although some of the cycles were performed after this date, they were gradually suppressed.

On the continent, a parallel movement was under way. The secessionist movements led to a demand for reformation in the Roman Catholic church. The Council of Trent, which was held intermittently between 1545 and 1563, attempted to purify the church of all objectionable practices. One result was the abandonment of dramatic entertainments as a means of religious teaching, except in the case of the Jesuits, who were permitted to have theatres in their schools. In 1548 religious plays were forbidden in Paris, and they were either prohibited or gradually abandoned elsewhere. It was only in Spain, where they were not outlawed until 1765, that plays continued to be an important part of religious festivals. For the most part, however, the drama of the Middle Ages had fallen out of favor by 1600.

Chapter 7

SPAIN AND ELIZABETHAN ENGLAND

Two European countries—England and Spain—developed strong popular theatres and major playwrights before the end of the sixteenth century. Although they were affected by the revival of interest in Greek and Roman culture, their theatres were logical outgrowths from Medieval practices. Since the English theatre is of greater importance than the Spanish, it will be considered first and in greater detail.

THE EMERGENCE OF THE PROFESSIONAL ACTING TROUPE

Although there were wandering players in England by the fifteenth century, all professional actors were, under existing law, vagabonds and rogues. The only exceptions were those groups attached to the households of the nobility, since such actors were classified as servants. The first record of the permanent employment of performers by a nobleman is found in 1482, and beginning with Henry VII (who reigned from 1485 to 1509) the rulers of England also maintained troupes.

Legally, the actor was recognized for the first time in a statute of 1572, which stated that all players must obtain a license either from a nobleman or from two justices of the peace. No other actors were permitted to perform. While this ruling seriously restricted the number of theatrical groups, it did give those able to obtain licenses legal status for the first time.

A costume design by Inigo Jones. From Cunningham's *Inigo Jones*. London, 1848.

The law of 1572 had allowed local officials (justices of the peace) to license companies, but in 1574 a new law assigned to the Master of Revels (a court official) the duties of examining all plays and licensing all acting companies. This placed control of the English theatre in the hands of central government.

To receive a license under the new arrangement, a troupe had to be under the patronage of a nobleman, who would allow it to use his name. Equipped with this protection and a license from the Master of Revels, a company had a clear legal right to practice its profession. Usually the nobleman contributed nothing to the financial support of the troupe which bore his name, except on those rare occasions when the company gave private performances at his request. In 1574 the first of these groups, the Earl of Leicester's Men, received a license from the central government. By 1600 there were always at least two companies playing in London, and frequently more.

Without the sanction of Queen Elizabeth and the nobles, the theatre in England might well have been stamped out, and certainly its growth would have been seriously hampered. For, unlike the upper classes who encouraged it, the middle class viewed the theatre with distrust. Many believed that it took people away from their jobs and thereby interfered with honest pursuits, that plays encouraged immorality, and that the theatre was only a camouflage for even more undesirable activities. The powerful town councils, largely composed of middle-class tradesmen, were opposed to professional theatrical activities of any kind.

The royal licensing of acting troupes did not quiet these objections to the theatre. Matters were complicated by the fact that the central government had neither a standing army nor a police force of any size, and had to depend on local authorities to enforce laws. Acting troupes, therefore, were tolerated rather than encouraged, and sometimes town councils paid actors not to perform.

The theatre was centered in London and it was there that the most strenuous objections were raised by local officials. They created so many obstacles that theatre buildings were erected outside the city limits to escape the jurisdiction of the London council. In spite of opposition, however, the protection of the central government permitted the theatre to develop, and by the 1580s it had established a strong foothold.

INFLUENCES ON THE DEVELOPMENT OF ELIZABETHAN DRAMA

The drama which emerged in the late 1580s may be traced to many influences: the schools and universities, the Inns of Court, and the popular theatre.

The revival of interest in classical learning began to be felt in England during the fifteenth century, but was not of major importance until the sixteenth century. As a result of this new interest, plays came to be studied and produced in schools and universities. This development of "school drama" may be divided into three phases: First, the plays of Plautus, Terence, and Seneca were read, studied, and performed in Latin. Second, Englishmen began to write plays both in Latin and English in direct imitation of the Romans. Third, English dramatists injected this classical influence into plays employing English subject matter and backgrounds. In this final phase, the imitation of classical models was largely unconscious, and the plays, although most frequently written and produced at universities, could easily be transferred to the public stage.

Some of the best early English plays were written and produced in the schools. *Ralph Roister Doister* by Nicholas Udall (1505–56) was probably performed at Eton while Udall was headmaster there between 1534 and 1541. *Gammer Gurton's Needle* (by "Mr. S") was acted at Cambridge University sometime between 1552 and 1563. Both of these plays belong to the second phase of development, for they show clearly the influence of Roman comedy.

Thus, schools and universities held a significant position in the development of Elizabethan playwriting, for they acquainted students with classical ideas of dramatic form and structure. Furthermore, English drama blossomed only after such school-trained dramatists as John Lyly, Thomas Kyd, and Christopher Marlowe began to write for the professional theatre.

The Inns of Court—combined residences and training centers for lawyers—were a second source of influence on the development of Elizabethan drama. Lawyers in this period came entirely from the upper classes, and many were interested in current trends in literature and the new classical learning. Like the schools, the Inns of Court produced plays for themselves and for important guests. The first regular English tragedy, *Gorboduc* by Thomas Sackville and Thomas Norton, was produced in 1561 for Queen Elizabeth. This work, which clearly shows the influence of Seneca's tragedies, is the first English play to be written in blank verse. Both Seneca and blank verse were to be of considerable importance to the later popular drama.

Although Elizabethan drama owes much to classical influence, to the schools, and to the Inns of Court, an equal or possibly greater debt is due the Medieval drama and the plays produced by the professional troupes in the sixteenth century. The latter plays were a bizarre mixture of elements from all the preceding native drama and often contained a smattering of the new classical learning as well. Perhaps the most famous of these plays was written by Thomas Preston in the 1560s. The full title indicates both its method and contents: *A Lamentable Tragedie Mixed Full of Pleasant*

Mirth, Containing the Life of Cambises, King of Persia, from the Beginning of his Kingdom, Unto his Death, His one Good Deed of Execution, after that Many Wicked Deeds and Tyrannous Murders, Committed by and through Him, and Last of All, his Odious Death by God's Justice Appointed. Set in Persia, it mixes local characters with abstractions typical of the morality play (such as Shame, Diligence, Trial and Proof), classical mythological figures (such as Cupid and Venus), and English low-comedy farcical types called Hob, Lob, and Marian-May-Be-Good. Probably no play demonstrates better the chaotic condition of popular drama between 1550 and 1585.

It was out of these various influences that a new drama emerged. The years between 1580 and 1642 in England saw the production of many of the world's greatest plays.

PRINCIPAL DRAMATISTS PRIOR TO SHAKESPEARE

Although many dramatists of importance had appeared by the time Shakespeare began to write for the theatre around 1590, the most influential were Thomas Kyd, Christopher Marlowe, and John Lyly.

Thomas Kyd (1558–94) was educated at the Merchant Taylor's School, where he studied Roman drama. His own play, *The Spanish Tragedy* (*c.* 1587), shows the influence of Seneca to a marked degree in such aspects as its sensational subject matter, the motive of revenge, and the use of ghosts and a chorus. It achieved unprecedented popularity and, as a result, became extremely influential. The "revenge" play (of which *Hamlet* is an example) became a popular type of Elizabethan drama, but, more important, Kyd showed his successors how to construct striking situations, startling reversals, and suspenseful plots. Compared to Shakespeare's plays, *The Spanish Tragedy* seems crude, but it represents a remarkable advance in dramatic technique over the English plays which preceded it.

Christopher Marlowe (1564–93) was educated at Cambridge University and began writing for the theatre at about the same time as Kyd. The most important of his plays are *Doctor Faustus, Edward II, Tamburlaine,* and *The Jew of Malta.* Marlowe is generally regarded as the finest English writer of tragedy prior to Shakespeare. His principal contributions to Elizabethan playwriting are: the perfection of blank verse as a medium for drama, and the organization of plays around one strong character whose motives are explored thoroughly. With the possible exception of Shakespeare, Marlowe developed the history play to its highest point.

John Lyly (*c.* 1554–1606) is noted principally for his prose comedies, written in an elegant and sophisticated style on themes taken from mythology. The plays have pastoral settings—a kind of "never-never land" where everything is delicate and graceful. They were widely admired and were

considered important advances over the rather crude farces of the preceding era. The influence of Lyly can best be seen in Shakespeare's *A
Midsummer Night's Dream, As You Like It,* and *Twelfth Night.*

THE ELIZABETHAN THEATRE STRUCTURE

Before considering how Shakespeare built upon the work of his predecessors, it is helpful to examine the theatre building and staging conventions of
the period in which he wrote—from approximately 1590 to about 1615. The
evidence is not always complete, and practice may have varied from one
company or theatre to another, but the probable conditions can be outlined.

Two kinds of theatre buildings—open-air structures (the one usually
designated as the "Shakespearean" theatre) and indoor halls—were in use.
The former are usually referred to as "public" and the latter as "private"
theatres. Both were public in the sense that they were open to any spectator
with the admission fee, but "private" theatres were smaller, charged higher
prices, and played to a more select audience. Beginning in the early seventeenth century, the same troupes played in public theatres in summer and
in private theatres in winter. Since the public theatres were more characteristic of the period, the following discussion will be confined to them.

A note of caution is in order. Since the early 1940s, many have
been led to believe that John Cranford Adams' reconstruction of the Globe
Theatre (the theatre used by Shakespeare's troupe) is an accurate one.
This reconstruction, however, is based largely upon conjecture and cannot
be regarded as authentic; in fact, it is highly questionable in most of its
details. The truth is that we do not know enough about the Elizabethan
theatre to make an adequate reconstruction of anything more than the
broad outlines.

A number of public theatres were built before 1615. The first,
erected in 1576, was called simply The Theatre. Others were: The Curtain (1577), Newington Butts (*c.* 1580), The Rose (1587), The Swan
(1596), The Globe (1599, rebuilt in 1614), The Fortune (1600), and The
Hope (1614). It is not certain that they were alike in their basic appearance; it is logical to assume that they differed considerably in details just
as theatres in any period do.

The theatres varied in size, but the most elaborate seated from two
to three thousand spectators. They were of differing shapes: round, square,
five-sided, eight-sided. Typically, they were laid out in this manner: A large
central unroofed space, called the "pit" or "yard," was enclosed by three
tiers of roofed galleries which formed the outside of the building. At the
door to the theatre each person paid the same admission price. This entitled him to stand in the yard; if he wished to sit, he paid an additional
fee and was admitted to the galleries.

Within the sketch the following labels appear: tectum, poeticus, mimorum ædes, orchestra, proscænium, planities sive arena.

Johannes de Witt of the Netherlands visited London in 1596 and made a sketch of The Swan Theatre. De Witt's friend, Arend van Buchell, made a copy of the sketch, which is reproduced above. De Witt's own drawing has not survived. Since this sketch is the only contemporary pictorial evidence, it influences attempts to reconstruct the Elizabethan theatre. From Bapst's *Essai sur l'Histoire du Théâtre*. Paris, 1893.

A raised stage (from four to six feet high) extended to the center of the yard. This large platform, sometimes called the forestage or main stage, was the principal acting area. Spectators could stand around three sides, and the galleries also commanded a view from at least three sides.

The greatest disagreement about the Elizabethan theatre concerns the "discovery" space (variously called the "inner below," the "study," and the "pavilion") at the rear of the forestage. In many plays of the period characters, objects, or places must be revealed or concealed. It is generally agreed, therefore, that there was an area at the rear of the main stage for this purpose. Its size and precise location, however, are disputed. The two major answers have been: (1) that this area was recessed into the back wall with a curtain across the front; and (2) that this area jutted onto the forestage like a pavilion and thus had curtains around three sides. Neither view can be established, though the weight of opinion is shifting toward the second. For our purposes it is sufficient to know that the large acting area jutting into the middle of the yard had two doors at the rear for entrances and exits, plus a space between these which could be used for revelations and concealments. It may have been large enough for scenes to be played inside it, or it may have been similar to the Medieval mansion (that is, only large enough to indicate a locale, while the forestage served as the *platea*).

Conclusions about the upper stage grow out of those about the discovery space. Those scholars who believe that there was an "inner below" state that there was a similar recessed space on the second level called the "inner above," while those who prefer the "pavilion" argue that there was an acting area on top of this forward projection. In either case, however, it is clear that there was an area on the second level which could be used by the actors. In addition, there were one or two windows on the second level out of which characters could lean or into which they might climb. The logical place for these would be above the two doors on the

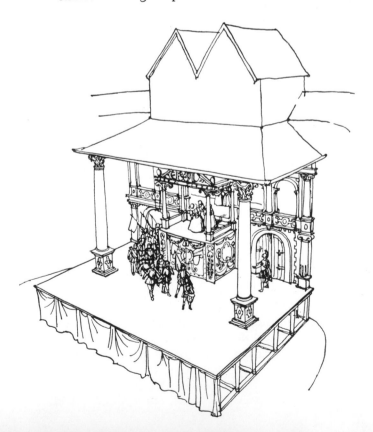

Left: The inner stage conceived of as a pavilion. From C. Walter Hodges' *The Globe Restored.* London: Benn, Ltd., 1953. *Right:* A reconstruction of the Fortune Theatre built in London in 1600. The contract, which still exists, for this building is another principal source of information about the features of the Elizabethan theatre. Also from Hodges. Both courtesy of Ernest Benn, Limited, London.

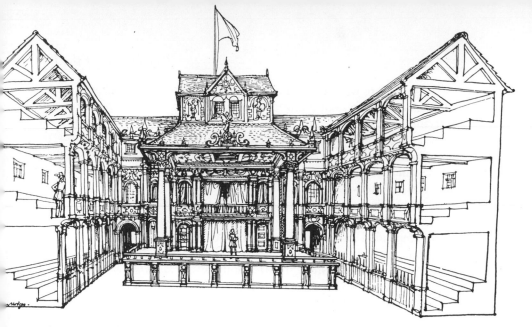

main stage. A third level was occasionally used by actors in scenes supposed to occur in very high places, but ordinarily this space was reserved for musicians.

The basic outlines of the stage, then, are simple: (1) a large platform (at the Fortune Theatre, approximately forty-three feet wide by twenty-seven-and-a-half feet deep) jutting to the middle of the theatre structure; (2) a door on each side at the rear of this stage; (3) a discovery space between these doors; (4) an upper acting area over the discovery space; (5) windows on each side of the upper stage; (6) a third level which might be used by actors, but which was usually reserved for musicians.

This stage seems to have been designed for a continuous flow of dramatic action. As the actors left the forestage by one door at the end of a scene, another group might enter at the other door and begin the next scene; or the discovery space might be opened and the stage would become a new place; or a scene on the forestage might be followed by one on the upper level; or more than one level might be used at the same time. One scene flowed into the next without pause. (The plays were not divided into acts; such divisions were made by later editors.)

It is usual today to assume that no scenery was used in the Elizabethan theatre, but the records kept by Philip Henslowe (a businessman associated with the Admiral's Men) list such items as rocks, trees, beds, a hell-mouth, and a cloth representing the "city of Rome." It is possible that there were a number of set pieces, or that mansions may have been put up occasionally as on the Medieval stage. It is also possible that mansions were used in the beginning and gradually were discarded. It seems unlikely that very much scenery requiring shifting was used, however, as it would have seriously interrupted the flow of scenes. The distinct possibility exists, nevertheless, that scenic elements were used at times.

Machinery was housed both below and above the stage. A number of trap doors in the floor allowed for grave scenes, for the appearances of ghosts and devils, for fire and smoke, and for other special effects. Typically, a roof (supported by posts at the front of the stage) extended over the stage. Cranes, ropes, and pullies for raising and lowering objects were housed there. Sound effects for thunder, alarm bells, cannons, and fireworks were also operated in this area.

The Elizabethan theatre, with all its originality, included many features similar to those of past structures. For example, the Elizabethan theatre depended primarily on a permanent stage facade for its scenic background as had the Roman theatre, and the acting area was surrounded by spectators as in the Greek theatre. Some features were clearly related to the Medieval stage: the generalized acting area, the practice of having spectators stand in the yard, the special effects, and the possible use of mansions—all of these recall Medieval theatre. But, the Elizabethan theatre combined these features in a unique structure which was both derivative and original.

LIGHTING AND COSTUMES

Since theatres were roofless and performances occurred in the afternoon, there was little need for artificial illumination. Night scenes in plays were usually indicated by the presence of candles, lanterns, or torches.

While not much scenery was used, the Elizabethan stage was certainly not devoid of color and pageantry. Banners and other devices were employed to distinguish between armies and knights; there were many battles, processions, and dances. Most important, costumes were an ever-present source of visual pleasure.

The costumes for the Elizabethan stage were of two basic kinds, contemporary clothing and conventional dress. By far the majority of roles were costumed in Elizabethan garments appropriate to the rank or profession of each character. Like the Medieval, the Elizabethan mind had little sense of history, and characters from almost any place or time could be dressed alike.

On the other hand, however, certain stereotypes of the period made it necessary to set off some roles. The principal uses of conventionalized costumes were for: (1) special foreign groups, such as Romans, Turks, or Spaniards, (2) supernatural beings, such as fairies, classical gods, ghosts, and witches, (3) certain professional types, such as clerics, senators, and clowns, and (4) animals, such as lions, boars, and bears.

In spite of this apparent complexity, however, the majority of costumes were basically Elizabethan garments, and most of the conventionalized costumes were created by superimposing a few simple elements

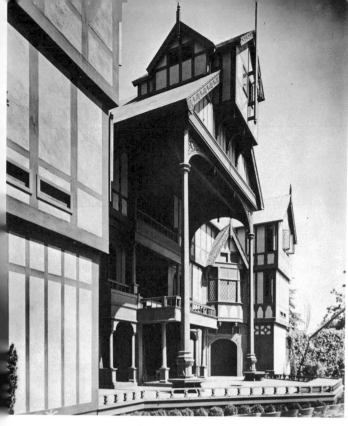

The stage at the Oregon Shakespeare Festival in Ashland, Oregon. Courtesy Oregon Shakespearean Festival Association. Photograph —Dwaine Smith.

on contemporary dress. For example, Roman characters were identified by the addition of a drapery to Elizabethan clothing.

Nevertheless, a large wardrobe was necessary, since each company changed its program almost daily and had a large number of plays in its repertory. An actor might wear his own clothing in some roles, but the company assumed primary responsibility for all other costumes.

THE ACTING TROUPES

Acting companies included from ten to twenty members, of which approximately ten were shareholders, the others were hired men. A company divided its receipts so that each shareholder was entitled to a specified percentage of the profits. The hired men (the "extras," doorkeepers, musicians, and stage hands) were paid a set wage (in this period their pay was comparable to that received by skilled laborers in other trades). Shareholders obviously had an interest in the financial success of the company, and the largest shares were usually allotted to the most important members of the acting company. Typically, when a troupe was formed the shareholders agreed to stay together for a stated period of time, and the conditions under which a member might leave or under which new shareholders might be taken in were specified. The hired men were usually engaged for a period of two years.

If a company did not have enough money to build a theatre, and to buy costumes and other necessary equipment, it might enter into an agreement with another person or group to furnish the necessary items. In return, these "householders" were given half of the gallery receipts, while the company retained the other half, in addition to all of the general admission fees.

Besides the regular members of the troupes, there were also apprentices. Each company needed from three to five boys to perform the female roles. A boy began his apprenticeship when he was between ten and fourteen and continued in it until he reached the age of twenty-one. At the end of his training, he might be taken into the troupe as a regular member, or he might join another company. Each boy was apprenticed to an individual actor rather than to the company as a whole. He lived with his master, who gave him room and board and trained him. Payment for the boy's services was made to the master by the company.

Each of the regular actors probably specialized in certain types of roles. The playwright, as a rule, wrote for a specific company and he knew who would play each character in his play. Thus he often wrote for the special capabilities of specific actors. This may have placed certain restrictions on the dramatist, but it also was an advantage since he knew what he could expect from each actor. Richard Burbage (*c.* 1567–1619) played most of Shakespeare's leading roles, and the range of these parts suggests that he was one of the great actors of the English stage.

The acting company performed a large repertory of plays, changing the bill almost daily. A play was repeated several times during a season if there was sufficient demand, and when it was no longer popular it was dropped from the repertory and a new work was added. Each actor had to be prepared to perform a great number of roles each season and was kept busy rehearsing and performing both new and old plays.

Some companies had dramatists under contract to furnish a set number of plays in a given period and paid them a weekly salary. Other companies bought plays outright. The playwright was expected to supervise the original production of his own works, although subsequent rehearsals were conducted by the bookholder, who combined the functions of prompter and stage manager. Since the actor was supposed to know his trade, the playwright probably confined himself chiefly to explaining his intentions, though he no doubt suggested specific pieces of business or line readings when he was not satisfied with an actor's inventions.

Before a play could be performed, it had to be approved by the Master of Revels. Each actor's part (complete with cues) was then copied and given to him. An over-all summary of exits, entrances, and the play's story line was posted backstage so that actors might consult it. The bookholder kept the master, or prompt, copy of the play in which were indicated exits and entrances, properties required for specific scenes, cues for stage hands and musicians. The bookholder probably stood behind one of the doors at the back of the stage and followed the performance through a grating.

On days when plays were to be presented, a flag was raised above the theatre. Performances were given regularly except during a siege of the plague, during certain religious seasons, or upon the death or severe illness of a ruler or important public official. The audience was composed of all sorts of persons: noblemen, merchants, workmen, men, and women. No doubt the level of appreciation varied considerably among audience members. Some playwrights wrote disparagingly of them, especially the "groundlings" who stood in the yard, while others praised their perceptivity. Each performance ended with singing, dancing, or a comic afterpiece designed to send the audience home in a jolly mood.

SHAKESPEARE

William Shakespeare (1564–1616) is generally conceded to be the greatest of Elizabethan dramatists. Little is known of his early life, but by 1590 he seems to have been established in London, and by 1595 he was a shareholder and actor in the Lord Chamberlain's company. He was later a

The stage of the Stratford Shakespearean Festival, Canada. Although it is an adaptation of many of the features of the Elizabethan stage, it is not an historical reconstruction. Courtesy of the Stratford Shakespearean Festival Foundation of Canada. Photograph—Peter Smith.

householder in The Globe theatre building as well. As householder, actor, director, and playwright, he was a versatile man of the theatre.

He began writing plays around 1590 and completed about thirty-six. It is difficult to date his individual plays, but they have been placed in approximate order through similarities in style, contemporary references to them, and other types of evidence. Like most of his contemporaries, Shakespeare borrowed much of his material from novels, older plays, histories, mythology, and other sources.

Shakespeare's works have been divided into three groups: histories, comedies, and tragedies. In the histories he dealt with the English past, especially the period of the War of the Roses. These plays (*Richard II, Henry IV*, Parts I and II, *Henry V, Henry VI*, Parts I, II, and III, *Richard III*, and *Henry VIII*) show his skill at reducing large masses of historical material to the demands of the stage.

His comedies represent a wide range of styles. *The Comedy of Errors* (based on Plautus' *Menaechmi*), *The Taming of the Shrew*, and *The Merry Wives of Windsor* tend toward the broad effects of farce; *A Midsummer Night's Dream, As You Like It*, and *Twelfth Night* are romantic comedies; *All's Well that Ends Well, Measure for Measure*, and *Troilus and Cressida* are plays so near to being serious that they are frequently termed *dark* comedies.

But it was in tragedy that Shakespeare displayed his greatest genius, though here too he used a wide range of subject matter and treatment. *Romeo and Juliet, Hamlet, Julius Caesar, Macbeth, Othello, King Lear*, and *Antony and Cleopatra* must be ranked among the greatest tragedies ever written. More problematical are *Titus Andronicus*, with its Senecan horrors; and *Cymbeline, The Winter's Tale*, and *Pericles*, which are tragicomedies. Since it is impossible to discuss all of Shakespeare's plays, a single work, *King Lear*, will be examined in detail.

KING LEAR

THEMES AND IDEAS. The basic theme of *King Lear* is the relationship of parents and children; it appears in the main plot, concerning Lear and his daughters, and in the subplot, dealing with Gloucester and his sons. Since the parent–child relationship is a basic part of human experience, *King Lear* has universal significance.

The second theme is appearance versus truth. Both Lear and Gloucester are deceived (with very little evidence) by an appearance of perfidy and lack of gratitude in children who are actually loyal and true, and both accept as truth the lies created by their false children. As in *Oedipus the King*, a contrast is also drawn between physical sight and spiritual blindness. Gloucester says, after his eyes have been put out, "I

The opening scene of *King Lear* at the Oregon Shakespeare Festival, 1958. Courtesy Oregon Shakespearean Festival Association. Photograph—Dwaine Smith.

stumbled when I saw." In Lear's case, madness is substituted for blindness. The perfidy of his daughters causes Lear to lose his reason, but in this state he grasps the truth more firmly than when he was sane. As Edgar points out, Lear has found "Reason in madness!" Near the end of the play Lear and Gloucester explore the meaning of their experiences.

> *Lear.*   . . . yet you see how this world goes.
> *Glou.*   I see it feelingly.
> *Lear.*   What! Art mad? A man may see how this world goes with
> no eyes.
>
> Through tattered clothes great vices do appear;
> Robes and furred gowns hide all. Plate sin with gold,
> And the strong lance of justice hurtless breaks:
> Arm it in rags, a pigmy's straw does pierce it.
> . . . .
> Get thee glass eyes
> And, like a scurvy politician, seem
> To see the things thou dost not.

Both Lear and Gloucester learn the difference between appearance and truth—the difference between those like Cordelia and Edgar and those like Goneril, Regan, and Edmund. In one sense, then, the play dramatizes the results of choices made on the basis of appearance. Through suffering comes wisdom, though in Lear's case it comes too late.

A third theme concerns the degree to which man's fate is determined by forces outside himself. For instance, Gloucester, early in the play, suggests that strange happenings in human affairs are caused by a dislocation in the planets; later he says: "As flies to wanton boys are we to th'gods;/

They kill us for their sport." Fortune also is considered a governor of man's fate.

In the Elizabethan period, Fortune was frequently pictured as a goddess with a wheel, which might raise a man to the pinnacle of fame for no demonstrable reason and just as inexplicably dash him down again. It is in this context that Kent says: "Fortune, good night; smile once more; turn thy wheel." On the other hand, there are numerous suggestions that man's fate is determined by his own decisions. It is Lear's first choice which makes all of the later events possible; similarly, it is Gloucester's hasty belief in Edmund's lies that leads to his downfall. In the final scene, Edgar states: "The gods are just, and of our pleasant vices/ Make instruments to plague us."

These opposing views of human destiny are partially explained by the Renaissance conception of the universe. Man, as the final creation of God, was thought to be the center of God's concern; God had created the earth and all its nonhuman inhabitants for man's use. Furthermore, it was believed that the entire universe revolved around the immobile earth. The planets were said to move in concentric spheres, one inside the other. Because all parts of the universe were connected like the cogs of a machine, the well-being of the whole was affected by each part. Harmony among all created a "music of the spheres," but chaotic conditions in any element were felt throughout the universe. This explains why physical manifestations of disorder play such a large part in Shakespeare's tragedies. The storm in *King Lear*, for example, is a metaphorical indication of the disruption of order.

To Shakespeare man is not a mere puppet, but an intelligent being free to choose his own path. Consequently, he frequently violates the divine order, and, when he does, he suffers accordingly.

No doubt there are other themes in *King Lear*, since the implications of such a great play cannot be easily exhausted. These three—parent–child relationships, appearance versus truth, and the degree to which man is free—are themes, however, which have interested men in all ages.

PLOT AND STRUCTURE.   Shakespeare's skill in play construction may be seen by examining the over-all movement of the main plot. The opening scene establishes Lear's position as an absolute monarch. He disposes of the kingdom as though it were his own private property, and passes sentence on his daughters and subjects without consulting anyone. He is accustomed to having every whim satisfied: he expects his daughters to express publicly their love for him, and he disowns Cordelia when she will not flatter him; he banishes Kent for presuming to offer advice. In this way Lear's character is established. Furthermore, without this scene it would be impossible to appreciate the extent of Lear's fall. The opening also prepares for later events by revealing the true motives of Goneril, Regan, Cordelia, and Kent.

Between this beginning and Lear's reunion with Cordelia near the play's close comes a series of humiliations for Lear which, though mild at first, lead to his abandonment in a raging storm and culminate in his madness. Although Lear's downfall is not undeserved, the undisguised evil of Goneril and Regan arouse indignation at his treatment and create constantly increasing sympathy for him. Compassion is aroused when Lear's growing recognition of his mistakes is accompanied by a loss of power to rectify them. In the storm scene he is completely stripped of authority and is forced to face himself as a man, alone, at the mercy of his inward torment just as he is at the mercy of the outward torment of the elements.

The scenes which follow the storm show Lear's attempts to re-orient himself. In his powerless state he comes to know the difference between freely offered devotion and that which is pretended for the sake of reward. But the evil forces which Lear has unleashed through Goneril and Regan prevent him from rebuilding a life based upon his new-found wisdom.

Much the same progression is found in the subplot. There are significant differences, however, for while Lear himself sets his destruction in motion when he divides his kingdom, Edmund is the moving force

King Lear at the Old Vic, London, 1958. Scene showing Goneril, Regan, the Fool, and Lear. Directed by Douglas Seale; setting and costumes by Leslie Hurry. Photograph—Angus McBean. Courtesy of the Old Vic Company and Angus McBean.

behind Gloucester's downfall. Gloucester's blindness (which parallels Lear's madness) is caused by his loyalty to Lear, and is not inflicted by his own children. Like Lear, however, Gloucester is forced to re-examine himself and experiences a spiritual rebirth.

Perhaps Shakespeare's structural skill can be seen most clearly in the intertwining of the two plots. This is accomplished in a number of ways: by having Gloucester and Edmund present at Lear's abdication; by having Gloucester serve as host to Regan and the Duke of Cornwall; through Gloucester's attempts to aid Lear; and through the relationships between Edmund, Goneril, and Regan. Furthermore, the resolutions of the two stories are made essentially one: Goneril and Regan kill each other over love of Edmund; Edmund orders the deaths of Lear and Cordelia; the revelation of Goneril's love for Edmund leads to a duel between Edgar and Edmund and to Edmund's death. Thus, while the subplot has its own intrinsic interest, it simultaneously serves to point up the themes found in the main plot and motivates much that happens to Lear. Gloucester's story, therefore, is essential to the main plot and not a distraction.

The unity of action found in *King Lear* is not of the same kind, however, as that in *Oedipus the King,* in which all attention is focused upon Oedipus and his search. Shakespeare uses a much broader canvas than Sophocles and includes more facets of the story, more characters, a wider sweep of time and place. Nevertheless, he has not sacrificed unity, for the various elements have been carefully integrated.

CHARACTERIZATION AND ACTING. The role of Lear is far more complex than any other in the play. It is sometimes difficult to distinguish between such characters as Goneril and Regan because of the few traits assigned each; both have the same motives, and the over-all impression is simply that each is completely depraved. Cordelia, on the other hand, is the perfect woman, and has as little trace of evil as her sisters have of good.

Shakespeare gives little information about the physical and social attributes of his characters and emphasizes psychological motives instead. Each of the secondary personages has one dominant drive which is placed in opposition to that of another character. Thus, Cordelia is contrasted with her sisters, Edgar with Edmund, Cornwall with Albany, Kent with Oswald, and France with Burgundy.

Although the secondary characters are not as complex as Lear, they are not poorly conceived, for they fulfill well their functions in the dramatic action. Furthermore, each role offers the imaginative actor a challenge to create a characterization of considerable depth. For example, Edgar must assume a series of disguises (a madman, a peasant, an unknown knight), change his speech from poetry to prose and from standard English to an accent, and convey a sense of deep emotional involvement when often

Dekker's *Shoemaker's Holiday* done in a setting which approximates an Elizabethan stage. Directed by Walter H. Trumbauer.

his disguise will not permit the open expression of his true feelings. Thus, a basic character type (the good son) is individualized by involving him in a series of unusual events. Nevertheless, the dominant impression created by Edgar is one of simplicity rather than of complexity, and actors who have played the role have sometimes experienced difficulty in making Edgar interesting to audiences. The same is true of Cordelia, but less so of Goneril, Regan, and Edmund, since evil characters always seem to fascinate audiences.

Gloucester comes near to being a copy of Lear. Both are old men, easily deceived, and they undergo many of the same experiences. Lear's role, however, is developed at much greater length and in more depth than is Gloucester's. In the opening scene, both Gloucester and Lear seem vigorous, but by the end of the play both are decrepit and broken. The decline from vigor to debility is dramatically right. Furthermore, visible physical change seems essential to the play's development.

Lear is difficult to interpret because the part encompasses a wide range of action, emotion, and psychological change. In the opening scene, Lear is in complete command; he is easily angered and insists upon having every wish satisfied. This habitual, and somewhat childish, behavior defeats him when he no longer has the power to enforce his desires. Impotence commences during his first clash with Goneril, and his sense of frustration grows until it leads to madness. Lear's insanity is portrayed with variety. At first he shouts imprecations, and then he becomes quiet and withdrawn; his dialogue shifts to prose, and he becomes preoccupied with sex, devils, and tortures. From this low point, Lear gradually begins a spiritual ascent, though he never regains his physical vigor. His psychological regeneration develops slowly, for he feels undeserving of Cordelia's love and he can comprehend her forgiveness only with difficulty. When he at last understands the extent of her devotion, he determines to make recompense for the past. Their reunion, which reaches heights of happiness only to descend to despair and death, requires consummate acting skill on the part of the actor portraying Lear.

Throughout the play, Shakespeare injects details to humanize Lear. Perhaps the most obvious of these comes in one of the final speeches, into which Lear injects, "Pray you, undo this button." Here, a figure fighting with overwhelming emotions is suddenly reduced to the level of common humanity. It is a simple touch, but one that arouses pathos more effectively than any description of Lear's feelings could.

The part of the Fool is used as a foil for Lear. His privileged state allows him to speak openly what others must leave unsaid, and it is significant that he is present only in those scenes which can profit from such outspokenness. When Lear himself is turned into a simpleton by insanity, he speaks in the same blunt fashion as the Fool. After the storm scene, the Fool does not reappear, for he is no longer needed.

Lear, thus, is the center of concern for Shakespeare. The other characters are adequate, but in no sense approach the complexity of the title role.

LANGUAGE. Shakespeare's dramatic poetry is generally conceded to be the greatest in the English language. His basic medium is blank verse, which allows much of the flexibility of ordinary speech while at the same time elevating and formalizing it. The final lines in a scene, usually written in rhymed couplets, serve to round off and brake the forward movement of the verse, like a *coda* in music.

This pattern (blank verse ending in a rhymed couplet) is broken frequently by the injection of passages written in prose, which, typically, are spoken by lower-class characters and are often used for comic purposes. In *King Lear*, however, both Edgar and Lear turn to prose in the mad scenes, for though they do not change rank in actuality, they look at life from the standpoint of the simple mind and speak as though they were members of the lower class.

Probably the most important element in Shakespeare's dialogue is figurative language. The principal purpose of a figure of speech in dramatic poetry is to set up either direct or indirect comparisons. Shakespeare's superiority over other writers of dramatic poetry lies in his use of comparisons which enlarge the significance without distracting the attention from a dramatic situation. For example, in the following passage he associates the storm with Lear's daughters and at the same time suggests that the storm is a sign of divine displeasure. Thus, the audience grasps the significance of the immediate event and its larger implications simultaneously.

> Rumble thy bellyfull! Spit, fire! spout, rain!
> Nor rain, wind, thunder, fire are my daughters.
> I tax not you, you elements, with unkindness:
> I never gave you kingdom, called you children;
> You owe me no subscription. Then let fall
> Your horrible displeasure. Here I stand your slave,
> A poor, infirm, weak, and despised old man.

Shakespeare often combines direct and indirect comparisons in a single passage. For example, both metaphors and similes are used to relate a character's mental state to that of a tortured soul in Hell.

> You do me wrong to take me out o'th'grave:
> Thou art a soul in bliss; but I am bound
> Upon a wheel of fire, that mine own tears
> Do scald like molten lead.

These examples, which by no means exhaust the range of Shakespeare's figurative language, also illustrate how his poetic devices partially fulfill the same function as the constant visual representation of Heaven and Hell on the Medieval stage. They relate human actions to the divine and demonic forces of the universe; and man's affairs are depicted as significant to all creation.

Shakespeare's language makes special demands upon the actor. Figures of speech are apt to seem contrived and bombastic if the actor does not appear to be experiencing a state of feeling sufficient to call forth such language spontaneously. All too frequently, Shakespeare's plays are damaged in performance when actors do not rise to the emotional demands of poetry. The very richness of expression can be a stumbling block for both performer and reader.

SPECTACLE AND SOUND. There are many opportunities for visual splendor in *King Lear*. The action occurs in a large number of places, and if all were depicted realistically the stage would present a constantly changing aspect. Our knowledge of the Elizabethan stage, however, suggests that Shakespeare envisioned the spectacle in terms of stage properties, costumes, and the movement of actors.

Although scenery is not important, the frequent change of stage place is. The forestage, inner and upper stages would allow the necessary flow of one scene into the next. For example, the storm scene, which is set consecutively in an open space, before a hovel, and inside a farm house, would require only the forestage and the discovery space.

The relatively bare stage is enlivened by processions, contending armies, and numerous attendants. The opening scene, for example, is an important state occasion which would demand an elaborate procession of officials and courtiers, all of whom would be dressed in their finest garments. In later scenes, banners and heraldic devices would be used to distinguish Albany's and Cornwall's forces from those of the French. In almost every scene minor characters enrich the stage picture.

The actors' stage business also creates spectacle. Gloucester's eyes are put out, Kent is seized and placed in the stocks, Edgar and Edmund fight a duel, Lear dies. Nearly every scene offers physical action of this sort. (A comparison of the onstage action of *King Lear* with that of *Oedipus the King* helps to define a principal difference between Elizabethan and Greek tragedy.)

The costumes are an important visual element. In Shakespeare's day, most characters probably wore contemporary garments but their necessarily large wardrobes would provide much variety in color and line. During the production some characters must change costumes several times. For example, Lear first appears in robes of state; in the following scenes, he wears the garments of a nobleman; after he goes mad he appears in tattered garments entwined with weeds and flowers; and, following his reunion with Cordelia, he is restored to clothes appropriate to his rank. Edgar changes from his gentleman's attire to rags, then to a peasant's garment, and finally to a suit of armor. Although most of the characters probably wear the same costumes throughout the play, the shifting combination of persons on stage lends constant variety to the picture.

Such sound effects as the storm, offstage fighting, and trumpet flourishes, are important in *King Lear*. Music is used in a number of scenes. But most important is the sound of the actors' voices speaking Shakespeare's poetry.

King Lear, because of its combination of universal themes, a compelling story, powerful characters, great poetry, and interesting visual and aural effects, is one of the world's great plays. Although it embodies the values of its own period, it is timeless in appeal and transcends the limitations of a particular era. Thus, it continues to move audiences today as it has since its first presentation.

SHAKESPEARE'S CONTEMPORARIES AND SUCCESSORS

Shakespeare's greatness diverts attention from his contemporaries and successors, many of whom are also among the world's best writers. Of Shakespeare's contemporaries, Ben Jonson (1572–1637) was the most important. He began his career in the theatre as an actor (around 1597), but did not continue long in that profession. In 1598 he wrote *Every Man in His Humour* (in which Shakespeare acted), and he soon became one of the most controversial authors of the day. He often accused his fellow playwrights of failing to understand the purposes and techniques of drama and of catering to the depraved taste of the "groundlings." Of all the authors of the period, Jonson was most attuned to classical ideas, and his work as a poet, playwright, and critic influenced many younger men to work for a more classical "regularity."

His most famous plays are *Volpone* (1606), *The Silent Woman* (1609), *The Alchemist* (1610), and *Bartholomew Fair* (1614)—all comedies. His tragedies were not well received. Jonson also wrote most of the masques (to be discussed later) which were presented at the courts of James I and Charles I.

Probably Jonson is best remembered for popularizing the "comedy of humours." Since classical times it had been assumed that there were four bodily "humours," blood, phlegm, yellow and black bile, and that health depended upon the proper balance among these fluids. Too much of any one was said to lead to illness. The practice of medicine, therefore, consisted of two basic treatments: purging (to eliminate excessive bile or phlegm), and bleeding (to eliminate excessive blood).

A number of Elizabethan authors applied this medical concept to human psychology, and Jonson, in particular, drew upon it in writing plays. He attributed the eccentricities of behavior to an imbalance of humours and created a wide range of character types based upon this scheme. The psychology of humours was much in vogue between 1598 and 1603, and, though it is seldom mentioned in plays after that time, many playwrights continued to base their characterizations on it. This approach to human behavior tended to produce character types rather than well-rounded individuals.

Jonson's most widely admired play is *Volpone*. The main character, Volpone, pretends to be rich and without heirs. Each of several persons is led to believe that he will inherit the fortune if he can stay in favor with Volpone. Consequently, each showers him with expensive gifts. At last Volpone tires of his deception, makes a will leaving all his wealth to his servant, Mosca, and pretends to die. Later, when he tries to reclaim his property, Mosca refuses to give it up. Eventually Volpone, Mosca, and the would-be heirs are exposed and punished.

Most of the characters have been given the names of predatory animals, birds, or insects, such as Volpone (the fox), Voltore (the vulture), and Mosca (the fly), and the names are descriptive of the characters. Into this network of corruption, Jonson introduces two sympathetic figures, Celia and Bonario, who are almost sent to prison through the collusion of the others. This complication threatens to make the play serious, but the truth is revealed in time to prevent injustice and to maintain the high level of comedy.

Jonson frequently used comedy to denounce vice and foolish behavior. His consistent purpose of reforming conduct has led many to describe his plays as "corrective comedies."

Francis Beaumont (*c.* 1584–1616) and John Fletcher (1579–1625), who wrote a number of plays in collaboration, were principally responsible for establishing the vogue of tragicomedy and romantic tragedy. Their chief works are *Philaster, The Maid's Tragedy, A King and No King,* and *The Scornful Lady,* all written between 1608 and 1613.

Tragicomedy and romantic tragedy are similar forms; both are essentially serious but tragicomedy ends happily and romantic tragedy unhappily. The subjects of Beaumont and Fletcher's plays were usually sensational. For example, in *The Maid's Tragedy* a wife tells her husband on their wedding night that she is the King's mistress, and that she has married him only as a means of continuing her affair. The rest of the play develops from this sensational revelation.

Both playwrights were particularly skilled in dramatic construction. They built complications to startling climaxes, alternated quiet and tumultuous episodes, and condensed complex material into far fewer scenes than Shakespeare employed. Their plays show more technical proficiency than do Shakespeare's, but their subjects emphasized the shocking rather than the significant. Until well into the eighteenth century, their plays maintained a reputation equal to those of Shakespeare and Jonson and were performed regularly until the nineteenth century.

All of the characteristics noted in the work of Beaumont and Fletcher formed a general pattern during the period from 1610 to 1642. Important writers of tragedy during these years include John Webster (? –1634) and John Ford (1586–1639). Webster's *The White Devil* (1612) and *The Duchess of Malfi* (1614) are among the most powerful of English tragedies. Ford is best known for *'Tis Pity She's a Whore* (*c.* 1625–33), in which a brother and sister are lovers. Since Ford treats them sympathetically, the play is frequently used as evidence of the decadence of English drama after the death of Shakespeare.

Other noteworthy playwrights of the time were Thomas Middleton (*c.* 1570–1627), Philip Massinger (1583–1640), Thomas Heywood (*c.* 1570–1641), Thomas Dekker (*c.* 1572–*c.* 1632), Cyril Tourneur (1575–1626), and James Shirley (1596–1666).

THE COURT MASQUE

When James I came to the English throne in 1603, he brought with him a taste for elaborate theatrical entertainment. He became the patron of Shakespeare's company, which was renamed the King's Men, and gradually all London troupes came under the direct patronage of the royal family.

The frontispiece to Kirkman's *The Wits* published in 1662. The book contains a number of "drolls," or short scenes extracted or altered from longer plays, which were probably performed during the Commonwealth. This illustration was long thought to represent the stage of the Red Bull, a public theatre which was used regularly from c. 1605–1642. More recently it has been argued that it represents a composite of the stages used for surreptitious performances during the Commonwealth. Note that the characters drawn are from a number of different plays. From *Londina Illustrata*. Volume II, 1825.

Unlike Elizabeth, who usually contented herself with performances by the public troupes, James also financed private court entertainments called "masques," which were performed on special occasions, such as weddings, births, and visits from foreign dignitaries. The English masque was similar in all important features to the Italian *intermezzo* and utilized Italian staging methods. (See Chapter 8 for a discussion of Italian materials.) Ben Jonson wrote a majority of the masques, which were designed by Inigo Jones (1573–1652), the court architect. Jones had studied in Italy, and it was he who initiated Italian staging methods in England.

The influence of the masque was soon felt in the public theatres, where processions, music, allegorical scenes and dances were employed with increasing frequency. For example, Shakespeare's *The Tempest* (1611) contains many masquelike elements. But the influence of the masque on scenery in the public theatre was not great until after 1660, when the proscenium arch and perspective settings were introduced.

CLOSING OF THE THEATRES

Although the theatre was a thriving institution and was encouraged by the royal family, Puritan opposition to it grew throughout the first part of the seventeenth century. In 1642, after Puritan forces had won the Civil War, all theatres were ordered closed and were not reopened until Charles II was restored to the throne in 1660. There were surreptitious performances during the Commonwealth, but the English theatre was virtually non-existent during these years. When it was revived in 1660, it bore little resemblance to the theatre of Shakespeare, for it had been altered in accordance with Italian staging ideals and new tastes in drama.

SPANISH THEATRE AND DRAMA IN THE GOLDEN AGE

As in England, the late sixteenth century brought a burst of activity in Spain. So fertile was the period between 1580 and 1680 that it has been designated the Golden Age of Spanish literature. Both the Spanish theatre

A conjectural reconstruction of a Spanish *corrale* as it might have appeared about 1660. From Ricardo Sepulveda's *El Corral de La Pacheca.* Madrid, 1888.

A reconstruction of a *carro* or wagon for an *auto sacramentale*. From Sepulveda's *El Corral de La Pacheca*, 1888.

and drama of this era have much in common with their English counterparts.

The first permanent public theatre (or *corrale*) was opened in Madrid in 1574, two years prior to England's first permanent theatre. It was remodeled from an already existing courtyard formed by the walls of houses. The balconies of the surrounding buildings were used to seat spectators, while standing room and benches were provided in the courtyard. The stage, situated at one end, did not jut into the middle of the yard as in England, and was viewed only from the front. Its plan was similar to that of the Elizabethan theatre, however, in most other respects: back of a large forestage, an inner area could be closed off by a curtain, while a balcony served as an upper stage. Later Spanish theatres used the same basic arrangement.

The connection between the church and the theatre remained close in Spain, and some of the *corrales* were under the control of *confradias*, or religious and charitable institutions. Furthermore, nearly all playwrights of the Golden Age wrote plays (*autos sacramentales*) for religious festivals, and professional troupes performed them. Religious dramas were not forbidden in Spain until 1765.

Although Lope de Rueda (1510–65), a dramatist, actor, and producer, is credited with establishing the professional theatre in Spain, it did not flourish until after 1580. The two great playwrights of the Golden Age were Lope Felix de Vega Carpio, usually called Lope de Vega (1562–1635), and Pedro Calderon de la Barca (1600–81).

Lope de Vega was a prolific playwright. Over four hundred extant works are attributed to him, and some accounts estimate his total output as more than eighteen hundred plays. His subjects were drawn from the Bible, the lives of the saints, mythology, history, romances, and from other sources. Although he was an inventive and skillful writer, his dramas fail to achieve that profundity which marks Shakespeare's work. Like Shakespeare, he made considerable use of song and dance, and intermixed the comic and the serious. Some of his best known dramas are *The Sheep Well*, *The Gardener's Dog*, and *The King, the Greatest Alcalde*. Because of his great output and popularity, Lope de Vega influenced almost all subsequent Spanish dramatists. His reputation in Spain is comparable to that of Shakespeare in England.

With the exception of structure, Calderon's plays bear little resemblance to those of Lope, for they are explorations of theological and philosophical ideas. He is said to have written more than two hundred plays, of which approximately one hundred survive. Many of his works are *autos sacramentales* written for religious festivals. Probably the best known of these is *The Great World Theatre* (c. 1645), while the greatest of his philosophical plays is *Life Is a Dream* (1673).

Other important playwrights of the Golden Age were Tirso de Molina (1584–1648), whose play *The Deceiver of Seville* is the first dramatic treatment of the Don Juan legend, and Juan Ruiz de Alarcon y Mendoza (c. 1581–1639). Unfortunately, with the death of Calderon, the Spanish theatre ceased to be a vital force.

Thus, both England and Spain developed strong dramatic traditions before the new Italian ideas of writing and staging were widely known in either country. Their theatres appear to be logical and gradual evolutions from preceding practices. And, in neither country was there a sharp division between the theatrical entertainment designed for the court and that intended for the common people. Possibly the vigor of Spanish and English drama may be attributed to the fact that it was written for all classes and was not the art of a select few.

Chapter 8

THE ITALIAN RENAISSANCE

Even before the theatres of Spain and England had developed, the Renaissance had begun to transform the Italian stage. Although Italy produced no drama of importance in this period, it introduced three innovations which were to influence the theatre throughout Europe: the proscenium stage, perspective scenery, and the *commedia dell'arte*.

BACKGROUND

Many forces helped to create the Renaissance. Probably the most important of these was the general secularization of thought. Men ceased to be preoccupied with the problem of salvation and devoted more attention to living in the present. Since Medieval learning was deficient in most practical subjects, guidance was sought in classical writings. Rome exerted far greater influence than Greece, because Latin was the language of the educated class; Greek was not widely known in the West until the sixteenth century.

The interest in classical learning soon extended to plays. Although the works of Terence had served throughout the preceding centuries as models of spoken Latin, they had not been studied for their dramatic qualities. In the fifteenth century, however, they became increasingly

A drawing by Jacques Callot (1592–1635) showing *commedia dell'arte* characters Razullo, left, and Cucurucu, right, and in the background a stage. From Pougin's *Dictionnaire Historique et Pittoresque du Théâtre* . . . , 1885.

popular as literary works. Attention was also attracted to the plays of Plautus and Seneca. Plautus' reputation was enhanced by the discovery in 1429 of a number of plays which had been lost. With interest in Latin drama well established, Greek plays gradually became known. When Constantinople fell to the Turks in 1453, many scholars fled to the West bringing valuable manuscripts, among them those of the Greek dramas. These plays were not widely disseminated, however, until the sixteenth century.

The spread of classical learning was aided by the invention of the printing press. Prior to this invention, all books had been copied by hand. But now Johann Gutenberg's press made it possible to reproduce an unlimited number of copies of the same work, reduced the cost of books and made them available to a much wider public. Printing was introduced into Italy in 1465, and classical dramas were printed shortly thereafter: Plautus' plays in 1472, Terence's in 1473, Seneca's between 1474 and 1484, Aristophanes' in 1498, Sophocles' in 1502, Euripides' in 1503, and Aeschylus' in 1518.

This new interest in classical drama was accompanied by an inquiry into literary principles. What is the purpose of drama? Are there rules for writing plays? What distinguishes comedy from tragedy? For answers to these and many other questions, Renaissance critics turned to the works of Horace and Aristotle. Horace's *Art of Poetry* (written in the first century B.C.) was published in 1470, and Aristotle's *Poetics* (written in the fourth century B.C.) was published in 1498. The theorizing based on these two works eventually crystallized into those neoclassical precepts which dominated dramatic writing for almost two hundred years. (These precepts will be discussed in Chapter 9.)

The theatre of Greece and Rome also attracted attention. The chief source of information was *De Architectura* by Vitruvius, a Roman architect of the first century B.C. This treatise was rediscovered in 1414 and was first printed in 1486; it was so popular that twenty-three editions had appeared by 1600.

Interest in plays of the past soon led to a desire to see them staged. Leadership in production was divided between the courts and the academies. Italy at this time was a collection of independent states, many of them quite small, each ruled by a Duke or Prince. The maintenance of a sumptuous court at which the arts were patronized became a common means of demonstrating the supposed superiority of one ruler over another. Court theatres, supported by almost limitless funds, thus developed those scenic conventions which were to dominate the European stage until the nineteenth century.

Although less wealthy than the courts, the academies also contributed significantly to the development of theatre in the Renaissance.

Many court spectacles were staged in gardens, courtyards, or streets. Here is a scene designed by Buontalenti for the courtyard of the Pitti Palace in Florence, for a wedding celebration in 1589. From a print in the University of Iowa Library.

An academy was an organization which had been formed for the purpose of studying a specific subject. Some were devoted to classical architecture, and these did much to popularize Vitruvius' work; others were formed to study classical drama, or literary theory. Many of them constructed theatres and staged plays. Their greatest influence, however, was exerted through their formulation and dissemination of theories about the physical theatre and drama.

The theatres of both the courts and academies were essentially amateur organizations designed for the entertainment of select audiences on special occasions. For example, at the courts scenery was designed by court architects, the plays were usually written by authors under royal patronage, and the actors were courtiers. Plays were produced at irregular intervals for such occasions as engagements, weddings, births, or visits by important personages.

Since Medieval drama was spurned as formless and old-fashioned, the plays staged by courts and academies were either classical or close imitations of the classics. They were called *commedia erudita* (or learned drama) to distinguish them from the popular, nonliterary *commedia dell'arte* productions.

COMMEDIA ERUDITA

Lodovico Ariosto (1474–1533) was the first important Italian comic writer, and his *Cassaria* (1508) and *I Suppositi* (1509) are regarded by many as the beginning of Italian drama. The play which has the greatest appeal today, however, is *Mandragola* (*c.* 1513–20) by Niccolo Machiavelli (1469–1527). It shows how a jealous old man is tricked into approving of an adulterous relation between his wife and a young man. It is an amusing comedy which combines classical form with the cynicism and subject matter of Medieval farce.

The first important tragedy in the *erudita* tradition is *Sofonisba* (1524) by Giangiorgio Trissino (1478–1550). Although such plays as *Orbecche*, *Dido*, and *Cleopatra* by Giambattista Giraldi Cinthio (1504–73) achieved considerable success, tragedy was never very popular in the Renaissance, and most of it seems lifeless today.

A third form, the pastoral, also came into prominence in the sixteenth century. Although it is like the Greek satyr play in the use of rural settings and of characters such as nymphs, satyrs, and shepherds, it is completely unlike the satyr play in its emphasis upon fine sentiments, delicate shades of emotion, and conventional love stories. The most popular of the pastoral plays were *Aminta* (1573) by Torquato Tasso (1544–95) and *The Faithful Shepherd* (*c.* 1590) by Giambattista Guarini (1538–1612).

THE INTERMEZZI AND OPERA

The love for spectacle could not always be satisfied by the *commedia erudita*, most of which required only a single setting. Therefore, in spite of the contemporary rejection of Medieval drama, the taste for allegorical devices, processions, and miraculous occurrences continued.

Out of this interest grew the *intermezzi*, which were at first short pieces played between the acts of regular plays. Their popularity, however, soon led to their expansion into separate pieces in which the love of spectacle was given full expression. Typically, their subjects were drawn from mythology, especially those stories which allowed the use of elaborate special effects, such as Hercules descending into Hades, or Perseus on his flying horse fighting a sea monster. Each character and event was given an allegorical interpretation which related it to the royal patron, his enemies, or friends. Music and dance also were emphasized.

The intermezzi were later absorbed into opera, which after 1600 became the favorite dramatic form in Italy. Opera received its first impetus

Another court spectacle, *Das Rossballet*, at the court of Vienna in 1667. From Alexander von Weilen's *Geschichte des Wiener Theaterwesens*. Volume I, Vienna, 1899. Joseph Furttenbach (1591–1667) studied in Italy from *c.* 1610–20 and took many of the Italian staging ideas back to Germany. The design below shows clearly the Italian influence. From Furttenbach's *Architectura Civilis*, Ulm, 1628.

at the Camerata Academy in Florence, a group especially interested in Greek tragedy. The members of the Camerata knew that Greek tragedy had had a chorus, that it had included music and dance, that at least part of the dialogue had been sung or chanted, and that the plots had been drawn from Greek mythology. Out of their efforts to write plays of this kind, opera began to take shape around 1597. By 1650 the new form was popular throughout Italy and was rapidly spreading to all of Europe.

After the development of opera, the intermezzo declined in popu-

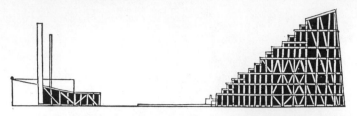

larity, since most of its characteristics were absorbed into the newer form. After 1600 opera became increasingly important in stimulating experiments with scenery and special effects. And it was through opera that Italian theatrical ideas were first imported into most European countries.

DEVELOPMENT OF THE ITALIAN STAGE

Although there were a number of theatrical centers in Italy, the principal ones were at Florence, Ferrara, Urbino, Mantua, Rome, and Milan. A stage was built in the Vatican as early as 1452, and there are scattered references to temporary theatres during the remainder of the fifteenth century. The major developments, however, had to wait until the sixteenth century.

From the very beginning, two traditions were at work: that which stemmed from the architectural treatise of Vitruvius, and that derived from the contemporary interest in perspective. Attempts to combine these two forces led eventually to the modern theatre.

Credit for formalizing the principles of perspective is usually given to the Florentine artist Filippo Brunelleschi (1377-1446). Although not the originator of perspective, Brunelleschi integrated previous knowledge into a method which allowed it to be taught. Consequently, most Italian artists had mastered it by 1450. It is difficult today to appreciate the reaction of the Renaissance mind to perspective, which was sometimes viewed as a form of magic, since through its use the artist created the illusion of space and distance where they did not actually exist. Perspective gave the artist a power which he had not previously possessed, and he applied it in all possible ways. It is not surprising, then, that he recognized its possibilities for stage scenery.

The joint influence of Vitruvius' work and of perspective are evident in the first treatise on staging in the Renaissance: a portion of *Architettura* (1545) by Sebastiano Serlio (1475–1554). In his treatise Serlio shows how a theatre is to be laid out, how the stage is to be erected, how scenery is to be arranged; he outlines the rules of perspective and discusses a number of additional topics. Like most of his contemporaries, Serlio assumed that theatres would be set up in already existing halls. His plan is an adaptation of Vitruvius' description of the Roman theatre to an indoor, rectangular space. Stadium seating is set up at one end of the hall, and a platform is constructed at the other end. The space between the stage and the seats is left free in imitation of the Roman orchestra. (See the accompanying illustrations.)

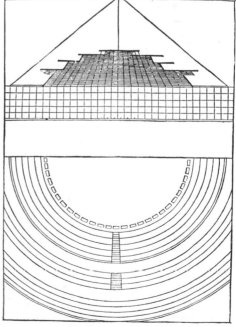

Left. A cross section of Serlio's theatre.
Right. His ground plan for a theatre, 1545.
Above. His design for the comic scene. From
Sebastiano Serlio's *Architettura*, 1545.

The stage floor is divided into two parts from front to back. The front is flat and is used for acting. The rear is sloped upward toward the back and is used principally for scenery. The floor is painted in squares, the lines of which diminish in size and converge toward the center of the back. The upward slope and the diminishing squares aid in the creation of perspective.

Houses constructed of canvas stretched over wooden frames are set up on both sides of the stage. The first two houses on either side are three-dimensional. Those farther back are painted on two-dimensional surfaces, and the stage is enclosed at the rear by a back cloth upon which is painted a perspective scene. All of the scenery is constructed and painted to give the illusion of diminishing size and distance as it nears the back wall of the stage. To help in this illusion the tops of the flats are shaped to slope downward just as the floor slopes upward toward the back.

Serlio envisioned the need for only three kinds of settings—one for tragedy, one for comedy, and one for pastoral. His book includes illustrations of these settings which were imitated by other designers all over Europe. Serlio's scenes for comedy and tragedy are essentially the street scenes of the Roman theatre translated into perspective settings. However, he tends to preserve the Roman façade in his use of a single setting for all tragedy, another for all comedy, and a third for all pastoral drama. In his arrangement it is almost impossible to shift scenery during a play. He also does not mention any framing device (or proscenium arch) to cut off the spectator's view at the sides or top. Presumably, the side houses continue until they meet the walls of the hall in which the stage is set up. Perhaps in execution a curtain cut off the view at the top.

Serlio and most of his contemporaries who designed stage scenery were court architects by profession who constructed stages and scenery as needed. This may explain why so many of the architectural details of scenery in the sixteenth century were three-dimensional rather than merely painted on flats. It was not until the houses became entirely two-dimensional in the seventeenth century that scene shifting was widely practiced.

The first permanent theatre of importance in Italy was the Teatro Olimpico. The Olympic Academy was formed in 1555 for the purpose of studying Greek tragedy, and its theatre was constructed with this type of play in mind. It was designed by Palladio and was begun around 1580. Palladio died before the theatre was completed, however, and it was finished by his pupil, Scamozzi. It was first used in 1585 and still stands.

The stage, the stage background, and the auditorium of the Teatro Olimpico more nearly follow Vitruvius' plan of a Roman theatre than any other edifice of the period. But even here the influence of perspective scenery is felt, for Scamozzi raked the floor upward behind the façade doors and constructed a street in perspective behind each. (See photograph

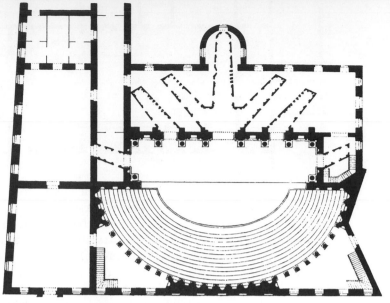

A ground plan of the Teatro Olimpico at Vicenza. From A. Streit's *Das Theater*. Vienna, 1903. A photograph of the interior as it appears today is on page 7.

page 7 and plan above.) The resulting stage picture is essentially a city square into which a number of streets emerge. The street scenes were entirely fixed and could not be shifted. The Teatro Olimpico, therefore, was not in line with the growing demand for more spectacle.

The form which the theatre was to take can be seen clearly for the first time in the Teatro Farnese built in the ducal palace at Parma in 1618. Its importance lies in the fact that it is the first theatre known to have been constructed with a permanent proscenium arch.

The origin of the proscenium arch is a much-disputed question. Some argue that it comes from the enlargement of the central doorway of the Roman stage background. Others claim that it comes from the triumphal arches which were used in many of the street pageants of the period for royal entries and processions of various kinds. Others argue that it is taken over from paintings in which buildings and other objects are used to frame the perspective picture. Any or all of these may be true, since the proscenium arch was adopted to fill a need felt clearly for the first time in the Renaissance theatre, and it may have been suggested by a number of different sources.

Regardless of its origin, however, the proscenium arch serves two basic functions. First, if perspective is to be effective there must be some means of restricting the view of the audience. For example, if the audience can see the back wall of the stage above the painted cloth, the illusion of place and of distance is destroyed. The proscenium frames the picture and focuses audience attention upon it. Second, if scenery is to be shifted (and by the seventeenth century there was a growing demand for more spectacle), some framework to hide the machinery and the offstage spaces is desirable. The proscenium helps to maintain the magic of the theatre by concealing the mechanics by which that magic is created.

Some kind of framing device had been used prior to the construc-

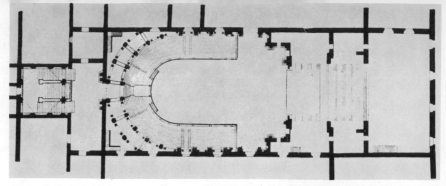

tion of the Teatro Farnese, but it had been temporary and used according to the demands of each play. The Farnese put into permanent form a device which had been evolving over a number of years, and thereby became the prototype of the majority of theatres up to the present day.

The new picture-frame stage was unlike any which had preceded it, for it attempted to create the illusion of a single place in its entirety. The Medieval stage had suggested symbolically a great number of places all seen simultaneously, while the classical theatre had made use of a permanent architectural façade which might serve as any number of places —a street, a temple, or a palace. The desire to create the illusion of more and more complex places and events in the Renaissance manner was largely responsible for later developments of the proscenium-arch theatre.

MAIN FEATURES OF THE ITALIAN THEATRE

By 1650 the theatre structure which was to dominate Europe for the next two hundred years had evolved in Italy. This structure had a number of important characteristics in auditorium, stage, lighting, machinery, and scenery.

The auditorium was basically an elongated U-shaped structure. Along the side walls and at the back of the auditorium, boxes were ranged in tiers one above the other. The number of tiers varied from one theatre to another, but there were usually at least two. The boxes were the most expensive seats, although the view of the stage was not good except from those at the rear of the house, and these were poorly situated for hearing. They were valued, however, for their relative privacy and were especially popular with well-to-do and would-be respectable persons.

Usually, there was a gallery above the top row of boxes. Here were the cheapest seats which were normally occupied by servants or members of the lower classes. The central floor space (the orchestra or pit) was not popular with the elite until the late nineteenth century. Except in England, there were no seats in the pit until near the end of the eighteenth century, and the spectators consequently stood and moved about freely. This area was usually occupied by the fashionable young gentlemen and would-be critics. The price of admission to this part of the house was less than that charged for boxes, but considerably more than that charged for the gallery.

The stage was divided from the auditorium by the proscenium arch.

The Teatro Farnese in Parma. *Left.* The ground plan. *Above.* The stage. *Below.* The auditorium. From A. Streit's *Das Theater.* Vienna, 1903.

The stage floor was raked upward toward the rear of the stage. Usually there was considerable space below the stage floor for operating machinery and for trap doors, and space above for suspending painted backdrops, curtains, and additional mechanical devices. There was only a small amount of space on either side of the stage.

Since the theatres were indoors, they needed artificial lighting. Candles or oil lamps were used until approximately 1825, when they were replaced by gas. Chandeliers hung in the auditorium, at the front of the stage, and sometimes over the stage itself. Lights were mounted behind the proscenium arch (both at the sides and above), footlights might be used at the front edge of the stage, and lights might be mounted behind each set of wings. Ordinarily, stage lights were concealed both for greater illusion and to avoid too much strain on the eyes of spectators.

Another important part of this theatre was its machinery and scene-shifting devices. As the demands for scene changes and spectacle increased, ways of meeting these demands had to be devised. It was difficult to shift the Serlian settings, since they were composed in large part of three-dimensional houses. Nicola Sabbattini (*c.* 1574–1654) published a treatise in 1638 called *Manual for Constructing Scenes and Machines for the Theatre* in which he describes various ways, all of which are rather clumsy, of shifting the Serlian type of scenery. Basically they involve sliding a new house around the one already there, or pulling a new piece of painted canvas over an old one.

Another device used in the sixteenth and seventeenth centuries was the *periaktoi*. These are made by putting three flats together in a triangle and mounting them on a central pivot. A different scene is painted on each side, and to shift sets the periaktoi are turned around to expose another side. These are difficult to construct and difficult to operate on a raked floor.

A much simpler scene-shifting method was eventually adopted. The three-dimensional pieces of the Serlian setting were replaced by two-dimensional frames covered with canvas upon which all details were painted. These flats, or wings, were set up parallel to the front of the stage in a series from front to back. At each wing position, as many different flats could be put up (one immediately back of another) as there were scenes to be depicted during the performance. To change from one scene to the next, the wings visible to the audience were pulled offstage, revealing another set of wings upon which was painted the new scene. The back wall of the set was formed by painted flats which met in the center of the stage, or a painted drop which might be pulled up into the overhead space. Several back scenes could be set up, one behind the other, and shifted in the same way as the side wings.

In addition to side wings and back scenes, there were borders (two-

A setting by Furtten-bach supposedly using *periaktoi*. From the title page of *Deutsche Schau-bühne*, Strassburg, 1655. *Below.* In his *Recreational Architecture*, 1640, Furttenbach shows the use of *periaktoi*. Note also the curved borders above the stage, and the pit for special effects at the rear of the raked stage. From von Weilen. Volume I, 1899.

dimensional framed cloths) which hung above each set of wings and continued the scene overhead. The borders might be painted to represent the sky or clouds in an outdoor setting, or the beams, ceiling, or vaulting of an interior scene. Not only did they block the audience's view of the overhead area, they also provided space between them for lighting and special effects.

The borders, the side wings, and the back scene were the three basic elements of every set. To shift them simultaneously and instantly was the ideal. The machinery to do this shifting differed on the Continent from that used in England (after 1660). The "chariot and pole" system became the standard on the Continent, while in England the "groove" system was used.

The chariot and pole system is rather complex. At each wing and

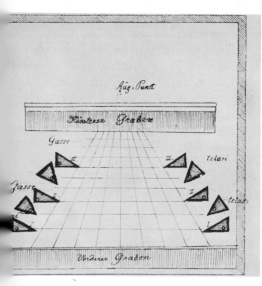

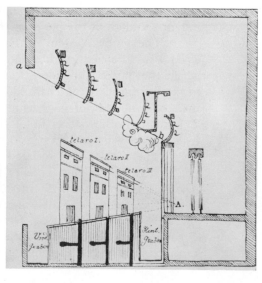

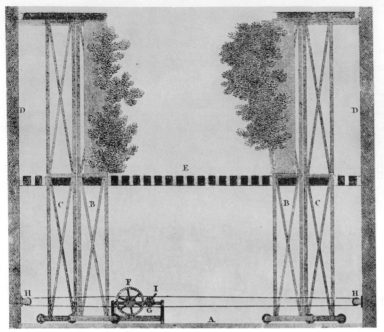

A diagram showing the operation of the chariot and pole or "continental" system of shifting scenery. A—the tracks in which the chariot rides; B and C—the chariots; D—stage walls; E—stage floor; F, G, H, and I—the lines, pulleys, and levers which operate the system. From Rees' *Cyclopedia*, XX, 1803.

back-scene position, slots were cut in the stage floor parallel to the front of the stage. At corresponding positions under the stage, tracks were set up. Frames on casters ("carriages") were placed in these tracks, and to each carriage were attached poles which extended upward through the slots in the floor. In turn, the wings and back scenes were attached to these poles. Moving the carriages in their tracks toward the center of the stage thrust a set onstage, while the reverse process moved it offstage.

This basic arrangement was further mechanized by a system of ropes and windlasses. Any carriage or border could be attached by rope to a windlass. When all of the wings, borders, and the back scene of a single setting were attached to the same windlass, one man could change the entire set by turning a single crank. The change could be accomplished instantly and all of the pieces of the set moved in unison.

The groove system of England was less complicated. Pieces of wood were attached overhead and to the stage floor to make grooves in which the flats could slide off and onto the stage. The scenic elements might be rigged to be changed by windlass, but the English depended more on a number of stage hands for making scene changes than did the Continent. Both systems fulfill the same function and were utilized so long as the "wing and drop" setting dominated the stage.

The man most associated with the perfection of the chariot and pole system is Giacomo Torelli (1608–78). He first worked with Aleotti, who designed the Teatro Farnese. Later in Venice, he perfected a system of winches for moving all scenic parts simultaneously; this allowed him to create seemingly magical feats which won him the nickname, "the Great Wizard." His reputation led to his employment in Paris, where his methods were largely responsible for transforming the French stage. Long after his time, Italian scenery and shifting methods continued to dominate the Continental theatre.

By Torelli's time scenery on the Italian stage had become relatively standardized. Behind a proscenium arch a series of wings on either side and overhead borders terminated in a back scene. On the flat surfaces of these elements was painted a perspective vista, the vanishing point of which was usually in the center of the back scene. If the actors came too close to the back scene, the perspective effect was ruined by the disparity between the size of the actor and the objects painted on the backdrop. As a result, actors performed principally at the front of the stage. The scenery thus became a background rather than an integral part of the characters' environment. This uneasy relationship between actor and scenic background remained until the mid-eighteenth century, when angle perspective was perfected.

In angle perspective, the vanishing point is placed offstage to either one or both sides. The audience appears to see the object at an angle, therefore, and a feeling of great space is created by suggesting the continuation of vistas offstage on either side. The backdrop itself may depict relatively close objects, and the actors may move near it without ruining the perspective.

A design by Giacomo Torelli for Act II of *Andromède* by Pierre Corneille, 1650. Note the "glories." From a contemporary engraving, courtesy of Alois Nagler.

The Bibiena family is usually associated with the development of angle perspective. At least seven members of this family devoted themselves to scenic design and worked in all the important theatrical centers of the day in Italy, Austria, Germany, Sweden, and Russia. The Bibiena family is typical of many in the seventeenth and eighteenth centuries. Italy was the traditional home and training ground for scene designers in Europe, and several families—among them the Quaglio, Galli, Galliari, and Mauro—made scene design their profession and sent members wherever designers were needed.

Machinery for special effects became an important part of the Italian theatre, and it is here that the Renaissance stage shows most clearly its Medieval heritage. The Renaissance perfected what the Medieval stage had developed to a high degree.

The stage floor of the Renaissance theatre had many trap doors through which special effects could be operated. Flames and smoke might emerge; devils and other characters might appear and disappear. Many plays called for earthquakes, the destruction of cities, and similar effects which could be achieved by machinery under the stage.

Overhead a similar amount of machinery might be used. One of the favorite effects during the Renaissance was the appearance of deities or other supernatural beings in clouds, astride mythical animals, or in chariots. These machines were called "glories." Essentially, all of the flying machines involved the use of a crane, or pullies and ropes, attached to a platform or to molded figures. Most frequently the "glory" base was a wooden platform. Around this was attached cloth painted to resemble clouds. Thus, characters appeared to be standing on a cloud. Animals or chariots were made from decorated wooden frames of an appropriate shape. Some of these machines were extremely elaborate—one in France in 1662 is said to have measured forty by sixty feet.

The front curtain was used only to keep the stage hidden until the play was ready to begin so as to heighten surprise. The changing of scenery was part of the performance and was considered to be a special effect in its own right.

By the mid-seventeenth century all elements of the picture-frame stage had developed: the wing-drop-border perspective setting, the proscenium arch, scene-shifting devices, and machinery for elaborate special effects. The auditorium also had become fixed in its features: the elongated semicircle with pit, boxes, and gallery. This theatre evolved in Italy, spread to all of Europe before 1700, and remained relatively unchanged until the mid-nineteenth century. Many of its elements still dominate the theatre today.

A drawing by Ferdinando Galli da Bibiena (1657–1743) to demonstrate perspective scenery for his students. At the bottom, the floor plan is shown reversed in relation to the drawing. Note the perspective points toward either side. From Bibiena's *Direzioni a'Giovani studenti nel disegno*. Bologna, 1731–32. *Below*. A design of 1719 by Giuseppe Galli da Bibiena (1696–1757) for an opera. Courtesy of the Metropolitan Museum of Art, Dick Fund, 1931.

COMMEDIA DELL'ARTE

Alongside the drama of the court and acadamy there grew up an almost diametrically opposite form called *commedia dell'arte*. *Arte* signified that the actors were artists or professionals in contrast to the amateurs who performed the *erudita* or learned drama. *Commedia dell'arte* was actor-centered, it was improvised, it made use of stock characters, and it was adaptable to almost any playing condition.

The actor was the heart of *commedia dell'arte* and almost the only essential element. His tools were largely himself and his imagination; he had to be able to improvise, to adapt to an audience and to the physical arrangements of the stage. At times he acted on makeshift platforms in the open air, at others on the elaborate stages of palace theatres, and at carnivals—anywhere that an audience would gather.

The play script for the *commedia dell'arte* consisted of a scenario which outlined the principal action, the twists and turns of the plot, and its outcome. The actors improvised the dialogue and developed the action as the situation seemed to demand.

A set of stock characters was used in all plays, and the same actor always played the same stock role. The characters were similar from one troupe to another: lovers, certain professional types, and servants.

The roles of the lovers were straight parts; they did not wear masks and were intended to be handsome and sympathetic. There was always one male and one female lover, though there might be an additional pair. Although the plot usually centered around their problems in overcoming some obstacle to marriage, they were not the center of interest, for typically comedy was generated by the antics of other characters. The lovers provided an excuse for the plot and served as the norm against which other characters could be judged; they were dressed in contemporary fashionable clothing and frequently spoke elegant and poetic speeches.

Three professional types appeared most frequently. Pantalone, an old merchant, was a miser and in many productions the father of one of the young women. Dottore, a pedantic bore, loved to spout long speeches filled with questionable learning. He might also be the father of one of the young men, or even a suitor to one of the young women. The Capitano was a soldier who boasted of his prowess in love and war, but was invariably proven a coward. Usually, he was a suitor to one of the young women. Each character wore the same mask and highly individualized costume and used the same characterization in all plays.

The principal comic roles were those of the servants, or *zanni*. They were employed by members of the first two groups and were involved in all sorts of machinations for helping or thwarting the lovers, for tricking the professionals, and so on. In the process, they managed to use a

Harlequin. An illustration by Maurice Sand from his *Masques et bouffons*, 1859.

multitude of comic tricks. They varied from the stupid to the clever, and might have marked physical characteristics, such as a large nose or a humped back. Each role had its own mask, costume, and fixed characterization. The most famous of the *zanni* were Harlequin, Coviello, Pulcinello, and Tartaglia. There were also one or two female servants who attended the women lovers and engaged in the play's intrigues. Frequently they carried on love affairs with the male servants. All female roles were played by women.

These were the basic types. While each play was improvised, the actors, after a time, developed a set of speeches, "sure fire" comic routines, and other dependable aids in holding audience attention. The most famous of these aids were the *lazzi,* or bits of comic business which might be utilized when appropriate, or when audience attention wandered.

There are many theories about the origin of *commedia dell'arte*. The supporters of one theory argue that the *commedia* was the direct descendant of the Atellan farce of Rome, and that actors in the Dark Ages preserved traditions which sprang back into prominence when times became more favorable to them. There are, of course, similarities between some of the *commedia* stock figures and some of those used in Atellan farce. There is no positive evidence of any direct connection between the two forms, however.

Another theory suggests that the *commedia* is an outgrowth of interest in the plays of Plautus and Terence, and that gradually these plays were transformed by the actors. Still another theory sees the *commedia* as entirely native to Renaissance Italy without any necessary forbears. Any of these theories may be right, for the beginnings of *commedia* remain obscure.

Regardless of origin, the troupes came into prominence around 1550. The first clear reference to improvisation by these actors is found in 1568. In the second half of the sixteenth century *commedia dell'arte* became extremely popular in Italy, and by the end of the century troupes were playing in France and elsewhere. In the seventeenth century, the *commedia* spread all over Europe. But it declined after 1750 and was virtually dead by 1800.

Probably the most important troupes were the Gelosi and the Accesi companies. The Gelosi was probably the most prominent of all the troupes because of the popularity of its leader, Francesco Andreini, and his wife, Isabella. The latter was a favorite with many of the literary figures of the day and was herself a poet. The Gelosi existed from about 1570 to 1604, during which time it played throughout Italy and France. The Accesi troupe flourished between 1590 and 1635. Its leaders were Pier Maria Cecchini, Tristano Martinelli, and Flaminio Scala, an important composer of scenarios, who was an actor in the company for a time. The Accesi paid at least two visits to France. Other notable troupes were the Confidenti, the Desiosi, the Fedeli, and the Uniti.

The *commedia* played for all types of audiences and produced a genuinely popular theatre movement. Many of its troupes were invited to play at the courts, but they were equally at home in the market place or at fairs. They at times performed regular drama, but were more famous for their improvised scripts.

After public theatres began to be built in Italy in the seventeenth century, the troupes made use of the kind of theatre which had been developed at the courts, and scenarios were written to take advantage of new scenic possibilities and special effects.

Almost eight hundred *commedia dell'arte* scenarios still exist. Since they only outline the action, however, it is difficult to get a clear picture of the actual quality of a *commedia* performance, though all accounts testify to the great skill of the actors. The popularity of the troupes for a period of over two hundred years also attests to their genuine audience appeal. The influence of *commedia* was great and may be seen in the work of a number of writers, perhaps most notably in Molière's comedies.

The renewed interest in classical drama, the development of the picture-frame stage, perspective scenery, elaborate machinery for special effects and scene shifting, opera, *commedia dell'arte*—all of these are contributions of the Italian Renaissance which were to have important effects on the theatre of the next two centuries.

Alfonso Parigi's (?–1656) setting for Prospero Bonarelli's *Il Solimano. Below.* The same setting with flame effects. From Pougin's *Dictionnaire* . . . , 1885.

Chapter 9

FRENCH CLASSICISM

French professional theatre had its roots in Medieval drama. While early trade guilds were staging plays in certain towns, special associations were created in others for this purpose. One of these amateur groups, the Confrérie de la Passion, was organized in Paris during 1402. By 1420 the Confrérie was established in a permanent indoor theatre in the Hôpital de la Trinité, and in 1518 it was given a monopoly on theatrical production in Paris. It became virtually the only producer of plays in Paris after this time. Thus, this troupe became the oldest permanent company in Europe, the first to have a permanent theatre, and the first to be granted a monopoly by a ruler.

In 1548 the Confrérie built a new theatre, the Hôtel de Bourgogne, which was to remain in use until 1783. Construction was barely completed, however, when the Confrérie was forbidden to produce religious plays, although its monopoly on theatrical production in Paris was reconfirmed.

Unable to maintain audiences with secular plays, the Confrérie began to rent its theatre to traveling troupes. Soon its activities were confined solely to those of a landlord, and each group desiring to perform in Paris had to pay a fee to the Confrérie whether or not it played at the Hôtel de Bourgogne—a monopoly not rescinded until 1675.

Farce actors at the Hôtel de Bourgogne in 1630. Notice the *commedia* costumes. From a contemporary engraving by Bosse reprinted in Arsène Houssaye's *La Comédie Française*, 1880.

THE FRENCH THEATRE BETWEEN 1600 AND 1630

Although there were many performances in Paris in the late sixteenth century, the professional theatre did not gain a strong foothold until the troupe headed by Valleran-Lecomte leased the Hôtel de Bourgogne around 1599. This group gained so much prestige that in 1608 it was allowed to call itself *Les Comédiens du roi* (The King's Players).

The principal French playwright of the early seventeenth century was Alexandre Hardy (*c.* 1575–*c.* 1631), who supplied Valleran-Lecomte with a large proportion of his plays. Hardy is said to have written between six and seven hundred works (of which thirty-four still exist), and he is probably the first French author to make a living by writing for the stage. Although his plays were of many types, he mixed elements so freely that his works are usually called tragicomedies. His emphasis was always upon a continuous sweep of action similar to that found in novels of chivalry and adventure. Hardy was an extremely popular dramatist, but his plays lacked depth, and he was unable to establish in France a strong tradition of "irregular" drama like that prevalent in England and Spain.

The staging of such plays as those by Hardy at the Hôtel de Bourgogne was quite different from the contemporary practice of either Italy or England. From the very beginning, the Confrérie had used an indoor stage. This stage was set up at the end of a rectangular hall in which there was not much room from side to side. At the Hôtel de Bourgogne the stage was only about thirty-five feet wide (as compared with a typical outdoor stage of over one hundred feet). When the mansions were set up, therefore, they had to be placed differently, and were arranged along the sides (one behind the other from front to back) and across the rear of the stage.

The resulting picture had a superficial resemblance to Serlio's stage, but in Serlio's settings all of the elements were considered to be part of the same location, while at the Hôtel de Bourgogne each structure represented a different place. The space in the middle of the stage was used as a generalized acting area in the manner of the *platea* of the Medieval stage.

This type of setting was termed the *décor simultanée* (or simultaneous setting), since all places were represented at once rather than consecutively. A number of designs by Mahelot for settings of this kind are still in existence. (See the illustration on page 164.) These simultaneous settings were used at the Hôtel de Bourgogne until around 1650. By that time, the Italian style was becoming dominant and the old method gradually fell into disuse. The simultaneous stage had been in keeping with Hardy's dramatic method, but was not adapted to the French classical drama which began to develop in the 1630s.

Mahelot's design for *La Prise de Marsilly* at the Hôtel de Bourgogne in the 1630s. Note the simultaneous representation on stage of a number of locales. Courtesy of Bibliothèque Nationale, Paris.

CHANGES IN FRENCH THEATRE BETWEEN 1630 AND 1650

The period from 1630 to 1650 saw sweeping changes in the French theatre, caused by more settled political conditions, a strong desire to raise the general cultural level of France, the importation of Italian ideas on staging and drama, and the appearance of strong native dramatists.

France was embroiled in civil wars over religion in the late sixteenth century and again in the 1620s. After Cardinal Richelieu became chief minister of France around 1625, however, the political situation gradually grew more calm as he extended the power of the central government over all phases of French life.

Richelieu and many other Frenchmen began to be concerned about France's cultural affairs around 1630 and set out to improve the status of literature and the arts. These men looked to Italy as a guide for their new programs. Italian ideas had been current in France as early as 1550, but they were little known except among the educated classes and did not become widespread until after 1630.

Up to this time, the professional theatre had only a precarious footing in Paris. While the Hôtel de Bourgogne was occupied frequently, no company performed there continuously. Beginning in 1629, however, there were always at least two professional companies playing in Paris.

Both of the public theatres in the 1630s (the Hôtel de Bourgogne and the Théâtre du Marais) were still using simultaneous settings. Cardinal Richelieu was not happy with this kind of staging, which emphasized

Medieval rather than classical ideals. In 1641, therefore, he built in his palace a theatre of the Italian type containing the first permanent proscenium arch in France. This theatre, called the Palais-Royal after Richelieu's death, was to become the home of Molière's troupe.

Richelieu died in 1642 and Cardinal Mazarin, a native of Italy, succeeded him as prime minister. Mazarin brought Torelli to Paris to stage operas. By 1650 Italian scenic methods and theatre structures were well understood and had become the standard against which others were judged.

The Théâtre du Marais was rebuilt in 1644 on a much larger scale and turned more and more to spectacle in the Italian manner. The facilities of the Hôtel de Bourgogne were too limited to allow much spectacle, so it moved more and more to a unified stage picture, and its simultaneous settings were largely abandoned by 1650.

The Italian influence may also be seen in the formation of the French Academy, which came into existence about 1629 when a small group of men who were interested in literature and language began to meet together informally. Richelieu encouraged them to form an official organization, which they eventually did about 1635. This group, whose membership is restricted to forty at any one time (supposedly the oustanding men of French letters), still exists. It always has had considerable prestige, most conspicuously so in the seventeenth and eighteenth centuries, and has exerted a decided influence on French literature and drama.

In 1641 Cardinal Richelieu's new theatre contained the first permanent proscenium arch in France. The illustration shows the setting for the first production, *Mirame*. Later this theatre was called the Palais-Royal and was used by Molière's troupe from 1660–73, and after that time was the home of the Opera. From Pougin's *Dictionnaire Historique et Pittoresque* . . . , 1885.

When the French Academy was formed it took as its province the principles and practices of literary composition and the rules of the French language.

THE BASIC PRINCIPLES OF NEOCLASSICISM

The French Academy took its standards of drama primarily from Italian critics. These standards are important to an understanding of the development of drama during the seventeenth and eighteenth centuries, for they are at the heart of what is normally called the Neoclassical movement.

Neoclassical criteria were really a synthesis of the work of many men in many countries, but were most consistently applied and defended in France. Italian critics of the sixteenth century (especially Minturno, Scaliger, and Castelvetro) laid the foundations upon which French critics of the seventeenth century (notably Chapelain, D'Aubignac, and Boileau) built.

The Neoclassicists looked to Greek and Roman criticism (principally that of Aristotle and Horace) for their ideals. Many conceptions, however, were based upon misunderstandings of these classical authors.

While there was, as in all movements, considerable variation in the ideas of individual writers, the basic principles of neoclassicism were consistent enough to allow a general summary. Neoclassicism was primarily concerned with a number of basic issues: the purity of dramatic types; the purposes of drama; the concepts of verisimilitude and decorum; and the unities of time, place, and action.

Only two kinds of drama, tragedy and comedy, were recognized as legitimate forms. These were thought of as pure, and no mixing of tragic and comic elements was allowed. Each form had its own rules. Tragedy drew its characters from rulers or the nobility; its stories dealt with affairs of state, the downfall of rulers, and similar events; its endings were always unhappy; and its style was lofty and poetic. Comedy, on the other hand, drew its characters from the middle or lower classes; its stories dealt with domestic and private affairs; its endings were always happy; and its style was characterized by the use of ordinary speech. Such distinctions meant, among other things, that tragedy could not be written about the common man, and that comedy could not be written about the nobility. Each of these rules is somewhat arbitrary, though each bears some resemblance to actual Greek and Roman practice. The neoclassic critic, nevertheless, viewed these demands as necessary and inviolable, and dramatists were denounced when they deviated from them.

In actual practice there were many other dramatic types in the seventeenth and eighteenth centuries. The usual justification of such deviations was that these forms were not serious efforts and were not

The court of France sponsored many spectacles similar to those of Italy. This illustration depicts *Circe* by Beaujoyeulx in 1581. The settings are by Jacques Patin. Note the galleries for spectators and the mansion-like arrangement of the scenery. The theatre was a hall in the Petit Bourbon and was later converted to conform to the Italian ideal by Torelli in 1645. Molière's company used the Petit Bourbon from 1658–60, when the building was demolished. From Germain Bapst's *Essai sur l'Histoire du Théâtre*. Paris, 1893.

worthy of critical consideration; they were said to be the products of poorly educated or tasteless writers, and the plays were called "illegitimate" dramas.

The Humanist movement in the Renaissance had had a special problem in justifying literature as a legitimate study. In breaking away from the former preoccupation with theology, the easiest route was to urge the usefulness of drama for teaching moral lessons. This was the line taken by almost all theorists between 1500 and 1800 (and which many take even today). Most theorists argued that the purpose of drama is two-fold—to teach and to please. However, the precedence was almost always given to teaching. If this teaching were to be obvious (as it should be, according to many), the plays would, as a rule, need to show characters being punished or rewarded for their behavior. (The term *poetic justice* was coined in the seventeenth century to indicate this meting out of justified rewards and punishments to the characters in a play.) Comedy was expected to ridicule behavior which should be avoided and tragedy to show the horrible results of mistakes and misdeeds.

It was also considered necessary that drama should please, for otherwise teaching would not be possible. This is sometimes called the "sugarcoated pill" function of art—entertainment to sweeten a moral lesson. Furthermore, only those plays which observed verisimilitude could teach and please effectively. Verisimilitude, "the appearance of truth," is a complex concept. To the Neoclassicist, verisimilitude had three basic aspects: reality, morality, and generality or abstraction. "Reality" was that aspect which demanded that the playwright rule out those things which could not actually happen in real life. It eliminated fantasy and supernatural occurrences. The only exceptions allowed were those in which supernatural events were an accepted part of the story (as in Greek myths or Biblical material). The playwright, however, was encouraged to minimize such aspects of a story.

But the demand to remain faithful to natural events was always modified by another for moral teaching. The dramatist was not to show merely what might possibly happen, rather he was to depict events in terms of an ideal moral pattern. On the surface, this demand may seem to contradict that for reality, but it was not so viewed by the Neoclassicist. His explanation was: The universe is ruled over by a just God; it is not conceivable, therefore, that wickedness will go unpunished and goodness remain unrewarded. Thus, while it may be possible to point out particular cases in which justice does not seem to prevail, these seeming injustices are really part of God's plan, which is beyond human comprehension. Such cases, therefore, should be considered abnormal and not suitable for drama. Justice and morality are inseparable parts of ultimate truth, and the dramatist should be concerned only with truth in this higher sense.

The demands for reality and morality were further modified by that of generality or abstraction. Basic to an understanding of the neoclassical ideal is this third aspect. It involves the following line of reasoning: Everything encountered in life is a "particular"—that is, no two things are ever exactly alike. On the other hand, all particulars of a given classification have certain characteristics in common which allow them to be grouped together. For example, human beings have certain common features which allow them to be set off from dogs or horses. Characteristics necessary to a thing before it can be categorized compose its "essence." In other words, although human beings have qualities in common with dogs and horses, there are some which are totally different and without which a being cannot be called human. The Neoclassicist defined truth as the essence of things, found in characteristics common to all individual cases making up a given group. Those characteristics which differ in individual cases are accidental qualities, and, therefore, not necessary parts of the truth.

In his early years Louis XIV was especially fond of the theatre. This shows his costume for "Le Ballet de la Nuit" in 1653 in which he appeared as the "Sun King," an image which he cultivated for the rest of his life. From Bapst's *Essai sur l'Histoire du Théâtre,* 1893.

The Neoclassicist believed that it was possible to determine these essences (or norms) for everything in existence, including human beings and literary types. These norms were said to be discovered through the rational and systematic study of all things and were not considered to be mere fabrications. It was further agreed that all rational men should accept these standards and that dramatists should base their works upon them. Those who did not were considered to be perverse or enemies of the truth.

Perhaps most important to the dramatist was the belief that human nature has its own governing patterns, which are the same in all places and in all periods. The dramatist, therefore, was expected to confine himself to writing about the permanent aspects of humanity. This meant cutting away all qualities which might be attributed to a particular time, place, or personal peculiarity. In neoclassical plays, therefore, there is little concern with individualizing details and great emphasis upon the more universal aspects of character and situation.

These criteria are most easily seen in characterization. Each age group, rank, profession, and sex was thought to have its own essence. The dramatist was expected to remain true to these norms in creating his characters, and the critic was expected to use them in judging the verisimilitude of the playright's creations. This principle of character portrayal was termed *decorum,* which in its broadest sense means "fittingness" or "appropriateness." Used in this broad sense, it is a helpful concept; but as employed by the Neoclassicist, it was frequently synonymous with the set of behavioral standards approved at the time.

Verisimilitude, then, as a concept, tried to reconcile realism, moralism, and abstraction in a conception of truth, and the dramatist was expected to embody this truth in his work. Both verisimilitude and decorum are indicative of the neoclassical attempt to achieve complete universality in drama by cutting away everything that is not true of all men in all times and all places.

Verisimilitude was further thought to dictate the adherence to the unities of action, time, and place. While some kind of unity of action has been demanded by critics in almost every age, the Neoclassical period normally interpreted the rule to mean that a play should have only one action, and that there should be no subplots.

The Neoclassical period is the only one which has placed great emphasis upon the unities of time and place. While Greek and Roman playwrights tended to observe these unities, there was no insistence by critics of the time that they were necessary to good drama. Castelvetro, writing in Italy around 1570, was the first critic to set down the unities in the form which was accepted for the next two hundred years. He argued that since an audience knows that it has been in the theatre for only a few hours, an author cannot convince it that several days or years have passed. Therefore, the time which has passed in the play should be equal to the time the audience has spent in the theatre, but in no case should it exceed twenty-four hours. Likewise, he argued that the audience knows that it has been in only one place and, therefore, it cannot be expected to think that the play's location has changed from Rome to Athens, or other widely separated places.

This utter confusion of clock time with fictional time and of actual place with fictional place is characteristic of the period and may be explained by that aspect of verisimilitude which demanded a close correspondence between reality and drama. The Neoclassical age, thus, normally demanded that a play have only one line of action, should take place within twenty-four hours, and should be confined to one place. The demand for unity of place was sometimes broadened to allow more than one location if all could be easily reached within the twenty-four hour time limit.

These, then, are the basic principles of neoclassicism: the strict separation of dramatic types; the insistence upon pleasurable teaching; the strict adherence to verisimilitude and decorum; and the observance of the unities of time, place, and action. These may seem artificial and arbitrary today, but to most persons in the seventeenth and eighteenth centuries they were meaningful concepts which seriously affected the writing and staging of plays.

CORNEILLE AND RACINE

The writer most closely associated with the transition to classicism in France is Pierre Corneille (1606–84). He began to write plays in the late 1620s, but his first great success came in 1636 with *Le Cid* (*The Cid*). The production of this play set off a controversy which brought the issues of classicism to a focus, for the play in many ways adhered to neoclassical demands, but in the very observance of them managed to raise serious questions about the validity of verisimilitude, decorum, and the unities.

The Cid is essentially a tragicomedy, for its serious action (dealing with love versus honor) is resolved happily. The unities are for the most part observed—the action is completed within twenty-four hours, the place is confined to the city of Seville, and there are no important subplots. But so many things happen in twenty-four hours that credibility—or verisimilitude—is strained. Furthermore, at the end of the play Chimène, the play's heroine, has agreed to marry Roderigue, who has killed Chimène's father in a duel less than twenty-four hours earlier. This ending both strains decorum and (since it is a happy one for the main characters) puts *The Cid* outside the neoclassical conception of pure tragedy.

The play was a great success in the theatre and was both denounced and extravagantly praised. The newly formed French Academy was asked to arbitrate the dispute which had arisen over the play's merits. Its decision was written by Jean Chapelain, the Academy's acknowledged leader (with Richelieu's help, it is sometimes said), and the play was judged in terms of how well it accorded with the neoclassical ideal. Chapelain decided that *The Cid* was not a tragedy, and that, while it had many things to recommend it, verisimilitude and decorum (the most important requirements) had been severely strained. The whole controversy seems somewhat ridiculous today, but at the time it served to make the public conscious of the new classical ideals which were shortly to dominate critical taste and dramatic writing. Corneille himself soon accepted the judgment passed on *The Cid*, and his subsequent plays (the most famous of which are *Horace, Cinna,* and *Polyeucte*) adhered to the new demands and helped to establish classicism as the standard of the period. In 1647 he was elected to the French Academy, a clear indication that he was by that time considered completely acceptable by that group.

The distinguishing characteristic of Corneille's drama is the hero with an indomitable will. While the hero constantly grows in strength throughout each play, he does not grow in complexity. Corneille needs a great number of episodes to demonstrate this increase in strength. His plots are relatively complex, therefore, while his characters are comparatively simple.

Although he did not reach the heights that Racine was destined to achieve, it is Corneille who made the important beginning and who marks the transition to the new vogue in drama. He wrote for the theatre only rarely after 1650 and even then his popularity was declining. He lived to see himself almost totally eclipsed in critical esteem by Racine.

The plays of Jean Racine (1639–99) mark the peak of French classical tragedy. Racine's first play, *La Thébaïde*, was produced by Molière in 1664. His reputation was firmly established in 1667 with *Andromaque*, and he rapidly surpassed Corneille in public favor. Among his most famous works are: *Britannicus* (1669), *Bérénice* (1670), *Bajazet* (1672), and *Phaedra* (1677). Racine's reputation rests most clearly upon *Phaedra*, which is usually considered to be the greatest of French tragedies. His plays contain little external action; their drama results from internal psychological conflict centered on a single character. This character wants to do the right thing, but is prevented either by circumstances or by his own nature. The essential qualities of Racine's plays may be seen by looking more closely at *Phaedra*.

PHAEDRA

Basically, *Phaedra* is concerned with the conflict between morality and rationality on one hand, and immorality and irrationality on the other. Against her will, Phaedra loves her stepson, Hippolytus. Although she is fully aware that this love is wrong, she is powerless to resist it. Racine is principally interested in depicting this conflict within Phaedra.

Most plays concerned with the conflict of good and evil have shown goodness at the mercy of some external evil, or as the victim of forces set in motion by some ill-advised decision. In *Phaedra*, good and evil are bound up in the same personality. Herein lies the power of the play, for it shows a person who is thoroughly moral in her convictions but whose will-power has been sapped by irrational emotional drives. Since the conflict is primarily an internal one, Racine needs little external action.

The opening act of the play reveals that Phaedra has been in love with Hippolytus for a long time and her inner torment has at last driven her to the point of suicide as the only means of maintaining her moral integrity. She is prevented from carrying out her decision, however, by the news of the supposed death of her husband, Theseus. Oenone, Phaedra's nurse and companion, convinces Phaedra that it is now no longer shameful for her to love Hippolytus.

Phaedra declares her love to Hippolytus, who reacts with disgust. Phaedra is filled with shame at her boldness and is again on the verge of despair. Her hopes are revived by Oenone, only to be completely dashed by the news that Theseus is not only alive but has arrived in Troezen, the scene of the play's action.

When Theseus enters with Hippolytus, Phaedra is faced with a moral dilemma: How can she greet her husband in the presence of his son, to whom she has just declared her love? Her hasty departure arouses Theseus' suspicion, and Oenone, to save Phaedra, accuses Hippolytus of having made advances to Phaedra. Theseus calls down a terrible curse upon Hippolytus and banishes him.

Phaedra is on the verge of telling Theseus the truth when he unwittingly reveals that Hippolytus is in love with Aricia. Her good motive turns to jealousy, and Phaedra refrains from speaking and thereby saving Hippolytus' life.

As Hippolytus leaves Troezen, a sea monster (sent by Poseidon, the sea god, in answer to Theseus' curse) frightens Hippolytus' horses and he is dragged to his death. Oenone commits suicide, and Phaedra, driven by grief, remorse, and self-disgust, takes poison. Before she dies, however, she confesses her guilt to Theseus.

As this brief outline shows, the character relationships in *Phaedra* are complex, while the external action is simple. The plot complications are important only because of the emotional reactions they arouse in the characters. The crucial factor at almost every point is Phaedra's uncontrollable passion for Hippolytus; it is this passion which brings misery to all characters in the play, for the deaths of Hippolytus, Oenone, and Phaedra, and the desolation of Theseus and Aricia all stem from this single source.

Racine uses powerful contrasts in story and characters. For example, Phaedra's confession of love to Hippolytus is placed immediately after Hippolytus' similar confession to Aricia. As a result, the innocent love of Aricia and Hippolytus is set against the illicit love of Phaedra, and the sweetness and youth of Aricia serves to point up the torment and maturity of Phaedra.

Act I of Racine's *Phaedra* at Northwestern University. Directed by Lee Mitchell; setting by Herbert Philippi; costumes by Paul Reinhardt; lighting by Joel Rubin. Courtesy of Northwestern University.

Each action in the play sets in motion a chain of events which is irreversible and which leads inevitably to the catastrophe: Phaedra's confession to Hippolytus makes it impossible for her to turn back; Hippolytus' confession to Aricia makes it impossible for him to turn back; Theseus' curse on Hippolytus sets another uncontrollable train of events in motion. Finally, there comes a powerful obligatory scene in which Phaedra forces herself to come face to face with Theseus after both know the full truth. There are no excess scenes; Racine achieves absolute clarity without any superfluous details.

Racine adhered to the neoclassical ideals of drama almost completely, but the audience feels no strain as a result of his remaining within these bonds. The unity of time is clearly observed, a few hours at the most elapse during the course of the play. The place is unspecified (it is in or around the palace), but this is typical of neoclassical drama, since what happens to the characters does not depend upon where it happens. The action is focused almost entirely upon Phaedra's passion and its results. The Aricia story forms a minor subplot, but it is made a necessary part of the main action.

Racine based his play on Euripides' *Hippolytus,* but he made many significant changes. In Euripides' drama the emphasis is upon Hippolytus' self-righteous vow to remain chaste all of his life. To punish him for denying her power, Aphrodite sets Phaedra's love in motion. The results are much the same as in Racine's play, but the causes and the implications are entirely different. In Euripides' work, Hippolytus is not in love with someone else, and Phaedra is a more or less innocent tool of the gods.

Racine eliminated the gods from his play and brought events into the realm of verisimilitude by showing only those occurrences which could happen in real life. The monster from the sea is the only supernatural element, and Racine could not omit it since this was an accepted part of a well-known myth. It is subordinated as much as possible, however, by placing the action offstage and by careful preparation before it happens.

Phaedra also departs obviously from its Greek model in elimination of the chorus. While some neoclassical critics favored use of the chorus, the weight of opinion, and certainly of practice, was against it. The typical argument against its use was that it is not natural for characters to reveal their innermost thoughts before such a large group of people. Thus *Phaedra,* like most neoclassical plays, substituted *confidantes* (close trusted companions) for the chorus. Each of the principal characters, except Theseus, has a confidant: Phaedra has Oenone, Hippolytus has Theramenes, and Aricia has Ismene. This is an important device since it realistically motivates the voicing of feelings and intentions.

Also in *Phaedra* the characters have very few passages to speak when they are alone on stage, and these are either prayers or are uttered under extreme emotion. Both the use of the confidant and the elimination of soliloquies are dictated by the demand for verisimilitude.

The role of Phaedra has always been considered one of the great acting parts in French drama; for a woman, it is a role comparable to that of Lear for a man. It is difficult to perform, for there is little external action, and audience attention must be riveted on Phaedra's internal conflict. The subtleties and changes of emotional states must be clearly portrayed; therefore a wide range in depicting the nuances of emotion is mandatory: her quiet resignation turns to hope in the opening scene; she is overcome by passion for Hippolytus; his rejection fills her with humiliation and rage; Theseus' return arouses abject shame and horror; she is overcome with jealousy when she learns of Hippolytus' love for Aricia; she turns on Oenone with bitterness and recrimination for the advice which has led to such a terrible situation; finally, on the point of death, she performs her duty with firm resolution. But this broad outline does not touch the gradations and subtle shifts of emotion within scenes which lay bare the heart and mind of a woman at the mercy of desires which are in conflict with her moral convictions. It is Phaedra's great capacity for moral feeling in conjunction with her uncontrollable love that makes her both admirable and pitiable at the same time. Her suffering and remorse redeem her in the minds of an audience.

While Phaedra is the main center of concern, each of the other principal characters is confronted with a psychological conflict of importance to the play. Hippolytus, for example, is torn in the beginning between his love for Aricia and his duty to his father; later, he is torn between his desire to maintain his father's honor and to vindicate his own. Hippolytus, like Phaedra, loves against his will, so there is no question that he will ever return Phaedra's love. All the characters desire to act rationally, but each is swayed by irrational forces. Phaedra's is merely the most extreme of the cases.

Almost nothing is said about the age or physical appearance of the characters. The emphasis is entirely upon their psychological and moral states. Decorum of character is observed for the most part, and it is the departure from decorous behavior which brings doom. Broad strokes rather than minute details have been used. The play is permeated with the aim for the universal (for the neoclassical idea of generalization) rather than for the particularities of time, place, and idiosyncrasies of character.

PLAY PRODUCTION IN FRANCE BETWEEN 1650 AND 1675

The Parisian acting troupes in the time of Racine and Molière were organized on a sharing plan similar to that used by Shakespeare's company. They were democratic organizations in which each member had an equal vote. The French companies included women, who also had equal rights with the men and who received comparable pay.

French plays were generally less complicated than Elizabethan dramas and acting troupes were consequently smaller. A French company was usually composed of from ten to fifteen members. As in the Elizabethan theatre, however, a number of persons were also employed by the troupe as supernumerary actors, as ticket takers, musicians, scene painters, scene shifters, candle snuffers, and so on.

At the end of each performance the costs of production were deducted from the receipts and the remainder was divided among the shareholders. Thus each actor's income depended upon the success of the company and was not determined by a fixed salary. All of the leading groups in Paris at the time, however, received some money yearly from the King, although this sum was not large enough to insure them against loss.

Plays were selected by having the author read his work to the troupe, which then voted on its acceptance or rejection. A play might be bought outright from an author, but a more usual practice was to give the author two shares of the receipts for a stated number of performances. After this time the play belonged to the troupe and no further payment was made to the writer. The playright supervised the first production of his work, after which the actors were presumed to be ready to perform it upon twenty-four hours' notice.

When a play was accepted, the troupe discussed and agreed upon the casting. This process was simplified by the fact that each actor was normally employed to play a particular kind of role. Thus, while there may have been some controversy over casting, there was a reasonably clear understanding about the rights of each actor to certain kinds of parts. When a new actor came into a troupe he learned his roles from the person he was replacing, or from someone else in the company who was acquainted with the way in which the parts had been played before. Roles came to be played, therefore, in a traditional manner passed on from one actor to another.

While actors might play in both comedy and tragedy, they usually specialized in one or the other. Molière, for example, was never successful in tragedy, although he was considered to be the best comic actor of his day. One additional convention should be noted: old women in comedies were usually played by men. For example, Molière's brother-in-law, Louis Béjart, specialized in this kind of role and played Mme. Pernell in the original production of *Tartuffe*.

The actors were responsible for furnishing their own costumes, which were part of their professional equipment. For the most part costumes were contemporary garments, and frequently noblemen gave clothing to actors for stage use. As on the Elizabethan stage, however, there were a number of conventionalized costumes. For example, by the end of the seventeenth century, a traditional garment for tragic heroes had evolved.

(See the illustration lower right.) It was Roman in derivation, although there was little historical accuracy in its treatment. Comedy, restricted as it most generally was to contemporary subject matter, used costumes more nearly like those worn in everyday life.

The scenic demands were simple. Ordinarily, the setting represented a single place, and even that was not indicated in detail. (The scenery was indicative of the neoclassical quest for generality.) Since place was not to be depicted with marked individualizing features, the same set (done in the Italian manner with wings, borders, and back scenes) could be used for a number of different plays. Furthermore, by the second half of the seventeenth century spectators were seated regularly on the stage itself (on chairs or benches at either side). The area left for acting was only about fifteen feet across at the front. The actor, therefore, was placed in the midst of spectators in a very confined space. The majority of plays as a result did not call for very much physical action, and there was little intention of creating the illusion of a specific place.

Occasionally, however, the troupes produced plays which depended on elaborate scenery and special effects. At such times, the spectators were forbidden to sit on the stage and great care and expense was invested in the scenic background. The stage, the auditorium, the scenery, and the special effects followed in all important respects that of the Italian theatre (see Chapter 8).

The best season for plays was from November to Easter. The usual days of performance were Sunday, Tuesday, and Friday, though other days were used at times. Three o'clock was the announced time for performances, but actual starting time was later. The bill for each performance was

Left. A shoemaker's costume (1670) by Jean Berain (1637–1711), the principal designer for the court in the last part of the seventeenth century—said to have created the style associated with the reign of Louis XIV. From Jullien's *Histoire du Costume* . . . , 1880. *Right.* The tragic hero's costume as it developed during the seventeenth century and persisted through most of the eighteenth. An engraving after a painting by Watteau. From Gillaumont's *Costumes de la Comédie Française,* . . . 1884.

composed of a long play (with incidental entertainment between acts)
and a short play (usually a comedy or farce) as an afterpiece.

MOLIÈRE

Jean-Baptiste Poquelin, who assumed the name Molière (1622–73), was
the son of a prosperous upholsterer of Paris. He received a good education
and entered the theatre in 1643. His first venture, the Illustre Théâtre,
failed and Molière and his companions played in the provinces of France
from 1645 to 1658. During those years the group obviously learned much,
for when they returned to Paris they rapidly became second only to the
Hôtel de Bourgogne troupe in the eyes of the Parisian public, and they
surpassed that group in comedy. Molière was a favorite of Louis XIV, who
allowed him to use the theatre which Richelieu had built, now called the
Palais-Royal, and protected him in many controversies.

Although Molière is noted today principally for his comedies which
emphasize character types and social criticism, he wrote other kinds of plays
as well. He was greatly influenced by the *commedia dell'arte*, and many of
his plays are farces which use the *commedia* character types. He also wrote
a number of comedy ballets for the court and even tried his hand at
tragedy. Throughout his work Molière borrowed as he saw fit from Plautus,
Terence, the *commedia*, and from Spanish and Italian sources. It is almost
solely through his efforts that French classical comedy was raised to a
level equal to that of French tragedy. His work has achieved a more universal appeal than that of his tragic contemporaries. He was the greatest
French comic writer of the seventeenth century and one of the great comic
authors of all time. His plays are still to be seen on the stages of almost

Molière was often called upon to provide entertainment at the court. Shown here is
a scene from *La Princesse d'Élide*, a comedy-ballet performed out of doors at Versailles
in 1664. The scenery was real shrubbery. From Pougin's *Dictionnaire . . .* , 1885.

every country, while the plays of Corneille and Racine are now seldom produced outside of France.

Molière's most famous works are: *The School for Wives* (1662), *Tartuffe* (1664), *The Miser* (1668), *The Doctor in Spite of Himself* (1666), *The Misanthrope* (1666), *The Would-Be Gentleman* (1671), and *The Imaginary Invalid* (1673). *Tartuffe* will be examined in some detail.

TARTUFFE

Tartuffe, or the Impostor was produced in a three-act version in 1664, in an altered form in 1667, and finally in its present five acts in 1669. It has remained a regular part of theatre repertories since 1669 and has been performed more often than any other play by Molière.

THEMES AND IDEAS. Tartuffe is obviously concerned with religious hypocrisy. While it is possible to place too much emphasis upon contemporary conditions, it may be helpful to look at some background factors which help to clarify the play.

The most likely target of Molière's satire was the Company of the Holy Sacrament. This was a secret society which had been formed in 1627 and which had achieved great influence throughout France. Its purpose included the repression of heresy, the promotion of charity and missionary work, and the improvement of morals. It was particularly in connection with the last of these aims that the Society offended many, for it maintained "spiritual police" who spied upon private affairs. As one critic said of the group: "They had for their agents fanatics who to save souls recoiled from nothing, 'sanctifying by the purity of their intentions' what simple folk would call dirty actions."

Molière read *Tartuffe* to certain persons before it was first produced in 1664, and the Society organized an attack against it immediately. So much controversy was aroused that Louis XIV forbade further performances. Molière revised the play in 1667 hoping to remove some of the objections, only to have it withdrawn again. By 1669 the opposition was largely gone.

Whether or not Molière had the Society in mind is not of great importance. It is clear that he was thinking of groups like the Society, which feel that they alone can tell true piety from false and who create conditions under which hypocrites can flourish. Molière, through the ending of the play, indicates that France would be better off without such groups, and the King is shown as being able to tell truth from falsehood without their aid.

As in all of Molière's works, the balanced view of life is upheld in *Tartuffe*. True piety, to Molière, does not demand the abandonment of pleasure but the right use of it. The truly devout try to reform the world by actions which set a good example rather than by pious speeches. Or, as it is put in the play, "They don't espouse the interests of Heaven with greater zeal than does Heaven itself."

Another favorite theme with Molière is the forced marriage. In part, this topic is a convention inherited from past comedy, especially *commedia dell'arte*, in which the plot frequently turns on the attempt of a father to arrange an unsuitable marriage for one of his children. On the other hand, Molière consistently argues in his plays that most of the evils of marriage can be traced to forced unions. In *Tartuffe*, as elsewhere, he argues that such marriages are sure to lead to adultery. But in this play, marriage is an entirely secondary concern. The main theme is hypocrisy.

PLOT, STRUCTURE AND CHARACTERIZATIONS. The plot of *Tartuffe* divides into five stages: the demonstration of Tartuffe's complete hold over Orgon; the unmasking of Tartuffe; Tartuffe's attempt to get revenge; the prevention of that revenge, and the happy resolution of affairs for everyone else. There are three important reversals, therefore. The first of these (the unmasking of Tartuffe) brings all of the characters to an awareness of the state of things. The brief span of hope is quickly dispelled, however, for Orgon, as well as the rest of the family, is soon discovered to be at the mercy of Tartuffe. Since Orgon's credulity has placed him in this position, it would serve him justly to be punished, but innocent members of the family also are involved.

The structure for the first two reversals (turning the tables on Tartuffe; Tartuffe turning the tables on Orgon) is carefully prepared, but the final reversal and the play's resolution are not. The contrived ending (in which Tartuffe is suddenly discovered to be a notorious criminal) has been the subject of much criticism. It is an emotionally satisfying ending, in the sense that justice is meted out and a state of normalcy is restored, but the contrivance cannot be explained away by any usual criteria of good dramatic construction.

Another score upon which Molière has been criticized is the long delay in the appearance of Tartuffe, who does not enter until the third act. This delay is not accidental, however, for Molière himself wrote:

> I have employed . . . two entire acts to prepare for the entrance of my scoundrel. He does not fool the auditor for a single moment; one knows from the first the marks I have given him; and from one end to the other he says not a word and performs not an action which does not paint for the spectators the character of an evil man.

Molière was attempting to prevent any confusion about Tartuffe's true nature. This is further borne out by the inclusion in the first act of a lengthy argument by his "common sense" character, Cleante (the character who most nearly represents Molière's point of view), in which true piety is distinguished from false. There is a similar discussion in most of Molière's plays, but as a rule it comes toward the end. The placement of this argument in the first act of *Tartuffe* further indicates Molière's desire to make his purpose clear to the audience.

The structure of *Tartuffe* may be seen clearly by looking at the use made of various characters. Orgon's is the only role which is of importance in every act (in terms of onstage action). Cleante appears in Act I, where he performs his principal function—to present the common sense point of view. He does not appear again until Act IV; in that act and in Act V he merely reenforces the ideas set forth in Act I. His presence in the play does not influence the action at all; it merely points up the theme.

While Dorine, the maid, appears in each act, her role is virtually completed after the beginning of Act III, even though she has been a major character up to that point. Her frankness and openness are used as a foil to show off Orgon's credulity, the lovers' petulancy, and Tartuffe's false piety. It is she who sets their exaggerated behavior in proper perspective with her wit and common sense. After Tartuffe's entrance, she is no longer needed.

Even Tartuffe is given rather strange treatment when he finally makes his appearance after two acts of preparation. He has one of the most famous entrance lines ever written: "Laurent, put away my hair shirt and my scourge, and pray heaven may ever enlighten you. If any one asks to see me, tell them I've gone to the prison to distribute the charity which others have given me."

But the majority of his role is given over to his two "love scenes" with Elmire. Molière seems to take it for granted that the audience will accept the picture of Tartuffe painted earlier by the other characters and that the play need only show one aspect of his hypocrisy. Tartuffe's first speeches to Dorine (those in which he asks her to cover her bosom with a handkerchief so as not to arouse evil thoughts in him) reveal his sensual nature, and it is this quality primarily that is developed onstage.

Tartuffe displays another important side of his character when being denounced by Damis. Rather than defend himself, he appears to accept the accusations with humility and as the lot of a pious man. This scene more than any other shows how Orgon has come to be taken in by Tartuffe.

While Act V shows Tartuffe's true nature, which has been masked under his hypocrisy, it is still true, nevertheless, that most of what the audience knows of Tartuffe comes from what other characters say about him rather than through what he actually does onstage.

The lovers, Valère and Mariane, appear in Act II and are unimportant thereafter. They serve merely to show how far Orgon has been influenced by Tartuffe, since Orgon is planning to marry Mariane to Tartuffe. The lovers' quarrel is a source of amusement but it is completely unrelated to the rest of the play. As in *commedia*, the lovers are handsome, upright, and admirable young people who deserve each other's love and who are being kept apart by a muddle-headed and perverse parent.

Elmire is also used when needed and ignored at other times. She appears in Act III (in which Tartuffe tries to seduce her), but she has only a few lines, and most of these treat Tartuffe's suggestions with an air of frivolity. The bulk of her lines come in Act IV, when she is of major importance as the instrument for unmasking Tartuffe. This uneven distribution of the role has led to some confusion as to her true nature, for some have argued that her moral character is questionable. It seems clear, however, that Molière had in mind a reasonably worldly but moral woman.

It is Orgon's role, however, which is most evenly distributed throughout the play and which is a key to it. While the Tartuffes of the world are dangerous, they can exist only because of the Orgons, for the prosperity of the wicked depends upon the gullibility of the foolish. Just as Molière emphasizes Tartuffe's calculated piety, so, too, he emphasizes Orgon's impulsiveness and stubbornness. Orgon is not a fool; he is a prosperous merchant with a substantial fortune. He goes wrong in his judgment of Tartuffe largely because he acts without considering sufficient aspects of a question. When Tartuffe is finally unmasked, Orgon's character remains consistent, for failing to see the difference between hypocrisy and piety, he says: "I give up all pious people. From now on I will hold them in utter contempt, and treat them worse than the devil himself." Thus, instead of returning to a normal position, he assumes an equally exaggerated, though opposite, one.

Tartuffe is usually classified as a comedy of character, which means that its principal interest lies in the revelation of character (as opposed to situation, customs, or witty conversation). Much has already been said about the individual roles, but some additional factors should be considered.

Little indication is given in the play of ages or physical appearances. Molière wrote with his own company in mind, directed the play, and must have filled in for them many of the details left unspecified in the script. The role of Tartuffe was written for DuCroisy, who was at that time forty-three years old. He was a large, tall man with a ruddy complexion, and not unhandsome in a rough way. This, no doubt, was one of the sources of humor. All of Tartuffe's talk about scourges, hair shirts, and fasting were contradicted by his obvious plumpness, rosy health, and lecherousness.

Orgon was played by Molière himself, who was noted for his expressive face and body. Elmire was acted by Molière's wife, who was twenty-nine years old at the time. Mme. Pernell was played by a man, and, therefore, was no doubt intended to be a figure of considerable fun in her

Tartuffe, with the time of the action changed to the Victorian era. Directed by Lee Mitchell at Northwestern University. Courtesy of the University.

exaggerated censure of everyone except Tartuffe, and in her denunciation of all pleasure. All of the characters were drawn from the middle or lower classes (in accordance with the neoclassical standard of comedy).

The humor of the play is derived principally from the psychological relationship of the characters to the situation. The basic point of view (the norm) is established in the roles of Cleante and Dorine. Deviations are treated in a ridiculous light. For example, Orgon's lack of concern over his wife's sickness in contrast with his concern over Tartuffe's health is used for comic purpose. Orgon's responses to the alternation of information about Elmire and Tartuffe dramatize the situation and Orgon's character—and they create laughter.

Molière's use of his material to accomplish several purposes simultaneously can be seen also in his treatment of the notary, M. Loyal. The notary's supposed good will and his name contrast comically with his obvious bigotry and pleasure in evicting Orgon and his family. This minor role could have been easily handled straightforwardly, but Molière individualizes the notary and achieves humor, while at the same time forwarding the plot.

Another example of Molière's comic technique can be seen in Orgon's scene with Dorine. She tries to reason with him, rouses his ire, and manages to make her points while still seeming to obey him. Again many functions are served simultaneously.

Probably the least challenging roles for actors are those of the lovers and of Cleante. They are meant to be straight parts created to achieve audience sympathy and regard; yet they are more nearly cardboard figures than the others. Tartuffe's role is challenging, but the actor playing it must be wary of becoming too villainous, for the comedy may disappear if he becomes too much of a threat. Orgon's is really the best acting role, for not only is it the longest, it requires the greatest comic technique. One test of excellence is found in the scene in which Orgon conceals himself under the table and overhears Tartuffe's attempts to seduce Elmire. The success of the scene depends almost entirely upon a highly skilled pantomimic performance by the actor playing Orgon.

The unities of time and place are strictly observed in *Tartuffe*. Only a single room is required and even that needs only a table—under which Orgon can be concealed—and a closet—in which Damis can hide—for no specific use is made of the setting except in these two instances. The action is continuous, or nearly so, and it occurs in the same day. All of the action, with the possible exception of the lovers' quarrel, is directly related to the main theme of the play. *Tartuffe* is clearly within the classical tradition.

Molière, nevertheless, has let dramatic need, rather than any preconceived notion of form, dictate his technique. That he is successful is shown by the fact that, in spite of the many objections raised to it, *Tartuffe* has remained one of the most popular plays ever written. If it has flaws, it rises above them.

AFTER MOLIÈRE'S DEATH

Molière died in 1673. His life and death illustrate the status of the actor in France at that time, for, while he was highly admired as an author, the fact that he was an actor kept many honors and rights from him. He could not be seriously considered for membership in the French Academy, and when he died he was forbidden a Christian burial, since the edict against the actor which had been issued in the sixth century was still in effect. Most actors renounced their professions when they saw death approaching and were reconciled to the church. But Molière died suddenly, being taken ill during a performance, and either did not have time or refused to go through the usual procedure. Unfortunately, while the actor's legal and economic status had improved by that time, he was still considered to be an inferior person and in some senses an outcast because of his profession. The English actor achieved full social status long before his French counterpart, but it is doubtful that the actor anywhere was fully accepted prior to the twentieth century, if then.

At the time of Molière's death, five theatrical companies were playing in Paris: Molière's, the companies at the Hôtel de Bourgogne and at the Marais, a company of Italian actors, and an opera troupe. The director of the opera, Lully, managed to gain control of the Palais-Royal, and Molière's company was forced to move. Soon afterward it was amalgamated with the Marais company. In 1680 this combined company was ordered to merge with the Hôtel de Bourgogne troupe.

This merger is one of the important events in French theatrical history, for the new group was called the Comédie Française, and as such became the first national theatre in the world. This organization is still in existence, and more nearly embodies a continuous theatrical tradition than any other single theatre. It is one of the great museums of the world, since its function has been to produce the most distinguished plays of the French

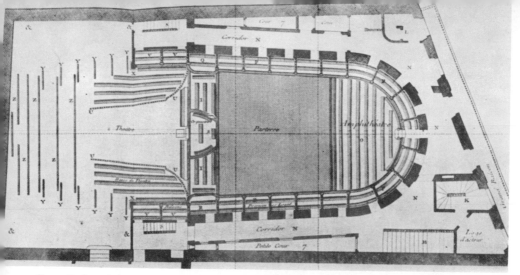

Ground plan of the theatre used by the Comédie Française between 1689–1770. Note the benches on the stage for spectators. From Mantzius' *History of Theatrical Art*. Volume IV, 1905.

repertory. It is sometimes called the House of Molière and takes justifiable pride in being a direct descendant of his troupe.

The order which created the Comédie Française also laid down the rules under which it was to be governed: like its predecessors, essentially it was to be a shareholding company, and it was to be governed democratically by its members. Rules governed admission of actors to the group, retirement, pensions, and all other matters. A yearly subsidy was to be paid to the group by the King.

In 1698 the Italian troupe was expelled from France because of a supposed satire against Mme. de Maintenon, whom Louis XIV had married secretly in 1684. By 1698 the number of troupes in Paris had been reduced to one dramatic and one operatic company. Each of these two companies was granted a monopoly on certain kinds of theatrical entertainment.

In the 1670s the Royal Academy of Music and Dance (more commonly called the Opéra) had been given a monopoly on the production of opera and all theatrical entertainment which utilized elaborate spectacle, dance, or music requiring trained voices or more than six instruments. At the time of its formation, the Comédie Française had been given a monopoly on the production of regular comedy and tragedy. An Italian troupe returned to Paris in 1716 and eventually was given a state subsidy, but its repertory was restricted to irregular drama. This arrangement, with minor adjustments, was to continue until the French Revolution.

The seventeenth century—the age of French classicism—saw the theatre come to maturity in France. It produced three great dramatists—Corneille, Racine, and Molière—who have set the standard for French theatre since that time.

Chapter 10

THE RESTORATION AND THE EIGHTEENTH CENTURY

ENGLAND

Charles II was restored to the throne of England in 1660 and with him the theatre regained its place in English life. Since then, although theatres have been closed during plagues, at the time of Royal deaths, and on similar occasions, English theatre tradition has remained a vital force.

Soon after theatres were reopened state control was established. Originally this control was exercised largely through the granting of patents or monopolies. Charles II issued two patents, one to William D'Avenant (1606–68), who headed the company called the Duke's Men, and one to Thomas Killigrew (1612–83), who headed the King's Men. For a time George Jolly held a third patent, but the number was confirmed at two in 1663.

Many attempts were made in the first part of the eighteenth century to circumvent the patents. These violations, coupled with numerous satirical attacks on government officials and policies, led to the passage of the Licensing Act in 1737. The law reconfirmed the patents and further provided that before production all plays must be licensed by the Lord Chamberlain, who thus became an official censor. Under the terms of

Marie Françoise Dumesnil in Racine's tragedy, *Athalie*. In spite of its Biblical setting, Dumesnil's dress is in the height of eighteenth-century fashion. From Pougin's *Dictionnaire Historique et Pittoresque du Théâtre . . .* , 1885.

the law the government came to control both the plays and the number of theatres. Although the enforcement of these provisions was relaxed from time to time, for all practical purposes the number of theatres licensed to produce legitimate drama in London remained at two until 1843, when the patents were rescinded. The provision for the licensing of plays, however, still remains in effect. Between 1737 and 1843 the two patent houses in London were Drury Lane and Covent Garden.

THEATRE STRUCTURE

When the English theatre reopened in 1660, performances were given at first in playhouses which had been built before 1642. Soon, however, new structures in the Italian manner were erected. The theatre building which evolved differed in only a few respects from that already worked out in Italy.

One of the differences lay in the size and use of the apron (that portion of the stage which extends forward of the proscenium arch). While there was an apron stage in the Continental theatre, it was not used as extensively and did not have proscenium doors (that is, doors opening onto the apron) as in the English theatre. In the Restoration period, there may have been as many as three proscenium doors on each side of the stage, but two appear to have been more usual. These doors allowed for great flexibility in staging. For example, an actor might exit through one door and re-enter immediately at another door on the same side, thus indicating a change in place or a passage of time. The apron stage was comparable in many ways to the forestage of the Elizabethan theatre and the *platea*, or generalized acting area, of the Medieval theatre.

The apron gradually diminished in size in the eighteenth century, but it and the proscenium doors were retained and used until well into the nineteenth century, when the demand for greater realism in scenery and acting gradually led to their abandonment. The use of the apron, or forestage, by the actor placed him forward of the set, which then became principally a background for his action, since he did not play in the setting so much as in front of it. The forestage, by projecting the actor into the auditorium, helped to create greater intimacy between audience and actor.

The auditorium was arranged in a manner similar to that used on the Continent, with boxes, pit, and galleries. From the Restoration on, however, there were always seats for spectators in the English pit. As in France, spectators sat on the stage, a practice which continued in England until 1762.

SCENERY

The scenery used in the English theatre between 1660 and 1800 differed in no important respect from that in current use on the stages of France and Italy. Scenes were painted in perspective on wings, borders and backdrops. The settings, in accordance with the neoclassical demand for universality, were generalized, and a large number was not needed. Plays were usually set in a palace, a garden, a prison, or some other generalized place, and consequently the same setting could be used in a number of different plays. Sometimes theatres even used a set of "neutral" wings which remained stationary throughout a play with only the back scene being shifted to indicate a change in place. The "groove" system of shifting scenery (explained in Chapter 8) was employed.

Pantomimes, operas, and certain plays, however, demanded more detailed scenery and elaborate special effects. In these cases, new scenery was specially designed and its unusual nature and any special effects were widely advertised. On such occasions, spectators might also be forbidden to sit on the stage.

In the eighteenth century the interest in settings gradually grew, and by 1800 considerable emphasis had come to be placed on the reproduction of specific places and upon the illusion of a given time of day or of weather conditions such as fogs, storms, and moonlight scenes.

The most important eighteenth century English scene designer was Philippe Jacques de Loutherbourg (1740–1812). He began staging spectacular pieces (he seldom designed for legitimate drama) for David Garrick in the early 1770s and his startling effects created a sensation. He compli-

The interior of the Covent Garden Theatre in 1794. The Covent Garden was one of the two leading theatres in London from 1732 until 1843. Since the middle of the nineteenth century it has been the home of opera. From *Londina Illustrata*. London 1819–25.

A scene from Elkanah Settle's *The Empress of Morocco* (1673) at the Duke's Theatre in Dorset Gardens, London. Although the forestage is not shown, a portion of the proscenium doors and stage boxes can be seen at the extreme sides. Note also the musicians' gallery above the proscenium. From *Londina Illustrata*, 1825.

cated the stage picture by adding ground rows (profile pieces shaped and painted to represent rocks, mountains, grassy plots, fences and similar objects) to the traditional wing-border-drop settings. Since these could be placed almost anywhere on the stage, he achieved more naturalness and the illusion of greater space and distance.

De Loutherbourg also reproduced likenesses of actual places on stage and thereby helped to create a demand for scenic illusion. He improved stage lighting and was able to give the effect of natural light at different seasons, times of day, and in varying weather conditions. He utilized transparent backdrops behind which special lighting devices could achieve the semblance of a rising moon, a volcanic eruption, changes from fair to stormy weather, and similar effects. His influence was all in a direction that would be thoroughly exploited in the nineteenth century.

THE ACTOR

When the English theatre was reopened in 1660 its financial structure was considerably altered from what it had been in Shakespeare's day. From the

The Drury Lane Theatre was one of the two major theatres in London from the Restoration until 1843. This engraving shows its appearance in 1792. The present Drury Lane is used primarily for musicals. From *Londina Illustrata*.

Restoration on, the theatre was to come more and more under the control of businessmen. After 1660 actors often served as managers of theatrical troupes, but most actors withdrew from the business aspects of the theatre. They became employees rather than active participants in the over-all affairs of a company.

Typically, in the English theatre (from the Restoration until the end of the nineteenth century) an actor was hired for a stated period, usually one or two years, at a specified salary with the additional guarantee of one or more "benefit" performances each year. At a benefit performance, the receipts (after deduction of operating expenses) go to an actor, author, charitable group, or other designated source. The first benefit performance for an actor dates from about 1685, and soon the prominent members of a company came to expect at least one benefit each season. While this occasion brought the actor additional income, it also offered the manager an excuse for paying him less salary. Benefits often were occasions for great rejoicing, but they were also sources of embarrassment if the attendance was small, for they became a test of the actor's popularity.

Although the English actor did not have the financial security or government subsidy enjoyed by his French contemporaries, his social status was higher. He was never excluded from the church; a number of actresses married into the nobility; some actors were even buried in Westminster Abbey, an honor reserved for persons of great national importance. On the other hand, the moral character of the actor continued to be questioned, and it is doubtful that he was viewed as entirely desirable by the general populace.

The "closet" scene from *Hamlet*, showing Thomas Betterton in the role of Hamlet. From an engraving in Nicholas Rowe's edition of Shakespeare's plays published in 1709. *Below.* David Garrick in a scene from *King Lear*. Note the eighteenth-century garments. From a contemporary engraving after a painting by Wilson. Courtesy of the University of Iowa Library.

Each actor or actress (actresses were introduced to the English stage in the 1660s and were accepted throughout Europe after that time) was usually employed for a "line of business." This meant that each was trained to play a specific kind of part. If his line of business included the young lover, he played such roles regardless of age until he retired from the stage. While this sometimes led to incongruous casting, it also allowed the actor to develop considerable perfection in his specialty.

An actor learned his profession from experience rather than at a school. He might begin in a provincial company and later be taken into a more important troupe, or he might learn a line of business while acting supernumerary roles in a London theatre. Once he was accepted as a full member of a troupe, however, his line of business was usually fixed for life.

Charles Macklin as Shylock. Macklin was the first actor to play Shylock as a serious role rather than as a low-comedy figure. From Doran's *"His Majesty's Servants,"* 1897. *Opposite page*. David Garrick as Macbeth. From the *English Illustrated Magazine*.

Each actor also "possessed parts." This meant that once he was given a particular role, it remained his until he left the company. An actor might have assigned to him up to a hundred roles, any one of which he might be expected to perform on twenty-four hours' notice.

Many of these factors were determined by the fact that the theatres were operated on a "repertory system" (a system by which a number of plays are alternated throughout a season). Between 1660 and 1900 the majority of any company's repertory was made up of standard plays from the past. A lesser part was composed of recent plays from previous seasons. Usually these recent plays were not popular enough to justify their continuation for more than a few years. The smallest amount of a company's offerings was made up of new plays. Those sufficiently popular were retained in the repertory, but many new plays were dropped after a single season or, if they were total failures, even after a single performance.

New plays were usually staged by their writers, while old plays were rehearsed by the stage manager, who was normally an actor in the company employed also for these additional duties. In any case, "the director" took it for granted that the actor knew his job, and he probably restricted himself to suggesting details of characterization or line readings. He probably spent very little time with the blocking (the positioning of actors on stage). Actors learned as part of their training to give the best stage positions to the leading characters and to move around them as inconspicuously as possible. The actor also learned to direct his speeches to the audience as much as to the other characters. The presence of the audience was constantly recognized and emphasized by the practice of leaving the lights on in the auditorium throughout a performance.

Rehearsals for plays not previously in the repertory normally extended from seven to twelve days. Meanwhile the actors were also performing nightly, and a short "refresher" rehearsal was probably held each day for the play that was to be performed that evening. By modern standards the rehearsal procedures were perfunctory, and great reliance was placed on the actor's stage presence and quick wit.

Acting style was no doubt much more exaggerated than modern

taste would approve. The actor was said to base his acting on life, but to idealize what he found there rather than merely to copy it. Thus there was careful selection, arrangement, and considerable exaggeration. Periodically during the eighteenth century, actors were said to have reformed acting in the direction of a more natural style. But naturalism in acting is a relative matter, and these actors undoubtedly only eliminated some of the exaggeration. The eighteenth-century actor was always an actor, and there was little likelihood of confusing his performance with real-life actions.

The eighteenth-century actor surpassed the playwright as the major artist in the theatre. Audiences in large part went to see a particular actor perform a particular role. The appeal was comparable to that of opera today, for, since the audience might already know the play, it attended to enjoy the technical skill and interpretation of a specific actor. After certain speeches or scenes the audience applauded as it does today when an opera singer finishes an aria. This constant interaction between audience and actor made for a more personal reaction than that encountered in theatres today.

The most famous actors in England between 1660 and 1800 were Thomas Betterton, Colley Cibber, James Quin, David Garrick, and Charles Macklin. Thomas Betterton (*c.* 1635–1710) dominated the English stage from about 1670 to 1710, during which time he played the leading roles in almost all of the plays in the repertory. Colley Cibber (1671–1757) is the best-known performer of the period from Betterton's death until the 1730s. He was primarily a comic actor and excelled in the role of the "fop," or fashionable man-about-town. His autobiography is one of the principal sources of information about the theatre of that period.

Between 1715 and 1740, James Quin (1692–1766), who was noted especially for his declamatory style, was considered the ranking tragic actor. It was partially due to Quin's acting style that David Garrick (1717–79) was said to have returned acting to a more natural mode when he came into prominence in the 1740s. Garrick was the major actor on the English stage between 1741 and 1776, and was the manager of the Drury Lane Theatre for a number of years. Through his sound judgment and taste, both in management and acting, he elevated the English theatre to a position of international esteem. Especially noted for his performance of Shakespearean roles, he is generally thought to have been the greatest of English actors.

Charles Macklin (1699–1797) acted for approximately seventy years and was probably the most realistic actor of the century. He was especially well known for his playing of irascible old men and is most famous for his serious portrayal of Shylock, a role which had been performed previously by low comedians.

The actor in an established theatre company in London in the eighteenth century enjoyed a comfortable life, though his counterpart in the provincial company still led a hazardous existence. Even in London, however, there was as yet no pension system (as in France), and many actors ended their days in poverty.

THE PLAYWRIGHT

But the actor's position was secure compared to that of the playwright. In the Restoration, writers of plays might be employed by companies on a fixed salary, but this practice soon gave way to the benefit system. Under this system, the author received the receipts of the third performance. If a play were especially popular he might also receive benefits on the sixth, ninth, and each additional third night of the initial run of a play. As a rule, however, he was fortunate to receive one benefit. After the initial run, the play belonged to the company and the author received no further payment.

The playwright could not copyright his works and frequently sold the publication rights of his plays for a small sum of money. It was not until well into the nineteenth century that the playwright was able to obtain a copyright and consequently demand a royalty for each performance.

The period from 1660–1700 is noted particularly for heroic tragedy and the comedy of manners. The heroic play was written in rhymed couplets, usually concerned the necessity of choosing between love and honor (the relative merits of which were debated in lengthy and bombastic speeches), and abounded in violent action and startling reversals. Today

A scene from Dryden's *All for Love*. From an engraving in *The Dramatick Works of John Dryden, Esq.*, 1735. *Right.* A scene from Farquhar's *The Beaux' Strategem*. From an engraving in *The Works of the Late Ingenious Mr. George Farquhar*, 1711.

these plays seem totally unreal and absurd, although they were extremely popular in their own period.

Alongside the heroic play another more vital strain of tragedy developed. It was written in blank verse and was more directly descended from the tragedies of Shakespeare. The outstanding works of this type are *Venice Preserv'd* and *The Orphan*, written by Thomas Otway (1652–85), both of which held the stage until the nineteenth century. Another type of Restoration tragedy can best be seen in *All for Love*, by John Dryden (1631–1700), a rewriting of Shakespeare's *Antony and Cleopatra* to make it conform to neoclassical ideals.

The Restoration is principally noted, however, for the comedy of manners, a kind of play in which characters and events are subordinated to the revelation or criticism of social values and customs.

There has been much argument over the moral tone of Restoration comedy. Since 1700 most critics have interpreted it as condoning or accepting behavior which is normally considered to be reprehensible. It is probably true that these plays waver between accepting and satirizing the age, but they should not be condemned too hastily. Before passing judgment, it is important to understand the basic view behind these plays.

Restoration comedies imply that man is corruptible, but that this fact must be accepted with an attitude of sophistication and tolerance rather than one of indignation and outrage. Restoration writers did not mean, however, that all forms of behavior are justified and that no distinctions are to be made between actions. The admirable man is considered to be the one who accepts as his guide the maxim, "Know thyself," for this will lead him to assess his own qualities and capabilities and to respect them in his daily life. The plays, therefore, satirize persons who are either self-deceived or who are attempting to deceive others. The humor is directed against the fop, the pretender at wit and sophistication, the old woman who is trying to be young, the old man who marries a young wife, and other similar types. The standard is represented by those characters who are truly witty and sophisticated, who see others and themselves clearly, and who act accordingly. These characters always accept everything with a worldly air, however, and for this reason the plays have given the impression to many readers of condoning immoral behavior. In a few plays immoral behavior is accepted, but in the majority of cases the rewards and punishments are meted out in accordance with how well the characters have been able to live up to the ideal of self-knowledge.

Restoration comedy originated with such works by George Etherege (1634–91) as *Love in a Tub* (1664), *The Man of Mode* (1676), and *She Would If She Could* (1668). It reached its perfection in the plays of William Congreve (1670–1729), especially *Love for Love* (1695) and *The Way of the World* (1700).

The Restoration comedy of manners was not calculated to please the Puritan elements in English society. After the return of Charles II in 1660 Puritan influence, which had dominated England during the Commonwealth, was little felt for some time. Theatre audiences were largely drawn from the upper classes or from the more liberal members of the middle class.

A change set in after 1689, however, when William and Mary were crowned rulers of England. They did much to forward the interests of the merchant class, which came to wield more and more power. In the 1690s many members of this rising middle class began to attend the theatre, were offended by what they saw there, and exerted pressure for reforms.

The rise of the middle class coincided with a resurgence of Puritan ideas, the most powerful statement of which appeared in Jeremy Collier's *A Short View of the Immorality and Profaneness of the English Stage*, published in 1698. In this work Collier attacked current plays, particularly the comedies of manners. While many of the dramatists of the day defended their own works and those of other writers, Collier was sufficiently persuasive that many playwrights reconsidered their views. All of these factors combined to bring about a change in the attitudes and spirit of English drama after 1700.

The transition to the new outlook can be seen most clearly in the comedies of George Farquhar (1678–1707), whose *The Recruiting Officer* and *The Beaux' Stratagem* are among the best English plays of the early eighteenth century. The new drama put a greater emphasis upon emotion and a clear-cut set of moral standards; the settings were more frequently placed outside of London, and the characters were less apt to be drawn from fashionable society.

While neoclassical tragedy continued to be written throughout the eighteenth century (the best-known example is *Cato* by Joseph Addison), the most important dramatic types were the sentimental comedy and domestic tragedy. The appearance of both of these types can be explained in part by the desire of the middle class to see itself and its ideals depicted on the stage.

SENTIMENTAL DRAMA

The term *sentimental* is sometimes used to describe almost all of the drama of the eighteenth century. It indicates basically an overemphasis upon arousing sympathetic response to the misfortunes of others.

Even comedy became preoccupied with the ordeals of sympathetic characters, and humorous portions were reserved for minor characters, usually servants. Plays could be called comedies largely because they ended happily, rather than because of their subject matter or its treatment. The expressed aim of the dramatist was to draw forth a smile and a tear, or, as one writer put it, to produce "a pleasure too exquisite for laughter." Characters were refined, filled with noble sentiments, oppressed by circumstances which they bore bravely, and from which they were eventually rescued and handsomely rewarded.

Today these plays seem highly exaggerated in their depiction of human nature. The characters appear too good and noble to be human, and the circumstances too contrived to be true. But these plays attracted large audiences, who were reduced to tears and who accepted the works as realistic pictures of human motivations. To understand the plays, therefore, it is necessary to examine the view of human psychology prevalent at that time.

The eighteenth century conceived of man as being good by nature. To remain good, a man needed only to listen to his instincts and to follow what they told him. Evil behavior was viewed as the result of circumstances or the failure to follow dictates of the heart. The person who fell into evil ways might be reformed, sometimes even in a moment's time, through an appeal to his basic goodness. The endurance of ordeals was looked upon as the test of true virtue; the rewarding by a just god of those who withstood hardships and temptations was a logical and necessary outcome.

One other factor—the encouragement of emotional display in the eighteenth century—helps to explain the contemporary appeal of sentimental drama. Man viewed as subject to all sorts of pressures from without, if he is not to be overcome by them, must exert counteracting pressures from within. The chief form of outwardly directed pressure was considered to be emotion. The display of emotion, then, became both a sign of a healthy mind and a means of maintaining health. Furthermore, the ideal emotions were thought to be those sympathetic responses aroused by the suffering of innocent beings. Emotional display, therefore, was proof of a virtuous nature (one properly moved at the sight of suffering), and, at the same time, this display helped to maintain health. To weep and to feel deeply, then, was desirable, and playwrights labored to fulfill that need.

Eighteenth-century sentimental comedy received its first full expression in 1722 in *The Conscious Lovers* by Sir Richard Steele (1672–1729). The vogue for this type dominated the theatre for a long time. Its later development is best exemplified in Hugh Kelly's (1739–77) *False Delicacy*.

Sentimental comedy had its serious counterpart in domestic tragedy, which deliberately avoided the kings and nobility of traditional tragedy and chose its characters from everyday life (principally the merchant class). It usually painted the horrible outcome of giving in to sin, just as sentimental comedy showed the rewards of resisting sin.

George Lillo (1693–1739) established the vogue for domestic tragedy with *The London Merchant* (1731). This play shows an apprentice who, led astray by a depraved woman, robs his employer and murders his uncle. It is clearly indicated that had he resisted temptation he could have married his employer's daughter and become a prosperous merchant. The virtues of the merchant class are praised and sin is denounced in the most obvious terms. Today *The London Merchant* seems overly simple, but it exerted great power over audiences throughout the eighteenth century and was a major influence on the drama of France and Germany. Although others tried to follow in Lillo's steps, *The Gamester* by Edward Moore (1712–57) is the only other notable English play of the type in the eighteenth century.

Sentimental comedy and domestic tragedy are indicative of the changes from neoclassical standards. Each represents a considerable departure from the "pure" dramatic forms, for each mingles elements formerly reserved solely for either comedy or tragedy.

BALLAD OPERA, BURLESQUE, AND PANTOMIME

Many other departures from the neoclassical ideal occurred in the eighteenth century as more and more "illegitimate" types appeared. The most important of these new forms were ballad opera, burlesque, and pantomime.

The emergence of ballad opera can be explained in part by the popularity of Italian opera. In the early years of the Restoration, opera was imported into England, and for a time there was a struggle between the Italian form and a native English opera. The Italian form triumphed and in the early years of the eighteenth century became one of the most popular types of theatrical entertainment. It reached its peak in the 1730s with the works of George Frederick Handel (1685–1759). The ballad opera built upon this enthusiastic response.

The first and most important example of this new development was *The Beggar's Opera* by John Gay (1685–1732); it appeared in 1728. In the ballad-opera form, sections of dialogue alternate with songs set to the tunes of popular ballads. *The Beggar's Opera* was so popular that the producers were forced to keep it running continuously for sixty performances, and it thus became one of the first long-run shows in history. Its popularity led to many imitations between 1728 and 1737.

While *The Beggar's Opera* treated the Italian opera humorously, it did much more, for it also satirized the contemporary political situation in England. At the end of the work one of the characters observes that it is difficult to tell whether the robbers are imitating the ruling classes or whether the ruling classes are imitating the robbers. The moral is said to lie in the demonstration that the lower classes, like the upper, have their vices, but that, unlike the upper classes, the lower orders are punished for their wrongdoings.

The ballad opera eventually gave way to the sentimental operetta, or comic opera. The principal writer of this new form was Isaac Bickerstaffe (1735–1812), whose most popular works were *Love in a Village* and *The Maid of the Mill*.

During the 1730s Henry Fielding (1707–54) turned to writing farces which burlesqued much of the drama of the day and frequently satirized the ruling classes more severely than had Gay. Fielding's *The Tragedy of Tragedies, or, The Life and Death of Tom Thumb the Great* makes a travesty of the tragedies of the time, while his *Pasquin* and *The*

A design by Cipriani and Richards for Charles Dibdin's pantomime, *The Mirror, or Harlequin Everywhere*, performed at the Covent Garden Theatre in 1779.

Historical Register for 1736 ridicule contemporary politics and social conditions. The combination of ballad opera and burlesque did much to bring about the passage of the Licensing Act of 1737.

The most popular new form in the eighteenth century, however, was pantomime. It came into being around 1715 and was perfected by John Rich (*c.* 1682–1761), manager of one of the patent companies. This pantomime was composed of dancing and silent mimicry performed to musical accompaniment and set against elaborate scenery and special effects.

Typically, the plot was composed of alternating comic and serious scenes. The comic plot usually involved Harlequin, who by some device had obtained a magic wand by means of which he could transform places, objects, and persons at will. The serious plot, normally, was derived from a mythological or historical subject already known to the audience.

Pantomime made its appeal largely to the eye, and great expense and much time was lavished on producing it. But the investment was repaid by audience attendance. It was largely through the visual requirements of opera and pantomime that stage machinery and scenery developed in England.

GOLDSMITH AND SHERIDAN

By the 1770s sentimentalism (in the form of comedy, domestic tragedy, comic opera, and pantomime) dominated the English stage. At this time two dramatists, Goldsmith and Sheridan, endeavored to reform public taste.

Oliver Goldsmith (1730–74) through his plays, *The Good-Natured Man* and *She Stoops to Conquer*, attempted to reestablish what he called "laughing" comedy. His plays are in the tradition of the more boisterous works of Ben Jonson or of Shakespeare's farces. The plays of Richard Brinsley Sheridan (1751–1816), on the other hand, are in the vein of Restoration comedy, but without its ambiguous moral tone. His most famous plays are *The Rivals*, *The Critic*, and *The School for Scandal*, the last of which is frequently said to be the greatest comedy of manners in the English language.

THE SCHOOL FOR SCANDAL

THEMES AND IDEAS. On the surface *The School for Scandal* and *Tartuffe* have striking similarities. These may be seen especially in the unmasking of the hypocrite, and the means used to make the husband realize that he has been deceived.

The differences between Molière's and Sheridan's plays are greater than their similarities, however. *Tartuffe* is much more restricted than *The School for Scandal* in the scope of its action and in the number of characters introduced. But the source of greatest difference lies in tone: *Tartuffe* shows the threat of religious hypocrisy to individual freedom and morality; *The School for Scandal* is largely confined to poking fun at sentimental comedy and to showing the comic results of scandalmongering. Unlike Tartuffe, Joseph Surface never becomes a serious threat to the welfare of admirable characters, and the "school" of scandalmongers tampers, for the most part, with the reputations of persons never seen by the audience. As a result, Sheridan's play is much more lighthearted in tone and seems far less serious in its purpose than Molière's work.

The School for Scandal is a comedy of manners, for it is primarily concerned with depicting the current fashions and customs of the day. The main action is set against the background of the "school for scandal" which embodies the contemporary social setting. The shallowness of this group allows hypocrites such as Joseph Surface to flourish, since it cannot tell the difference between pious statement and virtuous action. Furthermore, the group's own shallowness prevents its members from perceiving the depths of character in others. Trifling with reputations, consequently, has become a game for those who are unable to distinguish between human behavior and character.

Sheridan places much of the blame for this state of affairs on the vogue for sentimentalism, and his principal unsympathetic character, Joseph Surface, is made a "man of sentiment"—that is, one who mouths moral maxims. His pious statements are accepted as proof of a virtuous character, while the frank and natural behavior of his brother, Charles, is taken as the sign of a lost soul. Sheridan is ultimately concerned with the distinction between true virtue and pious remarks—between ingrained character and "sentiment." His sophisticated and humorous treatment of this theme, however, never allows its serious aspects to come to the fore, for he concentrates on the comic results of human shortsightedness and frailty. Much of the humor in the play results from the way in which the plans and methods of the rascals serve as traps in which they themselves are caught.

While Sheridan satirizes sentimental comedy, he has not been able to free his own play from many of its characteristics. His admirable characters are inclined to moralize or fall into "sentiments" such as Maria's line: "Wit loses its respect with me when I see it in company with malice," and the play as a whole illustrates the typical lesson of sentimental comedy—true virtue will be rewarded (and with a sizable fortune). Furthermore, characters have been divided into the truly virtuous, who act from the dictates of their hearts, and the misguided, who behave according to current fashion. Lady Teazle's actions demonstrate at first the results of following fashion; her reform is brought about by listening to the dictates of her heart.

PLOT AND STRUCTURE.   *The School for Scandal* has both a Prologue and an Epilogue, as did almost every play written during the Restoration and eighteenth century. The Prologue is used to put the audience in the right frame of mind and to suggest the mood of the play, while the Epilogue contains an appeal for audience favor along with a summation of the play's basic intention. Both Prologue and Epilogue are short and not essential as aids in understanding the play.

The School for Scandal is structurally complex since it weaves together the schemes, desires and cross-purposes of so many characters: the underhanded machinations of Joseph Surface and Lady Sneerwell, the cross-purposes of Sir Peter and Lady Teazle, the attempts by Sir Oliver to discover to whom he should leave his money, the desires of Charles and Maria to marry each other, and the rather generalized desire of the scandalmongers to interfere in the affairs of everyone else.

Sheridan has solved his problem in part through the relationship he has set up among the characters. All move within the same social circle in London and all know each other well. Furthermore, Sir Peter is the guardian of Maria and has been the best friend of the now-deceased father of Charles and Joseph Surface. The close tie among characters allows Sheridan to maneuver them more freely and to motivate their presence whenever needed on stage. It also allows him to bring together logically the various strands of the plot as the play progresses.

The scandalmongers are among the least important characters, but they are used to great advantage in the play's structure. First, Sheridan establishes the social background by showing the school in action. Second, the school is used for expository purposes, for their gossip reveals many important facts and sets up the conditions out of which the conflicts arise. Third, their gossip and intrigues affect the other characters. It is they who have almost ruined Charles Surface's reputation with Sir Peter and Maria, and it is Snake's defection from the group which eventually clears the final obstacle from the path of Charles and Maria. Fourth, the school is one of the principal sources of comedy through its witty and malicious conversations. It is a mark of Sheridan's greatness as a comic writer that the group always remains ridiculous and, while complicating the action, does not seriously threaten the welfare of the sympathetic characters.

Sheridan's structural method has some elements in common with the technique used by Shakespeare. The similarity is especially evident in the way the subplot and the main plot are integrated. In *The School for Scandal* the Sir Peter–Lady Teazle story has little connection with the Joseph–Maria–Charles story in the beginning. As the play progresses, how-

The screen scene from *The School for Scandal* at the Drury Lane Theatre, 1778. Note the forestage, the proscenium doors, the stage boxes, the clearly defined wings, and the similarity of the actor's costumes to those worn by the spectators. Courtesy of the Yale University Library.

ever, the two stories move closer and closer together, and in the "screen" scene the revelation of Joseph's relationship with Lady Teazle leads to the resolution of both the subplot and the main plot.

Sheridan, like Shakespeare, also moves the place of action in accordance with the needs of his story. *The School for Scandal* has fourteen scenes which occur in four different houses. This freedom of movement makes the complex plotting much easier, for it would be almost impossible for all of the events to occur believably in a single place.

Sheridan, like both Shakespeare and Molière, constantly strove for clarity in characterization and situation. For example, in the opening scene he makes it quite plain that Joseph Surface is a hypocrite who is attempting to ruin his brother. The situation between Sir Peter and Lady Teazle is made equally clear in the second scene. Asides to the audience are used throughout the play whenever an action or a motivation might be otherwise ambiguous. In addition, many of the characters have been given names which point to their basic natures: Snake, Sir Benjamin Backbite, Lady Sneerwell, and so on.

While Sheridan makes the situation completely lucid at any moment, he does not let the audience foresee the way in which it will be resolved. He arouses expectations that Joseph Surface will be unmasked, that the school will be put to rout, that Lady Teazle will be brought to her senses, and that Maria will be made happy, but the play's complications serve to keep the truth sufficiently concealed to make the outcome doubtful. Thus, Sheridan achieves clarity and suspense simultaneously.

The high point of the play is the screen sequence, which is frequently said to be one of the most skillfully constructed scenes ever written. There are good reasons for such a judgment, since it brings to a climax almost all of the preceding conflicts and uses them to build a series of increasingly important comic reversals which culminate in the discovery of Lady Teazle behind the screen. This discovery leads to an obligatory scene involving Lady Teazle, Sir Peter, and Joseph that serves to bring Lady Teazle to her senses and to unmask Joseph's hypocrisy. This is the decisive moment in the play, leading directly to the unwinding of complications and the play's resolution.

The unities of both time and place are observed, since all action occurs within twenty-four hours and all places are within easy reach of each other. The close connection between the main plot and the subplot creates unity of action also. *The School for Scandal* is a good example of the neoclassical standard, which was more liberally interpreted in England than in France.

CHARACTERS AND ACTING. Remembering the neoclassical notion of decorum is helpful in understanding the characters in *The School for Scandal*, for they are drawn largely as types. Charles Surface is the natural young man, who does those things which are appropriate to men of his age. He is frank, honest, rash, unthinking, hasty, and fundamentally good-natured. Joseph, on the other hand, pretends to have the characteristics of the older, mature person and thus is unnatural and ludicrous. Sir Peter adheres to the ideals of decorum for a man of his age except in his marriage to a young woman, and he is made to suffer for that lapse.

Maria, Sir Oliver, and Rowley constitute the standard of behavior in the play, for each embodies the ideals of appropriate behavior and moral conduct. It is the ideals of these characters that are vindicated in the play. On the other hand, the school of scandalmongers and Joseph Surface clearly deviate from these patterns and are punished. Charles, Lady Teazle, and Sir Peter deviate only in a few respects and, at the end of the play, they acknowledge their shortcomings.

Sheridan uses only a few broad strokes to differentiate his characters. For example, the scandalmongers are distinguished from each other principally through age, sex, and methods of gossip. Sir Benjamin and Crabtree differ from each other primarily through age and from the other members of the school by sex. Mrs. Candour is unlike Lady Sneerwell mainly because of her distinctive method of murdering reputations.

All of the characters—except Old Rowley, Moses, and the servants —are from the leisure class. None is concerned about making a living. Charles and his companions worry about getting enough money to live pleasurably, but they would not consider working for it. The characters' world, therefore, is that of the aristocracy. They are preoccupied with such matters as marriages, the making of proper impressions, the maintenance and destruction of reputations. To live life pleasurably is the ideal. Sheridan satirizes those who murder reputations and those who are hypocrites, but he does not raise any doubts about the essential rightness of the social system itself. This restricted concern gives the play a tone of lightness and frivolity which is only slightly modified by the moralizing of Maria and Sir Oliver and by the play's ending.

A kind of sophistication and urbanity, therefore, are required of its actors. The members of the school must display an artificiality which contrasts sharply with the down-to-earth qualities of Sir Oliver, Sir Peter, and Old Rowley. Maria's straightforwardness contrasts with Lady Teazle's unthinking behavior, and Charles' frank enjoyment of life with Joseph's pretense of sobriety. All of the roles offer acting parts of substance, with the possible exceptions of Maria, Old Rowley, the minor roles of servants, and Charles' companions. Most of the characters are allowed to be delightfully malicious, to undertake a series of disguises, or to undergo experiences which demand a wide range of responses. Maria, however, remains constant throughout the play and serves more than any other character as the ideal against which the others may be judged.

Visual and Aural Appeals. *The School for Scandal* is set in the London of the time in which it was written (1777). This is reflected especially in its costumes, which were those worn by the upper classes of the day. The accompanying contemporary engraving of the "screen" scene shows the production's costumes and setting, the theatre's apron stage, proscenium doors, and its audience members seated in boxes. The actor's dress corresponds closely with that worn by the audience, and the division of the scenery into two sets of wings and a back scene is evident.

By this time spectators had been banished from the stage and more emphasis was being placed on the settings, a large number of which are traditionally used for *The School for Scandal*. Most of the places are not specific in their requirements, however, being designated merely as a room in Sir Peter's house, or at Lady Sneerwell's, and so on. The more specific settings are required for the scene in which Charles sells the family portraits and for the screen scene. All of the settings were at that time changed in full view of the audience.

The School for Scandal contains a considerable amount of rather precisely specified action. For example, at Charles Surface's house a supper is in progress during which toasts are drunk and songs are sung. This is followed by an auction of the pictures. Many other scenes require an equal amount of clearly specified business. Much of the action obviously took place on the forestage, and a large number of exits and entrances were logically made through the proscenium doors. The use of the forestage kept the action close to the audience and made the use of asides much easier and more acceptable.

The language of the play serves as much as any other factor to give *The School for Scandal* its appeal. Sheridan follows in the tradition of the comic writers of the Restoration by making his characters speak with great polish and wit. He uses a kind of idealized conversation in which each turn of phrase seems exactly right, though spontaneous. It is sophisticated and sparkling; it reflects the same detachment from socioeconomic concerns as does the subject matter. It shows the English language at its peak in conversational usage. Sheridan's polished prose demands a precise delivery, and when it is properly spoken, it becomes a special source of delight for an audience.

The School for Scandal has maintained a more consistent popularity than any other comedy in the English language. Its story, its wit, and its comic inventiveness have kept it understandable and thoroughly enjoyable to each generation.

By the time Sheridan's play was produced, neoclassicism was being undermined by new forces which were to come together shortly in the Romantic movement. Before turning to these new developments, however, the broad outlines of the eighteenth-century theatre on the continent will be reviewed briefly.

FRANCE

Although today the English theatre of the eighteenth century may seem more interesting than that of other countries, at the time the French theatre dominated Europe. In the last part of the seventeenth century France became the major world power and the center of culture, a position it was to maintain throughout the eighteenth century.

By 1700 the neoclassical ideal, as embodied in the tragedies of Corneille and Racine and the comedies of Molière, had become the standard for European drama. The insistence upon remaining true to the tragic ideal of Racine did much to freeze dramatic invention in the eighteenth century; the only French tragic writer of note was Voltaire (1694–1778). He began writing plays in 1718, but after spending a few years in England in the 1720s decided that French drama should be liberalized. His chief innovations were the introduction of crowd scenes and ghosts, more emphasis upon scenic background, and greater realism in acting and costuming. He also allowed a small amount of violent action on stage. But Voltaire's reforms seem slight today, and his influence operated principally to preserve the ideals of Racine. His best plays are *Zaïre* (1732) and *Alzire* (1736).

But while tragedy remained rather close to the Racinian mold, comedy departed considerably from Molière's pattern as the eighteenth century progressed. The changes in comedy parallel rather closely those already noted in England.

The works of Pierre Carlet de Chamblain de Marivaux (1688–1763) are important forerunners of sentimental comedy. Marivaux wrote principally for the Italian players, who, after the death of Louis XIV in 1715, were allowed to return to France. This troupe played at first in Italian, but, finding this unprofitable, soon turned to plays in French. It was restricted in the kinds of plays it could do, however, since the Comédie Française had a monopoly on regular drama. The Italians, therefore, performed short plays and "irregular" dramas. Many of Marivaux' plays were written in three acts to conform to this demand, since all regular dramas of the period employed the five-act form.

The dominant theme of Marivaux' plays is the awakening of love. Typically, the main characters are a man and a woman who have no intention of falling in love. Gradual and subtle changes are traced as the characters are moved to a point at which they must confess the love that has overtaken them. Earlier comedy treated lovers already firmly in love when the plays opened; the complications arose from their attempts to overcome the opposition of parents or some other external force. In Marivaux' plays, however, the obstacles are psychological and within the characters themselves.

The plays are written in a highly polished, carefully wrought, subtle style which has come to be called *marivaudage*. The most famous of the

A setting by Jean Nicolas Servandoni (1695–1766), one of France's leading designers of the eighteenth century. This setting was used at the Opéra in Paris around 1730. From Bapst's *Essai sur l'Histoire du Théâtre,* 1893.

works are *The Surprise of Love* (1722), *The Game of Love and Chance* (1730), and *False Confidences* (1737). Although they contain many sentimental elements, they concentrate primarily upon the revelation of universal psychological states. For this reason, Marivaux' works are today among the most frequently produced plays in France.

True sentimental comedy appeared first in the works of Pierre Claude Nivelle de La Chausée (1692–1754), whose plays *The False Antipathy* (1733) and *The Fashionable Prejudice* (1735) established the vogue for *comédie larmoyante* (tearful comedy) in France. These plays differed from their English counterparts only by being written in verse, but even this distinction was not maintained by many of La Chausée's successors.

Domestic tragedy had no strong advocate in France until Denis Diderot (1713–84) espoused it in the 1750s. Diderot argued that the traditional classifications of drama into tragedy and comedy should be supplemented by two "middle genres" (which correspond roughly to sentimental comedy and domestic tragedy).

It was the middle genres which interested Diderot most, and he advocated many reforms in contemporary staging methods designed to increase the appeal of these dramatic types. He believed that the best drama is that which arouses the greatest emotional response in an audience, and that the degree of emotion aroused is in direct proportion to the illusion of reality created. He argued, therefore, for the use of prose dialogue, for characters and situations drawn from everyday life, and for the "fourth wall" approach to staging.

According to the fourth-wall theory, the stage is to be treated as a room with one transparent wall through which an audience views what transpires. The actors should act as they would in a real-life room and situation without taking any cognizance of the audience's presence. To achieve this effect, the stage picture must be conceived in terms of complete naturalness. Although Diderot's idea of the fourth wall was not to be carried out completely until the late nineteenth century, it is an important concept in the movement toward realism.

Diderot also wrote one of the important treatises on acting, *The Paradox of the Actor*. In this work he argues that on stage the actor should feel nothing himself but should render the external signs of emotion so compellingly that the audience is convinced of the reality of the fictional situation. Diderot's treatise is frequently placed in opposition to the works of Stanislavsky, in which it is suggested that the actor should become emotionally involved in the dramatic situation. In their writings both Diderot and Stanislavsky are concerned with arousing the maximum response in the audience, both want the actor to understand fully the emotions to be projected, and both demand a high degree of technical skill

A scene from Beaumarchais' *The Marriage of Figaro*. From an engraving made in 1785. From Pougin's *Dictionnaire* . . . , 1885.

from the actor. They differ in the extent to which they wish the actor to be emotionally moved himself. Diderot argues that personal involvement deprives the actor of control over his performance, while Stanislavsky believes that some degree of involvement is essential in achieving spontaneity and is necessary in avoiding a merely mechanical display of skill.

Although Diderot's ideas have remained important, they exerted little influence on his contemporaries. His plays, *The Illegitimate Son* and *The Father of a Family*, were not successful, although they did help to establish the term *drame* as a designation for a serious play which does not fall into the category of traditional tragedy.

The most important French playwright of the late eighteenth century is Pierre Augustin Caron de Beaumarchais (1732–99). He wrote some *drames* in the fashion of Diderot, but he is remembered primarily for two comedies, *The Barber of Seville* (1775) and *The Marriage of Figaro* (1784). Both center around the character of Figaro. In the first play he is a barber and the epitome of all the clever servants of comedy as he aids Count Almaviva in his plan to marry Rosina, the ward of Doctor Bartholo, who wishes to marry Rosina himself. The scene in which the Count, disguised as a music master, gives Rosina a lesson while Figaro shaves Doctor Bartholo is comparable in quality to the screen scene in *The School for Scandal*.

While social satire plays only a small part in *The Barber of Seville*, it is a major concern in *The Marriage of Figaro*. In the later play Figaro

Henri Louis LeKain as Orasmane in Voltaire's *Zaïre*. From Frederic Loliée's *La Comédie Française* Paris, 1907.

is in Count Almaviva's service and on the point of marrying Suzanna, a serving girl in the household. The Count is tiring of Rosina and is attempting to seduce Suzanna. The action of the play is principally taken up with uncovering and thwarting the Count's schemes, which offer many opportunities for comment upon the relative worth of the aristocracy and the lower classes.

Comic opera also developed in France in the eighteenth century. Alain René LeSage (1668–1747), its originator, began his career by writing for the Comédie Française, which produced his great comedy of manners, *Turcaret*, in 1709. A disagreement with the Comédie left him with no outlet for his plays, since there was no other legitimate theatre in Paris at that time. He turned, therefore, to the small theatres which had been set up at the Fairs. These theatres, which were illegitimate and contrary to the monopoly held by the Comédie Française, managed to remain in operation, nevertheless, throughout the eighteenth century. For them, LeSage wrote short pieces in which spoken dialogue alternated with songs set to popular tunes (just as Gay was to do later); the characters were the stock *commedia* figures and the subject matter was frequently topical and satirical. These short pieces gradually evolved into comic opera.

In the 1740s comic opera came under the sentimentalizing influences of the eighteenth century. The new trend can best be seen in the works of Charles Simon Favart (1710–92), who not only dispensed with *commedia* characters but also used original music and subject matter similar to that normally found in sentimental comedy. In this new guise,

Claire Hippolyte Clairon as Medea. Detail of an engraving after a painting by Van Loo. From Loliée.

comic opera was taken over in 1762 by the Italian troupe (by now a state-subsidized group).

France produced a number of outstanding actors in the eighteenth century, the most famous of whom were Clairon, Dumesnil, and LeKain. Claire Hippolyte Clairon (1723–1803) played in a number of small theatres before making her debut at the Comédie Française in 1743 in the role of Phaedra. Her success was immediate and lasting. Diderot thought her the ideal actress, and she was also a favorite with Voltaire, who worked with her in making many of his reforms in acting and costuming. Her acting was the essence of carefully planned, controlled, "natural" style.

In opposition to Clairon's approach to acting, Diderot placed that of Marie Françoise Dumesnil (1713–1803), who made her debut at the Comédie Française in 1737. Dumesnil excelled in emotional roles but lacked the control of Clairon. She had no interest in reforming the stage and thought the actor should always be magnificently dressed regardless of part. Her great emotional intensity led many to rank her above Clairon.

Henri Louis LeKain (1729–78) made his debut at the Comédie Française in 1750 and soon was acclaimed the greatest tragic actor of the day. Although he had a rough voice, was small and not handsome, he overcame these handicaps completely. He was closely associated with Clairon and helped her carry through many reforms in acting and costume.

At the time of the French Revolution the monopolies held by the Comédie Française, the Comédie Italienne, and the Opéra came to an end. For the first time since the fifteenth century governmental restraints were removed. But the 1790s were a time of chaos in the theatre just as in politics. Order was not completely restored until Napoleon became Emperor in 1804, but he reinstated governmental control of the theatre and used his influence to encourage the old neoclassical standards. It was not until the 1820s that romanticism was to break the hold of neoclassicism, which had dominated the French stage since the mid-seventeenth century.

ITALY

In Italy during the seventeenth century public theatres began to replace court theatres. The first was built in Venice in 1637, and soon others were opened all over Italy. Opera and *commedia dell'arte* dominated the repertory. But while opera continued to grow, *commedia dell'arte* came to an end during the eighteenth century. By about 1750 it had become repetitious, somewhat vulgar, and decadent. Its farce did not really suit the new taste for sentimental drama. Two of Italy's most famous playwrights, Goldoni and Gozzi, attempted to reform it but with little lasting effect.

The first of these writers, Carlo Goldoni (1707–93), began writing plays for a *commedia* troupe in his native city, Venice, in the 1740s. He came to the conclusion that *commedia* could be reformed by substituting written scripts for its improvised action. At first he wrote out only a single part completely, but soon he was able to get the actors to accept plays in which all of the speeches were written out. He continued to use traditional characters but sentimentalized them and removed whatever indecency he had found. *The Servant of Two Masters* is an example of his type of *commedia* play.

Had Goldoni's work been restricted to his reforms of *commedia*, he would not be remembered today. But he also wrote many other kinds of plays, and became Italy's greatest comic writer of the eighteenth century and one of its greatest dramatists of all times.

Goldoni's comedies usually concern women, who are treated as

A scene from a play by Carlo Goldoni; from an engraving in the edition of his plays published in Venice in 1789. Note the *commedia* costume right.

The auditorium and stage of the Comédie Française in 1789. From *L'Ancienne France: Le Théâtre . . . et la Musique. . . .* Paris, 1887.

being much more sensible than men, and the middle and lower classes, who are almost invariably depicted as superior to the upper class. Sentimentalism pervades most of his work, but a spirit of fun and lightheartedness keeps it from being overly sentimental. Many of his plays are still highly regarded and frequently performed; the most notable are *The Mistress of the Inn* (1753) and *The Fan* (1764). Goldoni's last years were spent in France, and a number of his more than two hundred and fifty plays were written in French.

Carlo Gozzi (1720–1806) was bitterly opposed to Goldoni's methods of reforming the *commedia*, to his sentimental treatment of *commedia* characters, and to his satirical picture of the aristocracy. Gozzi's works, which were calculated to counteract Goldoni's influence, are fantasies and fairy tales in which imagination is given free rein, and in which many events and practices of the day are satirized. Gozzi wrote out some of his scenes in their entirety, but most were improvised. Because they are incomplete and topical, it is difficult to a appreciate his plays today. Neither Gozzi nor Goldoni was able to stop the decline of the *commedia*, and by 1800 one of the most interesting theatrical forms had come to an end.

Italy has produced few great dramatists. Of these, two appeared in

A design by Vincenzo Mazzi. From Mazzi's *Capricci di Scene Teatrali*. Bologna, 1776. *Opposite page*. A design by Giuseppe Galli da Bibiena. From Bibiena's *Architettura e Prospettiva*. Vienna, 1740.

the eighteenth century: Goldoni in comedy, and Alfieri in tragedy. Conte Vittorio Amedeo Alfieri (1749–1803) was born in Turin of a wealthy and noble family. Most of his early life was spent in traveling about Europe without any fixed purpose until in 1775 he turned to writing plays and rapidly became Italy's greatest writer of tragedy.

His plays are a curious mixture of social consciousness and classical subject matter and form. Most of his works deal with questions of freedom, equality, political consciousness and responsibility. His ideas are embodied in stories taken from classical or Biblical sources. In his attempt to recapture the spirit of Greek drama, he cut away every detail that was not absolutely essential. He employed very few characters, used no chorus, and observed the unities strictly. His plays have great power because they concentrate upon the dilemma of a single individual in a compelling situation. His greatest plays are *Saul* (1784) and *Mirra* (1786).

Saul shows the Biblical character at the end of his life, aware of his decline in power, and jealous of David's strength. He alternates between exerting his authority autocratically and being led by others; he vacillates between madness and sanity; he is both pathetic and terrifying. The total interest of the play is centered in the role of Saul, which is considered in Italy to be the ultimate test of the tragic actor.

But Alfieri was writing at the end of the neoclassical tradition. Although his plays served to revive the national spirit in Italy and continue to be highly regarded, they have had little influence on subsequent writers.

In spite of its great contributions in shaping the European theatre, by the end of the eighteenth century Italy had ceased to develop new ideas. In the nineteenth century it remained the center of the operatic world but played little part in the development of theatre and drama.

NORTHERN AND EASTERN EUROPE

The eighteenth century saw the development of theatre throughout northern Europe and in Russia. Prior to 1750, there were only sporadic theatrical performances in Russia. Although there was some Church drama in the Medieval period, it was slight in comparison with that of Western Europe. Russia also produced a "school" drama, and professional companies from the West performed irregularly from the seventeenth century on.

Russian rulers alternately patronized and forbade a court theatre. But the Russian theatre as a professional institution dates only from the mid-eighteenth century. The first dramatist of any note was Alexei Petrovich Sumarokov (1718–77), whose tragedy *Khorev*, written in the French neoclassical style, was first performed in 1749 by students at the Cadet College. At about the same time Fëdor Grigorievich Volkov and his brother achieved some success with an amateur company in Yaroslavl. The Empress Elizabeth heard of them and summoned them to St. Petersburg in 1752. They remained there and by 1757 had been given a state subsidy and were performing regularly for the public. The Volkov troupe formed an alliance with Sumarokov, and the Russian public theatre dates from that time. It did not produce any great drama, however—or even a theatre of any stature when compared with Western Europe—until the nineteenth century.

The theatre and drama of northern Europe also achieved prominence for the first time in the eighteenth century. Norway and Denmark were united as a single country from the fourteenth century until 1814. Danish was the official language of both countries, and there was no Norwegian drama of note until the nineteenth century. Denmark's drama

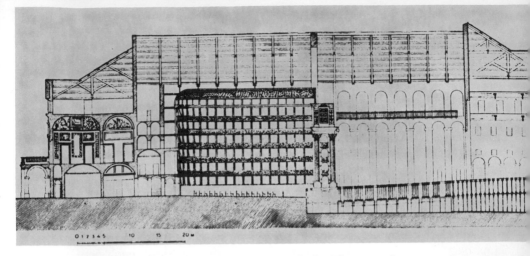

A ground plan and cross section of La Scala. The opera house was designed by Giuseppe Piermarini and built in Milan in 1778. Note the seven tiers of boxes. Although the stage is approximately a hundred feet deep, this depth may be increased by opening the doors at the rear of the main stage. La Scala has long been one of the principal opera houses of the world. From Piermarini's *Teatro della Scala in Milano*, 1826.

went through many of the same stages as that of other countries. There was probably a Medieval church drama (though little evidence remains), and there was a school drama in the sixteenth century, but no plays were written in the Danish language until the eighteenth century. The culture of Denmark was largely derivative, with France its chief influence. The language of polite society was French, the academic language was Latin, and Danish was used only in business and other daily transactions.

The theatre in Denmark at the beginning of the eighteenth century was restricted to a resident French company at the court and to small touring groups from Germany which played at fairs or for special occasions. About 1720 Frederick IV dismissed his French actors, but the leader of the troupe, René Magnon de Montaigu, had been in Denmark for thirty-five years and petitioned to be allowed to open a public theatre. Permission was granted, but there were no plays in the Danish language. Montaigu commissioned Holberg to furnish him with Danish plays and the theatre opened in 1722. Danish theatre may be dated from that time.

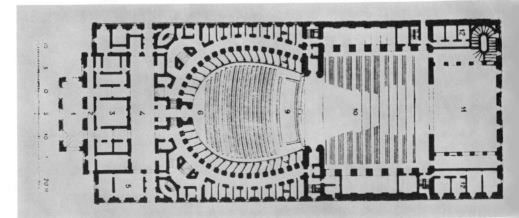

Ludwig Holberg (1684–1754) was born in Norway, was well educated and widely traveled. He became a professor at the University of Copenhagen in 1717 and around 1719 began writing satires in Danish which are usually considered to be the beginning of literature written in the Danish language. Holberg was thus a natural choice when a need was felt for Danish-language plays. He wrote a large number of comedies, the most famous of which are *Jeppe of the Hill,* and *Erasmus Montanus.* Holberg said that his models were Plautus and Molière; in actuality, his plays seem much closer to Medieval farce, although this comparison must be qualified since Holberg used his plays to teach morality. Because Holberg created Danish drama almost single-handedly there is a tendency to praise him too highly. He is a good but not a great writer, and much of his work still seems fresh in its treatment of Danish types and farcical situations.

Sweden also developed drama in the Medieval period, had a "school" drama in the sixteenth century, and eventually developed a professional theatre in the seventeenth century. But it did not produce a dramatist of any stature until Strindberg began writing at the end of the nineteenth century. Sweden's theatre and drama up to that time were primarily a reflection of influences from other countries, though plays were written in the Swedish language as early as 1550. As in other European countries, the Court cultivated opera and ballet. Although there was a public theatre in Sweden as early as 1690, it was not until the reign of Gustav III (1746–92) that the theatre flourished. A National Theatre was established in 1773, and the Swedish theatre has been a relatively vigorous institution since that time.

It was Gustav III who built the theatre at Drottningholm (a summer residence of the court). This theatre was closed up at the end of the eighteenth century and left unused after that time. It was rediscovered in the 1920s and has become one of the great theatrical museums, since it is the only eighteenth-century theatre in existence which has been left unaltered and which is complete with all of its scenery and machinery. It is generally considered one of the primary sources of information about the theatre of that day.

AMERICA

The theatre in America is also a product of the eighteenth century. Although there was sporadic theatrical activity even in the seventeeth century, American theatre can be said to date from 1752, when Lewis Hallam (1714–56) brought a company of actors to America. They played first in Williamsburg, Virginia, but went on to perform in most of the major cities on the Atlantic seaboard. Many later groups were outgrowths of this company.

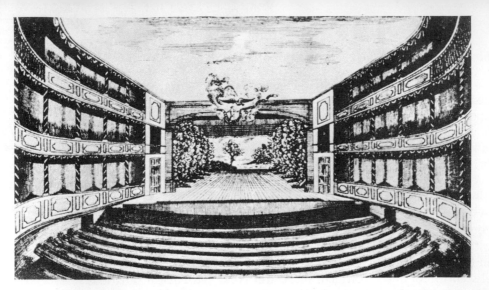

Although the theatre in America underwent considerable opposition, it was beginning to be accepted when the American Revolution put an end to all theatrical activities. In the 1780s the theatre was revived and by the end of the century was firmly established from Charleston, South Carolina to Boston. After this time the theatre followed the westward movement of American settlers, and actors soon traveled to whatever settlements could support even a few performances.

The American theatre was a frank imitation of the English system, and most of its early workers came from England. Probably the major figure in the late eighteenth century was William Dunlap (1766–1839), a playwright and manager. He worked principally in New York and did much to establish a theatre of some importance there. His *History of the American Theatre*, written in 1832, has remained an important source of information on the early theatre in this country.

GERMANY

The most striking changes in eighteenth-century theatre occurred in Germany. In 1700 Germany was composed of many small states divided by religious and political differences. The Thirty Years' War (1618–48) had depleted both Germany's population and its resources. There were few large cities and the country was generally poor. The theatre was divided between private court productions and public traveling companies, with little connection between the two.

Court theatres arose under the influence of Italian opera. The first opera in German-speaking territories was given at Salzburg in 1618, and the court at Vienna had productions of opera regularly after 1631. Gradually this vogue spread over all of Germany, and each court maintained, as well as its financial condition would allow, theatres patterned after those of Italian courts. Although these theatres served to set a standard for

later practice in public theatres, professional touring companies were the actual foundation of the German stage.

The oldest known traveling players in Germany came from England around 1590. Gradually the English actors were replaced by Germans, and by 1650 all-German companies existed, although the conditions under which they worked did not change essentially until after 1750. None of the troupes had a permanent base since no town could as yet support a professional theatre. Touring, therefore, was a necessity. But touring was costly and time-consuming, and the companies varied their programs as much as possible so as to achieve a maximum appeal to the limited audience in each town. For example, one company in 1735 produced seventy-five different full-length plays and ninety-three one-act plays in a period of eight months. The working conditions and the pay were poor, and the troupes were generally scorned by the educated classes. Actors, therefore, were frequently drawn from those persons who had no other work open to them.

The low state of the theatre was reflected in the kinds of plays performed. They were filled with violence, improbable actions and characters, and bombastic dialogue. Hanswurst, a character based on the Harlequin of *commedia dell'arte*, crept into all plays, even serious ones.

All these factors conspired to keep the German theatre in a state of low repute, and it was not until about 1725 that Johann Christoph Gottsched (1700–66) and Carolina Neuber (1697–1760) made the first serious effort to reform the German stage.

Gottsched was interested in improving the level of German literature and in elevating taste and morals. He saw in drama one means for reaching the poorly educated classes, and formed a liaison with the acting troupe headed by Carolina Neuber as a means of putting his ideas into practice.

Gottsched's ideals of drama were taken almost entirely from the

Hanswurst, the Harlequinlike character who appeared in numerous German plays of the eighteenth century. From an eighteenth-century print; courtesy of the University of Iowa Library.

French neoclassical plays, which were completely unknown to the audience who frequented the popular theatres. Gottsched and his associates, nevertheless, set out to provide a new repertory for the theatre, much of which was to be composed of translations or adaptations of French works.

Carolina Neuber tried to raise the level of acting and the reputation of the theatrical profession by insisting upon careful rehearsals and a high level of personal morality. She banished Hanswurst from her theatre and revised her repertory to bring it into closer accord with Gottsched's aims. In none of her attempts was she entirely successful, however.

Although Gottsched and Neuber never achieved their aims, their work marks the turning point in the history of German theatre. From this time on there was a steady rise in the fortunes of the theatrical profession, and by the end of the eighteenth century German drama and theatre could be compared favorably with that to be found anywhere in the world.

Germany's first important dramatist, and one of the great drama critics of the world, was Gotthold Ephraim Lessing (1729–81). It was Lessing who turned attention away from French neoclassicism and directed it to English drama as more compatible with German tastes and as a better model upon which to base German practice. His own plays influenced later writers and helped to raise the status of German drama in the eighteenth century. *Miss Sara Sampson* (1755), which is set in England, established the vogue for domestic tragedy in Germany. Today, probably his most popular play is *Minna von Barnhelm* (1767), a comedy which

Friedrich Ludwig Schroeder as Falstaff. From *Literatur und Theaterzeitung*. Berlin, 1780.

shows how a rich young girl maneuvers a man into marriage, though he wishes to decline because he has lost his own wealth. It is a tender and romantic play which has much in common with the sentimental comedy of the period, but which, like the works of Goldoni, is saved from the extremes of its type by its over-all good humor and spirit of fun.

Lessing's *Nathan the Wise* is a dramatic poem not originally intended for the stage, although it has achieved a continuing reputation in the theatre. The play combines Christian, Moslem, and Jewish characters to illustrate that the best religion is one capable of achieving the most humanitarian results. It is a testament to religious tolerance, a fact that has helped to insure its lasting reputation.

Lessing uses a strict cause-to-effect structure in his plays. Each event grows naturally out of the one preceding it, and everything that happens is carefully prepared for in advance. He observes the unities (except in *Nathan the Wise*) and seeks to return to what he calls "true" classicism, as opposed to the "false" classicism of the French.

Lessing's plays and his critical writings, especially the *Hamburg Dramaturgy* (1767–68), turned attention away from French drama, but with results which Lessing did not foresee or approve. Many concluded from his arguments and practice that all rules were meaningless, unnecessary, and contrary to German needs. As a result, much of the German drama of the late eighteenth century is chaotic, formless, and almost incapable of communicating with an audience. Out of these new experiments and ideas, however, romanticism was to develop.

Just as German drama found a more adequate expression in the works of Lessing, so too actors appeared who were able to raise the status of their profession. Most of these actors were in some way descended from the Neuber troupe. Johann Friedrich Schonemann (1704–82), originally a Hanswurst actor, later joined the Neuber troupe and then formed his own. Into this company he took Ekhof, Ackermann, and Sophie Schroeder, all of whom were to play an important part in German theatre. Konrad Ekhof (1720–78) joined Schonemann's company in 1740. He did more than any other actor of the eighteenth century to establish a high reputation for the acting profession. He reformed the contemporary acting style in the direction of greater naturalness, and ran a short-lived training school for actors; he worked with and greatly influenced most of the other principal performers of the day and became universally admired throughout Germany.

Konrad Ackermann (1710–71) was married to Sophie Schroeder (1714–92). They began their acting careers in Schoenmann's company, but later formed their own troupe and played throughout Germany, in Russia, and in Switzerland. Ackermann's good nature made him a favorite with audiences and his managerial skill kept the company in good financial condition.

Friedrich Ludwig Schroeder (1774–1816), the son of Sophie Schroeder by an earlier marriage, is generally considered to have been the greatest German actor of the eighteenth century and perhaps of all time. He grew up in the Ackermann troupe, but it was from Ekhof that he learned most. Schroeder did more than any other actor to popularize the new drama which came into vogue after Lessing, and he introduced Shakespeare to the German stage. Because of his acting, his managerial skill, and his personal charm, he was for many years considered to be the head of the theatrical profession in Germany.

By the time of Schroeder's retirement, in 1798, the theatrical profession (in comparison with its state in 1700) had been revolutionized. Permanent theatres housed important troupes in a number of German cities, the profession was widely respected, and German drama was beginning to assume world importance. Furthermore, Germany was already in the process of developing a Romantic drama which would totally overthrow those neoclassical ideals which had dominated the stages of Europe for more than a century and a half.

Chapter 11

ROMANTIC DRAMA AND MELODRAMA

In the first part of the nineteenth century a number of previous trends culminated in two related developments: the Romantic drama and melodrama. The Romantic movement was mainly confined to the period between 1800 and 1850, but melodrama continued to dominate the stage throughout the century. Since melodrama is in part an outgrowth of the general Romantic movement, the basic Romantic outlook will be considered first.

ROMANTICISM

The forces which led to romanticism were all evident in the eighteenth century. First, there was a growing distrust of reason as the principal means for achieving man's highest goals. Neoclassicism had been based in large part upon the belief that man can discover, through rational analysis, adequate criteria for everything, whether in life or in literature. In the eighteenth century, however, this view was gradually replaced by the belief that man should be guided by his natural instincts, which might be trusted to lead him to right feelings and right actions. (Sentimental drama owes much to this outlook.)

Second, there was growing doubt about the rightness of the existing social and political order. The rise of the middle class served to emphasize general subservience to the nobility. The justice of such an arrangement

An audience at the performance of a melodrama. From Paul Ginisty's *Le Mélodrame*. Paris, 1901.

was brought into question, and men were led to reconsider the sources of class and political structures. Primitive society came to be idealized as a condition in which man was free to follow the dictates of his conscience without economic and political strictures. The equality of man and the freedom of action became battle cries of the new movement. (Both the American and the French revolutions were clearly related to these ideas).

Third, the notion that truth is to be defined in terms of "norms" was replaced by the notion that truth is to be seen in the infinite variety of creation. According to the Romanticists, the universe was created by God out of himself so that he might more easily contemplate himself. Everything in existence, therefore, is a part of everything else, for all has a common origin. To know ultimate truth, then, one must know as much of creation as possible. Rather than eliminate details so as to arrive at a norm, one must seek to encompass the infinite variety of things.

Fourth, since all creation has a common origin, a thorough and careful study of any part may lead to a glimpse of the whole. Thus trees, grass, rivers, and mountains reflect something about man, just as man reflects something about nature. The more unspoiled a thing is—that is, the less it deviates from its natural state—the more suitable it is for use in the search for truth. Romantic writers, therefore, showed a marked preference for poetry about natural objects and landscapes, and for drama about unspoiled men living in primitive times or for those who were in rebellion against the false restraints of society.

Fifth, it was believed that it is impossible ever to grasp all of reality, though one may and should continually strive to do so. Since the ultimate source of creation is God, truth is infinite and beyond complete comprehension or adequate expression. Therefore, no matter how the writer may strive to embody truth, he is doomed to failure.

Sixth, the person most capable of grasping and expressing truth is the "genius." During the neoclassical period it had been implied that if a writer followed the rules he could produce good drama. In the eighteenth century, however, the need for some special, indefinable quality was suggested. At first this quality was called "taste," but gradually the term *genius* was used to include all those factors which account for greatness. Originally genius was viewed as capable of supplementing the rules (which were still considered necessary to good writing), but eventually genius came to be spoken of as though it were in conflict with the rules, which in turn were seen as serving to restrict genius to too narrow confines. Genius, therefore, was acknowledged as capable of making its own rules and laws.

In addition, genius was thought to include an innate ability to grasp intuitively the greatness of the universe; this capacity sets the individual possessing it off from his fellow men, who, because they keep their eyes on the material, everyday world, are blind to the true nature of reality. The

A design by Alessandro Sanquirico (1780-1849) for the ballet "L'Alunno della Giumenta" at La Scala in Milan, 1812. Sanquirico was one of Italy's leading scene designer's in the first part of the nineteenth century. From Sanquirico's *Raccolta di Varie Decorazioni Sceniche*. Milan, 1810-28.

genius, then, is different from other men, and consequently is at times in conflict with his society. The true writer, however, is driven to express truth regardless of the consequences. Genius is, therefore, both a gift and a curse.

Seventh, the artist must search for forms which are adequate for the expression of great truths. Given the conceptions of the period, it was only natural that the artist abandoned and denounced the neoclassical rules for writing. New forms were needed which would allow the maximum freedom in expressing the infinity of creation. Shakespeare's plays most nearly fit the new conceptions, and they came to represent the ideal form for the writers of the Romantic period, just as the Greek and Roman drama had served as models for the writers of the Neoclassical period.

Romantic writers frequently saw in Shakespeare's works, however, only a freedom from restraint. As a result, they adopted a very loose structure in which the unities (sometimes even of action) were abandoned. Frequently, their plays were written without any consideration for the requirements of the stage (since genius was thought too great to be confined by such practical needs). Consequently, many of the plays were never produced, and others had to be adapted before they could be staged. About much of the work there is an air of impracticality. But the new ideas freed writers from the often arbitrary demands of neoclassicism.

Along with the rebellion against the old ideas of form went the abandonment of old subject matter. Greek myths gave way to Medieval tales, historical legends, and stories about folk heroes or rebellions against social and moral codes. This subject matter was used to embody themes showing man's attempts to achieve freedom of ideals or behavior, to find personal peace of mind, or the secret of existence. The new form, subject matter, and themes combined to create a drama almost opposite in its characteristics from that of the Neoclassical period.

MAJOR ROMANTIC PLAYWRIGHTS

Most of the ideas which eventually comprised the Romantic standard were first set forth in England. The philosophical ideas and dramatic forms evolved slowly over most of the eighteenth century, so that it is impossible to speak of a Romantic "revolution" in England as it is in most other countries. Furthermore, in England the neoclassical ideas were never so firmly entrenched as they were elsewhere, and the transition to romanticism was more easily accomplished.

England's Romantic movement led to little significant drama, however, perhaps because a ready-made Romantic writer was found in Shakespeare. The best known of the nineteenth-century playwrights of the Romanticist school are James Sheridan Knowles (1784–1862) and Edward George Bulwer-Lytton (1803–73). Knowles, an actor as well as a dramatist, is remembered primarily for *Virginius* (1820), a play which mixes elements reminiscent of Shakespeare with melodramatic devices. Bulwer-Lytton's *The Lady of Lyons* (1838) and *Richelieu* (1839) held the stage continuously until the twentieth century. Today, they too seem closer to melodrama than to tragedy, but they are still among the most vital English plays of the period. A number of the poets of the time—Byron, Shelley, Browning, and others—wrote plays, but they either did not or would not adapt their works to the needs of the stage and many of their plays remained unproduced.

By 1800 a well-defined Romantic movement was under way in Germany and was to prove far more productive than its counterparts elsewhere in Europe. Two of the most important dramatists of the period were Johann Wolfgang von Goethe (1749–1832) and Friedrich von Schiller (1759–1805). Both men denied being Romanticists, and each wrote some plays in the classical style. Each, however, also wrote truly Romantic plays and helped to establish a taste for the new drama.

Goethe is to German literature what Shakespeare is to English, for he is universally considered to be the greatest of German writers. His first play, *Göetz von Berlichingen* (1773), deals with the attempts of a German baron of the sixteenth century to remain free in the midst of political and religious intrigues. Around him swirls the life of the times much in the manner of a modern movie scenario. It was not conceived with stage presentation in mind, and contains fifty-four scenes with over forty named characters (in addition to soldiers, peasants, gypsies, judges, jailers, courtiers, and so on). The play was soon adapted for the stage, however, and became enormously popular and influential.

Goethe underwent a change in the 1780s and came to the conclusion that true greatness lies in an idealized art similar to that of the Greeks. He wrote a series of plays in the classical manner, the most famous of which is *Iphigenia in Tauris*. But Goethe is best known today for *Faust*,

A setting by Karl Friedrich Schinkel for a production of Schiller's *The Maid of Orleans* at the Royal Theatre in Berlin, 1801. About two hundred actors were used in this scene. From Weddingen's *Geschichte der Theatre Deutschlands*. Berlin, 1904.

a play which is in many ways the very epitome of the Romantic outlook. It too was not conceived with the stage in mind, though it was soon adapted for theatrical presentation and has been performed continuously since its own day. It is a work of enormous scope, about which more will be said later.

Schiller had a much surer feeling for the theatre than did Goethe. His first play, *The Robbers* (1782), was an immediate success and was played throughout the world until the end of the nineteenth century. Beginning with *Don Carlos* (1787), Schiller turned principally to great moments of crisis in history for his subject matter. *Don Carlos* deals with the aspirations of the Spanish prince to free the Netherlands from Spain and to encourage the development of freedom throughout the world. He is opposed by the intrigues of the court and the church, and eventually his father, Philip, is forced to give him up to the Inquisition for punishment. Schiller also used English history in *Maria Stuart*, French history in *The Maid of Orleans*, Swiss history in *William Tell*, and German history in his Wallenstein trilogy. Few dramatists have combined such a sweep of historical material with such theatrical power. If he falls short of Shakespeare it is because of his too obvious attempt to set forth philosophical ideas. In other respects he is probably the greatest serious dramatist between Racine and Ibsen.

Of those writers who are now identified with the German Romantic movement, the best is Heinrich von Kleist (1777–1811). Yet he never saw any of his plays produced. They were not published until 1821 and only later found their way into theatrical repertories, of which they have remained a part. Today he is remembered principally for one comedy, *The Broken Jug,* and two tragedies, *Penthiselea* and *The Prince of Homburg.* The last play must be ranked among the best of German Romantic dramas. It concerns a young officer who is so bent upon gaining renown that he defies military orders when he sees the chance of winning a victory. Although he is successful, he has endangered the entire army. He is sentenced to die and is reprieved only after he comes to recognize that his personal ego must be subordinated to that greater good which is to be found in self-renunciation and service. It is a compact and moving drama.

The plays of Georg Büchner (1813–37) are illustrative of the growing disillusionment with romanticism. The excesses of the French Revolution had called into doubt many of the social and political ideas of the movement. The doubts were increased when Napoleon, who originally had been envisioned as the savior of Europe, was crowned Emperor and became as despotic a ruler as those he succeeded. As the belief in the possibility of unselfish service to others was shaken, pessimism began to replace the former optimism. Büchner's *Danton's Death* concerns an idealist who, seeing his highest aims wrecked by the pettiness of his fellow men, comes to question the validity of the ideals themselves. He is unable to decide whether life has any meaning, and he goes to his death with dignity but still in doubt. *Woyzeck* shows a man who is little better than an animal led inevitably to his downfall by the social circumstances under which he is forced to live. Both plays are pessimistic in outlook and peculiarly modern in their views of human psychology.

The Romantic movements in both England and Germany were already declining before Romantic drama was accepted in France. Although all strictures on the theatre were removed at the time of the Revolution, Napoleon reinstituted censorship in 1804 and openly favored neoclassical drama. In 1812 he issued a decree which reinstated the rights of the Comédie Française, though at the same time he also established three other state theatres (one for minor dramatic forms, one for comic opera, and one for opera). In many ways, therefore, Napoleon reinstated the situation which had existed before 1790. There was one important difference, however—Napoleon allowed a number of private theatres. These nonstate theatres were located largely on the Boulevard du Temple and the secondary theatres of Paris have been called the Boulevard theatres since that time.

In spite of Napoleon's efforts, however, Romantic ideas were in the air. They were given currency largely through *On Germany* by Mme. de Staël, an enemy of Napoleon who had lived her years of exile in Germany. Her book was published in 1810 but was suppressed almost immediately. When Napoleon was overthrown in 1814 the book was quickly reissued and had an enormous circulation.

But it was not until Victor Hugo (1802–85) published the Preface to his play *Cromwell* in 1827 that the aims and ideas of the French Romanticists were clearly set forth. Romanticism did not triumph in France, however, until Hugo's *Hernani* was produced at the Comédie Française in 1830.

The French plays of the new movement differ considerably from their German counterparts, and in actuality are more closely related to the melodramas of the day. *Hernani* and many other Romantic dramas made use of such devices as disguises, secret panels, hidden staircases, and hairbreadth escapes. They differ from contemporary melodramas only in greater depth of characterization, the use of verse, the five-act form, and a preference for unhappy endings.

Hernani concerns a man who has been forced to become an outlaw because his father has been accused unjustly of treason and has had his lands confiscated. He loves Doña Sol, who is also loved by her guardian, Don Ruy Gomez, and by Don Carlos, the future Holy Roman Emperor. Don Carlos comes searching for Hernani while he is a guest in the house of Don Ruy. When he cannot find Hernani, who is hidden in a secret chamber behind a portrait, Don Carlos takes Doña Sol away as a hostage. Before Hernani sets out to rescue Doña Sol, he gives Don Ruy a horn and promises that, if he is ever needed—even if it requires his life—Don Ruy need only blow the horn. In the final act, which takes place on the wedding day of Doña Sol and Hernani (now forgiven and no longer an outlaw), Don Ruy, filled with jealousy, blows the horn. Hernani drinks poison, as does Doña Sol, and Don Ruy then kills himself. It is a plot in which love and honor are pushed to the extreme, but it is also a play filled with melodramatic devices, suspense, and powerful poetry.

Other important French romantic dramatists were Alexandre Dumas, Alfred de Vigny, and Alfred de Musset. Alexandre Dumas *père* (1803–70) is remembered today chiefly for his novels, *The Count of Monte Cristo* and *The Three Musketeers*, but in the 1830s he was famous as a dramatist of the new Romantic school. He wrote a number of plays, among them *Henri III and His Court* and *The Tower of Nesle*, which display the same essential characteristics as those of Hugo.

Alfred de Vigny (1797–1863) translated many of Shakespeare's plays into French and helped to popularize them. He is best remembered today for his play *Chatterton*, which depicts a poet who is too delicate and refined in spirit to find happiness in the materialistic world into which he is thrown. He eventually dies rather than compromise his own values. In many ways the play epitomizes the Romantic genius at war with his world but refusing to give in to it.

The works of Alfred de Musset (1810–57) are almost totally unlike those of his French contemporaries. Musset was concerned with the psychological investigation of characters, especially in relation to love. The human ego is the real source of complications in most of Musset's plays. He frequently writes of two people in love (or who think they are in love). Each is so afraid of being hurt that he disguises his true feelings, but this disguise serves only to wound the other person, who strikes back in a way which widens the breach. Sometimes the breach can be healed and the play ends happily, at others it cannot and disaster results. The psychological orientation of Musset's plays have kept them fresh for modern audiences. They are still widely produced in France and are the most universally admired of French Romantic dramas. His most famous plays are *No Trifling with Love, A Door Should Either Be Shut or Open,* and *Lorenzaccio.*

Out of the various manifestations of romanticism in the early nineteenth century, the drama of Germany has proven most important. Part I of Goethe's *Faust* will be examined in detail as an example of Romantic drama.

FAUST

Although Goethe frequently denounced romanticism, much of his work epitomizes the movement. This is especially true of *Faust,* which is conceived in dramatic terms but which is too vast to be contained in the theatre. It must always be adapted and condensed when produced. Partially because of this very complexity, *Faust* is considered by many to be the greatest literary work in the German language.

Goethe worked on *Faust* throughout his life. He began writing Part I in the 1780s and did not complete it until 1808; Part II was not published until 1831. *Faust* is, then, in a sense a record of Goethe's own growth and change.

Themes and Ideas. *Faust* is a play about man's aspirations and capabilities, a hymn to his essential greatness and ability to work out his own salvation. Taken in its entirety, it is an extremely optimistic work.

The "Prologue in Heaven" establishes the basic theme. God says that man cannot avoid making mistakes in his search for fulfillment, but that continuous striving will lead him to the truth. *Faust* dramatizes the search itself. Mephistopheles makes a pact to aid Faust, whose soul he may take whenever Faust finds that moment about which he can say: "O stay! thou

A scene from Goethe's *Faust*, Part I, at Yale University. Directed by Frank MacMullan; designed by Frank Bevan; lighting by Stanley Mc-Candless. Courtesy of Yale University, School of Drama.

art so wondrous fair!" This will be the moment of fulfillment toward which Faust has directed all of his energies and beyond which there will be no point in living.

Part I shows Faust's discontent, his pact with Mephistopheles, and his search for fulfillment in physical pleasures. This is the clearest and most dramatic part of the work. Part II becomes more difficult to understand, but it shows the completion of Faust's striving. Having found sensual pleasure inadequate in Part I, Faust then seeks for meaning in ideal loveliness and poetry; eventually he finds the moment for which he has been searching when he renounces his own selfish interests for service to others. But Mephistopheles is thwarted when he comes to take Faust's soul, for Faust has been led to salvation and truth through that very striving for fulfillment with which Mephistopheles has aided him.

Goethe is concerned in Part I, however, only with the first phase of this story. The beginning depicts Faust's deep discontent and his longing to encompass the infinite meaning and activity of life. Faust then makes his pact with Mephistopheles, who sets out to show him pleasure. Faust falls in love with Margarete; she is disgraced and dies; Faust and Mephistopheles flee. This rather straightforward story is complicated by a number of seemingly irrelevant scenes. Each scene contributes to Goethe's purpose, however, for his main interest always lies in depicting the philosophical and spiritual development of Faust.

The second scene is an excellent illustration of Goethe's methods and interests. It shows a day of revelry in which a cross-section of humanity participates. Faust's psychological state is delineated through a pointed contrast between Faust, a group of peasants, and Wagner, the scholar. Faust admires the peasants, who are at peace with their world and can find pleasure in music, dance, and drink. But Faust knows that these pleasures are fleeting; he wants to find lasting and complete satisfaction.

Wagner, on the other hand, seeks his pleasures in books and in the past. Faust wants to live life intensely as the peasant does, he wants to encompass knowledge as the scholar does, but he is also searching for something more, something indefinable. The scene serves principally, therefore, as a means of outlining Faust's psychological state rather than as a means of forwarding a dramatic action. It is a moment suspended in time and analyzed with care, but it does not arouse the kind of expectations of future developments which are typical of dramatic composition. *Faust* alternates such static scenes with more dynamic ones.

Goethe is also concerned with man's relationship to good and evil. At one point, Mephistopheles says that God lives in eternal light, that the witches and evil spirits live in eternal darkness, and that man lives in both light and darkness. Man thus exists somewhere between good and evil and though he longs for eternal light, his own nature and circumstances keep him in partial darkness. It is not surprising then that many of the scenes in the play use night and day symbolically. For example, the Walpurgis Night scene points up Faust's dilemma as a man who has given himself up to darkness in his attempt to achieve the light.

Darkness is related to Faust's false search for fulfillment in sensual pleasures, which are part of man's animal nature. Such physical pleasures are also essentially selfish. For example, Faust's love for Margarete is primarily carnal, and he displays no real concern for her welfare until it is too late. He does not talk of marrying her, he only dreams of possessing her. Her death and the dilemma of Faust at the end of Part I show the limitations of sensuality as a way of life. Mephistopheles, furthermore, is the very incarnation of a sadistic sensuality, which Faust accepts as his guide throughout Part I, although he is continually tormented by the difference between the ideal he had set out to find and the actual situation.

The Walpurgis Night scene illustrates in part the darker side of man's nature, and in part the range of creation. Everything has been created out of God (it is He who has separated the light and the darkness) and everything is part of his plan. The witches and evil spirits, then, are part of Faust; they represent sensuality without moral standards, unrestrained whim and selfishness.

Goethe shows that sensuality is eventually self-defeating. At the end of Part I, Faust is left more dissatisfied than when he began his search. A higher power can save Margarete, but Faust can only stand by helplessly. He must search elsewhere for the answer.

PLOT AND STRUCTURE. The structure of Faust is extremely loose. Although it bears certain superficial resemblances to Elizabethan drama, it does not have the economy of Shakespeare's plays and it lacks any compelling unity of action. For example, Shakespeare always made his basic dramatic situation clear in the opening scene, but it is not until the fourth

A nineteenth-century setting for *Faust*. From Germain Bapst's *Essai sur l'Histoire du Théâtre*. Paris, 1893.

scene of *Faust* that the pact with Mephistopheles sets the play in motion. If the two Prologues are included, almost one fourth of Part I is taken up with introductory material.

The principal dramatic questions raised in the play concern Faust's ability to find completion and to save his immortal soul. These questions hold the play together, but the nature of the first is such that Faust may look anywhere for its answer. Goethe chooses to have Faust seek first for fulfillment in sensual pleasures, but this is not a necessary development out of what has gone before. Any other choice could have been made, though Goethe's is not illogical. Furthermore, any phase of Faust's search could be illustrated at length or briefly. The decision is largely arbitrary and grows almost entirely out of the author's preferences, rather than out of any demands of the play's action itself.

The only sequence which is developed in terms of a clear cause-to-effect relationship is the Faust–Margarete story. But even this sequence is broken up by the insertion of scenes which illustrate Faust's psychological and philosophical attitudes. Although all of the scenes are thematically related, they are by no means all dramatic. Many could be eliminated without any confusion to an audience, and their removal might actually lead to greater clarity in performance.

Part I does not complete the story of Faust. It concludes the Margarete sequence and Faust's search for fulfillment in sensual pleasure, but the central questions remain unresolved and are continued throughout Part II. Thus, while Part I reaches a climax and resolution of one phase of the story, it marks only the beginning of Faust's search.

Part I consists of twenty-five scenes (plus two prologues) and requires about sixteen settings. Time and place change rapidly, and many special effects are demanded (such as a dog which grows in size and is transformed into Mephistopheles, the Walpurgis Night scenes, the Witch's Kitchen in which monkeys stir potions, and so on). Its production stretches the demands of the stage as far as they have ever been extended, but these demands are a clear outgrowth of Goethe's aims to encompass as much of life as possible and to dramatize man's search for meaning, his varying states of mind, and the vastness of his aims and abilities. Many different kinds of scene are necessary to fulfill all of Goethe's intentions. The constant variety keeps the work from becoming boring, but if Goethe's purposes remain unclear, *Faust* may appear to be a jumble of disconnected scenes. It is a lofty conception which requires a special effort from the reader for comprehension and a very high degree of interpretive and technical skill from the director for audience appreciation.

CHARACTERS AND ACTING. The cast of characters in *Faust*, Part I is too vast to count, for it is made up in large part of crowds, choruses, and unspecified numbers of witches, wizards, and spirits. Those given any degree of psychological development are few: Faust, Mephistopheles, Wagner, Margarete, Martha, Valentine, and Lieschen. The rest are types or abstractions. For example, in scene 2 a large number of people are celebrating a holiday outside the city walls, but these are designated only as soldiers, peasants, maids, apprentices, students, and the like.

Goethe is interested in the range of creation but he is not concerned with individuals except in a few cases. His principal effort has gone into Faust, and it is only as the other characters illustrate his condition that they are important to the play. It is evident that the role of Faust is the most difficult one for an actor. This is true not only because of Faust's central position, but because the role consists so much in the expression of longing, of dissatisfaction, of unbounded aims. An actor may easily become bombastic and ridiculous since what Faust wants is so intangible and is expressed in such lofty speeches.

Mephistopheles' role is much easier to encompass. It consists largely of displays of cynicism, cunning, and deprecation. It does offer an actor considerable scope to display his talents, nevertheless, since it must embody the threat to Faust's success.

Margarete is primarily the young and innocent girl brought to ruin by her own too-loving and credulous nature. She is required to display a wide range of emotions, however, for she goes from awakening love, to happiness, to shame, to madness and death. Hers is the most clearly conceived and most concrete role in the play.

The actors portraying the type characters must bring to the play extensive talents—for movement, dance, song, and pantomime. The extras in this play make the difference between a good and a bad production, for they supply a background for the action and illustrate some of the complexity of creation.

VISUAL AND AURAL APPEALS. There is probably no play which allows designers to utilize their gifts so thoroughly as does *Faust*. The costumer must create suitable garments for will-o'-the-wisps, witches, monkeys, wizards, personifications of abstract qualities, and evil spirits, in addition to those for human characters. The lighting designer must suggest the ranges of night and day, fiery furnaces, and the wonders of Walpurgis Night. The scene designer must either provide a single background capable of suggesting the great variety of places or innumerable scenes which, at the same time, will permit the flexibility necessary for rapid changes of scene.

The audience's senses are assaulted through all possible means: the spoken word, song, music, dance, natural and supernatural visions, witches' frolics, folk festivals, and disembodied voices. There is an almost endless variety of attractions. The proper staging and coordination of all of these elements strain the powers of any director, even with the full assistance of choreographer, musicians, costumer, lighting designer, and set designer. The task is stupendous, but if properly done *Faust* shows the theatre in its fullest splendor, for it extends the resources of the stage to their breaking point. In its attempt to embody the infinity of experience, *Faust* is a perfect example of romanticism.

MELODRAMA

At the same time that Romantic drama was developing, melodrama was also emerging; it was eventually to become the most popular form in the nineteenth century. It appealed to a much wider audience than had Romantic drama and continued to develop and to hold the stage long after the Romantic movement had ended.

Plays have exhibited melodramatic qualities since the earliest times; examples may be drawn from every period. But it was not until the eighteenth century that various factors came together to create the conditions out of which a distinct dramatic form called "melodrama" was to emerge.

Perhaps the most important feature of melodrama is its observance of strict moral justice. No matter how horrible the trials of the virtuous characters or how powerful the villainous, the good are always rewarded and the evil are always punished. The world depicted is one in which deeds and characters are separated by clear-cut moral distinctions. The emotional appeals are basic: the arousal of pity and indignation at the wrongful oppression of good people, and of intense dislike for wicked oppressors. A melodrama also, typically, brings in "comic relief" through a minor character. This character is usually rather simple-minded or severely frank. The action, which progresses almost entirely through the machinations of the villain, is generally definite and simple in outline, for too many subtleties would confuse the moral issues. Normally, it is composed of a series of incidents which show the hero or heroine undergoing superhuman trials at the hands of one or more totally unscrupulous characters. Suspense assumes major importance and the reversal at the end of the play is extreme (from almost certain death to safety, from near-disgrace to complete vindication, and so on). To keep the plot moving, there is usually a series of unexpected discoveries or of hairbreadth escapes (frequently utilizing concealed hiding places or disguises). Since the characters do not change psychologically or morally, interest is centered almost entirely upon the manipulation of events and upon the visual elements.

The melodrama of the nineteenth century developed a set of stock characters which appeared in almost all plays: the hero and heroine, the comic character, and the villain. Sometimes there were more than one set of these in the same play. Although their specific traits and circumstances differed from play to play, the basic pattern of characterization and action remained remarkably constant.

The term *melodrama* means a combination of music (melo-) and drama. Throughout the nineteenth century this type of play was accompanied by a musical score just as a movie is today. This music underlined the emotional qualities of the scenes and helped in achieving the desired response from the audience. Most melodramas included incidental songs and dances and, depending upon the capabilities of the actors, these portions might be expanded or contracted in any given production.

Most of the characteristic features of melodrama were present in eighteenth-century drama, though they had not all been brought together. It merely remained for these elements to be recombined in a new way and recognized as a separate dramatic form. The credit for the formalization goes to two men: August Friedrich Ferdinand von Kotzebue (1761–1819) and René Charles Guilbert de Pixérécourt (1773–1844). Kotzebue, a German, wrote over two hundred plays, the most famous of which are *Misanthropy and Repentance* (played throughout the English-speaking

A setting by Gué for one of Pixérécourt's melodramas. The play is set in Scotland in the sixteenth century. From Paul Ginisty's *Le Mélodrame. Paris*, 1901.

world as *The Stranger*) and *The Spaniards in Peru*. Thirty-six of his plays were translated into English, and there was a Kotzebue craze in almost every country between 1790 and 1810. He was a master of sensationalism, with which he mixed sentimental philosophizing and startling theatrical effects. His success led to many imitations.

But it was Pixérécourt, a Frenchman, who consciously fashioned his plays as melodramas. All of his works show those characteristics which have become the accepted marks of melodrama. His first full-length play, *Victor, or The Child of the Forest* (1798), established both his success in the theatre and the melodrama as a type. He wrote over one hundred plays, almost all of which were enormously popular. According to his own statement, he wrote for a public which could not read. He did not labor so much over the dialogue, therefore, as he did over creating easily identified character types and startling theatrical effects. His plays brought vast new audiences into the theatre, and in his own day he was one of the most successful dramatists who has ever lived. But his fame was not lasting, for others learned to manipulate the same kinds of effects and to invent even more startling stage tricks.

Melodrama soon eclipsed all other dramatic forms in box-office appeal. Its subject matter was drawn from a wide variety of sources: history, lurid or provocative newspaper articles, popular stories and novels, and domestic problems. Regardless of its subject matter, however, the basic characteristics remained unchanged.

UNCLE TOM'S CABIN

The most popular melodrama of the nineteenth century was *Uncle Tom's Cabin*, based on a novel by Harriet Beecher Stowe published in 1852. Mrs. Stowe was opposed to having her work adapted for the stage, but was unable to prevent it because of the inadequate copyright laws of the period. And, in spite of the enormous popularity of the play, she never received any financial remuneration from her novel's stage version.

A number of dramatizations of *Uncle Tom's Cabin* appeared, but the one to achieve lasting success was that by George L. Aiken, an actor who later became famous as a writer of pulp fiction. Aiken's adaptation was first produced at Troy, New York, in September, 1852. Originally Aiken constructed a three-act play which ended with the death of Little Eva. He then wrote a second play which continued the story until the death of Uncle Tom. These two were soon put together to form the six-act play which was presented after that time.

The six-act version was produced in New York in 1853 and played continuously for 325 nights, a phenomenal run for the period. The play was so long that it was performed without the usual afterpiece and helped to establish the single-play entertainment which was to become standard.

THEMES AND IDEAS. Mrs. Stowe was principally concerned with showing the plight of the Negro, and her novel was in large part a plea for the abolition of slavery. Much of this is retained in the play. It can best be seen in the story of George Harris and Eliza, which shows how slave owners (even the good ones) could part families by selling members, and how the Negro was forced to become a fugitive because of his status as a piece of property. The Negro's plight is also shown in the story of Uncle Tom, who—too—is parted from his family (though this is not emphasized), and who eventually dies at the hands of the inhumanly cruel Simon Legree.

The rights of slave owners versus the natural rights of man is debated sporadically in the play. The institution of slavery is shown to be an evil, even though all slave owners might not be evil. The precariousness of the Negro's position is demonstrated by St. Clare's death, for this good slave owner has planned to free Uncle Tom but fails to do so in time, and Uncle Tom is condemned to a terrible fate under Simon Legree's brutality.

Uncle Tom's Cabin is also concerned with religion. (Mrs. Stowe was married to a minister and came from a family famous in religious circles.) Uncle Tom is sustained in his trials by his religion, which is said to explain his trustworthiness and perfection as an individual. He teaches his religion to Little Eva, aids in St. Clare's conversion, and comforts Cassy with his picture of God's love. This emphasis is summed up in the final tableau in which Little Eva, riding on a "milk white dove" among clouds bright with sunlight, blesses the kneeling figures of St. Clare and Uncle

Tom. This final scene seems to suggest that religious faith, patience, and goodness will bring about eternal salvation.

Along with religion, love plays a large part. Topsy is reclaimed by love, St. Clare reforms because of his love for Little Eva, Eliza and George are made strong by love, and Phineas Fletcher is converted to abolitionism through his love for a Quaker girl. The evil characters are depicted as totally devoid of love for others.

But the ideas expressed are decidedly subordinate causes for the play's appeal. Ultimately, it must have been the spectacle of good and evil in conflict that accounted for the strong emotional response which this melodrama elicited from generations of playgoers.

PLOT AND STRUCTURE. *Uncle Tom's Cabin* is composed of a number of stories which are only loosely connected. For example, the subplot dealing with Eliza and George Harris is connected with the main plot only by the fact that Eliza and Uncle Tom are owned by the same family. The decision to sell Eliza's child and Uncle Tom to a slave dealer initiates both plots, but the two are totally unrelated after that time except thematically, for both do illustrate the evils of slavery. The looseness of the plot may also be seen in many of the play's elements. Uncle Tom's life with Little Eva and his fate through Simon Legree's domination are connected only by the fact that each reveals the character of Uncle Tom. The scenes between Miss Ophelia and Deacon Perry have no discernible purpose in the play except as comic relief.

The organization of *Uncle Tom's Cabin*, therefore, is not that of a cause-to-effect relationship between the various parts (though this kind of organization is used within the individual subplots), but is largely determined by the play's themes and by a desire for variety. The parts are held together by a series of coincidences and the most tenuous of circumstances —the characters meet at just the right moment, and their personal lives are manipulated as needed for the story with little attempt to justify the startling fluctuations (for example, Shelby loses and regains his money, and Little Eva and St. Clare die to motivate the plot complications).

But the sprawling form and the poorly motivated occurrences obviously did not detract from the play's appeal. The variety was in itself one of the chief sources of attraction. The story of Topsy serves as an antidote to what today seems Little Eva's almost cloying perfection; George and Eliza are suitable contrasts to Uncle Tom in their attitudes toward slavery; and Simon Legree is a striking contrast to St. Clare and Shelby as slave owners. Variety is also to be found in the alternation of comic and serious tone, of quiet, peaceful scenes with those of great activity, and in the many reversals of fortune.

The unity of the play is to be found in its themes and characters. But even here there is a wide range of appeal aimed at all segments of the audience. The goodness of Little Eva and Uncle Tom constitutes one appeal, others may be seen in the rebellion and success of George and Eliza, the comic and pathetic actions of Topsy, the schemes of Gumption Cute, and the villainy and punishment of Simon Legree.

The play's six acts are subdivided into thirty scenes, a number of which are tableaux (scenes without words). The most striking is the final one in which Little Eva blesses Uncle Tom and St. Clare. (The tableau was advocated by Diderot in the eighteenth century and was widely used in minor entertainments by the end of that century, but did not come into great prominence until the nineteenth century, when no play was considered complete without a series of striking tableaux.)

Uncle Tom's Cabin pays no attention whatever to the unities of time and place. It is set in Kentucky, Ohio, Louisiana, and Vermont, and it is obvious that a great length of time has elapsed between the first and last scenes. It shows many of the same characteristics as *Faust* reduced to the most popular terms.

CHARACTERS AND ACTING.   The play includes approximately twenty-five characters, though a number of additional actors could be used to advantage in such scenes as the slave auction. While this is a large cast, it is kept as small as it is only through the coincidences of the plot, for the same characters come together frequently even though the scene of the action may change from Kentucky to Louisiana to Vermont. Since many characters disappear for scenes at a time, roles can be doubled with ease.

All of the characters are types. (The names Uncle Tom and Simon Legree have passed into popular usage as names for types of behavior.) The demands on the actor, therefore, are not great, for each needs to show only a few specific characteristics. Uncle Tom never wavers in his loyalty and convictions; Little Eva is constantly good; George Harris is in rebellion throughout his scenes; and though Topsy becomes less rambunctious she remains essentially the same. St. Clare is said to reform but, since he is never shown intoxicated on stage, this change has little meaning to an audience.

The character of Simon Legree demonstrates one of the chief differences between nineteenth-century melodrama and that of today. Although Legree is totally brutal, he does have a scene in which he shows fear of damnation. In a modern play such a scene would be used to explore the psychological bases for his brutality, but in *Uncle Tom's Cabin* the psychological causes are ignored and he is shown to be totally depraved. The difference in approach to characterization is the principal change in modern melodrama from its forebears of a century ago.

Interesting hints are given about two characters who remain undeveloped. Marie, Little Eva's mother, is petulant, has frequent headaches, and displays other signs of being demanding and childish. After one scene she is completely neglected, however, and no action stems from these characteristics. Similarly, Cassy is shown to be relatively complex. She has compromised her principles, but still knows the difference between right and wrong. She seems to have some strange power over Simon Legree and torments him. But she remains a minor character, for these hints are never developed.

The characters, then, as is typical of melodrama, are simple. They are characterized physiologically, sociologically, and in terms of basic attitudes. Much is made of physical appearance, and the division into white and Negro is important to the play's theme. Furthermore, the characters have significant "looks" about them—Little Eva is said to have an unworldly appearance; George Harris is spoken of as having a look of courage and conviction; and Topsy's appearance is an important element in her characterization.

Sociological factors are also a major means of characterization, since the division into slaves and free men, owners and overseers, workers and the leisure class is important. The chief emphasis in characterization, however, is on the fundamental attitudes of each role. But these attitudes are confined largely to clear-cut moral qualities—either good or bad. No character needs to deliberate about what he should do, for his action is predetermined by his basic moral nature. The characters are kept simple, therefore, by the restriction of differentiation to appearance, social position,

Eliza crossing the ice in *Uncle Tom's Cabin*. Produced by William Brady at the Academy of Music, New York, 1901. Courtesy of the Harvard Theatre Collection.

and basic attitudes and habits of mind. Clarity is the result, although the lack of complexity in the play's personages makes them appear over-simplified.

LANGUAGE. By the mid-nineteenth century prose was coming to be used more and more as the medium of drama. Melodrama especially turned to a simple, straightforward prose in which characters openly state their feelings and motives. While clarity is achieved, the characters frequently seem unduly self-conscious about their own moral qualities—the good people appear self-satisfied and pious, while the bad seem thoroughly aware of their own evil natures. It is such sharply chiseled, stilted statements of moral purpose which make nineteenth-century melodrama so easy to satirize.

But if the language is simple, it is, for this very reason, also capable of arousing intense emotional response. Uncle Tom's death can still be a touching one, and the plight of Eliza and George can arouse indignation and admiration.

The language of melodrama helped to move the standard more and more toward the pattern current today—the attempt to approximate every-day speech rather than to idealize it. Poetry was increasingly supplanted by the prose of lifelike conversation.

VISUAL AND AURAL ELEMENTS. Melodrama, like Romantic drama, placed great emphasis upon the visual elements of production. The settings for *Uncle Tom's Cabin* range from the comfortable interiors of wealthy homes to rough cabins, from the idealized landscape of St. Clare's garden to the ice-filled river over which Eliza escapes; there are city streets and desolate country scenes. The contrast is made more clearly evident by rapid changes, for no act of the play has fewer than four scenes. Comic or quiet and restrained scenes such as the idyllic scenes of Uncle Tom and Little Eva contrast sharply with the flight of Eliza and George, a slave auction, or the beating of Uncle Tom.

The basic scenic elements were still the wing and drop, with special pieces added as needed. The illusion of reality was the aim, however, and much effort was taken to make such scenes as that in which Eliza crosses the ice as realistic as possible. The popularity of the play led many com-panies to mount rival productions in which they attempted to outdo each other in realistic stage effects. Mules, horses, and bloodhounds were added in the pursuit of Eliza and George, and every effort was made to convince the audience of the terrible plight of the characters. Melodramas of this sort pushed the demands made on the physical stage to the extreme and served as the foundation upon which motion pictures were eventually built.

The costuming was related to the contemporary dress of daily life, but was modified to emphasize the particular qualities of the individual characters. Simon Legree was made terrible in part because of his appearance. Little Eva no doubt was costumed as the nineteenth-century idea of perfection.

Uncle Tom's Cabin was accompanied by an orchestral score. At various points a number of songs were inserted. After the play achieved its great popularity, productions vied with each other in the amount of incidental entertainment (in the form of songs and dances) added. Undoubtedly, the spectacle, music, and dance of *Uncle Tom's Cabin* coupled with its strong, simple, emotional story explains in large part its success and the popularity of other melodramas of the nineteenth century.

Melodrama combined the infinite demands made upon the stage by Romantic drama with the moral outlook of much of the eighteenth-century drama; it put into popular terms most of the trends of the preceding hundred years. It must also be remembered that while melodrama is frequently thought of principally in terms of the nineteenth century, it actually remains the most popular form of entertainment today, since the majority of motion-picture and television dramas are of this type. They differ from their nineteenth-century counterparts mainly in their use of modern subject matter and in a greater attention to the psychological motivations of character.

One of the favorite types of theatrical entertainment in America in the nineteenth century was the minstrel show. This portion of a cover for a piece of sheet music shows some figures associated with one of the best known troupes, Christy's Minstrels. Courtesy of the University of Iowa Library.

MAJOR TRENDS IN THE NINETEENTH-CENTURY THEATRE

The period between the late eighteenth and the late nineteenth centuries saw a number of changes in the theatre, most of which were elaborations upon previous trends. The basic organization continued to be the resident stock company, which performed a large repertory of plays each season. Although this arrangement continued throughout the nineteenth century, it was gradually undermined by the "star" system and the "combination" touring company.

DECLINE OF THE STOCK COMPANY

Repertory companies had always had their leading players, and the most powerful companies were able to attract the best actors, but the exploitation of "stars" was largely an innovation of the nineteenth century. In America around 1810 actors with great reputations began to find it profitable to accept starring engagements with local companies, with each of which they would remain for a week or two playing their most famous roles. The rest of the cast was composed of members of the local group. Originally the star system lifted the level of local productions, since touring actors were those of the first rank. After 1830, however, those with lesser talent also began to tour, and members of the local troupes became merely supporting players. This, in turn, led the better local actors to try their fortunes on the touring circuit. After a time managers found it difficult to maintain a first-rate company.

By 1870 the railroads extended from coast to coast and offered reasonably dependable transportation to almost any place in the United States. After this time the star system gradually gave way to the "combination" company, in which a star toured with a complete cast, scenery, and costumes. The combination company normally performed only one play, rather than a repertory of attractions. The resulting success of these touring groups gradually undermined the local theatres, and by 1900 the resident stock company was quite rapidly declining in America. Along with it, lines of business, the possession of parts, and the repertory system also were vanishing. By 1900 the ideal had become the "long-run hit."

The expansion of "the road" created new problems. New York increasingly became the center of production from which all touring companies originated. Actors, therefore, had to go to New York to seek employment, just as local managers did to book attractions for their theatres. By the 1890s the booking situation was on the verge of chaos, since a manager might have to negotiate with as many as forty different producers, each of whom was simultaneously dealing with numerous other local managers. Often touring companies defaulted on their contracts, leaving the local theatres without attractions.

It was out of this situation that the Theatrical Syndicate grew when six theatre managers and booking agents joined together in 1896 for the purpose of gaining a monopoly on "the road." The Syndicate promised local theatres a full season of plays complete with stars, on the condition that they book all of their attractions through the Syndicate. Although many local managers welcomed the new stability, others rebelled against the monopoly. In these cases, the Syndicate bought, rented, or built rival houses and gradually drove the recalcitrant managers out of business. Then, because the Syndicate controlled a majority of the theatres, they could also force New York producers to sign exclusive contracts with them, since otherwise the road companies would find it difficult to obtain enough bookings to make tours profitable. Through such devices, the Syndicate dominated theatrical production in America between 1896 and 1915, when its power was finally broken.

The combination system triumphed in Europe toward the end of the nineteenth century as well, but Europe in general has been reasonably successful in maintaining a few repertory companies in addition to the long-run hit shows which have become the desired goal everywhere.

THE AUDIENCE

The eighteenth century had seen the middle classes flock increasingly to the theatre, and to this group the nineteenth century added the lower classes. The Industrial Revolution which greatly increased the number of workers in the large population centers was partly responsible for expanding theatre audiences. The working classes, however, had somewhat different tastes from the earlier audiences, and the total range of entertainment offered in the theatre was constantly enlarged to attract as many persons as possible.

The number of theatres also was vastly increased in the first half of the nineteenth century. Many of these new theatres performed regular drama, but a large percentage was devoted solely to "variety" entertainment. For a time regular stock companies competed with the variety theatres by combining the variety show with regular dramatic fare. Singing, dancing, and miscellaneous entertainment were inserted between the acts of the main play of the evening, and the performance was concluded by a lengthy afterpiece, usually a comedy or a comic opera. Performances were lengthened until they lasted from seven in the evening until well after midnight.

In the last half of the century, however, there was a gradual separation of regular drama from the variety-hall atmosphere. Theatres came to specialize in a particular kind of entertainment and regular drama became again the province of a more sophisticated group, a trend which was accelerated in the twentieth century by the development of motion pictures, which consciously attempted to attract that mass audience which had constituted a large part of the nineteenth-century theatre-going public.

As the theatres turned to greater specialization in one type of performance, the evening's bill became less complex. Theatres offering dramatic entertainment turned more and more to a single play as the sole attraction. The amount of time needed for performances changed correspondingly, and by 1900 only two to three hours were normally required.

The changes in the audience led to corresponding changes in the

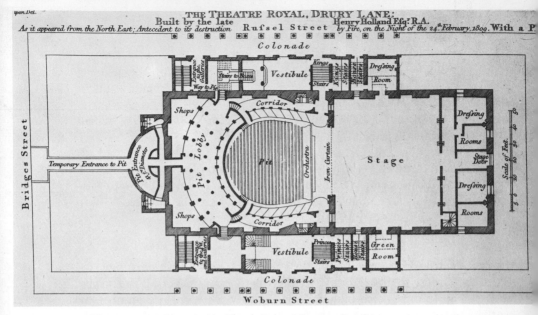

The ground plan of the Drury Lane Theatre, London, as it was prior to the burning of the theatre in 1809. From *Londina Illustrata*. London, 1819-25. *Right.* Interior of the Drury Lane Theatre in 1808. Note the five tiers of boxes. Courtesy of the Metropolitan Museum of Art, Dick Fund, 1917.

theatre auditorium. In the late eighteenth and early nineteenth centuries many theatres were built which seated three thousand or more spectators. The old box, pit, and gallery arrangement continued to be used until late in the nineteenth century. The increased size of the auditorium, however, made hearing and seeing from the boxes more difficult, and around the middle of the century the practice was begun of placing comfortable armchairs in what formerly had been called the pit (now the orchestra). Gradually, except in opera houses, the orchestra replaced the boxes in prestige and desirability. In theatres built after the late nineteenth century boxes were often omitted and the space formerly occupied by them was devoted to mezzanine or balcony seating.

THE STAGE

The developments in staging are primarily outgrowths of an increasing interest in historical accuracy and in realism. Prior to the late eighteenth century, history was not considered to have any relevance to art. Universal truth, which was thought to be independent of time and place, was said to be the aim of drama, and neoclassicism in general was almost totally antihistorical in its ideals. The eighteenth century, however, began to develop a concern for the circumstances of time and place. As a result, the changes and developments through which society has gone became as important (if not more so) than those factors which had remained constant. Interest began to shift from the ideal or universal qualities to the individualizing details of man's existence. The national origins and devel-

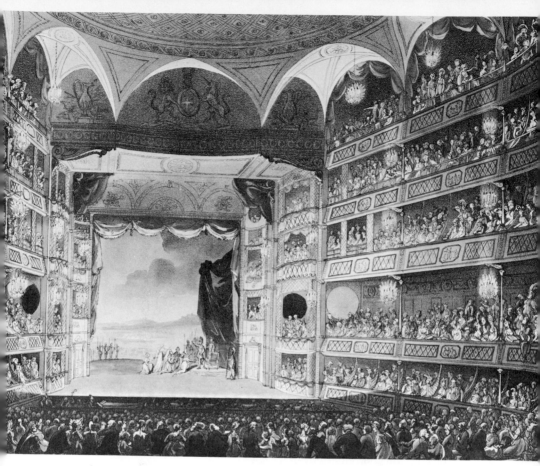

opments of architecture, literature, dress, and social customs began to be studied with enthusiasm. The first history of costume appeared about 1775 and antiquarianism in general came to the fore after this time.

A desire to see this new knowledge used in the theatre soon developed, and plays were written which demanded settings using known historical buildings and in which the details of time and place were of interest. Older plays, such as those of Shakespeare, were given historically accurate settings as well.

The interest in time and place also carried over into concerns for the unusual or the exotic. Authentic dances and costumes of other countries began to creep into plays, and unusual or picturesque settings became popular. This kind of background detail came to be called "local color," since it rendered the characteristic and individual features of a specific locale.

Such historically accurate details and local color were used only sporadically and inconsistently, however, up to about 1825. Charles Kemble's production of Shakespeare's *King John* (produced in London in 1823) was the first to claim complete historical accuracy in every detail of setting and costume. Both scenery and costumes for this production were

the work of J. R. Planché (1796–1880) who, through such productions and through his histories of costume and other antiquarian studies, did more than any one else to forward the movement toward historical accuracy in the theatre. By 1850 it had become a point of pride and of box-office appeal to offer productions in which every detail was certified to be accurate.

Quite frequently the historically accurate details and local color were used only as interesting visual embellishments which had no effect upon the action of the play. It did not bother audiences or producers that historical accuracy was most often irrelevant to the spirit of the plays themselves. Nevertheless, it was through such visual details that realism began to enter the theatre. Realism in subject matter and characterization were not to be exploited until after 1850, but the ground work had been laid.

Once realism of detail had been accepted as a standard, however, more and more aspects of the setting had to be treated accordingly. The wing-and-drop setting obviously could not render an interior realistically, and by the 1840s experiments were under way with the "box" set (a setting in which the back and projecting two side walls are joined together as in a house). This new kind of setting was used sporadically during the remainder of the century and had become standard by 1900.

Before the box set could be used with great efficiency the stage floor itself had to be revised, for in the nineteenth century it sloped upward toward the back. Such a slope was well suited to wings and drops placed parallel to the front of the stage, but was not satisfactory when scenery was placed at any other angle. In the late nineteenth century, theatres with

William Capon (1757-1827) was one of the first English designers to be interested in historical accuracy. Much of his work was done for John Philip Kemble, and his scenery remained in use until about 1840. The illustration at left shows one of his street scenes used in a number of Shakespearean revivals at the Covent Garden Theatre beginning in 1809. From *The Magazine of Art*, 1895. *Right*. A costume design by J. R. Planché for Shakespeare's *King John* in 1823. This production is supposed to have been the first one which was historically accurate in every detail. The costumes in the design are for Philip Falconbridge and Hubert De Burgh. Courtesy of the Stark Collection, University of Texas Library.

level stage floors began to be built, but they did not become typical until the twentieth century.

Such a revision of the stage floor was inevitable, as it had become increasingly difficult to create realistic effects solely through wings and drops. More and more special units were needed, and it became increasingly desirable to set up scenic elements at any angle and at any point on the stage floor. The old groove and chariot-and-pole systems became too restrictive, and new methods of shifting scenery had to be devised. Toward the end of the nineteenth century producers experimented with such devices as the revolving stage, the elevator stage, and the rolling platform stage. (A revolving stage is created by mounting a large circular segment of the stage floor on a central pivot. A number of settings may then be mounted on this portion of the stage floor, and scene changes are effected by merely revolving the stage until a new setting comes into view. An elevator stage is one on which various portions of the stage floor may be raised or lowered. Scenery may be mounted on a segment of this floor while it is in the basement and it may then be raised to stage level. A rolling platform stage is one mounted on tracks parallel with the front of the stage. Entire settings may be mounted on the platforms in the wings and then rolled onstage. The revolving stage, the elevator stage and the platform stage are only three of the many mechanical devices which have been used to shift scenery since the mid-nineteenth century.) In theatres which did not have such aids, scene shifting was normally done by a large number of stage hands who moved each unit manually.

The trend toward realism brought about changes in many other theatrical conventions. For example, in the last part of the nineteenth century, the front curtain began to be closed regularly to mask scene changes. Several factors brought about this change. The increasing complexity of settings demanded that stage hands do much of their work on stage and their visible presence would have been a distraction. Probably more important, however, was the growing demand for the illusion of reality, an illusion easily destroyed for most audiences if settings are assembled before them.

Diderot's theory of the fourth wall also began to be applied with some consistency. Auditorium lights were extinguished during the performances, and the actors played more and more within the settings rather than on the forestage. The separation between the actor and the audience was emphasized further by a kind of playing in which the actors concentrated upon creating the illusion of being in a real room in a real house. Again, however, such realism in acting and in staging was not universally applied, although the trend was clearly and definitely in that direction.

Developments in stage lighting also aided in the development of realism. Gas began to replace candles and oil lamps by 1820 and was in use almost everywhere by the 1830s. For the first time since the theatre had moved indoors the stage could be as brilliantly lighted as desired. Furthermore, by 1850 the "gas table," a central panel of gas valves, permitted complete and instantaneous control over all of the stage lights. This new power led to numerous experiments in achieving realistic effects. The invention of the lime light and the carbon arc aided in these experiments since they provided means for creating concentrated beams of light for the first time. Both devices were exploited beginning around 1850; at first

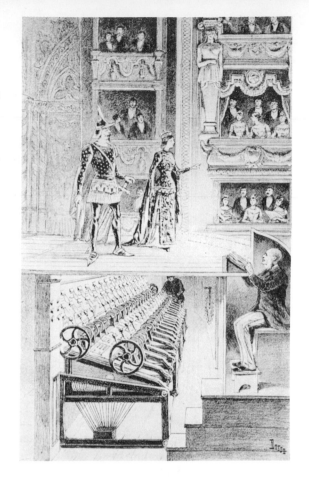

Left. Scene from a production of Shakespeare's *Anthony and Cleopatra* at the Sadler's Wells Theatre, London, 1849. Although the men seem to be clad in Roman attire, Cleopatra is clearly wearing a fashionable dress of the nineteenth century. From *The Illustrated London News*, 1849. *Right*. A lighting control board in the last part of the nineteenth century. Note also the prompter at the front of the stage. From G. Moynet's *La Machinerie Théâtrale*, 1893.

they were used for such special effects as rays of sunlight or moonlight, but gradually their potentialities for lighting the acting areas were also realized. About 1880 electricity began to replace gas as the chief means of lighting the stage. It offered even greater flexibility without the great danger of fire, which had been the chief drawback of gas. By 1900, electricity had almost completely replaced gas for lighting the stage.

The brighter stage light, however, emphasized the falseness of the painted scenery and props, and by the 1830s three-dimensional details began to appear. Door knobs were added to doors, real molding was attached to the walls, carpets were laid over the floors, and artificial fires realistically glowed in fireplaces. Such details began to be demanded by the action of plays, and in the second half of the nineteenth century actors were asked for the first time to perform such everyday tasks as boiling water, brewing a pot of tea, serving and drinking it.

THE ACTOR

The increasing attention to details and to realism carried over into acting as well. Many of the developments can best be seen by looking briefly at the careers of certain outstanding English actors.

The stage of the early nineteenth century was dominated by the Kemble family, the most famous members of which were John Philip Kemble (1757–1823) and his sister, Mrs. Sarah Siddons (1755–1831). Kemble made his debut at Drury Lane in 1783 as Hamlet and remained on the London stage until 1817. Mrs. Siddons, frequently said to be the greatest English tragic actress (Sir Joshua Reynolds' portrait of her is entitled "The Tragic Muse"), was established in the London theatre by 1782, retired in 1812. The Kembles aimed at achieving grace, dignity, and beauty in movement, gesture, and voice. Thus, they tended to idealize characters.

By 1820, however, the "classical" style of the Kembles was being replaced by the Romantic ideal, which was epitomized in the acting of Edmund Kean (1787–1833). He made his debut at Drury Lane in 1814 and remained on the stage until his death. He often sacrificed dignity and beauty in order to portray emotions more realistically. On the other hand, he so neglected the dispassionate moments in a play that he was often inaudible. This alternation of intensity with indifference led Coleridge to remark that to see Kean act was like reading Shakespeare by flashes of lightning. Kean was undisciplined and lived a wild and unrestrained life, but he could magnetize audiences and he set the standard for the actors who succeeded him.

William Charles Macready (1793–1873) made his debut in 1810 and retired in 1851. Macready's acting style was a compromise between those of Kemble and Kean, since he worked for beauty and dignity combined with emotional intensity. Furthermore, like the Kembles he gave much thought and study to his roles and planned each detail with care. Also like Kemble, Macready was a theatre manager for a number of years, during which he introduced many Romantic plays, especially those of Bulwer-Lytton, to the public. He was noted for his painstaking rehearsals, an illustration of the growing interest in the details of theatrical production.

Mme. Lucia Elizabeth Vestris (1797–1856) achieved fame in light comedy and musical entertainments at the Olympic Theatre in London beginning about 1830. With her husband, Charles Matthews (1803–78), she did much to return comic acting to a more natural style. Mme. Vestris is probably more important as a theatrical manager, however, in which capacity she is credited with a number of innovations. She is thought to have used the box set for the first time in England (in 1841); she introduced real (rather than fake) properties, abandoned the practice of costuming comic characters in ludicrous garments, and shortened evening programs so that audiences could be out of the theatre by eleven. Almost all of her changes moved the theatre toward greater realism.

With his wife, Ellen Tree (1806–80), Charles Kean (1811–68), son of Edmund Kean, achieved fame as an actor and manager, principally

Edwin Forrest as King Lear.   John Philip Kemble as Cato in Addison's tragedy.

From Lewis C. Strang's *Players and Plays of the Last Quarter Century*. Volume I. Boston, 1902.

Edwin Booth as Hamlet.   Edmund Kean as Othello.

William Charles Macready in the grave-digger scene from *Hamlet*. From *The Illustrated London News*, 1846. *Below*. Sir Henry Irving's production of *King Lear*, 1892. A sketch by Hawes Craven. From the souvenir program.

through his Shakespearean productions at the Princess' Theatre in London between 1850 and 1859. Kean prided himself on the historical accuracy in every detail of his settings, costumes, and properties. No time or expense was spared in achieving the utmost perfection, and his productions marked the triumph of historical accuracy as the standard for English staging. The patronage of Queen Victoria further served to elevate Kean's work in the eyes of the English public.

François Joseph Talma in 1791 as Titus in Voltaire's *Brutus*. From Adolphe Jullien's *Histoire du Costume du Théâtre*. Paris, 1830.

Squire Bancroft (1841–1926) and his wife, Marie Effie Bancroft (1839–1921), were noted for many reforms which they carried through at the Prince of Wales Theatre between 1865 and 1880. They were famous for their staging of plays about contemporary English life, especially the plays of Tom Robertson (1829–71), to which they applied rigorous standards of realism in every element of production. Just as Charles Kean triumphed with the realism of history, the Bancrofts succeeded with the realism of modern life. Their practices helped to popularize the box set, realistic costumes, properties, and acting. Furthermore, they made acceptable that innovation which has transformed the orchestra into the most desirable seating area in the theatre.

English acting reached its peak in the nineteenth century with Henry Irving (1838–1905). He was the first actor to be knighted, a sign that the acting profession was at last socially acceptable. With Ellen Terry (1847–1928) he achieved great renown during the final decades of the century in his productions of Shakespeare's plays, Romantic drama, and melodrama. Irving was also a theatrical manager, and it was he who finally abandoned the groove method of shifting scenery. He placed scenic units onstage wherever needed and employed a vast number of stage hands to make the necessary changes. He was the first manager who consistently concealed scene changes from the audience. Irving, more than anyone else in England, integrated all the trends toward complexity and realism in staging.

This survey of English actors by no means exhausts the list of great actors of the nineteenth century. Others were: François Joseph Talma

(1763–1826), Rachel (1821–58), Benoit Coquelin (1841–1909), and Sarah Bernhardt (1845–1923) in France; Mikhail Shchepkin (1788–1863) and Prov Sadovsky (1818–72) in Russia; Tommaso Salvini (1829–1916), Adelaide Ristori (1822–1906), and Eleanora Duse (1859–1924) in Italy; Ludwig Devrient (1784–1832), Emil Devrient (1803–72), and Fanny Janauschek (1830–1904) in Germany; Helena Modjeska (1844–1909) in Poland; and Edwin Forrest (1806–72), Charlotte Cushman (1816–76), and Edwin Booth (1833–93) in America.

THE PLAYWRIGHT

The nineteenth century saw the playwright achieve a measure of financial security at last. Prior to this time he lost all control over the production of his plays after their initial performances. He might be paid a fixed sum for the play or he might be given the receipts from a number of its performances. He might also retain publication rights, but once these were sold he received no further payments.

The "royalty" system of paying authors (a payment either of a fixed sum or of a percentage of the receipts for each performance) was first used in France in the late eighteenth century. This system was not universally accepted, however, until the last quarter of the nineteenth century.

The first copyright law was passed in England in 1833, but it applied only to those works written after that time, and it did not protect the author outside of England. Thus, an American might produce an English play without paying its author any fee. Furthermore, he might translate foreign works and claim them as his own. An international copyright agreement was negotiated in 1887, and all countries subscribing to it promised to protect the rights of foreign as well as domestic authors.

With rare exceptions, by 1900 the playwright had achieved adequate legal protection throughout the world. He might still have difficulty in getting his plays produced, but when they appeared, either on the stage or in print, his rights were guaranteed by law.

As is usual, the culmination of one trend sets in motion forces which lead to another. And so it was to be in the nineteenth century, for drama of the Romanticist movement, melodrama, and the realism of stage spectacle laid the groundwork for that movement which is usually called realism, and which marks the beginning of modern theatre. By the last half of the nineteenth century those ideas and practices which are typical of the modern theatre were already emerging and were merely waiting to be exploited.

Steele MacKaye (1842-94) was a playwright, inventor, actor, director, *régisseur*, and reformer in the American theatre. The illustration above shows his Madison Square Theatre in New York which opened in 1880. It featured a double stage, one above the other, on elevators. Settings could be changed in less than one minute. From *The Scientific American*, April 5, 1884.

PART THREE

THE MODERN THEATRE

Chapter 12

REALISM AND NATURALISM

By the mid-nineteenth century the Romantic standard had come to seem meaningless. The belief in man's idealistic nature had received setbacks. For example, after the downfall of Napoleon around 1815, most European countries reinstated political conditions which were in many ways more oppressive than those in existence during the eighteenth century. The ideals of liberty, equality, and fraternity no longer seemed to have any reality. Furthermore, the general misery of a large part of humanity was being emphasized in the results of the Industrial Revolution. The factory system was pouring workers into the centers of population where living conditions were daily more inadequate. Crime and poverty were all too prevalent.

THE BACKGROUNDS OF REALISM

In the face of such political and economic conditions the Romanticist's tendency to search for a solution to problems in an idealized notion of man's capacity for infinite good seemed both too vague and too impractical. Many came to argue that dreams must be abandoned for a systematic and scientific search into man's actual state and for solutions based upon discoverable facts. Observation, prediction, and control of society became the new ideals.

Facing Part Three: A scene from Eugene Ionesco's *The Chairs*. Directed by James Clancy.

Above. A scene from *The Wild Duck*. Directed by John Terfloth; setting by Carleton Mollette.

Among the major influences on the new thought were the writings of Auguste Comte (1798–1857), whose philosophy came to be called *positivism*. In his writings, published between 1830 and 1854, he argued that sociology is the highest form of science and that all knowledge should ultimately be used for the improvement of society. He found the key to such improvement in observation and experimentation precise enough to explain all happenings in terms of natural cause and effect. Comte's concept places primary emphasis upon those facts which can be experienced through the five senses, and it thereby limits concern to the observation of contemporary events.

Positivism was re-enforced by *The Origin of the Species* by Charles Darwin (1809–1882). The doctrine set forth there had two main parts: (1) evolution, or the idea that all forms of life have developed gradually from a common ancestry; and (2) the survival of the fittest, as an explanation of the reason for the evolution.

This point of view has several consequences. First, heredity and environment become the determining factors of existence. Everything that man is or can be is the result of the physical make-up with which he is born and of the conditions under which he lives. Second, heredity and environment become explanations for all character traits and actions. Furthermore, since behavior is determined by factors beyond the individual's control, he cannot be blamed for his behavior. If blame is to be assigned it must go to the society which has allowed such undesirable hereditary and environmental factors to exist. While few believers in these theories advocated trying to control heredity, many turned their attention to ways of improving the social environment.

Third, the ideas of evolution and the survival of the fittest cast considerable doubt upon the existence of God as conceived in most religions. If He existed, according to the new views, it was as a totally indifferent and impersonal force. The idea of immortality was seriously challenged at the same time. If there is no future life, man can reach fulfillment only in the present one, and, to many, science seemed to offer the greatest possibilities of achieving the maximum human good.

Fourth, Darwin's ideas strengthened the idea of progress. If man has evolved from an infinitesimal grain of being to the complex creature he now is, greater and greater improvement and inevitable progress seemed to him to be clearly indicated. Although progress came to be thought of as inevitable, it was also believed that desirable change can be hastened by the consistent application of the scientific method to all phases of human life.

Fifth, man treated as a natural object is subject to the same laws and conditions as all other things in nature. Prior to the nineteenth century man had been viewed generally as somehow distinct from and superior to the rest of creation. Now, by this concept, he tended to lose this privileged status and to become merely another object for study and control.

Like most movements, then, realism was attempting to improve the lot of mankind by coming to grips with truth. The new school, however, saw truth as being limited to knowledge gained through the five senses (sight, hearing, taste, smell, and touch). Such a marked change in the view of truth inevitably influenced the conception of art and the theatre.

REALISM IN THE THEATRE

By 1850 a conscious movement toward realism in art was emerging. It developed first in France, and before 1860 the following precepts about the writing of plays had already been set forth. The playwright should strive for a truthful depiction of the real world. Since he may know the real world only through direct observation, he should restrict himself to writing about the society around him. Furthermore, he should strive to be as objective as possible in his work and avoid distorting the truth.

Given such an outlook, it was only natural that playwrights came to emphasize the details of contemporary daily life. They avoided historical subject matter and the idealization of human motives and actions. Many writers turned to themes and character types which had not previously been treated on the stage, and conservative critics of the day charged that the theatre had become little better than the tavern or the sewer. To such charges of immorality and decadence, the supporters of realism replied that the plays were truthful depictions of life and, therefore, were moral since truth is the highest form of morality. To prefer an idealized picture of life, they argued, is to elevate falsehood over truth and is itself immoral. Furthermore, the supporters of realism suggested, if audiences did not like the pictures of contemporary life which they saw on the stage, they should strive to change the society which had furnished the models rather than denounce the playwright who had been fearless in his treatment of what he saw around him.

The visual elements of staging were the aspects of drama most easily brought into accord with the new demands, for the groundwork had already been laid by Romantic drama and melodrama. These forms had developed with ever-increasing accuracy the details of costuming and scenery, but had used settings primarily to idealize place, historical period, or characters. It was a simple task to extend the previous practices to meet the demands of realism.

A suitable dramatic form also was already in existence in the "well-made" play. Although all its elements had been utilized before the nineteenth century, the credit for perfecting the technical form of the well-made play goes to Eugène Scribe (1791–1861), one of the most prolific and successful writers of his day. Scribe's plays, numbering over four hundred, are lacking in depth, and are important now only because they epitomize the dramatic structure adopted by the new realistic school of writers.

The basic characteristics of the well-made play are: clear exposition of situation and characters; careful preparation for future events; unexpected but logical reversals; continuous and mounting suspense; an obligatory scene; a logical and believable resolution. This kind of structure has been used for almost all types of plays, but it was especially adapted to the needs of realism because of its dependence upon a clear cause-to-effect relationship and the logical progression of complications.

Although prior uses of settings and dramatic technique were easily adapted to the needs of the new school, earlier movements provided little guidance in the treatment of subject matter and characterization. Two French playwrights, Alexandre Dumas *fils* (1824–95) and Émile Augier (1820–89), were among the first to direct attention to contemporary social problems as suitable subjects for drama.

Dumas *fils* came to the attention of the public in 1847 with a novel, *The Lady of the Camellias*, which he dramatized in 1849. Because of its subject matter, however, the play was not granted a license for production until 1852. One of Dumas' biographers has said this of the play:

> Now came a young man who dared to depict not a courtesan of historical legend, not an adventuress surrounded by a halo of poetic symbolism, but a "kept woman" of everyday contemporary life, and this author made his subject even more realistic by writing in ordinary prose.

The play, generally known today as *Camille*, was an instantaneous success, and its heroine, who dies of tuberculosis, has become a legendary character. Although the language and subject matter show a movement toward realism, the treatment was still a romanticization of the "prostitute with a heart of gold."

Dumas soon became dissatisfied with his own work and turned to a more realistic treatment of his subject matter. In 1855 he wrote *The Demi-Monde*, which denounces the same kind of characters he had idealized in *Camille*. From this time on he attempted to establish a theatre of "social utility" by writing plays which discussed contemporary social problems such as divorce, unscrupulous business practices, and the plight of illegitimate children. But as Dumas became more and more concerned with social problems he also became more and more an obvious moralist, and his plays came to be called *pièces à thèse* (or thesis plays). Dumas' work seems dated now because the social problems he treated have changed and because of his excessive preaching, but he probably did more than anyone

Many of Ibsen's early plays were written in the romantic style. Probably the best known of the early plays is *Peer Gynt* (1867). The scene shown is from the production in Christiania, Norway, in 1876. From T. Blanc's *Christiania Theaters Historie 1827–1877*. Christiania, 1899. *Opposite page*. A scene from *Ghosts* as produced at the Burgtheater in Vienna in 1904. From *Bühne und Welt*. Berlin, 1904–5.

before Ibsen to establish a drama based upon contemporary social situations and problems.

Augier is noted principally for his political and social satires of contemporary French conditions. Many of his plays deal in a less didactic way with the same problems treated by Dumas: the power of money, the dangers of churchmen in politics, fallen women. The dramatic power of Augier's plays on realistic themes did much to popularize the new style of playwriting.

But it is to Ibsen that credit must be given for the full exploitation of the realistic mode and the ultimate triumph of the new methods. "Modern" drama is usually dated from around 1875 when Ibsen began to write in the realistic vein.

Henrik Ibsen (1828–1906), Norway's first important dramatist, began writing about 1850. His work up to about 1875, much of which is based on stories drawn from Norway's legendary past, is clearly related to Romantic drama. In 1875 Ibsen turned to the problem play with *The Pillars of Society* and continued in that vein with *A Doll's House*, *Ghosts*, and *An Enemy of the People*.

The subject matter and dramatic technique of these plays demonstrate many of the characteristics for which Ibsen became famous. Each play shows how the false values of society force individuals into lives based upon lies. For example, *Ghosts* presents a woman who was persuaded to remain with a depraved husband whom she did not love. The son born to this relationship has inherited a venereal disease from the father and at

the end of the play loses his mind. The mother's world, thus, is shattered by her acceptance of the values of her society.

Ibsen has embodied his subject matter in the well-made play form. His characters speak lifelike prose devoid of such nonrealistic devices as asides and soliloquies. The effect is that of an objective view of real people who do not indulge in heroics either in language or in action. The honesty and power of these plays shocked and fascinated audiences. In many countries Ibsen's works were banned, and it was not until well into the twentieth century that they could be freely produced anywhere.

Ibsen was not content to continue writing such social problem plays, however, and his later work took a different direction. Beginning with *The Wild Duck* (1883) he broadened his approach through the extensive addition of symbolism. The focal interest in such plays as *Hedda Gabler* and *The Master Builder* is shifted from society to the individual. The use of symbolism and the concentration upon individual characters increased in Ibsen's late work, culminating in his final play, *When We Dead Awaken* (1899).

Ibsen's changing dramatic interests and methods during the fifty years covered by his writing sum up many nineteenth-century trends. His wide range, his mixture of realism and symbolism, and his great power in characterization affected almost all drama after his time. The qualities of his work can probably best be seen in *The Wild Duck*, which combines many characteristics popular with audiences.

THE WILD DUCK

In *The Wild Duck*, Gregers Werle returns home after an absence of fifteen years, decides that the lives of all his acquaintances are based on lies, and determines to make them face the truth. His efforts lead to catastrophe.

The principal characters are Old Werle (Gregers' father), Hjalmar Ekdal (Gregers' childhood friend), Old Ekdal, Gina, and Hedwig (Hjalmar's father, wife, and daughter respectively). Old Werle is prosperous, while the Ekdals live in comparative poverty, although years ago Werle and Ekdal were business partners. Ekdal was sent to prison for illegal dealings and Gregers suspects that his father let Ekdal accept blame which was partially his. Gregers also believes that Old Werle arranged Hjalmar's marriage to Gina, a former maid in the Werle household, because Gina was pregnant by Werle. Thus, he thinks that Hedwig is not Hjalmar's child.

Gregers takes a room at the Ekdals, in spite of Gina's protest, so that he may force them to face the reality which all are avoiding. Through insinuation and leading questions, Gregers gradually brings his "truth" out into the open. After Hjalmar rejects Hedwig, she decides, with a child's simplicity of reasoning, that only some great sacrifice can prove her love for Hjalmar; and in consequence she kills herself.

Essentially, *The Wild Duck* is a play about the necessity of illusions. Dr. Relling, another tenant in the Ekdal house, says the majority of persons need "a saving lie" upon which to base their lives, to enable them to retain a degree of self-respect and a sense of purpose.

All of the play's characters serve to illustrate this theme, but the opposing positions are most obviously represented by Relling (who believes in the necessity of illusion) and Gregers Werle (who believes that everyone must be forced to face the truth). Relling appears to represent Ibsen's own point of view, for Greger's self-righteous meddling brings only disaster to others.

Ibsen has strengthened his theme through the symbolism of the wild duck. The wild duck is a living creature, but around it are built up a series of relationships and concepts which suggest wider meanings for the events and characters than would be possible without it. The symbolism of the duck pervades the entire play and to understand it fully the different stages in the duck's existence must be reviewed. First, the duck, happy and carefree, lives in a wild state. Then it is shot down by a rather awkward hunter. In its pain and desire to hide, the duck dives to the bottom of the sea; it is sought out, however, and brought to the surface by a dog. The duck survives but does not thrive in the hunter's house. It is given to another family who construct an artificial environment for it and, though crippled, the duck appears to be as happy as in its wild state.

Transferred to a human pattern this scheme results: In his early years a man may live a relatively carefree existence; then one day, wounded by circumstances, he tries to run away, to hide, or to die because of his feelings of inadequacy and disgrace; but he is forced to return to his daily existence and constructs a set of delusions by means of which he can regain his self-respect and sense of purpose; he becomes relatively happy in this artificial environment. Every major event and character in *The Wild Duck* is related to this pattern. Ibsen would seem to indicate that it is the basic outline of human existence and that it can be tampered with only at great risk.

CHARACTERS AND ACTING.   Ibsen has related each of his main characters to his major ideas. The entire Ekdal family is reflected in the wild duck, while Old Werle is the hunter, and Gregers aspires to be the dog. The attic, in which the Ekdals live, is comparable to the ocean depths into which the wounded duck dives, and this comparison may be extended to the entire house, since each of its tenants, with the exception of Hedwig, is seeking to hide within his own particular illusion.

Old Ekdal lives in an illusory state which has become part of his nature. It is implied that he has always been childish, that when he was in business with Werle he spent most of his time hunting. This neglect of responsibility brought on his disgrace. Since his release from prison he has reconstructed his life around the attic, its "forest," and "wild life." He prefers the safety of this make-believe world to the real one. Like the wild duck, he too has been wounded and now lives in an artificial environment.

Gina is one of the most enigmatic characters in the play, for the real truth about a number of events in her life is left unclear. She is the character most capable of forgetting the past and of living life moment by moment. She is the most stolid and down-to-earth person in the play, but she too is one of Werle's victims.

Ibsen has drawn a number of interesting parallels and contrasts between Old Werle and Hedwig. It is possible that Hedwig is the daughter of Old Werle (this is never clarified), both have weak eyesight, both try

The setting for *The Wild Duck* used by André Antoine. Courtesy of Bibliothèque de l'Arsenal, Paris.

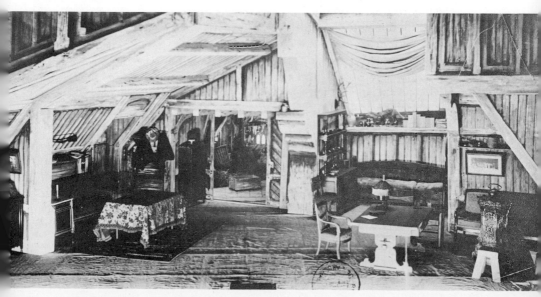

to make amends to others. But Old Werle has treated life as though it were the sport of hunting, and when he wounds he makes amends with money, arranges marriages, and attempts to rebuild illusions. Hedwig responds to life with her whole being, and, in contrast, kills herself rather than wound others. She is representative of the wild duck in its free and natural state. She is open, frank, without artifice. Old Werle shot the wild duck in sport (just as he had seduced Gina and used others all of his life); he wounds, but he does not kill. But Hedwig shoots herself in the heart; hers is an act of sacrifice and love. Old Werle faces up to his shortcomings at the end of the play, but he still lives under the illusion that money and material gifts can atone for the wounds inflicted on others.

Ibsen's principal effort has gone into the roles of Hjalmar and Gregers. Hjalmar speaks as a man of sensitivity, of ambition, and of high ideals might, but his actions show that he is insensitive, lazy, and self-centered. Gina handles the business; she and Hedwig sacrifice every comfort for Hjalmar. Old Ekdal's disgrace is to Hjalmar an excuse for easy sentiment, just as Hedwig's death will be in the future. But Hjalmar is perfectly happy in his illusions, for he can indulge himself and, at the same time, find excuses for being basically ineffectual.

That Gregers accepts Hjalmar as a hero demonstrates his own impracticality and lack of experience. He has hidden away from the world for fifteen years, has thought much about life, but has avoided becoming involved in it. He never really attempts to change his own life, but feels free to meddle in the affairs of others. He is the "dog" who drags those at the bottom of the sea to the surface to make them face reality squarely.

Relling is used as a foil for Gregers. His ability to anesthetize the pain of disillusionment is demonstrated in Molvik, the theology student who rationalizes his failures under the belief that he is "demonic." Relling, the doctor, has administered to the wounds of the characters by providing them with the "saving lie," while Gregers destroys these illusions that have made life tolerable.

But in spite of the obvious use of characters for the purpose of illustrating ideas, Ibsen's techniques for building roles are realistic ones. Every characteristic of importance is shown through action. For example, Hjalmar's character is built up through a series of contrasts between actions and statements. The audience sees his awkwardness at the dinner party and then hears his self-glorifying account of it; he leaves the picture retouching to Hedwig in spite of her bad eyes and his own expressed anxiety about her eyesight. Similar techniques are applied to each role.

Furthermore, each character's traits are brought out through well-motivated and lifelike speech or action. The audience learns about the characters as it would in a real-life situation and there is seldom any feeling of contrivance in presentation.

Ibsen has been careful to fill in the sociological backgrounds of his characters, for each attitude and trait has been given a clear and logical explanation which depends in part upon particular social circumstances. For example, Hjalmar's selfishness is explained in a measure through the inserted information that he was reared by two doting maiden aunts.

Ibsen has also made his characters complex personalities by showing both the good and bad aspects of each. None is perfect (with the possible exception of Hedwig), but none is villainous. This complexity makes each role a good acting part requiring subtlety of playing. An actor must avoid overemphasizing any of the many qualities given to his role, for this would reduce its three-dimensional complexity.

PLOT AND STRUCTURE. Ibsen took the well-made play form and removed from it the sense of artificiality which had resulted from the use of asides, concealed hiding places, overheard conversations, the fortuitous arrival of letters, and similar devices. He retained its basic outline of sound preparation and the logical development of an action out of previous occurrences and clearly demonstrated character traits. His effect of reality results from a meticulous selection and arrangement of detail.

Ibsen typically uses a late point of attack, and in most plays no more than two or three days elapse, for the stage action is the culmination of a long chain of events. In *The Wild Duck* the most important previous events have occurred at least fifteen years before the play opens. This demands a careful handling of exposition, since these prior occurrences are essential to an understanding of the present. Ibsen's favorite device for realistically motivating the revelation of past events is the return of a character who has been absent for a considerable length of time. In *The Wild Duck* Gregers Werle has returned home after a fifteen-year absence during which he has lived in virtual isolation and without any real contact with home. Thus, he can believably inquire about past events. At the same time, however, Gregers' attitude and his purposeful air arouse curiosity about his motives and create suspicion that the truth is being concealed. As the past is revealed, therefore, expectations about future developments are also evoked.

Although this exposition of the past occurs throughout the play, it is concentrated especially in the first two acts. Many of Ibsen's plays are written in four acts, but *The Wild Duck* uses five, in part because two are required to establish the past and present situations out of which the succeeding three acts grow. Ibsen's need for two acts of preparation is also illustrated by the use of two settings for establishing the contrast between Old Werle's situation and the Ekdals'. By the end of the second act, both situation and characters have been clarified, the symbolism of the wild duck has been established, and Gregers has indicated his intention of rectifying the errors of the past. Everything that occurs in the final three acts is a logical outgrowth of the first two.

Ibsen's skill can be seen in the great economy of this play. There are no extraneous scenes and almost nothing could be removed without destroying clarity. At the same time, there is no feeling of haste, for each event seems to develop as it might in real life. Nevertheless, each of the acts is built on a series of complications leading to a point of high suspense near the end of the act, and the whole play builds to the climactic scene of Hedwig's death. Ibsen, thus, achieves great dramatic power (which can result only from careful craftsmanship) while giving the effect of naturalness.

Although it might be argued that there are a number of plot strands —almost one for each character—all are so tightly woven together that the action is one. It is the effect of each character on all the others that motivates the action and leads to its logical and believable outcome.

VISUAL AND AURAL EFFECTS. Ibsen's realistic technique can be seen in the visual elements of *The Wild Duck* also. Detailed descriptions of the settings are given in stage directions. Furthermore, unlike most earlier plays, the details of setting are important to the play's action. The characters are heavily influenced by the physical conditions which surround them, and this can be made clear to an audience only through an adequate and accurate representation of environment. The characters seem to live in the settings, for they do everything there that they would do in a real room. In the studio they eat, retouch photographs, entertain friends, and carry on their daily existence in countless ways. The settings are never merely a garnishing added to the play, but are vital to its action.

Although environment helps to create character, the characters in turn help to create environment. The garret, for example, has been remodeled into an artificial forest to meet the psychological needs of those who people it. Unlike a neoclassical play in which settings are generalized, *The Wild Duck* demands a stage environment singularly its own—one determined by the specific action which occurs there and the particular characters who live there. Instead of merely supplying a typical and normative environment, the set designer is now being asked to create a highly individualized environment.

The actions performed in *The Wild Duck* are all such as might be seen in daily life. The audience is inclined to judge the believability of the action, therefore, in terms of how well the actors recreate the conditions of daily living. For example, in the third act the table is set, a meal is served and eaten. Although on stage not everything is done exactly as in real life, it must correspond with normal action closely or much of the play's effect will be undermined. Stage production in such plays as *The*

A scene from Shaw's *Man and Superman*. Directed by Harold Crain.

Wild Duck, therefore, must be based in part upon a direct observation of life. The aim is that of creating an illusion of reality through the accumulation of details, rather than through the idealization of reality and elimination of details, as had been true under neoclassicism.

The same realistic ideals are reflected in the speech of *The Wild Duck*. Gina relapses into her lower-class speech in moments of distress, and Old Ekdal is inclined to become more aristocratic in his expression under similar circumstances. Hjalmar alternates between flights of fancy and mundane expression. Ibsen, thus, has tried to capture an illusion of daily speech colored by individual characteristics.

Ibsen in many ways epitomized the realistic ideal: subject matter and themes drawn from contemporary life; a serious attempt to present a truthful picture based upon observation; the avoidance of any appearance of contrivance. His embodiment of these aims through effective dramatic techniques became the model for realistic drama after his time.

ENGLAND

The spirit of realism was felt throughout the world. For example, in England the works of such playwrights as Arthur Wing Pinero (1855–1934), Henry Arthur Jones (1851–1929), John Galsworthy (1867–1933), and George Bernard Shaw (1856–1950) show in varying degrees the influence of Ibsen and the ideas of the new trend.

Pinero began his career by writing farces and sentimental plays, but adopted the new realistic mode around 1889. His best-remembered play, *The Second Mrs. Tanqueray* (1893), concerns a "woman with a past." Pinero's approach helped to break down the strictures against such frank subject matter, for his treatment was such that it remained acceptable to conservative audiences.

Jones started writing plays in the 1870s and made his principal impression in the 1880s and 1890s. He was a moral and somewhat melodramatic playwright who, along with Pinero, helped to pave the way for more realistic drama. His best-known works, all highly successful in their own day, are *Saints and Sinners* (1884), *Michael and His Lost Angel* (1896), and *Mrs. Dane's Defence* (1900).

Galsworthy won fame first as a novelist and did not begin writing plays until 1906. His realistic social-problem dramas, especially *Strife* (1909), *Justice* (1910), and *Loyalties* (1922), were among the most powerful plays of the early twentieth century. Galsworthy in many respects follows in the footsteps of Dumas *fils*, for he too, typically, argues for a specific point of view, or thesis.

George Bernard Shaw was probably the most vociferous and certainly the most important of Ibsen's admirers. But Shaw was interested in comedy more than in serious drama, and his approach shows a marked departure from that of Ibsen. While all of Shaw's plays are ultimately serious in their intention of influencing human behavior, they use comedy to make serious points. Shaw takes what he thinks to be the audience's position on a problem and turns it upside down. In the process he shows the shortcomings of the usual point of view and sets forth his own opposing ideas. Eventually he establishes the validity of his own ideas as the solution to the problem dramatized. But Shaw is more than a mere propagandist, for his plays have remained effective even though the social problems he treated have changed. While he wrote plays from the 1890s until near the time of his death, his major work was over by 1925. Among his most important plays are *Man and Superman, Caesar and Cleopatra, Candida, Major Barbara, Pygmalion, Androcles and the Lion, Heartbreak House,* and *Saint Joan.*

RUSSIA

The plays of another writer of the late nineteenth century, Anton Chekhov (1860–1904), were to become almost as influential as those of Ibsen. Unlike Ibsen's plays, however, which are clearly related to those of his French predecessors, the works of Chekhov are outgrowths of influences native to Russia.

Nikolai Gogol (1809–52) had previously established a kind of grotesque and farcical realism with *The Inspector General,* which satirizes the small-town officials of his day. This beginning was further developed by Alexander Ostrovsky (1823–86) and Ivan Turgenev (1818–83).

Ostrovsky was the first important Russian writer to confine himself solely to the dramatic form. He wrote forty-eight plays and is credited with having created a Russian drama not modeled on that of western Europe.

Act I of Turgenev's *A Month in the Country* at the Moscow Art Theatre in 1909. Stanislavsky appears at the left in the role of Rakitin. From *Moscow Art Theatre, 1898–1917*. Moscow, 1955.

In his realistic dramas and satires of the merchant class and the lower aristocracy he copied the speech of everyday life and treated his material in an objective manner. He also used symbols in much the same manner as Ibsen and Chekhov were to do. *The Thunderstorm* and *The Forest* show his work at its best.

Turgenev as a dramatist is remembered today almost solely for *A Month in the Country* (written in 1852 but not produced until 1872). As the title suggests, the characters are connected with a household on a country estate. Natalya, the principal character, falls in love with the young tutor of her son. But Natalya's young ward is also in love with the tutor, and another man is in love with Natalya. The play is a study in boredom, jealousy, heartbreak, and compromise. The characters are in no sense heroes, but all are portrayed with deep understanding as Turgenev reveals the inner psychological motivations of each. In the end all of the characters are disappointed and have had to make compromises. It is a quiet but intense drama.

Chekhov began by writing short stories and humorous sketches, and his first plays were vaudeville skits or one-act farces. His long plays, which he began to write in 1887, were not successful until Stanislavsky and the Moscow Art Theatre presented *The Sea Gull* in 1898. This theatre also produced *Uncle Vanya, The Three Sisters*, and *The Cherry Orchard*. It is upon these four plays that Chekhov's reputation rests.

Chekhov's dramas have many qualities which place them in the realistic-naturalistic vein. The subject matter and themes are drawn from contemporary Russian life and show the way daily living gradually breaks the spirit and drains the will. The characters long for happiness and wish to live useful and full lives, but they are constantly thwarted by circum-

Act I of the original production of Chekhov's *The Cherry Orchard* in 1904. From *Moscow Art Theatre, 1898–1917*. Moscow, 1955.

stances, their own personalities, and the desires of others. Frustration and compromise are the lot of most of his characters.

Chekhov's realism is further seen in his dramatic form, for the plays have a surface quality of aimlessness which matches the aimlessness of the character's lives. There is no sense of hurry, of theatrical trickery, or even of normal dramatic structure. Chekhov is nevertheless an excellent craftsman, for each moment is carefully constructed to contribute to the over-all effect. He is so skillful at concealing the machinery of his plays that they give the effect of events happening as they might in real life.

Chekhov's realism is also to be seen in the ambiguous tone of his plays. In spite of the generally pessimistic outlook of his characters, humor plays a large part in his works. Arguments have raged from the beginning as to whether the plays are comedies or serious dramas. Chekhov's own point of view is sufficiently subordinated so that both interpretations of the plays have been given. Actually they are both comic and serious simultaneously, and one mood succeeds the other in rapid order. As with life itself, the comic and the serious are not rigidly compartmentalized but occur in close juxtaposition and sometimes simultaneously in the same event.

But Chekhov cannot be seen only as a realistic writer, for like Ibsen, he also uses symbolism in his works, especially in *The Sea Gull* and *The Cherry Orchard*. In the latter play, the orchard becomes a symbol of the Old Russia and of the aristocracy. The orchard is preserved though it no longer yields any fruit. The owners cling to it and fail to sell it even though its sale would save the rest of the estate, which the owners love. In the end the orchard is bought by a newly rich peasant and is subdivided for a housing development, an action which illustrates the changing social order.

The orchard, thus, enlarges and extends the meaning of *The Cherry Orchard* just as the duck does in Ibsen's *The Wild Duck*.

Chekhov's plays have exerted a strong and lasting influence on succeeding playwrights. Many critics see all modern realistic drama as stemming from the joint influence of Ibsen and Chekhov.

NATURALISM

Thus far only realism has been considered. At the same time that realism was developing, however, another more extreme movement, naturalism, was also emerging. Realism and naturalism were closely related through their mutual demands for a truthful depiction of life and in their beliefs that ultimate reality is discoverable only through the five senses. Naturalism, however, went much further than realism, for it insisted that art must become scientific in its methods, and it placed greater emphasis on the idea that all behavior is determined by the forces of heredity and environment.

The major spokesman of the naturalistic school was Émile Zola (1840–1902). He argued that art, if it is not to perish, must become scientific both in its subject matter and methods. Subject matter, therefore, might be of two kinds: that taken over from scientific findings; or that which records with absolute fidelity events observed in real life. In the former case, the dramatist sets up characters and a situation and then lets them interact according to the inevitable laws of heredity and environment. The results should demonstrate those facts about human behavior already discovered by science. If the dramatist does not wish to deal with already discovered scientific laws and facts, Zola then suggests the following approach:

> Instead of imagining an adventure, complicating it, preparing stage surprises, which from scene to scene will bring it to a final conclusion, one simply takes from life the history of a being, or of a group of beings, whose acts one faithfully records.

The dramatist, thus, is restricted either to dramatizing scientific laws or recording case studies.

Zola also argued for a scientific approach through the complete objectivity of the writer, who should never allow his own ideas or outlook to intrude. He should observe, record, and experiment with a complete sense of detachment and with the sole aim of demonstrating the truth.

Because the dramatist should be objective about his subject matter, he should feel free to treat whatever seems most fruitful for arriving at truth. In practice, naturalism tended to emphasize the more degraded aspects of lower-class life. These were brought onto the stage in the name of "truth" and "facts." As a result, much of naturalistic drama seems to be preoccupied with human maladies. On the other hand, it has broken down many of the barriers against the treatment of "unpleasant" subjects and characters. Zola was fond of comparing naturalistic art with medicine, and to him the dramatist should have the same interest in examining and defining human social illnesses as the doctor does in physical ailments. Just as dramatists of the eighteenth century had turned to material taken from the lives of the middle class, so those of the nineteenth century tended to enlarge subject matter to include the lives of the lower classes. But whereas the life of the middle class had been idealized, the life of the lower classes was shown to be debased.

Zola and his followers also argued for a completely objective dramatic method. Selection and arrangement of material, they concluded, served only to distort the truth rather than to reveal it. "The word *art* displeases me: it contains I do not know what ideas of necessary arrangement," Zola said. One member of the movement suggested that a play should be a "slice of life." By this he meant that a dramatist should transfer to the stage as faithfully as possible a segment of real life. To avoid distortion, the point at which the story was to be taken up should be selected at random and the point at which it ends should be equally arbitrary. A concern for complications, crises, and resolutions was to be strictly avoided.

Because of the emphasis upon environment as a determinant of character and action, the stage setting was given greater importance under naturalism than in any previous movement. Every detail was reproduced accurately on stage so as to make actions occurring there understandable. Perhaps the most famous setting in the naturalistic vein was that used by André Antoine for a one-act play, *The Butchers* (1888). For this work real carcasses of beef were hung up on stage and the interior of a butcher shop was reproduced in every detail. Similar care was extended to costumes, furniture arrangement, properties, and stage action.

Zola stated that the actors should "not *play*, but rather *live*, before the audience." The stage was arranged as much like a room in a real house as possible, therefore, and the actors tried to speak and move as they would in real life—to "live" onstage. Sometimes in these attempts the actors became inaudible and their action incomprehensible because of a lack of concern for the audience. While such an approach increased the effect of reality, it also frequently led to confusion.

The extreme demands of naturalism lost sight of the differences between the theatre and life itself. A dramatist must select, arrange, and heighten his material if he is to hold the interest of an audience. Reality cannot be transferred to the stage; reality must be interpreted there. For these reasons, naturalism attracted a great deal of attention in the late nineteenth century but it produced few dramatists of note.

Zola was much more famous as a theorist and as a novelist than as a playwright. His best-known drama is *Thérèse Raquin* (1873), an adaptation of a novel. A more successful dramatist in the naturalistic vein was Henri Becque (1837–99), who is remembered chiefly for *The Vultures* (1882) and *La Parisienne* (1885).

Naturalism as a conscious movement was largely ended by 1900. It was important in focusing attention upon the need for accurate, first-hand observation of life, in pointing out relationships between environment and events, and in encouraging greater attention to the details of stage production. In its demands that reality be reproduced on stage, however, naturalism was advocating ideas that could not be carried out. As such extreme demands were abandoned, naturalism itself was gradually absorbed into the larger and more acceptable realistic movement.

REALISM IN THE TWENTIETH CENTURY

Realism has continued to be the most powerful force in the twentieth-century theatre. Many of its conventions have been modified, however, by those movements discussed in Chapter 13. These modifications illustrate one of the principal characteristics of the modern period: its eclecticism, that is, its willingness to borrow and to utilize material drawn from a wide variety of sources and dramatic styles. Many writers who are primarily realistic in their outlook have written plays which fall into other categories, and many of their realistic works display some characteristics of other approaches. Nevertheless, realism, in spite of all influences and modifications, has remained dominant in twentieth-century playwriting. Its present-day characteristics will be discussed more fully in Chapter 14.

THE EMERGENCE OF THE DIRECTOR

The same forces which produced realism and naturalism also led to corresponding changes in the theatre arts. Historical realism and local color had already been accepted by 1850. So, too, there had been a movement away from the wing-and-drop setting toward the box set. But the realism of 1850 was largely achieved by adding to a play details which were not integral to it. For example, Shakespeare's plays were produced in historically accurate settings, but this did not make them realistic—it merely added realistic spectacle to nonrealistic dramas. Only when plays were written which made scenic background an integral part of action did true realism begin to develop.

As the demands for greater realism in all aspects of theatrical production increased, so did the need for more careful rehearsals and the better coordination of all elements. These needs in the late nineteenth century led to the emergence of the director.

Antony's oration over the body of Caesar in Saxe-Meiningen's production of *Julius Caesar*. From *Die Gartenlaube*, 1879.

The history of the modern director is usually traced from the time of Georg II, Duke of Saxe-Meiningen (1826–1914), the ruler of a small German state. The Duke's troupe came into public prominence through a series of tours between 1874 and 1890, and the force of its presentations established the importance of the director in bringing about effective theatrical production.

Saxe-Meiningen's troupe performed the same standard plays (such as those by Shakespeare and Schiller) which appeared in the repertory of almost every company of the day. Nevertheless, this obscure troupe, composed solely of unknown actors, gave performances of such electrifying power that it eclipsed the work of the major theatres. It became clear that the unique qualities of the Saxe-Meiningen troupe were to be traced to its staging methods.

The most important factors in the Duke's approach were his complete control over every aspect of a production, and his long and careful rehearsals. A painter and draftsman, he designed the scenery, costumes, and every movement of the actors. He did not utilize stars and each actor was subordinated to the over-all effect. He insisted on absolute obedience and drilled his troupe until it met all of his demands. He paid as much attention to the crowds and supernumerary parts as he did to the principal roles. Furthermore, stage scenery and properties were carefully designed in terms of the action, and the total stage picture as it developed moment by moment was worked out with extreme care.

The effectiveness of the Saxe-Meiningen troupe was largely a result of careful planning and integration of all theatrical elements. Nothing like it had been seen before, and it stimulated the imagination of those men who were to become important in later years. Saxe-Meiningen's realism, however, was largely restricted to pictorial elements, for he was not interested in the new realistic plays. Nevertheless, he demonstrated how scenic environment and stage action can be integrated to achieve powerful effects.

The well-established acting troupes were not willing to undertake Saxe-Meiningen's methods, however, for they depended upon star actors for their appeal, and such established actors were not willing to subordinate themselves to the demands of a director. Also, the long rehearsals needed for the perfection of a production were costly. It remained for newly organized and largely unknown groups to build upon Saxe-Meiningen's example. Furthermore, few well-established theatres were willing to produce the new realistic and naturalistic drama, particularly as censorship in many cases forbade the presentation of these plays.

THE INDEPENDENT THEATRE
MOVEMENT IN EUROPE

To meet the challenge of the new drama and new theatrical methods, independent theatres began to be established in the late 1880s. These theatres were private, being open only to members, and, therefore, were not subject to censorship. Membership, however, was open to anyone. The actors and other workers were amateurs or little-known professionals who were willing to subordinate themselves to the needs of the total production. Independent theatres, therefore, were able to accomplish what the more important theatres could not, for these newer groups were primarily responsible for exploiting and developing the new staging techniques and giving the new drama its chance to be heard.

The first of the independent theatres was the Théâtre Libre, founded in Paris in 1887 by André Antoine (1858–1943). Antoine, a clerk in a gas company, began his work with amateur actors and with stage furniture taken from his own home. He was an enthusiastic follower of Zola and was heavily influenced by the Saxe-Meiningen troupe. Unlike the latter troupe, however, Antoine's theatre bent all of its efforts toward achieving absolute fidelity to real life. Since he believed that environment determined character and action, Antoine worked out every detail of background and action with great care. He designed interior settings as though they were real rooms, arranged everything in them as it would be in real life, and only then decided which wall should be removed for stage production. He did not rearrange furniture to accommodate the audience's view, but rather tried to achieve an absolute naturalness in the stage picture. He used real properties (such as carcasses of beef, bottles of wine, running water, and so on), and tried to reproduce every detail of an environment. He applied the same standards to the actors' movements and speech, and held long and painstaking rehearsals to achieve the effects for which he was striving.

Many realistic and naturalistic plays were seen in Paris for the first time at Antoine's theatre, and it was to such plays that his approach was most suited. Although his original audience was a special and private one, the fame of the Théâtre Libre gradually grew and soon others wished to see productions of this kind. By 1900 most of the old barriers against realism had been broken down and many of Antoine's methods were being adopted by more conservative theatres.

Antoine's was only the first of a number of important independent theatres. In 1889 the Freie Buehne was founded in Berlin by Otto Brahm (1856–1912). This theatre, like the Théâtre Libre, was founded for the purpose of producing the new realistic and naturalistic drama. The chief difference between Brahm and Antoine seems to lie in the greater emphasis placed on the individual actor by Brahm. In 1894 Brahm became affiliated with a commercial theatre, and after this time his methods were gradually assimilated into the popular theatre of Germany.

In London the Independent Theatre, founded by J. T. Grein (1862–1935), opened in 1891 with Ibsen's *Ghosts*, which had previously been banned from the English stage. The Independent Theatre was organized to produce plays of a "literary and artistic rather than a commercial value," and was not concerned with the new realistic and naturalistic drama to the degree that most of the other independent theatres were. Nevertheless, this group paved the way for the new drama, and was the first to present Shaw's work in England.

The Moscow Art Theatre was founded by Constantin Stanislavsky (1865–1938) and Vladimir Nemerovich-Danchenko (1859–1943) in 1898. This group derived much of its original inspiration from the Saxe-Meiningen company. Like the older troupe, the Moscow Art Theatre also had few trained actors, and Stanislavsky tried to compensate for this fact through long rehearsals and careful attention to external detail. As time went by, however, Stanislavsky became more and more concerned with the problems of the actor. Although he sponsored many experiments with other approaches to theatrical production, he always remained a realist at heart and his "method" is aimed at producing an intense psychological realism.

Ultimately the Moscow Art Theatre exerted its greatest influence through its work with the actor. Interest was first aroused in America in 1923 when the troupe visited the United States, and increased with the American publication of Stanislavsky's books, the most important of which are *My Life in Art* (1924), *An Actor Prepares* (1926), *Building a Character* (1950), and *Creating a Role* (1961).

There is much argument over the essence of Stanislavsky's system of acting. Basically, however, it consists of the following principles: (1) The actor must have a thoroughly trained and flexible body and voice which are capable of responding to all demands.

(2) The actor needs to be skilled in the observation of reality. Out of the knowledge gained through observation he can build his role truthfully by the careful selection of lifelike action, stage business, and speech.

(3) The actor needs to be thoroughly trained in stage technique. While he should always strive to avoid any appearance of artificiality, the actor must be able to project his characterization to an audience.

(4) The actor must undergo psychological training of a rather complex nature. He must be able to imagine himself in the situation of the character he is playing as it is outlined in the script. To play such situations truthfully the actor needs to develop "emotion memory" (the ability to recall out of one's own experience how it feels to be in an emotional situation such as that being acted).

(5) If the actor is not merely to play himself on the stage, however, he must have a thorough knowledge of the script. The actor, therefore, needs to define clearly his character's basic desires and motivations in each scene, in the play as a whole, and in his relation to other characters. The character's primary motivation is called "the spine" of the role since the rest of the characterization must be built upon it. The actor must understand his role so thoroughly (every detail of background, feeling, and action) that he can believe in its truth. To make the character thoroughly comprehensible and believable, the actor at times may have to fill in or invent details omitted from the script. A complete understanding of the play must also lead the actor to subordinate his own role to the demands of the production as a whole and to cooperate in achieving an ensemble effect for the entire troupe.

(6) All of his work onstage should be welded together through

The interior of the Moscow Art Theatre about 1910. From *Moscow Art Theatre, 1898–1917.* Moscow, 1955.

concentration. The actor must focus his entire attention upon the situation and characters as they unfold moment by moment. He should strive to convince the audience that he is involved in a situation which is occurring spontaneously and for the first time. To do this he concentrates upon imagining, feeling, and projecting the truth of the stage situation.

(7) The actor must be willing to work continuously for the perfection of himself as an instrument and for the perfection of his performance in each play.

Stanislavsky's entire system seeks to establish the need for devoted and constant effort on the part of the actor in his profession. To Stanislavsky the actor is successful only when he can convince the audience of the truth of the stage situation, and such conviction results only from intense training and endless striving for perfection.

Each of the major independent theatres stood for extreme care in production, and each contributed to the establishment of the director as the key artist of the theatre. In almost every case, however, these theatres attempted to produce all plays, regardless of type, in as realistic a manner as possible. In this sense, they continued those trends which had begun under romanticism and melodrama.

THE DEVELOPMENT OF ECLECTICISM, OR "ARTISTIC" REALISM

Around 1900, however, the idea began to emerge that each type of play, and even each individual play, has its own style and demands its own distinctive stage treatment. This was a revolutionary idea in many respects, for prior to this time a single standard of stage production was applied to all plays in each period. For example, in 1850 a Greek drama, a play by

The auditorium and stage of Reinhardt's Grosses Schauspielhaus in Berlin. Reinhardt remodeled the Circus Schuman into this structure which resembled a Greek theatre. From G. B. Barkin's *Arketechtura Teatra*. Moscow, 1947.

A design by Norman Bel Geddes for Max Reinhardt's production of *The Miracle*. The theatre was transformed into a cathedral for this production. Courtesy of the Bel Geddes Collection, a gift of the Tobin Foundation, Hoblitzelle Theatre Arts Library, The University of Texas.

Shakespeare, and a melodrama would all have been given the same kind of settings, and would have been acted in the same style. Even Antoine approached each play with the same ideal—the creation of scenes as near those of real life as possible.

The ideals of realism which governed Antoine, however, came to be modified into an "artistic" realism, or the creation of a "stage environment" exactly right for each individual play. The new approach did not attempt to reproduce scenes from real life, but instead concentrated upon the appropriateness of all elements to the particular play. The style of a play was also thought to result in part from the theatrical conventions and the actor–audience relationship which had existed at the time it was written. In stage production, therefore, the conventions of all periods came to be used. This eclecticism has become one of the principal characteristics of the twentieth-century theatre.

Eclecticism is in some ways only a new twist on historical realism, since it often substitutes historical knowledge of theatrical production for historically accurate details of daily life, architecture, or dress as the basis of stage production. While eclecticism had led to sound artistic results, it is, nevertheless, a logical extension of historical realism.

The beginnings of the new trend may be seen in the work of William Poel (1852–1934), who founded the Elizabethan Stage Society in 1894. He constructed a version of the Shakespearean stage and produced a number of Elizabethan plays on it. More than anyone else he was responsible for convincing theatre workers that realistic settings only interfered with Shakespeare's true qualities. After this time it became more and more common to produce Shakespeare's plays on a stage which attempted to approximate the one for which he wrote. Poel worked entirely with plays of a single period, however.

True eclecticism, or "artistic" realism, was established through the work of Max Reinhardt (1873–1943) in Germany. He began his career as an actor under Brahm, but turned to theatrical production around 1900. Reinhardt produced plays from all periods and of all types, and each play was to him a new problem which demanded a new solution. He constructed or modified theatres to achieve the kind of physical arrangement he thought best for each type of play: he transformed a theatre into a cathedral, and built another which approximated the arrangement of a Greek theatre; he thought some plays required large theatres, while others fared best in small houses; he experimented with all kinds of stage machinery and theatrical devices to aid in the creation of the right atmosphere for each play.

With this eclecticism, Reinhardt coupled the idea of the director as the supreme artist of the theatre. He always made a *Regiebuch*, or prompt book, in which every detail of movement, lighting, scenery, costume, and sound was recorded with exactness. He dictated the gestures of his actors, and similarly controlled each element of a production. A script was for him the meager outline offered by the playwright which the director must complete. For Reinhardt the director was, without question, the principal artist of the theatre.

Reinhardt, thus, contributed many ideas to the modern theatre: the need for a different approach to each play; the influence upon each other of theatre architecture and dramatic styles; the need for a detailed prompt book which has been prepared before rehearsals begin; the director as the supreme artist of the theatre and as the completer of the playwright's work. Most of these ideas form the basis for the teaching of directing in America. Reinhardt's continuing influence may also be seen in the present-day experimentation with theatres-in-the-round, open stages, and other new audience–actor relationships.

Reinhardt was not interested in realism as such, but in each of his experiments with styles of production he attempted to achieve an artistic realism. His influence and methods, therefore, frequently had much in common with those nonrealistic approaches which will be discussed in Chapter 13.

THE UNITED STATES

The new ideas on staging were widely practiced in Europe before they were known in America. Between 1896 and 1915 the conservative Theatri-

Eugene O'Neill (1888–1953) continued the tradition of realism in a number of his plays. Here is a scene from his *Anna Christie*, written in 1922. Directed by Paul Davee.

cal Syndicate maintained control of theatrical production. By 1910, however, the new spirit of the European theatre was making itself felt in the United States.

Between 1910 and 1920 the little theatre movement blossomed and began to fill the void left by the decline of the resident stock company. Most of the new theatres were noncommercial and were more concerned with artistic excellence than with financial success. They combined the European idea of an independent theatre with the new concept of the director (each group needed a strong guide since its actors were usually amateurs).

The little theatre movement eventually divided as some organizations were transformed into professional theatres while others became community theatres. Important among these early groups were: The Little Theatre of Chicago, founded in 1912 by Maurice Brown; The Toy Theatre of Boston founded by Mrs. Lyman W. Gale in 1912; The Washington Square Players of New York, founded in 1914; The Provincetown Players, founded in Provincetown, Massachusetts, in 1915 but later moved to New York; and The Arts and Crafts Theatre of Detroit, founded in 1916.

Of these groups The Arts and Crafts Theatre, The Provincetown Players, and The Washington Square Players were to exert the greatest influence. Sheldon Cheney started *Theatre Arts Magazine* at The Arts and Crafts Theatre in 1916. This magazine became the spokesman for the new movement in America and did much to popularize its ideals and to acquaint Americans with European developments. Between 1916 and 1948 it was one of the most important influences on American theatrical ideas.

The Provincetown Players consciously aimed to develop new American playwrights and to produce the best European plays as examples for American theatre artists. It was the first to recognize the talent of Eugene O'Neill and to foster it consistently thereafter. Many of O'Neill's most unusual works were first produced by The Provincetown Players, which offered an opportunity for experimentation impossible to find in the commercial theatre.

The Washington Square Players became The Theatre Guild in 1919 and set out to produce the best American and European plays. More than any other group it was able to carry the new ideas into the commercial field and to influence the American theatre as a whole. Furthermore, The Theatre Guild, along with The Provincetown Players, did much to encourage the "New Stagecraft" in America.

Between 1910 and 1930 *New Stagecraft* was used to designate those ideas on staging which had developed in Europe in the late nineteenth and early twentieth centuries. Shortly after 1910 a number of young Americans traveled and studied in Europe. When they returned to the United States they brought with them an enthusiasm for what they had seen, and actively sought ways of transforming the American theatre along European lines. They were welcomed principally in the little theatres, but only gradually was the validity of the new concepts established. The "New Stagecraft" was not generally accepted in the commercial theatre until the late 1920s.

Among those most intimately associated with the new movement were Robert Edmond Jones (1887–1954), Lee Simonson (1888–   ), and Norman Bel Geddes (1893–1958). It is probably significant that all of these men were designers, for the chief influence of the "New Stagecraft" in America was exerted upon the visual aspects of stage production.

The Theatre Guild also gave birth to another important organization, The Group Theatre. The latter began as a workshop of The Theatre Guild but became independent in 1931. The Group Theatre was a repertory company consciously modeled on The Moscow Art Theatre, and it attempted to apply consistently the Stanislavsky method of acting and stage production in its work. During the 1930s it produced some of the most interesting plays to be seen in New York and was especially successful in producing the works of Clifford Odets (1906–1963).

The Group Theatre also fostered the talents of a number of important directors such as Harold Clurman and Elia Kazan and actors such as Lee J. Cobb, John Garfield, and Morris Carnovsky. The members of this troupe were the principal popularizers of the Stanislavsky system of acting in America. Such former members as Lee Strasberg (at the Actors' Studio) and Stella Adler (at her own studio in New York) have continued to teach this method.

The realistic and naturalistic movements at the end of the nineteenth century had many and far-reaching effects. Not only did they establish new ideals for writing but they also gave rise to new concepts of staging. Many of these ideas have undergone important changes in the twentieth century under the impact of other movements. These changes and developments are the subject of the chapters to follow.

Chapter 13

REVOLTS AGAINST REALISM
SYMBOLISM, EXPRESSIONISM, AND EPIC THEATRE

Although realism has continued to dominate the theatre, it has not been universally accepted. Revolts against its ideas and methods appeared almost immediately and have continued. Each protest, however, has been short-lived, although each has served to modify realism. The most important of the revolts prior to World War II were symbolism, expressionism, and the epic theatre.

SYMBOLISM

Symbolism (sometimes called neoromanticism or impressionism) developed in France in the 1880s, and as a conscious movement was over by 1900. Symbolism is antirealistic in its denial that ultimate reality is to be found in the evidence of the five senses, or through rational thought processes. On the contrary, it holds that truth is to be grasped only by intuition.

Since ultimate truth cannot be logically understood, it cannot be expressed in logical language. It can only be suggested through symbolic

A stage design by Adolphe Appia entitled "Dessin de Rhythmique—l'Ile des Sons." Courtesy of Fondation Adolphe Appia, Berne.

objects or actions which serve to evoke in the audience feelings and states of mind which correspond to the dramatist's intuitions of reality. The surface dialogue and action in a Symbolist play, therefore, are not of primary importance. As Maeterlinck put it:

> Side by side with the necessary dialogue you will almost always find another dialogue that seems superfluous; but examine it carefully, and it will be borne home to you that this is the only one that the soul can listen to profoundly, for here alone it is the soul that is being addressed.

He went on to say:

> Great drama, if we observe it closely, is made up of three principal elements: first, verbal beauty; then the contemplation and passionate portrayal of what actually exists about us and within us, that is to say nature and our sentiments; and, finally enveloping the whole work and creating the atmosphere proper to it, the idea which the poet forms of the unknown in which float about the beings and things which he evokes, the mystery which dominates them, judges them, and presides over their destinies. I have no doubt that this last is the most important element.

Thus, while a play portrays human actions, its ultimate aim is to convey intuitions about a higher truth which cannot be adequately expressed in words and which can only be suggested through symbols.

Unlike the Realists, the Symbolists chose their subject matter from the past, and avoided any attempt to deal with social problems or to recreate the physical environment of its characters. Like the Neoclassicists, they aimed to suggest a universal truth which is independent of time and place. Unlike the Neoclassicists, however, the Symbolists did not believe that truth can be logically defined or rationally expressed. A Symbolist drama, consequently, tends to be vague, mysterious, and puzzling.

By far the most famous Symbolist playwright was Maurice Maeterlinck (1862–1949). He was born in Belgium, but spent most of his life in France and wrote in French. His most important works are those written in the 1890s during his association with the Symbolist school. *Pelléas and Mélisande* (1892) is considered perhaps the greatest Symbolist drama.

PELLÉAS AND MÉLISANDE

On the surface *Pelléas and Mélisande* is the melodramatic story of a young wife who falls in love with her husband's younger brother. The husband kills his brother and the young wife dies of grief. This simple story of awakening love and its consequences holds the play together, but it is the ideas and feelings behind this façade which are of most importance to Maeterlinck.

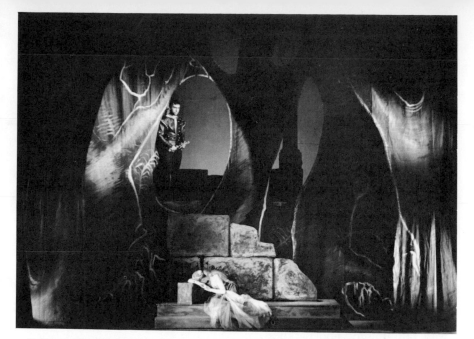

Pelléas and Mélisande at the Belgian National Theatre. Photograph—Carl Hensler. Courtesy Hensler, Brussels.

Fate, a sense of presentiment, and an air of mystery dominate each scene. The characters are somewhat like puppets, for they do not understand their own actions and the causes which lie behind them. The backgrounds of these characters are never filled in, the time and place of the action is left unspecified, and events do not occur in terms of cause and effect. Instead of realistic and logical action growing out of character and situation, the play depicts a fairy-tale world in which inexplicable forces control human destinies.

Maeterlinck suggests that life is a mystery, both in terms of its meaning and of the forces which control it. He does not state his ideas directly but uses recurring motifs and symbols to imply them. Because the ideas are only suggested, it is impossible to isolate them with any definiteness. Nevertheless, some of the more obvious symbols can be examined. Those which recur most often are water, light and darkness, height and depth.

Water plays a part in almost every scene. Mélisande is first discovered by a pool; she and Pelléas play by a fountain into which she loses her wedding ring; later Pelléas and Mélisande declare their love for each other and Pelléas is killed by the same fountain; they search for her ring in a grotto, which must be approached by a narrow path between two lakes; Pelléas and Golaud find bottomless pits filled with water under the castle; the sea is spoken of in almost every scene; and the women try to wash away the stains on the threshold of the castle with water.

In each scene some important use is also made of light or darkness. The forests surrounding the castle produce darkness, and light may be seen only by looking toward the sea; characters sit in darkness or try to find a pool of light; lamps refuse to stay lighted.

Other ideas or feelings are suggested through the use of low and high places. Mélisande sits in a tower; Pelléas and Golaud penetrate into the bowels of the castle to investigate the stench which arises; soaring towers and bottomless pits appear in almost every scene.

It is impossible to assign a definite meaning to each of these motifs or symbols. Rather, the play must be read in terms of the connotations suggested by the context in which the symbols occur. The sea, for example, seems to suggest the only avenue of escape, while the forest is constantly encroaching on the castle. The sea is also associated with light, while the forest is always spoken of in terms of darkness. Light is used to suggest frankness, the known truth, lightheartedness, and happiness. Darkness on the other hand implies secrets, the unknown, untruths, and unexpressed thoughts and fears. Love, happiness, and light struggle throughout the play with fate, misery, and darkness.

Pools of water are used to suggest many different things. The characters try to see the bottom of pools of water, just as they try to peer into the depths of each other's eyes and souls; in neither case can they ever penetrate the mystery. A fountain is also used to indicate the difference between Mélisande's feelings for Golaud and for Pelléas: Golaud has discovered her by a fountain in a dark forest; Mélisande comes to Pelléas by a fountain in an open park and in full moonlight.

Behind all the happenings, however, there is a sense of mystery and fate. Love comes to Pelléas and Mélisande against their wills, just as the sheep are led to slaughter against theirs; doors will not stay open and lamps will not stay lighted in rooms when Pelléas and Mélisande are alone. They are led by forces greater than themselves.

The powers of love and light are pitted against those of fate and darkness. At the end of the play both the enigma of the human soul and the meaning of life remain as mysterious as when the play began. Arkël, speaking of Mélisande and her baby, makes it clear that this mystery is the essence of life and will continue to be so.

> 'Twas a little being, so quiet, so fearful, and so silent. . . . 'Twas a poor little mysterious being, like everybody. . . . I shall never understand it at all. . . . Come; the child must not stay here in this room. . . . She must live now in her place. . . . It is the poor little one's turn.

Maeterlinck, thus, while rebelling against the outlook of the Realists and Naturalists, is as deterministic as any of his opponents. His characters are at the mercy of forces just as destructive and far more mysterious than those of heredity and environment. In many ways, Materlinck's world is more frightening than that of Zola, for it is unknowable and beyond human control.

PLOT AND STRUCTURE. *Pelléas and Mélisande* has sometimes been termed *Shakespearean* because of its free use of time and place and its lack of specificity about the details of background. These surface similarities, however, almost exhaust the likenesses between Maeterlinck and Shakespeare, for Shakespeare always told a coherent story in thoroughly understandable terms, while Maeterlinck merely uses a story as a means for suggesting intuitions about life and the soul.

Although *Pelléas and Mélisande* on the surface is constructed around a love story, its content and organization is determined ultimately by its themes and ideas. Many scenes are only loosely connected with the main story line. For example, the opening scene in which the women try to wash the stains from the castle steps sets a mood of mystery and hopelessness, but has nothing to do with the story's action. Likewise, such scenes as that in which the sheep are led to slaughter are extraneous to the main plot. The mood and theme, therefore, are as important in determining the play's structure as is the action.

Furthermore, the number of scenes between the first meeting of Pelléas and Mélisande and their deaths could be expanded or contracted without seriously affecting the story. Awakening love is suggested early, but its existence is denied until the moment before Pelléas is killed. Thus, while all the scenes are connected, they do not develop through a clear chain of cause and effect.

Although Maeterlinck has used the five-act form, his act divisions are entirely arbitrary since they do not mark any important break in the action or any point of high suspense. The individual scene is the major structural unit, for each is used to suggest one aspect of the theme.

Premonition is used to build and maintain suspense. There is a continual hint of a mystery behind the events which may be revealed. The characters seem to be led on inevitably toward some important discovery which is never forthcoming. They meet death but they are not enlightened about the mystery of existence. Even the audience is led only to the conclusion that life is mysterious and will remain so.

CHARACTERS AND ACTING. The characters are almost as vague as the ideas. They yearn, they love, and they die without knowing why.

All of the main characters are of the ruling class, but this fact has little effect upon their personalities or the action of the play. Their ages and physical appearance are also of little importance: Arkël is an old man; Genevieve is his daughter and the mother of Golaud and Pelléas; Golaud's hair is beginning to turn gray; Yniold is a child; it is implied that both

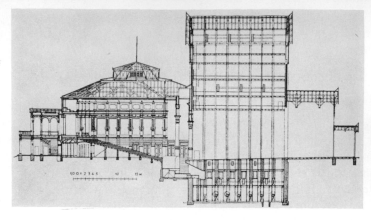

Left. A cross section of Wagner's theatre at Bayreuth, which opened in 1876. From Sachs' *Modern Opera Houses and Theatres.* London, 1896–98. *Right.* The stage and auditorium. Note the absence of a center aisle or side boxes; deeply raked auditorium, double proscenium. From Barkhin's *Architectura Teatra.* Moscow, 1947.

Pelléas and Mélisande are young and attractive. All of this information is pertinent, but it is slight in detail.

The psychological attributes are left vague as well. Arkël is compassionate and constantly attempts to see into the depths of being. Genevieve wants everyone to be happy. Golaud is a hunter, a man of action who loves quickly and steadfastly; he has a deep sense of honor which drives him to kill Pelléas. Neither Pelléas nor Mélisande performs any positive action or displays any positive psychological traits prior to the scene in which Pelléas dies. Until that time they sigh, they resist love and preserve a sense of propriety. None of the characters fully understands his own motivations, and each is driven by forces stronger than himself.

Maeterlinck, therefore, is not interested in portraying lifelike characters, but rather is attempting to suggest states of feeling which come upon characters mysteriously and which lead to mysterious consequences. His concept is further illustrated by the original production of the play in Paris in 1893. The actors chanted their lines and used unnatural gestures to emphasize the gulf between everyday occurrences and the world explored in the play. It is not the texture of daily living which is important, therefore, but the realm of the spirit which lies beyond the physical facts of existence.

VISUAL AND AURAL EFFECTS. The language of *Pelléas and Mélisande* is extremely simple. Its simplicity and repetitiveness suggests a beginner's textbook in reading. But this repetitiveness helps to emphasize the recurring motifs, and the simplicity is designed to prevent too much interest in surface reality. The very lack of complexity suggests that the audience needs to seek penetratingly for the play's significance.

The quality of unreality was made clear in the original production through a number of devices. All stage lighting came from directly overhead and was kept very low in intensity. A gauze curtain was hung at the front of the stage so that the entire action seemed to be occurring in a mist. The scenery was painted in grayed tones to emphasize the effect of distance and mistiness. The actors wore costumes modeled on the paintings of Memling which would locate the action in the fifteenth century. These stage devices were further emphasized by a sing-song delivery of lines and

the use of unnatural gestures. The entire production was designed to re-move the action from the physical world of everyday life; it was as unlike the productions of the Realists as possible.

Pelléas and Mélisande, thus, was not concerned with those con-temporary problems which excited the Realists, and it did not attempt to render truth through a depiction of the external details of daily life. Rather, it wished to deal with such universal but vague ideas as love, life, and death, and to suggest perceptions and intuitions through symbols and motifs. Symbolism took as its sphere of interest the spirit of man and consequently had to resort to means quite different from those of the Realists.

Perhaps because of its lack of concreteness, symbolism was able to appeal only to a limited audience. It produced extremely few plays of lasting interest and its ultimate importance lies in its influence on other approaches to writing and staging.

THE SYMBOLIST THEATRE

The revolts against realism also produced new attitudes toward the theatre, and when symbolism became important new ideas on staging soon fol-lowed. The Symbolists drew their principal inspiration in staging from the work of Richard Wagner (1813–83). Wagner is remembered today pri-marily as an operatic composer, but in his lifetime he dedicated himself to the fusion of all the arts into a master art work: music drama. He was opposed to realism and argued that music is necessary in drama so as to "distance" it from actual life. Furthermore, according to Wagner, music offers a means whereby the dramatist–composer can control the perform-ance of the actor–singer, for the music can dictate the pitch, duration, and tempo of the words. Since this master-artist also should specify the scenery, costumes, lighting, and all other theatrical elements, a unified production was foreseen.

Wagner believed that the greatest truths are not subject to the kind of analysis and observation advocated by realism, and that art can communicate the ultimate truth only by freeing man from all conventions. He, therefore, used a double proscenium, a curtain of steam, and a darkened auditorium to increase what he called the "mystic chasm" between the spectators and the stage. He wished to lift the audience out of its humdrum daily existence through an idealized drama "dipped in the magic fountain of music."

While Wagner stood for many of the same ideals as did Saxe-Meiningen, the latter had attempted to make all plays as "real" as possible. Wagner, on the other hand, wished to increase the distance between reality and art, so as to make the audience aware of those higher values which he thought lay beyond those envisaged by the Realists. It was only natural, therefore, that the Symbolists found inspiration in Wagner's ideas.

The Symbolists encountered many of the same difficulties in getting their plays performed as the Realists and Naturalists had. The established theatres were not interested in such unusual works and the Symbolists, like the Realists and Naturalists, finally had to resort to the establishment of independent theatres.

The first of these was the Théâtre d'Art, founded by Paul Fort in 1890, which was succeeded by the Théâtre de l'Oeuvre. The latter opened in 1892 under the direction of Aurélien-Marie Lugné-Poë (1869–1940) with the premiere of *Pelléas and Mélisande*. The Théâtre de l'Oeuvre did not confine its interests to Symbolist drama, though it is chiefly remembered for its work with such nonrealistic plays. It survived until 1929 and introduced many new and important writers to the French public.

Lugné-Poë called his theatre the l'Oeuvre to indicate his desire to make the theatre a work of art. He did not wish to create an illusion of reality, but only to suggest a background and to provide a mood in which the spoken word could create its own environment.

The Symbolists in general believed that scenery should be confined to draperies or undefined forms which give the impression of infinite space and time. Any historical detail serves only to limit the play to a specific time and place rather than to extend it and to suggest universal qualities. Decor should be confined to elements which create an over-all impression and should emphasize the ideas and feelings of the play without attracting attention to itself.

Similarly, costumes should be simple, draped garments of no particular period or place, and should use colors suggestive of the play's mood. The Symbolists, thus, advocated a simplicity of setting and costume which would attract as little attention to the physical elements of production as

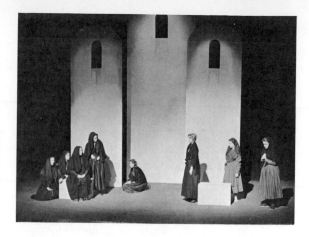

Federico Garcia Lorca (1899–1936) shows the influence of symbolism in such plays as *Blood Wedding* (1933), a scene from which is shown here. Directed by Ronald Gee; setting by Joe Zender.

possible. Everything should be designed to concentrate attention upon the words of the playwright.

APPIA AND CRAIG

Although not of the Symbolist school, two major theatre theorists, Adolphe Appia (1862–1928) and Gordon Craig (1872–   ), were clearly in the tradition of Wagner and the Symbolists.

Appia set out to embody Wagner's ideas, and his efforts led to many of the accepted ideals of theatrical production in the twentieth century. He began with the notion that artistic unity is the fundamental demand, but he found that this demand is difficult to achieve because of the diverse elements involved: the moving actor, the horizontal floor, and perpendicular scenery. He eventually concluded that light and music are the means whereby the various elements can be fused into a unified work of art.

The unity Appia sought, however, demanded many changes in existing approaches to theatrical production. He rejected scenery with painted details and called for three-dimensional pieces as the only environment in which the three-dimensional actor might properly move without destroying unity. To reveal the shape and three-dimensionality of the scenery and the actor, light which comes from various angles and directions is required, and must be capable of changing as action and mood change. This constantly changing light fuses the various elements into a unified whole, for it reveals and reflects shifting emotions, shapes, and moods. Light becomes the visual equivalent of music, which welds the elements together aurally just as light does visually.

Appia advocated an approach to stage production which begins by finding the essential qualities in a script and then searches for the means whereby these qualities may be embodied in theatrical terms. Since the aim is an interpretation of the script, and since a unified and artistic performance must always be sought, the entire production must be seen through the eyes of one person. This controlling artist is the director. Appia, thus, re-enforced the trend toward a theatre under the control of a

director, while suggesting new approaches to the entire art of stage production.

Although few of Appia's stage designs were ever executed, his ideas
were made available through a number of books and sketches. His designs
are simple, all unnecessary details having been removed. The emphasis is
upon the mood, light, mass, and line which interpret the essential character of a scene. His ideas and his examples have exerted a continuing influence on modern staging.

Craig believed in many of the same ideas which Appia had set forth,
but he was much more militant in his statements and did a great deal
more to popularize these ideas. Craig had little interest in plays, as such.
He was more concerned with the theatrical product which is created by
the "super theatre artist," who blends action, words, line, color, and
rhythm into a work of which the play is only a part. Everything must be
seen through the eyes of the master artist and everything must be made
to conform to his vision. For this reason, Craig once suggested that the
actor should be replaced by the marionette, since the marionette cannot
inject its own personality into the work and thereby ruin the director's
over-all conception.

Craig was opposed to realistic drama, which he called "the theatre
of sermons and epigrams." He wanted an artistic product which would
appeal directly to the senses and which would transform the theatre into
"a place for visions."

Craig, like Appia, stood for extreme simplicity in scenery, costume,
and lighting, and depended upon line, mass, and color for his effects rather
than on historical accuracy or detailed ornamentation. Also like Appia, he
helped to strengthen the demand for the director as the supreme theatre
artist.

Craig realized that his work would not find immediate acceptance
in the commercial theatre and sought for places in which he might experiment. He established a school in Florence, Italy in 1913, but his work
there was interrupted by World War I. He also propagandized for his
ideas through his magazine, *The Mask*. As with Appia, few of Craig's scene
designs were ever carried to completion, but his writing inspired many
theatre workers and has had untold influence on the modern stage.

The continuing influence of the Symbolists and of Appia and Craig
may be seen in the desire for a simple decor appropriate to the mood of a
play (as opposed to the demand by the Realists for a background based on
everyday life). Their ideas merged with those of Reinhardt to re-enforce
the eclectic approach to theatrical production and to elevate the director
to the position of supreme artist in the theatre.

Although symbolism as a conscious movement was largely over by
1900, it continued to exert important pressures on drama and the theatre.
Its primary significance probably rests in its belief that art should function

through implication and suggestion rather than through direct statement. This belief has permeated all of modern art.

Even realism in the twentieth century has become less insistent upon the need to be explicit about all environmental factors and has come to rely in part upon suggestion and imagination. The influence of symbolism has also been increased by the wider acceptance of Freudian psychology, which emphasizes an interior psychological realism. Since Freud demonstrated that the human mind frequently substitutes one experience or object for another, the symbol has achieved considerable use even for the realistic depiction of states of mind and feelings.

As will be seen, the methods of symbolism have also been utilized by other revolts against realism. Thus, while symbolism as an organized movement has ceased to exist, its influence has continued in much of twentieth-century art.

EXPRESSIONISM

The most important revolt against realism in the early twentieth century was called "expressionism." Although expressionistic elements may be found in earlier art, as a movement expressionism emerged in Germany around 1910. The name was first applied to the paintings of a group which modeled their work on that of Van Gogh and Gauguin. Soon, however, the term was applied to other art forms. The first successful use of expressionism on the stage came with Walter Hasenclever's *The Son* in 1914. The movement reached its peak of popularity during World War I, and disintegrated under the impact of the disillusionment which followed. As a conscious movement it was over by 1925.

The term *expressionism* designates the central aim of the move-

Craig's setting for *Hamlet* at the Moscow Art Theatre in 1911. From *Moscow Art Theatre, 1898–1917.*

ment's members: to express a personal vision of reality. The Expressionists assumed that Nature is anthropomorphic (that is, they ascribed human characteristics to Nature) and they portrayed it in such a way as to suggest human feelings, ideas, or perceptions. Thus, the Expressionist was not concerned with reproducing external appearances, but rather sought to interpret all objects, actions, and experiences in strictly human terms. The dramatist expressed his vision of happenings, no matter how personal and subjective that view might be.

Truth for the Expressionist, therefore, is to be sought in the personal vision of life. Unlike the Realist who seeks truth in the observation of external facts, the Expressionist seeks truth within the human mind. What the human mind finds to be true, therefore, may not be in accord with objective appearance at all, and may even contradict the Realist's conception of truth.

Since the author must embody this interior truth, he seeks for means which are capable of adequately expressing his vision. He may distort the normal appearance of objects, he may use disconnected and telegraphic speech, he may call for actors to use mechanical movement, or he may use symbols. Any device which aids the playwright in expressing his view may be used, for the Expressionist is not bound to an attempt to create the illusion of daily life.

The Expressionists ultimately divided into two camps—the Activists and the Mystics. The latter group was content to express its views of man and its states of feeling, but the former sought to transform man and society through a program of action. It was the Activists who were of principal importance in the theatre, and the discussion which follows deals primarily with the work of this group.

Man is always the center of the Expressionist's interest. He is seen as being capable of nobility and as a creature who strives for greatness. But industrialism and science have kept man's eyes on the ground and have reduced him to a machinelike creature through the ideals of mass production and conformity of behavior. Furthermore, the Expressionist argued, realism accepts the machinelike state as ultimate reality and seeks to understand man through a study of these external factors. On the other hand, the Expressionist wished to begin by understanding man's soul or spirit and then to transform society so that man's greatness might be fully realized. Society and all external phenomena must be viewed from the standpoint of man's soul, therefore, rather than the soul being interpreted from the evidence of external reality.

The Expressionists saw the world in which they lived as having been distorted by inhuman forces. Sometimes they argued that man's soul itself has been distorted by these forces. They tended to employ two approaches in their depiction of man's plight. First, much of the drama concentrates upon the negative aspects of the present. It attempts to show how current

A scene from Strindberg's *The Dream Play*. Directed by Philip Benson; setting by Thad Torp; lighting by David Thayer.

ideals have distorted man's spirit and have made him into a machine through false values. Second, a smaller proportion of the drama looks forward to the transformation of society and to a time when harmony between man's environment and his spirit can be achieved. Expressionist drama, then, usually either aims at making the audience aware of the present's shortcomings, or suggests a program for accomplishing a more perfect future.

EXPRESSIONISTIC DRAMATISTS

One of the major influences on Expressionist drama is the work of August Strindberg (1849–1912), the first Swedish playwright to achieve international fame and one of the major dramatists of the modern world. Strindberg wrote over fifty plays, in addition to novels and nonfictional works. Up to about 1895 his writing belongs to the realistic school, and his plays *The Father* (1887) and *Miss Julie* (1888) are among the best works of the time.

Personal crises drove him to the edge of insanity, however, and as a result his outlook on life and art underwent profound changes. In the late 1890s he began to write a number of plays which may be considered to be the forerunners of expressionism. These include *The Dream Play* (1902) and *The Spook Sonata* (1907). In his Preface to *The Dream Play* Strindberg says:

> The author has tried to imitate the disconnected but seemingly logical form of the dream. Anything may happen; everything is possible and probable. Time and space do not exist. On an insignificant background of reality, imagination designs and embroiders novel patterns: a medley of memories, experiences, free fancies, absurdities and improvisations.

In other words, in *The Dream Play* Strindberg tries to destroy the limitations of time, place, and logical sequence by adopting the viewpoint of the dream. One event flows into another without any logical explanation, characters dissolve or are transformed into other characters, and widely separated places and times blend together. It is this dramatic method which many of the Expressionists adopted.

The most widely known Expressionist playwrights are Ernst Toller (1893–1939) and Georg Kaiser (1878–1945). Toller's first play, *Transfiguration* (1918), written while he was in prison as a pacifist, is an antiwar drama. Among his later works the most important are *Man and the Masses* (1921) and *The Machine Wreckers* (1922). *Man and the Masses* shows how the machine and factories have come to dominate men's lives. Toller realizes that the machine is here to stay, but argues that the soul of man must conquer the factories so that the machine may become the servant of man rather than man being reduced to the role of servant to the machine.

More importantly, however, *Man and the Masses* shows a heroine, who stands for the Expressionistic ideals, betrayed by the mass of workers, who are not yet ready for the new vision. It points out the great gap between the ideal and actuality, and between the Expressionists and the great mass of workers, whose lives the Expressionists hoped to transform. But while the play is pessimistic in its outcome, it still looks forward hopefully to the day when the masses will be ready for a better life.

Kaiser began writing in 1911, but his early work is principally satirical and without any strong conviction. World War I, however, made him question the whole foundation of a society which could indulge in such acts of destruction. In the process of this questioning he wrote some of the most powerful of Expressionistic plays.

His best-known works are *From Morn to Midnight, Gas I* (1918), and *Gas II* (1920). In *Gas I* the Expressionist view is seen in much the same light as that in Toller's *Man and the Masses* (it is defeated, but hope for the future is expressed). By the time he wrote *Gas II*, however, Kaiser had abandoned his belief in the ideal and predicted man's ultimate destruction.

From Morn to Midnight will be examined in more detail as an example of Expressionistic drama. It was written in 1912, published in 1916, and was first produced in Munich in 1917.

FROM MORN TO MIDNIGHT

Ashley Dukes subtitled his translation of *From Morn to Midnight* "A Modern Mystery in Seven Scenes." While this designation was not made by Kaiser, it suggests something of importance about the play through its implied comparison with Medieval drama. Other writers have re-enforced this comparison by stating that the play shows the "stations of martyrdom" in the life of modern man. The play's central character, the Cashier, may be viewed, then, as an Everyman of the modern world, and the time span of the action, from morn to midnight, suggests the span of human life.

The play is also related to *Faust,* since both are concerned with man's search for meaning and fulfillment. Like Faust, the Cashier ultimately finds an answer, but unlike Faust, he becomes a martyr to the debasement of modern man.

From Morn to Midnight shows man reduced to a machinelike existence, devoid of any purpose except material gain. The Cashier is jarred out of this pattern by the exotic and sensual appeal of the Lady from Italy. He realizes for the first time that he has been buried alive and sets out to live life to its fullest. Along the way he makes several stops: one involving home and family, another symbolic of society and the state (the race track scene), another showing personal and sensual pleasure, and finally one involving religion. He ultimately recognizes the rightness of the soul's claims, but the debasement of the masses is such that they are not ready for his answer and he dies a martyr.

While the ending is pessimistic, it suggests that since "the new man" has emerged in the Cashier, it might also emerge in the masses. Were this to occur, a rebirth of society would ensue.

PLOT AND STRUCTURE. The seven scenes of *From Morn to Midnight* are held together by the presence of the Cashier in each and through his search for fulfillment. Everything is focused upon the experience of the central character. As in *Faust,* the areas of experience into which the Cashier searches for fulfillment are entirely arbitrary, for the number and order might easily have been quite different. The sequence and the choice are never explained in the play. The unity, therefore, is not to be found in a causally related action, but must be sought in the play's theme and in the Cashier as the focus of events.

The first two scenes are primarily preparatory and expository. Scene 1 establishes the dehumanizing effects of materialism and demonstrates the values of the society out of which the play's events grow. The bank is the embodiment of materialism, since money is both a symbol and a goal of materialism. The Stout Gentleman and the Bank Manager, representatives of the established order, are convinced that money can buy everything and is the answer to all of man's problems.

The result of such values on the common man is seen in the Cashier. He has no lines until the end of the first scene, for the playwright wishes to show the Cashier's machinelike qualities: he raps when he wants attention, he takes in and pays out money like an automaton, he

The race track scene in *From Morn to Midnight* at Cornell University. Directed by Darkes Albright.

enters sums in a book mechanically. For all practical purposes he has become a soulless machine.

But this routine of existence is broken by the appearance of the Lady from Italy. Her strangeness jars him out of his machinelike state and in his desire to possess her he responds as his society has conditioned him to act—since money is the key to success, he steals an amount which should be sufficient to accomplish any aim.

Scene 2 shows that the Cashier's simple view of the road to happiness is in error. The Lady is respectable, and the Cashier has irrevocably lost his old place in society.

Scene 3 marks the major transition between the old life and the new. The Cashier cannot go back and, therefore, he must decide what is to be done in the future. For the first time he realizes the emptiness of the past: "With my own hands I have accomplished nothingness." He adds, however: "But I am inquisitive. My appetite is whetted. My curiosity is hugely swollen. I feel that great discoveries lie before me." Although he determines to explore life, he still believes that his stolen money will be the key to success.

Scene 3 also prepares for all those which are to follow, for it is out of his decision to search for the meaning of life that each of the succeeding scenes grows. The scheme of the play is seen further in the appearance of Death. The Cashier declines Death's invitation to go with him by saying, "Ring me up again toward midnight," and, "I see stretching ahead of me a host of calls to pay before this evening." In the scenes which follow, the Cashier pays his "host of calls" and then at midnight re-encounters Death.

Although Scene 4 marks the first of the Cashier's "calls," it is still related to the past since it involves his own home and family. These institutions, which might logically contain an answer to man's search for happiness, are shown to have been as completely mechanized as the bank. All activity, even sentiment, has been thoroughly standardized. The Cashier's decision to leave the house before he eats dinner marks such a disruption of order that his mother dies. It is not surprising then that the Cashier decides that the home "is not a halting-place, but a signpost; the road leads farther on."

Scene 5 shows the Cashier's attempt to find meaning through the political and social structure of society, which are symbolized in the race track. Here the people assemble to watch the contestants, who, no matter how tired they may be, race whenever a monetary prize is offered; the higher the prize the more exciting the race becomes. All eyes in the stadium (except those of the Cashier) are on the races and the winning of prizes. Again, therefore, the race symbolizes the materialistic drive for monetary gain.

The stadium, however, is also segmented in terms of the social classes. "The frothing is least at the bottom, among the well-bred public in the stalls. There you see nothing but looks—but what looks! Round stares. Eyes of cattle!—One row higher the bodies sway and vibrate, the limbs begin to dance. A few cries are heard. Your respectable middle class! Higher still all veils are dropped. A wild fanatic shout, a bellowing nakedness, a gallery of passion!" The Cashier sets out to break down all the barriers of class and feeling by offering the highest prizes ever heard of. "Gates and barriers vanish in smoke. The trumpets blare and the walls come tumbling down. No restraint, no modesty, no motherhood, no childhood—nothing but passion! There's the real thing. That's worth the search. That justifies the price!"

At this stage in his search, thus, the Cashier is attempting to break down class barriers and to achieve a universal brotherhood of man. He is trying to induce the fullest expression of emotion, which he thinks will bring freedom from the regimentation of society. But just as the Cashier is about to succeed, the Emperor arrives and all the spectators are reduced again to their former regimented responses. The Cashier has still been using the lure of money as the principal means to find happiness. He has not yet been able to rid himself of the values of his society.

Scene 6 explores the search for happiness through sensual pleasures. The most exotic foods and the suggestion of a sexual orgy are used as representatives of this goal. This road, too, proves to lead nowhere. When the Cashier lifts the mask of one of the women she is so ugly that he is repulsed, and another proves to have a wooden leg. The anticipated joys of the flesh turn into disgust and the Cashier rushes out. Kaiser emphasizes the emptiness and soullessness of material pleasure through the complete selfishness of the frequenters of the cabaret. They steal the money left by the Cashier for a poor and tubercular waiter, who must, then, pay the bill himself.

Scene 7 brings the Cashier to the end of his journey, as he searches for fulfillment in religion. He has been brought to a Salvation Army hall by the same Salvation Lass who has appeared fleetingly in Scenes 5 and 6, in both of which she has gone about her business as mechanically as the Cashier did in Scene 1. It is not surprising, therefore, that she too turns out to be as corrupt as the rest of society.

The Cashier has come to the Salvation Army hall because he has lost all sense of purpose. In the meeting which follows the testimonials of repentant sinners sum up the Cashier's experiences in the play and each makes the Cashier see himself more clearly.

Finally he realizes that the call of the soul is the true road to happiness. But when he repents of his past and scatters his absconded money about him, the total materialism of society is reconfirmed. The supposedly repentant sinners become beasts striving to tear the money from each other. Only the Salvation Army Lass does not enter the fight, and the Cashier thinks that he has found his true mate. She is merely more cunning than the others, however, for she turns him over to the police for the reward.

In the darkness of the hall a tangle of wires outlines the skeleton of Death, whom the Cashier had eluded in Scene 3. "From morning to midnight I run raging in a circle—and now your beckoning arm shows me the way—whither?" He dies with his arms outstretched on the Cross and his dying sigh echoes words associated with Christ, *Ecce Homo* (Behold the Man). The lamps explode, and the Policeman says, "There must be a short circuit in the main"—a remark which the audience should interpret as referring to society.

Although the Cashier has seen the way to truth, the people (as in the history of Jesus) are blind to his values and prefer materialism to his spiritualism. He has changed nothing, but he has shown the way. Kaiser expected his audience to see the difference between two sets of values, and to prefer those of the Cashier.

CHARACTERS AND ACTING. Each of the characters in *From Morn to Midnight* is given only a social designation or "type" name. Each is intended to embody the characteristics of a group rather than an individual. The speeches of most of the characters are made up of a series of clichés and they perform only stereotyped actions. This machinelike quality is essential to Kaiser's attitude toward modern life, and it must be reflected in the acting.

Only the Cashier (beginning in Scene 3) and the Lady escape from this pattern. The Lady is from another world and it is her unusualness which jars the Cashier out of the mold into which his life has been forced.

The burden of the play falls on the Cashier. He is the only truly articulate character and the only one who is able to escape from that machinelike existence which dominates the lives of the others. His speech and action must undergo a change beginning in Scene 3, therefore, and they must contrast with that of the other characters. He should grow in humanity and strength as his search comes nearer and nearer to fulfillment. Only if his role is made to seem sympathetic and his search superior can Kaiser's intentions be realized. A mechanical quality must be worked for in all characters except the Lady and the Cashier. On the other hand, however, the Cashier must be made to seem universal for he represents mankind in its search to escape the stultifying results of modern life.

VISUAL AND AURAL FACTORS. The mechanical qualities of action and speech must be reflected in the scenery, lighting, and costumes, and each of these must represent modern life in its most stereotyped form. Scene 3 offers one of the best clues for the proper approach to the visual elements of the play. In that scene a tree turns into a skeleton and then reassumes its normal appearance. The visual elements, therefore, are intended to express the Cashier's (or the playwright's) vision of reality, rather than to reflect the everyday appearance of objects.

In their efforts to find visual counterparts for a play's actions and characters, the Expressionists frequently used scenery composed of fragments rather than full-stage sets. The scenic elements might have jagged lines, the walls might tilt or lean, unnatural color might be used; details might be enlarged or diminished in size to emphasize the relative importance of each to the play's ideas. Reality, then, was distorted to make the usual elements expressive of feelings and ideas.

A scene from Elmer Rice's *The Adding Machine*. Directed by Gregory Foley.

Costumes, lighting, and stage properties were treated in similar fashion. Many characters might be dressed identically so as to emphasize the uniformity of modern man. (See, for example, the treatment of the Jewish Gentlemen in the race track scene of *From Morn to Midnight*.) Unnatural colors in lighting might be used to point up the distortion of human values in the script.

From Morn to Midnight attempts to express the playwright's personal vision of the plight of modern man: the mechanization of feelings and activities and the denial of the human spirit. It demonstrates the horrifying results and suggests a way out of the dilemma. As with much modern art, *From Morn to Midnight* requires a special intellectual effort for comprehension. Once the scheme is apprehended, however, the play is a simple one aimed at achieving complete universality. Today it seems oversimplified in its analysis of human ills and in its recommendations for a better future.

THE DECLINE AND LATER INFLUENCE OF EXPRESSIONISM

Expressionism reached the height of its popularity during and immediately following World War I. Its desire to transform the world into a place where man's highest spiritual potential might be realized appealed to many persons. But the high hopes which reigned at the close of the war were soon dissipated by the wranglings over peace settlements and by other factors which seemed to prove man's basic selfishness and urge for destruction. The foundations of expressionism were gradually undermined and the movement had ceased to be productive by 1925.

Although primarily a German movement, expressionism exerted considerable influence elsewhere. American dramas which show indebtedness to this movement include: Elmer Rice's *The Adding Machine*, Eugene O'Neill's *The Hairy Ape* and *The Great God Brown*, and Marc

O'Neill experimented a number of times with expressionistic techniques. Here is a scene from his *The Hairy Ape*, which was influenced by expressionism. Directed by A. Dale Riley

A scene from André Gide's and Jean-Louis Barrault's adaptation of Franz Kafka's novel, *The Trial*. This play shows many characteristics of expressionism. A Stanford University production. Directed by F. Cowles Strickland; settings by Wendell Cole; costumes by Lenyth Brockett.

Connelly and George Kaufman's *Beggar on Horseback*, all of which were written in the 1920s.

The later influence of expressionism is to be seen largely in a freer treatment of the visual elements of stage production, in the introduction of dream sequences into otherwise realistic plays, and in similar devices. Its dramatic techniques and its approaches to staging have been absorbed into the general eclecticism of the twentieth-century theatre.

THE THEATRE OF SOCIAL ACTION

Although the Expressionist movement came to an end, its intention of revolutionizing society did not. New theatrical outlooks emerged which combined features of both naturalism and expressionism.

Naturalism had recorded the externals of environment as faithfully as possible since it believed that these factors determined character and action. Its plans for social reform, therefore, looked forward to a transformation and control of environmental factors as a key to desired changes in society and the individual.

Expressionism, on the other hand, believed that a recording of the externals of existence only prevented man from perceiving the deeper reality which lay embedded in the human soul. It distorted external reality, therefore, in order to reveal an inner reality. The Expressionists looked forward to social reform which would come from desires generated within man. Any change in society would need to stem from a prior change in man's conception of himself and the possibilities of the human spirit.

Thus, while both Naturalists and Expressionists desired change, they disagreed about the sources and the methods for bringing it about. But the twentieth century brought another trend which lay somewhere between the two and shared ideas common to both. There is no generally accepted name for this movement as a whole, but, for the sake of convenience, here it will be called the "Theatre of Social Action." It has been most thoroughly exploited in Soviet Russia, but has also been developed elsewhere, most notably in the "Epic Theatre" of Bertolt Brecht which will be discussed in detail later.

The Theatre of Social Action typically has accepted the idea that man's actions are in large part determined by economic and political forces. It has abandoned the Expressionists' mystical belief in the human soul while retaining their faith in the possibilities of human greatness. Like the Expressionists also, it has tended to work for reforms by seeking to move the individual to a realization of the need for change and the desire to work for change.

Although the Theatre of Social Action has seen itself as being "realistic and down-to-earth," it has abandoned the Naturalists' demand for objectivity and the faithful recording of reality. It has adopted a partisan view of its subject matter and has used many of the theatrical devices associated with expressionism—such as fragmentary scenery and the distortion of visual elements. It seeks to entertain, to teach and, most of all, to move the spectator to practical action outside the theatre. Thus, while the movement has viewed society in much the same light as the Naturalists, it has sought to depict reality and to work for its transformation through many of the same means used by the Expressionists.

THE RUSSIAN THEATRE AND MEYERHOLD

The most obvious attempt at using the theatre to transform society was that of Soviet Russia after the Revolution of 1917. The theatres, which had been frequented principally by the privileged classes, were thrown open to the workers, many of whom had never attended a theatre before. To reach the new audience and to use the theatre as an instrument for the Revolution, many argued that new methods were needed. Consequently,

Opposite page. Design for a Constructivist setting used by Meyerhold. *Above.* A scene from the same production.

a number of experiments were undertaken to meet the needs of a "people's theatre."

Much of the so-called "new" theatre was merely melodrama in which the forces opposed to the Revolution were depicted as villains and in which the Communists were shown to be heroes. This type of drama still dominates the Russian stage and is called "socialist realism." Many of the older theatre workers, such as Stanislavsky, attempted to meet the needs of the new audiences by making the plays as intensely real as possible. Stanislavsky's methods eventually triumphed and have had the official support of the Soviet regime since the 1930s.

On the other hand, there were many who felt that the revolution in political and economic matters demanded a similar revolution in the theatre. The most extreme and influential exponent of this view was Vsevolod Meyerhold (1874–1942). He began his career as an actor in Stanislavsky's company, and in 1905 was put in charge of an experimental group to seek ways of enlarging upon the realistic methods of the Moscow Art Theatre. But Meyerhold was fundamentally opposed to realism and soon left the troupe. Between 1905 and the Revolution he attempted to explore all the possibilities of the theatre as an artistic medium. In many ways his work parallels that which was going on in painting at the time and is analogous to abstract art.

After 1917 Meyerhold tried to adapt his methods to the needs of the Revolution. In the late 1930s he was denounced as being too "formalistic" (that is, as not being sufficiently understandable to the masses and as not being in line with "socialist realism") and was removed from his post as a theatre director. By that time, however, his work had become famous throughout the world and had influenced the theatre in general.

Three concepts are normally associated with Meyerhold: biomechanics, theatricalism, and constructivism. First of all, however, it is necessary to understand that to Meyerhold the director was the only true artist of the theatre. He rewrote or adapted plays to fit his own conceptions, he insisted on absolute obedience to his directions, and he shaped every element of the theatre in accordance with his own ideas. His was entirely a director's theatre.

To facilitate his work, Meyerhold devised a system for training actors which he called "biomechanics." Meyerhold was not interested in portraying psychological realism on the stage, but wanted rather an actor whose body was as efficient as a machine in carrying out the orders of its operator. The actors, therefore, were trained through ballet, gymnastics, and other means until they were capable of responding instantly to the needs of the director. (In performance they were frequently asked to swing from trapezes, to turn somersaults, and to shoot up through trap doors.)

Meyerhold worked to achieve "theatricalism." Instead of striving for the illusion of real life, he wished the audience to remain conscious that it was in the theatre. He believed that, since the theatre is an art, all its means should be used self-consciously and to their fullest capabilities. Consequently, he removed the front curtain from the stage, placed lighting instruments in full view of the audience, used a "gymnastic" approach to acting, juxtaposed many contrasting dramatic elements, and used totally abstract settings called "constructions." Meyerhold never allowed his audiences to confuse the theatre with real life, but sought to comment upon social, political, and economic situations, to stir up thought, and to incite the audience to desirable social action outside the theatre.

Meyerhold's work is sometimes referred to as "constructivistic." The name "constructivism" was first applied to the work of a group of Russian sculptors around 1912. It refers to the completely abstract nature of their products, which did not attempt to represent anything but which were merely "constructions" composed of intersecting planes and masses. Meyerhold adopted many of the ideas of this group, especially in his stage settings which were completely nonrepresentational, being composed of platforms, ramps, trapezes, and other elements designed as a "machine" upon which the actors might perform most efficiently. Ultimately, the stage, the actor, and all theatrical elements were viewed by Meyerhold as a single, complex machine to be used by the director in his interpretation of society. His was a totally dictatorial approach, even though he thought of himself as being in the service of a socialist revolution. And although these methods proved too abstract for most theatregoers, Meyerhold's application of completely nonrealistic means to the treatment of realistic social problems has had continuing effect upon the theatre.

BRECHT AND "EPIC THEATRE"

A more successful attempt to achieve a Theatre of Social Action can be seen in the work of Bertolt Brecht (1898–1956). Brecht began his work in the German theatre at the time when the Expressionists were at the peak of their popularity, and much of his early writing is obviously influenced by that school. He went on to develop his own independent ideas, which continued to mature and change up to the time of his death.

Brecht called his work "epic" theatre to distinguish it from that of the past—the "dramatic" theatre—against which he was in revolt. He thought that the old theatre had outlived its usefulness since it reduced the spectator to a role of complete passivity. In it, according to Brecht, events are presented as fixed and unchangeable, since even historical subjects are treated in present-day terms; this approach encourages the audience to believe that things have always been the same. Realistic staging gives the actions an air of stability which contributes to the idea that society is solidly entrenched and cannot be altered. The spectator, therefore, can only watch in a hypnotized and uncritical way; his senses are lulled, and he cannot participate "productively" in the theatrical event.

In the place of this old theatre Brecht envisioned a new theatre in which the spectator will become a vital part. But to bring about this change both drama and theatrical production must be altered. To describe the desired conditions, Brecht used three key terms: *historification, alienation,* and *epic.*

Unlike the Realists, Brecht thought that the theatre should not treat contemporary subject matter in a lifelike manner. Rather, the theatre should "make strange" the actions it presents. One avenue to strangeness lies in historification. Ordinarily this means using material drawn from other times or places. But unlike the old theatre which handles historical material in today's pattern, Brecht argued that the dramatist should emphasize the "pastness"—the removal of past events from the present. He should attempt to arouse in the spectator the feeling that if he had been living under the conditions shown in the play, he would have taken some positive action. The audience should then go on to see that, since things have changed, it is possible to bring about desirable social changes in the present.

Historification is a part of the larger term *alienation.* (Alienation is not an accurate translation of Brecht's original term, *verfremdung,* but it is the one which has been popularized in America. A more accurate translation would be "to make strange.") In addition to historification, the playwright may use other means for making things strange. He may deliberately call the audience's attention to the make-believe nature of the work (rather than trying to convince the audience of the play's reality).

Songs, narrative passages, filmed sequences, and other devices may be used for this purpose. The audience should never be allowed to confuse what it sees on the stage with reality. Rather the play must always be thought of as a comment upon life which is to be watched and judged critically.

Although Brecht always insisted that the theatre should bring pleasure, he thought the greatest pleasure is to be found in "productive participation," which involves the active judgment of the spectator and his application of what he sees on the stage to conditions outside the theatre. To make him critical and capable of watching productively, the spectator must be "alienated" from the play's events.

Alienation does not mean that the spectator should not become emotionally involved with the characters and the action; if he is to respond as Brecht desired ("If I had lived then I would have done something") emotional response is essential. This emotional response is always part of the larger, critical response, however.

Each element of production was designed to contribute to the "alienation" of the spectator. Brecht did not envision, as have most twentieth-century theorists, a synthesis of all the arts in the theatre, but rather the independence of each. Music, for example, should make a comment upon the action rather than merely underscoring the meaning of the words. For example, in *Mother Courage* the satirically bitter words of a song which tell of the gradual moral degradation of a character are set to a consciously "pretty," light-hearted tune. The contrast between words and music achieves alienation and forces the spectator into a thoughtful consideration of the song's significance.

Likewise, scenery in his plays is not intended to create the illusion of place. It may suggest a locale, but it does not depict it in detail. Brecht advocates the use of projections, fragmentary set pieces, and similar devices for indicating the location of action, but in each case the elements are intended to comment upon the action as well. In his writings Brecht advises the actor to think of his role in the third person. In this way the player avoids trying "to become the character" (as he might under the

A scene from Brecht's *The Caucasian Chalk Circle*. Directed by John Terfloth.

Stanislavsky method) and remains in a position to comment upon the role while presenting it to an audience.

As a further aid in "alienation" Brecht wishes to keep the action "theatrical" by letting the mechanics of the theatre remain visible. He suggests letting the lighting instruments be seen, changing the scenery in view of the audience, and placing the musicians on stage. The theatre, by such devices, is prevented from lulling the audience into a feeling of security and timelessness, and is aided in engaging both the emotions and the judgment of the spectator in such a way as to alert his powers and his sense of responsibility to society.

Brecht calls his theatre "epic" for a number of reasons. First of all, he wishes to distinguish his ideas from those of the traditional, or "dramatic," theatre. Second, he thinks that his theatre resembles the epic poem more than it does the drama of the past. The epic poem is composed of alternating sections of dialogue and narration, and the entire story is presented from the viewpoint of a single storyteller. The epic poem also has almost complete freedom in changing place and time; it tells about some scenes and shows others; it bridges great passages of time with a single sentence or a brief narrative passage; it may easily cover the entire sweep of an historical period. (It is easier to see Brecht's point if such a work as *The Iliad* is kept in mind and contrasted with normal dramatic works.)

As with other forms of Theatre of Social Action, Epic Theatre sees the ultimate effect of drama as occurring outside the theatre. The play stirs up thought and incites the spectator to act for desirable social reforms. In this way it escapes becoming an opiate and assumes a vital and productive role in men's lives.

Many of the approaches to staging used by the Epic Theatre resulted from the work of Erwin Piscator (1893–   ) in Berlin in the 1920s. The most famous of his productions is *The Good Soldier Schweik* (1927), a bitter satire on the German war machine. The experiences of the common soldier, Schweik, are depicted through a swirl of events that cover an enormous number of places and a lengthy stretch of time. Piscator used treadmills, projections, scenic fragments, giant caricature drawings, and many other devices which allowed him to reduce the vast demands of the action to the stage and to comment upon it simultaneously. Like Brecht, Piscator did not intend to be objective in his stage presentations; he wished to comment upon society and to arouse the critical faculties of his audience.

Among Brecht's more important plays are *The Three-Penny Opera*, *The Caucasian Chalk Circle*, *Mother Courage*, *Galileo*, and *Mahagonny*. Another important work, *The Good Woman of Setzuan*, will be examined as representative of Epic Theatre.

THE GOOD WOMAN OF SETZUAN

The Good Woman of Setzuan was written between 1938 and 1940 and was first produced in 1943 in Switzerland. It is a "parable" which has been "historified" by placing it in China, although the time is more or less contemporary with that of its composition.

In this play Brecht is concerned with the possibility of goodness. Shen Te, the heroine, wants and tries to be good, but as she points out:

> *When we extend our hand to a beggar, he tears it off for us*
> *When we help the lost, we are lost ourselves*
> *And so*
> *Since not to eat is to die*
> *Who can long refuse to be bad?*

Two factors have created this situation—society and human nature. It is difficult to know which of these Brecht thinks most responsible. Most of his nonfictional writing suggests that society is the culprit, and that a different economic system (presumably some form of socialism) would remove many of the incentives for immoral behavior which Brecht sees as existing under capitalism. In *The Good Woman of Setzuan* the capitalist class is represented by Shu Fu, Mrs. Mi Tzu, and Shui Ta, who exploit the others. The methods of the class are most graphically illustrated in Shui Ta, the disguise Shen Te takes to preserve herself from the demands of her relatives.

But this is not the whole picture, for the capitalists are no less admirable than the representatives of the working classes. Shen Te's relatives are liars, thieves, and parasites. While they may have been forced into such behavior by social conditions, their vindictiveness and cruelty (for example, the enjoyment they get from seeing the Carpenter deprived of pay for honest work) make them as callous as the others. Ultimately Brecht shows human nature as consistent regardless of social class—all are ready to tear off the hand that is extended in help.

The exceptions are to be seen in Shen Te and Wong, and even here the exception in each is a matter of desire rather than accomplishment. Shen Te wants to be good, but she is eventually driven to take on the disguise of Shui Ta. When Shen Te sins, however, it is out of love for others and not out of self-love.

So much evil set against so little good gives the play a sense of hopelessness, and makes it difficult to believe in the possibility of change outside the theatre (as Brecht would desire). Herein lies one of the basic contradictions in Brecht's work as a whole. He was a moral person who felt deeply man's inhumanity to his fellow creatures and deplored the failure of all men to live in love and harmony; he longed for the fulfillment

A scene from Brecht's *The Good Woman of Setzuan* at the University of Texas. Directed by Francis Hodge; settings by John Rothgeb; costumes by Paul Reinhardt.

of his hopes for a better existence; but, at the same time, his plays imply that such ideals are hopeless because of man's essential selfishness.

Brecht is not entirely pessimistic, however. He never gives up the notion that man is one of the principal determinants of his own fate rather than being determined entirely by his heredity and environment. He believes that if an audience can be made to watch critically it can come to conclusions about itself and contemporary society and can take steps to alter what it does not like. Thus, the pessimism found in his plays is altered by Brecht's optimism about the possibilities of action outside the plays. A sense of ambiguity always remains, nevertheless.

PLOT AND STRUCTURE. The "epic" nature of *The Good Woman of Setzuan* is made clear by the prologue in which narration and dialogue are freely mingled and in which time and place are considerably telescoped. The irony which permeates the whole work is also established by the disparity between Wong's assurances to the Gods that everyone is waiting to receive them and the fact that they must accept lodgings with a prostitute.

The prologue also establishes the basic situation: the Gods find their good person and enjoin her to remain good. At the same time, however, they refuse to be concerned about how such a difficult assignment is to be carried out—they "never meddle with economics." Herein lies the basic conflict, for economic factors are the very ones which stand in the way of goodness. Thus, the Gods' demand that man be good and their refusal to be concerned with the determinants of morality are clearly at odds. By this means Brecht implies that the solution to human problems is not to be sought in divine intervention.

The Good Woman of Setzuan alternates short and long scenes. The short scenes serve two main purposes: to break up the action, and to comment upon the action. Both contribute to Brecht's aim of forcing the audience to think by giving it clues about the significance of what it has seen and time in which to reflect upon it.

The long scenes are basically devoted to the conflict between good and evil as seen in the two aspects of the "good woman." Her true self is shown in the person of Shen Te, and her evil self is embodied in Shui Ta. She assumes the disguise of Shui Ta whenever her goodness has brought her to the edge of destruction. At first the impersonation is for brief periods, but, as the play progresses, she must become Shui Ta for longer and longer periods. Brecht uses this device to show the progressive deterioration of morality under the circumstances. The play ends in a stalemate for the Gods leave Shen Te with the same message they gave in the prologue, "Be Good." She is still no nearer to knowing how this is to be accomplished, and they are still unconcerned over such practical matters.

The long scenes have been broken up by the insertion of songs and speeches delivered directly to the audience. The songs are ostensibly about subject matter different from that of the scenes they accompany; some are parables in themselves. All comment, directly or indirectly, upon the action, however.

Brecht makes no attempt to create the illusion of real happenings. For example, when Wong says he will find a place for the Gods to spend the night, he suggests the attempt, although the various houses need not be represented on stage at all. The action, thus, is outlined, but many of the details are omitted.

This approach allows Brecht to telescope events and to eliminate transitions. For example, in the prologue the Gods are taken into Shen Te's house and the lowering of stage lights designates the passing of night. This device is analogous to the narrative technique in which a writer might bridge a transition with, "The next morning——." This technique can be seen more clearly in the scene in which Shen Te meets Yang Sun and falls in love with him. There is no preparation whatever for this turn of events, and again it is much as if a storyteller had said, "One day Shen Te was out walking in the park when she saw a young man trying to hang himself." The need to motivate her presence or to show the connection of this scene with those which preceded it is eliminated.

Again, however, Brecht's structural techniques are explained in part by his belief that scenes should be clearly separated as part of the "alienation" process. They are further explained by his insistence that the basic social content of each scene should be capable of expression in one simple sentence. (For example, scene three of *The Good Woman of Setzuan* might be expressed by "Shen Te falls in love with a young aviator.") All parts of a scene should be clearly related to this simple statement. Brecht is not concerned with inner psychological truth but concentrates upon what he calls "social gestures"—or the manifestations of attitudes in social behavior. The clear depiction of a "gesture," then, is the aim of each scene.

Although Brecht aimed at simplicity and clarity, his techniques have puzzled many since they do not accord with normal dramatic structure. The introduction of songs, the failure to make clear connections between scenes, and many of the devices designed to achieve "alienation" frequently seem to conflict with the traditional ideas of dramatic action. For these reasons, Brecht's hoped-for clarity has become only obscurity for many spectators.

Given some understanding of Brecht's aims, however, the same devices which some find distracting become effective sources of contrast and vigor. The alternation of long and short scenes, of narration and dialogue, of song and speech, of direct appeal and oblique reference—all of these serve to increase interest and at the same time relate to those basic social gestures with which Brecht is concerned.

CHARACTERS AND ACTING. Brecht considerably oversimplifies characters, for he is principally concerned with their social relationships. He is not interested in rendering total personalities or the inner lives of his characters, but rather with showing their relationship to a social situation. The majority of speakers in *The Good Woman of Setzuan* do not have names, but have been given social designations such as Gods, Wife, Grandfather, and Policeman. All represent types of behavior more than they do individuals. Their desires are also put in terms of social action: Shen Te wishes to treat all persons honorably, to make it possible for Yang Sun to become a pilot, to provide proper food for the children, and so on. The social and economic facts are the most important ones in each characterization.

These social factors are supplemented by Brecht's basic attitude that men are almost universally selfish. In the social situations, therefore, the actions are in large part determined by each character's attempt to better his own situation even at the expense of others. Brecht has not been accused of distorting human psychology as much as he might since his view of humanity is basically in keeping with Freudian theories and with determinism. The modern world has come to accept the idea that everyone is basically selfish and that even good deeds fulfill some selfish need within the individual. Thus, Brecht's picture of humanity has not offended as it would had his exaggeration been in the direction of showing the goodness of men. Nevertheless, Brecht's characterizations are based on only a few traits and are confined principally to social factors and a limited number of psychological attitudes.

Brecht, however, did not intend to portray well-rounded individuals. He set out to present an interpretation of social reality, and his characters are important only insofar as they aid in that presentation. The action does not exist to display character, but character is used to demonstrate a social action.

The only character who rises to the level of moral decision is Shen Te, and the plot depends in large part upon the series of choices which she makes: to accept the God's injunction to be good; to become Shui Ta in order to preserve her well-being; to help Yang Sun; and so on. These choices are necessary to demonstrate one of Brecht's basic concerns: the moral dilemma of man under the existing economic conditions.

Brecht's ideas on acting are in keeping with his general approach to the theatre. The actor should not impersonate a character so much as he, from the standpoint of a third person, should narrate the behavior of a person in a specific situation. He wishes actors to avoid identifying with the characters or trying "to live the part." He suggests that the actor should analyze the basic social qualities of his role and concentrate upon "presenting" these to the audience in a kind of demonstration which comments upon the action and the characters. The actor, thus, aids in creating the alienation effect and in arousing a critical response in the audience.

The actor performing in Brecht's plays should be familiar with Brecht's ideas on acting, although it is doubtful that they can always be carried out. The members of Brecht's own acting troupe have stated that they were not aware of approaching the roles in his plays differently from those in other plays, and that Brecht himself was not insistent upon the application of his ideas. Nevertheless, his intentions are important to an understanding of his over-all approach to the theatre. The more introspective approach of Stanislavsky is of limited value in acting Brecht's plays.

VISUAL AND AURAL ELEMENTS.   Brecht once suggested that his approach to the visual elements of the theatre was one of naïveté. "The opposite of a naïve approach is naturalism." He strives for a childlike simplicity, a make-believe quality. "The natural must be made to look surprising."

The sweep of events and the rapid changes of time and place would in themselves prevent the full-stage representation of all the locales indicated in any of Brecht's plays. But Brecht desires neither historical accuracy nor the accumulation of naturalistic details in his settings, but wants only elements which aid in the alienation effect. Scenery and costumes, therefore, remain only outlines or suggestions. Fragmentary settings, projections, and captions are his favorite devices in settings. Costumes may use some historically accurate elements but others may be modern or merely expressive of social factors rather than the historical period.

The Good Woman of Setzuan is set in ten different places. Each of these, however, can be indicated by a few scenic elements. For example, Scene 4 is set in a square onto which three shops open. Each shop may be suggested by a single flat and these may be carried on stage by the actors in full view of the audience. As Brecht wrote:

> . . . *let the spectator*
> *Be aware of busy preparations, made for him*
> *Cunningly; he sees a tinfoil moon*
> *Float down, or a tiled roof*
> *Being carried in; do not show him too much,*
> *But show him something!*

While little scenery is needed, that which is used should be designed with great care so that it makes a definite contribution to the play's effect. In Brecht's theatre it is not enough to copy reality; reality must be clarified by transforming it and by making it strange. The right kind of scenery allows the spectator to view reality critically and to understand it—something which would not be possible were it presented in its everyday and familiar guise.

With every aspect of drama, then, Brecht seeks to transform the old theatre into a new one in which the spectator can participate rather than merely observe passively. He wishes to make plays both enjoyable experiences and critical exercises. He takes it for granted that audiences are capable and eager to perform the intellectual and critical feats he envisions. Many, however, have declined to accept his kind of theatre, and the masses (the audience he most wanted to attract) have usually misunderstood him, while he has achieved his greatest popularity with the educated classes, for which he frequently expressed scorn.

Another factor which sets Brecht off from most of his contemporaries is his frank commitment to a point of view. Most modern playwrights have professed to be objective observers of life, but Brecht is a consciously moral and propagandistic playwright. It is clear that he thinks Shen Te is right in trying to be good, and that man's happiness is to be found in living with others in harmony and according to the Golden Rule. While he satirizes the Gods and their lack of concern over practical matters, he does not call into question the ideals they embody. Brecht shows the results of ignoring these ideals but at the same time the impossibility of achieving them under existing conditions. In this way he forces the audience to ask, "What must be done to make it possible for men to be good?" He doesn't answer, but he compels his audience to consider the question and to apply it to the social situation in which it lives.

Perhaps Brecht's ideas are called most into question by the fact that thus far he has been the only playwright who has achieved distinction in the Epic Theatre. He has influenced a number of other writers, nevertheless, and other epic dramatists of importance may yet appear.

One of the forms most obviously related to Brecht's Epic Theatre is the "Living Newspaper" which grew out of the Federal Theatre project in America. During the depression the United States government created the Federal Theatre as part of its Works Progress Administration program to relieve unemployment. It was in operation between 1935 and 1939, and had units in various parts of the country. It was most active in New York, however, where the unemployment situation in the theatre was most serious. While the New York groups produced many kinds of plays, they are best remembered for the Living Newspaper productions. The Living Newspaper, as the title indicates, aimed at achieving in the theatre a product similar to the printed newspaper. In actuality it was more closely related to the documentary film, for, as it developed, each play was confined to treating a single problem in a manner which combined factual information with an entertaining presentation. The most famous works are *One Third of a Nation* (on slum housing), *Triple-A Plowed Under* (on the farm program), and *Power* (on public utilities and flood control). These plays combine scenes illustrating social conditions with narration; these more typical dramatic devices are supplemented by statistical tables and filmed sequences projected on screens. The plays are the combined work of many authors and display a definite point of view (in favor of social reform and corrective legislation). This combined political and social bias aroused much criticism, and the Federal Theatre ceased to exist after 1939 because of the refusal of Congress to appropriate funds to support it. It marks the United States government's only attempt at directly subsidizing the theatre.

The Living Newspaper shows quite clearly the use of many of the same devices, and much the same point of view, as projected by Brecht and Piscator. This "epic" approach has not attracted many imitators since 1940, however, and most of the plays dealing with social problems have been written in the dramatic form popularized by Ibsen. The "theatricality" of epic staging, nevertheless, has served, in conjunction with other movements, to move the ideals of staging away from illusionism.

Symbolism, expressionism, and the Theatre of Social Action are each revolts against the realistic ideal which has dominated the theatre since the late nineteenth century. While they have not been able to overthrow realism, they have served to show its shortcomings and have altered its outlook and methods. The results will be examined in the chapter which follows.

Chapter 14

THE THEATRE SINCE WORLD WAR II

The theatre since World War II can best be described as eclectic in nature. That is to say it has borrowed, combined, and modified elements from all of the modern movements, and has adapted staging devices from all past periods for use in the production of both period and modern plays. The diversity of the present-day theatre can be illustrated by considering three of its most representative forms: modified realism, musical drama, and the "theatre of the absurd."

MODIFIED REALISM

Realism still dominates the theatre of today, although it has been modified by the ideas and methods of symbolism, expressionism, Epic Theatre, and musical drama. Modern art in general has conditioned audiences not to demand an absolute fidelity to nature, and to accept simplification, suggestion, and distortion as basic techniques in art. In the theatre the result has been a greater willingness to emphasize theatricality or, put another way, to depend less upon the illusion of reality and more upon the frank recognition that the theatre is different from reality.

The Ascot Gavotte scene from the original New York production of *My Fair Lady.* Courtesy of Friedman-Ables, Inc., Photographers.

Stage settings, for example, have relied more upon the suggestion of reality than upon the complete representation of the details of period and place. The locale may be sufficiently indicated but the audience is frequently asked to use its imagination in filling out details.

Similarly, play structure has become much freer and much less dependent upon the techniques of the "well-made play" which governed the realistic writing of the late nineteenth and early twentieth centuries. There has been a trend toward using a larger number of scenes and toward paying little attention to the division into acts. Experimentation with dramatic techniques has become common. There is today great leniency and freedom both in dramatic structure and in staging.

The modifications in the methods of realism have been brought about in part by changes in man's view of the world in which he lives. The discoveries of science (which in the late 19th century were thought to free man from dependence on spiritual ideals) have only emphasized the need for moral and spiritual values which can guide the use of these discoveries. New knowledge, such as that about atomic energy, may be used for good or for evil purposes, and science cannot give answers to questions about such moral values. As the realization has grown that many of man's most important problems cannot be solved (or even dealt with) by science, the conviction that observable phenomena alone contain truth has lost some of its power.

Furthermore, psychology has shown increasingly that many of man's most powerful motivations are subconscious and cannot be seen through purely external signs. Reality, then, is no longer thought of as being so easily perceived as in the late nineteenth century, and the means for representing it in the theatre have consequently become much more flexible. Techniques have been borrowed from any source so long as they serve to reveal and interpret life more accurately. By becoming more flexible,

Eugene O'Neill's *Long Day's Journey into Night* is one of the most searching plays of the post-war era. Shown here is the final scene. Directed by Lael Woodbury.

Tennessee Williams' *Summer and Smoke*. Directed by David Schaal; scenery by Arnold Gillette.

modified realism has absorbed much that has been learned through the many revolts against the realism of the late nineteenth century.

CONTEMPORARY REALISTIC DRAMATISTS

The fusion of a number of modern movements may be seen most clearly perhaps in the work of Tennessee Williams (1914–   ), whose best known plays include *The Glass Menagerie, A Streetcar Named Desire, Summer and Smoke, The Rose Tattoo, Orpheus Descending, Suddenly Last Summer,* and *The Night of the Iguana.* Williams came into prominence in 1945 with *The Glass Menagerie* and has contributed regularly to the theatre since that time.

Many nonrealistic elements are used frequently by Williams. Symbolism, of the type employed by Ibsen and Chekhov, is to be found in almost every play of his and the titles of his works are indicative of their deeper and symbolic meanings. He also, normally, demands settings which are fragmentary, although the parts included may be treated realistically. Frequently, they show interiors and exteriors simultaneously so as to allow great fluidity in playing without requiring scene changes. A good example may be seen in *Summer and Smoke,* which requires that two interiors and a fountain in a park be visible continuously. Such use of scenery has been made possible in part by earlier nonrealistic movements.

Time is also fluid in many of Williams' plays. *The Glass Menagerie* is especially noteworthy for the use of memory as the chief device for selecting scenes from the past, and the play shows a distant resemblance to the works of Strindberg in this aspect.

But while these plays may be extremely theatrical, they also are intensely real in their treatment of character. Williams is concerned principally with those inner psychological realities which can best be depicted by the manipulation (rather than the mere recording) of external elements. It is the complex motivations of Freudian psychology which lie at the root of most of Williams' work.

The conflicts of his characters, however, are frequently made representative of larger issues in the world. Spirituality and materialism are almost always at odds and the resolutions of conflicts depend upon the characters' abilities to reconcile the demands of these two sides of human nature. For example, in A *Streetcar Named Desire*, Blanche's desires for beauty and love are set against Stanley Kowalski's materialism and lust. In some of Williams' plays the conflict is put in terms which makes them seem too abstract and schematic, but in others it is embodied in intensely powerful and lifelike portraits.

Another aspect of Williams' realism is to be seen in the juxtaposition of comic and serious elements in the same scene. Like Chekhov, Williams is able to show multiple aspects of character and differing moods simultaneously. Amanda in *The Glass Menagerie*, for example, is admirable, pathetic, and ridiculous, and consequently the scenes in which she appears shift mood rapidly and in a lifelike manner. Williams portrays human limitations in constant contrast with the highest aspirations in such a way as to produce both pathos and humor. His plays, consequently, are at once compassionate and bitter.

All of these qualities show both the continuing power of the realistic outlook and the modifications which have been made in realism by other views. In many ways, Williams' plays are a summation of the various influences that have gone into the twentieth-century theatre.

The works of William Inge (1913–   ), such as *Picnic, Bus Stop, Come Back, Little Sheba,* and *The Dark at the Top of the Stairs,* show many of the same characteristics as those of Williams, though in general they are more limited in both range and depth. Inge is concerned with internal psychological problems as they demonstrate the difficulty of coming to grips with the truth about oneself—with facing "the dark at the top of the stairs." The resolutions of his plays are more optimistic than Williams', for Inge seems to indicate that all one needs to do to obtain happiness is to face up to psychological realities. Since he is much less interested in both the wider implications of psychological conflicts and with theatrical devices, his work remains much more clearly in the main stream of realism than does that of Williams.

The Ibsen tradition has been most clearly exemplified in contemporary drama by the work of Arthur Miller (1915–   ). Miller achieved prominence first with *All My Sons* (1947), and has continued to contribute to the theatre with such plays as *The Crucible* and *A View from the Bridge.* But it is *Death of a Salesman* (1949) which has insured Miller's position, for many consider this to be the finest American play of

William Inge's *Picnic*. Directed by Ronald Gee.

the post-war era. It will be examined in more detail as an example of modern American drama and of modified realism.

DEATH OF A SALESMAN

Death of a Salesman explores Willy Loman's obsessive desire to succeed. Willy wants to be recognized, liked, and admired. It is his perplexity over the gulf between his accomplishment and his ideal that precipitates the play's action.

Success as Willy conceives of it, however, is largely material success, for to be well liked and to be materially successful are inextricably linked in his mind.

Material success seems so necessary to Willy that he cannot believe that his sons can love him if he is not successful. Love becomes an item to be bought rather than something to be freely given. Willie has conditioned his sons to believe that they do not deserve to be respected unless they are successful on his terms. It is only when Willy understands that Biff loves him, even though both of them are failures, that he achieves a certain amount of insight. It is too late to change the course of events, but he goes to his death as near to peace as he has been in the play.

The conflicts, then, arise out of the passion for success and the need to be loved and understood. Miller has used two characters to represent the poles between which Willy operates: Uncle Ben epitomizes material success, while Linda represents love given without question and without any conditions attached. Willy's conflict grows out of his unconscious assumption that success is necessary before love is possible.

Many have seen in *Death of a Salesman* a condemnation of American business practices. Miller has stated elsewhere that he did not have such a purpose in mind and a consideration of the play's characters bears out his contention. Charley, another businessman, is one of the most admirable characters in the play and the one who has most nearly achieved success in both his private and his business life. Charley has never worried about being "a success," however, while Willy has thought of little else. Willy has condoned stealing, lying, and cheating so long as these lead toward his goals. His failure, therefore, does not result from the fact that he is a salesman, but rather stems from the means he has adopted to get ahead. His failure in business is important only because it reflects his failure as a father, as a husband, and as a human being.

PLOT AND STRUCTURE. Miller has said that he conceived of the action of *Death of a Salesman* as occurring within Willy's mind, and that Willy's psychological states have dictated the structure of the play. This is only partially true since Willy does not participate in several scenes and could know nothing about them. These exceptions, however, are scenes which take place in the present; those which go backward in time invariably grow out of Willy's psychological associations.

The present action occurs within twenty-four hours (with the exception of the funeral), but the scenes from the past range over twenty years. Past and present flow together as Willy tries to find the answers to his questions: Why have I failed? Where did I go wrong? What is the secret of success?

It is interesting to compare Miller's play with works from earlier periods. Both *Death of a Salesman* and *Oedipus the King* involve a search into the past to find the roots of present evils. The scenes in *Oedipus the King*, however, are all drawn from the present and the past is revealed only through speech; *Death of a Salesman*, on the other hand, uses Willy's psychological states to transport the audience backward in time to witness the scenes. As in *Faust*, there is a search for an answer to the meaning of life, but whereas Faust projects forward in time to fulfillment through his quest, Willy goes backward in time to seek the causes of his failure. *Death of a Salesman* also recalls Medieval drama in its use of a kind of simultaneous setting and in the complete fluidity of time.

The only unusual feature of the structure of *Death of a Salesman* is the "flashback" technique, for otherwise the play is organized conven-

Scene from the original New York production of *Death of a Salesman*. Setting by Jo Mielziner. Courtesy of Graphic House, Inc.

tionally in terms of exposition, preparation, complications, climax, obligatory scene, and resolution. Each flashback is carefully prepared for by wandering talk, offstage voices, sound effects, music, or a similar cue. Most productions of the play have also used a change in stage lighting to aid the audience in the transition from present to past action. The flashbacks are carefully engineered so that each reveals only a small part of the past. The outline gradually emerges but it is not complete until the climactic moment.

In *Death of a Salesman* psychological realism has replaced external realism and a greater freedom in dramatic structure has resulted. Many of the scenes of *Death of a Salesman* materialize out of a character's mind and are treated only in fragmentary form. The aim, nevertheless, remains much the same as that which moved Ibsen—to depict with fidelity a contemporary situation.

CHARACTERS AND ACTING. By far the most important character in *Death of a Salesman* is Willy Loman. But Biff serves as a strong secondary interest since the major issues of the play are worked out between him and Willy.

Willy is sixty-three years old, a man on the verge of a physical and psychological breakdown. He has been trying to sell himself all of his life, and he has lied both to himself and to others in his desire to believe that he is a success. Recent developments, however, have forced him to face the fact that he is in actuality a failure. Yet he cannot see where he has taken the wrong path. The play shows his search to find the causes for his lack of success.

Willy is tired, puzzled, touchy, quick to get angry, ready to hope; he cajoles his sons, offers advice when it isn't wanted; he is always looking for the secret that will "open doors." Above all he is dominated by the ideal of success, and he has tried to instill the same ideal in his sons.

Uncle Ben personifies success, and in many ways is merely an extension of one aspect of Willy's personality. He represents the mystery of success, for he has gone into the jungle and come out rich; he has been to far-away and dangerous places and thus gives a romantic aura to success. Ben also implies that success is bound up with the "law of the jungle," with shady deals and quick-wittedness.

Willy, however, wants to triumph on his own terms—as a salesman who is liked by everybody. He can never accept completely Ben's advice, therefore, even though he can never give up Ben's ideal. This split in Willy's desires is at the root of his character and can be seen even in his death, which is an attempt to achieve material gain and the love and gratitude of his family simultaneously. He is both a pathetic and a powerful figure.

Biff is thirty-four years old but is still an adolescent in his attitudes. He is irresponsible and a wanderer; he is incapable of happiness because of the sense of guilt aroused in him by Willy. From Willy he learned early that the way to success lies through lying and stealing, and through knowing the right people. But the lure of success has been short-circuited in Biff by his disillusionment with Willy, which dates from the discovery of his father's unfaithfulness to Linda. Consequently, Biff rebels against success, constantly flouts authority, and enjoys hurting his father.

Biff is more honest than Willy, nevertheless, for he tries to face the truth and has a sense of moral responsibility which is totally lacking in his brother, Happy. It is Biff who finally makes his father face the truth and they both come to understand that love is not earned through material success, but is a gift freely bestowed. Miller gives no indication of what the future may hold for Biff, but it will no doubt be more peaceful than the past.

Linda understands what both Willy and Biff learn during the play: love has no conditions. She knows all there is to know about Willy, but she loves him, accepts him, and fights fiercely for him even against her own sons. Her sense of decency and rightness makes her put Willy above everyone, for to her it is not a matter of whether Willy has earned love and respect—his right to them is unquestioned. Because she loves so unconditionally, Linda cannot understand why Willy commits suicide or why the boys have turned out as they have.

Success has no magic for Linda. She fears Ben and his lures. Willy cannot choose between the positions represented by Linda and Ben, and it is only Biff who is eventually able to make Willy even consider Linda's point of view.

Happy has inherited the worst of Willy's traits without the saving possibility of love. He is entirely selfish and unfeeling; lying and cheating are integral parts of his nature. He is a materialist and sensualist beyond redemption, devoid of Ben's vision and strength.

Charley and Bernard have succeeded where Willy and Biff have failed and their principal function in the play is to serve as contrasts. Charley says he has succeeded because he has never been passionately dedicated to anything. Yet the play shows that Charley is dedicated to being a "good man" as opposed to being a success in Willy's terms. Charley is not aware of his dedication, but his unconscious commitment to "human" above "material" factors is the key to his happiness just as the reverse is the key to Willy's failure.

Many have seen in Howard an indictment of "businessman morality." Miller has denied this and has said that Howard is a man of common sense and that he acts as he must. More important for the play, however, Howard serves to spur Willy on in his search for an answer. In real-life terms it might have been more humane for Howard to make a place for Willy in the home office, but in terms of dramatic action his decision is necessary to make Willy face himself more completely.

Miller is interested in his characters principally as they relate to his basic themes. He concentrates upon their sociological and psychological attitudes, and other details have been cut away in an attempt to achieve universality. Miller's success is indicated by the general tendency of audiences and critics to see in the play an indictment of modern society.

SPECTACLE AND SOUND. Miller's ideas for the staging of *Death of a Salesman* are clearly indicated in the script. The continual presence of the house helps to re-enforce the convention that the flashbacks are fragments of the past which Willy recalls, and it helps to make clear the simultaneity of the past and the present in Willy's mind.

Miller has stated that the motion picture version of *Death of a*

Salesman was not successful in large part because of the realistic depiction of the physical surroundings in the flashback scenes. He believes that in this way the emphasis was shifted from the psychological conflict in Willy's mind to the physical setting of the action.

The fragmentary and schematic setting preferred by Miller eliminates all external and purely illusionistic details. Such a setting is entirely in keeping with the dramatic techniques used in the play.

Sound has also been used most effectively. Music helps to set the mood and it marks the transition to the flashback scenes. Ben has his own special music which is played each time he appears; honky-tonk music accompanies Willy's scenes with the Other Woman; music helps to set the locale of the restaurant scene. The method used by Willy for committing suicide is made clear only through the offstage sound of a car driving away.

Audiences have accepted as realistic the fragmentary setting and novel staging conventions of *Death of a Salesman* and have never been puzzled by them. But it is a realism which has been modified by making a bold use of the means of the theatre; it is a realism in which the surface has been cut away so that the inner workings of a mind may be seen more clearly.

The methods used by Miller are representative of the way in which realism is practiced in present-day theatre. It continues to be the dominant mode of dramatic expression, but it is increasingly open to influences from nonrealistic approaches.

THE MUSICAL PLAY

The musical play is the most popular form of entertainment in today's American theatre, and is becoming increasingly important throughout the world. Many have maintained that it is the only distinctively American contribution to the theatre.

The current musical is a descendant of many minor theatrical forms of the nineteenth century, notably the extravaganza, the variety show, burlesque, and vaudeville. The extravaganza depended upon music, dance, and lavish scenic display for its appeal. Its subject matter was most frequently drawn from myths or fairy tales and, unlike most of the other minor dramatic forms, was seldom topical or satirical. It was a favorite form with nineteenth-century audiences.

The variety show, as the name suggests, is composed of a collection of short acts of various types, most of which involve singing, dancing, or comic routines. Although no attempt is made to weld the acts together with a plot, the various parts of entertainment are similar to those found in a musical.

` Burlesque has had a long and complicated history. Originally a burlesque was a parody of some well-known play, literary work, or social custom. For example, Buckingham's *The Rehearsal* (1671) and Sheridan's *The Critic* (1779) parodied the drama and theatrical conventions of their times. In the nineteenth century burlesque was converted into a travesty (or a farcical retelling) of any well-known play, which at the same time ridiculed theatrical conventions and contemporary affairs.

It was not until around 1870, however, that modern burlesque emerged in America. It took its inspiration from an extravaganza, *The Black Crook* (1866), which became notorious because of its scantily clad (for that time) dancers. Soon burlesque had become a collection of monologues, comedy sketches, songs, and dance numbers which featured a female chorus. The emphasis was upon beautiful women and jokes with sexual implications. It rapidly came to be thought of as an entertainment intended only for a male audience.

This form of burlesque reached the height of its popularity just prior to World War I, and it was not until the 1920s that the strip tease became its main feature. Since that time it has existed on the fringes of legality and in many places has been banned. It is, nevertheless, one of the forerunners of the musical in its use of chorus numbers, comic acts, music, and dance.

Scene from *Once upon a Mattress*. Book by J. Thompson, Marshall Barer, and Dean Fuller. Music by Mary Rogers and Marshall Barer.

A scene from *Finian's Rainbow*. Book by E. Y. Harburg and Fred Saidy. Music by Burton Lane. From a production directed by Willard Welsh; scenery by Warren Hovious; choreography by Carolyn Morgan.

Like burlesque, Vaudeville has had a long and varied history. Originally the word vaudeville meant a satirical song. Later it was used to designate a play which contained songs set to well-known tunes. In the nineteenth century *comédie-en-vaudeville* was used to indicate a comic play interspersed with incidental songs. At times such a work was also called a musical comedy.

Vaudeville in the sense most commonly used today, however, developed in the late nineteenth century. Tony Pastor (1837–1908) is credited with developing vaudeville through his attempt to make the newly popular *Black Crook* form of burlesque into an entertainment which would appeal to a mixed and respectable audience. He began to experiment around 1880 and soon proved successful in turning the emphasis away from sex and the off-color joke to a "family" type of entertainment which had much in common with the variety show.

The transition had been made successfully by the 1890s and the popularity of vaudeville continued until the 1930s. The decline of the form is usually attributed to the rise of the sound motion picture which could furnish the same kind of entertainment at lower admission prices. Vaudeville and burlesque were the training grounds for many of the great entertainers of the twentieth century: Jack Benny, Jimmy Durante, George Burns, Bert Lahr, and many others.

It was usual also in the nineteenth century to introduce singing and dancing into the performance of legitimate dramas, especially melodramas.

Furthermore, singing and dancing were to be seen in every theatre as entr'actes or in afterpieces. Singing, dancing, and spectacle were standard parts of every program, therefore. But the movement in the late nineteenth century toward greater realism and the one-play bill gradually eliminated such incidental entertainment from the legitimate theatres. It was at this time that many of the elements of older forms came together to create musical comedy.

The origin of musical comedy is usually traced to the work of George Edwardes at the Gaiety Theatre in London in the 1890s. His series of works, in which farcical plots were used to hold together songs, dances, and chorus-ensemble numbers, proved so popular that a number of imitations soon appeared. Most of these early musical comedies were set in mythical places or in European countries in which Barons and Counts abounded. The stories had little to do with everyday life, and emphasized instead the romantic and exotic appeals of far-away places and unusual happenings.

Around the time of World War I the vogue for ballroom dancing and "ragtime" music turned attention to more familiar characters and surroundings. The plots still remained unimportant, however, and served principally as excuses for spectacular settings, songs, dances, and the presence of beautiful chorus girls.

In the 1930s another important change occurred when more concern began to be paid to plot and psychological motivations of characters. The new stature of the musical is indicated by the fact that *Of Thee I Sing* was awarded the Pulitzer Prize as the best play of the year in 1931, the first time that a musical had ever won such an honor. The new direction can also be seen in such musicals as *Lady in the Dark* and *Pal Joey*, both of which were psychological studies of characters and both of which attempted to integrate all of the elements of the musical into a unified whole. The new trend was not completed, however, until the 1940s in such works by Oscar Hammerstein II (1895–1960) and Richard Rodgers (1902–   ) as *Oklahoma, Carousel,* and *South Pacific.*

While Rodgers and Hammerstein consolidated earlier gains, they did not remain unchallenged for supremacy. Innumerable fine musicals have been written since 1950, such as *Guys and Dolls, Pajama Game, Damn Yankees, West Side Story, The Music Man,* and *How to Succeed in Business without Really Trying.*

One of the most successful writing teams has been Alan Jay Lerner (1918–   ) and Frederick Loewe (1904–   ), who have contributed such works as *Paint Your Wagon, My Fair Lady,* and *Camelot.* The most popular musical comedy (in terms of length of run) of all time is *My Fair Lady,* which opened in New York in 1956. This work will be examined in more detail as an example of the modern American musical.

MY FAIR LADY

My Fair Lady is adapted from George Bernard Shaw's *Pygmalion* (1912), "A Romance in Five Acts." It is a retelling in modern terms of the legend of Pygmalion, a sculptor, who falls in love with one of his statues. He prays to the goddess of love to bring the statue, Galatea, to life. His wish is granted and he marries Galatea.

Shaw uses this legend only as point of reference, for his principal interest lies in showing that differences in speech are in large part responsible for maintaining the social and economic class structure of England. He argues that if everyone were taught to speak English properly the mainstay of the class system would be gone. He makes his point by showing how a flower girl can be passed off as a Duchess by changing her speech. Other factors (how she dresses and walks, her topics of conversation, and so on) are also changed, but Shaw argues that all of these alterations would be useless unless the speech were changed.

Although Shaw's points have relevance in Europe where class structure is much more rigid than in America, it is doubtful that the play's social message has contributed to its success. Most audiences have seen in it only the romance which the title indicates—a Cinderella story in which the transformation of speech serves as a device upon which the plot turns.

To *Pygmalion* Shaw eventually added a postscript in which he denies that Higgins marries Liza (Eliza in *My Fair Lady*). In spite of this denial, however, most persons have seen the play in a more sentimental and romantic light, and Shaw's association of it with the Pygmalion legend invites such a view. *My Fair Lady* changes the story line of *Pygmalion* chiefly in making the love story more definite. The ending of the musical seems much more in keeping with the over-all tone of the play than does Shaw's own postscript.

PLOT AND STRUCTURE. Although *My Fair Lady* follows Shaw's play rather closely in basic outline, many structural changes have been made. *Pygmalion* is written in five acts, while *My Fair Lady* contains eighteen scenes divided into two acts. The conversion from play to musical has been accomplished by breaking up the acts into short scenes, by adding scenes which dramatize events only talked about in the play, and by condensing Shaw's speeches to allow time for the addition of songs and dances.

In actuality, the musical is much closer to the motion picture version of the play than to the original work. For example, while the stage play does not show any of Eliza's voice lessons, both the movie and the musical contain a series of short scenes in which her training is dramatized; likewise, both the movie and the musical show the ball at which Eliza triumphs, while this is not seen in the play.

Well over half of the eighteen scenes of the musical have no direct counterpart in Shaw's play, though almost all are based upon material in the play. Many of the additions allow for greater variety and spectacle. For example, the slum background from which Eliza comes is shown, thereby creating opportunities for chorus numbers. Some emphasize the love story. A new final scene has been added, and the part of Freddy, who falls in love with Eliza, is built up to show Eliza's desirability and to create a threat to Higgins.

Some scenes are also added to create suspense. For example, the break between the two acts follows a scene which is not shown in Shaw's play. At the ball, Karpathy, an expert on speech, over and over questions Eliza's identity and the authenticity of her title. He vows to find out the truth and as the curtain falls he is seen dancing and talking with her. Thus, the act ends on a note of doubt and suspense which carries interest over intermission and contrasts with the exultation of the opening scene of Act II.

The act division of *My Fair Lady* is also indicative of a shift of interest in the plot. Act I is concerned with the decision to make over a flower girl and to pass her off as a Duchess. This purpose has been accomplished when Act II begins. The last part of the play shows the results of Eliza's refusal to become merely an object to be used and then abandoned.

Many departures from the original play have been dictated by the conventions of the musical. In its original form the play requires almost as much playing time as does the musical. Some changes had to be made, therefore, to allow for the addition of music, song, and dance. A chorus is an accepted feature of a musical and occasions must be created for its inclusion. In *Pygmalion* only Act I (outside the Covent Garden Theatre) would allow such a treatment. Some of the most obvious changes, such as the addition of the slum and ballroom scenes, have already been indicated. Another is the substitution of a race track sequence for a drawing room. In Act III of Shaw's play Higgins takes Eliza to his Mother's home for tea, at which only seven persons are present. In the musical the same purpose (to allow Eliza a trial appearance in the fashionable world) is served, and most of Shaw's dialogue is preserved, but the change in setting to a race track allows much fuller scope for spectacle and the full use of the chorus. This change led to one of the most admired scenes in *My Fair Lady*.

Other conventions of the musical are a marked emphasis upon settings, costumes, and other visual elements (which will be discussed later), and a large number of scenes. Considerable variety is gained in *My Fair Lady* by the alternation of short and long scenes. Some involve only one or two characters, others include the entire cast.

Thus, while the differences between *Pygmalion* and *My Fair Lady* are numerous, the musical has managed to maintain the essence of Shaw's play while transforming it to meet the demands of the musical stage.

CHARACTERS AND ACTING. The writers of a musical face a dilemma since excellence in both acting and singing can seldom be found in one person. They are frequently forced, therefore, to subordinate one demand to another. In *My Fair Lady* the decision in most cases was made in favor of the actor. Only four of the major characters (Higgins, Eliza, Doolittle, and Freddy) are required to sing solo numbers and only two of these (Eliza and Freddy) need to be trained singers.

The songs written for Higgins and Doolittle lie within so limited a vocal range that almost anyone can sing them. On the other hand, those written for Eliza and Freddy demand considerable vocal ability. Since Freddy's acting is of only secondary importance, ultimately only the role of Eliza demands outstanding ability in both acting and singing.

In terms of the action, *My Fair Lady* has only five roles of importance: Higgins, Eliza, Pickering, Doolittle, and Freddy. Of these Higgins and Eliza are of primary importance, while Pickering, Doolittle, and Freddy are of secondary importance.

Higgins has been made more polished and urbane in the musical than he is in Shaw's play, where he was inclined to be unfashionable in his dress and unconventional in his behavior. The Higgins of the musical is still an individualist, but the rough qualities are gone. Nevertheless, he is still self-confident, selfish and unfeeling where others are concerned. Throughout the musical he is passionately devoted to his work and blind to other human needs. It is only at the end that Eliza is able to force him to recognize the power of love. The last line of the play indicates, however, that he will not change very much, for instead of rising to embrace her he merely says, "Eliza? Where the devil are my slippers?"

The greatest range in acting ability is required for the role of Eliza. She must be able to give a convincing portrayal of a Cockney flower girl from the slums and must be able to transform herself gradually until the audience is willing to believe that she might pass as a Duchess. Her emotions are varied: outrage, defiance, frustration, dejection, longing, triumph, love, and so on. Eliza's principal motivation is the desire to be loved and respected. This drives her in the beginning to accept Higgins' offer to transform her, and later to leave Higgins because he has merely used her for his own purposes instead of considering her feelings as a human being. Ultimately it is her personal integrity that forces Higgins to see himself more clearly and to recognize his need for Eliza. When he can come to respect and love her, both have reached a new kind of satisfaction upon which to build the future.

Although Pickering is onstage during a large part of *My Fair Lady* he serves principally as a foil for Higgins. It is he who bets with Higgins that he cannot pass Eliza off as a Duchess; it is he who treats Eliza as a lady and points up Higgins' indifference to her as a human being. Pickering

Scene outside of the Covent Garden Theatre from the original New York production of *My Fair Lady*. Rex Harrison as Henry Higgins, Julie Andrews as Eliza Doolittle. Courtesy of Friedman-Ables, Inc., Photographers.

has only one principal characteristic: he acts as a gentleman would at all times. While he serves to aid in the advancement of the plot, the events have no effect upon him personally and he plays little part in the last act.

Doolittle is almost the opposite of Pickering. He is a wastrel, a near-drunkard, and a person who avoids marriage and all responsibility. He represents lower-class morality and attitudes, but eventually falls victim to respectability. His complete lack of conventionality and his frankness have made the role a popular one with audiences.

Freddy serves as another contrast for Higgins, for he sees Eliza almost completely from a sentimental point of view. He offers Eliza love and respect in large part because she has the strength which he lacks. Higgins on the other hand has the strength that Eliza wants in a man, but is lacking in the love and consideration which Freddy offers. It is only when Higgins can make some compromise that the possibility of happiness for Eliza materializes.

The other characters have little effect upon the outcome of the play and serve principally to supply the background of the action. Most of these are played by members of the singing or dancing choruses. Thus, while *My Fair Lady* has great variety and dramatic strength, it requires only a few outstanding performers. The lesser members of the cast are obviously still of importance, but need not be performers of the first rank.

LANGUAGE AND MUSIC.   Shaw has long been recognized as a master of the English language. The speeches in his plays are always sharply outlined and marked by clarity and grace. A large part of the dialogue in *My Fair Lady* is taken directly from *Pygmalion*; the rest has been written with Shaw's style in mind, and has been successfully blended with the original.

Shaw was not afraid to make his characters express themselves clearly and at length. He accepted the idea that good speech is an essential part of the theatre, and had little patience with that school of modern writing which makes its characters inarticulate "mumblers." Shaw's relish for the English language and good speech is carried over into the lyrics of *My Fair Lady*. Higgins especially is a master of the well-turned phrase, of sophistication and urbanity.

Of course, much of Shaw's dialogue has been eliminated so that songs and dances may be included. The songs, therefore, must supply much that has been left out. For example, the first three solos (Higgins' "Why Can't the English Learn to Speak?"; Eliza's "Wouldn't It Be Loverly"; and Doolittle's "With a Little Bit of Luck") establish the basic characterizations of the persons who sing them.

Much time may also be saved in a musical by capitalizing upon the fact that an audience readily accepts direct statements of feelings and intentions in a song, while these might need to be motivated and revealed slowly in a more realistic kind of drama. The song, thus, may be used as a device comparable to the soliloquy or aside and may convey a great deal of information in a brief amount of time. When good use is made of songs, then, the time which they take away from the dramatic portions is more than made up.

Music also makes the condensation of time more acceptable. For example, the lesson scenes in *My Fair Lady* are run together and the entire sequence builds to the song of triumph, "The Rain in Spain," which is based upon a phrase which has formed the motif of the lessons.

Time may also be saved effectively by the use of the reprise (the repetition of a song) or the repetition of musical phrases. Such repetitions associate events separated in time and make a comparison or establish a connection between events without the need for lengthy or explicit statement.

Music also gives the audience many kinds of clues by establishing moods and building expectations. Even before the curtain opens the overture has already given some idea of the general mood and the melodic qualities of the work to follow. Music also helps to establish the mood of individual scenes and serves to create audience expectation.

Music further aids in achieving variety. *My Fair Lady* contains musical numbers of widely contrasting types: songs of delight, such as "The Rain in Spain" and "You Did It"; love songs, such as "On the Street Where You Live," "I Could Have Danced All Night," and "I've Grown Accustomed to Her Face"; songs of rage and defiance, such as "Just You Wait," "Show Me," and "Without You"; songs of boisterous enjoyment of life, such as "Little Bit of Luck," and "Get me to the Church on Time"; of longing, such as "Wouldn't It Be Loverly"; descriptive musical numbers, such as the "Ascot Gavotte," and the "Embassy Waltz."

In spite of its great effectiveness, the amount of music in *My Fair Lady* is relatively small, for while many musicals include over thirty numbers, *My Fair Lady* has only twenty-one. Its superior effectiveness in underlining, adding to, and supplementing the drama is clearly attested to by the play's great and lasting popularity.

SETTINGS.   The musical almost always offers great scope to the imagination of designers. The mixture of song and dialogue automatically places the production outside the restrictions of realism and indicates the need for an imaginative use of pictorial elements to match the musical and dramatic qualities of the script.

A listing of the settings needed for Act I of *My Fair Lady* indicates some of the demands made on the set designer: outside the opera house; the tenement section; Higgins' study; the tenement section; Higgins' study; near the race at Ascot; inside a tent at Ascot; outside Higgins' home; Higgins' study; promenade at the Embassy; the ballroom. Not only is a wide variety of places indicated, but the alternation and frequent repetition of some of them indicates that they must be capable of quick changes so that the flow of one scene into another will not be impeded. The designer's problem is simplified somewhat by the fact that some sets need only accommodate a few persons, while others must contain the entire cast. Some sets may be small, therefore, while others must occupy the entire stage.

The costumes are also numerous and equally a source of great visual variety and beauty. The time of *My Fair Lady* is stated as 1912 and serves to place them in a period noted for its elegance. Cecil Beaton, who designed the costumes for the original production, made effective use of the many possibilities of the period. Upper-class characters are used in the Ascot race scenes and at the Embassy Ball, while lower-class characters are seen in the flower market and tenement scenes. Not only did Beaton distinguish between the two classes but he also used great imagination in commenting upon the scenes. In the Ascot setting, for example, he put all characters in shades of black and white and thereby emphasized the lack of variety in their characters. On the other hand, in the flower-market scene he took his inspiration from the paintings of Renoir and through the use of subtle gradations of pastel colors the characters themselves came to look like bouquets.

Since *My Fair Lady* covers a period of over six months in time, many costume changes are needed. The transformation of Eliza must be indicated in what she wears as well as in how she sounds. Furthermore, the chorus must change its identity often and, therefore, needs a great variety of costumes: sometimes they represent slum dwellers, at others they are dancers at the Embassy Ball, or are loungers outside the opera house, and so on.

Dance adds to the visual effectiveness of the musical play. Like the music, it too can comment upon the action and through its expressiveness help to forward the plot. It is not used extensively for this purpose in *My Fair Lady*, but in other musicals it has played an extremely important part. Here, nevertheless, it is a source of considerable charm and visual beauty.

My Fair Lady combines an extremely effective story with interesting and unusual characters, memorable music, and charming and colorful spectacle. As a result it has achieved unprecedented popularity in the theatre, and is both representative and a superior example of the musical form today.

The musical is by far the most popular type of theatrical entertainment in America. Its dramatic appeals coupled with the pleasure of music, song, and dance attract a wide range of audiences. Since greater and greater strides are being made toward integrating dramatic and musical values, the old objection that the musical is empty in content is no longer valid. Not only has the musical been strongly influenced by serious drama but it in turn has been a powerful force in the movement of drama away from realism toward a greater theatricalism. The musical, therefore, is not merely a form of entertainment, but is coming more and more to be a significant part of dramatic literature.

THE THEATRE OF THE ABSURD

While schools of thought differ about the ultimate meaning of existence, most have agreed that life has meaning. The 1950s saw a movement emerge, however, which seriously questions that there is any meaning, at least in an objective and verifiable sense. This outlook in drama has come to be called the "Theatre of the Absurd." (Absurd in this usage does not mean ridiculous, but rather irrational, unreasonable, or illogical.)

The basic assumption of the Absurdist school is that the world is entirely neutral. Facts and events do not have meanings, therefore; rather man assigns meanings to them. Thus, if men choose to regard an action as immoral, it does not denote that the act is in actuality immoral, but only that men have chosen to see it as such. The concept of morality itself is viewed as a human fabrication not based upon any logical proof.

Within such a framework of thought one action is ultimately as significant as another. All of the ways man uses in trying to improve himself are absurd and irrational, for the system of values upon which man's ideals are based is without foundation.

The Absurdist, thus, finds ultimate truth in chaos, formlessness, the welter of contradictions, and the inanities which make up everyday existence. Truth becomes the lack of logic, order, and certainty. Since there is no objective truth, each man must find a set of values by which he can live his own life, but he must be willing to face the fact that his values are also absurd. The values he chooses help him to bring some kind of order to his day-to-day living, but they have no more ultimate truth or logic than those chosen by any one else.

The Absurdist movement is a logical extension of the nineteenth-century insistence upon viewing the world scientifically. The Naturalists argued that the only truths are those apprehended through the five senses and tested and verified by the scientific method. But the only aspects of man's existence which have thus far yielded consistently to such scientific treatment are the physical and biological sciences. The facts covered in these studies, however, make up only a very small part of daily existence and man's most difficult decisions are normally concerned with moral

A scene from Samuel Beckett's silent play, *Act without Words, I.* Directed by James Gousseff.

A scene from Luigi Pirandello's
Henry IV. Directed by Dan Calder.

questions (that is, the rightness or wrongness of possible courses of action).
But morality is not subject to scientific treatment and verification, and from
a strictly naturalistic point of view, therefore, it cannot be brought within
the realm of truth.

The Naturalists never faced up to this dilemma for, in spite of their
attempts to restrict truth to scientific fact, they still believed for the most
part in objective standards of morality. Nevertheless, the implication of
a strictly scientific outlook is that morality has no objective foundation
and, thus, that it is based upon a set of accepted conventions—on conformity to a code of behavior which is convenient rather than truthful.

The Absurdists have chosen to see all aspects of human existence in
this light, for to them all of the ideas about man's importance, his knowledge, and his behavior are equally fictitious and illogical. Man is seen as
being adrift in a chaotic universe, and as constructing whatever fictions he
needs to help him survive under those conditions.

FORERUNNERS OF THE ABSURDISTS

While absurdism has gained prominence only since World War II,
it is not without important forebears. The first expression of an "Absurdist"
outlook by an organized movement (though certain individuals had ex-
pounded such a view prior to this time) came in the Manifesto of the
Dadaists in 1918.

The name "Dada" was chosen by this group because of its meaninglessness. As a movement it was essentially negative, since its members were
more interested in denying the validity of older views than they were in

affirming any positive position. Much of their work, therefore, was satirical in nature. They also elevated the illogical and the irrational to positions of primary importance. For example, they believed in automatic writing (that is, setting down thoughts as they came into the mind regardless of connection or relevance), the formless nature of which was thought to be a truthful expression of the writer's subconscious mind. Dadaism did not last long and was generally looked upon as a fad rather than as a serious artistic movement.

Dadaism gave way to surrealism which began to emerge around 1919 and which reached its peak of popularity in the 1920s. For the Surrealists the principal source of truth lies in the subconscious mind, which is frequently thought to be at its freest (that is, least subject to control by the conscious mind) when man is dreaming. Thus, the dreamlike state, in which the subconscious mind reorganizes everyday reality and evades the normal processes of thought and perception, is considered to be the surest approach to truth.

In 1924 André Breton, the movement's principal spokesman, defined surrealism as "pure psychic automatism, by which is intended to express, verbally, in writing, or by other means, the real process of thought. Thought's dictation, in the absence of all control exercised by the reason and outside all esthetic or moral preoccupations." Truth, then, is to be sought by freeing the mind from rational control and by activating the subconscious mind through a dreamlike state.

Both dadaism and surrealism see the world as essentially irrational and they seek to express this irrationality through artistic means. Neither movement, however, produced any drama of merit, and they are important only as forerunners of other schools and as influences on other movements in drama and the theatre. Many persons today refer to the Absurd drama as surrealistic.

Another important forerunner of Absurdist drama is the work of Luigi Pirandello (1867–1936), one of the outstanding dramatists of the twentieth century. His plays, such as *Right You Are, if You Think You Are* (1918), *Six Characters in Search of an Author* (1921), *Henry IV* (1922), and *As You Desire Me* (1930), are all based upon the idea that truth is a matter of one's point of view. Typically, all of the main characters in a play by Pirandello have been involved in the same event or with the same person, yet each has a quite different version of what has happened; each is convinced that he is right. Pirandello does not settle these arguments since to him there is no objective truth–there is only each individual's view of it. Out of such ideas Pirandello fashioned powerful plays that achieved wide renown and have remained popular. His influence has been widespread and his view of reality is clearly similar to that of the Absurdists.

The most significant forerunner of the Absurdist school, however, is existentialism. Many of the plays now labeled Absurdist were originally called Existentialist, and the beginnings of Absurd drama are clearly associated with the existential school of philosophy.

The central problem in existential philosophy is the meaning of "existence." (What does "to exist" mean? What are the implications of answers to this question for man's actions in daily life?) This problem has concerned philosophers since the beginning of time, but twentieth-century existentialism has given it a special emphasis. The modern movement began to be recognized in Europe in the years following World War I and achieved great popularity during and following World War II. It has been especially concerned with the problem of moral values in a civilization which has engendered two world wars and which has produced the atomic and hydrogen bombs.

The most widely known writers of this school are Jean-Paul Sartre (1905–   ) and Albert Camus (1913–1960), although Camus denied belonging to any particular philosophical school. Sartre has been one of the principal spokesmen for existentialism. He has stated that all of his work is an attempt to draw logical conclusions from a consistent atheism. He argues that there are no universal and absolute moral laws or values and that man is adrift in a world devoid of purpose. Therefore, each man is free (since he is not bound to a god or to a set of verifiable principles for behavior) and is responsible only to himself. It is each man's duty to find his own values and to act in accordance with them. This viewpoint is set forth in a number of essays and philosophical treatises, but it also forms the basis for such plays as *The Flies* (1943) and *The Devil and the Good Lord* (1951).

Camus had much the same view of man's condition but he called it "the absurd" and supplied the label by which the entire movement has come to be called. Camus said that absurdity arises from the clash between human hopes and desires and the meaningless universe in which man lives. Man's problem, then, is to find his way through a world of chaos. Among Camus' plays which illustrate this idea are *Caligula*, *Cross-Purposes*, and *The Just Assassins*.

Both Camus and Sartre, however, emphasized the necessity for each man to find his own personal set of values in an otherwise chaotic world. Man, thus, determines his own course rather than being at the mercy of heredity and environment. Both dramatists also expressed their ideas in plays which utilize conventional dramatic structure and techniques.

The "Absurd" dramatists who came after Camus and Sartre differ from them in two important respects. The later writers have concentrated upon demonstrating the absurdity of existence rather than the necessity of bringing order to absurdity, and they have embodied their chaotic subject matter in an equally chaotic dramatic form. It is these later dramatists which most persons have in mind when they speak of the Theatre of the Absurd.

The first of the Absurd dramatists to come into prominence in America was Samuel Beckett (1906–   ) with *Waiting for Godot* (1952). The play has been translated into over twenty languages and has become one of the most controversial of the postwar period. Beckett, Irish by birth, has never acknowledged his allegiance to any formal school of philosophy and *Waiting for Godot* has as many religious as Absurdist connotations. In it two tramps wait for Godot, who never appears. It is a play about the act of waiting and of hope, but it is also a play about the nonfulfillment of hope. Some interpret it as indicating that the hope of salvation gives meaning to life; others see it as a statement about the absurdity of such hope.

Beckett's work as a whole suggests that it is impossible ever to be certain about anything. Since the meaning of life and of all experience is ambiguous, the playwright, therefore, must reflect this ambiguity in his subject matter and dramatic techniques. Beckett's works are rich in suggestions about the nature of human existence, but, as with Symbolist drama, the essential mystery which lurks behind the action and characters remains unexplained. Beckett leaves it up to each member of the audience to find his own meaning in the events seen on the stage. Among the more important of Beckett's later plays are *Krapp's Last Tape* and *Happy Days*.

A French dramatist who has recently come into prominence in America is Jean Genet (1910–   ), best known for *The Balcony, The Blacks, The Maids,* and *The Screens*. Genet sees existence as an endless set of reflections in mirrors. Each image may for a moment be mistaken

A scene from Beckett's *Waiting for Godot*. Directed by William Reardon.

for reality, but upon examination it always proves to be an illusion. Truth (or the beginning of the set of reflections) can never be found. Genet's characters assume roles, but when the disguises are removed the true persons are never discovered for each appearance is found to be only a new disguise. Through these means Genet attacks and undermines the accepted conventions of the modern world. Like most of the other Absurdists, however, he is unable to offer any positive ideas to replace the old conceptions, since this would necessitate arguing for the truth of his own views.

Eugene Ionesco (1912–   ), is another Absurd dramatist who has achieved considerable renown. His first play, *The Bald Soprano,* was produced in Paris in 1950. To indicate his attempt at writing something as unlike conventional drama as possible, Ionesco called *The Bald Soprano* an "antiplay." In it no action is developed, many of the characters are so much alike that they may be interchanged, and the dialogue is made up almost entirely of clichés. The meaninglessness and repetitiousness of the subject matter is paralleled in the dramatic techniques, for the plot does not progress to a climax and the dialogue degenerates until the characters are merely repeating the letters of the alphabet. Ionesco's dramatic form thus becomes a suitable parallel to the content of his play.

Ionesco has continued to write in much the same vein. Among the more important of his later plays are *The Chairs, The Lesson, Victims of Duty, The New Tenant, The Killer,* and *Rhinoceros. The Chairs* will be examined in more detail as an example of Ionesco's work and of Absurdist drama.

THE CHAIRS

Ionesco labeled *The Chairs* "a tragic farce," and elsewhere he has said that the theme of the play is nothingness–which is reflected in the empty chairs, the empty stage, and the emptiness of the life portrayed. The play also suggests the impossibility of communicating anything about experience to others, for the speech of the deaf-mute orator is as specific about the meaning of life as one can be. The inanities of everyday conversation, the repetitiveness of daily existence, the thwarted hopes and ambitions of mankind are depicted. The play is a summation of the typical Absurdist view of the human condition. Ionesco does not offer any solution or plan for change; he is content merely to set forth the situation.

PLOT AND STRUCTURE.   The principal thread which holds *The Chairs* together is the promise of a revelation about the meaning of life. The delay of the message until the end of the play arouses and maintains expectation and suspense.

The majority of the play, however, is taken up with an exploration of different aspects of human experience, ranging from childhood to old age. The Old Man sits on the Old Woman's lap and becomes a child, while she assumes the role of a mother. Later they talk about their court-ship and marriage, and many scenes from their past married life are suggested, as when one of the invisible characters tries to seduce the wife, while the husband conceives an idealistic attachment to one of the in-visible women. The Old Man and Old Woman show many facets of old age, and death itself is seen in the suicide of these two old people.

Furthermore, the play explores an equally wide range of human emotions and attitudes. The characters laugh uncontrollably, cry, go into states of dreamy forgetfulness, become angry and outraged, cajole and fawn, have love scenes, greet visitors, and do obeisance to the Emperor; they juxtapose talk about the significance of existence with the sale of programs for the occasion. The universal desire to discover the meaning of life is demonstrated through the vast and almost endless crowd that inundates the couple when the Old Man announces his intention of revealing the secret.

One of the keys to the play's structure is to be found in the use of chairs. When the play begins there are only two chairs on stage. This introductory scene establishes the basic situation of two old people living alone in a house completely surrounded by water. Into this setting other, invisible characters begin to appear. Each arrival is matched on stage by an empty chair. The first arrivals are treated at some length and are rather clearly individualized, but after a time the pace quickens as more and more people enter. The later arrivals are identified only by a name or a professional designation and the identity of many is not specified at all. Chairs eventually take up so much of the floor space that the old people must elbow their way about.

In several of Ionesco's plays objects grow and multiply. He is probably trying to suggest that human lives are dominated by an increasing number of details, all of which are essentially alike and ultimately mean-ingless. This is one of the devices which has led many to call Ionesco a Surrealist. The nightmarish quality of *The Chairs* is emphasized by the fact that, although the chairs are real, the people remain invisible. Objects, thus, have greater reality than do people. The multiplication of chairs seems to be pointing toward some goal, but the goal is never reached.

It is significant that the Old Man hires someone else to give his message about the meaning of life since he cannot articulate it himself—a fairly sure sign that he does not know what it is he wants to say. Ionesco has specified that the Orator should be costumed as a caricature of the nineteenth-century conception of a poet. He undoubtedly meant in this way to satirize the idealistic Romanticist playwright who always had a positive idea about the meaning of existence and of man's importance in the universe.

The expected message never comes. As in *Pelléas and Mélisande*, life remains an enigma, but while Maeterlinck implies that a mysterious force presides over the universe, Ionesco merely derides the notion that life has any significance. His ridiculous and pathetic treatment of human attempts to resolve the riddle make a dramatic form which corresponds to his view that existence is chaotic and without meaning.

CHARACTERS AND ACTING.   The Old Man and the Old Woman in *The Chairs* are, in a sense, representative of all mankind. Ionesco has made them old to emphasize the idea that they have experienced all of life. At the same time he parodies the custom of asking old people to what they attribute their long lives and for any message they may have for others.

Equally important, the Old Man and the Old Woman serve as mirrors in which the audience sees everything else. Their actions and reactions create the invisible characters and serve to people the stage. The play is a *tour de force* for two actors and taxes to the utmost the players' abilities in pantomime and in portraying a vast range of human emotions and attitudes. While all plays need to be skillfully performed, *The Chairs* is especially dependent upon excellent acting for its effectiveness in the theatre.

Ionesco has little interest in character consistency and he does not attempt to explain his characters' reactions. Rather, he has shown them responding in ways which are typically human in a series of commonplace human situations. This typicality is manipulated so as to point up the uniformity of existence and to make comments upon human experience as a whole.

The characters are asked to shift rapidly from one kind of situation or emotion to another without any kind of logical explanation for the change. Again, this points up the essential lack of logic in life. The various parts are held together principally by the play's theme and by the fact that the same actors perform them all.

The dialogue of the characters is made up largely of clichés. It serves to emphasize the conformity and repetitiveness of life. It satirizes man's illusion that he is communicating with others when in fact he is only repeating meaningless banalities.

Although Ionesco's ultimate aim is to show the absurdity of existence, he has provided two actors with extremely rewarding roles. The theatricality of the play is only heightened by the demand that the actors give convincingly lifelike portrayals of a wide range of human attitudes.

VISUAL AND AURAL EFFECTS.   Ionesco places so much importance upon the staging of *The Chairs* that he has found it advisable to furnish a diagram showing the arrangement of the setting. A close study of his diagram and a careful reading of his stage directions in relation to it is extremely helpful in understanding the spirit of the work. He has indicated a number of doors and one window on each side of the stage. During the play the Old Woman frequently goes out a door on one side and reappears with chairs through another door on the opposite side of the stage. Yet in the script the house is said to be surrounded by water and the old people commit suicide by jumping out the windows into the water. The Old Woman, then, would have had to go through the water in order to get to the other side of the stage. The action, thus, contradicts the logic of the setting and Ionesco uses this contradiction deliberately to show his lack of concern for illusionistic stage conventions. By this means he is able to comment upon theatre itself and at the same time achieve a comic effect. Consequently, his use of the stage is itself "absurd" and forms a perfect parallel for the play's action.

Other aspects contribute much to the play's effect. The visible multiplication of chairs is extremely important. The actors must create the feeling that every inch of stage space has been usurped by the invisible crowd—the invisible must be made to seem visible. This desire is emphasized by the final stage directions which specify that, after the old people have committed suicide and the orator has failed to communicate his message, the noises of the invisible crowd should become audible—through laughter, murmurs, coughs.

Ionesco has thus been able to achieve a union of content and form. His subject is the absurdity of human existence and he has utilized character, action, and setting in such a way that absurdity is paralleled in dramatic techniques. Although many of the features of *The Chairs* are distinctive, Ionesco's play is nevertheless representative of the outlook and the methods of the Absurd school of dramatists.

RELATED DRAMATISTS

Although the Absurdist movement has been centered in France, it has had adherents in other countries. In England the work of Harold Pinter (1930–   ) and N. F. Simpson (1919–   ) fall into this general category. Pinter began writing plays in 1957, and his *Birthday Party* (1958) and *The Caretaker* (1960) have achieved considerable success. Simpson's best-known work, *One-Way Pendulum*, is a satire on contemporary British life in the form of nonsensical farce.

In America the Theatre of the Absurd has found less of a foothold than in many other countries perhaps because Americans are less inclined to be pessimistic about life. Another explanation may be the comparative difficulty of getting productions for "off beat" plays. Thus far the most

A scene from Friedrich Duerrenmatt's *The Visit*.

successful Absurd dramas in America have been Edward Albee's (1928–) *The Zoo Story, The American Dream,* and *The Sandbox.* His full-length play, *Who's Afraid of Virginia Woolf?,* suggests that Albee is moving away from the Absurdist school. Jack Gelber's *The Connection* and Arthur L. Kopit's *Oh Dad, Poor Dad, Mama's Hung You in the Closet and I'm Feeling So Sad* are other American dramas in the Absurdist style.

In Switzerland Friedrich Duerrenmatt (1921–) has achieved fame with plays that are clearly related to the Absurdist movement. He is known principally in America for *The Visit, The Marriage of Mr. Mississippi,* and *Romulus.* Duerrenmatt has stated that plays should frighten audiences and make them face up to the grotesque world in which they live. Such an experience he hopes will make men attempt to find some order, although he seems to have little faith in the possibilities of positive action since he has said, "The universal for me is chaos." The most that men can hope for, therefore, is the courage to endure life.

The Absurdist movement may be seen as entirely pessimistic, but this is a superficial view. Many persons in the nineteenth century saw realism and naturalism as negative and as dedicated to denying man any ideal qualities. While this estimate was partially true, it was not the whole truth, for these movements were concerned with portraying a new perception of reality and in making way for a better world by facing facts. The Theatre of the Absurd also is essentially an attempt to face squarely the implications of modern thought. Like many movements, it began by denouncing older views and gave the appearance of being only negative. But it now shows signs of growing and becoming a mature art movement, one that will contribute significantly to the theatre of the future.

The theatre of today is complex and takes many forms. Only three of these—modified realism, the musical, and the Theatre of the Absurd— have been considered as representative of the whole. Its many complexities, however, are already creating the conditions out of which the theatre of the future will grow. The theatre of our day will soon give way to other movements and will take its place in the long and continuing history of one of man's great creations—theatre.

PART FOUR

THE THEATRE ARTS
IN AMERICA TODAY

Chapter 15

THE PLAYWRIGHT
AND
THE PRODUCER

The playwright's script is normally the starting point for any theatrical production. The work of the playwright, therefore, is of primary importance in any consideration of the operation of the contemporary theatre. The playwright's means have already been discussed in Chapter 3, but something needs to be said about his working methods.

THE PLAYWRIGHT'S WORKING METHODS

There are many approaches to writing plays. Sometimes a writer starts with an idea. For example, he may be struck by the double standard of morality which demands different behavior for men and women. He may then work out an action, either comic or serious, illustrating this idea.

Other writers may start with a character or set of characters. An unusual, amusing, or abnormal character may raise a question about the results of putting him into a situation in which his peculiarities would lead to conflict. Still other playwrights may be aroused initially by a story. A newspaper article, a personal experience, or an anecdote may set the playwright to thinking about the significance of events, or the possibilities for comedy or tragedy in a particular situation.

Part-title illustrations. Productions by the New York City Ballet; choreography by George Balanchine. Photographs—Martha Swope. *Left: Liebeslieder Walzer.* Music by Johannes Brahms; costumes designed and executed by Karinska; scenery and lighting by David Hays. *Right: Movement for Piano and Orchestra.* Music by Igor Stravinsky. Reproduced by courtesy of Martha Swope.
Above. Design by Inigo Jones. From Peter Cunningham's *Inigo Jones . . .* 1848.

Regardless of the original impetus, however, the good playwright is seldom content merely to set forth an idea, to outline characters, or to tell a story. In most cases he does all of these things in the same play, for it is difficult to reveal characters except through an action which tells a story. Similarly, story and character revelation inevitably have implications, profound or trivial, and so illustrate an idea. The initial interest which gave rise to the play is not always evident from the finished play, therefore, and writers themselves do not always know how they first became interested in writing a particular work. The possibilities for drama are to be found everywhere and any event may arouse a response in the writer which results in a play.

Just as plays arise from various impulses, so too the methods followed in the actual process of writing are equally varied. Some dramatists prefer to work from a scenario. This involves making an outline of the story prior to writing the dialogue. The playwright then follows this scenario systematically. There are many variations on this procedure. Some writers prefer a very brief outline which merely indicates the major developments, while others prefer a sketch which traces all the details of the plot and characters so that the writing of dialogue merely fills out these details. Regardless of how complete the scenario may be, however, this procedure implies that the playwright has clearly in mind what he wishes to do before he begins writing. While this is true for some playwrights, it is not true for all.

Other writers find a scenario too inhibiting, since it seems to direct thought along a rigid channel. Writers frequently find that their interests shift after they begin writing. As the play develops, a minor character may take on such stature that the playwright may decide to shift the focus to him. In such a case the entire scenario will probably need to be reworked. Therefore, the scenario must remain flexible until the play is finished.

Another procedure which has worked well for many consists of writing the scene of crisis first and then working out those scenes which precede and follow it. The argument for this method is that, since the crisis is the scene toward which the entire play moves, all the rest must be constructed to make it convincing and effective. Having written this scene, then, the dramatist can more clearly see what must go before and what must follow it. Again, however, as the play takes shape the dramatist may change his mind about his over-all purpose and a different crisis may be needed, and then the whole process will need to be repeated.

Other writers prefer to make a large number of notes about characters, situations, and ideas. These notes may be read over and over until the play gradually evolves from these random jottings. The actual writing of the play may not start until the whole has taken shape in the author's mind and may then be done very quickly.

A favorite method, especially with beginners, is to "think on paper."

That is, the writer begins composing with only a vague idea of how he wishes the play to conclude, and lets the characters and situations develop as he goes along. This is one way of thinking through situations, but it is apt to be a lengthy process, since it may necessitate a great number of attempts and may never result in an organized story.

No doubt there are many other ways in which playwrights work. The central purpose of all, however, is to organize and reduce to an effective form the many elements which go into a play. It is possible that every dramatist must "feel his way" toward the final product; he may not be entirely clear himself what it is he is trying to capture until he finds it. This may be true even of those who start with a clear-cut scenario, since each play is a great deal more than the bare outline of its plot.

Seldom does a playwright hit upon the final version of his play in the first draft. Most finished works represent many revisions and may take shape over a period of years. Furthermore, since plays are intended for the stage, most writers need to see their works in performance before they can be sure that no further revisions are needed.

Although there is a constant need for good scripts, a playwright seldom finds the steps easy in getting his work performed. The goal of most playwrights is professional production, which is becoming increasingly difficult to achieve because of the great financial risks involved.

If the dramatist wishes a Broadway production of his play, however, a producer must be found. Negotiations with potential producers have become so complex that most writers work through agents, who understand the problems and who can devote a great deal of time to selling a play.

If a producer becomes interested in a work he may take an option on it. This means that a given amount of money is paid to the playwright for the possibility of performing the play and to prevent others from doing so; a time limit is specified and if the play is not produced during that period all rights revert to the playwright, who is then free to negotiate with others. Options may be renewed but they are never a guarantee of production, for the same play may be optioned many times without ever being presented.

Before his play can be produced in New York the playwright must become a member of the Dramatists Guild of the Authors League of America. Although it is a "closed shop," anyone who has had a play optioned for production may join the Dramatists Guild. The purpose of the Guild is to protect the author and to secure for him the best possible working conditions and financial arrangements.

If a producer decides to present a play, the dramatist is given a contract specifying the amount of his royalties and the limit of the producer's control over the play (most of the terms of the playwright's contract are part of a standard form worked out by the Dramatists Guild). The play-wright seldom relinquishes the television, motion-picture, or foreign rights in his play to the producer. The playwright's contract specifies that he must be available for consultation and possible rewriting throughout the rehearsal period. His duties are over only when the play opens in New York. His contract also states that his is the final decision on any proposed changes in the script. Legally, in most cases, he does not have to make any revisions in his work after the contract is signed.

On the other hand, the playwright is constantly under pressure to make changes. Even before a producer sees a play a dramatist's agent may suggest a number of changes. A producer may express an interest in a script on the condition that certain revisions be carried out. The financial backers ("angels") may specify certain alterations. Frequently a "big name" star will agree to appear in a play if it is rewritten to show off his abilities to greater advantage. Rehearsals may show up real or imagined weaknesses in the script, and rewriting may go on up to the opening night in New York.

It has become customary to have a series of "out-of-town" (that is, out of New York) tryouts. This means that plays are opened in such cities as Philadelphia, New Haven, Washington or are given a pre-Broad-way road tour. Critical notices and the response of audiences are carefully studied after each tryout and the play is reworked in accordance with these reactions. The process is continued until the production is considered ready for New York. Sometimes a play is almost completely rewritten during this time.

Such a procedure dismays many, who feel that the playwright is reduced to the status of a "hack" writer; that is, he must write what is demanded of him and for the ultimate aim of achieving financial success. Whether this is true or not, it is certain that the playwright is subject to a great number of pressures, and his ability to assess the validity of the many suggestions is of prime importance. No one knows what makes a successful play; otherwise there obviously would not be so many failures in the New York theatre. Yet the playwright is bombarded with advice and demands from many sources—all of which claim to have the answer which will turn the playwright's work into a successful venture.

The penalties for failure (both financial and artistic) have become so great that everyone strives to avoid them at any cost. Regardless of the source of the failure in a New York production the blame is almost always placed on the playwright.

This pressure on the dramatist is more pronounced in the United States than in any other country. The costs of production are not nearly so high in most other countries, and as a result the pressure to achieve commercial success is not so great. Where theatres are subsidized a commercial failure is absorbed, and repertory companies do plays with the intention of performing them from time to time and gradually recovering their investment. In the United States, on the other hand, a playwright is always under extreme pressure to succeed. One failure, even after a series of successes, raises doubts about a dramatist's future work and makes producers wary of doing his plays.

In spite of all these factors, however, most playwrights refuse to let any nonprofessional group present their works so long as there is any hope for professional production. Most of the original plays produced by nonprofessional companies are written by students, local residents, or the winners of playwriting contests. While these may be good plays, as a rule authors do not even enter plays in contests unless they have been unable to interest an agent in the work.

This situation is in many ways unfortunate. A playwright needs to see his work performed if he is to learn his profession well. Frequently the nonprofessional theatre offers more freedom for experimentation than the professional, and certainly the pressures are fewer. Playwrights seem to feel, however, that any incompetence in production will make their work appear so bad that all chances for commercial production will be ruined. It is certain, however, that many nonprofessional organizations in America could produce original plays effectively, and could offer the playwright an opportunity to see his work on the stage. This is only one area in which the professional and nonprofessional theatre have failed to achieve a working relationship which could be profitable to both.

THE PRODUCER

The ultimate fate of a play depends much upon the producer, who is concerned primarily with its financing and sale. It is the producer who contracts for the play, secures a director, a theatre, and the necessary financial backing; it is he who publicizes the production, sells tickets to it, and makes all other necessary arrangements of this kind. While he is not directly responsible for the artistic aspects of a performance, his position is such that he exerts considerable influence on all theatre workers. The producer, therefore, is one of the most important persons in the theatre.

The way in which the producer's function is carried out varies according to the situation—professional, summer stock, community, or educational theatre. The responsibilities are most clearly defined in the professional theatre.

The producer of a play in New York may be a group, such as the Theatre Guild, or an individual, such as David Merrick. If a producer has been in business for some time, he may maintain a permanent office and staff, but many producers are concerned with only one show at a time and many maintain no office except when they have a play in production. In most cases, a special corporation or partnership is formed for each play so as to protect the investors in the production. In this way no investor is responsible for debts beyond a specified amount.

Before money can be raised, the producer must have a play under option. The majority of plays performed in New York are new plays or foreign plays not previously seen in America. New plays are normally secured by the producer through a playwright's agent, though some will read scripts which have been submitted directly by the author. If he is sufficiently interested in a script, the producer takes an option on it. With a play in hand he seeks to raise money for its production. The cost of producing a play on Broadway has become exceedingly high, and even a simple show today requires between $75,000 and $100,000 to meet all expenses up to the opening performance, and a musical may run to $500,000. Few individuals can afford to invest so much money in such a risky venture and it is usual for a producer to solicit funds from a number of individuals or groups. One of the producer's first jobs, then, is to interest others in the script and to convince them that the play constitutes a worthwhile investment.

If the author is well known, or if the producer has a reputation for being successful, or if actors of enough box-office appeal are secured, the job of raising money may not be difficult. But it is frequently necessary to send out brochures along with copies or summaries of the play to likely investors. Sometimes readings are arranged for interested parties. In raising money the producer must submit to prospective investors a proposed budget for the play up to its Broadway opening and a statement as to how profits are to be divided. (The producer is usually entitled to fifty percent of the net profit, regardless of how much money he has invested.)

After the required amount of money has been secured, the producer may then proceed with the actual business of getting the play on. He usually needs a considerable number of secretarial, financial, and legal assistants since his responsibilities may become extremely complex. He must negotiate contracts with all of the persons involved in the production: the director, the actors, the designers, the stage manager, and so on. He must rent space for tryouts and rehearsals and must secure a theatre (which is not always easy since the number of New York theatres is relatively small). The producer arranges for out-of-town tryouts (including theatres, transportation, and publicity). He must keep financial records which are submitted to all investors at regular intervals. He handles the payroll and closes down the show at the end of its run.

The producer must give his approval to all changes in plans made after the contracts are let. He may participate in conferences about alterations in the script, settings, costumes, lighting, music, and dance—any factor which affects the show as a financial investment.

The producer's job is made difficult in part by the fact that he must deal with eleven different unions representing the following groups: the playwrights (though some deny that the Dramatists Guild is a union); the directors and choreographers; the actors; the musicians; the stagehands; the wardrobe attendants; the press agents and managers; the treasurers; the ushers and doormen; the porters and cleaners; and the engineers. Each of these groups has its own minimum demands which the producer must meet.

The League of New York Theatres, the producers' organization, requires that each production have a company manager and a theatrical press agent (who must belong to the Association of Theatrical Press Agents and Managers). The company manager works with the producer in carrying out the provisions of the budget. He aids in letting the contracts and is usually in charge of the payroll; he makes arrangements for rehearsal space, for the theatre, the out-of-town tryouts, and similar matters.

The press agent is concerned principally with selling the show. He is responsible for all news releases (though these must be approved by the producer) and advertisements; he makes sure that pictures of actors and of scenes from the play are available to the press; he works with the newspapers in those towns in which the show is tried out. He must decide upon the most strategic time for making the major drive for ticket sales. He arranges for the playbills which are given to all customers and any souvenir programs which are to be sold. He must know the order of billing for the stars and must see that everyone is given proper credit. After the show opens he chooses the quotations from the reviews which appear in the ads and does all that he can to keep the public interested in the play.

The producer's work, then, is largely concerned with the financial aspects of play production. It has become fashionable in recent years to blame the producer for the state of the American theatre and to argue that he has turned it into a business venture. Given the handicaps under which he works, however, it is remarkable that anyone attempts to stage a play in New York, and it is certain that a sound business sense is required to keep the theatre alive under the present conditions.

In summer stock, community, and educational theatres the position of the producer is not so clearly defined, although his responsibilities must be assumed by someone. Such groups are normally organized to perform a number of plays over a long period of time rather than being concerned with only one play. Many of the duties, therefore, may be simplified. For example, a group may use the same theatre for several years and will not need to rent one for each play. The producer's work is also frequently divided among several members of the permanent group.

Most of the semiprofessional and summer stock groups use variations on the procedure outlined above in the discussion of the New York theatre. As a rule, they must raise money from investors, but usually the sum is a great deal less than that needed to produce a play in New York and the investment is made in the organization rather than in a specific play. The financial pressures on semiprofessional groups are not usually so great since most are not subject to the demands of many of the unions which function in New York. These organizations also tend to produce plays already proven elsewhere; therefore, there is not so much risk involved, and the previous success of the plays may be used to advantage in publicity.

Similarly in the community and educational theatre the group is the producer and the various duties may be divided among many persons. The community theatre as a rule hires only a director (and sometimes a designer-technician). All other work is done by volunteers under the supervision of the director or of unpaid, elected members of the group (such as the board of directors, the president, or some specified committee or officer).

In the educational theatre, the responsibilities are divided in still other ways. Frequently the director of a play must take primary responsibility for choosing the play, working out a budget, and arranging for publicity. Since his salary is usually paid by the school and since most of the other work is done by students or by faculty members, the expenses are confined to such items as royalties, and the materials for building costumes and scenery. Furthermore, the use of the theatre building does not normally cost the group anything. Thus the financial risks are not great in the educational theatre, and for that reason more experimentation is possible than in other groups.

Most permanent organizations present from three to eight plays each year. In planning such a season, a group may take the following factors into consideration: (1) the need for variety in the type of play, (2) the available actors, (3) the production demands in terms of scenery, costumes, and lighting, (4) the total cost, and (5) the taste of local audiences. The amount of weight given to each of these factors varies from group to group.

The majority of plays done in semiprofessional and nonprofessional theatres falls into two categories: (1) plays which have been recently produced in New York, and (2) the "classics," or plays from the past which are thought to be still meaningful. Relatively few original plays are done by these groups, though the educational theatre is more apt to present original plays than the semiprofessional or community theatre.

If a nonprofessional group produces an original script, the arrangements are usually made directly with the author. The nonprofessional rights to plays recently produced in New York are handled by agencies (such as Samuel French and Dramatists Play Service), which collect a royalty fee for each performance of the play. Older plays may not require any royalty payment as the copyright of a play lasts for twenty-eight years and may be renewed only once. Translations and adaptations of older plays may be copyrighted by persons other than the author, however, and it is the responsibility of any producing group to determine the copyright status of any script.

THE AGENT

Many theatre workers—playwrights, directors, designers, choreographers, musicians, dancers—have agents. The agent's function is to sell his client's services to the producer. An actor (and to a lesser extent other theatre workers) may have difficulty in getting a tryout or an interview if he does not have an agent who is known to the producer.

The agent may work alone or he may be employed by an organization. There are a few very large organizations which represent hundreds of persons in various phases of the theatre. Most agencies, however, are relatively small and maintain a rather close contact with their clients.

An agent is usually not willing to accept a client unless he has seen his or her work. The agent's own earnings depend upon selling the talents of his clients, and he does not wish to represent anyone unless he is reasonably sure that the person has the talent to fill a job satisfactorily. For his services he is paid a percentage of the worker's earnings on each contract negotiated.

Like other careers in the theatre, the agent's also has come under stronger and stronger regulations as more attempts have been made to protect theatre workers from unethical practices. Today an agent must normally be approved by the client's union (in other words, an actor's agent must be approved by Actors' Equity, and so on). In the complex world of the professional theatre, a good agent is well worth the fee and frequently makes the difference between employment and unemployment.

Securing a producer for a new play is a difficult task, and the commercial aspects of the theatre are frequently bewildering and complex. It is the producer, nevertheless, who makes it possible for other theatre workers to translate the written script into a staged performance.

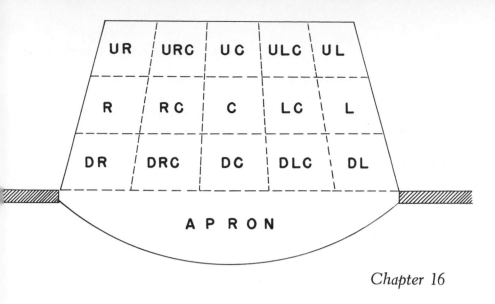

Chapter 16

THE DIRECTOR

Just as the producer is the person most concerned with the financial aspects of play production, the director is the one most responsible for all artistic elements. He must decide how the script is to be interpreted, and he must coordinate the efforts of all the other theatre artists into a unified performance. A good director, therefore, is of primary importance in the success of any play.

Although the director's exact duties may vary from one organization to another, ordinarily he performs these functions: (1) he decides upon the interpretation to be given the play, (2) he casts the actors, (3) he works with the playwright, designers, and technicians in planning the production, (4) he rehearses the actors, and (5) he coordinates all of the elements into the finished stage performance.

UNDERSTANDING AND INTERPRETING THE SCRIPT

The length of time available to a director for the study and analysis of a script varies greatly. Many educational theatres each spring select the bill of plays for the following school year. In this case, a director may have several months in which to prepare. On the other hand, many organizations choose plays one at a time, and in the professional theatre a director may be chosen at the last moment. In these cases the director has little time in

The working subdivisions of the stage are the ground on which the director plans and fuses the myriad elements of the play.

which to study the script. Regardless of the length of time available, the director must familiarize himself as thoroughly as he can with the play if he is to cast and rehearse the actors intelligently, and if he is to guide the designers and technicians in their interpretation of the script.

The kind of analysis undertaken varies from director to director and with the complexity of the play. The principal elements of play structure, characterization, thought, language, and spectacle have already been outlined in Chapter 3, and will be reviewed only briefly.

The director should study the play's construction by examining the pattern of preparation, complication, crisis, and resolution; he should study the devices used to build suspense and those used for exposition. In making an analysis it is helpful to divide a play into short scenes marked off by the entrance or exit of characters (since each entrance or exit usually brings about a shift in character relationships). Each short scene may then be examined in terms of its major functions. What are the motivations of the characters in the scene? What is the predominant mood? How is the scene related to those which precede and follow it? What is its significance in the play as a whole?

Answers to these and similar questions will help the director to understand the play's meanings and to see why the play is constructed as it is. He will become aware both of the strengths and weaknesses of the script and of the problems to be solved.

The director must also understand each character, both in terms of its function in the play and the demands made upon the actor who will play the part. He must be aware of the physical characteristics, dominant qualities (such as wistfulness, strength, or cunning), emotional range, and the vocal qualifications needed for each character so that he can cast and rehearse the play intelligently.

The director must analyze a script in terms of the scenic, costume, and lighting requirements. He must try to envision the stage setting in terms of its mood and atmosphere, its arrangement for the proper flow of action, and as an appropriate environment for the characters and events. He must be in a position to talk intelligently and persuasively with the designers and technicians about these and any other factors which are involved in design.

In addition to analyzing the script carefully, the director may need to acquire considerable background information about the author, the period of the play (if it is not modern), and the environment depicted (if it is one unfamiliar to the director); or he may wish to read what critics have said about the play, and find out how it has affected audiences in the theatre. Each of these inquiries should help the director to understand the play's qualities, and to decide what approach he needs to take in his embodiment of the script on the stage.

The problems of interpretation vary according to the kind of play the director is working with. Scripts may be divided roughly into three categories: period plays, recent Broadway successes, and original plays.

The director encounters special problems when he undertakes plays from the past. To ensure that they will be comprehensible and moving, he may choose to make changes. He may substitute words and phrases for those that have become obsolete and meaningless in modern terms. Sometimes he may omit subplots; sometimes cut speeches; sometimes rearrange or combine scenes.

A director may decide that a play can be made more meaningful to a modern audience by changing its time and place. As examples, *Hamlet* has been done in modern dress and *Much Ado About Nothing* has been set in the southwestern part of the United States. A director may change the emphasis in a play so as to give a new interpretation to a character. For example, the comic aspects of Shylock in *The Merchant of Venice* were emphasized in Shakespeare's time, but recently the sympathetic qualities in the role have been played up. Hamlet has been played as a man of action and one too introverted to act. The director must be clear about what he expects to achieve by such interpretations and must be convinced that they are justified.

A director may also seek to make a play more comprehensible by building his interpretation around a central visual device or a key image. For example a director might take the S-curve, which was the dominant decorative shape in the eighteenth century, and apply it in the production of plays from that period to the settings and costumes, to the movement and gestures of the actors. Meyerhold built his production of *The Inspector General* around the image of spying and eavesdropping. In one scene the stage was completely surrounded by doors, at each of which a character tried to overhear the onstage conversations.

The style and period of a play can frequently be made understand-

Directors may change a play's period to point up parallels. Shakespeare's *Troilus and Cressida*, of the Trojan War era, is shown set in the 1640s (English Civil War). Directed by James Gousseff; setting by Arnold Gillette; costumes by Iris Brooke.

Adaptations of stage conventions of a past era to present tastes are often employed. *Noah*, a Medieval cycle play, as performed at the Mermaid Theatre, London.

able to a modern audience through the adaptation of the staging methods—the acting techniques, the costumes and scenery, and the stage—in use at the time when the play was written. For example, the Elizabethan stage and its conventions are frequently utilized in productions of Shakespeare's plays. Theatrical conditions of the past, however, must always be comprehensible and should be adapted until they can serve as a bridge between the past and the present.

In working with a recent Broadway success, the director usually finds that the printed copies obtained from the play agency contain a floor plan of the setting, a property list, clear indications of the actors' movements, and many suggestions for interpretation. Most of this information is taken from the prompt copy of the original production script (that is, it describes what happened in the New York production). Many directors follow these suggestions as closely as possible, but most directors are more inclined to interpret the play themselves and to adapt the floor plan and other elements to their own particular situations rather than merely copying the New York production. Regardless of the amount of information given in an acting edition, however, a director must always add much, since it is impossible to specify in writing all of the subtleties which go into any competent production.

When producing a new play, the director's duties are made more complex by the necessity of working directly with the playwright. Frequently the script is in a constant state of flux up to the opening night. Changes are made for the purpose of achieving greater clarity and believability. Sometimes entire acts are rewritten; sometimes only individual speeches or short scenes are changed; sometimes only transitions are reworked.

The director should look upon himself as a critic and adviser to the playwright, and should avoid being autocratic and arbitrary in his demands. If the director and the playwright are too much at odds, either the director or the production will have to be dropped. Neither the playwright nor the director should assume that he is infallible; suggestions by each should be made and listened to in the spirit of helpfulness.

The director of the new script is aided in arriving at an understanding and interpretation of the play by the dramatist, who normally is present to help clarify doubtful points or ambiguities. On the other hand, while he must seek to embody the playwright's conceptions whenever he can, the director must not accept the playwright's word that something is in the script which the director cannot see. The playwright's ideas must be expressed in a dramatic form which can be projected to an audience, and when they are not the director must point this out and must work with the playwright in seeking solutions to such problems.

The director, thus, must seek to understand the script through all of the means at his disposal. He must know what he wishes to emphasize so as to bring out the values he finds there. It is only after he has done this preliminary exploration and planning that he is ready to work with the other theatre artists.

THE DIRECTOR AND THE DESIGNERS

Usually before rehearsals begin, the director meets with the designers and discusses his approach to the play with them. They, too, should have read and studied the play prior to this time and, therefore, should be able to discuss it intelligently. They may not have arrived at the same interpretation as the director, however, and the first task for all is to reach a general agreement about the basic treatment of the script. The director should be willing to listen to ideas and suggestions, some of which may alter his previous conception of the play. Ultimately, however, the director must decide on the interpretation to be used, and the designers must attempt to work within these limitations.

Royall Tyler's *The Contrast* performed in a wing-and-drop setting adapted from the stage usage of the eighteenth century. Directed by William D. Coder.

If the director has any specific requests, he should make them at this first meeting. For example, the floor plan of a setting in large part determines the movement pattern of the actors. The director may desire, therefore, to have a door, or a desk, or a sofa in a particular place. He may also have specific suggestions about costumes and lighting. The director's requirements should be made clear to the designers before they begin work on their designs.

After deciding upon the basic approach and understanding necessary requirements, the designers must then be allowed some time in which to visualize the production and to make sketches. There may be a series of meetings between the designers and the director in which proposals are talked over and revisions are suggested.

Before giving final approval to any plans, the director must be sure that he has taken into consideration all of the pertinent factors. He must assure himself that the proposed setting will mirror adequately the action, mood, theme, style, characters, and period of the play. He must be convinced that it will be functional in terms of the movement he envisions. If there are to be scene changes, he needs to know how long each will take. He must believe that the proposed costumes will enhance the actors' movement, and that they will reflect sufficiently the psychological and sociological attributes of each role. The director must also know the kind of lighting he desires, and he must be specific about the size, shape, and general appearance of all properties.

Sketches and drawings of various kinds are mandatory, since words are inadequate for communicating about visual elements. Every designer must be capable of demonstrating the color, shape, and stage appearance of each item he proposes, and the director usually insists upon this demonstration as a way of insuring himself that everyone has the same conceptions in mind. Unless the designers are specific, the director may discover at dress-rehearsal time that a number of elements do not function as he had envisoned. Last-minute changes are not only costly, but sometimes impossible due to insufficient time.

Of course the director must be in a position to make the final decision on all elements which go into a production, but he should not assume the role of a dictator. Each designer has important contributions to make and should be allowed as much freedom as possible. Too many restrictions may serve to discourage an artist and may not bring out his best work.

After all plans have been approved, the designers and technicians execute the scenery, costumes, and properties, while the director turns more and more to his work with the actors. There may be conferences at regular intervals throughout the rehearsal period, but the work of the designers and of the director and actors progresses more or less independently of each other until dress rehearsal.

CASTING

By far the greatest amount of a director's time is devoted to working with the actors. Normally, one of his first tasks is the selection of actors to portray the various roles. Occasionally, a director must accept a cast which has been selected by someone else. Some producing organizations employ a casting director to select actors for its various productions. Sometimes a star is employed before the director is selected and casting must be worked around the star. Usually and ideally, however, the director sets out to find actors who fit his conception of the characters.

Various methods are employed in casting. One of the most usual is the open tryout, the purposes of which are to secure as wide a choice as possible of the available actors, and to give all interested persons a chance at being cast. In New York City, where the supply of actors overwhelmingly exceeds the demand, open tryouts are almost never used. When they are, the director and producer may set up a list of specifications and let an agent, a stage manager, or an assistant eliminate those actors who do not fit the basic requirements. The director may see those who remain, but, since time is limited because of finances, each applicant may be given only a very few minutes in which to display his talents. Much casting under such circumstances is done on the basis of personal qualities and physical characteristics rather than on demonstrated acting ability. Open tryouts in the nonprofessional theatre usually proceed at a more leisurely pace, and there are normally fewer candidates for roles. Even here, however, decisions may have to be made on the basis of very limited knowledge about the acting ability of those trying out.

A typical variation on the open tryout is that in which initial sessions are open to all but in which final sessions may be attended only by those who have been specifically invited. In this case, the early tryout periods are used to eliminate unlikely candidates.

Another basic approach to casting is the closed or invitational tryout. Most New York producers will see only those actors already known to them or their staffs or those sent by agents known to the producers. Many educational institutions and community theatres assemble card files which indicate the experience, personal characteristics, and the estimated acting ability of candidates. Such records are usually compiled in part from a large open tryout held early in each theatrical season. In casting each play after that time, only those persons whose records show them to be likely candidates for roles are invited to try out. Some educational institutions restrict casting to those who are majors in theatre or those whose work is known to the directors. Many community theatres restrict casting to their members.

The way in which tryouts are conducted also varies widely. Sometimes actors are able to read and study the play in advance; at other times, actors may be asked to read material which they have not previously seen. Some directors ask that actors memorize scenes from other plays and perform them. Sometimes actors are asked to prepare pantomimes so that abilities in movement and business may be tested. Sometimes a director may give a detailed explanation of characterizations and situations and then ask the actors to read a scene with these explanations in mind. He may stop the reading to give further instructions or to suggest changes in characterization, and so on. In such a case, the director is attempting to find out how flexible the actor is, or how easily he can assimilate criticism.

The director is seldom able to find actors who are ideally suited to the play, and he must adjust his ideas of the roles accordingly. Some parts are more important than others, however, and the director usually casts the major roles first and then selects the remainder of the cast with the qualities of the leading actors in mind.

Many factors determine the final casting. Some roles demand specific physical characteristics in terms of height, weight, handsomeness, a particular voice quality or accent, and so on. This may limit the choice considerably. Another important factor in casting is the possibility of growth in a role. Sometimes an actor has the right qualities for a part but may be unable to move well or to adopt instructions. On the other hand, another actor, who may not be as well suited to the role otherwise, may be quick to respond and may show greater likelihood of developing a more convincing characterization than the first actor. Some actors give very good readings at tryouts but never develop beyond that point. The director, therefore, must assess the possibilities of eliciting finished performances from each candidate.

The directors must also consider the range of characteristics which each actor must portray. Although each part will have a dominant quality, it also must have other attributes which give it subtlety and variety. A great tragic role such as that of Lear has many facets of characterization and the director must seek an actor who is capable of portraying as many of these as possible.

Casting must also be done with all of the other actors in mind. Sometimes a tall girl must be rejected because of the necessity of using a short man in another role. Two actors may not work well together and one may have to be eliminated. The director also tries to avoid too many persons of the same physical type or with the same vocal qualities, since contrast is needed. He, therefore, seeks actors who are both right for particular roles and who combine to make up a balanced ensemble.

Casting may be further complicated by the necessity of designating "understudies." An understudy normally plays a small part in the play, but also learns a larger role so that he may play it in case the originally selected actor becomes ill or must be absent from a performance for any reason.

When an understudy takes over a larger role, the part which he has vacated must be filled; therefore, many productions have an elaborate system of understudying designed to avoid disruption of performances. This policy is always used in professional productions, but is seldom used in the nonprofessional theatre. Most nonprofessional productions are performed for only a few nights, while the professional production is often planned to run indefinitely and the producer cannot afford to cancel performances because of the unexpected absences of actors.

Many professional productions also employ "standbys." This means that a well-known actor is paid to be available in case the star is not able to go on. A standby does not perform in the play at other times.

Some theatres also use a system of "double-casting" (that is, two actors alternate in performances of a major role). This practice has been used especially for musical shows in which the vocal demands are great. Some educational theatres also have used double casting to give opportunities to more actors.

Understudies, standbys, and the double-casting system all raise difficulties in rehearsing a play, however, since each actor must be given a reasonable amount of time in which to grow and develop in his role. These practices also complicate the problems of casting since an effort must be made to find two actors for each part who can keep the quality of performances reasonably even and the over-all pattern of the show unchanged whenever substitutions are made.

Casting is almost always a difficult task for the director, and he is seldom able to assemble an ideal cast. Taking all factors into consideration, however, out of the actors available to him, the director eventually chooses those whom he believes most capable of projecting the qualities he sees in the script.

WORKING WITH THE ACTOR

While the director acts as a guide and interpreter to all members of the production, his own efforts at carrying out plans are restricted primarily to his work with the actors. He supervises rehearsals, explains the script, criticizes performances, and makes suggestions for improvements. He attempts to create an atmosphere in which actors can feel freedom from unnecessary tension while exploring and developing their roles.

The director must try to see each actor as an individual who has his own working methods and problems. For example, some actors accept criticism gracefully in the presence of others, while such public comments make other actors self-conscious or argumentative. Some actors must work first on the psychological aspects of a role, while others prefer to learn the lines and movement first. Some actors need to be handled firmly, others gently. The director must be flexible, therefore, if he is to get the best performance out of each member of his cast.

The director must also remember that the actor's ego is unusually involved in his work. In creating a role, the actor uses his own body, his own voice, his own mind and emotions. He can never put his creation at a distance and look at it as can most other artists. The inadequacies of a performance are in many respects due to the actor's lack of comprehension or perception of a part or even to his own personal inadequacies, and any attack upon his work may be interpreted as a personal affront. The director, therefore, must be tactful and understanding.

The director must also assume the role of the ideal audience. Since an actor can never see his own performance from the point of view of the audience, the director must try to do this for him. The director attempts to assess the probable effect of the acting performances, both individually and as a whole. He seeks to alter, correct, or intensify characterizations wherever necessary so as to achieve the desired response. A director is not infallible, however, and he must be willing to listen sympathetically to the actors' ideas. Although as an efficient executive he must make all important decisions, he should seek always to avoid a dictatorial approach. Much of the success of a production depends upon the director's ability to win the respect and cooperation of the actors. He must be a critic, a teacher, a leader, a friend, and at times a disciplinarian.

THE DIRECTOR'S MEANS

The means available to the director in staging a production encompass the entire resources of the theatre: the script; the voice, speech, and movement of the actor; the stage space, scenery, and properties; the costumes and makeup; the lighting; the music and sound. Since each of these elements is discussed elsewhere in this book, the primary emphasis here is on the director's use of the actors for interpreting the script. Three major problems will be considered: (1) the creation of the stage picture, (2) the use of movement, gesture, and business, and (3) the use of voice and speech.

THE STAGE PICTURE. Each moment of a performance may be thought of as a picture capable of communicating with the audience even apart from the spoken word. If this ideal is to be put into practice, the director must arrange with care the available visual elements at each instant. He must seek to indicate pictorially the center of attention, the situation, the dominant emotion, and the character relationships. Furthermore, he must arrange the picture with due regard for esthetic composition, and for the mood, the style, the period, and the type of play.

In creating the stage picture, the director is always faced with the problem of focusing attention on important elements and subordinating unimportant ones. He must be especially aware of the various devices for achieving emphasis, therefore.

One of the most important of these is the bodily positions of the actors in relation to the audience, for all other factors being equal, the actor most nearly facing the audience at any given moment will be the most emphatic. The director, then, may manipulate the actors' positions to achieve emphasis. (The various bodily positions are explained in greater detail in Chapter 17.)

A second source of emphasis is height. All other factors being equal, the tallest character will be the most emphatic. To vary height, the director may have actors sit, stand, kneel, sit on the floor, lie down, climb steps, stand on platforms, and so on. The possibilities are many but depend in part upon the setting being used and the type of play. Some settings contain no furniture, others may have no steps or platforms; actions, such as lying on the floor, might be inappropriate in tragedy, but quite acceptable in a modern domestic comedy.

A third device for achieving emphasis is the use of specific areas of the stage. It is generally believed that an actor becomes more emphatic by moving closer to the audience, or by moving toward the center of the stage, and that he becomes less so when he moves away from the audience or to the sides of the stage. The director, therefore, may change emphasis by manipulating the actors in relation to the audience or the stage space. (The usual division of the stage into areas may be seen from the chart on page 363.)

Emphasis may also be gained through focus. If all of the actors look at the same thing or person, so will the audience. In this way attention may be shifted rapidly from one character to another or from one part of the stage to another. It is one of the easiest methods of changing emphasis.

Also, emphasis may result from spatial relationships. If a number of actors are grouped on one side of the stage and a single actor is placed on the other side, attention will be directed to the isolated character. This is an extreme example, but any change of spatial relationships may aid in focusing attention upon the desired character. Contrast may also be used.

A scene from Thornton Wilder's *Our Town*. Note the variety of bodily positions. Directed by Lewin Goff.

A scene from Maxwell Anderson's *Elizabeth the Queen* which illustrates several directorial problems. In this scene the protagonist must be seated, although emphasis must at times go to other characters. Note the various use of levels, both in terms of the stage setting and of the actors' positions—seated, kneeling, standing. Note also how the lighting serves to focus attention on the center of the stage. Directed by E. C. Mabie; lighting by Hunton Sellman; setting by Charles Elson.

If all of the actors except one are facing in the same direction the contrast will direct attention to the one who is different.

Other ways of gaining emphasis include the use of costume (a brilliantly colored garment in the midst of drab clothing will become a center of interest); lighting (contrasting colors or a spotlighted area may create a point of emphasis); and scenery (placing a character in a doorway or against a piece of furniture may put a frame around him or strengthen the visual line sufficiently to call attention to him). In addition to these visual means of gaining emphasis, a number of others are available to the director, although they are not directly related to creating the stage picture. These include movement, gesture, business, voice, and speech—all of which will be discussed later.

Seldom does a director depend upon a single device for gaining emphasis. He may use several of them simultaneously and he should avoid too much repetition of the same device. Furthermore, emphasis may need to be divided between two or more persons in some scenes.

A discussion of emphasis automatically assumes that some elements must be subordinated just as some are brought forward. After the focal point of a picture is determined, therefore, all of the characters can be arranged in terms of their relative importance in the scene. In the subordination of characters, all of the devices used for emphasis may be reversed. For example, a subordinate character may be seated while the focal actor is standing; the lowering of height is thus the reverse of the procedure one might use if emphasis were desired.

Emphasis and subordination are important, however, only insofar as they depict the situation, the character relationships, and the dominant emotion of a scene. The stage picture should be composed with these aims in mind. For example, a love scene may make use of nearness in space to indicate the emotional relationship of the characters; it may use bodily attitudes to indicate the internal state of each character; it may use bodily position to indicate which character's response is the most important at the moment; and so on.

The stage picture must also be arranged with due consideration to its composition. It should be balanced in terms of line, mass, and proportion, and should create a harmonious effect. A concern for good composition often leads the director to adjust the positions of the actors onstage. For example, an actor may be directed to move from one place to another merely for the sake of the composition, which would otherwise become unbalanced when an actor leaves the stage or changes his position.

Many directors feel that too much attention to composition will lead to a self-conscious posing of actors and will draw attention to the stage picture as such. Others feel that if the actors understand the dramatic situation well enough they will group themselves properly and that no specific attention need be given to composition. Obviously, it is possible

The first German production of *Hamlet* (Berlin, 1778). Note the directorial use of emphasis. From Otto Weddigen's *Geschichte der Theater Deutschlands*. Berlin, 1904.

to overemphasize composition, but the director must exercise his function as a critic and judge the effectiveness of the pictorial elements as viewed from the auditorium.

The stage picture depends to a large degree upon the setting, the costumes, and the type of play. The placement of doors, windows, and furniture allows one pattern of development and impedes others. The absence of furniture in some period plays (such as Greek and Shakespearean tragedies) rules out certain kinds of pictures which would be used normally in plays set in modern living rooms. The costumes of some periods do not lend themselves to kneeling or lying down; in others, skirts may be so large that they do not allow close physical contact. In discussing plans with the designers, a director must be conscious of the kind of stage picture he would like to achieve and the effect that any given design will have on his aims. Pictorial composition is made much easier by a thorough consideration of its relationship to the proposed designs. The stage picture is also affected by the type of play. A tragedy, for example, will not normally use many of the ludicrous arrangements which would be entirely appropriate to a farce.

Although a properly composed stage picture will not in itself insure success for a play, no director can afford to be unaware of the importance of this aspect of staging. A good visual sense, which must be improved constantly by study and practice, is a strong element in the effectiveness of any director's work.

MOVEMENT, GESTURE AND BUSINESS. While the stage picture has been discussed as though each moment in the play were frozen in time, in performance an impression of movement, rather than of stillness, is usually dominant. Movement is the means used for blending one stage picture into another and to create the sense of flow, change, and development. It is one of the director's most powerful tools of expression.

Movement may be broken down into three main types: movement

A scene from Giraudoux's *The Madwoman of Chaillot*. Note the S-curve composition ending with the central focus on the figure down left. Directed by David Lanphier; setting by Jerry Emery.

Obey's *Noah*. The visual elements in this scene divide the stage into a number of areas, and the line of actors leads the eye to the kneeling figure facing full front. Directed by Sidney Spayde; setting by Charles Elson.

from place to place on the stage, gesture, and business. Any of these types may be dictated by the script or may be invented by the director and actors. Many movements (such as entering and exiting, ringing for a servant, closing curtains, lighting lamps) may be specified by the stage directions or lines in the play. Frequently these are so clearly indicated that a failure to perform them would contradict the sense of the scene.

Many scripts, however, indicate no action beyond the arrival and departure of characters. Yet a completely static stage picture would soon become boring, and the director is often forced to seek logical motivations for moving the actors. Even in plays which specify a considerable amount of movement, the director also must move characters arbitrarily for the purpose of balancing the stage picture and creating interest.

Regardless of the reason behind any movement, the director seeks to make it appear motivated rather than aimless. In designing the pattern of movement, therefore, the director must always take his cues from the play. For example, every scene involves shifting character relationships. While the script may not indicate these in terms of movement, the director may dramatize the changes by this means. Furthermore, the majority of moments in a play have some emotional connotations which may serve as motivations for movement. For example, surprise, extreme anger, and eagerness are responses which normally serve to bring one person closer to another, while disgust, fear, and reluctance may move characters apart. In such ways, movement can illustrate the emotional responses of the characters at any moment.

Several factors may help the director to determine what characters need to move and how they should move. First, movement may be used to achieve emphasis. It catches the eye of the spectator and serves to direct attention to that actor whose movement is greatest; it is almost universally more attention-getting than speech. Since all of the actors in a scene need to react visibly, however, movement must be controlled so as to create the proper focal point. For example, after a surprising announcement, the focal actor may rise, while a subordinate actor may show his response merely by sitting more erect. All actors must respond appropriately and all may use some movement, but the amount and type must be selected so as to direct attention to the actor requiring attention.

Second, movement should be appropriate to the characters. An elderly person normally uses fewer and slower movements than a young person; the nervous or angry person has a different pattern of response than the casual or relaxed person. Sometimes a character must attempt to appear relaxed when he is not, and in such a case movement must make this clear. Movement, then, becomes an important means of characterization.

Third, movement should be indicative of the situation. Highly emotional scenes normally demand more movement than others, and the movement used is more apt to be rapid and clearly defined. Conversely, a casual atmosphere may call for slower and more curved movement. Guarded, careful movement may be needed in a scene in which characters are trying to outwit each other, while movement which conveys an air of spontaneity is required in scenes of relaxed family life.

Fourth, movement must be appropriate to the type of play. The movement for *Oedipus the King* should be more stately and formal than that for *The Chairs*. Furthermore, certain kinds of movement may be associated with a given period. For example, *The School for Scandal* deals with a society noted for its elegance of dress, walk, and gesture. Other plays, such as *From Morn to Midnight* and *Pelléas and Mélisande*, deliberately distort or stylize movement in their conscious departure from realism.

Fifth, movement may be used for building scenes to a climax, for achieving contrast, and for rhythmical effects. An increase in the amount and size of movements will help to achieve a sense of growing confusion or conflict, and of development and change. The effect of movement is greatly increased if one group of actors moves across the stage in one direction while another crosses in the opposite direction. Confusion can be emphasized by having actors run, stop, change direction, and run again. Even in a production with a small cast, the feeling of growth and development toward a high point of interest in a scene may be achieved by the careful increase of movement. Scenes also need to be clearly differentiated from each other, and a use of contrasting movement will point up differences in mood and situation. Repetition, growth, climax, and resolution are important in the achievement of emotional effects in the theatre and all may be aided by the proper use of movement. In his use of movement, however, the director must never lose sight of the standards of appropriateness and effectiveness.

In addition to movement from place to place on the stage, the director must also be concerned with action which does not require a change of stage area. The actors' gestures, facial expressions, and bodily attitudes are of special importance in achieving subtlety and clarity.

Gestures are normally spoken of as restricted to the use of the hands and arms, but they may also include movements of the torso, the head, feet, or legs. Gesture is especially important as a subtle means for gaining emphasis, since a gesture by an actor prior to his speaking is frequently sufficient to shift attention to him.

Gesture may also be used effectively in those scenes in which the situation must be clarified for the audience, but kept obscure for characters in the play. For example, in a crucial scene in which one character questions another, the interrogator might be placed upstage of the actor he is questioning. The downstage actor may be facing the audience with his back turned to the questioner. Upon being asked a particularly revealing question, a slight movement of the hand in front of the body (such as upward toward the throat) tells the audience that the question has made a deep impression, though the questioner may not be aware of any reaction at all.

Gesture is indicative of basic psychological qualities. A large number of spontaneous gestures helps to create the impression of an uninhibited,

The handling of crowd scenes is a difficult problem. In this scene from Aeschylus' *Agamemnon* the group facing the woman stage left makes that figure emphatic. The secondary emphasis is on the man stage right. Note the variety of movement. Directed by F. Cowles Strickland; scenery by O. G. Brockett, costumes by Lenyth Spenker.

extroverted personality, while few and awkward gestures may have the opposite effect. Gestures which are appropriate to the particular character must be sought after, therefore, even when their primary purpose may be for achieving emphasis and clarity.

Bodily attitude and facial expression are especially useful means for displaying the emotional state of characters and for indicating immediate reactions. Bodily attitude refers to the over-all tone and configuration of the human figure—stiffly upright, slumping, relaxed, and so on. When not obscured by a costume, bodily attitude is one of the most telling indexes to the actor's relative tension or relaxation (so much so, in fact, that the actor frequently has difficulty in demonstrating the character's, rather than his own, state of feeling by this means). Facial expression is not always visible to the entire audience, but it should not be overlooked as a supplementary aid in projecting emotion. By themselves, facial expression and bodily attitude are not sufficient for conveying the substance of a scene, but they support and clarify other means.

Another aspect of movement is stage business (those detailed actions, such as filling and lighting a pipe, arranging flowers, wrapping packages, eating and drinking, dueling and fighting). Business has to be carefully staged with timing of action and speech sufficiently rehearsed, as the actors involved normally must at the same time carry on a conversation or react to other characters. Each step in the business, therefore, must be planned and timed to make appropriate points and to avoid distracting the audience's attention from more important stage action or lines.

Much of the business in a play is prescribed by the script, but much of it may also be invented by the actors or the director. It is one of the chief means for clarifying and enriching those characterizations which may have been left somewhat vague by the playwright. Actors and directors frequently strive to build up a strong sense of character by adding details which seem appropriate and probable for the particular characters and situation. Although business should never be allowed to interfere with the

A scene from Sherwood's *Abe Lincoln in Illinois*. The woman at center remains dominant in spite of her profile position because of her spatial relationship to the other characters, the stage area, and the emphasis received from the doorway behind her. Directed by E. C. Mabie; setting by Arnold Gillette.

A scene from Synge's *The Playboy of the Western World*. Directed by James Haran; costumes by Lenyth Brockett.

"build" of a scene or with important lines, when properly used it is a great aid in clarifying reactions. For example, a pipe-smoking character might, in a moment of great tension, break the stem on his pipe and thus indicate his inner emotional state.

Movement, then, since it encompasses the total physical action, is probably the most powerful visual means available for affecting the audience. The director must know how to use it, therefore, with maximum effectiveness.

VOICE AND SPEECH. Although the director may also use sound and music, his principal means for audible expression are the actor's voice and the playwright's words. The problems associated with voice and speech in most cases fall into the province of acting, but the director must understand and know how to use these elements for his purposes of interpreting the script on the stage.

The variable factors in voice are pitch, volume, and quality. All of these may be used for purposes of characterization and as indications of changing emotions and relationships. For example, in moments of stress, the pitch and volume of the voice normally rise and the quality may become strained. The actor needs a trained voice so that he may effectively use it for projecting varying psychological states and dramatic situations.

Little attention has been paid during the past quarter of a century to adequate voice training. The result is that the actor now too often ignores one of his most powerful means for affecting an audience and for achieving variety and a wide range of effects. In spite of this neglect, audiences are affected by vocal factors. A high-pitched male voice arouses different connotations in an audience than does a low-pitched masculine voice; similarly, different associations are aroused by loud-mouthed and soft-spoken characters. A director must understand vocal factors and their effects on audiences sufficiently to know what is desirable for each character and to be able to give aid to those actors who are not capable of accomplishing by themselves the proper vocal attributes. An actor can achieve a permanent improvement in his vocal characteristics only over a long period of time, however, and, therefore, most directors cast their plays using those actors who already most nearly fit the proper vocal qualities for each role.

The variable factors of speech are articulation, pronunciation, duration of phonation and unvoiced segments, inflection, and voice projection (or audibility); each of these may also be manipulated for the purpose of achieving specific results. Articulation involves the production of the various sounds, while pronunciation has to do with the selection of sounds. A person may articulate sounds clearly, but mispronounce words. A well-trained actor should understand both articulation and pronunciation and should be able to utilize both in the production of standard stage speech. But he also should be able to alter articulation and pronunciation to suit the demands of character and situation.

Poor articulation is caused by careless use of tongue and lips in forming sounds, and is associated with lack of education or a dialect. Mispronunciation has many of the same associations, but it is sometimes used to indicate naïveté or inexperience (as when it results from the person's never having heard the words pronounced). A knowledge of the International Phonetic Alphabet symbols (I.P.A.) can be of great help in demonstrating in what way sounds should be altered from the actor's normal speech.

Duration refers to the length of time assigned to any sound, while inflection refers to the pattern of rising and falling pitch. Both duration and pitch may be used to emphasize some syllables and to subordinate others. Stress of one or more syllables is usually necessary if the audience is to recognize a word. For example, in *probably* the first syllable is normally given the greatest stress through duration; however, if the stress is shifted to the second syllable the word becomes almost unrecognizable.

Duration also refers to the rate of words per minute in an over-all speech pattern. Slowness and speed in speaking have definite value in characterization. For example, slow speech may help to create the impression of laziness, sickness, and weakness, while a rapid rate may suggest tension or vivacity.

Inflection is one of the principal indicators of meaning. Surprise, disgust, indifference, and other reactions are frequently indicated by the "tone of voice." The sense of a speech may be altered completely sometimes by changing the inflections. Dialects are distinguishable in part by their pitch patterns. That of the southern United States, for example, is characterized in part by a stress on the verb and by a rising inflection at the end of sentences.

In working with voice and speech, the director must strive above all for audibility (projection) and intelligibility, for unless the audience can both hear and understand the actors the play will have little chance of success. Dialects frequently need to be altered in order to make them understandable (a completely accurate rendering of the Irish dialect is often gibberish to an American audience). Some actors may also mumble lines with the excuse that they are striving for greater naturalness. The director must decide when the competing demands for naturalness and communication have been satisfactorily resolved, but he should never accept speech which is unintelligible to the audience.

The director must also seek for variety in voice and speech. Nothing is more monotous than the delivery of all lines at the same speed and with the same emotional intensity. Each scene in a play usually has a dominant tempo and emotional tone, but these dominant patterns need to be broken up if monotony is to be avoided. Many devices may be used for achieving variety. Among the most powerful of these is contrast. For example, a character who has delivered an emotional, rapid, and loud speech may pause and then, in a quiet, slow and very controlled manner, go on to his next lines. The pause may also be used with great effect to mark transitions in thought, changes in emotion, a shift in tempo, and so on. Pauses, however, must be made meaningful to an audience, for unless the significance of the pause is clear the effect will be merely one of slowness or a suggestion that the actors have forgotten their lines. All of the variable factors in voice and speech—pitch, volume, quality, articulation, pronunciation, duration, and inflection—may be manipulated for the purpose of achieving variety.

The director must make sure that the dominant ideas and emotions of each scene are reflected in voice and speech. Some ideas and emotional responses need to be stressed and others subordinated. Solutions to this problem can normally be found by working with the actors until each understands his motivations, his relationship to all the other characters, the significance of each moment to the particular scene and in the play as a whole. From such understanding proper emphases usually result, although some technical aid in phrasing, intensity, and inflection may be needed, especially when the director is working with inexperienced actors.

The director must strive for believability in voice and speech. Actors may sound false and be unconvincing in their roles. Such shortcomings may be corrected by working on those factors discussed in the preceding paragraph. Sometimes difficulty arises from the failure of one or more actors to respond "in key." (That is, response may seem inappropriate to the stimulus.) "Overacting" and "underacting" are usually judged in terms of the adequacy of response to the situation. The director must help the actor to find the right "key." Sometimes an actor's speech may seem too artificial and studied. In such cases, the director must help the actor to achieve more nearly a quality of spontaneity, or a more conversational tone. Conversely, for Shakespearean and other verse plays a director may need to help actors get away from the typical phrasing used in everyday speech and into the sweep of the poetic lines.

The director may also use voice and speech in building a scene or an entire play toward a climax. A crowd scene may be built in part through the increasing volume and intensity of vocal sounds. While large groups offer the most obvious examples, voice and speech may be used in all plays to advantage for establishing progression, building a climax, and forming a sense of resolution.

The devices available to the director for embodying his interpretation of a script are many and varied, but regardless of which he chooses he must strive for clarity and for harmony of effect through emphasis and subordination, and through the creation of progression through beginning, middle, and end. He must be both a sound technician and an impeccable critic.

REHEARSING THE PLAY

Rehearsals can seldom be held in surroundings which will approximate those to be used in performance. As a rule the scenery, costumes, lighting, and properties are not available prior to dress rehearsals, and the place where rehearsals are held is seldom the stage upon which the play will be presented. The director and the actors must rely heavily upon their imaginations in working toward a finished performance.

One of the first problems which must be solved is that of adequate rehearsal space. A room at least as large as the stage setting is required, though more space is desirable. The ground plan of the set is usually marked out on the floor with chalk, paint, or adhesive tape. If there is more than one set, each must be indicated (lines of different colors may be used to distinguish different settings). Chairs, tables, and other improvised furniture may be brought in to help the actor become familiar with the floor plan and the stage space in which he will be performing. Difficulties are greatest when the setting has a number of levels and steps upon which the actors must move. It is sometimes impossible to duplicate these levels in the rehearsal space, and the actor must keep himself aware of the demands of the setting by forcing himself to go through the motions of climbing stairs, by standing on chairs to simulate raised platforms, or by similar devices.

Further problems arise in connection with stage business. If actors must serve tea, wrap packages, or perform other complicated actions of this type, it is usually necessary to find temporary properties which approximate those to be used on stage, for such complex business cannot be put off until dress rehearsals. Comparable difficulties occur with costumes in those plays in which clothing differs markedly from modern dress. The comfortable and convincing use of long skirts, trains, complicated headdresses, swords, and similar articles requires considerable practice by the actor. Many theatres, therefore, maintain a supply of rehearsal garments to aid the actor in becoming accustomed to unfamiliar dress. Without such help the actor may become awkward and even self-conscious when he encounters his costumes for the first time at dress rehearsal.

Rehearsing plays under these conditions creates a number of additional problems. It is difficult in a small space to get a clear view of the action as it will appear in a large auditorium; it is difficult to judge the volume of sound and the size of gestures—the degree to which the play is being projected adequately. For these reasons, it is important to have as many rehearsals as possible on the stage and in the auditorium in which the play will be performed.

The director must know approximately how much rehearsal time will be available to him. In the nonprofessional theatre actors are usually available for rehearsals only in the evenings or on week ends, and for periods of time not in excess of three hours. It is typical to restrict rehearsals to five evenings each week over a time span of from four to six weeks. In the professional theatre a rehearsal period of about four weeks is usual, but actors must be available approximately eight hours each day. Knowing the situation in which he must work, a director can predict with reasonable accuracy how much rehearsal time he will have.

The director must then work out a rehearsal schedule which will utilize the available time to maximum advantage. A number of factors must be considered in constructing a schedule. First, the director should strive to make the most efficient use of his actors. It is unfair to ask an actor to attend a number of rehearsals in which he is never used. If the director has broken the play down into short scenes, he will usually find that he can schedule all of those scenes which use crowds on the same evening, that other periods may be devoted to working with the principal characters, and so on. If the script is complex, the director may want to make use of assistant directors and to schedule more than one rehearsal simultaneously. He may also plan his time so that some actors can rehearse difficult pieces of business or lines elsewhere while another scene is being run through in the rehearsal room.

Second, the schedule should be broken down in terms of objectives. The director cannot work on all problems simultaneously. For example, the actors cannot work on detailed pieces of business as a rule until they have learned the lines well enough to dispense with the script. For this reason, the director usually designates certain phases of the rehearsal period as being concerned primarily with specific objectives. Other problems are not ignored, but they are not of primary concern at that time.

The first phase is usually devoted to reading, analyzing, and understanding the script. The amount of time devoted to these problems varies from director to director, with the complexity of the action and the characters, and with the experience and ability of the cast. During this period the director is principally concerned with making sure that each actor understands his own role and its function in the play; he seeks to make clear his own interpretation of the script and to clarify the objectives toward which everyone must work. The director may also strive to stimulate the imagination of the actors by raising questions about the motivation of characters, by pointing out the relationship between scenes or characters, by clarifying symbolic devices, and by indicating key speeches. Some directors give the actors specific directions for the reading of lines at this time, but most prefer to defer such details until later in the rehearsal schedule.

The next period of time is usually taken up with blocking (that is, with indicating movement from place to place on the stage and with positioning each actor at each moment). For example, an actor might be directed to enter up center, to cross slowly to the sofa down left, and to stand facing front. Normally the director is concerned at this point only with the gross patterns of movement; subtleties and refinements are left until a later time.

There is considerable disagreement about how much preplanning a director should do prior to attending the rehearsals devoted to blocking. Some argue that the director should have every movement charted out and written down. Blocking rehearsals then consist merely of relaying these directions to the actors, who perform the prescribed movements and note them in their own scripts. Others argue that it is impossible to decide with any accuracy what movement patterns are needed until the actors are present, and that movement should evolve out of the actors' feelings rather than from a mold imposed by the director. This method usually results in a considerable amount of trial and error with fixed patterns developing only after a considerable length of time. Eventually, however, the pattern of movement must become set if performances are to be perfected.

The majority of directors use a method which lies somewhere between the two extremes outlined above. Much thought has usually been given to blocking before rehearsals begin and much of the movement will be used exactly as planned. On the other hand, most directors find that many adjustments must be made and that many improvements occur if the director encourages suggestions from the actors and if he views his own blocking critically. Time will be saved by preplanning, but rigidity should be avoided.

Regardless of how the blocking is arrived at, the patterns of movement should be rehearsed until they are entirely clear to all the actors.

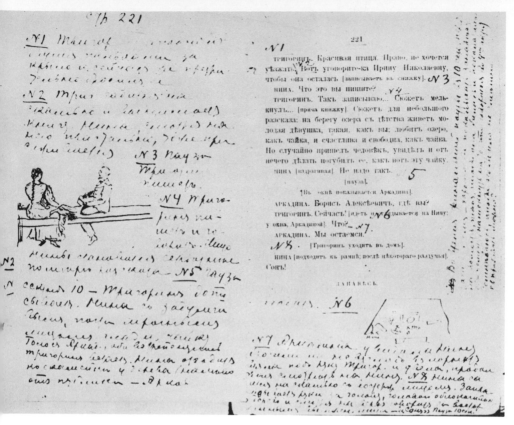

A page from Stanislavsky's prompt book for Chekhov's *The Sea Gull*. Note the floor plan of the setting at the bottom right, and Stanislavsky's apparent interest in bodily position as indicated by the sketch of the seated figures at the left. From *Moscow Art Theatre*, 1898–1917.

It is usual to block an act or a few scenes at a time. When the blocking for a segment is clear, the director moves on to the next part and repeats the process until the entire play is blocked. One or more rehearsals may be devoted to blocking each act.

The next period is normally devoted to lines. At this time the director is concerned with the actors' ability to repeat their lines without the aid of a script or a prompter. The director normally sets a date by which the actors must know their lines. (Usually he designates a deadline for each act.) Lines should be learned as early as possible, for it is extremely difficult to work for subtlety and polish if the actors are still concentrating upon remembering blocking or speeches.

Once the actors are sure of movement and lines, the director may proceed to the next phase in rehearsals—detailed work on characterization, line readings, business, transitions, build, and ensemble playing. The director may need to spend much time with actors exploring the motivations for certain actions or speeches; he must see that the timing is just right; he may wish to question the reading given to certain lines; and so on. It is frequently necessary to go over and over the same piece of business to ensure that it is integrated precisely with the lines and that it is being utilized to make the desired points. He may have to run the same scene through many times to achieve the proper build in intensity. He must make sure that there is variety; he must work for ensemble playing, as opposed to a series of isolated individual performances.

In any phase of the rehearsal schedule the director may stop the cast frequently to comment or criticize and to rerun a scene in whole or in part. He must allow the actors to play entire scenes or acts through as often as possible, however, so that they develop a feeling for the continuity of scenes, the shifts in mood, and the build of each scene and of the play as a whole. The director must avoid letting too many days elapse between rehearsals of the same scene, for if actors forget too much, valuable time must be spent in accomplishing all over again the gains of a previous rehearsal.

The final phase of the rehearsal schedule is devoted to integrating all of the elements of production as they will be seen on the stage. For the first time the actors are allowed to rehearse in their costumes, in make-up, with the scenery, lighting, sound, and music which will be used in performance. Frequently these rehearsals also mark the first time that the actor has rehearsed on the stage. Many adjustments may need to be made at this time.

The process of integration will be eased considerably if proper planning was done at the early conferences between the director and the various designers. Further steps may also be taken to ease the tensions of final rehearsals. For example, a dress parade, at which all of the actors appear together in their costumes, will allow the director to see how the actors look individually and as a group in each scene. It also allows the actors to become familiar with their costumes, to try out movements, to discover the possibilities and problems in their garments. Difficulties may be discovered at this time which can be corrected without taking valuable time at dress rehearsals.

In addition, a technical rehearsal—the purpose of which is to work out problems of scene changes, lighting cues, costume changes, sound, music, and properties—may be scheduled. All needed adjustments cannot normally be made during this rehearsal, but difficulties can be noted and often can be corrected before dress rehearsals begin.

Lighting and sound are apt to present the greatest problems of integration. While the lighting may be planned in advance, it cannot really be adjusted and finished until the scenery is in place and until the actors use the stage area. It is not always possible to know exactly how large an area a lighting instrument will cover, or exactly what level of intensity is desirable until all other elements are present. Much time is normally spent,

A scene from *The Trespassers* by Ralph Arzoomanian performed in the round. Directed by Philip Benson.

therefore, in adjusting the lighting instruments, in setting the exact level of light, in getting light cues recorded, and so on. Sometimes this process takes more than a full day. Likewise, sound must be adjusted in terms of other elements. It is impossible to know exactly how loud it should be, exactly when it should be begun, how it should build and fade away until it is tried out in the auditorium to be used for performances.

Dress parades and technical rehearsals, thus, can uncover difficulties which may be remedied before dress rehearsals start. Sometimes such rehearsals are not used and dress rehearsals must also serve this additional function. Regardless of when the various elements are introduced, the process of integration must take place, and it is almost always a source of stress.

Most directors attempt to have two or three dress rehearsals. These are intended to approximate the conditions of performance as nearly as possible. Difficulties are noted and corrected. The wise director uses those crises which almost always arise as a means of preparing his cast for coping with emergencies which may occur during public performances. Some directors invite a number of people to the dress rehearsals as a way of getting some indication of probable audience response and as a way of preparing the actors for a larger audience. He may make some adjustments in the light of this response.

In the professional theatre, the out-of-town tryout may function as a series of dress rehearsals, after each of which changes may be made. These changes in turn are tried out on other audiences before the play is officially opened in New York.

As a rule, there are no further rehearsals after the play is opened officially. There are many exceptions to this rule, however. The stage manager of a professional company may call a rehearsal at any time that he feels the company needs it. The understudies are rehearsed regularly in their alternate roles throughout the run, and touring companies may have run-throughs in order to acquaint the actors with the particular stage and auditorium. In the nonprofessional theatre, the director may discuss each performance with the actors and may make suggestions for improvements. Sometimes such groups play only on week ends and several days may elapse between performances. In such cases, refresher rehearsals may be held. Normally, however, the director's work is over and his responsibilities are completed with the opening performance.

SPECIAL PROBLEMS

The director's responsibilities and problems vary with the particular situation in which he finds himself. For example, his work is considerably complicated if he is staging a musical. In this case, a choreographer normally designs the dance movements and rehearses the dancers; the musical conductor rehearses the singers and chorus. The director, however, must still integrate song and dance into the whole and must devise the transitions from spoken lines into song, and from stage movement into dance. Many of these problems will be dealt with in Chapter 21.

Most of the problems of directing are usually discussed in terms of the proscenium stage. More and more, however, arena and open stages are being used. It should be obvious that, if the audience is to view the action from three or four sides (rather than one), adjustments must be made for achieving emphasis, in composing the stage picture, in patterns of movement, and even in voice and speech. What is near one part of the audience will be far away from another; an actor, while facing one group of spectators, will have his back to another group. The director, therefore, must find motivations for turning his actors more often so that each segment of the audience can see more clearly. Furthermore, greater attempts must be made to use the entire body more expressively, so that the back view can also be used to communicate. While the same devices for achieving emphasis will suffice, several may need to be used in combination because of the altered audience–actor relationship.

The arena theatre must dispense with most scenery, and the director, consequently, must find other ways of communicating. Properties and costumes may take on greater significance, and, since they are normally seen at much closer range than on the proscenium stage, they may need to be selected and executed with more care. Facial expression, subtle reactions, and business can be used with far greater effect, however. While the director may be unable to use some of the devices which work well on the proscenium stage, he will find that many which were of little value in the proscenium theatre are of great importance in the arena situation. The basic problems of projecting a script and the director's basic techniques remain the same; it is only the selection of the specific means to be used which must be adjusted in terms of the altered situation.

EMPLOYMENT

In the professional theatre, the director is employed by the producer. If the director is well known, as a selling point, his services may be put under option before the producer attempts to raise money for financing the production. On the other hand, the director may be employed after the show has been cast (though this is unusual). Since many producing organizations have a permanent casting director, the director of a particular play may have less control over casting than does his counterpart in the nonprofessional theatre. The director in professional theatre, nevertheless, may request that an actor be replaced if he does not find him competent. (The conditions under which an actor may be replaced are clearly specified by Actors' Equity.) Until recently the professional director did not belong to a union. In 1959, however, the Society of Stage Directors and Choreographers was formed and recognized in 1962 as an official bargaining agent. In the future, the director's rights and working conditions will be more clearly outlined by union contracts.

It is customary for the director to be paid a part of his fee when the contract is signed and the rest during the rehearsal period. It is also customary for the director to receive a percentage of receipts throughout the run of the play. The director's responsibilities normally end with the opening of the play in New York, though he may be called in periodically to approve replacements and to make sure that performances are reasonably close to his original intention. He may also be asked to direct road companies of the play (though this is entirely optional).

In the semiprofessional theatre and in summer stock, directors are usually employed to direct a specified number of plays within a stated period of time. In such organizations the director's duties are apt to be less precisely stated than in the professional theatre, and, if there is more than one director, each may have other responsibilities when he is not actively directing a show.

In the community theatre it is typical for one director to be responsible for all productions. He must either direct all of the plays himself or find other competent persons to do so (frequently without pay or for a nominal fee). In many groups, the director is the only paid staff member and must assume primary responsibility for all aspects of the theatre's operation. If there is also a designer–technician, the director's duties are usually restricted to the directing and acting program, and to the business management and publicity for the group.

In the educational theatre directors are normally also teachers. Directing may be considered as part of the director's teaching load, or it may be looked upon as an extra-curricular activity. The position of the director varies widely in educational theatre. Frequently a single faculty

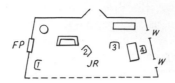

Left margin notes (handwritten):

∧ *X1 Back \ to open up.*

∧ *Puts portfolio on CH2 to steady it. Takes picture out of portfolio, Xing to R of Ch. 2 as she does so.*

He looks at her.

Savoring them slowly. After P. he X R to below RC of sofa.

(loud)

X ✗ RJ

∧ *X1 R*

∧ *Indicates sofa X1L*

Script page:

88   The Doctor's Dilemma   ACT I

saving. ∧ Oh, doctor, I married him just to help him to begin: I had money enough to tide him over the hard years at the beginning— to enable him to follow his inspiration until his genius was recognized. And I was useful to him as a model: his drawings of me sold quite quickly.

RIDGEON.   Have you got one?

MRS DUBEDAT ∧ [*producing another*]   Only this one. It was the first.

RIDGEON [*devouring it with his eyes*] ∧ Thats a wonderful drawing. ∧ Why is it called Jennifer?

MRS DUBEDAT.   My name is Jennifer.

RIDGEON. ∧ A strange name.

MRS DUBEDAT.   Not in Cornwall.   I am Cornish. It's only what you call Guinevere.

RIDGEON [*repeating the names with a certain pleasure in them*] ∧ Guinevere.   Jennifer.   [*Looking again at the drawing*] ∧ Yes: it's really a wonderful drawing. ∧ Excuse me; but may I ask is it for sale?   I'll buy it.

MRS DUBEDAT. ∧ Oh, take it.   It's my own: he gave it to me.   Take it.   Take them all.   Take everything; ask anything; but save him.   You can: you will: you must.

REDPENNY ∧ [*entering / with every sign of alarm*] Theyve just telephoned from the hospital that youre to come instantly—a patient on the point of death.   The carriage is waiting.

RIDGEON [*intolerantly*] ∧ Oh, nonsense: get out. [*Greatly annoyed*] ⊂What do you mean by interrupting me like this?

REDPENNY. ∧ But—

RIDGEON.   Chut! cant you see I'm engaged?   Be off. *Redpenny, bewildered, vanishes.*

MRS DUBEDAT [*rising*] ∧ Doctor: one instant only before you go—

RIDGEON. ∧ Sit down.   It's nothing.

Right margin notes (handwritten):

∧ *He X close to her L. She holds the picture for hi—*

He places his hand on the picture to hold it with her. They are close together.

Turns L to her.

∧ *She X to his L below sofa*   *RJ ✗*

Opens both C. doors. Slams in.

Redpenny X to UL Ch 2.

∧ *Puts drawing on R arm sofa, backing R1 ✗ to clear sightline.*

∧ *X R 1, hand out in appeal.*

A prompt book page showing ground plan for French scene, script cuts, and blocking notes. From Curtis Canfield's *The Craft of Play Directing.* New York: Holt, Rinehart and Winston, Inc., 1963. Courtesy of the author.

member must bear the burden of the entire theatre program, but in others he may be one of a large and specialized staff and may have no production duties other than directing.

THE DIRECTOR AND HIS ASSISTANTS

The director may have a number of assistants who aid him in carrying out his duties. The most important of these are a rehearsal secretary, an assistant director, and a stage manager.

The rehearsal secretary sits near the director at rehearsals and takes down whatever notes and comments he wishes to have recorded. Sometimes the director may see the need for a particular prop; he may wish to be reminded of a weak point in the script, or some deficiency in the acting. At the end of a scene or a rehearsal he may ask the secretary to read these notes to him and he may relay his comments on acting directly to the performers. Sometimes he may ask the secretary to type out the notes and to give appropriate sections to the persons concerned. He may need to inform the designers of small changes in plans or requirements not anticipated before the rehearsals began.

Sometimes the duties of the rehearsal secretary are combined with those of the assistant director, whose over-all responsibilities are difficult to define since he may be called on to do almost anything. Sometimes he is asked to rehearse specific scenes or to coach actors. He may serve as a liaison between the director and the designers; he may attend all conferences and be given specific tasks to carry through. On complex productions, there may be a number of assistant directors, each with his own area of responsibility.

The duties of the rehearsal secretary, assistant director, and the stage manager may all be combined into a single job (though this is not usual). The stage manager's is the most important executive post after the show has opened, for it is his responsibility to see that each performance proceeds as planned. Because of his great importance to the proper running of a show, he is selected with considerable care in the professional theatre. He is hired by the producer and he must be a member of Actors' Equity. A large show may have one or two assistant stage managers, each with a specific area of responsibility (such as being in charge of the chorus in a musical). An assistant stage manager may also act in the production, but a stage manager may not. (In the rarest of emergencies such as a sudden accident to a player a stage manager has been known to walk onstage reading from the prompt script, but this is most unusual.)

In the professional theatre the stage manager helps in organizing and running the tryouts; he attends all rehearsals and records all changes in the lines, all blocking, and other directions in a master copy of the play; he posts the rehearsal schedule and keeps all notices up to date; he may be asked to notify the designers of any changes in plans which affect their work. If the company goes on tour he must see that all belongings are shipped and received.

Since the stage manager is in charge of the performance, he must know as much as possible about every aspect of the production. As a guide, he compiles a prompt book, which records everything that affects the performance (all cues for lights, scene changes, sound, actors' entrances, curtains, and so on), and he must see that all directions are carried out. After the show is opened he rehearses the understudies each week and may call a rehearsal of the entire cast if he believes that performances are deviating too far from the director's conception. If replacements in the cast must be made, the stage manager may, in consultation with the casting director or director, employ them.

In the nonprofessional theatre the stage manager's job is much less demanding, since the director usually remains on the job and can take care of many of the problems which arise. The stage manager is still responsible for running the show during each performance, however. In some theatres he does not attend rehearsals from the beginning, but comes in only a few days before the first technical or dress rehearsal (that is, just in time to familiarize himself with the problems of running the show). Regardless of when he assumes his post, however, the stage manager is one of the most important persons for assuring the proper running of a performance.

While the preceding discussion does not cover every one of the problems and responsibilities of the director, the broad nature of his duties should by now be clear. The director cannot make bad or inferior acting good, nor can he entirely overcome the handicaps of inappropriate scenery, costumes and lighting, but his guidance is frequently the key to the proper realization of the artistic qualities of a script. It is the director who can create a truly integrated performance in which all elements are utilized to maximum advantage and who can prevent a production from remaining merely an aggregation of separate arts. His job requires artistic insight, taste, tact, organizational ability, leadership, and the capacity for endless hours of hard work.

Chapter 17

THE ACTOR

Of all the theatre workers, the actor is the one who most nearly personifies the stage for the general public. Other artists, especially the playwright, may gain considerable recognition, but the actor's fame is, as a rule, more widespread. This is to be explained in part by the fact that the actor is the only theatre worker an audience sees. It is the actor who lends his body and voice to the character and makes it live and breathe. Except in rare cases, however, the actor's fame does not outlive him for his is an interpretative art, and there are always new interpreters ready to step into the roles he has vacated.

The actor's problems are in many ways unique. He is one of the few artists whose principal means of expression cannot be separated from himself, for he must create with his own body and voice, his own psychological and mental endowments. The director, the designers, and the playwright may sit in the auditorium and watch the product of their work, but the actor can never completely dissociate himself from that which he creates. Only through a filmed performance can he ever see himself from the viewpoint of others, and even then the experience of working in a theatre before a live audience cannot be duplicated.

The actor, nevertheless, must attempt to evaluate his own work, and, as a consequence, he develops a kind of double vision of himself—as the creator of a role and as the embodiment of a character. In performance, he must be attuned to the response of the audience as a measurement of

A scene from Sherwood's *Abe Lincoln in Illinois*. Here level, bodily position, the focus of the other actor, all "give" the stage to the standing actor.

the effectiveness of his work, but at the same time he must seem to be thoroughly absorbed within his character. Like any artist, if he is to grow and mature in his profession, he must develop the capacity for assessing his own accomplishments, although for him the task is extremely complex.

It is often difficult to separate talent, skill, and creativity from the personality of the actor. Stage presence (being at ease on the stage), the knowledge of tricks which please or amuse an audience, and the ability to project one's own personality are often taken as signs of good acting. Acting, however, while it may make use of all of these, is ultimately distinguished by the ability to embody and project the essence of a given role regardless (or in spite of) the actor's own personal characteristics.

It is too commonly assumed that there are no requisites for becoming an actor beyond a few striking personality traits. Acting, however, is an art, and as with any art there are three requisites—native ability, study, and practice. As with any other artist, the actor can achieve perfection only through hard and continuous work. His native ability cannot be increased, but it can be cultivated and developed through discipline and constant practice.

THE ACTOR'S TRAINING AND MEANS

The actor's principal means of expression are his body and voice, the role he is playing, and the stage environment in which he works. These means have been discussed in part in the preceding chapter dealing with the director. The material which follows supplements the discussion to be found there and considers many of the same points again from the actor's point of view.

THE BODY.   Since it is one of his principal means of expression, every actor must attempt to develop a flexible, disciplined, and expressive body. Flexibility is needed so that the actor may instantly and more or less subconsciously express physically a wide range of attitudes, actions and reactions. If he is to be able to utilize this flexibility, however, the actor must be able to control it, and control comes only through practice and discipline.

Some actors can achieve these ideals with comparative ease, but for others they remain sources of trouble. An actor may receive much help by taking courses in stage movement, dance, fencing, and acrobatics, and by participating in activities which demand physical control and coordination. Dance and fencing may be of special help, not only because of the gracefulness and discipline which result, but also because the growing importance of the musical has opened many opportunities to the actor who can also dance, and because fencing is a skill demanded in many period plays.

Regardless of the source of his training or his relative skill in movement, the actor must be capable of physically embodying a role. The actor with a well-trained body has mastered his principal means for doing so.

THE VOICE. In training the voice, the same ideals—flexibility, control, and expressiveness—also apply. The actor should understand how the vocal instrument functions, and he should strive to achieve the maximum control over pitch, volume, and quality. He should learn how to breathe properly, how to achieve variety, how to insure that he will be audible and intelligible. He should train himself to speak standard American speech habitually, and should acquire a sound knowledge of phonetics as an aid in recording and learning dialects and all deviations from normal stage speech. To develop flexibility, control and expressiveness, constant practice is necessary. Training in oral reading, acting, and singing may be of help, but years of drill are usually required. Changes cannot be wrought overnight and normally an actor without a good foundation in voice training can do little to transform his vocal characteristics during the four to six weeks of the typical rehearsal period. In every role the actor has a greater chance of success if his voice can be manipulated to achieve desired results.

OBSERVATION AND IMAGINATION. While the body and voice are the actor's principal means of expression, to determine their appropriate uses he must develop other abilities which may be grouped together roughly as observation and imagination. Except in rare cases, the characters an actor is asked to portray are recognizable human types (occasionally an actor may be asked to assume the role of an animal, flower, or even an inanimate object; in such cases, however, the nonhuman roles are still assigned human traits). To portray a role well, then, the actor must have a considerable understanding of human emotions, attitudes, and motivations, and he must know how these are manifested externally.

In understanding others, the actor must rely principally upon observation. The actor, therefore, must develop the habit of observing and remembering the behavior of others. For example, if an actor is called upon to play an old man, a close and minute observance of the behavior of old men is one of the best preparations for the role. The actor, however, cannot observe all aspects of behavior at once, and he must study one detail at a time. In looking at old men, he should analyze the walk, the posture, the use of the hands and arms, the manner of sitting and rising, and so on. Furthermore, it is not sufficient as a rule to observe only one person of a type, for that person might be an exception to more normal behavior. The actor should observe many people and try to see the typical.

This type of observation should also be applied to the display of emotions (the way in which people respond when they are happy, grieved, surprised, terrified, and so on). While such observation cannot always be transferred directly to the stage, it should form the foundation for characterizations; it is through such means that believable, lifelike portrayals develop.

Observation of others must be restricted to external behavior. The actor, however, does have his own internal states of feelings, emotions, and attitudes and he can, in effect, observe these. He can analyze how he felt in a given situation, his motivations, and the behavior which resulted. As a rule, the actor assumes that his own reactions are normal and typical, and that he, therefore, may utilize what he has learned through self-analysis in the portrayal of stage characters. He may strive to develop what has been called "emotion memory" so that he may easily recall how he felt in a given situation (presumably one similar to that called for in the play) and utilize this memory in building character motivations and reactions. One of the principal problems of the actor is that of "feeling himself into" the place of another, and the solution is much easier to find if he can recall how he has felt under like circumstances. The actor, thus, comes to know others by knowing himself thoroughly, and he embodies roles in part by calling upon his knowledge of himself.

The actor is asked to create fictional rather than real-life situations, however, and to do this he must develop his imagination. In utilizing his observations and his memory of emotions, he must keep in mind the circumstances which are dictated by the play. He must be able to project himself imaginatively into the situation and make it believable to himself. Unless he can imagine himself as the character in the situation, it is unlikely that he will be able to convince an audience that his performance is an honest one.

CONCENTRATION. If the body and voice are to be directed by understanding and imagination in the creation of a believable stage performance, concentration is also needed. Concentration refers to the actor's ability to immerse himself in the play and to shut out all distractions.

Many actors, because of their overfamiliarity with the lines and movements of a play, seem to be mere automatons. They respond on cue, but it is clear that they have not actually been listening or watching. The good actor, on the other hand, creates "the illusion of the first time," no matter how often he has performed the role. To give such performances he must concentrate on what is happening around him, not in a general sense but upon the specific phrases, intonations, gestures, and movements, and must respond in the appropriate key and at the appropriate moment. Concentration is a difficult skill to develop, but it is a necessary one for the actor.

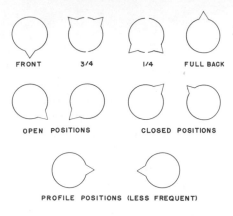

Diagram showing various bodily positions. See page 365, Chapter 16, for a diagram of stage areas.

FRONT   3/4   1/4   FULL BACK

OPEN POSITIONS   CLOSED POSITIONS

PROFILE POSITIONS (LESS FREQUENT)

TECHNIQUE. Experience has shown that some ways of doing things on the stage are more effective than others, and over the years many of the actor's routine tasks have become standardized. These mechanics of acting are normally referred to as technique.

Sometimes all actors are separated into two broad categories: those who depend primarily upon technique, and those who depend primarily upon feeling. The "technical" actor is the one who understands what devices are needed for achieving the desired results and who applies these devices systematically in the creation of a role. The actor who works from feeling is thought to depend upon the sincerity of his own responses to arouse belief in the audience. Either method may work, but the best actor actually draws upon both approaches. At any rate, a thorough knowledge of technical devices should never be disparaged, and every director hopes that his actors will know the basic mechanics of acting. Many of these are elementary.

First, the actor needs to be thoroughly familiar with the designation of stage areas since directions are usually given in relation to them. *Upstage* means away from the audience; *downstage* means toward the audience; *right* and *left* refer to the actor's right or left as he faces the audience. The stage floor may also be spoken of as though it were divided into squares, each with its own designation: *up right, up center, up left, down right, down center, down left,* and so on. The actor's knowledge of this terminology is taken for granted and it is assumed that he will know what to do if he is told, for example, to enter up right and cross to down center.

Second, the actor should be familiar with the designation of body positions. *Full front* means facing the audience; the *one-quarter* position means turned approximately 45 degrees away from the audience; *one-half* or *profile* means turned 90 degrees away from the audience; *three-quarter* means turned 135 degrees away from the audience; and *full back* means turned completely away from the audience.

In addition, other terminology may be used to supplement area and body position designations. *Open up* means to turn slightly more toward the audience; *turn in* means to turn toward the center of the stage; *turn out* means to turn toward the side of the stage. Actors are also sometimes told to *share a scene*, which indicates that both should play in the one-quarter or profile position so that they are equally visible to the audience. *To give a scene* means that one actor gives the dominant stage position to another by changing his own bodily position so as to face more away from the audience than the other actor. In most scenes the emphasis shifts frequently from one character to another, and the actors may constantly be giving and taking the scene according to which needs to be most emphatic at any given moment. This requires skill so as not to attract attention to the device, but it is a basic technical accomplishment which is expected of all actors.

An actor may also be told to *dress stage*, which means that he should move so as to balance the stage picture. This usually involves moving to a position just vacated by another actor. Experienced actors make such movements almost automatically and without being obtrusive. To *focus* means to look at or to turn toward a person or object in order to direct attention to it. Stage terminology, such as that given here, summarizes a large number of the technical devices which the actor must know, and it serves the director as a kind of shorthand in his directions to the actors.

Other technical problems cannot be reduced to such basic terminology, but solutions to them must be learned nevertheless. Many of the mechanics of stage technique have been devised to keep the actors as visible to the audience as possible. For example, the actor normally gestures with his upstage hand so as not to cover his face; he learns to kneel on his downstage knee so as to keep his body more visible to the audience; he opens doors with whichever hand is on the offstage side as he faces the audience; he stands upstage of doors and windows if he must call through them.

Other technical devices are designed to help emphasize some actions and to subordinate others. For example, a letter which is to be important later may have to be "planted" in an earlier scene. While its placement may need to be emphasized, its handling must not seem unnatural. The actor, therefore, might hesitate, or start to put it somewhere else and then change his mind, before selecting the final spot. On the other hand, many actions need to be masked from the audience. Eating, for example, must be faked to a large degree since actors can seldom eat the amount or the actual kind of food designated in the script. Scenes of violence (such as stabbings, shootings, and fist fights) must also be faked. These require careful planning and rehearsal so that they appear convincing even while the details are hidden from the audience.

The actor, furthermore, normally strives to be graceful, since gracefulness is usually unobtrusive, while awkwardness calls attention to itself. The actor must learn to sit without looking to make sure that he is in front of the chair; he must rise without effort, be able to turn without seeming awkward, and avoid calling attention to anything unless emphasis should be directed to it. For example, if the actor turns and looks at a chair before sitting in it, the chair and the act of sitting receive an emphasis which is normally inappropriate.

The actor must learn to make movements which are precise and clear. Vagueness of movement creates the impression of indefiniteness. If the actor understands the purpose of his movements and gestures, he can usually make the purpose clear to an audience by selecting those actions which are expressive and by executing them with precision.

Only a few of the most common technical problems which face an actor have been touched upon. Every actor should acquire the soundest technical training possible, however, for an adequate technique is always necessary for the projection of characterizations to an audience. There is no reason to assume, as some have, that a knowledge of technique will result in mechanical performances.

SYSTEMS OF ACTING. No matter how well trained the actor is in those basic skills which have been discussed, he will not be able to use them adequately without some consistent working method. Without system, results are spotty and accidental. A person cannot set out merely to become a good actor; he must define his objectives and then try to find some means for achieving them. Only in this way will his work have a focus and will he be able to measure his progress and accomplishments.

There are many systems of acting. No actor should adopt a method, no matter how highly recommended by others, until he has given it a thorough trial. He should try as many different approaches as possible and adopt those elements from each which most effectively aid him.

While each actor must find that method which best fits his own needs, systems of acting tend to have many elements in common. The two poles are usually called the "psychological-internal" and the "mechanical-external." The controversy which has raged between the advocates of the two extremes is centered in the question: Must the actor be emotionally moved himself in order to act convincingly?

Exponents of the "external" school argue that the actor need not feel anything himself and that, in fact, feeling may interfere with his acting since it may cause him to lose control. The principal sources of good acting are said to be observation and technique, and the actor is advised to study human behavior and to learn how each emotion in a situation is typically manifested. When called upon to portray an emotion, then, he need merely recreate all of the external signs, since the audience does not know whether the actor feels anything or not.

Believers in the "internal" school argue that it is only through feeling that an actor can project himself into the situation of the character, and that the ability to re-create feeling states through the memory of emotion is the only way to avoid mechanical performances.

In their extreme forms, both of these schools are of questionable value. While Stanislavsky's name is popularly associated with the "internal" school, in actuality his theory represents a sound middle ground between the two extremes. It gives equal stress to the actor's psychological and technical training; in the system feeling gives force and meaning to technique, while technique allows the clear and expressive projection of feeling. Even Stanislavsky's system, however, must be judged by the degree to which it works for a given actor.

ADDITIONAL SKILLS AND TRAINING.   Ultimately the actor must apply all of his knowledge for the creation of a specific role in a given stage environment. To be effective, therefore, he should also acquire the ability to analyze plays, since he may apply his skills to advantage only if he understands thoroughly the motivations, attitudes, and function of the character he is to portray.

Since he must create within a stage rather than in a real-life environment, the actor should also seek to understand all aspects of theatrical production. The more he knows about the possibilities and limitations of scenery, costumes, and lighting, the better he will be able to utilize them in his work and to appreciate the conditions under which other theatre artists work. Such understanding is vital to the necessary teamwork involved in a production.

CREATING THE ROLE

Regardless of his experience and training, however, the actor must solve a number of specific problems each time he assumes a new role. Some of the typical problems will be treated under the following headings: analyzing the role; psychological and emotional preparation; movement and pantomime; vocal characterization; memorization and line readings; conservation and build; ensemble playing; and dress rehearsals and performances.

ANALYZING THE ROLE.   Before the actor begins work, he must understand his role thoroughly. Since any character must be approached in part according to its function in the play, the actor should seek first to understand the script as a whole. Not until then should he concentrate upon the study and analysis of his own role. Play analysis was discussed in Chapter 3, and only the most pertinent points about characterization will be reviewed here.

First, it is helpful to look at a role in terms of levels of characterization. What does the playwright reveal about the character's physical

A scene from Christopher Fry's *The Lady's Not for Burning* showing variety in the use of bodily position. Directed by Henderson Forsythe; setting by Andrew Stasik.

make-up; his profession, social class, economic status and family background; his basic attitudes, likes, dislikes, and general emotional make-up; his ways of meeting crises and conflicts? Which characteristics are most important, and how is each used in developing the story? Some traits will be of primary importance, while others may scarcely affect the play at all. The actor should strive to embody as many of the characteristics as possible, but above all should make those believable which are most essential to the story.

At times the actor may find that the script is not specific in filling in all the details which would make a well-rounded character. In fact, no script is ever entirely complete in this sense, and the actor is forced to invent much. For example, the character's physical appearance may not be specified. The actor must then decide upon certain appropriate physical characteristics. In working on psychological characterization, many actors find it essential to reconstruct the life of the character prior to the beginning of the play, although the playwright may have given little indication about the character's upbringing or social background. In filling in missing details, the actor must be careful to take his cues from the script and to invent nothing contradictory to the information supplied by the author. Some actors become so engrossed in inventing business and details that they lose sight of the main function of their roles. Appropriateness should always be the actor's guide when he fills out a character left vague by the author.

Second, the actor must define the goals of the character he is to play. He should seek to isolate the over-all goal first, but then he must see how it is manifested in each scene, how it evolves and changes. In defining the character's goals, it is usually helpful to break the play down into short units or scenes and to isolate the character's principal motivation in each. This will aid in giving focus to the actor's performance within the scene. Furthermore, if he will determine how the scene is related to those which precede and follow it, he can recognize the kinds of transitions which will be needed. The examination of each scene in relation to the whole play will show him the desirable emphases within a given scene and how his characterization as a whole should change and grow.

Third, the actor should study character relationships. He must determine how his character is viewed by all the other characters. What the character thinks of himself may not accord with the image he tries to create for others (he may try to mask his true self); each of the other characters may have differing conceptions of his nature. The actor also must analyze his character's feelings and attitudes toward every other character he encounters.

Fourth, the actor must examine how his role relates to the play's story and structure, its ideas and themes. He must understand the function of his character in relation to each of these elements in each scene and in the drama as a whole.

If the play is from a past period, an unfamiliar environment, or if it deviates from the realistic mode, the actor may need to make a special effort at understanding the script, his role, and its demands. He may need to study the period or place, or he may have to determine the desirable acting style. Playwrights have normally written with a given theatre structure and acting style in mind, and it may aid the actor in his search for the playwright's intention if these factors are explored.

Some period plays may make special demands on the actor's movement. For example, men in the eighteenth century usually wore swords, carried walking sticks, snuff boxes, lace handkerchiefs, and other accessories which the modern man would find embarrassing to use. A satisfactory and convincing performance, however, will be possible only if the actor can project himself imaginatively into the world portrayed in the play. The actor, therefore, must find out what functions these accessories filled in the life of the eighteenth century, how they were used, and how they affected movement and gestures.

The actor is normally trained to perform in a realistic style. He may be confronted, however, with creating a role in an expressionist or epic drama, or one written in some other deviation from realism. He must be willing, therefore, to study the appropriate acting techniques. Most frequently his understanding of nonrealistic acting styles must come from printed accounts, for he is seldom able to see a given nonrealistic style on the stage often enough to learn it through direct observation. Background reading and other forms of inquiry may be necessary before the actor's conception of his role can be complete.

While the actor must do extensive work toward understanding his role, his interpretation must always be adjusted to that of the director. If the actor and the director are in disagreement, they should discuss their differing conceptions. Each should be willing to listen carefully to the reasoning of the other, but ultimately the actor must subordinate his interpretation to that being given to the play as a whole. The actor may have to change his interpretation or, if this is impossible, he should give up his part, for no satisfactory performance can result when there are basic disagreements between a director and an actor. After he is sure that he understands his role and that his interpretation will fit that of the director, the actor may then proceed to the problems of embodying the character on the stage.

PSYCHOLOGICAL AND EMOTIONAL PREPARATION. While the actor's analysis of the script may lead to an intellectual understanding of the play, he must still be able to project himself imaginatively into the circumstances—the situation, the setting, and any conditions laid down by the director—before his understanding is complete.

Sometimes an actor may find it difficult to imagine himself as the character, and he may need to experiment with ways of inducing belief in the given circumstances. The use of emotion memory, and the observation of similar persons and situations are the most commonly used aids. When these do not work, improvisations based upon more familiar circumstances may help the actor to get the right feeling for a role. With this foundation secure, he may then proceed to the less familiar circumstances found in the script.

Even in moments of stress the actor must remain "open" to the audience. Note how the kneeling figure keeps his face visible. A scene from Lope de Vega's *Fuente Ovejuna*. Directed by Francis Hodge.

The degree to which this kind of preparation is undertaken varies from actor to actor, but, regardless of approach, a good performance usually depends upon the actor's ability to understand every motivation and to imagine how the character would feel at any given moment. Although the actor may never actually feel anything himself, he must at least know how the character would feel. The effective use of every means of expression—movement, gesture, business, voice, and speech—depends upon that full knowledge of the character which is a combination of the actor's intellectual understanding of the script and his imaginative projection into the circumstances.

MOVEMENT, GESTURE, AND BUSINESS. As a rule an early phase of rehearsals is devoted to establishing movement patterns. The director may indicate positions for each moment. Some directors are very specific about these, while others give only general suggestions. The actor, however, should feel that all his movements are motivated and he should indicate to the director whenever he finds a direction contrary to his understanding of the role. Conflicts over movement can frequently be resolved through a discussion of the interpretation of the character, since disagreements most often come from the actor's feeling that certain actions are not in keeping with the role.

Even when the director specifies stage and bodily positions, the actor must still fill in a large number of details—the character's walk, his posture and bodily attitudes, and his gestures. The purposes and kinds of movement have already been discussed in Chapter 16, and need be reviewed only briefly here.

Movement is either specified by the script or invented. In either case it may be used for several purposes: to tell the story; to establish character, and to clarify motivations, attitudes, and emotional responses; to establish mood and style; to create variety; to secure and hold attention; and to achieve pictorial composition. While some of these uses may not be directly related to characterization, all movement must be executed by the actors and, therefore, must be performed "in character." The better the actor understands the purpose behind each movement, the more he will be able to make effective use of it.

The actor's physical characterization has at least three levels. First, a role must be approached in terms of its permanent physical qualities. While some roles require considerable changes from the first to the last act, as a rule the broad outlines (such as age, habitual ways of walking, sitting, and performing daily tasks, and typical gestures) remain unchanged. These are the over-all qualities for which an actor must work.

Second, out of these factors the actor must be able to select and use those appropriate to any given moment without ever violating the basic outlines. In finding appropriate action it is sometimes helpful to

A moment from Maxwell Anderson's *Elizabeth the Queen*. Note the effective use of gesture.

think of the play as though it had no words. The actor then must decide how the situation, the character relationships, emotional responses, and motivations can be expressed visually. Much of what he would do under such circumstances is redundant and would need to be discarded when words are added, but this approach may serve to stimulate his imagination and help him to find many helpful devices for his physical characterization.

Third, within the limitations imposed by the script and role, the actor should work for distinctiveness. While a characterization should always be clear, good acting always seems original and free from clichés. The actor can achieve this effect only after a rather careful consideration of the various ways by which a given point might be expressed and by a thoughtful choice of one which has both clarity and unusualness.

No rules can be laid down for physical characterization, but the broad criteria of appropriateness, clarity, expressiveness, and distinctiveness should be kept in mind. The specific ways of carrying these through must be found by the individual actor.

Vocal Characterization. An actor's analysis of a role should also involve a consideration of the vocal qualities and mannerisms appropriate to the character. For one role a high-pitched voice might be helpful; another might profit from a jerky delivery; another might require loudness and boisterousness; another may need a dialect.

The actor cannot always change his own voice sufficiently to give an ideal vocal characterization. For this reason, directors normally cast actors who already possess the vocal qualities they are seeking. The actor with a well-trained voice, however, can certainly modify his own vocal patterns to achieve desirable effects.

Every actor should be thoroughly familiar with his normal way of speaking (a tape recorder will help in this analysis). With this knowledge in mind when he begins a role, he can decide what vocal changes are desirable and which changes are possible. The actor must always be careful not to put undue strain on his vocal mechanism, however, for serious damage can result if changes are incorrectly made.

Not only should the actor analyze the over-all vocal characteristics of a role, he should also look at each scene for its own individual demands. Some scenes are relaxed, others are emotionally high-keyed, and still others display much variety. The basic quality of a scene and all changes can be made clearer through well-thought-out vocal patterns. For example, tension, which is typical of high-keyed scenes, may be manifested in raised pitch, greater volume, and faster tempo. A clear understanding of the function and the emotional content of each scene will tell the actor what he should work for in the use of his voice.

Voice is also an important element in clarifying ideas and emotions. Any change of thought or feeling may be indicated by a change in volume, pitch, or quality. Such uses of the voice should, of course, be done in character and be entirely appropriate both to the situation and to the persons involved.

Much of his vocal characterization may come naturally to an actor if he understands his role thoroughly and if he has been able to project himself into the situation imaginatively. Such automatic characterization should never be taken for granted, however, and the actor should constantly assess the degree to which his use of voice embodies the individual he is portraying.

MEMORIZATION AND LINE READINGS.   One of the technical problems facing every actor is memorization. It is usually helpful to memorize speeches and action simultaneously, for lines help to recall movement and movement to recall lines. It may be difficult to coordinate these two elements in the beginning, but, since blocking is always given in relation to specific speeches, ultimately their conjunction becomes fused in the actor's memory.

In solving the problem of memorization there are only a few simple rules. First, it is impossible to memorize everything at once. It is necessary, therefore, to divide the play into sections and to master one at a time. Second, it is extremely difficult to memorize disconnected words. The actor, therefore, should begin by familiarizing himself thoroughly with the sequence of ideas and motivations—the sense of each scene. After he is able to recall this sequence, he may then proceed to the memorization of actual words. This contextual approach is an aid to the actor in performance if he forgets the specific wording of a speech, for he can continue by improvising its sense. Furthermore, this enables him to assist other actors should their memories fail. This kind of familiarity with a play makes it possible for actors to dispense with the service of a prompter as a rule. Third, the actor should listen carefully to and be familiar with the lines of all the other actors in the scene, and he must memorize his cues (the lines or actions of others which precede each of his own speeches) as thoroughly as he does his own speeches.

There is some difference of opinion about the best time to memorize lines. The sooner the actor learns his lines, the earlier he will be able to polish and work for subtlety. On the other hand, if an actor memorizes his lines before he is clear about his interpretation of the role or the significance of his speeches, a mechanical delivery may result. All things considered, however, it is better to learn lines too early than too late, for nothing destroys the believability of a performance more quickly than "shakiness" in lines.

In addition to merely knowing the lines, the actor must be concerned with those patterns of stress, intonation, and duration which serve to project meaning. A thorough understanding of all the implications of a line is necessary before it can be properly "read." The good actor normally concentrates upon the over-all thought and emotion rather than upon individual words. He knows where one idea ends and another begins, and makes transitions with care so that each thought is clear to the audience.

To indicate progressions and transitions, the actor uses changes in pitch, volume, and duration so as to set off one unit or idea from another. This is especially important in long speeches where both monotony and confusion of thought or feeling are most apt to occur.

In the majority of plays, the actor must work for the effect of spontaneity, for his speeches should appear to arise without any forethought from the situation and emotion. Falseness in line readings or in tone makes the audience question the sincerity of the actor or of the character. Spontaneity and believability must be judged in terms of the specific play, however, for the demands of *King Lear* differ from those of *Death of a Salesman* because of the dissimilarities in language and phrasing.

Regardless of the type of play, the actor's standard for the reading of lines should be: clarity of ideas and emotions, spontaneity, believability, variety, and distinctiveness. In addition, he must project his voice to the most remote seat in the auditorium.

CONSERVATION AND BUILD. Still another technical problem which faces every actor is the necessity of conserving his powers and building his role in a climactic order. Every play progresses from the less to the more interesting—it builds in intensity or suspense. Likewise every actor's performance should also grow and progress. Many actors fail because, while they play individual scenes well, their performances as a whole are not properly planned and articulated to develop in intensity and complexity.

The need to sustain and build a part is most clearly seen in highly emotional roles. If the actor begins his performance at an emotional pitch which is too high, he may soon find that he can build the intensity no farther. The rest of the performance, then, remains on a level and becomes monotonous. The actor, therefore, must learn to judge his power and to plan his performance so that it continues to evolve in interest throughout the play.

ENSEMBLE PLAYING. No acting performance (except in those rare plays written for one actor) is complete by itself. It is only one of many characterizations, and its effectiveness must be judged in part according to how well it is integrated with the other performances. An actor, therefore, must be able to relate himself convincingly to all the characters on stage. The sense of artistic wholeness which results from the cooperative efforts of the entire cast is frequently called "ensemble playing."

Ensemble playing is the result of a number of factors. First, it can come about only when each actor is willing to subordinate himself to the demands of the play. He must be able to fade into the background when this is desirable; he must refrain from trying to "steal" scenes; he must put the good of the production above winning plaudits for himself.

Second, ensemble playing depends in part upon each actor's awareness of the working methods, strengths, and weaknesses of his fellow actors. He learns what he can expect of the others, where he needs to compensate for their shortcomings, and how they may help him. Such cooperative acting is one of the distinctive marks of a company whose members have worked together over a long period of time. While this kind of awareness is limited in a cast which works together for only one play, it should be developed as far as possible.

Third, the most important factor in ensemble playing is the ability of the actors to concentrate. Listening, seeing, and responding with subtle and properly timed reactions are the most powerful forces for believability in the theatre. They create "the illusion of the first time." The best performances come about when all the actors concentrate so completely on the stage events that they compel the audience to concentrate in a like manner upon the action which seems to be unfolding spontaneously before their eyes.

DRESS REHEARSALS AND PERFORMANCES. As a rule it is not until dress rehearsals that an actor is confronted with all of the properties, the setting, his costume and make-up, and the stage lighting. The surer he is of his performance by this time the less distracting the new elements will be. He can do much to ease the transition from rehearsal to performance if he has taken time earlier to familiarize himself as thoroughly as he possibly can with the stage environment. Normally, there are sketches and models of the stage as it will appear in performance, and the actor can study these so that the visual background will not seem strange. Throughout rehearsals he should have become at home with the floor plan, or

Scenes of eating pose difficult problems for both the actor and the director. Here, in a scene from Garcia Lorca's *The House of Bernarda Alba*, is an effective solution. Directed by Shirley Ahern.

general layout, of the scenery. Of special importance is his costume. He should find out everything he can about it—what movements it enhances, which it restricts, its possibilities for business, and so on. A costumer is usually delighted when an actor takes a genuine interest in his costume and is always willing to help the actor explore its intricacies and potentials. If stage garments are significantly different from those which the actor normally wears, he should be provided with a rehearsal costume which simulates the qualities of the clothing to be worn in performance.

The actor should also have given considerable thought to his make-up before dress rehearsal. He should be clear as to what effects he wishes to create, and he should have experimented with achieving them if they are in any way unusual.

If the actor has business with swords, guns, packages, food, or other items which may create difficulties in use, he should rehearse frequently with reasonable facsimiles of those which will be used in performance.

Performance, of course, is the goal of the actor's work. The better trained and rehearsed he is the more certain he will feel when opening night comes. It is a rare actor, however, who does not experience some stage fright. This is actually a benefit, however, for it keeps the actor keyed up, alert, and ready to meet any emergency.

If all goes well on opening night, there is a tendency for actors to relax and to give a poorer performance on the second night. Actors playing in long-run shows frequently experience difficulty in keeping up their interest in their roles, and the level of performance suffers as a consequence. The actor must remember, however, that each performance is the first one for the particular audience for which he is playing. The ability to maintain a high and reasonably even quality, however, depends ultimately on the ability of the actors to concentrate upon their work.

The actor will find it easier to maintain a high level of interest if he develops the habit of assessing the effectiveness of his own acting in each performance, and if he looks upon each night as an occasion for overcoming the shortcomings he has uncovered. Performance offers the actor his greatest opportunity for learning, since his ability to affect an audience is the ultimate test of his skill. Each audience should be viewed as a new judgment on his strength.

After a show has closed, the actor should take stock of his abilities and achievements. He needs to re-evaluate his goals and his working methods. The development of acting ability is a never-ending process and only the conscientious actor ever succeeds in perfecting his art.

THE ACTOR'S EMPLOYMENT

In America today most actors enter the theatre after attending colleges, universities, or professional schools. This marks a major break with past practice. Previously the actor had been trained "on the job." He entered a company at an early age, learned his trade as he played minor roles, and eventually graduated into that "line of business" which he filled for the rest of his life. This kind of training was possible, however, only so long as there were a number of theatres with resident repertory or stock companies. The repertory system began to die out in America near the end of the nineteenth century. Stock companies (later called "winter stock" as a differentiation from summer stock), which ran about fifty weeks a year and provided a wide range of experience for actors, virtually disappeared in the early 1930s with the intense popularity of motion pictures. New ways had to be found to train actors. As early as 1884, the American Academy of Dramatic Art had begun to provide professional training, and with the diminishing of stock a number of professional theatre schools sprang up. About 1915 theatre training began to be offered in colleges, but the inclusion of theatre courses in college curricula did not become widespread until well after 1920.

Today a very large percentage of colleges and universities in America offer at least one course in acting. These courses usually give a sound introduction to the principles, techniques, and goals of acting. The student often wrongly views such course work, however, as being sufficient to equip him for a professional career. Few colleges and universities offer enough work to train the actor adequately for the professional stage.

Within the framework of the educational theatre, the actor with real talent seldom finds it difficult to be cast in a show, although the supply of available actors is almost always greater than the demand. The

A scene from Congreve's *Love for Love*. Note the cane, lace, wigs, fan, and other accessories which affect the actors' movements. Directed by Peter Arnott; costumes by Margaret Hall.

actor who has been trained in a college and who does not wish to work in the professional theatre can almost always find an outlet for his talent in the community theatre after he has left school.

Professional theatre schools, most of which are located in New York, give the actor more intensive training in his craft than does the educational theatre. They also allow him to become familiar with the professional theatre at close range (though the degree to which this is true is often exaggerated). Unfortunately, however, graduation from a professional school gives little more guarantee of work in the professional theatre than does any other training.

Since the 1920s summer stock companies have flourished in the United States, and many actors have found these to be good sources of training and of employment. All Actors' Equity approved companies pay scaled salaries. Certain of these Equity-controlled companies accept apprentices who are considered to be in training. Unfortunately most of them have such short rehearsal periods that the actor is apt to learn tricks for covering up inadequacies rather than the solid foundations of acting. Because of its intensive schedule and because of the widespread practice of employing a varying proportion of experienced actors, summer theatre may serve as a kind of bridge between the educational and the professional theatre, even if it is not an entirely satisfactory one.

Regardless of training, the young actor who wishes to work in the professional theatre almost invariably goes to New York. Few realize that there may be somewhat longer but more promising roads to eventual success. For example, there is an increasing number of semiprofessional and professional theatres operating outside of New York, and the aspiring actor might well consider them as means for acquiring further training and experience. These organizations include The Actors Workshop in San Francisco, The Alley Theatre in Houston, The Mummers in Oklahoma City, The Front Street Theatre in Memphis, The Cleveland Playhouse, The Tyrone Guthrie Theatre in Minneapolis, the Association of Producing Artists in Ann Arbor, Michigan, the Pittsburgh Playhouse, and the Arena Theatre in Washington, D.C. As long as New York remains the center of theatrical activity in America, however, the majority of would-be actors will flock there, in spite of the fact that up to eighty-five percent of the members of Actors' Equity are frequently unemployed.

Since the majority of Broadway productions do not use open tryouts in casting, an actor, as a rule, must have an agent before he can hope to be employed in New York. The supply of actors is so much greater than the demand that most casting offices restrict themselves to interviewing those actors whose talents can be vouched for by someone they know (an agent who is well known and trusted, therefore, may be of invaluable aid to an actor). Most agents are notified by producers when casting is about to begin and agents, in turn, try to secure a hearing for those clients who seem suited to the roles. Even off-Broadway producers are depending increasingly on agents as a means of screening applicants.

It is not easy for an actor to obtain an agent, however, for few agents are willing to represent clients whose work they have not seen. A role in a nonprofessional or a summer-stock production is frequently used by an actor as a means of displaying his ability to an agent, who has been invited to witness the performance. The actor, on the other hand, should make sure that a prospective agent is on the approved list which Actors' Equity maintains in its attempt to protect its members from unethical agents.

Occasionally a Broadway production is cast by open tryouts which anyone may attend. News about casting (whether open or closed) is printed in the newspapers, especially *Variety* and similar "trade" papers. Many actors who are trying to "break in" to the theatre feel it essential to make the rounds of casting offices every day on the chance that some job may have opened up. Many aspiring actors work at other jobs at night so as to have days free for "making the rounds." Such persistence pays off frequently enough to keep up the hope of others.

Before an actor can perform in a Broadway production he must become a member of Actors' Equity Association. (He may be cast without being a member, but he must join before he can be given a contract.) There are actually a number of unions to which actors may belong and these are banded together in a larger organization, the Associated Actors and Artistes of America. Sometimes an actor belongs to more than one of the affiliates so as to increase his possibilities of employment. The Associated Actors and Artistes of America is composed of the following member groups: Actors' Equity Association; American Federation of Television and Radio Artists; Screen Actors Guild; Hebrew Actors Guild; Italian Actors Union; American Guild of Variety Artists; Screen Extras Guild; Burlesque Artists Association; Hebrew Chorus Union; and American Guild of Musical Artists.

Actors' Equity controls most contracts in the legitimate theatre, however. (Actors' Equity classifies acting companies according to production conditions; the percentage of the company which must be Equity members and the minimum wage scales are determined by a company's classification. Non-Broadway companies are most frequently governed by regulations which differ from those applied to Broadway productions.) Actors' Equity specifies minimum wages and working conditions, and it maintains a legal staff to advise its members on deviations from standard contracts.

There are three basic kinds of contracts in the New York theatre: "standard minimum"; "run of the play"; and "conversion." The normal contract is the "standard minimum," which specifies that an actor may leave the show after giving two-weeks' notice and that he may be let go in a similar manner. "Run of the play" contracts are more often used for stars, who agree to remain with a production for a given length of time. The contract also specifies the financial arrangements should the play close or the star leave the show before the stated period has expired. The "conversion" contract contains an option for converting a "standard minimum" contract to a "run of the play" contract, and is used when the producer is in doubt about an actor's abilities. If the contract is converted,

A scene from Tennessee Williams' A *Streetcar Named Desire.*

the actor's salary must also be increased; after the conversion is made the contract is governed by all the conditions of a "run of the play" contract.

Any contract may have special clauses which indicate additional duties (such as understudying a role), privileges, billing, and so on. No Equity contract may be made, however, which violates the minimum standards set up by Actors' Equity.

Most touring shows are also cast in New York, and it is frequently easier to obtain a role in a touring company than in any other kind of production because of the reluctance of so many actors to leave New York. A number of summer stock companies also cast their plays in New York in the early spring. New York, therefore, has become a casting center even for the professional theatre which operates outside of New York. It is largely for this reason that New York and the American professional theatre have become synonymous for the aspiring professional actor.

Acting is one of the most glamorous professions in the world, but at the same time it is one of the most exacting in its demands and one of the most difficult in which to secure a foothold. Yet the actor is the artist most necessary for the existence of a theatre. Given the conditions under which he must operate in America today, he needs not only great talent, but tremendous perseverance and dedication as well.

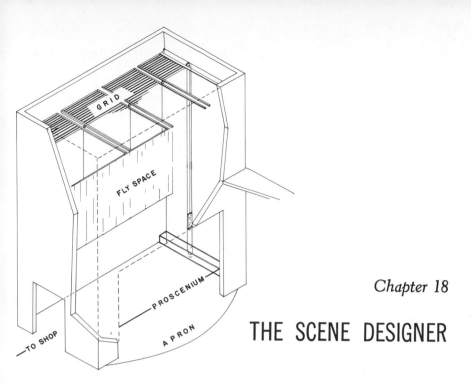

Chapter 18

THE SCENE DESIGNER

While the director and the actors make considerable use of the stage environment in their work, they normally depend upon others to design the scenery, costumes, and lighting which compose this environment. The designers, thus, are concerned with the visual embodiment of the period, the place, the socioeconomic background, the mood and atmosphere, the themes, and the style of the play.

All design for the theatre has a number of common aims and means, and frequently the same person designs the scenery, the costumes, and the lighting. Each of these elements, however, has its own distinctive features and will be discussed separately so that the principal functions and methods of each may be more fully clarified.

The scene designer is concerned principally with defining and characterizing the stage space. Through the placement of scenic elements he outlines those areas which will be used by the actors and he limits the vision of the audience to that portion of the stage which is needed for the production. He determines the desirable qualities for each part of the setting and the over-all visual characteristics of each scene and of the play as a whole. He must see that the setting is properly "dressed" with the appropriate furniture, draperies, pictures, and other properties which are part of the stage setting. He must see that all of his plans are properly executed and that his settings function in the performance of the play as envisioned.

Section of a proscenium stage.

The various aspects of the scene designer's work will be considered under the following headings: the purposes of design; the elements and principles of design; working procedures and plans; standard scenic pieces; assembling scenery; painting scenery; shifting scenery; furniture, decoration, and properties; rehearsals and performances.

THE PURPOSES OF SCENE DESIGN

The two basic purposes of scene design are: to aid audience understanding, and to express the play's qualities. As an aid to understanding, the stage setting may define the time and place of the action, it should clarify the relationship of the offstage and onstage space, and it should assist in establishing characterization.

The amount of emphasis placed on period and place varies considerably from one play to another. Some plays (such as *The Wild Duck* and other plays in the realistic mode) specify a large number of details associated with a particular period or place. The designer may need to include furniture, pictures, and other properties which will create an environment similar to that of real life at the time of the play's action. Other plays, such as those by Molière and Sheridan, indicate the time and country in which the action occurs but place no emphasis upon details. In such cases, the designer may use decorative motifs of the period, or a wing-and-drop setting such as that in use in the seventeenth and eighteenth centuries, but may make no attempt at creating the real-life environment of the time. In other cases, such as in Shakespeare's plays, time and place may be of still lesser importance and the locale may be left indefinite. In this case, however, the stage setting tells the audience immediately that the place of the action is of little consequence. Regardless of the importance of period and locale, the designer depends largely upon architectural forms and properties for defining time and place as they will be used in the production.

The physical arrangement of the setting should aid understanding in a number of ways. Whenever characters enter or exit, the script usually implies the place from which they are coming or to which they are going. The floor plan of the setting, therefore, should help to clarify both the onstage and the offstage space. In designing a realistic living-room setting, the arrangement of the rest of the house must be kept in mind (the location of the main entrance, the kitchen, and the bedrooms is usually important). In other plays the exact nature of the offstage space may not be specified, but the designer must make sure that his set allows the action to be clear (for example, if one character must enter immediately after another has left the stage and if the two are not supposed to see

A setting for a play about the search for happiness, Maurice Maeterlinck's *The Blue Bird*, in a production by the Moscow Art Theatre. From *Moscow Art Theatre, 1898–1917*. Moscow, 1955.

each other, the arrangement of the stage must permit this action if the audience is not to be confused).

The stage space can also aid understanding by allowing variety in the grouping of actors. Platforms and steps permit the director greater scope than does the one-level setting in achieving those emphases and stage pictures which will clarify character relationships and situations. Furthermore, since the floor plan of any setting allows certain patterns of movement and restricts others, it should be arranged to encourage the smooth flow of action. For example, the setting called for in *Death of a Salesman* includes three different rooms and an exterior. This arrangement permits one scene to flow smoothly into the next while helping at the same time to define clearly the location of each scene. The practice of using nonlocalized settings in the staging of Shakespeare's plays has in large part grown out of the desire to keep the action moving so as not to interrupt the audience's concentration.

The stage setting also helps to establish character. A living room setting, for example, should reflect the socioeconomic status and the tastes of its owners. Even the ungeneralized settings frequently used for Shakespearean plays should permit some differentiation from one scene to another which will be indicative of the characters in the scene. Furthermore, as has already been pointed out, sets should afford the director a maximum number of possibilities in grouping the actors for the purpose of revealing character and character relationships. The mutual influence on each other of character and environment should be kept in mind constantly.

The stage setting must also be expressive of the play's basic qualities.

It should help to create and heighten the proper mood. When the curtain opens the stage setting should give the audience a clear indication of the level of probability which is being created by the performance. The setting should help to answer the question: With what kind of world are we in contact (a reasonable facsimile of everyday existence; a world like our own but one in which all except the essential details have been stripped away; a world of fantasy; an absurd world)? The setting should give some indication of the type (tragedy, comedy, melodrama), the style (expressionism, naturalism, epic, and so on), and the theme of the play. The design should embody the qualities of the play through line, color, forms, and spatial relationships just as the actor seeks to embody the play's qualities through the use of his body and voice. A good setting is a visual statement of the values of the script.

THE ELEMENTS OF DESIGN

In carrying out the purposes of scene design, a number of basic design elements—line, shape, space, color, texture, and ornament—are used singly or in combination.

Line indicates the boundaries of objects. In reality, a tree, for example, does not have lines; it occupies a given amount of space. But, in drawing a tree, its shape is indicated by a series of lines. Line must be distinguished from the shape or mass it outlines, for a line has only one dimension—length—whereas mass gives the quality of two- or three-dimensionality.

While a line has only one dimension, it may go in any direction. There are two basic kinds of lines—straight and curved. These may be combined, or the direction of each may be altered to form zigzags, scallops, or any other variation. The dominant lines in stage scenery are the horizontal lines of the stage floor and ceiling, and the vertical lines of the setting. This basic pattern is broken, however, by the lines of furniture, draperies, foliage, and other scenic elements.

Line is normally thought to have the power of eliciting emotional responses. Straight lines may give a quality of stability, curved lines of grace. Zigzag lines set up an opposition which has a dynamic quality. Two lines which get farther apart as they rise vertically may create a feeling of openness, while those that come close together may create a sense of oppression since they seem to be falling inward. Although the emotional value of a line will depend in part upon the context in which it is seen, it serves, nevertheless, as an important means of creating mood and atmosphere, as well as for defining shape.

Shape and space are closely related factors and are frequently treated together as a single element—mass. While line has only the dimension of direction or length, mass involves two or three dimensions. It identifies the shape (square, round, oblong, and so forth) and the size (height, width, and thickness) of objects.

Each part of the setting, each piece of furniture, and each prop has a shape and occupies a certain amount of space. Mass must be considered in relation to each individual element in a setting, therefore, as well as in terms of the entire setting, which also has a dominant shape and occupies a given space.

The setting may be thought of as a hollow cube, the inside of which can be organized in a variety of ways. By altering the shape and size of the individual elements and their relationship to each other, almost any desired effect may be achieved. Thick, horizontal forms (for example, a room with a low ceiling and thick beams) may create an effect of compression, while narrow, vertical, and pointed forms (such as a room with thin, tall columns and high Gothic arches) may create a feeling of airiness, openness, and grace.

The shape and size of objects may be emphasized by making sharp distinctions between their different planes and surfaces (for instance, one side of a cube may be made very dark, another side very light). This treatment gives a quality of harshness to a setting. On the other hand, if the differentiations between planes and surfaces are subtle, a feeling of softness or diffusion will result.

Mass, then, involves the shape and size of the total setting and its various elements, and the organization of the stage space. It can be perceived in such factors as the height of a setting in proportion to its width and depth; the thickness of door frames and beams; the size and shape of furniture, trees, platforms and stairs. It creates impressions of openness or compression, of heaviness or lightness, of great space or of confinement.

In addition to line and mass, color is also an important element in design. Color may be described in terms of three basic qualities, dimen-

A setting for Act II of *The Importance of Being Earnest*. Note the symmetrical arrangement, which is emphasized by the grouping of the actors. Designed by Arnold Gillette.

sions, or properties: hue, saturation or intensity, and value. Hue is the name of the color. Saturation or intensity refers to the relative purity of a color, or its freedom from gray or its complementary hue. Value is the lightness or darkness of a color—its relation to white or black. A color which is light in value is usually called a tint, while dark values are called shades.

Colors may be classified as primary, secondary, and intermediate. The primary colors are those which cannot be created by mixing other colors, but from which all other colors may be derived. The primary colors in pigment are yellow, red, and blue. The secondary colors—orange, violet, and green—are those which are arrived at by equal mixtures of two primary colors. The intermediate colors are those which result from the mixture of a primary with a secondary color. They are yellow-orange, red-orange, red-violet, blue-violet, blue-green, and yellow-green. All of the colors may be arranged around a wheel to indicate their relationships. Those opposite each other on the wheel are called complementary colors, while those next to each other are called analogous colors. Colors may also be described as warm or cool. For example, red, orange, and yellow are warm colors, while green, blue, and violet are cool colors.

Almost any combination of colors may be used together if saturation, proportion, or value are properly controlled. Two colors which seem to clash when used in their full intensity or in equal quantity may be made harmonious by graying one or both of the colors (that is by lowering the saturation), by lightening the values, or by using a small amount of one color in proportion to the other.

Color schemes may be monochromatic, analogous, or contrasting. The simplest is the monochromatic scheme. This means that a single hue is used, and variety is gained by combining differing intensities and values. An analogous color scheme is one in which all of the hues have one element in common. For example, blue-green, green, and yellow-green all have green in common.

Another approach is the use of contrasting colors. The most obvious contrast is to be found in complementary hues: orange and blue, yellow and violet, blue-green and red-orange. If such a color scheme is not to be unpleasant, it must be used with considerable care for the proper saturation, value, and proportion. Sometimes a split-complement is used. This means that, instead of using the hue directly across the color wheel, those

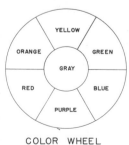

COLOR WHEEL

A designer's sketch for Goldoni's *The Mistress of the Inn*. Note the asymmetrical balance, the variety of line, shape, decoration, texture, the pleasing proportions and the flow of movement encouraged by the floor plan. Design by A. N. Benya. From *Moscow Art Theatre, 1898–1917*.

two hues which lie on either side of the complementary hue are selected. For example, instead of using yellow and violet, as one might in a simple complementary arrangement, the split-complement would use yellow with red-violet and blue-violet. Another common color scheme is called the triad; that is, three colors which are equidistant from each other on the color wheel are used together (for example, yellow-orange, red-violet, and blue-green).

The three properties of color may be manipulated in many different ways to achieve the effects desired by a scene designer. Mood and atmosphere, for example, depend much on the use of color. Many persons believe that light, warm colors are much more conducive to evoking the comic response than are dark, cool colors. Furthermore, colors may be associated with specific kinds of emotions. Red and orange may connote heat and passion, whereas green and blue are frequently associated with coolness and restraint. There is no way to determine with exactness the response which will be elicited by any given color, for much depends upon the context in which it appears. Nevertheless color does have the power to affect audiences emotionally, and the designer must consider this in his use of it.

Other effects may also derive from color. A hue of light value can help to create a feeling of openness and space while a dark color may aid in arousing the sense of depression and confinement. Dark objects seem bulkier and heavier than those which are light in value. Some color combinations are garish, while others are sophisticated. The designer, therefore, may use color in creating the right mood and atmosphere for arousing emotional response and for establishing the taste of the characters who inhabit the settings.

Texture is another element of each design. In stage settings, texture is often used to indicate the supposed material of which the setting is made. In actuality, the visible surface of most scenery is painted canvas. Nevertheless, in most cases it must appear to be of some other material (brick, stone, rough or smooth plaster, or wood) or to be some natural object (a tree, the ground, or outcroppings of rock). Each material and object is recognized in part by its texture.

Most frequently a setting makes use of more than one texture. The walls of a room may be plaster, but the doors and windows may be wood and glass. Other textures are brought in through rugs, the upholstery on the furniture, the draperies, and the pictures on the wall.

Texture may be used for any number of purposes. It may help to establish a period. For example, Elizabethan houses are often depicted as composed of half timbering (that is, a combination of heavy timbers and of plaster or stucco). Texture may help to establish the appropriate feeling for an environment. Adjectives such as smooth, rough, shiny, soft, and grained are often applied to texture and such descriptive words frequently seem equally applicable to the qualities inherent in a script. Some plays seem to demand rough textures, whereas others may call for smooth textures. The qualities of sleaziness, or fragility, or of richness depend in part upon the textures used. Texture, thus, may be chosen and manipulated by the designer to achieve his purposes.

Ornament is also an element in design. It includes the pictures on the walls, decorative motifs, wallpaper patterns, molding, and similar items. Ornament is one of the chief means for achieving distinctiveness in a setting for it is used principally to add the touches which complete the picture. For example, even if all the other elements of design have been used skillfully, the walls of a living room setting will appear barren without the proper use of ornament. This ornamentation, however, must clearly distinguish the living room of a wealthy person from that of a person of modest means, of the person of good taste from that of the person devoid of taste. Ornament, thus, is a subtle but important element of design.

The scene designer must be thoroughly familiar with each element of design and with what may be accomplished with each. Through his manipulations of these elements he externalizes the qualities inherent in the script.

THE PRINCIPLES OF DESIGN

In the application of the elements of design, certain principles must be adhered to if the results are to be pleasing and effective. These principles are harmony, balance, proportion, emphasis, and rhythm.

Harmony is the principle which creates the impression of unity. All of the elements of each setting must be harmonious and the various settings should be related in such a way that all are clearly parts of a single ordered whole. If monotony is to be avoided, however, variety is required both within a single setting and among the various settings. The elements of design may be manipulated so as to accomplish this double effect of unity and variety simultaneously.

Balance is that sense of stability which results from the apparent equal distribution of weight on either side of the center line. The stage may be thought of as a fulcrum with the point of balance at the center of the stage. The scenic elements placed on each side of that line should appear to be equal in weight; if they are not, an uneasy response may be aroused. Apparent weight has no direct relationship to actual weight. It is perceived in such factors as color, size, placement, and texture. A large, light-colored object may appear to weigh the same as a small, dark-colored object. Furthermore, the placement of objects on stage has much to do with the sense of balance. A small object near the outer edge of the set may be used to balance a large object near the center of the stage. A small object which appears to be made of stone may balance a larger one which appears to be made of wood. Each of the elements of design may be manipulated to achieve a sense of balance in the stage setting.

There are two basic kinds of balance: symmetrical and asymmetrical. Symmetrical balance means that each side of the stage is a mirror image of the other (that is, the same elements are repeated on each side of the center line). Obviously symmetrical balance can be easily achieved, but it is not always desirable since it creates an impression of formality and often of contrivance. Asymmetrical balance uses a more random placement of elements with the resultant effect of greater informality. It requires a more subtle manipulation of the elements of design, however, for it must give the appearance of being unplanned while nevertheless being perfectly balanced.

Proportion involves the relationship between the parts of a design: the basic shapes utilized (squares, rectangles, free-form, and so on); the scale of each element in relation to that of all the others; and the division of the space (for example, if a wall is to be painted two colors, how much of the space is to be used by each?). Proportion can be manipulated to elicit a wide variety of responses. It can help in achieving effects of stability or of instability, of grace or awkwardness. Furniture that is too large in proportion to the size of a room may give a cramped feeling, whereas furniture that is too small in scale may appear meager and poor. Each element of the stage setting must be properly proportioned both in itself and in relation to each of the other elements. The beauty or ugliness of the whole depends in large part upon the proportions of the individual items.

A design must also have a focal point, or center of emphasis. A well-composed design will direct the eye to the most important point immediately and then to each of the subordinate parts in the order of their importance to the whole picture. There may be a number of points of interest in the same design, but one should be dominant.

Emphasis may be achieved in several ways. Line may be used. For example, a triangular platform with its apex at center stage will lead the eye to that point. The lines of walls, furniture, steps, and decorative motifs may all be utilized to create focal points.

Emphasis may be achieved by the grouping or placement of objects. For example, a sofa may become an emphatic object through its position on stage, or a series of similar objects may be used to lead the eye to the last in the series or to contrast with an unlike object.

Color may be used effectively for achieving emphasis: a brighter saturation, a hue which contrasts with others around it, or a difference in value may serve to direct the eye to a point of interest. Unusual texture or decoration may also serve as a means of gaining emphasis.

Rhythm in visual design is that factor which leads the eye easily and smoothly from one part of the picture to the others; it makes one part flow into the next. All of the elements of design may be used in achieving a sense of rhythm. Lines and shapes may be repeated; the size of objects may be changed gradually so as to give a sense of progression; gradations or alterations in hue, saturation, and value of coloration may lead the eye easily from one part of the composition to another; changes in texture and ornament may give a sense of flow and movement.

The ways in which the elements and principles of design may be utilized are infinite in number. The scene designer must be thoroughly aware of the possibilities open to him so that he may vary his means according to the qualities and specific effects he wishes to achieve. A mastery of these elements and principles is part of the education of a designer and is assumed when he begins work on a show.

WORKING PROCEDURES AND PLANS

Like other theatre workers, the designer must begin by attempting to understand the script. He should make as thorough an analysis of the play as does the director or actor, although he will not always be looking for the same things. He should begin by studying the play in terms of its action, characters, themes, language, and spectacle. Only after he understands the play as a whole should he proceed to an analysis of its scenic demands, for unless the designer has a thorough understanding of the play he has little chance of providing the best visual statement of its values.

The designer analyzes the script with several points in mind: the number of settings required; the kinds of settings (interior, exterior, living room, courtyard, prison, and so on); the size of settings needed for the action; the desirable physical arrangement of the settings (number and placement of doors and windows, the kind of furniture needed, the need for platforms and steps); indications of period, place, social and economic factors; indications of type and style (tragedy, melodrama, comedy; symbolism, expressionism, realism, and so on).

The designer may need to do research into the manners and customs, the principal decorative motifs, the common architectural forms, the typical furnishings and household equipment, the materials normally used in buildings, and the uses made of color in the period of the play's action. He may wish to find out all he can about the staging conventions at the time when the play was written. He may not use all of this information when he designs his sets, but study of this kind can stimulate the imagination as well as provide accurate knowledge when authenticity is desired. With a thorough knowledge of the script in mind, the designer is ready for his first conference about the play.

Before the designer actually begins to make sketches and plans, he should meet with the director and the other designers. These conferences may also include the producer, the playwright, the choreographer, conductor, and principal actors. The purpose of the initial conference is to clarify the interpretation being given the play and the kind of production toward which all workers should aim. Differences in interpretation of the script should be resolved, but when they cannot, the director's point of view should be adopted.

At the initial conference the scene designer should also find out any specific requirements which the director wishes to make. For example, must the entrances and exits be at particular places on the stage? How much floor space does the director envision using for each scene? Are there any pieces of business which will demand a specific property or which will require a given arrangement of the set or furniture? If he does not already know, the designer must also find out answers to such questions as the following: How much money has been set aside for the scenery? Upon what stage is the play to be performed? What is the physical layout of this stage and with what equipment is it provided?

His knowledge of the script, of the director's interpretation, and of the financial and physical arrangements provide the limitations within

A designer's sketch for Molière's *Tartuffe*. Design by Charles Watson.

which the designer must work. With these in mind he can proceed to make sketches of his ideas.

The designer's principal means of communication are visual and he must put his ideas into visual form before they may be assessed. In the early stages of his work the designer may make numerous sketches before he arrives at one which pleases him. These "idea" sketches may be

The floor plan for *Tartuffe*. Note that this plan encourages curved movement.

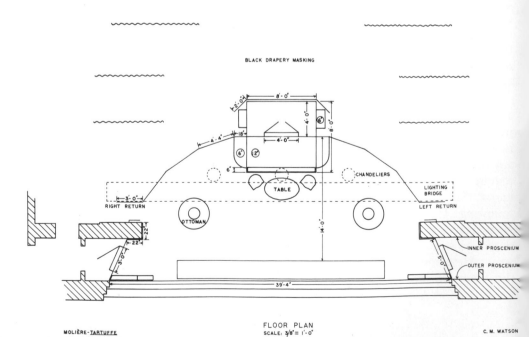

BLACK DRAPERY MASKING

CHANDELIERS

TABLE

LIGHTING BRIDGE

RIGHT RETURN

LEFT RETURN

OTTOMAN

INNER PROSCENIUM

OUTER PROSCENIUM

MOLIÈRE-TARTUFFE

FLOOR PLAN
SCALE: 3/8" = 1'-0"

C. M. WATSON

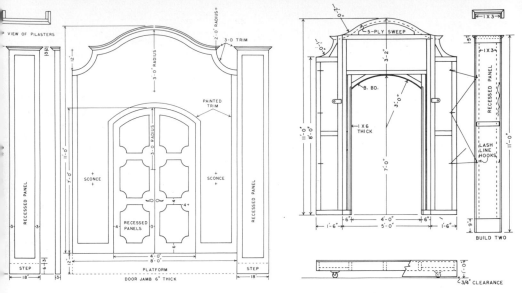

Left. Front elevation—center unit. *Right.* Working drawing, rear elevation—center unit for *Tartuffe.*

pencil or ink line drawings. After he has settled upon designs which he thinks right for the play, there are other conferences with the director and designers at which the ideas are discussed. Some sketches may need to be eliminated and new ones brought in. Before final approval can be given, however, the designs must be rendered in color and drawn in perspective to show how the finished settings will look on stage when lighted. Since sketches can be deceptive, the designer must also, as a rule, supply floor plans which show the layout of each setting, and in addition he may be asked to construct three-dimensional scale models which show in miniature each set as it will appear when completed. Revisions are made until agreement can be reached. No plans for scenery should be approved, however, without consideration of the lighting and costumes to be used, since the total stage picture is a combination of these elements.

After his visual conception of the scenery has been approved, the designer must make a series of working drawings. The number of these

A photograph of the finished setting for *Tartuffe.*

depends in part upon who is to execute them. If the designer must also build and paint the scenery, few drawings may be needed since he may carry all of the necessary information in his mind. If other persons must carry out the plans, however, numerous drawings may be needed. Working drawings are instructions which show what is to be done and the methods to be followed. The likelihood of errors is greatly diminished by complete plans.

In the professional theatre, scenery is built under contract by scenic studios and every detail of construction, assembling, and painting must be indicated. The designer's plans are used much as an architect's blueprints are. Any errors or omissions in the plans are chargeable to the designer. In the nonprofessional theatre, organizations may own a large amount of scenery which is used over and over. Under these circumstances, construction drawings are needed only for new pieces.

Although the number and type of drawings needed for a production vary from one organization to another, the following list indicates the typical kinds of drawings and plans which the designer may be asked to provide: (1) perspective color sketches showing the finished settings; (2) a floor plan for each setting; (3) a scale model of each setting; (4) rear elevations, which indicate the construction, materials, and methods to be used in assembling each unit of scenery (a rear elevation shows the unit from the back and in two dimensions only); (5) front elevations, which show each unit in two dimensions from the front with indications of any features (such as molding, baseboards, or platforms) which would be seen when looking at each unit straight on; (6) side elevations, which show units in profile and indicate the thickness and shape of each unit as viewed from the side; (7) detailed drawings, which show the methods by which such units as platforms, steps, trees, columns, and similar objects are to be built (some may be so complex that a separate drawing, possibly on a larger scale, is needed to clarify details of construction); (8) painter's elevations

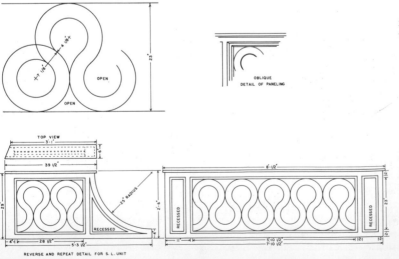

A detail drawing of the balustrade for *Tartuffe*.

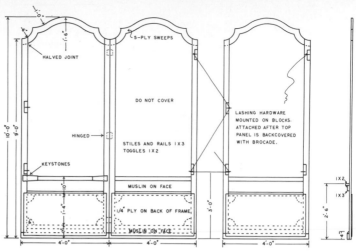

A working drawing for the screen units in *Tartuffe*.

HALVED JOINT

5-PLY SWEEPS

DO NOT COVER

LASHING HARDWARE
MOUNTED ON BLOCKS.
ATTACHED AFTER TOP
PANEL IS BACKCOVERED
WITH BROCADE.

HINGED

STILES AND RAILS 1 X 3
TOGGLES 1 X 2

KEYSTONES

MUSLIN ON FACE

1/4" PLY ON BACK OF FRAME

MUSLIN ON FACE

1 X 2

1 X 3

BUILD TWO SETS — REVERSE SECOND

of each unit, showing the color of the base coat and any overpainting which is to be used. With the exception of the perspective sketches, all of the plans are drawn to a specified scale so that the exact size of any object may be determined. In addition to the above list of drawings, the designer may also need to provide special plans showing how the scenery is to be shifted, where it is to be stored when not in use, or to indicate the solution to other problems. Ultimately the designer must be able to answer by means of sketches or drawings any question which arises about the size, shape, construction, assembly, painting, rigging, and operation of his settings.

The designer, therefore, must have a wide variety of abilities. He must be familiar with the elements and principles of design, he must have facility in sketching to show others his ideas, he must be able to make accurate scale drawings of every aspect of his settings, he must know what materials are to be used and be able to give the exact specifications for them, he must specify how everything is to be built, assembled, painted, and operated. The designer must be a man with artistic talent, but one with highly specialized practical knowledge as well.

After all of the plans are completed, the process of execution begins. While he may not be directly involved in carrying out the plans, the designer must eventually approve all work, for it is his responsibility to see that the finished settings conform to the approved plans.

BASIC SCENIC ELEMENTS

In carrying out his plans, the designer utilizes a number of basic scenic elements. These may be divided into standing units (those that rest on the floor or on other parts of the set) and hanging units (those suspended from above).

STANDING UNITS. The basic standing unit is the flat; that is, a frame, made of white pine or similar wood, over which canvas or muslin

Left. A plain flat. *Right.* A door flat and a window flat.

DOOR FLAT   WINDOW FLAT

has been stretched. Flats of almost any width or height may be made, but if they are too large they become unstable. Therefore, the typical height of flats ranges from eight to sixteen feet, and the normal widths range from one to six feet. In the professional theatre, the widest flats have been standardized at 5 feet 9 inches, since this is the maximum size which can be fitted into a railroad car (most shows do some touring even if it is only for the out-of-town tryouts).

The most common piece of scenery is the plain flat—a rectangle without any opening. Other types of flats include: the door flat (one with an opening into which a door frame may be set); the window flat (with an opening into which a window frame may be set); a fireplace flat (against which or into which a mantelpiece and fireplace frame may be set); and arch flats (variations on the door flat, with openings shaped to simulate Roman, Gothic, or other kinds of arches).

There are many variations on these basic types of flats. For example, for a setting which calls for double doors, it is possible to construct two flats with one half of the desired opening in each of the two. These two flats may then be hinged together to complete the full-sized opening. Similar procedures may be used for extra-wide windows or arches. Flats may also be constructed with slanting sides, with edges shaped to follow the contours of trees, foliage, rocks, ruined walls, decaying arches, and so on.

Flats are used in almost all settings, but they are of special importance for interior settings. A living-room set, for example, is normally assembled by hinging together a number of flats. Since flats are made in various widths, walls of any length may be constructed and the door and window openings may be placed exactly where needed by selecting flats of the right type and size.

Other standing units, in addition to flats, are: door frames, with doors; window frames, with windows; fireplace units; platforms; steps and staircases; rocks; built-up ground; tree trunks; and columns. While there are accepted methods for constructing each of these units, the procedures vary according to the intended appearance and use. For example, windows may be hinged to open outward or inward, they may slide up and down, or they may not need to be opened at all in a play. Doors may vary in appearance from the intricately-paneled to the rough-hewn; they may scarcely need to be closed throughout the play or they may need to be slammed, or forced open. Rocks may be used merely as a place behind which characters may hide, or a large number of actors may stand on them. Size, shape, and practicability, then, determine in part how each of these items is to be constructed. It is not within the scope of this book to indicate how scenic units are built; the process is described in detail in a number of good books on stage scenery.

Another typical standing unit is the ground row. It is used, as a rule, to show in profile such objects as walls, rocks, mounds of earth, distant hills and mountains, rows of buildings, and shrubbery. Ground rows are in actuality flats which have been placed on their sides, with the tops and ends shaped appropriately according to the object being represented; the details are painted on this flat surface. Ground rows may be placed anywhere on the stage, but most often they are set up near the back of the setting, since they generally are used to represent distant objects. They break up the line of the stage floor, create the effect of depth and distance, mask the bottom of the cyclorama, and hide lighting instruments and the bottom of drops.

HANGING UNITS. Hanging units include ceilings, drops, curtains, borders, and cycloramas. Ceilings are usually constructed in two parts approximately equal in size. Each of these parts is a rectangle with the length approximately equal to the width of the proscenium opening (that is, enough to cover the widest set which will be used on the stage), and its width equal to one half the depth of the deepest set to be used on the stage. These two rectangles are then covered with canvas, in the same manner as a flat, and hinged together on the face. The hinges are then covered with a muslin strip and the whole surface painted the desired color. The ceiling is suspended above the setting and let down on top of the flats which compose a room. The hinges allow the ceiling to be folded and drawn up out of sight when not in use. Ceilings may be made in other ways as well, but the one described here is the most typical.

Ceilings are used in interior settings to limit the overhead view of the audience and to create the illusion of a real room. Other devices may be used with interior settings, however, and must be used in exteriors, where a ceiling would be out of place. The most common substitution for the ceiling is the border—a short curtain or piece of painted canvas. Borders are hung parallel to the front of the stage and in a series from the front to the back of the stage. They may be made of black cloth, or they may be painted and shaped to represent foliage, the beams of a ceiling, or other objects.

A setting for Sir James M. Barrie's *The Admirable Crichton* using a cut drop through which the sky cyclorama is seen.

For almost three hundred years drops were a basic part of all stage settings, and still appear regularly in exteriors. Drops are made by sewing together enough lengths of muslin or canvas to create an area of the desired size. This piece of cloth is then attached at the top and bottom to wooden battens which support the cloth and keep it free of wrinkles. This cloth surface can be painted to represent any desired scene.

Draperies and curtains of various sorts are standard parts of scenery. Draperies may be hung parallel to the proscenium on either side of the stage from front to back in a series so as to mask the sides of the stage much as flat wings are employed. They are also used at times to divide the stage into two parts, and also may be an integral part of the scenic background.

The scrim is a special kind of curtain. It is made of net or theatrical gauze and appears to be opaque when lighted only from the front, but becomes transparent when light is turned on behind it. It is used for sudden appearances and disappearances, for showing first the outside and then the inside of a building or other object, for creating effects of fog or mist, and for a number of other purposes. In recent years Broadway musicals have made great use of scrims on which plastic has been sprayed. The plastic-covered areas can be painted to represent any object, and parts of the scrim may be cut away. In this way, settings of great delicacy and apparent depth can be achieved with materials of very light weight.

One of the most useful of hanging units is the cyclorama. Technically, a cyclorama is any arrangement of curtains or other materials which surround the stage area on three sides. For example, it may be composed of draperies, or a plaster dome. Most typically, however, the cyclorama is a continuous, tightly-stretched curtain suspended on U-shaped battens which curve around the back and sides of the stage. It is usually neutral or a grayish blue so that its apparent color may be changed through lighting. It is employed to represent the sky, to give the effect of infinite space, and to allow the maximum amount of the stage space to be used without the necessity of scenic units to mask the audience's view of the offstage areas.

In addition to the standard scenic units, many scripts demand highly specialized pieces. For example, many children's plays call for such objects as giant toadstools on which a character may perch. How such an article is to be constructed depends upon its use, but standard construction practices may be adapted to meet these special demands. As a rule, however, the basic scenic units assembled in varying combinations will meet the needs of most plays.

ASSEMBLING SCENERY

The designer must decide not only what scenic units he will need for carrying out his design, but also how these units are to be put together. The assembly will depend in large part upon how the scenery is to be transported from the scene shop to the theatre, and whether or not it needs to be shifted. Sometimes scenery must be transported from one town to another by truck or train and, therefore, needs to be assembled in units small enough to permit easy transportation. If the scenery is to be shifted manually, it may need to be put together in smaller units than if it is to be moved by other methods.

The typical methods of assembling scenery are hinging, permanent joining, and lashing. Hinges are used most often to join flats. Almost every interior wall is composed by joining two or more flats to create a continuous surface of the desired length. In this case, the flats are hinged together on the face, after which the hinges and the cracks between flats are covered with a strip of muslin (called a "dutchman"). This wall is then ready for painting. Wooden battens may be attached to the rear surface of the assembled units to make them rigid and to prevent folding. The battens or stiffeners may be attached permanently, or they may be removable so that each wall may be folded for easy storage when not in use. The hinging just described is permanent, since the units remain joined throughout the production. Other units may be held together temporarily by hinges during the time when the sets are in use and then taken apart for shifting and storage. Temporary hinging requires loose-pin hinges (those using a removable pin to hold the two halves of the hinge together); when the pins are lifted out of the hinges the two pieces of scenery may be separated. Temporary hinging is often used where two units meet at ninety-degree angles, or for joining platforms and steps together or to other units.

Permanent joining is done with screws, bolts, and nails. This kind of assembly is used for heavy units which do not need to be shifted, or for those that are shifted by means which do not require that the units be taken apart. Such joining gives more stability to a setting and is used whenever the situation will allow.

Lashing is a method of joining scenic units (especially the walls of an interior setting) by the use of lines or ropes. A line is permanently attached to the top, outer edge of one unit; this line is drawn around cleats which are attached at intervals to the outer frames of the units being joined; the line is pulled tight and tied near the bottom of the units. Lashing and unlashing may be done quickly and this process allows the rapid assembly and dismantling of settings on stage.

Technicians, or the employees of scenic studios, assemble the basic units of each setting in the scene shop. The scenery is then ready for painting.

PAINTING SCENERY

Scene shops normally stock dry pigment in a wide range of colors, from which any hue, saturation, and value may be mixed. When the desired color has been achieved, the dry pigment is combined with a binder— that is, a liquid solution which allows the paint to be applied to the scenery and which "binds" the pigment to the surface after it is dry. The most common binder is a glue and water solution, but others may also be used under special circumstances.

For a number of reasons, a mixture of dry pigment and glue "size" has become the standard medium for painting scenery. It is relatively economical in cost; has a low gloss when dry; the colors are easily duplicated if touching up or repainting is needed; and it may be easily removed with warm water, which loosens the glue.

After sizing, a prime coat, which is normally near in color to the final coat, is applied. This is usually mixed from cheap pigments so as to keep down the cost. A prime coat is not always used but it is desirable since it insures a reasonably uniform surface over which the base coat may be applied.

The base coat is added after the prime coat is thoroughly dry. The result is a uniform color of smooth texture. The final step is usually to modify the base coat through overpainting designed to give the appearance of other textures (such as those of plaster, brick or wood), or to alter the "flat" appearance of the surface. Overpainting may also be used for other purposes: to shade the upper portions of settings so as to decrease their prominence; to emphasize the shape and form of objects by giving emphasis to corners or curves; to counterfeit three-dimensional details, such as molding, paneling, the bark of trees, and mortar.

Painting may be done with a variety of techniques. The prime and base coats are normally done with a technique called flat painting, since the purpose is to give an even surface. It is usually done with a large brush or with a spray gun. Overpainting as a rule requires more specialized techniques than flat painting, since it aims to add texture, shading, or details over the base coat to achieve special effects. The colors used in over-painting, therefore, must contrast with the base coat; the degree of contrast depends on the purpose. For example, the texture of relatively smooth plaster may be achieved by "spattering" (that is, by flicking small drops of paint from a brush onto the base coat) with one color which is slightly lighter and a second which is slightly darker in value than the base coat itself. This creates the effect of raised and receding surfaces.

On the other hand, rough plaster may be simulated through the painting technique called "rolling." This involves the use of a rolled-up piece of ragged burlap or other rough-textured cloth. This cloth is dipped into paint, partially wrung out, and then rolled over the surface of the base coat in irregular patterns. This may be repeated with a variety of shades of paint.

Other common painting techniques include "sponging" and "scumbling." In sponging a natural sponge is dipped into the paint and patted onto the surface of the base coat. It may be used to achieve a variety of patterns and effects. Scumbling involves the simultaneous application and blending of more than one shade of paint on the same surface. This gives a mottled effect and may be used for foliage, or to simulate walls on which the paint is fading, mildewing, or crumbling.

The appropriate painting technique must be specified by the designer on his painter's elevations. The designer, as a rule, must be able to do the painting himself or to supervise the work of others. In all cases, he must approve the finished job.

THE ASSEMBLY AND SHIFTING OF SCENERY ON STAGE

After the scenery has been painted, it is transported to the stage upon which it will be used. In the nonprofessional theatre and in most summer stock organizations, this may merely involve moving the scenery from one part of the building to another. In the professional theatre, however, transportation by truck or train is usually involved. The typical New York production has an out-of-town tryout period and this requires that the scenery be moved from one city to another and that it be used on a number of stages before it is assembled on the stage for which it was intended.

How it is to be assembled on stage depends upon the method of shifting to be employed. A one-set show can be set up permanently, whereas a multiple-set production may require much planning so that the individual units can be assembled and disassembled quickly and quietly, moved easily, and stored economically.

There are many methods of shifting scenery, of which the most common are: by hand, by flying, and on wagons, jackknife stages, elevators, or revolving stages.

The simplest procedure (in the sense that no mechanical devices are needed) is to change all of the scenic elements manually. In this case, each part of a set is moved by one or more stage hands to some prearranged storage space offstage, and the elements of a new setting are brought on stage and assembled. Parts of almost every setting must be moved manually, even when the major shifting is accomplished by complex mechanical devices. Since manual shifting can be used on any stage, however simple or complex, a designer can always rely on it, though a large crew may be required to carry it through efficiently. Its drawbacks are its relative slowness and the necessity for breaking the setting into units which are small and light in weight.

The second most common method of shifting scenery is flying. In this case, the elements are suspended on battens or lines over the stage and are raised and lowered as needed. With an adequate gridiron and strong enough lines, entire settings can be flown. It is extremely unusual to do so, however, and flying is normally reserved for such elements as drops, curtains, ceilings, borders, cycloramas, and small units composed of flats.

A number of problems arise in connection with flying: (1) scenic pieces can only be flown parallel to the front of the stage, as a rule, since the battens to which they are attached are permanently installed in that manner; (2) extremely heavy units may offer too much danger of falling unless the flying apparatus is in excellent condition; (3) the stage space above the top of the proscenium opening must be at least one and a half times as great as the height of the proscenium arch if full-sized scenery is to be flown completely out of sight (for example, if the proscenium arch is twenty feet high, there should be an additional space of thirty feet above that).

Most stages provide some means for suspending short curtains and lighting equipment overhead. This space may be inadequate for shifting of scenery, however. When the overhead space is not sufficient to allow drops to be flown out of sight, "tripping" is sometimes used. This means that the top and bottom of a drop are attached to adjacent sets of lines. When both sets are raised, the drop is folded in the middle and drawn up. In this way only half as much overhead space is required. Drops may also be rolled up if there is not sufficient flying space overhead, but such a method is time consuming and is apt to damage the painting on the drop.

For proper flying, a gridiron (that is, a network of steel girders) is installed at the top of the stage house to serve as the basic weight-supporting structure. The lines for flying scenery are normally attached to steel pipes or battens which extend across the width of the stage (three or four lines are needed to support each batten). The scenic elements to

A scene from Paul Green's *The House of Connelly* mounted on a wagon stage. Note the use of foliage and other real objects. It is difficult to shift such a setting except on a movable platform. Setting by Lewis McFarland.

be flown are attached to these battens. For maximum efficiency, battens should be hung at regular intervals from the front to the back of the stage, so that scenery may be flown at any desired spot.

The lines (usually steel cables) which support the battens run up to the top of the stage house where they pass over pulleys resting on the gridiron; after passing over these pulleys they continue to one side of the stage house where they pass over another set of pulleys; they then turn downward toward the stage floor and are attached to the top of a cradle or frame; into this cradle, weights in sufficient amount to counterbalance the scenery are placed. To the bottom of the cradle are attached ropes which continue downward to the fly rail, where stage hands can raise and lower the battens on which scenery is being flown. The ropes may be tied off securely when not being used. This method of flying scenery is called a counterweight system, since it allows the even balancing of offstage and onstage weight. With a good counterweight system, a single stage hand can easily raise and lower scenic elements of almost any size.

A somewhat out-of-date variation on the counterweight system is a "rope and sandbag" arrangement. Here the lines are hemp ropes and the weights are bags filled with sand. This is a more cumbersome method, however, and most modern theatres have abandoned it. Its purpose and basic principle of operation, however, is the same as the counterweight system.

Some recent experiments with flying systems have utilized electronically controlled winches without counterweights, and a more flexible arrangement of the lines which allows scenery to be flown at angles rather than always parallel to the front of the stage. This method, however, is still in the experimental phase.

A continuous setting for Paul Claudel's *The Tidings Brought to Mary* mounted on a wagon stage; a different portion of it is used for each change of scene. Note that the stage is surrounded by a sky cyclorama. Low flats in the background mask the instruments used to light the cyclorama. *Opposite page.* One portion in use. Setting by Arnold Gillette.

Rolling platforms, or wagons, are another common device for shifting scenery. Platforms of almost any size may be placed on casters and rolled on and off stage. The larger the platform the more scenery may be placed on it and the less dependence need be put on manual shifting. On the other hand, wagons require a considerable amount of offstage space in which they may be maneuvered and stored. Many stages do not afford enough wing space to allow the use of this shifting device. The top surface of a wagon is normally raised off the stage floor from six to twelve inches—about one step—so that the platform does not become too noticeable and so that the actors may step on and off of it easily.

Most commonly, wagons are freely maneuverable and may be moved to any spot on the stage. This is not always the case, however, for some stages have tracks permanently installed (or temporarily laid for a particular production) in which the casters of the wagons move. This guides the platforms on and off stage with precision, but does not allow for flexibility in the positioning of the wagons at other places on the stage. Tracks of this kind may be used most efficiently for very large wagons on which entire settings are mounted. Such platforms are very heavy and, consequently, are difficult to maneuver; tracks guide them to the desired position onstage with the minimum effort.

The jackknife stage is another variation on the wagon. It normally requires a platform which is approximately as wide as the proscenium opening. When the wagon is in position onstage (that is, set up facing the auditorium as for a performance), it is attached to the stage floor at a single point—one of the downstage corners—to provide a pivot. It may then be rotated on and off stage much as a jackknife blade is opened and closed. Normally two jackknife stages are employed in conjunction—one attached to each side of the stage—and are especially useful in productions where two complex settings alternate. This arrangement, however, requires a considerable amount of wing space on each side of the stage.

It is also possible to mount the supporting braces of walls and heavy pieces of scenery on casters and to roll them on and off stage. These devices—which include the tip jack, the lift jack, and the outrigger—are not platforms but rather are devices by which a scenic unit can be lifted off the floor sufficiently (an inch or so) by means of braces and casters to allow the units to be rolled about. Any good book on stagecraft will show the methods of constructing and operating these rather complicated devices. The basic principle, however, is much the same as that of a wagon, but without the platform surface afforded by a wagon stage.

The revolving stage and the elevator stage are among the less common methods for shifting scenery. Each is costly and complex.

A revolving stage may be either a permanent or a temporary part of the theatre. In the case of the permanent revolving stage, a large circle of the stage floor (normally larger in diameter than the width of the proscenium opening) is mounted on a central supporting pivot, so that the entire circle may be rotated. Since the weight of this "revolve" is considerable, it is normally rotated by means of an electric motor. A temporary revolving stage may be constructed by mounting a low circular plat-

form on casters and attaching it at the center to the stage floor. One or more small revolving units may also be used at almost any place on the stage.

The revolving stage allows a number of settings to be erected on the stage simultaneously; the individual sets are placed so that each faces outward toward the circumference of the circle. To shift scenery, the stage is revolved until the desired setting faces the audience. It is also possible to change the settings on the backstage part while another setting is being used onstage.

The elevator stage is the least common method of shifting scenery in America. In this arrangement, sections of the stage floor may be raised and lowered like an elevator. In some theatres, portions of the stage may be lowered to the basement and scenery may be mounted on them and then raised to the stage level. Each segment may also be moved in tracks up- and downstage. In other words, as that part of the floor at the front is lowered, the upstage part may move forward with another setting and a third portion may rise from the basement to occupy the position just vacated by the upstage part. In this manner, scenery may be changed in the basement.

In some theatres each segment of the stage floor is mounted on lifts which allow that section to be raised, lowered, or tilted. This permits the creation of platforms and levels without the necessity of building and shifting them in the usual ways. Also a number of recent theatres have placed the floor of the orchestra pit on lifts. Since this floor can be set at

Steps and platforms used to create numerous playing areas. A scene from Webster's *The Duchess of Malfi*. Directed by Lael Woodbury.

A stage floor each segment of which is on an elevator. The segments also may be joined to form revolving stages. The stage of the Red Army Theatre in Moscow. From G. B. Barkhin's *Arketectura Teatre*. Moscow, 1947.

any level, it may be raised to form a forestage, it may be used for extra audience seating, or it may be used for its more normal function as a pit for the musicians. Such an arrangement allows for much greater flexibility in the use of an area that is often wasted in theatres.

All of these shifting devices may be combined in various ways, and seldom is one means used alone. The designer must know what methods are available to him and he must decide how each unit is to be moved. His scenery must be designed, constructed, and assembled with these requirements in mind.

SET DECORATION, PROPERTIES, AND FURNITURE

When the scenery is assembled on stage, the set decoration, properties, and furniture are added. These are all a part of the basic design of each set, but, with the exception of certain props, they are not normally built in the scene shop. They are not structural parts of the settings.

Into the category of set decoration and properties come such items as banners, pictures, draperies, books, vases, and lamps—all items which complete a setting. Properties are frequently subdivided into "set props" and "hand props." A set prop is one that is attached to the setting or which functions as a part of the design. A hand prop is present principally as part of the actor's business. Sometimes a set prop is used in business, but it may be classed as a set prop if it is a part of the setting and remains on stage.

The designer is always responsible for the selection of set properties. He may also choose the hand props, but more frequently hand props are considered to be the director's responsibility since they are so intimately connected with the acting. In the nonprofessional theatre, the responsibility for obtaining properties of both types may be assigned to a property crew.

The set decorations, properties, and furniture may be obtained in a variety of ways. Since they must be appropriate to the setting, the style and the period of the play, and may need to meet other demands, it is not always possible to find the desired shape, size, or general appearance. In such cases, the properties or furniture may have to be made. On the other hand, appropriate pieces may be bought, rented, or borrowed for most productions.

In the professional theatre, the designer must plan for a long run and, therefore, it is usually necessary to purchase all items to be used in the show. In the nonprofessional theatre, or in the case of short-run shows, it may be possible to rent items or to borrow them.

Regardless of how properties and furniture are obtained, however, the settings cannot be considered complete until these decorative and practical features are present. They are an important part of the over-all visual design.

TECHNICAL REHEARSALS, DRESS REHEARSALS, AND PERFORMANCES

Many theatres regularly schedule technical rehearsals for the purpose of checking the operation and problems of the scenery, costumes, lighting, and sound. Other theatres make this a part of dress rehearsals. Regardless of when it is done, however, provision must be allowed for determining whether the settings function as planned and to familiarize all those concerned with the procedures to be used in running the show.

It is extremely difficult to make major changes in settings after dress rehearsals begin. A costume may be altered with relative ease, lights may be adjusted, and even the movement of actors may be changed, but alterations in the size and basic appearance of a setting are difficult to make because of the rigidity of scenic units and of stage space. Neverthe-less, at times entire settings are abandoned and new ones are constructed and painted at the last moment if it is deemed necessary. In the profes-sional theatre, the designer receives extra pay for making any changes in the settings which are not due to his own mistakes.

The designer must be available for consultation and changes until the play opens. If the play has a long run he may be consulted occasionally about the replacement of elements which are becoming shabby. He may also be asked to redesign the show for touring companies. Generally speaking, however, responsibility for the scenery passes to the stage crew and the stage manager after the opening night.

THE DESIGNER'S EMPLOYMENT

The scene designer in the professional theatre is placed under contract by the producer of the play. To be so employed, the designer must be a mem-ber of the United Scenic Artists Union. It is more difficult to get into this organization than into any of the other theatrical unions. The applicant for membership must pay an examination fee and if accepted must pay an initiation fee of $500. His rather severe examination involves the ability to make sketches, working drawings, costume and lighting designs. While the requirements may be rigorous, they serve to insure the capability of union members.

Many beginning professional designers work as assistants to well-established designers and gain experience in this way. Some Off-Broadway theatres, many semiprofessional organizations, and a number of summer stock companies employ nonunion designers, and such experience is fre-quently important in the preparations of those who aspire to become union members.

In the community theatre, a designer-technician is often responsi-ble for all areas of design and for the execution of the designs. It is not unusual, however, in such organizations to find the director, as the only salaried worker, in charge of design. In such cases, he normally attempts to secure the services, free of cost or for a nominal fee, of a competent person in the community.

In the educational theatre, situations vary from those in which one person is responsible for all aspects of the theatre program to those in which there are separate and specialized designers in each of the areas of scenery, lighting, and costumes. Some educational theatres employ more than one person in each of these areas, and, consequently, a staff member, often called the Artistic Director, may be appointed to supervise the work of this large staff and to insure continuity and a reasonably uniform work-ing policy from one production to the next.

The working conditions of the designer, thus, vary considerably from one type of organization to another and even within the same kind of organization. His basic responsibilities as a scene designer, nevertheless, remain relatively constant.

THE DESIGNER'S ASSISTANTS AND CO-WORKERS

In carrying out his duties, the designer is aided by a number of persons: the assistant designer, the technical director, the master carpenter (or the heads of the scenery, property, and rigging crews), the stagehands, and the property crew.

In the professional theatre, well-established designers usually employ one or more assistants. These assistants are for the most part younger members of the United Scenic Artists Union. They may be asked to do almost anything: make working drawings, search for furniture and properties, act as liaison between the designer and the scenic studios—anything the designer may request. Designers outside the professional theatre may at times have an assistant, but such a position is not typical outside of New York.

In the nonprofessional theatre, the technical director may perform many of the functions of the designer's assistant. In many theatres, however, the technical director's job is considered to be quite independent of the designer and of an equal status. Nevertheless, the technical director, as a rule, merely assumes part of the duties which are performed by the designer in the professional theatre. Usually, he is responsible for constructing, assembling, rigging, and shifting the scenery—in other words, he carries out the designer's plans. In many organizations he is also in charge of lighting. The technical director's position has been created in many educational theatres because the tasks performed by the professional scenic studios in New York must be done in the theatre itself. When a theatre produces a large number of shows each year the designer's job may become too great for one person. In this case, it may be divided into its artistic and its practical aspects. A designer then assumes responsibility for the conception and the technical director for the execution of the designs. The technical director may also be asked to purchase all materials and to administer the backstage operation of the theatre.

The scenery is built, assembled, and painted in a scene shop (or some work space which fills that function). In the professional theatre, all persons involved must be union members, and the painters must have passed an examination given by the United Scenic Artists Union. In other types of organizations, the workers may be paid but are not always union members. Much of this work is done by apprentices in summer stock companies, while in community and educational theatres assigned or volunteer helpers work under the supervision of the designer or technical director.

When the scenery is delivered to the stage for rigging and shifting, scenery and property crews are brought in. In the professional theatre, all such persons must be members of the International Alliance of Theatrical Stage Employees and no one else is allowed to handle these items. A master carpenter travels with the show if it is on tour, and makes sure that the scenery is kept in good condition. In the nonprofessional theatre, scenery and props are usually handled by volunteers or assigned crews. Some organizations pay the persons in charge of the scene and property crews a small fee. In all types of theatre organizations, the head of the stage crews must operate under the supervision of the stage manager. Regardless of how these crews are secured or paid, however, their duties include the efficient movement and accurate placement of the scenery and properties during performances and the upkeep of materials throughout the run of the show.

The designer's helpers frequently go unnoticed by the public since little is done to draw attention to them. They are, nevertheless, important members of every theatrical organization since they make possible the efficient execution of the designer's plans.

Shakespeare's *Twelfth Night*. The setting, on a revolving stage, suggests a Renaissance city. This scene shows Maria, Sir Toby, and Feste teasing Malvolio who is imprisoned. Directed by George Kernodle; setting by Jerry Emery; costumes by Janice Wroth.

THE DESIGNER AND THEATRE ARCHITECTURE

One of the most important influences on the designer's work is the theatre building itself. The size of the auditorium, the relationship of the audience to the acting area, and the equipment of the stage determine to a large degree what scenic elements can be used and the treatment they must be given.

Every theatre has three basic parts: that intended to meet the needs of the audience; the stage; and the work areas. That designed for the use of the audience includes such facilities as the box office, lobby, coat-check rooms, rest rooms, corridors, entrances and exits, and refreshment facilities. Not all of these are incorporated into every building, but the most complete theatres normally are designed to provide the maximum comfort for the audience.

From the standpoint of theatrical production, however, the auditorium is the most important of the audience facilities. It should be designed so as to insure the optimum conditions for seeing and hearing. Unfortunately for audience members, these demands frequently are subordinated to others, the most common of which are: that a certain number of removable seats be included because the theatre must also be used as an assembly hall, a gymnasium or for some other function; that the seating capacity be as great as possible so as to bring in the maximum box-office receipts; that the auditorium be fitted into an already existing structure or into a space of a specified shape.

Auditoriums, therefore, vary widely in their basic characteristics. They may be large or small; all seats may be on the same level (although normally the floor is raked to allow for better sightlines), or there may be a series of balconies; the audience may view the acting area from one side, or it may be seated on two, three, or four sides; the distance of audience members from the acting area may vary from one or two feet to hundreds of feet; sightlines may be such that all members of the audience may see practically all of the acting area, or they may prevent some members of the audience from seeing large portions of the stage. The relationship of the audience to the acting area is of primary importance to the designer, since it determines in part the amount and type of scenery he can use, and where it may be placed.

Today there are in wide use three basic types of stages: the proscenium stage, the open (or platform) stage, and the arena (or theatre-in-the-round) stage. Each of these makes for a different audience–actor relationship, each has different facilities, and each demands a different approach to production.

The proscenium stage is designed to be viewed from the front only. Since the scenery and the action are oriented in only one direction, the

TYPES OF THEATRES

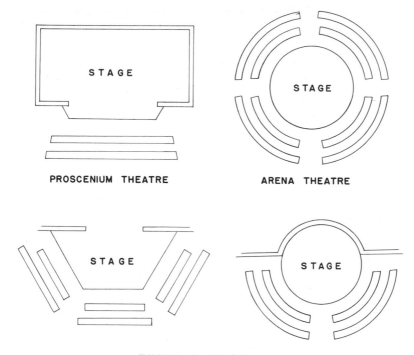

PROSCENIUM THEATRE

ARENA THEATRE

TYPES OF OPEN STAGES

designer may utilize three sides of the stage for the scenery, and entrances and exits may be placed at any point. The scenery may be as tall as the designer wishes and he may use few or many units. There is only one basic restriction: the view of the audience must not be blocked from the front.

The proscenium stage is equipped with a curtain which may be used to conceal or reveal the stage and the scenery as desired. The curtain may be closed to permit the shifting of scenery, and the stage ordinarily has a counterweight system, wing space, and other features which allow for a wide variety of shifting methods. There may also be trap doors in the floor for special effects or for entrances and exits from beneath the stage.

Usually the action and scenery are removed a greater distance from the audience in the proscenium theatre than in other forms of staging. There may be an orchestra pit or forestage between the first row of seats and the point at which the scenery begins. Therefore, the scenery is not seen at close range, as a rule, and may require a different treatment than were it intended for viewing from a distance of a few feet. The work of the designer in the proscenium theatre is a cross between that of the architect and the painter: while the scenery is created in three dimensions, it is viewed from only one direction.

With an open stage, the seats are usually arranged around three sides of a raised platform which juts into the auditorium. A good example may be seen on page 125. Less frequently, an open stage is viewed from only one side, but in this case it is essentially the traditional stage without its proscenium arch.

Most open stages permit only a restricted use of scenery, usually small units, and sometimes a shallow cyclorama. Some have a permanent architectural façade at the back, as in an Elizabethan theatre, which can be altered slightly to meet the demands of a particular script.

The open stage has no proscenium arch, and there may or may not be a curtain. If there is one, it is usually mounted in the ceiling on a recessed track, which is shaped to follow the contours of the stage. The ceiling of the stage is normally continuous with that of the auditorium, and there is no provision above the stage for flying scenery, drops, or curtains (with the possible exceptions already noted of a front curtain and a backcloth of some kind). Lighting instruments are accommodated in recesses in the ceiling.

The acting areas and the auditorium of the open-stage theatre are more unified than in the proscenium theatre, for the basic purposes of the open stage are to bring the audience and the actors into a more intimate relationship and to do away with the trappings of realism. Consequently, there are fewer provisions for the use of traditional scenery, and the size of the auditorium is usually smaller. Since three sides of the stage are usually surrounded by seats, however, even if the auditorium is large the audience members can be brought closer to the actors than they would be in a proscenium theatre with the same seating capacity.

Since the open stage is seen from three sides, it is in most respects a more three-dimensional medium than is the proscenium stage. The action, the scenery, and all the elements of theatrical production must be designed to project in three directions simultaneously. On the other hand, the designer cannot use large units of scenery except along the back, or on the sides near the back. Any scenery used at other points must be low enough not to interfere with the audience's view of the stage. Furthermore, as a rule, all scenery must be shifted manually. Occasionally a revolving stage may be installed, and there may be a number of trap doors, but scenery must be kept relatively simple and small in amount. The designer, therefore, must compensate for the restrictions upon his means by greater ingenuity.

In the typical theatre-in-the-round, there is no stage as such (that is, there is no raised platform). Rather, an open space is left at floor level in the middle of the auditorium. The seats for the audience are set up in a bleacherlike arrangement around all four sides of the acting area. Since in theatres of this type the acting area and the seats are not permanently installed, as a rule, the arrangement may be varied at will. The seats may be placed around three sides (thereby creating a variation on the open stage), or they may be placed on two sides. In the latter case, the seats may be set up so that the two halves of the audience face each other across the acting area, or they may be arranged in the shape of an L with the acting area located in one corner of the auditorium. Many arena theatres with fixed stages and permanent seating arrangements have been built, however. In some cases, raised stages have also been installed. The theatre-in-the-round typically has a small seating capacity, ranging from fifty to three hundred. It thus provides intimacy between the actors and the audience.

An arena theatre obviously restricts the scene designer considerably in the amount and kind of scenery he may utilize. In the true theatre-in-the-round (that is, one in which the audience is seated on all four sides), all scenery must be kept low enough to allow the entire acting area to be seen from every angle. The designer, therefore, must make his points principally with furniture and properties, or with flats not higher than two or three feet placed around the outer edge of the acting area. Since there is no curtain, all changes must be made either in darkness or in full view of the audience. All shifting, as a rule, must be done manually and units must be moved through the aisles of the theatre. While lighting instruments are suspended overhead, no provision is usually made for hanging scenic elements.

The designer, therefore, may suggest a locale, period, mood, and style, but he must do so with only a few set-pieces or properties. This enforced economy in materials, however, makes it necessary that the designer choose each element with great care, since each must suggest all that cannot be shown. Furthermore, because of the closeness of the audience to the acting area, the units must be executed with attention to each detail. Above all, the scenery, like the actors, must be expressive when viewed from any angle.

Each of the basic kinds of actor–audience relationships—proscenium, open stage, arena stage—determines in large part the amount, size, and type of scenery which can be used. While the basic purposes of theatrical production remain unchanged in each, the particular means to be employed must be varied with the conditions imposed by theatre architecture.

The amount of work space provided in a theatre also varies widely. A well-designed, self-contained theatre (that is, one which provides space for preparing all of the elements of production as well as for performing plays) will include the following: a scenery construction shop (with space to store the necessary equipment and materials), painting facilities, an area for the assembly of scenery, sufficient offstage space for the storage and shifting of scenery during performances, and provisions for the permanent storage of scenery when not in use; a property room near the stage, and another area for the permanent storage of furniture and bulky props; a costume-production shop; laundry, dyeing, cleaning and pressing facilities, and an area for the permanent storage of costumes; a work space for lighting personnel, a storage area for lighting equipment, a large room designed to house the remote-control lighting board, and a lighting booth for the control-board operator during performances (ideally with a full view of the stage); a number of large rehearsal rooms; a number of dressing rooms, each with make-up facilities (unless a separate make-up room is provided); adequate showers and rest rooms for the actors and crews, and an area where all of the actors and crew members can assemble to receive instructions or to relax (usually called the "green room"); space to house sound equipment and from which to operate it; adequate office space for the carrying on of the business of theatrical production.

Not all theatres, of course, are ideally equipped, but all must make some provision for each aspect of production. Unfortunately, theatre workers often perform their duties in nooks and crannies within the theatre plant or in improvised quarters in other buildings totally unsuited to their needs. One of the remarkable things about the theatre, however, is the ability of its practitioners to "make do" with whatever facilities are at hand, and the amazing results which sometime come from the necessity of rising above difficulties.

Chapter 19

THE COSTUMER

While the scene designer creates the proper stage environment in which the actors may perform, the costumer is concerned with the visual appearance of the actors themselves. At times, the same person serves as both scene and costume designer, but costumes and scenery can be separated profitably for greater clarification of each.

The costumer and the scene designer seek to fulfill many of the same purposes and they utilize the same elements and principles of design. In the concrete application of the purposes, elements, and principles of design, however, they work with entirely different materials and they create completely different products.

THE PURPOSES OF COSTUME DESIGN

The ultimate purposes of costume design are the same as those of scene design: to aid understanding, and to express or interpret the play. Each of these purposes may be achieved in a number of ways.

Costumes may aid understanding by identifying the period in which the action occurs—ancient Greece, Elizabethan England, or present-day America. In a particular script the exact period may be unimportant or unspecified, in which case the costumer (with the approval of the

Two costumes designed by Lodovico Burnacini in the late seventeenth century. From Alexander von Weilen's *Geschichte des Wiener Theaterwesens*. Vienna, 1889.

director) usually selects that period which seems best for the themes, characters, and action.

Costumes may also establish the locale. For example, they help to distinguish a farm from a city, one part of the country from another (southern California from New England), and may be indicative of a particular nation.

Costumes may identify the time of day and clarify the occasion: an informal morning at home with the family, a party, or a formal dance.

Costumes may establish the social and economic status of the characters by distinguishing between the lower and upper classes, between the rich and the poor, or between the decaying and the affluent members of the same class. Costume often identifies an occupation: the maid, the nurse, the milkman, the office worker, the soldier, and so on.

Costumes may establish the age of the characters, since some garments are appropriate to the young and others to the old. In some cases, garments may show that characters are trying to appear older or younger than they actually are.

Costumes may help to clarify character relationships. For example, in many of Shakespeare's plays, warring factions may easily become confusing to an audience because of the difficulty of identifying individual characters. One common solution of this problem is to clothe the members of each faction in the same color scheme and to contrast the two groups. Similar devices may be used to show either a sympathetic or an antipathetic relationship among characters in other kinds of plays. Likewise, changes in costume may be used to indicate a corresponding alteration in the relationships among characters, or in the psychological outlook of an individual character. For example, an increasing dishevelment in dress may parallel a growing discouragement within a character.

The relative importance of characters to the play's action may be shown in costume through emphasis and subordination. For example, if a woman dressed in black enters a scene in which all the other women are clothed in pastel colors, she immediately becomes an emphatic character. The costumer may use a number of similar devices to distinguish the major from the minor roles.

In addition to clarifying points which are largely factual in nature, the costumer must also seek to express a number of intangible qualities, such as mood, style, and theme.

Costumes should be expressive of the over-all mood of a play, and, in some cases, the mood of each scene. A play which is somber in feeling will probably fare best if the costumes are of grayed, subdued colors, while the mood of a farce may demand bright hues.

Costumes should also be expressive of a play's style. For example, a play such as *The Wild Duck* demands a closer fidelity to real-life gar-

A scene from *Alice in Wonderland* showing the use of fanciful and unusual costumes. Costumes by Aline Felton.

ments than does *Pelléas and Mélisande*. The costumes should always reflect the level of reality embodied in that particular script.

Costumes should seek to lead the audience to recognize the play's themes and ideas. This is accomplished largely through emphasis and subordination, through the revelation of character relationships, through the expression of the psychological qualities of individual characters, and through the proper expression of mood and style.

Each costume should be expressive of the psychological nature of its wearer. (Is he extroverted or introverted? Is he fastidious or careless? Is he open and frank, or is he trying to appear to be something he is not?) The costumer must try to project the truth about the character while at the same time allowing him to wear the clothing that he would choose for himself.

The costumer must also see that the progression and climax of the play's structure is paralleled in the costumes. If the same costumes are to be worn throughout, they must be designed with the needs of each individual scene as well as the play's over-all qualities in mind. Furthermore, if the same costumes are to be used throughout, they must be capable of sustaining interest for a long period of time, unlike the costume which is to be worn in only one scene. If costume changes are required, garments which are entirely appropriate for each scene but which also build in interest should be used.

The costumer, thus, is faced with fulfilling many objectives. The ability to meet the maximum number of demands marks the truly outstanding designer.

THE ELEMENTS OF COSTUME DESIGN

Like the scene designer, the costumer utilizes the basic elements of design: line, mass, color, texture, and ornament. Each costume represents a combination of these various elements.

Line has direction only. It may be curved, straight, or a combination of the two; the direction of the curved or straight lines may be alternated to form scallops, zigzags, or other patterns. Line in costume is manifested primarily in the silhouette of garments, but it may also be seen in the darts, the ornamentation, the seams, or other factors which create a visible line.

Mass involves the shape and size of objects—their general, over-all configuration and the amount of space they occupy. It will be most profitable here to consider the elements of line and mass together since they are so intimately connected in costuming.

Each period has its own distinctive silhouette. For example, the Greek woman wore a garment which fell in loose folds about the body, whereas the mid-nineteenth century woman wore a tight-fitting bodice and a bell-shaped skirt. In describing the silhouette of any period the characteristic lines of each of the following parts must be considered: the head, the arms, the upper body, the lower body, the feet, and the legs.

Hair styles and head coverings vary markedly from one period to another. For example, the man of today has little in common with his late-seventeenth-century ancestors, who wore plumed hats and full-bottomed wigs which hung in curls about the shoulders. In considering the head, the presence or absence of beards and mustaches should not be forgotten.

Arms may be uncovered, partially covered, or fully covered with close-fitting material, with puffed sleeves, or with sleeves as full as those of an academic gown. The covering of the upper body may be tight or loose fitting. Shoulders may be bare or covered; the bust and waist may be emphasized or masked. In many periods, corsets have altered considerably the natural shape of the body.

The appearance of the lower body may be changed more easily than that of the rest. Tights or bathing suits may reveal the form, or garments of various shapes and lengths may mask it. For example, skirts may be hung over variously shaped foundation garments to make them resemble bells, barrels, or a variety of other objects.

Foot and leg coverings have also varied widely through history. Men have worn high-heeled shoes, sandals, and wide-topped, knee-length boots. At times the legs have been revealed and at others covered.

Although the foregoing discussion emphasizes the differing silhouettes of various periods, it also illustrates that the natural lines of the

A costume and set design by Filippo Juvarra (1684-1735) for the court opera *Giunio Bruto overa La Caduta de Tarquinii*. From von Weilen's *Geschichte des Wiener Theaterwesens*. 1899.

human body may be altered in many different ways. The costumer, there-fore, can select those lines, shapes, and masses which convey the qualities he thinks most appropriate.

The basic properties of color—hue, saturation, and value—have al-ready been discussed at length in the preceding chapter. The reader's familiarity with this previous discussion will be taken for granted, and here only some of the costumer's specific uses of color will be considered.

All the colors of the spectrum are available to the costumer, but, if he is to achieve unity, he must limit his palette. The limitations may be set in a number of ways. The designer may choose to costume a play in the style of a particular painter. In this case he will use the favorite hues, the characteristic saturations and values found in that artist's works. A costumer may choose a particular color scheme (such as green, blue, and orange). By combining these colors in differing amounts, saturations, and values, he can achieve considerable variety while remaining within the unifying limits he has established. In addition to these methods of selecting the colors for a particular play, several others could be used equally well.

Color is one of the most powerful means for expressing mood and character. Although it is difficult to establish with exactness the connotations aroused by specific colors, different colors normally arouse different responses. Hues which are grayed in saturation and dark in value may aid in establishing a somber mood, while those which are light in value may suggest a mood of gaiety, delicacy, or frivolity. At the same time, the colors of each costume must be expressive of the personal qualities of that individual. A character's basic lack of taste may be indicated through the inharmonious colors of his costume. A defiant nature may be suggested by clothing of a color which is deliberately at odds with the occasion; the relative conservatism of an individual can be implied by subdued tones.

It has already been stated that color can be used to point up the relationship between characters. Those who are closely related through sentiment or politics may wear costumes of the same basic color scheme, while antipathy may be indicated through the use of contrasting colors.

Line, mass, and color are abstractions, however, until they are embodied in materials, each of which has its own texture and weight. The appearance and behavior of velvet and taffeta, for example, are very different. Velvet has a pile which gives it depth and, consequently, a low sheen; it is bulky and hangs in large folds; only with difficulty can it be shaped into intricate pleats or compressed into a small space; it has qualities which are associated with opulence and solidity. Taffeta, on the other hand, has a light, crisp, somewhat glossy surface; it may be shaped with relative ease; and it connotes brittleness and femininity.

Materials with heavy threads and loose weaves may give a homespun quality and be associated with the working classes, whereas the smooth texture of silk more often suggests the upper classes. Each material has its own texture, which the designer can use to capture the desired effects.

Ornament includes such items as ruffles, buttons, fringe, feathers, lace, and piping. It may not be essential to good design for different textures or colors to be incorporated into a garment, or for the line of the costume to be intricate, but in most cases the addition of ornament adds a special touch which brings the whole to life. For example, it is the white collar and cuffs which give variety and distinction to the dress of the Puritan. A red rose attached to a black mourning dress not only sets off the black, but it may indicate that the wearer is not totally engrossed in her grief. Feathers may give a dashing appearance to an otherwise uninteresting hat and transform it into a symbol of gaiety and high spirits.

Ornament can also be used to indicate a lack of taste. Too many ruffles, or too much ornamentation of any kind, indicates a person without restraint. Likewise, too many kinds of ornament may create a cluttered and disorganized effect.

Ornament, thus, can give variety, sharpen effects, and help to characterize. It must be used with considerable discrimination and taste by the costumer if it is to be effective.

Costumes are complemented or completed by accessories, such as canes, swords, purses, and jewelry. In many cases, accessories perform the same function as ornamentation. Accessories, like the costumes themselves, must be designed through the combination of the elements of line, mass, color, texture, and ornament. They must be entirely appropriate to the character and the accompanying costumes. Frequently, the design of accessories is dictated by their usage, since they normally serve as properties for the actor as well as being part of a costume.

THE PRINCIPLES OF DESIGN

The costumer must also understand and utilize the principles of design—unity, balance, proportion, emphasis, and rhythm. Unity means the harmonious relationship of all the parts of a costume; it is that factor which makes the garment seem a complete whole, rather than a collection of disparate parts. Each of the elements of design may contribute to a sense of unity. As with other artistic products, however, monotony must be avoided. Not only must unity and variety be achieved in each individual costume, but in the complete collection of costumes for the production as well.

The principle of balance is relatively easy to apply in costuming since in most cases garments are symmetrical—that is, both sides are alike. Not all clothing is symmetrical, however, and the costumer must understand asymmetrical balance as well. As examples, a drapery may hang down only one side of the back, and ornamentation or accessories may serve to alter an otherwise symmetrical arrangement.

Proportion is of great importance in the design of clothing. The amount and distribution of color, the length of the bodice in comparison to that of the skirt, and the width of the shoulders in relation to that of the hips, bust, and waist are some of the factors involved in proportion. Through the manipulation of proportions much can be done to change an actor's natural appearance. By emphasizing the vertical lines (that is, by increasing apparent height in proportion to width) a plump actor may be made to appear more slender, while emphasis on width may make an actor appear to be stocky. Grace and beauty in large part result from right proportions, whereas awkwardness and ugliness derive from poorly proportioned elements.

As with all artistic objects, a costume needs a center of interest—a point to which the eye is directed first. It may be created by a patch of color, by converging lines, by a change in texture, or through ornament or accessories. The skillful costumer can direct attention to an actor's good points and disguise his poor features through emphasis. He can also lead the audience to see the basic psychological qualities in each character. Furthermore, when the costumes are viewed together, some should be more important than others, since attention should be directed to the principal rather than to the subordinate actors.

Finally, the parts of a costume should be related in such a way that the eye travels easily from one part to another, from the major point of interest to each of the subordinate parts. Rhythm is closely related to unity and emphasis since the easy flow of vision comes about in large part because of the unified relationship of all the elements, and because some are pointed up and others played down.

As with the scene designer, the costumer should have a thorough knowledge of the elements and principles of design before he sets out to create costumes. In the actual process of design, he organizes the elements (line, mass, color, texture, and ornament) in accordance with the principles (unity, balance, proportion, emphasis, and rhythm) in such a way that the purposes of costuming (to aid understanding, and to express the play's values) are accomplished. The process and the final product (the costumes) vary with each production, since they must be adapted to meet the demands of the script and the limitations of the working conditions.

WORKING PROCEDURES AND PLANS

As with other theatre workers, the costumer should make a thorough analysis of the script in terms of plot, character, thought, language, and spectacle, for not only should the costumes be appropriate to the individual characters, they must also project the over-all qualities and values found in the script. Only after he has analyzed the play as a whole should he proceed to a more minute study of its costuming demands. The costumer's study of a play should most resemble that of the actor, since his designs, like the actor's performance, must be expressive of the characters. But whereas the actor seeks to embody his understanding of character through movement and voice, the costumer uses line, mass, color, texture and ornament to create a visual counterpart for the action.

The costumer may also need to study many background factors which aid in understanding the play and the period in which its action occurs. He must be thoroughly familiar with the garments worn in that age, the characteristic silhouettes, typical textures and materials, favorite

A rough sketch by Inigo Jones for costumes. From Peter Cunningham's *Inigo Jones*. . . . London, 1848.

colors, ornamental motifs, and the usual accessories. He should know as much as possible about the manners and customs of the day so that he will know how each garment and accessory was used. He should become thoroughly saturated in both the play and any background information which might be helpful.

Before he begins to design costumes, a conference should be held with the director, the scenic designer, the lighting designer, and possibly the producer, the playwright, and some of the actors. The play should be discussed at length and the interpretation being given the script should be clarified for all those present.

If he does not already know, the costumer should find out how much money is available for costumes, how many costume changes are envisioned for each character, and any special demands which must be met (for example, actors sometimes refuse to wear certain colors, or the director may have specific business in mind which requires a costume of a particular cut). The costumer must know the kind of theatre in which his work will be seen, since small details might be used to advantage in a theatre-in-the-round, but would be totally ineffective in a large, more conventional auditorium. He must find out as much as he can about the plans of the other designers, since the scenery, costumes, and lighting should be unified.

After he is sure that he understands the limitations under which he must work, the costumer is ready to make sketches. Like the scene designer, he may begin with idea sketches in pencil or ink, and he may need to do many before he finds those designs which he considers right. After he is reasonably well satisfied that he has arrived at designs appropriate to the script, additional conferences are held with the director and the other designers. The sketches are discussed, revisions may be requested, and still other conferences may be needed before final agreement is reached. In any case, before the designs can be approved, they must be

ORESTES

HELEN

rendered in color and in such a way that they clearly indicate the final product.

The designer is then asked to provide working sketches and certain other plans. The basic working drawing of the costume designer is a color sketch which shows clearly the basic lines and details of each costume. If there are any unusual features the details are shown in a special drawing (usually in the margins of the color sketch). It is also necessary at times to show more than one view of the costume if the front and back (or the sides) have distinctive features. Samples of the materials to be used in making the garment are attached to each drawing. The sketch, then, shows the lines and cut of the garment, clarifies any unusual details, and shows the materials from which it is to be made.

A costume chart is also needed. This chart is made by dividing a large sheet of paper, or cardboard, into squares. Down the side the name of one character (and that of the actor playing the role) is listed alongside each square. In like manner each scene (or act) is listed across the top. Thus, there will be one square for each actor in each scene of the play. In each square the designer indicates the costume items (including accessories) to be worn in that scene, and he may, in addition, attach color samples of each garment. The range of colors and the over-all color scheme, thus, can be seen at a glance, and the list of costume items can be used as a guide for dressing the actors and for keeping the costumes organized for efficient running of the production. A sample costume chart is printed on page 465.

Three costumes designed by Paul Reinhardt for Euripides' *Orestes. Opposite page: left*, Orestes; *right*, Helen. *Right.* Electra. *Below.* A scene showing the costumes in use from the University of Texas production.

ELECTRA

CARRYING OUT THE DESIGNS

Costumes may be borrowed, rented, assembled from an existing wardrobe, or made new. When costumes are borrowed, the designer attempts to find already existing garments which fit his conceptions. Often, however, he must accept clothing which is not ideal.

Borrowed clothing can be altered only slightly, since, as a rule, its owner will wear it again after the performances are over. Much can be done, however, through the imaginative use of accessories or through the addition of ornamentation to achieve the desired effect without altering the basic garment in any way.

The practice of borrowing clothing is restricted almost entirely to the nonprofessional theatre and to short-run productions. Because older garments are not available for borrowing, this practice is also restricted to twentieth-century clothing in most cases. Male actors in the professional theatre often are asked to provide their own wardrobes in modern, realistic plays. This is not the same as borrowing costumes, however, since in such cases the actor's contract specifies that he will wear his own clothing.

Costumes from rental houses fall into a number of categories. Some of the larger agencies buy the costumes of a Broadway or road show when it closes, and then rent these costumes as a unit. The fact that the costumes from the original production are available is often used as an inducement. At other times, a house has a staff designer (all major costume houses employ at least one) who creates costumes for specific plays which are produced frequently. In such cases, the costumes are designed according to the agency's conception of the period and style most likely to be used in the greatest number of productions. In still other cases, costume houses merely assemble a large variety of costumes for each period. From this stock, the most appropriate garments are selected to make up the wardrobe for any given show.

When costumes are rented, the costume house in effect becomes the designer for the show. The director may write at length about his interpretation of the play, may request specific colors and kinds of garments, but eventually he must accept what is sent, for rental agencies often make substitutions in the requests. Only rarely is a costume house near enough to the producing organization that the costumes can be selected or approved on the spot. Rented costumes normally arrive at the theatre in time for one or two dress rehearsals, and there is seldom time to secure replacements, or to do more than make minor changes in the costumes.

The better costume houses provide good service, but seldom can the work of even the best rental agency provide an adequate substitute for garments designed and made with the needs of the specific production in mind. It should be added, however, that even groups which normally make their own costumes sometimes rent articles which are extremely difficult to construct, such as uniforms, male clothing of the nineteenth century, animal costumes, and other unusual items.

Permanent theatre organizations which make their own costumes usually maintain a wardrobe composed of items from past productions. In this way, a large stock of garments is built up over a period of time. The justification for such a practice is that the costumes can be reused in a

ROLE	I-1 (184 Lines)	I-2 (99)	I-3 (410)	II-1 (321)	II-2 (12)	II-3 (394)	III-1 (60)	III-2 (6)	III-3 (479)	III-4 (201)	IV-1 (293)	IV-2 (252)	IV-3 (106)	V-1 (129)	V-2 (371)
DUKE OF VENICE			Duke 1 Red												
BRABANTIO	1 Change to 2 add Jerkin, Hat, Gloves	Bra.	Bra.												
GRATIANO														Grat. 1 Black Gown	Grat.
LODOVICO											Lodovico 1 Gown Boots		Lod.	Lod.	Lod.
OTHELLO		Othe. 1	Othe. White & Gold	Othe. 2 Armor		3 Brown Dressing Robe		Othe. 4 Armor	Othe. 5 White Doublet	6 Dark Brown Doublet-Jerkin	Othe.	Othe.	Othe. Jerkin Off	Othe.	Othe.
CASSIO		Cas. 1	Cas. Olive & Gold	Cas. 2 Armor		Cas. Stripped of Rank	Cas.		Cas.	Cas.	Cas.			Cas.	Cas.
IAGO	Iago 1 Black Cape	Iago	Iago Black & Green	Iago 2 Armor		Iago	Iago	Iago	Iago	Iago	Iago	Iago		Iago in Shirt	Iago
MONTANO				Mont. 2 Armor		Mont.									Mont.
RODERIGO	Rod. 1 Black Cape	Rod.	Rod. Brown & Coral	Rod. 2 Armor		Rod.						Rod.		Rod.	
CLOWN				Clow.		Clow.	Clow.			Clow.					
DESDEMONA			1 Brown with Red Trim	1a Blue Gown over Brown		2 Tan Negligée			3 Rose with Tan Jacket	Des.	Des.	Des. Remove Jacket	Des.		Des. 4 Night-gown
EMILIA			Emi. 1 Green Dress	Emi.		2 Negligée	Emi.		Emi.	Emi.		Emi. Remove Over-sleeves	Emi.	Emi.	Emi.
BIANCA										1 Bian. Dk. Red & Brown	Bian.			Bian.	

INTERMISSION (between III-3 (479) and III-4 (201))

A Costume Chart.

number of future productions. The organization, in effect, becomes its own rental agency.

There are important differences between reusing costumes from one's own wardrobe and renting them from another source, however. When garments are to be taken from the theatre's own stock, the costumer will design the play with this in mind. He knows what is available and can choose in advance. Furthermore, existing costumes can be remade or altered to fit new conceptions. As a rule, some costumes are taken from stock while those to be worn by the principal characters may be made new.

The procedures and working conditions for creating new costumes vary from one kind of organization to another. In the professional theatre, the designer's sketches are turned over to a costume house which executes the designs under a contract with the producer. The designer must approve the finished costumes, but has little to do with the actual work itself beyond supervising the fitting of the garments.

Unlike the scene designer, the costumer does not have to furnish technical working drawings which show how his designs are to be carried out (that is, the costumer does not have to supply patterns, or cutting, sewing, and fitting directions). He depends upon the costume house to fill in this information.

In the nonprofessional theatre, the designer most frequently supervises the construction of his own costumes and must know as much about pattern drafting, draping and fitting as he does about design. Every costumer should understand thoroughly the techniques for carrying out his designs so that he will know what effects can be accomplished and by what means. Furthermore, such knowledge permits him to speak with authority and to give guidance to those who aid him in carrying out his plans.

Regardless of who actually makes the costumes, however, a number of standard procedures are involved. First, accurate measurements must be made of all the actors. (The stage manager or assistant director usually makes the appointments for these measurements and fittings.)

Second, the necessary materials must be bought. While it is expected that the designer will specify materials, it is not always possible to find precisely the same cloth or color. Either the designer, or some authorized person, may need to search at length for the right materials.

Next, patterns need to be drafted as guides for cutting and shaping the material. Many good books print patterns for garments of various periods. These must be adapted to fit the particular actor, however, and in some cases patterns must be made without any help from existing diagrams. It is at this point that the technical knowledge of the tailor and seamstress is of greatest value.

Patterns are needed for most garments, especially those tightly

King John 1st dress

Left. A costume design by J. R. Planché for Shakespeare's *King John*, 1823. Courtesy of the Stark Collection, University of Texas Library. *Right.* A. N. Benya's design for Mirandolina in Goldoni's *The Mistress of the Inn.* From *Moscow Art Theatre, 1898-1917.* Moscow, 1955.

fitted or intricately shaped, although some costumes are easier to make by draping. For example, the typical Greek garment hangs from the shoulders in folds and is not fitted to the body. It is easier, therefore, to drape the material on the actor or on a dress form. In this way, the folds may be arranged as desired, and many possibilities can be tried out.

After the patterns are completed, the material is then cut and the parts are basted together. Before the sewing is completed, however, the first fitting occurs. Each garment is put on the actor who is to wear it and its fit and appearance is checked by the designer. It is easy to make many alterations or changes at this stage which will be impossible (or extremely troublesome) after the garment is entirely finished.

After the preliminary fittings, the necessary changes are made and the garment is finished, and ornamentation and accessories are added. Another fitting is arranged at this time to assure that the costume looks and functions as planned. This process is repeated for each costume.

THE COSTUME PARADE, REHEARSALS, AND PERFORMANCES

When all of the costumes are finished, it is a wise idea to hold a dress parade. At this time, each scene of the play is covered in sequence so that the actors may appear in the appropriate costumes under lights which simulate as nearly as possible those to be used during performance. The actors then may be asked to perform characteristic portions of each scene.

The dress parade, which is attended by the director and the other designers (as well as the producer and the playwright in the professional theatre), allows everyone to see and evaluate the costumes without the distractions of a complete performance. Any difficulties can be noted and corrected before dress rehearsals.

In the professional theatre the dress parade is held at the costume house, while in other organizations it usually occurs on the stage. It is normally supervised by the costumer.

After any difficulties have been corrected, the costumes are moved to the dressing rooms in the theatre where the performances are to take place. If no dress parade as such is held, its functions must be accomplished during the dress rehearsal period.

Dress rehearsals allow the costumes to be seen under conditions as near as possible to those of performance. Changes at this time should be few, but those which are necessary must be carried out speedily so that the actor is not confronted with new details on opening night.

Once dress rehearsals begin, a wardrobe mistress (or costume-crew head) usually assumes responsibility for seeing that the costumes are in good condition and that each actor is dressed as planned. In the nonprofessional theatre, the costumer frequently assumes these duties. Technically, the costumer's work is over after opening night. In the professional theatre, he may be asked to supervise the replacement of costumes when they become shabby, and he may be asked to redesign the costumes for road companies.

THE COSTUMER'S EMPLOYMENT

The costumer's function may be performed by persons who are employed in other capacities as well. A very large number of nonprofessional organizations do not have a special costume designer. Sometimes his duties are filled by the director; more often, however, a designer-technician assumes responsibility for all the visual elements of a production. On the other hand, many organizations have a costumer who has no other responsibilities, and some have more than one costumer.

Even in the professional theatre, however, the scene designer may also design the costumes. In fact, scene designers who belong to the United Scenic Artists Union must be able to design costumes before they can be admitted to the union. In recent years, however, it has become more and more common for one person to design the costumes and another the scenery. Like the professional scene designer, the costumer must also belong to the United Scenic Artists Union, although he is not required to pass those parts of the examination dealing with scenery, unless he wishes

Costumes worn in 1732 for a comedy at the Comédie Française. Note the use of a similar print for the man's costume stage right and the woman's left center. From Frederic Loliée's *La Comédie Française*, Paris 1907.

to be qualified in that field as well. His entrance examinations and his responsibilities are otherwise the same as those for the scene designer.

Union rules forbid a designer to submit any designs for a prospective production until he has signed a contract (he may, however, show previous work). His fee is based on the number of costumes required. His contract specifies his billing and any special arrangements which are to apply. He must be available for consultation throughout the rehearsal period, and must accompany the show on its out-of-town tryouts if the producer desires.

Off-Broadway theatres, summer stock companies, and professional companies outside of New York frequently employ nonunion costumers. It is difficult to specify with any exactness the working conditions in such organizations, since the situation in relation to unionization varies according to the status of the organization.

THE COSTUMER'S ASSISTANTS

In carrying out his work, the costumer needs a number of helpers, the most important of which are: an assistant costumer; cutters, fitters, and seamstresses; the wardrobe mistress; the dressers.

The costumer's assistant does whatever is asked of him. He may make sketches, search for the appropriate materials, supervise fittings, or act as liaison between the costumer and other theatre workers. He must be as versatile as the costume designer himself, but he must be prepared to perform the less exciting tasks.

Cutters, fitters, and seamstresses make the costumes. Skilled workers at this stage can save time and can make the difference between ill-fitting and correctly fitting garments. Furthermore, if the designer is not to make the patterns and supervise the sewing himself, he must depend upon workers who have sufficient knowledge to carry out his plans. In the professional theatre, such workers must be union members. In the non-professional theatre, much of this work is done by volunteer or student labor, though occasionally a paid seamstress may be hired, either on a permanent or temporary basis, to sew and to supervise the work of others.

When the costumes are finished, a wardrobe mistress takes charge. She is assisted in her work by a crew of dressers. It is the responsibility of the wardrobe mistress to see that costumes are ready for each performance. They may need to be mended, laundered and ironed, or cleaned and pressed. She must see that garments are replaced when they begin to look shabby, so that the show will continue to look as nearly as possible as it did on opening night. She is directly responsible to the stage manager during performances. Some permanent producing organizations employ a full-time wardrobe mistress to supervise the upkeep of the stock as well as to supervise the preparation of costumes and the running of particular shows.

The number of dressers needed for a production depends upon the size of the cast and the complexity and rapidity of costume changes. Sometimes actors need very little help, but quick changes and complicated garments may require more than one dresser to aid a single actor. There must be a sufficient number to keep the show running smoothly during performances and to keep the costumes in shape at all times.

In the professional theatre, both the wardrobe mistress and the dressers must be union members. In the nonprofessional theatre, the costumer may serve as wardrobe mistress, but a paid or volunteer assistant may serve in this capacity. Dressers are normally students or volunteers.

THE COSTUMER AND THE ACTOR

The costumer must work very closely with the actor, for many of their problems are shared. First, the costumer should consider the strengths and weaknesses of each actor's figure when designing costumes. It is possible, of course, to design an appropriate and expressive costume without considering the actor who is to play the role, but this leads to questionable results when the on-stage effect is destroyed by the performer's physical appearance. Thus, if an actor's thin legs are out of keeping with the role he is playing, the costumer can conceal this shortcoming. Boots, a cape, or some flowing garment can be used to cover the legs or to draw attention away from them. Of course, there are limits to what the costumer can do for an actor, but he should always strive to make him look as nearly as possible the embodiment of the role he is playing.

The costumer should also keep in mind the actions demanded of the actor during his performance. For example, it is difficult to climb steps in a tight skirt, and fencing may be dangerous to an actor wearing billowing sleeves. On the other hand, these same garments might enhance movement in other situations.

Almost any unfamiliar garment will seem awkward to the actor, however, until he becomes familiar with its possibilities. Every costume, except one that is skin tight, allows some movements and restricts others. The characteristic features of clothes in each period emphasize qualities which were admired at the time, and allow movements which were socially useful, beautiful, or desirable. For example, the sleeves on a fashionable man's coat in the eighteenth century will not allow the arms to hang comfortably at the sides; rather, the arms must be bent at the elbows and held away from the body. On the other hand, the modern suit coat is cut so that the arms are most comfortable when hanging at the sides, while outward and upward movement is restricted. Each of these coats is adapted to the needs of its period. The costumer should understand the relationship between the cut of garments and movement. Also, if he will make these garments from authentic period patterns, the costumes will help the actors to get the feel of the time and the character.

In like manner, the costumer may aid the actor by proper attention to such objects as shoes and undergarments. The height of the heel on shoes is of great importance to stage movement. A high heel throws the weight forward on the balls of the feet, while heelless shoes bring the weight to the back. The right kind of footwear, therefore, can aid the actor in achieving appropriate period movement.

Undergarments also affect movement. Corsets, for example, are of various kinds and each is designed to force the body into a specific shape. By doing so, it encourages some actions and makes others impossible. A hooped, crinoline underskirt will not allow the same kind of movement as modern underwear.

If the costumer takes care to make sure that suitable movement is encouraged by the clothes he designs, he can be of enormous help to the actor in achieving the desired results. For maximum effectiveness, however, the actor and director must be willing to explore the possibilities of each garment and to allow sufficient time for rehearsal in it.

A scene from Molière's *Don Juan* showing costumes from a period (*c.* 1660) seldom used on the stage because of the typical male garment of the time called "petticoat breeches" (seen here on Don Juan at center stage). Here they have been effectively designed with the actor in mind. Costumes by Elizabeth Parsons.

MAKE-UP

Make-up is normally used to cover all parts of the actor's body not concealed by his costume. It is, therefore, an essential part of his physical stage appearance. Nevertheless, the position of make-up in the theatre is ambiguous—it is considered by all to be of great importance, but its mastery is frequently taken for granted and it is often given little consideration in the planning of a production.

Traditionally, make-up has been considered to be within the actor's province, and it is often assumed that each actor is entirely capable of designing and executing any kind of make-up. This is not always true, however, and it is especially questionable in the nonprofessional theatre. For this reason, in many nonprofessional organizations make-up is considered to be part of the costumer's duties; in others, the director's; in still others, a person skilled in make-up is recruited to supervise the make-up for each production. In the professional theatre, each actor is expected to take care of his own make-up.

Make-up is discussed here in connection with costuming because of its intimate connection with the actor's appearance. Furthermore, it is actually desirable that make-up be planned in advance just as much as any of the other elements of a production, and that it should be designed with the costumes, settings, lighting, and the characterizations in mind. It is not entirely logical to leave each actor to decide upon his own make-up when all other elements of a production have been planned with considerable care.

Regardless of how it is administered, however, make-up is an essential part of each production. The following brief discussion sets forth some of the principal considerations in its use.

PURPOSES.   Like the other aspects of production, make-up should aid understanding and should be expressive of the play's qualities. It should help to establish the age of a character, his general condition of health, and his race; within limits it may also aid in establishing profession (for example, persons who work outdoors may have different coloration from those who work indoors), basic attitudes (a grumpy person may have different facial wrinkles and lines than a cheerful one), and his self-regard (how well he takes care of his personal appearance).

Make-up may also be indicative of the style of a play. In a realistic drama, such factors as age and health are modeled as much as possible after life, whereas in an expressionistic play, more attention may be given to establishing an idea (for example, the faces of all the actors might be painted a grayish green to indicate that they are, in effect, living corpses).

Make-up may be used to establish psychological qualities and to make the face more expressive. A character can be made to look like the stereotype of the villain; or certain features may be emphasized to give an impression of secretiveness or of naïveté. The nose, mouth, eyes, or any other feature may be emphasized or minimized as needed.

Certain practical purposes are also served by make-up. For example, stage lighting is usually more intense than normal lighting and without make-up most persons appear pale and flat under stage lights. Make-up restores color and form to the face. It must also be applied, however, with the size of the theatre in mind, for while it should be seen, it should not appear grotesque and distorted, unless these qualities are needed for the production.

THE MAKE-UP PLOT. In those situations in which make-up is designed in advance and supervised by a responsible person, a make-up plot is normally used. A chart is made with a space left to indicate the basic information about the make-up of each actor: the color of the base, liners, eye shadow, and powder; any plastic features, such as a beard; any changes which must be made during the play. It serves both as a guide for application and as a check on how the make-up of each actor relates to that of all the others.

In designing make-up, the actor's facial characteristics and coloration must be compared with those which would be ideal for the character he is playing.

TYPES OF MAKE-UP. In make-up, effects may be achieved in two basic ways: by painting, and through the addition of plastic, or three-dimensional, pieces. Painting involves the application of color, high lights, and low lights on the face or other parts of the body. Plastic make-up includes such objects as beards, wigs, false noses, and warts. All make-ups use some painted effects, while plastic pieces are utilized more rarely.

Painted make-ups may be divided into a number of subcategories: the various age groups; straight and character make-ups; racial types; and special effects.

If an actor is to portray a character whose age is significantly different from his own, he must alter his appearance accordingly. Like the actor, then, the make-up artist should observe with care the characteristic distinctions between childhood, youth, maturity, early-middle age, middle age, late-middle age, and differing degrees of old age. He must study each part of the face separately to see the typical coloration, highlights, shadows, and lines; he should observe the forehead, the eyes, the nose, the mouth, the cheeks, jaws, and neck. He should not neglect the hands, arms, and other parts of the body; youthful looking hands, for example, sometimes destroy the illusion created by the facial make-up.

Make-ups may also be classified as "straight" or "character." With a straight make-up, the actor's own basic characteristics are utilized without

A make-up room showing actors in the process of applying make-up. *Opposite page.* A scene from Tagore's *King of the Dark Chamber.* The two actresses are wearing "straight" Hindu make-up, the actor at the rear an "old-age" make-up, and the man in the foreground a stylized painted make-up. Make-up by Donald Rosenberg.

any significant changes in age or over-all features. A character make-up is one in which the actor's appearance is significantly altered. The change may be one in age, but it might also be for the purpose of making the actor seem fatter or coarser, more lean and wizened, or to emphasize some peculiar facial characteristic.

Frequently scripts require a clear differentiation between characters on the basis of race. Again, the make-up artist must observe or discover the characteristic differences between such races as the Chinese, Indian, Polynesian, and Negro. He also needs to study the typical facial characteristics, coloration, and manifestations of age within each of the races.

Special painted effects include clown make-ups, those which distort or ignore the features of the face for the purpose of achieving some stylistic effect, or those in which decorative designs are painted on the face (in the manner of a primitive tribe).

The number of effects which can be achieved by painting are almost limitless. Most of them, however, are used to give a clear indication of age, character, and race, although the actor's own facial features may be altered or emphasized in the process.

While all make-up has painting for its basis, significant transformations in an actor's appearance may be more easily accomplished by the addition of three-dimensional elements. For example, a change in the shape of the nose with putty and the addition of a beard and bushy eyebrows can mask an actor's features more completely than painting can.

Gauze over cotton can be glued to the actor's face to form prominent cheeks, hanging jowls, a protuberant forehead, or fleshy jaws. Warts and large scars may be used to give the actor an unsightly appearance.

The actor may grow his own beard and mustache if he desires, but these can also be made with relative ease. There are many styles of hair, however, which the actor can assume only with the aid of a wig. For example, in the late seventeenth century, men wore loose, curled wigs which hung about the sides of the face and down the back. Baldness can also be simulated with a bald wig. Wigs may be made or rented in almost any style or color. Within limits much can be done to alter the appearance of the actor's own hair.

Make-up Materials. To accomplish the desired effects, a variety

of make-up materials are available from the manufacturers of make-up and from costume supply houses. In the professional theatre and in many non-professional organizations the actor is expected to furnish his own make-up supplies. It is not unusual in colleges and universities, however, for the theatre to supply the make-up. The following discussion indicates the principal materials most frequently used.

Every make-up begins with a base (pigment suspended in an oily base; most base make-up comes as a pastelike substance in tubes). A very wide range of base colors is available: various shades of pink, suntan, yellow, beige, brown, and even black and white. Each color may be used as it comes or it may be mixed with one or more additional colors to achieve the exact shade desired. The base color is applied over the exposed portions of the face, neck and ears. (A range of color equal to that of the tube colors is available in liquid form for application to larger surfaces of the body, such as the arms, legs, and torso.)

A base color alone is apt to make the actor's face appear flat and uninteresting. Over this base, therefore, lines, highlights and shadows are applied. For this purpose, a thick paste is available in small tins. This paste, normally called "liner," comes in a wide variety of colors, such as white, light brown, dark brown, blue, green, red, gray, and black. Like the base colors, these may be mixed to achieve any desired shade. They may be used for creating shadows under the eyes, hollows in the cheeks or temples, for making furrows in the forehead, or for outlining the creases which spread outward and downward from the nose—for achieving any desired high- or low-light. Red liner may be used for lipstick or rouge.

Crepe hair is used to make beards and mustaches. It comes in a wide range of colors, which may be combined to achieve more accurate representations of human hair, which is frequently mottled. Crepe hair is sold in long, plaited strands. When it is unplaited it is extremely crinkled, but it may be straightened by holding it over steam or by stretching it tightly for some time.

For making beards (and similar items such as mustaches and bushy eyebrows) liquid adhesive is needed. This is a plastic substance which becomes solid, though it remains flexible, when exposed to the air. It may be applied to the face (usually several layers are built up) to form a base upon which crepe hair can be attached (with the same liquid adhesive).

When the desired shape and size of beard has been made, the whole structure, including the base and the hair, can be removed. This permanent beard can be re-used at each performance by reattaching it to the face with liquid adhesive.

Nose putty is used for changing the shape of the nose, chin, cheek bones, or forehead. It may be shaped as desired and then attached to the face. It is not very successful when applied to flexible parts of the face, however, since it is apt to be loosened by movement and may fall off. For plastic effects on the flexible parts of the face, gauze may be stretched over pieces of cotton and glued to the face with liquid adhesive. These plastic elements are then covered with the same base color as that used on the rest of the face. Liners may be used to make them more realistic in appearance.

Various materials may be employed to alter the color of the hair. A white liquid, usually called hair whitener, may be combed through the hair to make it gray. It frequently gives an unnatural appearance, however, and much more realistic effects can be achieved by combing metallic powders through oiled hair. Aluminum powder makes a convincing gray, while copper and bronze give a reddish cast.

Wigs may be made from the kind of plastic hair used on store-window models. It may be bought in a wide variety of colors and can be sewn or glued to a cloth base which has been fitted to the actor's head. The hair can then be shaped into any desired style. Natural-hair wigs may be rented from costume supply houses. Wigs made from anything other than plastic or human hair are seldom satisfactory if a natural appearance is desired. If naturalness is not a consideration, wigs may be made from hemp, crepe hair, or a variety of other materials.

After the make-up is complete, the painted portions must be powdered, for otherwise the actor, when seen under the bright stage lights, will appear to be greasy. Powder comes in the same variety of shades as the base. It should be applied freely and the excess brushed off. Those parts of the body covered with liquid make-up need not be powdered since this kind of make-up has a low sheen. For removing make-up a good supply of cold cream and facial tissues is needed.

This brief outline does not explain the techniques needed for the proper application of make-up. These may be learned, however, from a number of good textbooks which cover the subject.

Since the actor's physical appearance is a basic part of his characterization, he should learn as much about his costume and his make-up as possible. It should also be the aim of the costumer and the make-up artist to aid the actor wherever possible to transform himself into the character he is playing. They must work together to make costume and make-up an integral part of the total design.

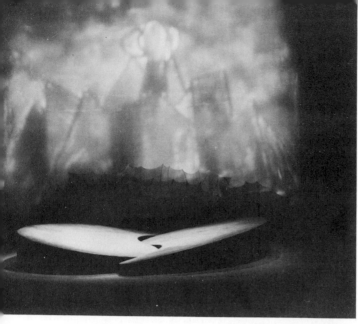

Chapter 20

THE LIGHTING DESIGNER

One of the least publicized, but most important, theatre artists is the lighting designer, for without his work that of the other artists would not be seen. Furthermore, his designs may either enhance or seriously distort the visual elements of a production—the action, the scenery, the costumes, and the make-up.

Perhaps his work is little known because light itself is intangible, takes up no stage space, and is visible only when it strikes a reflecting surface, such as an actor or a piece of scenery. Thus, while light must be present, it tends to be ignored unless it is obviously inadequate or obtrusively spectacular. Since lighting also requires a knowledge of complex instruments and control boards, of electricity and electronics, of optics and physics, to many it appears to fall more into the province of the electrical engineer than that of the theatre artist. In actuality, the lighting designer must be both a sound technician and an artist of high caliber.

FUNCTIONS OF STAGE LIGHTING

The functions of stage lighting, like those of the other areas of design, are to aid understanding and to be expressive of a play's values. First, and most basically, lighting aids understanding by making the other elements

A setting for Strindberg's *The Dream Play* showing the use of projected stylized shapes for a scenic background. Lighting by David Thayer.

visible. It need not make everything on stage equally visible, but it should reveal whatever the audience needs to see for an adequate understanding of the play.

Lighting also aids understanding in a number of other ways. It may establish the time of day (early morning, midday, late afternoon, or night), the source of the light (sun, moon, lamps, fire light), the weather conditions (a sunny, overcast, or stormy day), and it may help to identify the time of year (the amount and kind of light may vary from one season to another). The period might be partially established by the lighting fixtures on stage (oil lamps, candles, electric lights). It may further aid understanding through the proper use of special effects (such as lightning, offstage fires, flashing lights, or rainbows).

Lighting must be expressive of the play's mood and atmosphere, of its style, and its themes. Brightness, color and distribution can be used to create almost any desired mood. Normally, bright, warm colors are associated with gaiety, while cool colors of low intensity may create a somber atmosphere. If a scene is lighted from the side with a single bright source, the resulting sharp contrast between light and darkness will give a harsh quality. The intensity, color, and direction of the light may be combined in additional ways to create widely varying moods.

Lighting may be made expressive of the style and theme of a play through its effect on form. The stage is a three-dimensional space and the actors, properties, and furniture are three-dimensional objects. This fact

A scene from Shaw's *Saint Joan* showing an effective balance between background and acting-area lighting. Note the use of projections to suggest extension of the cathedral in the background and of a light pattern on the column to suggest light coming through a church window. Lighting by Hunton Sellman.

A setting for Richardson's *Dark of the Moon* showing the use of background lighting to aid in establishing mood.

may be emphasized or distorted, however, depending upon the style and themes of the play. If the illusion of real people in a real environment is important (as it usually is in realistic dramas), then natural light and shadow, careful attention to the source of light, the time of day, and similar factors can serve to reveal the scenery and the actors in all of their dimensions. On the other hand, if it is desirable to emphasize a theme such as the emptiness of life or the shallowness of existence, everything can be made to appear two-dimensional by lighting all of the visible surfaces with the same amount of light. The distortion of reality can be shown in many ways. For instance, if the majority of light comes from directly overhead, unnatural shadows will be cast on the face and the entire setting may appear distorted.

Lighting can aid in the expression of themes and style by serving as a compositional element. It can reveal what needs to be emphasized; it can select single objects and actors, or small groups or areas, and focus attention upon them, or obscure them; it can lead the eye to see what is important at any given moment.

THE CONTROLLABLE FACTORS OF LIGHT

In fulfilling the purposes of stage lighting, the designer has four factors which he may manipulate and control: intensity or brightness, color, distribution, and movement.

Intensity is determined basically by the number and wattage of the lamps in use. This original intensity is modified, however, in a number of ways. If a color medium intervenes between the light source and the stage (as is typical) the amount of light is reduced, for a color medium does not allow all of the light rays to pass through it. Distance is also a great destroyer of brilliance, and the farther a lamp is placed from the stage the lower will be the intensity of its light on the stage. The brightness of the light on any portion of the stage may further be controlled by the placement of the lighting instruments—all may be directed at the same spot, or they may be placed so as to distribute the light either evenly or unevenly over the stage. In addition, dimming devices can be employed to vary the brightness of the lights as desired.

Intensity, thus, is principally a matter of how much light reaches the stage. It can be controlled and used in the creation of mood and atmosphere or to meet the changing dramatic needs of the script. High intensity is often associated with comedy, whereas a lower intensity is thought to be appropriate for more serious plays. Brightness may be adjusted in accordance with the supposed source of the light, the hour of the day, or the psychological or atmospheric needs of the moment.

The visible spectrum of light is composed of the following colors: red, orange, yellow, green, blue-green, blue, and violet. Each is separated from the others by virtue of being composed of light waves of a given length. The waves which create the sensation of red are the longest of the visible rays, while those of violet are the shortest. "White" or "natural" light is a mixture of all the visible wave lengths. Color is attributed to objects because of their capacity for absorbing some wave lengths and for reflecting others. Without light there is no color.

Each light source has its own spectrum of color. The incandescent lamp (the most commonly used in stage lighting) is preponderantly yellow, with lesser amounts of other colors, while the fluorescent lamp most frequently gives a bluish light. Thus, the apparent color of objects, such as scenery and costumes, is affected by the light source, even when color filters are not employed.

To prevent the distortion of color in scenery, costumes, and make-up and to allow for color changes indicative of mood or time of day, it is desirable that the color of the lights be as variable as possible. To permit such control, color filters are used.

A color filter operates through a process of selective transmission— that is, it allows light of certain wave lengths only to pass through. For example, a blue filter screens out the majority of the red, orange, yellow, and violet rays. At the same time, however, this process reduces considerably the amount of light which reaches the stage. Furthermore, if a red object is lighted only with blue light, its apparent color will be changed to magenta.

To avoid such distortions, filters of different colors are placed on other lighting instruments, so that light from a number of sources may be mixed on the stage. For example, the primary colors of light—red, blue, and green—may be mixed to give white light. More frequently, however, a variety of subtle tints and shades are employed to achieve the desired results.

Color in light has three basic qualities: hue, saturation, and brightness. Hue is a basic term for describing a color (such as red, green, or violet). Saturation is the relative purity of the color—its concentration around a specific wave length. Brightness is the darkness or lightness of the color, or its component of white light. The addition of white light produces tints, while taking it away makes shades. Since color filters are manufactured with these three qualities combined in a wide variety of ways, it is relatively easy to find filters which are entirely appropriate to almost any script.

Distribution has to do with the direction from which light comes and the way it is spread over the stage: illumination may come from overhead, the front, sides, or back; and it may cover a portion or all of the stage. Direction is determined by the position of the light source. Almost any placement is possible, for instruments may be mounted in the ceiling of the auditorium, on the front of the balcony, or on pipes over the stage; they may be placed on the floor, or mounted on vertical pipes or stands.

Differences in the direction of light are important in establishing mood and visibility. For example, if all the light striking a character comes from behind him, his actions will be visible while his identity may remain unknown, since his face is not revealed. Such lighting can be used effectively for creating a sinister atmosphere or a mood of mystery. Furthermore, the audience's perception of dimensionality depends in large part upon the direction of the light, for illumination which strikes all surfaces of an object equally will make it appear flat, whereas that which lights some parts more than others emphasizes the various planes and surfaces.

The area covered depends upon the number of instruments being used (a number of light sources are normally required to light the entire stage), and upon what parts they are focused (all instruments may be concentrated on a single area, or their beams may be distributed over several parts or all of the stage). For example, in part of a scene a single spotlight may be used to light the face of one character while the rest of the stage is in darkness; in other parts of the same scene the entire acting area may be lighted by a large number of spotlights. It is possible, at least

A scene from Sidney Howard's *Yellow Jack* showing the use of light to isolate scenes in space.

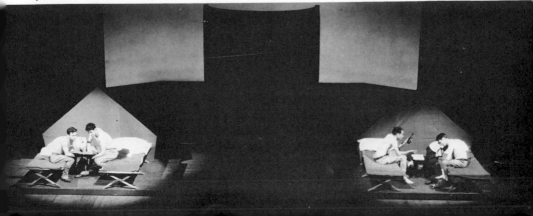

in theory, to distribute light exactly as desired, both in terms of its direction and of the areas lighted.

Movement refers to alterations in intensity, color, or distribution during a performance. The principal device for achieving the effect of movement is the controlboard. Through its use lamps may be brightened or dimmed to control intensity, to change the color, or the distribution of the lighting. Movement allows the light to change in accordance with the shifting moods and developments in the dramatic action. Because it can be altered moment by moment, light is probably the most flexible of all the elements of stage production, with the possible exception of acting.

The lighting designer must understand thoroughly the controllable factors of light—intensity, color, distribution, and movement—and how they may be manipulated to achieve the purposes of good stage lighting.

THE PRINCIPLES OF DESIGN

Stage lighting is governed by those same principles of design employed in other visual arts: harmony, balance, proportion, emphasis, and rhythm.

The lighting for an entire production must be planned as a unit so that all of the parts are harmonious with each other. It must be entirely appropriate to the style, period, characters, actions, and ideas of the play. This principle of unity must be applied both to individual scenes and to the play as a whole. Unity, however, can lead to sameness and monotony if due care is not taken to insure variety. Thus, while all of the elements should constitute a harmonious whole, a wide range of appropriate elements should be employed in the process.

Balance, proportion, and emphasis are closely related principles in lighting design, for each is achieved largely through the proper handling of the others. Lighting must be designed so that primary emphasis is given at most times to the acting areas. Since brightness always gives emphasis, the most intense lighting is usually focused on those parts of the stage used by the actors, and a proportionately lesser amount of light is employed for the background. The acting areas and the background must seem unified, however, and consequently the proportion of the intensity used on each part of the stage must be governed so that they blend together smoothly. Furthermore, as a rule the light on the acting areas should be equally distributed so that the actors do not pass through distracting dark and bright spots as they move about the stage. This usual balance, however, may be altered to meet the demands of the script, for it is often essential that one area be more brightly lighted than another. Proportion and balance, thus, create the necessary points of emphasis.

Rhythm is that factor which makes attention flow effortlessly from the main center of emphasis to the subordinate parts and back to the main center again. In lighting it is the result of gradations in intensity, and the proper handling of color and distribution. Since light can reveal, conceal, or alter any of the other visual elements of a production, rhythm in lighting design is one of the most important factors for welding all of the parts into a unified composition.

The lighting designer, then, shapes the controllable factors of light in accordance with the principles of design so as to realize the purposes of stage lighting. In doing so, however, he must work within the limitations imposed by the script and the particular theatrical conditions.

WORKING PROCEDURES

The lighting designer should have a thorough understanding of the play as a whole before he searches for its specific lighting demands. He should begin, therefore, with an analysis of the action, characters, ideas, and spectacle so as to clarify the basic intentions of the script, its meanings, and its style. After he is satisfied that he understands the play as a whole, he is ready to investigate how he may embody its specific qualities in the lighting.

The designer should look for any indications of the physical nature of the light: the sources of illumination (lamps, candles, moonlight, sunlight); changes in the intensity of the light (indications of growing darkness or light, of lamps being lighted, or shutters opened); variations in the light required for different parts of the stage; the direction of light (moonlight through a window, sunlight from one side of the stage); any special effects (such as lightning, rainbows, or fires); and the coloration of light (firelight, moonlight, lamplight, sunlight). Such practical considerations must be taken care of in the design and cannot be ignored if they are essential parts of the script.

The designer must be especially concerned with mood, for lighting is one of the most important contributors to the proper atmosphere for a play's action. Lighting may be bright or low, and warm or cold; it may blend the parts of the setting together or it may isolate the elements. Mood can be established or enhanced through varying combinations of intensity, color and distribution.

The designer must understand the style of the play. For a realistic drama the designer may need to make the light appear to come from specific light sources, and to change in accordance with realistic motivations. If the script is nonrealistic, the lighting can be more arbitrary in its changes, its color, and distribution. The lighting should always reflect the level of reality depicted in the script.

The designer should also seek to underline the structure and development of the play. For example, a play may move from happiness to despair and gloom, and lighting can aid subtly in showing this change.

The lighting designer may need to do background research into the typical lighting fixtures of a period, the specific qualities of the light derived from each, and the way each fixture was used. If the production seeks to adapt the staging techniques of the period in which the play was written, the designer will need to study the stage-lighting practices of that time. As a rule, however, the lighting designer's work is less affected by historical considerations than that of the set and costume designers.

The lighting designer's study of the play should be reasonably complete before his first conference with the director, the other designers, the producer, and the playwright. At this meeting, he should discuss his understanding of the play with the others and should outline his ideas for lighting the production. He must make certain that he understands the director's interpretation, the qualities being sought, and as much as possible about the plans of the scene designer and the costumer. There may be a series of conferences before final accord is reached.

In the professional theatre, the lighting designer must make sketches showing the stage as it will look when lighted. In the nonprofessional theatre, a general (sometimes vague) agreement is reached about the qualities of the lighting to be used—its relative intensity, its coloration and distribution—but the specific design is often left somewhat tentative.

This situation is dictated in part by the nature of light. A great deal of time must be spent in adjusting the lighting, and it is frequently assumed that the lighting designer can at the same time make alterations in his plans to compensate for unforeseen problems in acting, scenery, or costumes. Furthermore, little can be done about carrying out the lighting designs until the theatre is available and the scenery in place. For these reasons, the major work of lighting a show is done in the last few days of the rehearsal period.

THE LIGHT PLOT AND INSTRUMENT SCHEDULE

Nevertheless, the lighting designer should be able to outline his plans by means of sketches, light plots, and an instrument schedule.

A light plot is drawn on a floor plan or on a vertical section plan. The floor plan should show, as if seen from above, the layout of the entire stage, the setting, and any pertinent part of the auditorium. A vertical section plan is drawn as though one side of the theatre had been removed. It shows the vertical arrangement of the stage, the scenery, and the auditorium. In making a light plot, the following additional information is shown: the type, size, and position of each instrument, and the approximate area to be lighted by each. Abbreviations and symbols may be used to indicate many of the specifications. (See the accompanying illustration.)

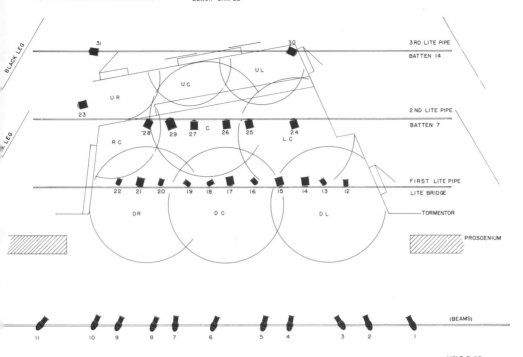

A light plot for Ibsen's *The Wild Duck. Below.* A photograph of the scene showing the lighting in use. Lighting by Ward Williamson.

It is usually necessary to make a separate light plot for each setting, since the area to be covered by the lights will vary in accordance with the scenic arrangement. It is also typical to make a composite plot which shows all of the settings simultaneously and the relationship of the lighting for each scene to that of all the others. This is especially helpful because the same equipment as a rule must be used to light more than one setting. Consequently, the areas to be covered must be worked out carefully so that the instruments will be effective in each situation.

Lighting for the stage may be divided into specific illumination, general illumination, and special effects. Specific illumination refers to that lighting which is confined to a very limited area; general illumination is light which spreads over a large part of the stage; and special effects are out-of-the-ordinary demands such as fires, rainbows, and lightning. Each of these must be given proper consideration in the design of the lighting and in the layout of the light plot.

Specific illumination is used principally for lighting the acting areas, since they need the greatest emphasis and often require much variety in the intensity, color, and distribution of light. The spotlight, the principal source of specific illumination, has been developed to meet the demands of lighting for the acting areas. It is designed to emit a concentrated beam of light which can be confined to a restricted portion of the stage; it cannot be used efficiently for lighting the entire setting.

Since a single spotlight can satisfactorily illuminate only a small segment of the stage, the total acting space is normally divided into smaller areas, the number depending on the size of the setting. For an average-sized setting, three or four areas are usual across the forward part of the stage, with an equal number at the rear. Each area may then be lighted separately. Ideally, at least one spotlight should be focused upon an area from each side so as to strike it at an angle of forty-five degrees in relation to both the horizontal and vertical axes. The lighting for each area must overlap sufficiently to prevent unduly bright or dark spots and to achieve an even distribution of light over the entire acting area.

Since the forward acting areas cannot be lighted effectively from behind the proscenium arch, some provision must be made for hanging instruments in the auditorium. The ideal angle for light (forty-five degrees) can best be achieved from apertures in the ceiling (frequently called the "beams") which permit instruments to be mounted across the entire width of the auditorium. Many theatres also have vertical apertures at the sides of the auditorium for housing lighting equipment. Not all theatres are designed with lighting needs in mind, however, and places for hanging instruments may have to be improvised. In many New York theatres, for example, spotlights are mounted on the front of the mezzanine or balcony.

The upstage acting areas are normally lighted by instruments hung back of the proscenium arch. In most theatres a light bridge is suspended just behind and above the proscenium opening, and there may be vertical pipes on either side of the proscenium, just back of the masking pieces known as "tormentors," to which lights may be fastened. Instruments may also be mounted on other pipe battens suspended over the stage at intervals from front to back, may be attached to the scenery, or placed on the floor or on stands.

A scene from Obey's *Noah*. The stylized rainbow effect is in keeping with the style of the play and the scenery used. Note also the cyclorama lighting.

In addition to the spotlights used for lighting the acting areas, others may be needed for special purposes, such as for following a ghost, for achieving momentary emphasis on a doorway, or for picking out the face of one actor as the rest of the stage is darkened. These may be mounted wherever needed.

General illumination serves three basic functions. First, it is used to light all of the background elements not illuminated by the instruments focused on the acting areas. The cyclorama, ground rows, or drops, for example, may not be lighted at all by the spots. Because it is usually desirable to light the background at a level of intensity lower than that used for the acting areas, general illumination is sufficient for this part of the setting. Second, it is used to blend the acting areas together, and to provide a smooth transition between the higher intensity of light on the acting areas and the lower intensity on the background. Spotlight beams often produce sharp, angular lines where they strike the walls of a set or the floor. The brightness of the spots further makes the cleavage between the acting areas and the rest of the stage conspicuous. It is therefore necessary to erase these distracting lines and to blend all of the lighting into a unified whole. Third, general illumination is used to enhance or modify the color or tone of the settings and costumes by the use of color filters.

General illumination is produced basically by striplights and floodlights, which are designed so that their light is diffused over a large area. Although this light cannot be confined to small areas, its direction can be partially controlled. Footlights are pointed upward and backward from the front edge of the stage. Border lights may be hung directly over the acting area and pointed downward, or they may be tilted to light the walls of

A scene from Shakespeare's *Julius Caesar*. The manipulation of light and shadow aids in creating a sense of conspiracy. Directed by A. N. Vardac; setting by Wendell Cole; costumes by Virginia Opsvig.

the setting. Other striplights may be placed on the floor to light ground rows or the cyclorama. Floodlights may be suspended on battens or placed on stands or the floor to illuminate drops or the cyclorama.

Special effects, as the name implies, are unusual demands and, therefore, cover a wide variety of miscellaneous lighting requirements and instruments. Still or moving clouds, stars, or even an entire scenic background may be projected. Prop fire logs, a machine for making bright flashes of light, or an instrument for producing realistic rays of sunlight may be needed. The demands and the solutions are many.

In making a light plot, the problems of specific illumination, general illumination, and special effects should be considered separately and then as a unit. The required instruments, the placement of each, the area to be lighted by each, and the color of filters to be used must then be decided and indicated on the lighting plan. The final solutions will be determined by the physical limitations of the theatre building, the arrangement of the settings (ceilings and walls, for example, rule out certain mounting positions), the color scheme of the settings, costumes, and make-up, and the other demands of the script.

It should be pointed out that many of the suggestions made here would need to be modified for an open stage or a theatre-in-the-round. In the latter case, for example, no background lighting is possible or necessary. On the other hand, the acting areas must be lighted from every side. The demands made on specific illumination are increased, therefore, while those on general illumination are decreased. Furthermore, all of the instruments must be mounted in the auditorium. For the open stage, a scheme between that for the arena and proscenium theatres is required. A larger proportion of effort will go to specific illumination than in the proscenium theatre, but some background lighting is still necessary. The basic principles for designing light plots remain unchanged, however.

CODE	AREA	INST. LOCATION	INSTRUMENT	WATTS	OUTLET	DIMMER	COLOR	NOTES
1	DL / DLC	BEAMS	8" ELLIPS.	750	B 1	A 2	62	
2	DRC	"	"	"	PROS L2	A 4	"	
3	"	"	"	1000	" L3	C 3	31	
4	DL	"	"	"	5	C 1	"	
5	"	"	"	750	6	A 1	62	
6	DC	"	"	1000	7	C 2	31	
7	DR	"	"	750	17	A 6	62	
8	"	"	"	1000	9	C 1	31	
9	DL	"	"	"	PROS R1	"	"	
10	"	"	"	750	" R2	A 3	62	
11	DC	"	"	"	12	A 5	"	
12	DLC	BRIDGE	6" FRES.	500	BR 3	D 5	70	
13	UC	"	"	"	6	B 7	62	
14	UL	"	8" OV. FRES.	1000	BR 4	D 3	31	
15	RC	"	"	"	C 6	C 6	"	
16	RC	"	6" OV. FRES.	500	8	B 3	62	
17	UC	"	8" " "	1000	15	C 4	31	
18	LC	"	6" " "	500	16	B 1	62	
19	DR SPEC.	"	"	"	17	B 5	"	
20	UL	"	"	"	19	B 6		
21	LC	"	8" " "	1000	22	C 5	31	
22	C	"	6" " "	500	21	B 2	62	
23	UL DOOR	2ND PIPE	"	1000	BR 11	B 8	62	
24	UL BACK	"	8" "	"	TORM L1	F 3	57	
25	UC . "	"	"	"	" L3	F 2	"	
26	UL "	"	"	"	BR 1	F 3	"	
27	LC "	"	"	"	BR 28	C 8	"	
28	C "	"	"	"	DS 4	F 2	"	
29	" "	"	12" FRES.	2000	DS 2	C 9	59	
30	BACKING	3RD PIPE	8" "	1000	DS 6	E 8	20	
31	"	"	"	"	DS 7	E 7	41	

An Instrument Schedule.

After the lighting plots are completed, an instrument schedule is made. This is a table which lists separately each lighting instrument to be used. For each, it indicates the specifications (wattage, lens, reflector, lamp, and any other pertinent information), the mounting position, the color filter to be used, the area to be lighted, the circuit into which it is plugged, the dimmer to which it is connected, and the scenes in which it is to be used. It provides a summary in tabular form of all the technical information needed for acquiring and setting up the lighting instruments for a production. It comprises a convenient checklist for much of the equipment to be used.

LIGHTING INSTRUMENTS, ACCESSORIES,
AND CONTROL BOARDS

To carry out his plans, the lighting designer must have at his disposal the necessary instruments and accessories, and a controlboard. If those desired are not available, his plans may have to be changed.

In the nonprofessional theatre, it is typical for an organization to own a supply of lighting equipment sufficient to meet the demands of its own productions. Also as a rule, such groups use buildings which have permanently installed electrical circuits and a controlboard. These facilities may be primitive or lavish, but the groups operate within the limitations of their own resources, except in those rare instances when they rent special items from a lighting supply house or are able to borrow them from other organizations.

The same conditions apply in most cases to permanent professional groups outside of New York. Commercial theatre buildings in New York, as well as the majority of those used by touring companies elsewhere, do not have controlboards or even permanently installed electrical circuits into which lighting instruments may be plugged. Since he cannot depend upon a theatre having any facilities beyond an adequate supply of electricity, the designer must list (with exact specifications) absolutely every item necessary for lighting a show. Some of this material may be rented, or all of it may be bought. Because most productions must do some touring (if only for out-of-town tryouts), the lighting equipment must be easily transportable and capable of quick installation. These requirements serve to keep Broadway productions from using certain complex equipment, especially some of the more recent controlboards.

Regardless of the type of organization for which he works, however, the designer should be thoroughly familiar with the available lighting supplies. He should know as much as he can about the potentialities and the limitations of each item so that he may plan wisely and efficiently.

LIGHTING INSTRUMENTS.   Lighting instruments may be divided into a number of categories: spotlights, striplights, floodlights, and special lighting equipment. The basic characteristics of each will be discussed briefly.

Spotlights are designed to illuminate restricted portions of the stage with a concentrated beam of light. Any good spotlight has a sturdy metal housing, a lamp socket, a reflector, a lens, a color-frame guide, mounting attachments, and some device for adjusting the focus. Each of these parts may vary considerably in design from one instrument to another.

Spotlights are available in a wide range of sizes, and are normally classified according to wattage, lenses, and reflectors. They range from

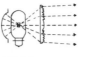

FRESNEL SPOTLIGHT

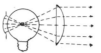

PLANO-CONVEX SPOTLIGHT

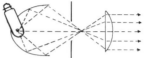

ELLIPSOIDAL SPOTLIGHT

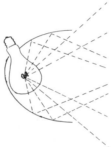

Diagrams showing the relationship among lenses, lamps, and reflectors in three types of spotlights and a floodlight.

FLOODLIGHT

100 to 10,000 watts in size. The average wattage is from 500 to 1000, although larger sizes are common.

A lens gathers the light coming from a lamp and bends it into parallel rays to create a concentrated beam. A lens, therefore, is essential if the spotlight is to fulfill its purpose. Three types of lens, the plano-convex, the Fresnel, and the step, are generally used in spotlights. A plano-convex, or condensing, lens is flat on one side and convex on the other. It gives a sharp, distinct beam of light. In a Fresnel lens, one surface is plane while the other is composed of concentric rings of differing diameters. The resulting lens is ridged on its convex side, and is much thinner than a plano-convex lens. It diffuses the beam of light and prevents the sharp edges which are typical of the plano-convex lens. In the step lens, the plane surface has been treated in much the same manner as the convex surface of the Fresnel lens and it produces similar optical results. Each spotlight is designed to take advantage of the peculiar qualities of one type of lens and will not operate efficiently with any other kind.

A Fresnel spotlight. Courtesy of Kliegl Brothers.

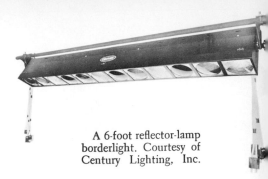

A 6-foot reflector-lamp borderlight. Courtesy of Century Lighting, Inc.

Lenses are also described in terms of diameter and focal length. They are available in diameters from three to twenty inches, although the most common sizes are six, eight, ten, and twelve inches. The focal length of a lens (also stated in inches) indicates the distance which the filament of the lamp should be from the axis of the lens. Each spotlight is designed to use a lens of a specified diameter and focal length and it will function efficiently only with the appropriate lens.

A reflector is placed behind or around the lamp to throw light forward which would otherwise be wasted. It serves, therefore, to increase the efficiency of an instrument. (Efficiency is the ratio between the amount of light emitted by the source and that which reaches the stage.) Reflectors are made of metal and are available in a number of shapes, although those used in spotlights are either spherical or ellipsoidal. The spherical reflector is placed behind the lamp, while the ellipsoidal reflector partially surrounds the lamp. Because of its shape and placement, the ellipsoidal reflector is far more efficient than the spherical.

Spotlights are frequently divided into three types: Fresnel, plano-convex, and ellipsoidal. The differences between the Fresnel and plano-convex spotlights result principally from the potentialities and limitations of the lenses, since otherwise their basic parts, including a spherical reflector, are similar. The ellipsoidal spotlight may be equipped with either one or two lenses of any type. Its distinctive qualities, however, are determined by its reflector.

The ellipsoidal spotlight is by far the most efficient type. It is also

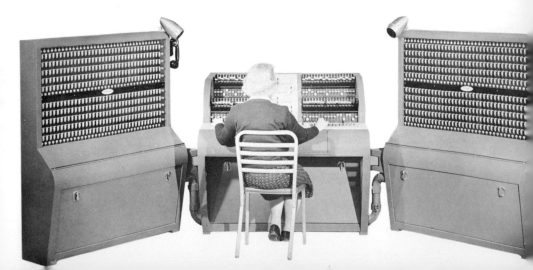

A 16-inch 750-1500 Watt diffuse alzac floodlight. Courtesy Century Lighting, Inc.

An ellipsoidal spotlight. Courtesy Kleigl Brothers.

much more expensive and much larger. It is used primarily where the distance between the instrument and the stage is great and where mounting space is not at a premium. Its primary application has been in lighting those acting areas which must be illuminated from the auditorium.

Fresnel and plano-convex spotlights are most frequently mounted behind the proscenium for lighting the upstage acting areas, since the throw of the light is short and hanging space is often minimal. The Fresnel spotlight is far more common now than the plano-convex because it is more compact and efficient.

All spotlights have a number of other features. Guides forward of the lens are used to hold color frames so that the color of the light may be controlled. All spotlights are equipped with a means of mounting which allows an instrument to be rotated from side to side and up and down. It can be pointed in any direction, therefore, and when the desired position is found, can be secured tightly. In every spotlight, the lamp, the lens, or the reflector (and sometimes more than one of these) is movable so that the focus of the beam of light may be adjusted.

Each of the spotlights in the wide variety now available has been designed with a specific kind of situation in mind. If the lighting designer understands the capabilities of each, he may select those capable of meeting his demands most efficiently.

A striplight is an instrument composed of a series of lamps set into a narrow, roughly rectangular trough. It is used as a source of general illumination.

Console and preset panels for the C.I. remote-control system. Courtesy of Century Lighting, Inc. See page 497.

A scenic projector. Courtesy of Kleigl Brothers. See page 495.

As a rule, each strip is wired so that there are three or four separate circuits. Each third or fourth lamp, then, will be on the same circuit and may be controlled together. All of the lamps on the same circuit are covered with filters of the same color. Thus, each strip will be able to produce three or four different colors when each circuit is used alone or all may be combined in various intensities to produce a wide range of additional colors. Frequently, one circuit is left free of color and can be used to alter (by the addition of white light) the colors produced by the other circuits. In this way, striplights may be used to "tone" the settings, costumes, and make-up.

Striplights vary considerably in length. Some are very short, having only three or four lamps, while others extend across the entire width of the stage. Short units are more flexible, since a number may be placed end to end to make a long section if needed and may be used individually where short units are sufficient.

Striplights also vary considerably in wattage, using individual lamps ranging from 25 to 500 watts. The size of the lamp depends upon the purpose for which the strip is being used. Most modern striplights (unlike their earlier counterparts) use a reflector, which combines a sphere and a parabola, behind and partially surrounding each lamp. The reflectors put each lamp into a compartment completely separated from all the other lamps in the strip. In some cases, however, striplights are designed to use reflector lamps (that is, the reflecting surface is a part of the bulb which surrounds the filament).

Striplights may be subdivided into three categories: footlights, borderlights, and miscellaneous striplights. Footlights are normally recessed in a slot at the front of the stage. Originally they were evolved to light the actors' faces from below so as to counteract the unnatural shadows caused by instruments placed at too sharp an angle overhead. After the development of better lighting instruments and techniques, however, footlights fell into disfavor and are now seldom employed. They may still serve useful functions, however, for eliminating shadows cast by large hats and similar objects, for blending the specific and general illumination together, and for enhancing color.

Borderlights are hung from battens above the stage. They may be short or they may extend the full width of settings, and they may be hung in several rows from front to back. They are used more often than any other instrument for blending the acting areas together and for "toning" the settings and costumes.

Miscellaneous striplights may be placed on the floor to light ground rows and drops, and around the base of the cyclorama (these are sometimes called "cyc foots") to create various sky effects. Small strips may be used to light backings for doors and windows and other small scenic units. Like spotlights, striplights are designed with specific uses in mind and they should be selected accordingly.

The floodlight is another common type of instrument designed to give general illumination. It uses a single lamp as the light source. This is set into a housing which has a large opening to allow the light to spread over a wide area; there is no lens. Most floodlights available today have either ellipsoidal (the most typical) or parabolic reflectors. The wattage varies from 250 to 5000. Each floodlight is also equipped to accommodate a color filter.

Floodlights may be used singly or in combination. They may be suspended above the stage to substitute for borderlights. Like striplights, they may also be placed on the floor for lighting drops and ground rows, and they may be used to light backings and other background scenic units. Perhaps the most frequent and important use of the floodlight, however, is in lighting the cyclorama. A series may be used to achieve a smooth, even illumination over the entire visible surface; with the aid of filters, any color may be produced.

It is impossible to specify all of the special effects which may be called for in the theatre. Instruments have been developed, however, to meet the most frequent demands.

Projectors of various kinds are employed for creating numerous special effects. Slide projectors are often used to project rainbows, stars, clouds, still pictures or captions. With the right equipment, the entire scenic background may be projected on a screen or on the cyclorama. Other projectors are designed for use with moving, circular disks on which images (such as clouds, waves, rain, smoke, or fire) have been painted. A motor revolves the disk at a constant speed past the projector lens and creates the effect of movement.

Lightning can be produced by bringing a carbon stick, to which one electrical terminal has been attached, into close proximity with a piece of metal, to which the other terminal has been attached. As the current leaps between these two points, a bright flash of light, like that seen in welding, results.

For fireplace or campfire effects, prop logs are constructed and painted appropriately. A lamp is then placed inside the logs and the light is allowed to shine through holes which have been covered with transparent red, orange, and amber material. Flames may be simulated by irregular strips of colored silk or plastic which are kept in motion by an electric fan.

These common special effects may be supplemented and adjusted by anyone with a knowledge of electricity and of stage lighting instruments and techniques. Additional equipment is also available from any stage lighting supply house.

ACCESSORIES. In addition to lighting instruments, a number of accessories—such as lamps, electrical cable and connectors, color frames and color media—are needed. Each instrument is designed to use a particular lamp. Similarly, each lamp employed in stage lighting is designed with its special uses in mind. Lamps vary in a number of ways and consequently must be described according to the type of base, the filament, the wattage, the shape, the treatment of the glass, and the position in which the lamp should be used (such as "base up" or "base down"). The catalogue of any lamp manufacturer gives complete details on lamps designed especially for stage use.

Electrical cable for the stage should be heavily insulated since it must withstand much wear (scenery may be moved over it and it is often stepped on). It is available in a number of sizes, each designed to carry a different maximum electrical load. Cable should be bought with its use in mind, therefore, and the designer must make sure that no cable is overloaded, for otherwise hazards to the equipment or danger of fire may result.

There are two principal types of stage connectors or plugs: the twist lock, and the pin connector. Both are of heavy-duty construction and are designed with the needs of the stage in mind. It should go without saying that every theatre needs an adequate supply of electrical cable and of connectors.

Almost every lighting instrument is provided with some means for using color filters. If this opportunity is to be utilized, a supply of color frames and of color media is required. A color frame is usually made of metal and has an opening of the same size and shape as that of the instrument with which it is to be used. The color medium is placed in the frame and then inserted into the color-frames guides on the instrument. A rigid color medium such as a glass roundel does not require a color frame and is inserted directly into the guides on those instruments designed to use this glass medium.

A number of color media are used in stage lighting. The most common is gelatin, a transparent plasticlike material which is available in a wide range of hues, saturations, and intensities. Almost any desired color can be achieved with it, and it may be cut to any desired shape. It is fragile, however, and fades with use. Some other plastic color media (such as cinemoid and cinabex) are also frequently used, but they are similar to gelatin in all important respects, the chief differences being only those of greater thickness and durability, and higher cost. Glass is commonly used as a color medium with striplights, although plastic media may be used on these instruments as well. Glass is the most durable color medium, but it is available in only a limited range of colors. Each color medium has its own qualities, advantages and disadvantages which should be thoroughly understood by the designer so that he may select his materials wisely. Color media and color frames may be bought directly from the manufacturer or from a lighting supply house.

A number of additional accessories are available, as a glance at the catalogues from lighting equipment manufacturers will quickly reveal. Those discussed here, however, are the most common and the most essential.

CONNECTING PANELS AND CONTROLBOARDS. No lighting arrangement is complete without some means for controlling the light. The type, size, and placement of instruments and the choice of color filters provides the possibilities for controlling intensity, distribution, and color. Before these opportunities can be thoroughly exploited, however, a controlboard is needed. A board permits some instruments to be used at maximum brightness, while others are off or partially dimmed out. Similarly, it allows the control of color by mixing the light from a number of instruments in varying proportions. In such ways, great flexibility can be gained.

If a controlboard is to be efficient, however, there must be some means for connecting each instrument to the desired control. For this purpose a connecting panel is required. To this panel run all of the stage circuits as well as all the controlboard dimmers. Any circuit may then be connected with any dimmer. Complete control can be achieved if there is a sufficient number of circuits and dimmers. Since the number of both is restricted in most theatres, however, careful planning is normally required to arrive at an arrangement suitably flexible for meeting the needs of a particular production.

In actuality, a controlboard might be merely a panel of switches for turning the lights on and off. If the lights are to be controlled with any subtlety, however, dimmers are required. Each dimmer is designed to accommodate a maximum electrical load and should never be used beyond its rated capacity. Since the load to be placed on dimmers differs from one production to another, theatres normally purchase a number of dimmers of varying capacities.

Dimmers are of many types, the most important of which are the resistance, the autotransformer, and the electronic. Each works on a different principle, but each allows a gradual increase or decrease in the electrical power reaching the lamps. This results in the dimming or brightening of the lights.

Dimmers vary considerably in efficiency, compactness, and price. The electronic dimmer, for example, will dim out completely a load of any size, while the resistance dimmer must be loaded to its approximate capacity before it is entirely satisfactory. On the other hand, the electronic dimmer is very expensive, while the resistance dimmer is inexpensive.

Although a large number of individual dimmers is desirable for efficient control, additional problems arise as the number of units increases. If each dimmer must be adjusted manually and individually, several operators will be required. To overcome this difficulty, all types of dimmers are now available with master controls which allow a number (or all) of the individual dimmers to be interconnected in such a way that a single handle can operate all. Any good board allows the dimmers to be interconnected in almost any desired combination.

Another problem arises in connection with the size of a bank of dimmers. Electronic units, for example, are so bulky that it is seldom feasible to house them in the immediate stage area. They are installed in another part of the building, therefore, and a small, compact, remote-control board is located in the vicinity of the stage. This places the bulky equipment out of the way, while allowing for its use. Resistance and auto-transformer dimmers must be installed in the stage area, since neither type can be operated by remote control efficiently enough for stage lighting purposes.

The placement of the controlboard is of considerable importance. The most common locations are: at one side of the stage near the proscenium, in the orchestra pit, at the back of the auditorium, and in a booth built into the face of the balcony. The ideal arrangement is one which permits the operator to see the stage from much the same vantage point as the audience. Such a location allows him to check the lighting and to perceive immediately when something is wrong. The controlboard should be located somewhere in the auditorium, therefore, whenever possible.

With the electronic controlboard, it is possible to preset dimmers. This means that the lighting for individual scenes, or for an entire show, may be set up in advance. Then, by means of a master dimming device, one scene may be faded out and another in simultaneously or the desired changes made within a scene. The ability to preset controls does away with the necessity for haste in going from one complex scene to another, and consequently eliminates many mistakes.

Probably no aspect of theatrical production has undergone so many changes in recent years as lighting control. It is advisable, therefore, to make frequent surveys of new developments which may make stage lighting more effective.

This brief survey of lighting equipment, accessories, and controlboards by no means describes all of the available equipment or the principles involved. It does cover the most common devices and their typical uses. The lighting designer, of course, should have as exhaustive knowledge as possible of both the range of equipment and its possible applications so that he may select wisely and work efficiently.

REHEARSALS AND PERFORMANCES

During the period when the actors are rehearsing and the scenery and costumes are being constructed, the lighting designer must assemble the materials for illuminating the production. If the theatre is available, many of the basic processes may be carried out at a leisurely pace. Typically, however, the theatre is not available until a few days prior to performances.

Regardless of time, the procedures are reasonably standard. By using the light plot and the instrument schedule, each instrument is mounted in the designated position and directed toward the indicated stage area. The correct color filter is added, the instrument is plugged into the right circuit and connected to the designated dimmer. The instruments may even be tentatively focused at this time. The work cannot be completed, however, until the scenery is in place.

The final setting and focusing of instruments is a time-consuming and sometimes disheartening task, for it is difficult to confine light exactly as envisioned. Unwanted lines, shadows, and bright areas may appear, and an even spread of light over the acting areas may be difficult to achieve. Furthermore, when the same instruments must be used to light more than one setting, an ideal adjustment for one scene may not be right for another.

In the professional theatre, the lighting designer often sits in the middle of the auditorium (where he may see the stage from the spectator's point of view) and calls out directions over a loud speaker to the lighting crew. Sometimes as many as twenty-four continuous hours may be spent in the adjustment of the lighting. In the nonprofessional theatre, this process is seldom compressed into a continuous session of such length, but its function must be carried out nevertheless.

Ultimately the goal is the precise adjustment of each instrument so as to achieve the desired lighting effects on stage. Furthermore, an accurate set of cue sheets must be constructed. A cue sheet indicates the setting of the lights at the beginning of each scene (this is done by listing those dimmers to be used, and the intensity setting of each), any changes to be made during the scene, and the cues for making those changes.

If there is a technical rehearsal, the lighting may be integrated more precisely with the other elements at that time. Changes in the lights may be required because of unforeseen problems with the scenery or costumes, or because more time is required for certain effects than had been envisioned. Further adjustments may be called for as a result of dress rehearsals. Previously unnoticed shadows may be discovered or the actors may move into an area not indicated in the plans. Any required changes should be made as quickly as possible and recorded on the cue sheets. Changes are seldom made after the opening night.

After the play is officially opened, the designer's responsibilities are over in most cases, and the lighting duties are passed on to the lighting crew.

EMPLOYMENT

Stage lighting is still viewed by some as an adjunct to scenic design, for the professional lighting designer must be a member of the United Scenic Artists Union, and is required to take an entrance examination covering many of the same requirements as that taken by the set designer. The demand for lighting specialists is, of course, comparatively recent. In some professional productions the scenic designer also designs the lighting. Nevertheless, the practice is changing with great rapidity and the lighting designer has definitely emerged as an artist in his own right.

In the professional theatre, the lighting designer is employed by the producer under a contract which must meet the minimum specifications of the United Scenic Artists Union. His responsibilities and his billing on the program are specified in his contract. His fee is determined by the number of settings which must be lighted and the relative difficulty of the task. He must be available for conferences throughout the rehearsal period, and his presence is absolutely mandatory for the setting up and adjustments of the lighting instruments. During the dress-rehearsal period, he must see that any necessary changes are made and that the lighting functions as planned. His job is considered to be over when the play opens in New York.

Off-Broadway and summer stock companies do not always hire lighting designers as such, and lighting is traditionally considered to be part of the scenic designer's job. In the community theatre, the designer-technician lights productions as a regular part of his duties. Where there is no designer, the director of the theatre must assume the responsibility for lighting, though the actual work may be done by volunteer helpers.

In many small educational theatres, conditions similar to those in the community theatre prevail. In organizations with a larger and more specialized staff, the technical director frequently serves as the lighting designer. In rare instances, a staff member may be able to devote his full attention to stage lighting.

THE LIGHTING DESIGNER'S ASSISTANTS

Like the other theatre artists, the lighting designer depends upon a number of other persons to aid him in carrying out his plans. His principal helpers are: an assistant designer, a master electrician (or head of the lighting crew), and members of the lighting crew (including the control-board operator).

The designer does not always have an assistant, but if he does the assistant may be assigned almost any of the tasks which the designer himself would otherwise perform. He may make the drawings for the light plots, compile the instrument schedule, find the necessary equipment, act as liaison between the lighting designer and the rest of the production staff, aid in setting up the lights and in compiling the cue sheets. In the Broadway theatre, the assistant designer must be a member of the union, but in other organizations he may be either a paid or a volunteer worker.

The master electrician (or lighting-crew head) is in charge of the lighting crew. He works closely with the designer during the period when the lighting equipment is being installed and the instruments adjusted. After the show opens, he must see that all equipment is properly maintained, and that the lighting operates as planned during performances. He is directly responsible to the stage manager.

Outside the professional theatre, the title of "master electrician" is seldom employed. A more common term is "head of the lighting crew." This may be a paid position or it may be filled by an assigned or volunteer worker. At times, the lighting designer himself serves in this capacity. In any case, the head of the lighting crew should be some one with sufficient knowledge and experience to supervise the work of others and to carry out plans efficiently.

Members of the lighting crew install, operate, and maintain all lighting equipment and shift any electrical equipment which must be moved during scene changes. The controlboard operator is of special importance since he is responsible for the actual manipulation of the lighting during performances. Not only must he be able to follow the cue sheets accurately, but he must also be capable of adjusting the controls to meet emergencies and the inevitable differences between one performance and another. In the professional theatre, the crew must be composed of union members. In the nonprofessional theatre, crews are usually recruited or assigned.

SOUND

The place of sound in the theatre is perhaps even more ambiguous than that of make-up, for, although it is an important part of production, its planning is often haphazard and may be done by several persons. In the professional theatre, sound produced by electricity is considered to be within the province of stage lighting, while that produced mechanically is classified with properties. This division is determined by union jurisdiction rather than by the needs of the theatre, but even outside the professional theatre the responsibility for sound is often assigned at random.

Like other theatrical elements, sound makes its greatest contributions when it is designed as a unit and carefully integrated with the production as a whole. Ideally, there probably should be a separate sound crew and the planning and execution of sound should not be considered a mere adjunct of some other phase of production. At the present time, however, the lighting designer, of all the usual theatrical personnel, is best qualified to cope with sound, since it is increasingly dependent upon electrical and electronic devices and since, like stage lighting, it requires technical knowledge normally considered to be an aspect of physics or engineering. For these reasons, sound is treated here in connection with lighting, although their ultimate relationship is more one of convenience than of likeness in theatrical terms.

The total sound of a production may be divided into three main categories: the actors' voices, music and other abstract sounds, and realistic noises. The first category is normally excluded in the treatment of sound, and has already been dealt with in previous chapters on acting and directing.

Music, if recorded, is considered to be sound, but if it is played "live" it comes within the province of the musicians. Since music is treated at some length in the next chapter, it will be excluded for the most part in the discussion here. Abstract sound is nonmusical and nonverbal noise which has no recognizable origin. Realistic sound effects are those which are readily associated with a natural or man-made phenomenon, such as thunder or an airplane.

Regardless of its type, sound fulfills two basic functions: it helps to establish such qualities as mood and style, and it serves as exposition. Music and abstract sound are used principally to serve the first function by establishing the proper atmosphere for action and for underlining the inherent qualities of scenes. For example, strange, hollow noises might be used in a nonrealistic play to parallel the subject matter. Realistic sounds, however, may also be used for their mood value. Thunder and rain can set the background for a murder mystery, while bird songs may establish a quiet, pastoral scene. Furthermore, realistic sounds may be performed in a variety of ways to accord with the appropriate mood and style. For example, a prolonged and distant train whistle can produce a mournful effect, while a staccato and brisk train whistle may produce a cheerful effect. In such ways, sound can be kept recognizable while being altered to give a variety of qualities.

The function of exposition is most frequently filled by realistic noises. Gun shots, automobile horns, crashing dishes, doorbells, and similar sounds may provide the necessary preparation for onstage action, or may be used to suggest offstage happenings.

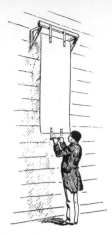

Three traditional devices for simulating thunder. *Left:* a thunderclap device; a sharp crack is produced by pulling the Venetian-blindlike slats together. *Center:* a "rumble cart"; it is filled with rubble, such as broken bricks, and the uneven wheels create a low rumbling sound when the cart is pushed across the floor. *Right:* a thunder sheet; the sound of thunder is created by shaking the thin sheet of metal. From G. Moynet's *La Machinerie Théâtrale.* 1893.

Sound may also identify time and place. Different noises may be associated with different times of the year and day, and sound may place the action in the city or the country, near a river or streetcar tracks. Regardless of which function it is fulfilling, sound should be entirely appropriate to the play as a whole and to the specific moment.

Sound for the theatre has a number of properties which may be controlled: pitch, quality, volume, direction, and duration. All of these factors, with the exception of direction, have been discussed already as they relate to speech, and they will be reviewed only briefly here.

The same basic sound may be repeated at a number of different pitches, each of which will affect an audience in a way different from the others. Doorbells, whistles, and gunshots may be quite varied in their pitches and it is possible to find whatever seems best for the particular production.

Sounds differ in terms of quality. Thunder is recognized in part by its rumbling, echoing quality, while an alarm clock may be distinguished by shrillness, or a gunshot by a sharp explosiveness. Since quality is the least understood of all the properties of sound, it is the most difficult to control with exactness. Nevertheless, it can be manipulated to achieve those distinctions which are indicated by such descriptive adjectives as harsh, pleasant, grating, crackling, soft, and shrill.

Volume is the relative loudness of sound. Any noise may be produced at any level of volume, although each sound may have its own characteristic loudness (thunder is normally louder than the sound of a ball being bounced). Distance, however, is also an important factor in our perception of sound. Thunder may be so distant that it is barely audible, while a ball being bounced on the side of a house may be very loud. Stage sound must be controlled, therefore, so that the typical qualities of the particular sound are maintained, while distance is also indicated. It is sometimes difficult to achieve the proper effect of distance with "live" sound. For example, it is often hard to find the right offstage spot from which to fire a blank cartridge which must simulate a distant gunshot. On the other hand, improvements in electronic equipment have made it increasingly easy to control the volume and effects of distance in recorded sound.

The volume of sound must be maintained at a level consonant with stage speech and action. It should not be allowed to override the actors' voices (unless this is intended) or to become distracting.

Sound also has direction, and illusion is often shattered in the theatre because a sound is obviously coming from the wrong side of the stage. For example, a telephone bell may ring off stage left when the phone is on stage right. Such a situation is frequently created by the necessity of having all of the sound equipment in the same place.

The best sound results when it may be projected from any direction: from any point in the visible setting; on either side, at the rear, or above the visible stage space; from either side, the rear, or overhead in the auditorium. This is possible only with a series of carefully placed loudspeakers or other sound equipment. With such an arrangement, however, a sound (such as that of a car) can be picked up on one side, seem to approach, pass behind the set, and out of hearing on the other side.

Since any sound can be prolonged or shortened, its duration is controllable. Furthermore, a sequence of sounds has timing as well as length. For example, if thunder is demanded, a decision must be made about when it should begin, how long it should continue, when it should reach its peak, and when it should die away.

All of the controllable properties of sound—pitch, quality, volume, direction, and duration—may be varied in relation to each other and to meet the particular demands of a script. Careful attention to each can lead to a successful sound score for a production.

Sound may be classified as live or recorded. Live sound is created anew at each performance, and consequently may vary considerably in any of its properties from one night to the next. It has the virtue, however, of being adaptable to the demands of individual performances. In recorded sound, the desired qualities are achieved and then placed on records or tape. Barring human or mechanical errors, recorded sound is exactly the same at each performance. On the other hand, it is not always sufficiently flexible in emergency situations or adaptable to the inevitable deviations from one performance to another.

Since there is scarcely a sound which cannot be produced either live or by recording, the choice of method must rest on a number of considerations. The factors of difficulty and efficiency may determine the choice. Such noises as doorbells and telephones can be produced so easily

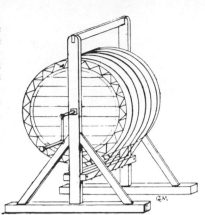
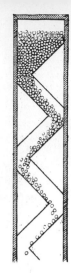

Wind and rain machines. *Left*: a device for creating the sound of wind; when the crank is turned, friction between the inner drum and the outside material produces the desired noise. *Right*: rain sounds are created by allowing shot, or dried peas, to run down a zig-zag metal chute. From Moynet's *La Machinerie Théâtrale*.

with electrical "buzzers" that a recording would be inefficient in most cases. On the other hand, where control over distance and volume (as with train noises) is important, a recording may be preferable.

The choice may also depend upon the availability and suitability of recorded sounds. A wide variety of effects can be obtained on commercial recordings, but these are not always adapted to the specific needs of a play. Many organizations, however, are equipped to record their own effects and can make them suitable in all respects. Conversely, while almost any effect can be created live, a great deal of experimentation may be required to produce some (such as bird calls and automobile engines) satisfactorily and it is normally easier to use recordings for such sounds.

The available sound equipment may also be a factor in the decision. Scratchy records and low-fidelity speakers may distort sound or call attention to the fact that it is recorded. On the other hand, high-fidelity speakers used with tape are in general entirely satisfactory.

Normally the only plan for sound is the cue sheet. It indicates each sound, when it is to begin, any changes, and when it is to end. It may also specify the method by which the sound is to be produced and, where electronic equipment is involved, it should specify sound levels. In those rare cases where elaborate and extensive sound equipment is available, it may be necessary also to make a table similar to an instrument schedule in stage lighting. It should list each piece of equipment (with adequate specifications), and should indicate for each its placement, use, and means of control.

In many ways, sound is analogous to stage lighting since each may be planned in advance but little can be done toward its final realization until the stage is available. As with the other elements, sound must be rehearsed and integrated carefully with the production as a whole. It must be adjusted and perfected in accordance with the demands of the particular stage and auditorium, the actors' voices, and the requirements of the script. When properly designed and executed, sound contributes much to effective theatrical production.

Chapter 21

MUSIC AND DANCE

Although music and dance are independent arts and assume many non-theatrical forms, they are employed sufficiently often in present-day theatrical productions to demand treatment as important stage elements. The following discussion, therefore, will concentrate on their stage uses, especially in musical comedy which relies so heavily upon them for its effectiveness.

TYPES OF MUSIC IN THE THEATRE

Two major types of music are found in the theatre: incidental and dramatic. Incidental music accompanies a play but is not considered to be part of it. It is used most frequently to set a mood, to underscore or heighten emotions, and to bridge scenes. Almost every motion picture uses incidental music extensively, just as did the melodramas of the nineteenth century. In the theatre today, incidental music is normally restricted to an overture and to music between acts; its purpose is the establishment of an atmosphere proper to the play. Occasionally, such music is introduced during a scene. For example, Tennessee Williams often asks for background music, and Miller's *Death of a Salesman* makes effective use of musical motifs.

In addition to purely instrumental music, incidental songs may also be added to scripts. Shakespeare's plays include many songs which underline the emotion of the moment or give added pleasure, but which seldom

A scene from Igor Stravinsky's *The Tale of a Soldier*.

forward the action. Most popular drama of the nineteenth century contained a variety of songs, the number of which might be extended or contracted as desired. Songs of this type are still occasionally employed in plays. Other incidental music may accompany dances.

Incidental music for professional productions may or may not be composed especially for the occasion, but if used it must be played by professional musicians, since union regulations are such that the use of recorded music is seldom possible. In the nonprofessional theatre, however, an orchestra is employed only rarely for nonmusical plays and recorded music is customary.

Dramatic music as an integral part of drama is found in such forms as opera and musical comedy. Here, the music is written with the specific needs of the action in mind, and the over-all effect of the drama is often dependent upon the power of the music. The musical portions of such plays are almost invariably performed "live." The dramatic functions of music have already been discussed in connection with *My Fair Lady*, and the reader may refer to Chapter 14 if he wishes to review these points.

THE COMPOSER

The composer of musical comedy usually works closely with a lyricist, who writes the words for the songs and frequently the "book" (that is, the dramatic structure and dialogue) though still another person may do this. Both the composer and the lyricist must work with the demands of the book in mind.

An agreement among composer, lyricist, and dramatist is normally reached as to where songs, musical interludes or dances are needed, and as to the basic qualities desired at each point. Either the music or the lyrics may then be composed first, but they must eventually be coordinated with each other and be entirely appropriate to the dramatic situation.

The composer of musical comedy creates at least the melodies (with their rhythms and tempos), while the complete musical score may have the collaboration of a special dance composer, who works directly with the choreographer, and the added assistance of an arranger and orchestrator.

The music used for dances in musical comedies today is composed more and more frequently around the dances, rather than the dances being fitted to existing music. Dances must be evolved in the dance studio and the composer of the main score does not normally have time to work with the choreographer in the way required to achieve good dance music. Consequently, some one else often does this work, and a number of persons in New York have become specialists in this field.

As the choreographer establishes his time and movement patterns, the dance composer sets down the rhythms and tempos. Themes and melodies from the main score may be added so as to integrate them with the rest of the music or the composer may then invent a melody which is suitable to the dance.

The work of both the main composer and of the dance composer is normally given to an arranger and orchestrator, who completes the musical score by adding harmony, developing variations, and choosing the musical instruments to be used and assigning parts to them. Although he must give his approval to the finished work, the composer of musical comedy may have neither the time nor the facility to orchestrate a score.

An example may clarify the arranger's job. The composer may supply only a melody as the basis for a ten-minute "production number." Were this melody merely played over and over again, extreme monotony would result. The arranger achieves the necessary variety, development and feeling through the instrumentation, and through modulations of key, rhythm, tempo, and volume. Much of the final texture and quality of the music, therefore, is the contribution of the arranger and orchestrator.

The overture to a musical comedy is also frequently put together by the arranger and orchestrator from the melodic themes of the main score. Therefore, it is frequently the last thing to be written, since the rest of the music must be set before the overture can be finished. It may also have to be tailored to fill a specified amount of time.

As a rule, more music is written for a show than is actually used. A production may need to be shortened, a song may be discarded and another substituted, or music may be added where none was originally

A setting for Pascal Colasse's opera *Les Noces de Thétis et Pelée* in 1689. From *L'Ancienne France: Le Théâtre . . . et Musique. . . .* Paris, 1887

Ford's Garden, Act I, scene 2, from Giuseppe Verdi's *Falstaff*. The Metropolitan Opera, New York, 1964. Book by Arrigo Boïto after Shakespeare's *Henry IV* and *The Merry Wives of Windsor*. Production designed and staged by Franco Zeffirelli. Courtesy of the Metropolitan Opera; Louis Mélançon photographer.

envisioned. Like other workers in the theatre, both the composer and the arranger must be available for making changes and alterations up to the opening night. Ordinarily the composer is consulted about the casting of the singing roles, and he must be available to work with the singing chorus and actors during rehearsals (though he is not in charge of these rehearsals).

THE CONDUCTOR

The conductor is responsible for the actual performance of the musical score. To assure its adequate presentation he must assume a number of responsibilities prior to the actual opening of the production.

First, he usually makes the final selection of the members of the singing chorus. Although preliminary tryouts may have eliminated many persons before he is brought in, and although his selections have to be approved by the director and producer, the conductor or musical director is asked to hear and approve each chorus member before he is employed for the show. The conductor must also assemble an orchestra for the production; an orchestra manager usually handles contractual details and insures that the music has been copied and that parts are available to all musicians.

Next, the conductor is in charge of all musical rehearsals and he must familiarize everyone—stars, chorus, and instrumentalists—with the music. These rehearsals are usually separate from those held for the dramatic portions of the script until late in the rehearsal schedule.

A number of difficulties may arise when the music and drama are put together, since the transitions may not be smooth. Furthermore, other difficulties arise when the entire orchestra is substituted for the single piano, which is, typically, the only accompaniment used in earlier rehearsals. The singers, for example, may have trouble hearing the melodies at this time. It is wise, therefore, to devote as many rehearsals as possible to integrating all of the elements of a musical comedy.

The conductor must work closely with the composer and the orchestrator. They must all agree upon the tempos and the interpretations of the music, and the conductor should feel free to make suggestions about orchestrations and all other musical matters.

The conductor, unlike other supervisory personnel in the theatre, is visible during all performances since he must conduct the musical portions. He cues in the singers and the orchestra, establishes the tempos, and keeps the musical interpretations as close as possible to those agreed upon during rehearsals.

In carrying out his duties, the conductor generally has an assistant who aids him in many ways. This assistant is usually a member of the orchestra, and may be the pianist at rehearsals (although this particular pianist is often hired for rehearsals only). He may be asked to assume any of the conductor's responsibilities.

The conductor is employed by the producer, although he must be entirely acceptable to the composer and the director of the show. He must be a member of the American Federation of Musicians.

Outside the professional theatre, the conductor's job may be divided into two—that of the musical director and that of the conductor. The musical director may help in casting the show and may supervise the musical rehearsals, while the conductor takes over beginning with dress rehearsals.

THE ORCHESTRA MEMBERS

In the professional theatre, orchestra members are secured through a musical contractor, or orchestra manager, who receives suggestions from the conductor. All must be members of the American Federation of Musicians.

Musicians in orchestras are assumed to be accomplished sight-readers of music and therefore rehearsals may not be held until a comparatively short time before the dress rehearsal. When a company travels, only a few key musicians go along and the rest must be hired locally. This means that the conductor and performers work essentially with a new orchestra at each place.

In the nonprofessional theatre more orchestra rehearsal time may be available and musicians are often not union members. Nevertheless, the orchestra is perhaps the least-rehearsed part of any musical production.

THE SINGERS

The principal (the nonchorus) roles in a musical may be cast in a number of ways. At times the musical requirements are such that only a person with a well-trained voice can cope with them; at others, the singing demands are slight. Sometimes a musical is written with the particular abilities of a star in mind and the music is tailored to fit his capabilities. The producer, the composer, and the director, however, assess the various requisites and agree upon the casting of the singers. Outside the professional theatre, or where the composer is not involved in the production, the director and the musical director must agree upon the choice of singers.

THE CHORUS

The members of the chorus in musical comedy are divided into singer-dancers and dancer-singers, all-singing choruses and all-dancing choruses. Those in the first category are employed because of their singing ability (with lesser skill in dancing), while the second group is hired with the reverse requirements in mind. Here, only the singer-dancer will be considered.

The employment of the chorus in the professional theatre is controlled under Actors Equity contracts similar to those used for dramatic actors. The standard contract may be altered after rehearsals begin and bit parts are assigned. Various chorus members (both singers and dancers) may be tried out in small singing or speaking roles until those most suitable are found. Chorus members may also be asked to serve as understudies. Any additional responsibilities must be reflected in higher salaries.

Chorus members work with the conductor for the musical portions and with the stage director for the dramatic portions. Dancers, of course, must work with the choreographer. Eventually all parts are combined and the orchestra added. Since so much of the quality of a musical depends upon the chorus, it should be selected and rehearsed with care.

DANCE

Dance has played a role in theatrical entertainment since earliest times. It was an integral part of Greek drama, but in later periods frequently became relegated to the minor dramatic forms or was used as incidental entertainment between the acts of plays. It has never been absent from the theatre, however, and has developed into such art forms as ballet and modern dance.

Although dance has been an important part of musical comedy from the beginning of the form, it was not until recent years that the position of dance changed from that of a mere embellishment to an integral part of the action. At the same time the demands on dancers and choreographers underwent a corresponding change, resulting in better training and a more imaginative use of dance forms.

THE TYPES AND USES OF THEATRICAL DANCE

Dance in the theatre is of two basic types: incidental and dramatic. Incidental dances are not an integral part of the dramatic action; they include ballets inserted into operas, and folk dances or "specialty" numbers which may be used to enliven a play or to set a mood but have no bearing on the progress of the action. Dances are also used at times as between-act entertainment. Incidental dance serves principally as a diversion. It may be extended, shortened, or omitted as desired since it is not essential to the play's development.

Dramatic dance, on the other hand, forwards the story, reveals character, or establishes mood and style. It cannot be left out without seriously damaging the effectiveness of the action. It includes certain ballets, modern dance compositions, and the danced portions of present-day musical comedy.

Theatrical dance serves a number of purposes. First, it always functions as spectacle and as entertainment with its own inherent interest. It adds movement and color which increase the audience's pleasure.

Next, dance helps to establish the proper mood. It may be carefree and comic, or it may be restrained and serious. The possible variations in dance are almost infinite and consequently it is possible to create sequences which generate those qualities of mood and atmosphere appropriate to the dramatic context.

Dance may aid in characterization. The kind of movement (angular, free, awkward, graceful) may reveal essential aspects of personality such as repressed desires or unstated feelings; it can make explicit many of the qualities only hinted at in the dialogue.

Dance can be used for its storytelling powers. Since the criterion of realism is seldom applied to dance, it can be used to suggest a great deal that would have to be enacted or discussed at length in a drama without music or dance. In this way, dance may serve as a device for condensing or elaborating upon situations or moods. For example, a young girl may have just discovered that she is in love; a dance may expand upon the emotion more effectively than spoken words.

A ballet in a London theatre in 1791. From Gaston Vuillier's *A History of Dancing*. London, 1898.

Dance may be used to make entertaining what might otherwise become a dull situation. For example, a reception or a presentation scene may form a danced sequence which accomplishes the dramatic purpose while achieving its own peculiar charm.

Dance is an important stylistic device, since it helps to establish the level of reality being presented, which is always more abstract and stylized than everyday experience. Dance, thus, aids the audience to accept departures from realism. On the other hand, it may be introduced into realistic or naturalistic dramas, but in such cases its presence must be motivated carefully.

Through a combination of other functions, dance may help also to establish the themes and ideas of a drama. By providing the proper mood, by characterizing, by condensing action or elaborating upon emotions, it gives emphasis to those themes which define a drama's ultimate meanings.

THE ELEMENTS OF DANCE

The choreographer works with three basic elements: space, time, and intensity. Dance, as a visual medium, must be conceived in terms of line, shapes, and spatial relationships. The lines formed by the movement of the individual dancers serve to define the shape of the dance and to mark out the total space involved.

While most dances combine straight and curved lines, it is possible to create a dance which utilizes one or the other almost exclusively. Lines may also be dominantly horizontal or vertical, depending upon the physical relationship of the dancers on the stage floor. Furthermore, a dance may be confined to a small area or may utilize the entire stage. All of the visual factors are affected by the number of dancers used. A single dancer creates something analogous to a line drawing, while a group of dancers may be thought of in terms of areas of color or masses of shapes. An analogy may also be made to music by relating the work of a principal or solo dancer to melody and the chorus of dancers to harmony. The choreographer must manipulate line, shape, and space in terms of each individual dancer and of the entire group. From the interaction he creates the visual patterns of dance. Space in dance is used dynamically, however, for the visual patterns are constantly being altered by movement in time.

Three factors are involved in time: rhythm, tempo, and the total time consumed by the performance of the dance. Regularly recurring pulses, or beats, combine to create rhythm. Beats are organized into measures, or into larger units composed of many measures. Dances are normally composed (and learned) in terms of these rhythmical units.

Tempo refers to the speed at which the pulses or beats are repeated. It may be fast or slow, and may change often. A lengthy dance may require greater complexity in the handling of rhythms, tempos, and spatial patterns than a short one, and may allow the development of more complex emotional states and ideas. Time factors, however, are flexible and allow many combinations for achieving desired results.

Intensity is a quality of dance. It results from the bodily attitudes, gestures, steps, and movements of each individual dancer and of the group as a whole. It is created by the tensions and relaxations of the dancers' bodies and may be described by such adjectives as restless, concentrated, free, restrained, and tense. The same basic spatial and time patterns may be infused with widely varying qualities through differing treatments of intensity.

The elements of dance—space, time, and intensity—must be organized according to the principles of design: unity, variety, proportion, balance, and emphasis. Since these have already been discussed extensively in Chapters 18–20, they will not be reviewed here. It is sufficient to say that the principles of design serve to weld the elements of dance into clearly defined relationships and esthetically pleasing patterns.

THE DANCER'S TRAINING

It is usually taken for granted that a dancer has, or will acquire, certain skills and knowledge. First, his body must be supple and disciplined to allow him to perform any physical action with predetermined control. His body is his primary means of expression and its complete mastery comes only with years of constant training.

Igor Stravinsky's *Movement for Piano and Orchestra*. A production of the New York City Ballet; choreography by George Balanchine. Stars—Suzanne Farrell and Jacques d'Amboise. Photograph—Martha Swope.

Second, the dancer should know as many different dance forms as possible. No one should need to explain to a trained dancer the distinctions among, for example, a waltz, a tango, or a minuet. In rehearsals many instructions are given with the assumption that the performer knows the standard dance forms and the steps which compose each.

Third, a dancer must know the basic ballet positions and movements. These have become standardized sufficiently to serve as a kind of shorthand for giving directions in rehearsals. For example, there are five basic foot positions, which are designated merely as "first position," "second position," and so on. In addition, there are accepted types of jumps, turns, lifts, and other movements.

If dancers have well-trained bodies and are familiar with basic dance forms and techniques, much time can be saved in rehearsals. For this reason, an effort is usually made to discover those dancers whose training will allow the most efficient use of rehearsal time and the greatest potentialities for successful performance.

THE CHOREOGRAPHER

The choreographer is a designer, or creator, of dances; his work, therefore, is analogous to that of the playwright or the composer. His working methods are such, however, that he must also fulfill functions similar to those of the play director or the musical conductor, for, since he has no universally accepted system of setting down his ideas, he must teach them to the dancers as quickly as possible. Creation and execution, thus, cannot be as clearly separated in dance as they can be in the other performing arts.

A choreographer may compose ballets, modern-dance pieces, incidental or dramatic dances for musical comedy or other theatrical forms. Here, however, only his work with musical comedy will be considered.

Like the other theatre artists, the choreographer must understand the script as a whole, its style, mood, characterizations, its patterns of development, and the director's interpretation. He must seek, then, to express this understanding through dance.

Before the choreographer begins work, there should be one or more conferences with the dramatist, composer, lyricist, director, producer, and the stage designers. Agreement should be reached about the points in the script where dance is to be used, the length of each dance, the basic qualities to be sought, and the number of dancers to be employed in each. The choreographer must also know how much stage space is available for each dance, what parts of each setting may be used, what costumes will be worn, and how these may affect movement. He should feel free to criticize those elements which affect his work and should seek changes when they might lead to adverse results. After he has clarified the conditions under which he must work, the choreographer is ready to begin the composition of the dances.

The choreographer for a Broadway musical may work directly with a composer or, as is becoming an increasingly more prevalent custom, design the dances apart from the music which eventually accompanies them. In this case he may employ a pianist to play a specified rhythm and tempo, but does not try to fit his dances to existing music. Instead, the music is then composed around the dances as they evolve.

The choreographer experiments with spatial relationships, rhythms, tempos, and intensities until he evolves the steps, postures, gestures, and patterns which compose the dances. Because rehearsal time must be used efficiently, he normally has the dances clearly in mind before he begins work with the chorus. Typically, he evolves the choreography by using his own body. He may work alone, or he may use an assistant choreographer or even a small group of dancers who can respond quickly and easily to directions and thus help him construct a highly complex dance.

Although Agnes de Mille and others have devised their own notational systems for recording movement, many choreographers must remember their dances until they can be taught to the performers. It is important, therefore, that the time be as short as possible between the conception of the dance and its execution.

In addition to creating the dances, the choreographer must also select and rehearse the chorus and any other members of the cast who dance. He must attend those rehearsals in which the choreography is integrated with the spoken and sung portions, and he may need to make alterations at that time to smooth out transitions or to eliminate problems not previously encountered. Adjustments may also have to be made because of the differing sizes of stages when a company is on tour. Furthermore, it is not uncommon for entire dance numbers to be eliminated and new ones substituted while a musical is on its out-of-town tryout tour.

When the show opens on Broadway the choreographer's job is finished. A dance captain, who is a member of the chorus, is selected and it becomes his responsibility to see that the dances remain as staged. He may hold rehearsals if he deems it necessary for returning the choreography or individual performances to the original conception. For this work, he receives additional pay.

In New York, choreographers have recently joined with the stage directors to form their own union, the Society of Stage Directors and Choreographers, and the status of the choreographer should be considerably strengthened by this organization. Previously there were no standard fees or working conditions for the choreographer and he was forced to accept whatever terms he could negotiate with the producer. Now, provisions for standard minimum fees and working conditions are governed by the union contract. This contract also specifies his billing and his duties.

Most choreographers receive their first professional training by working as members of dance troupes. Summer stock companies or off-Broadway productions often provide opportunities for breaking into the theatre as a choreographer.

In the nonprofessional theatre, the choreographer is most often a local dance teacher. Frequently there is little choice since the number of qualified persons is extremely small, and in many cases neither choreographer nor dancers are highly skilled. Under such conditions the dances must be composed with the limitations of these dancers in mind and the choreography should be such that the dances can be carried out by the available dancers in the allotted rehearsal time. It is seldom possible in the nonprofessional theatre to duplicate (even if this were desirable) the dances used in the New York production of a musical comedy.

THE DANCERS

Of all tryouts in New York, those for dancers are most often openly announced. Casting notices are printed in theatrical papers and posted at dance schools and studios.

Many dancers are never allowed to demonstrate their capabilities at auditions, however, for a large number are eliminated on the basis of physical appearance. This weeding out process may be conducted by an assistant who has been instructed by the choreographer and director as to the qualities they are seeking.

Those applicants who remain may be asked to carry out directions or to repeat dance steps and movements which are demonstrated to them. The instructions may become increasingly complex so that the choreographer can determine the extent of the dancers' training.

Applicants are eliminated until a reasonably small number (though greater than that needed for the show) remains. Then comes the process of pairing dancers and of assessing the relative merits of each. Finally the exact number of dancers needed for the production is selected. Although

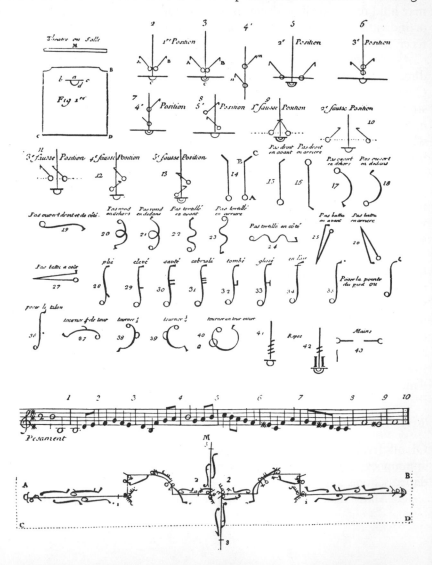

Opposite page. An eighteenth-century attempt to devise a system for recording dance steps. At the bottom of the illustration the steps are recorded in relation to a musical score. From *L'Ancienne France: . . .* Paris, 1887. *Above.* A nineteenth-century attempt to set down dance figures. From G. Moynet's *La Machinerie Théâtrale.* 1893.

the choreographer must approve all dancers, the director, producer, and authors may also be consulted. Dancers in the professional theatre are employed under Actors' Equity contracts which specify rehearsal conditions and salary.

The majority of rehearsal time is spent on dance, since the choreography must be learned entirely by rote through continuous repetition. It is taught to the dancers in sections and in terms of beats (or counts) to aid memory. A lesser amount of time is devoted to dramatic and musical rehearsals. Dancers may be cast in small speaking roles and may also serve as understudies.

In the nonprofessional theatre, it is usually necessary to use those untrained or minimally trained persons who volunteer their services. Frequently the choreographer must teach the dancers the most elementary steps. Under these circumstances, dance patterns must be kept simple, although vigor and interest may still be maintained within a limited range of movement. Good results are usually possible if the choreographer is willing to accept the limitations of his dancers and to capitalize upon their capabilities.

In their own right, music and dance are complex arts. When they are used in the theatre, they make production even more difficult than it normally is, for, like the other theatre arts, they must be conceived and rehearsed with care and must be integrated skillfully with the other elements of production. Their presence in theatre is amply justified, however, by their ability to heighten and project dramatic values and to bring added pleasure to audiences.

Chapter 22

THE THEATRE AS A PROFESSION

The American theatre today is a mixture of professional and non-professional workers, of professional and nonprofessional organizations. Such a situation is not unusual in the history of the theatre, however. For example, the Greek theatre of the fifth century B.C., one of the greatest of all theatres, was largely nonprofessional. In its organization and operation it was probably more closely related to the community theatre than to the professional theatre of our day. In the modern era, nonprofessional organizations rose to fill the gap left when the professional theatre began to decline outside New York. Today there are more theatrical producing groups in America than at any time in its history, although by far the majority of them are nonprofessional. The professional theatre continues to be small by comparison, and it is able to offer employment to relatively few persons. Nevertheless, the theatre remains a glamorous profession and numerous persons are continually searching for ways to find a foothold in it.

TRAINING FOR THE THEATRE

There is considerable controversy over how the prospective theatre worker should be educated. Some argue that he should receive a liberal education first (with little or no theatre training) and that this should be followed

A community theatre production of *Dark of the Moon* at the Theatre of Western Springs, Illinois. Mary Cattell, director. Theatre designed by James Hull Miller. This illustration shows the audience-stage relationship in an open-stage theatre.

by concentrated work in the theatre arts; others believe that professional training should be given from the very beginning and that little attention need be paid to a general education; still others state that liberal arts courses and theatre training should be mixed throughout the student's education. These ideas are embodied in two basic training grounds for the theatre: colleges and universities, and professional schools.

Although more and more colleges and universities have established programs which give some training in the theatre arts, many of them still do not include "performance courses" in the undergraduate curriculum. These schools normally offer work in dramatic literature and theatre history, and they give a sound liberal education, but they insist that theatrical training should be left to professional or graduate schools.

Other colleges and universities have taken the position that a liberal education can be combined effectively with theatre training. Consequently, playwriting, acting, directing, scenic, costume, and lighting design, technical production, music, and dance are all now regularly taught in these schools. The student, of course, is still required to take a course of study sufficient to provide a sound liberal education. Within a four-year program approximately one-fourth to one-third of the course work may be devoted to the theatre arts. If there is a graduate program, an additional one to three years of training may be available.

A professional school normally allows students to devote all or most of their time to theatre training. Some of these schools do not have a program of study leading to a certificate or degree. Rather, a student may enroll in any class he desires for as long as he wishes. Thus, he may study acting exclusively for a number of years. Others give certificates for the satisfactory completion of a prescribed program, and still others give academic degrees (usually the BFA or MFA). The length of a course of study varies from one to four years in the last two categories and includes such traditional subjects as history of the theatre, dramatic literature and kindred studies. If the school offers both undergraduate and graduate training, an additional one or two years of study may be possible.

Another subsidiary type of training—the apprenticeship—is available to limited numbers. In-service apprenticeships are most commonly offered by summer stock companies. As a rule, formal class work is minimal and experience is the principal source of learning. A few permanent companies have established longer apprenticeships, but these are still rare. In most cases, then, in-service training is available for periods of about three months out of each year. Consequently, this is a supplementary rather than a primary means of preparation.

Each of these approaches has its strengths and weaknesses. Most persons will concede that a broad liberal education is of value no matter what the student's future goals, and that a liberal education has special relevance to theatre and drama, which are ultimately concerned with all aspects of man's experience. The more the theatre artist understands about mankind, the more experiences he will be able to enter into imaginatively and project to others. A liberal education serves to broaden horizons, break down prejudices, and build inquiring and open minds.

On the other hand, the time spent in acquiring a liberal education cannot be devoted to developing professional skills. Some persons argue that the theatre arts must be studied and practiced constantly over long periods of time if they are to be perfected. Consequently, it is said that adequate professional training leaves too little time for obtaining a full academic education. Some believe that a truly professional artist is single minded in his concern for his work and that he has neither the interest nor the time for anything else.

The goals in any kind of theatre training may vary widely. The student may have no intention of pursuing the theatre (except as an avocation) after he completes his education, while others may be training to enter either the educational, the community, or the professional theatre.

THE THEATRE AS AN AVOCATION

The majority of students who receive theatrical training in colleges do not pursue the theatre as a profession after graduation. To most, courses in theatre and drama serve as one means for acquiring a liberal education of the same basic type as that received by students of English, philosophy, or history. Few persons expect that a major in one of the last-named subjects will lead to a profession as a literary critic, a philosopher, or a historian. In like manner, a major in theatre is sufficiently justified apart from any specific professional goals or focus on practical considerations.

Most of the students who major in theatre retain their theatre-going interest and may participate actively in nonprofessional productions. The opportunities for working in the theatre as an avocation are almost limitless, since the majority of theatrical organizations in the country rely upon unpaid personnel. The demand for actors is great, and almost anyone with an interest in scenery, costumes, lighting, properties, make-up, sound effects, dance, or music can find ample outlet for expression.

EDUCATIONAL THEATRE

Probably the largest number of opportunities for paying jobs in the theatre are to be found in connection with education. As a rule, theatre workers are employed in such situations for two purposes: to teach and to produce plays. Occasionally, schools employ persons who do only one of these, but the typical situation is one in which the working hours are divided between these two functions. A staff member may be allowed to specialize in one type of activity, such as directing or costuming, but to be assured of employment in the educational theatre he should be prepared to undertake almost any kind of assignment.

In most cases the person who decides to enter the educational theatre should have a sincere interest in teaching and should be willing to spend a large part of his energies in preparing and carrying out demonstrations, projects, and classroom lectures. The training for working successfully in the educational theatre must be broader in scope than that for other types of theatre organization. A good educational theatre usually attempts to educate students about the history of the theatre and the range of dramatic literature. As part of this education, plays representative of almost all periods and styles are produced. Personnel for the educational theatre, therefore, need to be familiar with production styles and techniques other than those of the contemporary theatre. Since they will be working almost exclusively with nonprofessionals who have had little or no training, they should also be able and willing to explain anything from the most elementary to the most complicated idea or practice. They must always keep in mind that they have the simultaneous responsibilities of educating students and of producing exciting performances.

Achievements must be viewed differently in the educational than in the professional theatre. While the aim should always be to give the best possible performance, in the educational theatre accomplishments must be measured in terms of the students' development, the problems mastered, and the handicaps overcome. High standards should be set, but it is unrealistic to expect that learners will be able consistently to accomplish as much as seasoned professionals.

The educational theatre may be divided in terms of levels: children's theatre, secondary school theatre, college and university undergraduate training, and graduate training. Each has its own peculiar opportunities and requirements. Because of its complex nature, children's theatre will be discussed last.

SECONDARY SCHOOL THEATRE

Almost every high school in the United States has some kind of theatre production program. Because there are so many, secondary schools present a major opportunity to those interested in the educational theatre. Relatively few high schools, however, offer courses in theatre and drama. On the contrary, the production of plays is frequently assigned to persons who have had no theatre training whatever. As a result the quality of production is often abysmally low. School administrators too often look upon the production of plays as simply a means of working off the excess energy of adolescents, or as a way of raising money for the band or some other activity quite unrelated to the theatre program. Until such attitudes change, there is little chance of raising standards.

On the other hand, there is an increasing number of secondary schools which have excellent theatre programs and large staffs. Many have outstanding facilities and teach a series of courses in theatre production, dramatic literature, and theatre history. Such schools are still atypical, however, and much remains to be done. Consequently, vast opportunities are open to qualified and energetic persons.

To work in the secondary school theatre, the teacher must bring an understanding of the adolescent and an ability to work with him, and must, as a rule, be certified to teach subjects other than theatre—such as speech and English, although any other subject may be acceptable. The secondary school is an important and open field, and one that must be cultivated if the majority of persons are to be reached, for most still receive no additional education. It is not an easy avenue to theatre work but it is a rewarding one.

UNDERGRADUATE THEATRE
IN COLLEGES AND UNIVERSITIES

More and more colleges and universities are offering courses in theatre for the undergraduate student. In most cases, the educational institution tries to hire properly qualified teachers, and the theatre at this level is generally in a more secure position than in the secondary school.

The varying approaches to theatre training on the college level have already been outlined, and the worker seeking employment in a college or university should investigate the goals of its specific theatre program before accepting a job. In most cases, theatre courses are considered as part of the liberal arts curriculum, while the production program is classified as extracurricular.

Typically, the students fall within the ages of eighteen to twenty-five, have had little experience, and few, if any, will enter the theatre as a profession. The teacher, therefore, must be prepared to compensate for the youth and inexperience of his students, and must not expect to have his classes or productions filled only with persons whose sole interests lie in the theatre. Most students view the theatre as recreation. The teacher, nevertheless, should hold up high standards and endeavor to establish a knowledgeable taste in future theatre audiences.

The worker in the undergraduate program may have a chance to specialize—for example, in directing or design—but most often he must be able to teach and to supervise all areas of theatrical production. He needs a broad background, therefore.

Working in college theatre has many rewards, but they are not necessarily those that come to the teacher in the professional school or to the worker in the professional theatre. Anyone who becomes a teacher in either college or university should be prepared to give both education and theatrical production their due; he should not look upon his job as "second best" to working in the professional theatre.

THE GRADUATE SCHOOL

The graduate school exists to give specialized training. Many of the institutions which offer undergraduate work also maintain graduate programs, but a few schools offer graduate work only.

Students in a graduate school are older and more mature than undergraduates, and they are securing further education as a rule because they expect to pursue some aspect of the theatre as a livelihood. Most of the course work they take is related to the theatre or drama. The teacher in this kind of situation, therefore, can expect a higher caliber of student, and can demand more devotion to the theatre and higher standards in production.

Those who obtain graduate degrees normally go into teaching or into community or children's theatre; a lesser percentage enter the professional theatre.

The nature of graduate education demands a staff of experienced specialists. Consequently, employment in this kind of situation is usually available only to persons who have demonstrated considerable ability in specific aspects of the theatre. In many ways this kind of job is one of the most crucial for the future of the theatre: since most theatre workers now receive their basic training in colleges and universities and since the graduate schools supply most of the teachers, the responsibility of the graduate school cannot be overestimated.

CHILDREN'S THEATRE

Children's theatre may operate in any framework: professional, community, or educational. Its distinguishing characteristic is its intended audience. Most theatre of the past has been directed at the adult audience; it is only in the twentieth century, and principally since World War II, that a theatre program has been developed to meet the needs of children. Today the children's theatre is a vigorous institution with promise of still further development. As it grows, so will the demand for qualified workers.

There are two principal kinds of children's theatre productions: those in which children perform for other children, and those in which adults perform for children. In either case the intended audience is the same, but the first type extends the benefits of theatrical performance to the children in the cast as well as to those in the audience.

A related activity is creative dramatics. Technically, this is not a theatrical activity. Rather, children are stimulated to improvise dramas out of stories, historical events, material taken from social studies, or from any other aspect of their lives or schoolwork. Each child is urged to express himself as fully as possible while keeping in mind the basic situation or story. The lines of the resulting drama are improvised, and theatrical aids, such as scenery and costumes, are not used. The aim of creative dramatics is the development of the child's understanding and imagination.

Children's theatre and creative dramatics are usually graded (or divided into levels) since the same experience will not appeal to children of widely varying ages. The plays and approaches, therefore, may vary somewhat with the age level of the intended audience or of the participants.

While children's theatre and creative dramatics are frequently coordinated with the elementary school curriculum, seldom is theatre work as such taught in elementary schools. Productions of children's plays are made available to school children in a variety of ways. The recreation program in most large cities usually makes some provision for children's theatre and creative drama; many community theatres produce a number of plays for children each year; the Junior Leagues of America do much in this field; and a large number of colleges and universities present one or more plays each season for child audiences.

It should be clear, therefore, that there is a fairly large demand for persons with some training in children's theatre and creative dramatics. Some colleges and universities have specialists in these areas on their staffs; school districts may hire a person who can demonstrate and supervise creative dramatics; some community theatres now employ a director whose sole responsibility is the production of children's plays; and public recreation programs often employ a specialist in this area. In addition, there are a number of professional troupes which perform only for child audiences.

The worker in children's theatre needs all of the basic training in theatrical production that any other worker should have. In addition, however, he should receive some specialized education in child psychology and in the techniques peculiar to this form of theatre and drama. The children's theatre carries a strong responsibility since it is in a position to mold future audiences, to generate a love for the theatre, and to instill an appreciation of art in general.

THE COMMUNITY THEATRE

The community theatre is a product of the twentieth century. It originated between 1910 and 1920 in response to a demand created by the disappearance of the resident stock company and the decline of traveling road productions. Today, almost every town with a population of more than 30,000 has a community theatre of some kind. In the total number of producing organizations, the community theatre is surpassed only by the educational theatre.

Many community theatres are operated entirely by volunteers, since they cannot afford to hire workers. Others are able to pay the director of each play a nominal fee and may also provide a small sum for the designer and certain other key workers. Typically, however, a community theatre employs a full-time director who supervises all of the productions. The more prosperous groups also have a full-time designer-technician, and some hire a children's-theatre director as well. A few employ more than one director and may have a number of part-time employees.

The purpose of the community theatre, however, makes it undesirable to hire persons other than in supervisory capacities. The primary function of community theatre, in addition to providing theatrical entertainment for local audiences, is to furnish an outlet for the artistic talents of its volunteer workers. While these persons need supervision and expert direction, as much initiative as possible is left to them.

Anyone who seeks employment in the community theatre, therefore, needs to be a leader. He should be diplomatic and capable of gaining the cooperation of diverse personalities. He should know a great deal about public relations and should have clearly formulated ideas about the role of the theatre in a community.

The typical volunteer in the community theatre holds a full-time job. Consequently, for him the theatre is an avocation to which he can devote only a few hours during the evening. The director and designer-technician must be willing to accept these limitations if they are to be successful. And the drawbacks are partially offset by the greater maturity of many of the volunteers, when compared to those in the educational theatre.

The typical season of plays in a community theatre is composed of recent Broadway successes. Even one classic each year is unusual for most organizations. The director, therefore, needs ample training in current theatre practice. On the other hand, the director should be able to change the traditional season's bill if he desires by gradually introducing plays other than recent hits and by demonstrating that his choices make rewarding evenings in the theatre.

Like all jobs, those of community theatre director and designer-technician have their disadvantages, but they provide the would-be professional with some of the best opportunities for fulltime employment.

STOCK COMPANIES

In recent years, the number of summer theatres has increased many times over. The majority are still found in the northeastern states, but the movement has spread throughout the country.

The summer stock company usually operates from late June until Labor Day, presenting a different play each week. During the run of a show, one or more additional scripts are being rehearsed. Under such circumstances there is little time for developing subtleties or for polishing characterizations. Rather, the intensive production schedule develops techniques for working rapidly, for covering up the shortcomings of inadequate preparation, and for quick thinking in onstage and backstage emergencies. These skills, plus the experience of performing a number of plays before a variety of audiences, and often with frequently changing casts, are the chief virtues of summer stock experience. On the other hand, shallowness and stage tricks may be substituted for sound study and care for details. Summer stock companies, under the usual circumstances which prevail today, are valuable as supplementary experience but can seldom fill all of the needs of the serious theatre worker.

There are many kinds of summer stock companies. Some are entirely professional and hire only professional actors, designers, and directors. Others employ varying percentages of professional personnel, while the rest are nonprofessional. Actors' Equity classifies companies according to the number of professional actors which must be employed, the minimum salaries which must be paid, and the working conditions. Companies employing professional actors may hire designers and directors who are not union members, however. Many companies pay all of their personnel even when none is a member of a union.

A number of stock companies not connected with educational institutions have apprenticeship programs. This means that a few relatively inexperienced persons are taken into the company to "learn while doing." Apprentices may receive room and board and even a small weekly salary; seldom is the remuneration more than that required for living expenses. Some organizations ask apprentices to pay a fee comparable to college tuition. This practice is generally frowned upon, however, and anyone interested in becoming an apprentice should be skeptical of a group which demands pay. The apprentice will put in long hours of hard labor, from which he will learn much, but he should not be expected to pay for working.

Summer stock has also been employed increasingly by educational institutions as a supplement to the training offered during the regular school year. Many schools operate such programs on campus, while others have theatres in resort areas far removed from the campus. College credit can be earned for the work done in most of these companies connected with colleges and universities. A large number of such groups offer either scholarships or a percentage of the season's profits as a means of paying the participants.

Typically, a summer theatre plays a season of recent Broadway hits. Those groups affiliated with educational institutions often mix older plays with recent successes. Some companies are devoted entirely to musicals, others perform only plays, while others do both. On occasions a new script is tried out.

There are a number of variations on summer stock. Some companies perform a single work for the entire summer. Notable are those groups in North Carolina, Kentucky, and Virginia that produce dramatizations of local history. The experience gained is roughly comparable to being in a long-run show in New York. Two stock companies operate "winter stock" in Florida.

Other groups have turned to repertory. This means that a number of plays are readied before the season begins and that the plays are then performed in rotation throughout the summer. While the scripts chosen may be of widely varying types and drawn from many periods, a number of organizations specialize in the plays of a single author, particularly those of Shakespeare.

The personnel for summer stock companies is usually interviewed and hired between January and May, and early application is advisable. Except in the completely professional company, workers are quite frequently expected to double in other capacities. Actors may be asked to help out with scenery, costumes, or lighting; technicians may assume small acting roles.

Since summer stock is seasonal its personnel is drawn from many sources: Broadway and off-Broadway, radio, television, motion pictures, semiprofessional groups, community, or educational theatres. Summer stock, therefore, supplements all of the other types of theatre and the amount and kind of available employment depends largely upon the orientation of the particular group. Because it is seasonal, however, it does little to relieve the chronic unemployment problem of the professional theatre or to eliminate the concentration of the professional theatre in New York. It is a temporary arrangement whereby the theatre goes to the resorts for a few weeks but without settling down there.

PROFESSIONAL COMPANIES OUTSIDE OF NEW YORK

Many plans have been proposed for decentralizing the American professional theatre, but little has been accomplished up to this time. Some promising beginnings have been made, chiefly through the financial support of such organizations as the Ford Foundation, toward enabling a number of groups outside of New York to make the transition from nonprofessional to professional status. Information about these theatres can be obtained from the Theatre Communications Group of the Ford Foundation in New York.

Most of these theatres are interested in auditioning outstanding performers from colleges and universities and they arrange interviews and tryouts at regular intervals. The young person aspiring to work in the professional theatre often would do well to apply to these companies rather than go to New York.

Most of the professional theatre groups outside of New York are permanent organizations which produce a season of plays each year. They do not try for long runs but rather present each play in a series for a limited engagement only. Because they perform a number of plays, they must strive for variety in programing and, consequently, they, like the educational theatres, are inclined to do scripts from a number of periods and representative of varying styles.

Normally, the same staff—designers, directors, business and promotional personnel, and, to a lesser extent, actors—is used throughout the season. Guest directors may be brought in for some plays, and it may be necessary to employ additional actors or to replace those who have left. Most of the organizations, however, seek to achieve that ensemble playing and production quality which is possible only when the same persons work together over a period of time.

Most of the professional theatres outside of New York are still comparatively new and are struggling for recognition and security. They cannot, as a rule, afford to employ well-known actors, designers, or directors, but they offer excellent opportunities to talented persons who are willing to work hard for limited pay. Some also accept apprentices.

It is too early to tell how successful these theatres will be, but they are among the most encouraging signs in the American theatre today. Because of their limited number, however, they cannot provide employment for more than a few hundred persons.

There is other professional theatre activity outside of New York, but most of it is accounted for by touring companies. Since these troupes are cast in New York, the "road" is merely an extension of the Broadway theatre.

THE PROFESSIONAL THEATRE IN NEW YORK

The conditions of employment in the New York theatre have already been reviewed in Chapters 15–21. Little has been said about the small number of jobs now available, however.

The situation may be illustrated by considering the actor's predicament. On March 31, 1963, Actors' Equity had 13,286 members. (This figure does not give a clear idea of the number of aspiring actors in New York, since the signing of an Equity contract is a prerequisite for admittance to the union.) Some figures compiled on the 1961–62 season show that the total number of actors employed in all of the productions which opened on Broadway between June 1, 1961 and May 31, 1962 was approximately 1250. This figure does not include Equity members playing in long-run hits which had opened previously, nor does it include those actors working in off-Broadway productions, road shows, in radio, television, and film, or outside of New York City. Nevertheless, it is safe to say that fewer than half of the members of Actors' Equity are employed at any one time, and occasionally as few as fifteen percent may be working. Approximately twenty-five percent of the membership can fill the normal demands created by productions playing in theatres within New York City.

As for designers, the Broadway productions of the 1961–62 season provided employment for twenty-six scene designers (some of whom did costume and lighting designs as well), twenty-two costume designers, and nine lighting designers. The majority worked on only one show each. Forty-five directors staged all of the plays of the 1961–62 Broadway season. Five directed two productions, and one directed three; none directed more than three.

The bleakness of this picture is relieved somewhat by the off-Broadway theatre, which provides approximately as many jobs now as the Broadway stage, although the pay and the recognition are less. Off-Broadway productions are often housed in inconveniently located buildings, most of which have small seating capacities and poorly equipped stages. Many are theatres-in-the-round or use open stages. Lobby space and other audience conveniences are minimal. Such shortcomings make for low rent and the small income potential has induced the unions to lower their usual demands. As a result, productions can be staged for much less money than on Broadway. The smallness of the theatres also means that these groups do not have to attract a mass audience but can exist on the patronage of smaller audiences.

The off-Broadway theatre is doing much to diversify the New York stage, and it offers many opportunities to lesser-known workers and to those who wish to work in a broader context than the mass-oriented Broadway theatre. The aspiring professional will find, however, that it is almost as difficult to secure employment off Broadway as on, and that the pay in most cases is the minimum permitted by the unions.

The outlook for the professional theatre worker in New York is very discouraging. A few persons make excellent livings and have fairly steady employment. Others work for a few weeks during the year, and still others find it impossible to secure any job in the theatre at all. Nevertheless, this does not prevent thousands of persons from migrating to New York each year. Of these, ninety percent or more fail in their goals. Enough succeed, however, to keep others hopeful.

The ingredients necessary for success in the American professional theatre today are debatable, but these are essential: persistence, luck, talent, skill. A person must be willing to "make the rounds" and to accept rejections day after day without becoming discouraged. Unless he has a continuing faith in himself in spite of constant disappointment, he is unlikely to succeed. There are so many aspiring and talented actors in New York that a certain amount of luck is often involved: being at the right place at just the right moment has started many actors on their careers. No amount of persistence and luck will keep an actor employed, however, if he does not have talent and skill. The rush of a production schedule in New York does not allow a director time to teach actors; he must assume that each already knows his trade. A knowledge of stage technique, an adequate working method, and flexibility in adjusting to a director's idiosyncrasies—all of these are essential to the actor. Designers, of course, will never have a chance to work in a professional status if they cannot pass the increasingly rigid examinations of the union.

Almost everyone does his best to discourage would-be professionals from going to New York. Nothing that anyone can say, however, will keep many from doing so. The true professional ultimately has a single-mindedness which cannot be discouraged by hardship. But no one should consider entering the professional theatre in America today unless he is willing to make many sacrifices and to undergo a great number of painful experiences.

SPECIAL EMPLOYMENT OPPORTUNITIES

In addition to the more obvious opportunities already discussed, a number of related activities should be mentioned. First, television and motion pictures offer additional possibilities to theatre workers. Without them, many professionals would lead a difficult life indeed. But these supplements to the theatre have their own unemployment problems and can do no more than relieve some of the pressures. For example, in 1962 the Screen Actors Guild had approximately 14,000 members. Of these, more than half earned less than $2000 each year, while approximately seventy-five percent earned less than $5000.

Second, a number of industrial and commercial firms stage special shows each year to publicize their products. Frequently such a production is extremely lavish and may tour a number of major cities. These shows normally play for invited audiences only; they pay extremely well, but provide little further recognition. Most are cast in New York and are, in effect, an extension of the Broadway stage.

Third, there is a considerable amount of employment available for stagehands, electricians, and dressers. Most persons trained in colleges and universities spurn such jobs, and perhaps rightly so, but these duties must be performed, and the salaries are substantial.

Fourth, theatre and drama have been adapted to a number of nontheatrical uses. For example, they are being used increasingly as therapy for emotionally disturbed persons. Improvised dramas allow patients to express their hostilities indirectly, and therapists often gain important clues about the causes of mental disorders from watching these dramas. To work in such a field, sound training in psychology as well as in drama and theatre is needed.

When the variety of theatrical activities—both in the nonprofessional and professional theatre—is considered, the number of employment opportunities are considerable. There are by no means as many jobs as there are applicants, especially in the professional theatre, but the situation could be worse. The theatre has never been an easy profession, and it probably never will be. There is always a demand for talented and dedicated persons, however, and the future of the theatre depends upon this select few.

Shakespeare's *Othello*. Directed by Harold Shiffler; setting by Keith Michael; costume by Elizabeth Hall.

POSTSCRIPT

The theatre of today is the inheritor of a tradition which began with the Greeks. Between its origins in primitive society and its present form many and complex changes have taken place, the most important of which have been surveyed in the preceding chapters. From this survey a number of conclusions seems warranted.

First, the theatre is a vital and organic part of society. The forms the theatre takes and the value placed upon it vary as historical and social conditions change. And, of course, the theatre can remain a healthy institution only when it is allowed to change along with these altering social conditions. When it is responsive to its age, the theatre fills a basic need in men's lives, but when it becomes static or too restricted in its scope, it ceases to be of importance in its time.

Second, the theatre is always a reflection of the ideas of its age. Every theatrical style has resulted from the attempt to find means adequate for expressing a view of reality and of man's place in the universe. As man's conceptions about himself and his world change his dramatic expression also changes.

Third, there is always a close relationship between the drama and the theatrical conventions of any age. The dramatist's conception of the theatre and its possibilities dictates in large part what demands his work makes on the theatre. The plays of any given period, therefore, have many common features which stem from use of the same conventions. Consequently, it is important for the understanding of a play to know the theatrical conditions for which it was written.

Fourth, while the historical and social conditions, the ideas, and the theatrical conditions are important determinants of dramatic expression, the individual playwright's vision is the ultimate source of greatness. A study of the Elizabethan period, for example, helps to clarify many of the characteristics of Shakespeare's work, but it does not explain why only one writer of Shakespeare's stature appeared.

Fifth, although every play is clearly a product of its age, the great plays are timeless enough to remain meaningful in later periods. Great drama provides a means by which the present can feel its way into the past, comprehend it, and perceive the continuity of human experience.

Sixth, the theatre and drama are important ways of knowing about man's ideas and feelings. Like history or science or philosophy, the theatre is a form of knowledge, but one which functions through feeling as much as through thought.

Seventh, the theatre should be studied in its total context, the scope of which is suggested by the preceding six points. A combination of the approaches outlined above yields a fuller understanding of the complex art of the theatre.

Eighth, the dramatic impulse is a natural human attribute and, therefore, it cannot be eradicated. The theatre may fluctuate in popularity, and the pleasures which it offers may be fulfilled at times by other activities, but the theatre in one form or another will always be a part of human society.

BIBLIOGRAPHY

This bibliography lists some of the more important works on the theatre, those that are either the most authoritative or the most representative of major points of view. All are in English.

The bibliography is divided into categories which correspond to the divisions in the text. Notes have been introduced occasionally for clarity. Additional works may be discovered easily by consulting the following bibliographical aids:

Baker, Blanch M. *Theatre and Allied Arts*. New York: H. W. Wilson Co., 1952.

Dramatic Index [1909–49]. Boston: F. W. Faxon, Inc., 1910–50. An annual list of books and articles on the theatre published in America and England.

Revue d'Histoire du Théâtre [1948–present]. This quarterly journal lists in each issue current publications on theatre throughout the Western world. English-language publications are given in English.

International Federation of Library Associations. *Performing Arts Collections: An International Handbook*. Paris: Centre National de la Recherche Scientifique, 1960. Guide to theatre collections.

Part One

Chapter 1: THE THEATRE AS AN ART FORM
Beardsley, Monroe. *Aesthetics: Problems in the Philosophy of Criticism*. New York: Harcourt, Brace & World, Inc., 1958.
Bentley, Eric. *What is Theatre? A Query in Chronicle Form*. Boston: Beacon Press, 1956.

A design by Andrea Pozzo. From Pozzo's *Perspectivae Pictorum atque Architectorum*. Augsburg, 1706.

Fergusson, Francis. *The Idea of a Theater*. Princeton, N.J.: Princeton University Press, 1949.

Greene, Theodore M. *The Arts and the Art of Criticism*. Princeton, N.J.: Princeton University Press, 1947.

Langer, Susanne K. *Problems of Art*. New York: Charles Scribner's Sons, 1957.

Munro, Thomas. *The Arts and Their Interrelations*. New York: Liberal Arts Press, 1949.

Rader, Melvin M. (ed.) *A Modern Book of Esthetics: An Anthology*. 3d ed. New York: Holt, Rinehart and Winston, Inc., 1960.

Vivas, Eliseo and Kreiger, Murray (eds.). *The Problems of Aesthetics; A Book of Readings*. New York: Holt, Rinehart, and Winston, Inc., 1953.

Young, Stark. *The Theatre*. New York: Doubleday & Company, Inc., 1927.

Chapter 2: THE AUDIENCE AND THE CRITIC

Boas, George. *A Primer for Critics*. Baltimore: Johns Hopkins Press, 1937.

Crane, R. S. *The Language of Criticism and the Structure of Poetry*. Toronto: University of Toronto Press, 1953.

Daiches, David. *Critical Approaches to Literature*. Englewood Cliffs, N.J.: Prentice-Hall, Inc., 1956.

Hamilton, Clayton. *The Theory of the Theatre and Other Principles of Dramatic Criticism*. New York: Holt, Rinehart and Winston, Inc., 1939.

Hollingworth, H. L. *The Psychology of the Audience*. New York: American Book Company, 1935.

Littlewood, Samuel R. *The Art of Dramatic Criticism*. London: Pitman, 1952.

Pepper, Stephen. *The Basis of Criticism in the Arts*. Cambridge, Mass.: Harvard University Press, 1949.

Chapter 3: DRAMATIC STRUCTURE, FORM, AND STYLE

Archer, William. *Play-Making: A Manual of Craftsmanship*. New York: Dover Publications, Inc., 1960.

Aristotle. *Aristotle's Theory of Poetry and Fine Art*. Critical Text and Translation by S. H. Butcher. 4th ed. New York: Dover Publications, Inc., 1951.

Bergson, Henri. *Laughter: An Essay on the Meaning of the Comic*. Tr. by C. Brereton and F. Rothwell. London: Macmillan & Co., Ltd., 1921.

Brooks, Cleanth and Heilman, R. B. *Understanding Drama*. New York: Holt, Rinehart and Winston, Inc., 1955.

Cook, Albert S. *The Dark Voyage and the Golden Mean; A Philosophy of Comedy*. Cambridge, Mass.: Harvard University Press, 1949.

Grebanier, Bernard. *Playwriting*. New York: Thomas Y. Crowell Company, 1961.

Heffner, Hubert. *The Nature of Drama*. Boston: Houghton Mifflin Company, 1959.

Lawson, John Howard. *Theory and Technique of Playwriting*. New York: Hill and Wang, 1960.

Lucas, F. L. *Tragedy in Relation to Aristotle's "Poetics."* New York: Harcourt, Brace & World, Inc., 1928.

Macgowan, Kenneth. *A Primer of Playwriting*. New York: Random House, Inc., 1951.

Meredith, George. *An Essay on Comedy and the Uses of the Comic Spirit*. New York: Charles Scribner's Sons, 1909.

Myers, Henry A. *Tragedy: A View of Life.* Ithaca: N. Y.: Cornell University Press, 1956.

Nicoll, Allardyce. *The Theory of Drama.* Rev. ed. London: Harrap & Co., Ltd., 1931.

Olson, Elder. *Tragedy and the Theory of Drama.* Detroit: Wayne State University Press, 1961.

Peacock, Ronald. *The Art of the Drama.* London: Routledge & Kegan Paul, Ltd., 1957.

Prior, Moody. *The Language of Tragedy.* New York: Columbia University Press, 1947.

Rowe, Kenneth. *Write That Play.* New York: Funk & Wagnalls Co., Inc., 1939.

Shipley, Joseph T. (ed.) *Dictionary of World Literature: Criticism, Forms, Techniques.* Rev. ed. New York: Philosophical Library, 1953.

Styan, J. L. *The Elements of Drama.* New York: Cambridge University Press, 1960.

Thompson, Alan R. *The Anatomy of Drama.* 2d ed. Berkeley: University of California Press, 1946.

General Works Applicable to Parts Two and Three

Altman, George et al. *Theater Pictorial; A History of World Theater as Recorded in Drawings, Paintings, Engravings, and Photographs.* Berkeley: University of California Press, 1953.

Bowman, Walter P. and Ball, Robert H. *Theatre Language; A Dictionary of Terms in English of the Drama and Stage from Medieval to Modern Times.* New York: Theatre Arts Books, 1961.

Cheney, Sheldon. *The Theatre; Three Thousand Years of Drama, Acting and Stagecraft.* Rev. ed. New York: Longmans, Green, 1952.

Clark, Barrett H. (ed.) *European Theories of the Drama.* Rev. ed. New York: Crown Publishers, Inc., 1947.

Duerr, Edwin. *The Length and Depth of Acting.* New York: Holt, Rinehart and Winston, Inc., 1962.

Freedley, George and Reeves, John A. *A History of the Theatre.* Rev. ed. New York: Crown Publishers, Inc., 1955.

Gassner, John. *Masters of the Drama.* 3d ed. New York: Dover Publications, Inc., 1954.

Hartnoll, Phyllis (ed.). *The Oxford Companion to the Theatre.* 2d ed. London: Oxford University Press, 1957.

Laver, James. *Drama, Its Costume and Decor.* London: Studio Publications, 1951.

Macgowan, Kenneth and Melnitz, William. *The Living Stage.* Englewood Cliffs, N.J.: Prentice-Hall, Inc., 1955.

Nagler, Alois M. *Sources of Theatrical History.* New York: Theatre Annual, Inc., 1952.

Nicoll, Allardyce. *The Development of the Theatre.* 4th ed. London: Harrap & Co., Ltd., 1958.

———. *World Drama from Aeschylus to Anouilh.* London: Harrap & Co., Ltd., 1949.

Southern, Richard. *The Seven Ages of the Theatre.* New York: Hill and Wang, 1961.

Stuart, Donald C. *The Development of Dramatic Art.* New York: Appleton-Century-Crofts, 1928.
Wimsatt, William K. and Brooks, Cleanth. *Literary Criticism; A Short History.* New York: Alfred A. Knopf, Inc., 1957.

Collections of Plays

Adams, Joseph Q. *Chief Pre-Shakespearean Dramas.* Boston: Houghton Mifflin Company, 1924.
Bates, Alfred (ed.). *The Drama; Its History, Literature and Influence on Civilization.* 22 vols. London: The Athenian Society, 1903–04.
Bentley, Eric. *The Classic Theatre.* 4 vols. Garden City, N.Y.: Doubleday & Company, Inc., 1958–61. (Vol. I—Six Italian Plays; Vol. II—Five German Plays; Vol. III—Six Spanish Plays; Vol. IV—Six French Plays.)
———. *From the Modern Repertoire.* Series 1–3. Bloomington: Indiana University Press, 1949–56.
———. *The Modern Theatre.* 6 vols. Garden City, N.Y.: Doubleday & Company, Inc., 1955–60.
Clark, Barrett H. *World Drama . . . An Anthology.* 2 vols. New York: Appleton-Century, 1933.
Dickinson, Thomas H. *Chief Contemporary Dramatists.* Series 1–3. Boston: Houghton Mifflin Company, 1915–30.
Duckworth, George E. *The Complete Roman Drama.* 2 vols. New York: Random House, Inc., 1942.
Gassner, John. *Best American Plays.* Series 1–4, and a supplementary volume. New York: Crown Publishers, 1939–61.
———. *A Treasury of the Theatre.* 2 vols. New York: Holt, Rinehart and Winston, Inc., 1960.
Grene, David and Lattimore, Richmond (eds.). *The Complete Greek Tragedies.* 4 vols. Chicago: University of Chicago Press, 1960.
Macmillan, Dougald and Jones, Howard M. *Plays of the Restoration and Eighteenth Century.* New York: Holt, Rinehart and Winston, Inc., 1954.
Matthews, Brander. *The Chief European Dramatists.* Boston: Houghton Mifflin Company, 1916.
Noyes, George R. *Masterpieces of the Russian Drama.* 2 vols. New York: Dover Publications, Inc., 1960.
Oates, Whitney J. and O'Neill, Eugene, Jr. *Complete Greek Drama.* 2 vols. New York: Random House, Inc., 1938.
Ottemiller, John H. *Index to Plays in Collections.* 3d ed. New York: Scarecrow Press, 1957.
Parks, Edd W. and Beatty, R. C. *The English Drama; An Anthology of Plays, 900–1642.* New York: W. W. Norton & Company, Inc., 1935.
Quinn, Arthur H. *Representative American Plays, from 1767 to the Present Day.* 7th ed. New York: Appleton-Century-Crofts, 1957.
Rowell, George. *Nineteenth Century Plays.* New York: Oxford University Press, 1953.
Stanton, Stephen. *Camille and Other Plays.* New York: Hill and Wang, 1957.
Tucker, S. M. and Downer, A. S. *Twenty-Five Modern Plays.* 3d ed. New York: Harper & Row, Publishers, 1953.
Ulanov, Barry. *Makers of the Modern Theatre.* New York: McGraw-Hill, 1961.

Part Two

Chapter 4: THE THEATRE OF ANCIENT GREECE

Allen, James T. *Greek Acting in the Fifth Century.* Berkeley: Univ. of California Press, 1916.

——. *The Greek Theatre of the Fifth Century before Christ.* Berkeley: University of California Press, 1920.

Arnott, Peter D. *Greek Scenic Conventions in the Fifth Century, B.C.* Oxford: Clarendon Press, 1962.

——. *An Introduction to the Greek Theatre.* London: Macmillan & Co., Ltd., 1959.

Bieber, Margarete. *The History of the Greek and Roman Theater.* 2d ed. Princeton, N.J.: Princeton University Press, 1961.

Cornford, Francis M. *The Origin of Attic Comedy.* London: E. Arnold, 1914.

Flickinger, R. C. *The Greek Theatre and Its Drama.* 4th ed. Chicago: University of Chicago Press, 1936.

Gaster, Theodor. *Thespis; Ritual, Myth and Drama in the Ancient Near East.* New York: Abelard-Schuman, Limited, 1950.

Greene, William C. *Moira: Fate, Good, and Evil in Greek Thought.* Cambridge, Mass.: Harvard University Press, 1944.

Hamilton, Edith. *The Greek Way.* New York: W. W. Norton & Company, 1952.

Harsh, Philip W. *A Handbook of Classical Drama.* Stanford, Calif.: Stanford University Press, 1944.

Kitto, H. D. F. *Greek Tragedy.* 2d ed. London: Methuen & Co., Ltd., 1950.

Jaeger, Werner. *Paideia: The Ideals of Greek Culture.* Tr. by Gilbert Highet. 3 vols. New York: Oxford University Press, 1939–44.

Lever, Katherine. *The Art of Greek Comedy.* London: Methuen & Co., Ltd., 1956.

Murray, Gilbert. *Euripides and His Age.* New York: Holt, Rinehart and Winston, Inc., 1913.

Pickard-Cambridge, A. W. *Dithyramb, Tragedy, and Comedy.* 2d ed. rev. by T. B. L. Webster. Oxford: Clarendon Press, 1962.

——. *The Dramatic Festivals of Athens.* Oxford: Clarendon Press, 1953.

——. *The Theatre of Dionysus in Athens.* Oxford: Clarendon Press, 1946.

Rees, Kelley. *The Rule of Three Actors in the Classical Greek Drama.* Chicago: University of Chicago Press, 1908.

Webster, T. B. L. *Greek Theatre Production.* London: Methuen & Co., Ltd., 1956.

Chapter 5: ROMAN THEATRE AND DRAMA

Allen, James T. *Stage Antiquities of the Greeks and Romans and Their Influence.* New York: Longmans, Green, 1927.

Beare, William. *The Roman Stage; A Short History of Latin Drama in the Time of the Republic.* 2d ed. London: Methuen & Co., Ltd., 1955.

Bieber, Margarete. See under Chapter 4.

Duckworth, George E. *The Nature of Roman Comedy.* Princeton, N.J.: Princeton University Press, 1952.

Hamilton, Edith. The Roman Way. New York: W. W. Norton & Company, 1932.

Hanson, J. A. Roman Theater-Temples. Princeton, N.J.: Princeton University Press, 1959.

Harsh, Philip W. See under Chapter 4.

Lucas, Frank L. Seneca and Elizabethan Tragedy. Cambridge: The University Press, 1922.

Norwood, Gilbert. Plautus and Terence. New York: Longmans, Green, 1932.

Chapter 6: MEDIEVAL THEATRE AND DRAMA

Chambers, E. K. The Mediaeval Stage. 2 vols. Oxford: The Clarendon Press, 1903.

Craik, Thomas W. The Tudor Interlude; Stage, Costume, and Acting. Leicester: The University Press, 1958.

Farnham, Willard. The Medieval Heritage of Elizabethan Tragedy. Berkeley: University of California Press, 1936.

Frank, Grace. The Medieval French Drama. Oxford: Clarendon Press, 1954.

Gardiner, Harold C. Mysteries' End; An Investigation of the Last Days of the Medieval Religious Stage. New Haven, Conn.: Yale University Press, 1946.

Hunningher, Benjamin. The Origin of the Theater. New York: Hill and Wang, 1961.

Nicoll, Allardyce. Masks, Mimes and Miracles. New York: Harcourt, Brace & World, Inc., 1931.

Salter, F. M. Medieval Drama in Chester. Toronto: University of Toronto Press, 1955.

Southern, Richard. The Medieval Theatre in the Round. London: Faber & Faber, Ltd., 1957.

Stratman, Carl J. Bibliography of Medieval Drama. Berkeley: University of California Press, 1954.

Stuart, D. C. Stage Decoration in France in the Middle Ages. New York: Columbia University Press, 1910.

Weiner, Albert B. Philippe de Mezieres' Description of the "Festum Praesentationis Beatae Mariae" Translated from the Latin and Introduced by an Essay on the Birth of Modern Acting. New Haven, Conn.: Andrew Kner, 1958.

Wickham, Glynne. Early English Stages, 1300–1660. 2 vols. New York: Columbia University Press, 1959–62.

Williams, Arnold. The Drama of Medieval England. East Lansing: Michigan State University Press, 1961.

Young, Karl. The Drama of the Medieval Church. 2 vols. Oxford: Clarendon Press, 1933.

Chapter 7: SPAIN AND ELIZABETHAN ENGLAND

Adams, John C. The Globe Playhouse: Its Design and Equipment. 2d ed. New York: Barnes & Noble, 1961.

Adams, Joseph Q. Shakespearean Playhouses; A History of English Theatres from the Beginnings to the Restoration. Boston: Houghton Mifflin Company, 1917.

Baldwin, T. W. The Organization and Personnel of the Shakespearean Company. Princeton, N.J.: Princeton University Press, 1927.

Beckerman, Bernard. Shakespeare at the Globe, 1599–1609. New York: The Macmillan Company, 1962.

Bentley, Gerald E. *The Jacobean and Caroline Stage.* 5 vols. Oxford: Clarendon Press, 1941–56.

———. *Shakespeare: A Biographical Handbook.* New Haven, Conn.: Yale University Press, 1961.

Boas, Frederick S. *An Introduction to Stuart Drama.* London: Oxford University Press, 1946.

Brooke, C. F. T. *The Tudor Drama; A History of English National Drama to the Retirement of Shakespeare.* Boston: Houghton Mifflin Company, 1911.

Chambers, E. K. *The Elizabethan Stage.* 4 vols. London: Oxford University Press, 1923.

———. *A Short Life of Shakespeare.* Oxford: Clarendon Press, 1933.

Crawford, J. P. W. *Spanish Drama before Lope de Vega.* Rev. ed. Philadelphia: University of Pennsylvania Press, 1937.

Ebisch, Walther and Schucking, L. L. *A Shakespeare Bibliography.* Oxford: Clarendon Press, 1931. Supplement, 1935.

Ellis-Fermor, Una. *The Jacobean Drama; An Interpretation.* 3d ed. London: Methuen & Co., Ltd., 1953.

Harrison, George B. *Shakespeare's Tragedies.* London: Routledge & Kegan Paul, Ltd., 1951.

Hodges, C. W. *The Globe Restored.* London: Ernest Benn, Ltd., 1953.

Hotson, Leslie. *Shakespeare's Wooden O.* New York: The Macmillan Company, 1960.

Joseph, Bertram. *Elizabethan Acting.* London: Oxford University Press, 1951.

Lawrence, W. J. *The Elizabethan Playhouse and Other Studies.* 2 vols. Stratford-on-Avon: Shakespeare Head Press, 1912–13.

———. *Pre-Restoration Stage Studies.* Cambridge: Harvard University Press, 1927.

Nagler, A. M. *Shakespeare's Stage.* New Haven, Conn.: Yale University Press, 1958.

Parrott, Thomas M. *Shakespearean Comedy.* New York: Oxford University Press, 1949.

——— and Ball, Robert H. *A Short View of Elizabethan Drama.* New York: Charles Scribner's Sons, 1958.

Ralli, A. J. *A History of Shakespearean Criticism.* 2 vols. London: Oxford University Press, 1932.

Rennert, Hugo A. *The Life of Lope de Vega (1562–1635).* Philadelphia: Campion and Co., 1904.

———. *The Spanish Stage in the Time of Lope de Vega.* New York: Hispanic Society of America, 1909.

Reynolds, George F. *The Staging of Elizabethan Plays at the Red Bull Theatre, 1605–1625.* New York: Modern Language Association of America, 1940.

Rosen, William. *Shakespeare and the Craft of Tragedy.* Cambridge, Mass.: Harvard University Press, 1960.

Rossiter, A. P. *English Drama from Early Times to the Elizabethans; Its Background, Origins and Developments.* New York: Hutchinson's University Library, 1950 (Reprinted, New York: Barnes and Noble, 1959).

"Shakespeare: An Annotated Bibliography," *Shakespeare Quarterly* (1924–present). [*SQ* was originally called *The Shakespeare Association Bulletin.*] Annual bibliography of writings about Shakespeare.

Shoemaker, William H. *The Multiple Stage in Spain during the Fifteenth and Sixteenth Centuries.* Princeton, N.J.: Princeton University Press, 1935.

Sprague, A. C. *Shakespearean Players and Performances.* Cambridge, Mass.: Harvard University Press, 1953.

Wickham, Glynne. See Chapter 6.

Chapter 8: *THE ITALIAN RENAISSANCE*

Bjurstrom, Per. *Giacomo Torelli and Baroque Stage Design.* Stockholm: Almqvist and Wiksell, 1961.

Burckhardt, Jakob C. *The Civilization of the Renaissance in Italy.* 3d ed. New York: Phaidon Publishers, Inc., 1950.

Campbell, Lily Bess. *Scenes and Machines on the English Stage during the Renaissance.* Cambridge: Cambridge University Press, 1923 (Reprinted, New York: Barnes & Noble, 1960).

Duchartre, Pierre L. *The Italian Comedy; The Improvisation, Scenarios, Lives, Attributes, Portraits and Masks of the Illustrious Characters of the Commedia dell'Arte.* Tr. by R. T. Weaver. London: Harrap & Co., Ltd., 1929.

Hathaway, Baxter. *The Age of Criticism; the Late Renaissance in Italy.* Ithaca, N.Y.: Cornell University Press, 1962.

Herrick, Marvin. *Italian Comedy in the Renaissance.* Urbana: University of Illinois Press, 1960.

Hewitt, Barnard (ed.). *The Renaissance Stage; Documents of Serlio, Sabbattini, and Furttenbach.* Coral Gables, Fla.: University of Miami Press, 1958.

Kennard, Joseph. *The Italian Theatre.* 2 vols. New York: W. E. Rudge, 1932.

Kernodle, George. *From Art to Theatre; Form and Convention in the Renaissance.* Chicago: University of Chicago Press, 1943.

Lea, Kathleen M. *Italian Popular Comedy; A Study of the Commedia dell'Arte, 1560–1620.* 2 vols. Oxford: Clarendon Press, 1934.

Mayor, A. H. *The Bibiena Family.* New York: H. Bittner, 1945.

Nicoll, Allardyce. *Masks, Mimes, and Miracles.* See Chapter 6.

―――. *Stuart Masques and the Renaissance Stage.* London: Harrap & Co., Ltd., 1937.

Schwartz, Isidore A. *The Commedia dell'Arte and Its Influence on French Comedy in the Seventeenth Century.* Paris: H. Samuel, 1933.

Smith, Winifred. *The Commedia dell'Arte.* New York: Columbia University Press, 1912.

Spingarn, Joel E. *A History of Literary Criticism in the Renaissance.* 2d ed. New York: Columbia University Press, 1908.

Symonds, John A. *The Renaissance in Italy.* 7 vols. London: John Murray, Ltd., 1909–37.

Vitruvius. *The Ten Books of Architecture.* Tr. by M. H. Morgan. Cambridge, Mass.: Harvard University Press, 1914.

Weinberg, Bernard. *A History of Literary Criticism in the Italian Renaissance.* 2 vols. Chicago: University of Chicago Press, 1961.

Chapter 9: *FRENCH CLASSICISM*

Hubert, Judd D. *Molière and the Comedy of Intellect.* Berkeley: University of California Press, 1962.

Lancaster, H. C. *A History of French Dramatic Literature in the Seventeenth Century.* 5 vols. in 9. Baltimore: Johns Hopkins Press, 1929–42.

Lawrenson, T. E. *The French Stage in the XVIIth Century: A Study in the Advent of the Italian Order.* Manchester: Manchester University Press, 1957.

Lockert, Lacy. *Studies in French Classical Tragedy.* Nashville: Vanderbilt University Press, 1958.

Lough, John. *Paris Theatre Audiences in the Seventeenth and Eighteenth Centuries.* London: Oxford University Press, 1957.

Palmer, John. *Molière.* New York: Brewer and Warren, 1930.

Tilley, A. A. *Molière.* Cambridge: University Press, 1936.

Turnell, Martin. *The Classical Moment; Studies in Corneille, Molière and Racine.* New York: New Directions, 1948.

Vinaver, Eugene. *Racine and Poetic Tragedy.* Tr. by P. M. Jones. Manchester: Manchester University Press, 1955.

Wiley, W. L. *The Early Public Theatre in France.* Cambridge, Mass.: Harvard University Press, 1960.

Wright, C. H. C. *French Classicism.* Cambridge, Mass.: Harvard University Press, 1920.

Chapter 10: THE RESTORATION AND THE EIGHTEENTH CENTURY

Beijer, Agne. *Court Theatres of Drottningholm and Gripsholm.* Tr. by G. L. Frolich. Malmo: J. Kroon, 1933.

Bernbaum, Ernest. *The Drama of Sensibility; A Sketch of the History of Sentimental Comedy and Domestic Tragedy, 1696–1780.* Cambridge, Mass.: Harvard University Press, 1915.

Boas, Frederick S. *An Introduction to Eighteenth Century Drama, 1700–1780.* New York: Oxford University Press, 1953.

Bredsdorff, Elias et al. *An Introduction to Scandinavian Literature from the Earliest Time to Our Day.* Copenhagen: E. Munksgaard, 1951.

Bruford, Walter H. *Theatre, Drama, and Audience in Goethe's Germany.* London: Routledge & Kegan Paul, Ltd., 1957.

Burnim, Kalman. *David Garrick, Director.* Pittsburgh: Pittsburgh University Press, 1961.

Campbell, Lily B. "A History of Costuming on the English Stage between 1660 and 1823," *University of Wisconsin Studies in Language and Literature,* II (1918), 187–223.

Cibber, Colley. *An Apology for the Life of Mr. Colley Cibber.* London: J. Watts, 1740. Reprinted many times.

Cook, John A. *Neo-Classic Drama in Spain; Theory and Practice.* Dallas: Southern Methodist University Press, 1959.

Dobrée, Bonamy. *Restoration Comedy, 1660–1720.* Oxford: Clarendon Press, 1924.

————. *Restoration Tragedy, 1660–1720.* Oxford: Clarendon Press, 1929.

Downer, Alan S. "Nature to Advantage Dressed: Eighteenth Century Acting," *PMLA* (1943), 1002–37.

"English Literature, 1660–1800; A Current Bibliography," *Philological Quarterly* (1926–present). Annual list of publications.

Fitzgerald, Percy H. *The Sheridans.* 2 vols. London: R. Bentley, 1886.

Goldoni, Carlo. *Memoirs of Carlo Goldoni.* Tr. by John Black. New York: Alfred A. Knopf, Inc., 1926.

Gozzi, Carlo. *The Memoirs of Count Carlo Gozzi.* Tr. by J. A. Symonds. 2 vols. London: J. C. Nimmo, 1890.

Hawkins, Frederick. *The French Stage in the Eighteenth Century.* 2 vols. London: Chapman & Hall, Ltd., 1888.

Hotson, Leslie. *The Commonwealth and Restoration Stage*. Cambridge, Mass.: Harvard University Press, 1928.

Kennard, Joseph. See Chapter 7.

Krutch, Joseph W. *Comedy and Conscience after the Restoration*. New York: Columbia University Press, 1949.

Lancaster, H. C. *French Tragedy in the Time of Louis XV and Voltaire, 1715–1774*. Baltimore: Johns Hopkins Press, 1950.

———. *Sunset; A History of Parisian Drama in the Last Years of Louis XIV, 1701–1715*. Baltimore: Johns Hopkins Press, 1945.

The London Stage, 1660–1800. Carbondale: Southern Illinois University Press, 1960–. Not yet completed.

Lynch, James J. *Box, Pit and Gallery; Stage and Society in Johnson's London*. Berkeley: University of California Press, 1953.

Nicoll, Allardyce. *History of English Drama, 1660–1900*. 6 vols. London: Cambridge University Press, 1955–59.

Odell, G. C. D. *Shakespeare from Betterton to Irving*. 2 vols. New York: Charles Scribner's Sons, 1920.

Palmer, J. L. *The Comedy of Manners*. London: Bell & Sons, Ltd., 1913.

Pascal, Roy. *The German Sturm und Drang*. Manchester: Manchester University Press, 1953.

Southern, Richard. *The Georgian Playhouse*. London: Pleiades Books, 1948.

———. *Changeable Scenery; Its Origin and Development in the British Theatre*. London: Faber & Faber, Ltd., 1952.

Summers, Montague. *The Playhouse of Pepys*. London: Paul, Trench, Trubner & Co., 1935.

———. *The Restoration Theatre*. London: Paul, Trench, Trubner & Co., 1934.

Thaler, Alwin. *Shakespere to Sheridan*. Cambridge, Mass.: Harvard University Press, 1922.

Theatrical Designs from the Baroque through Neo-Classicism. 3 vols. New York: H. Bittner, 1940.

Willoughby, Leonard A. *The Classical Age of German Literature, 1748–1805*. London: Oxford University Press, 1926.

Chapter 11: *ROMANTIC DRAMA AND MELODRAMA*

Abrams, M. H. *The Mirror and the Lamp; Romantic Theory and the Critical Tradition*. New York: Oxford University Press, 1953.

Arvin, Neil S. *Eugène Scribe and the French Theatre, 1815–60*. Cambridge, Mass.: Harvard University Press, 1924.

Bernheim, A. L. *The Business of the Theatre*. New York: Actors Equity Association, 1932.

Birdoff, Harry. *The World's Greatest Hit: "Uncle Tom's Cabin."* New York: S. F. Vanni, 1947.

Clement, N. H. *Romanticism in France*. New York: Modern Language Association of America, 1939.

Coad, O. S. and Mims, Edwin, Jr. *The American Stage* (Vol. XIV of *The Pageant of America*). New Haven, Conn.: Yale University Press, 1929.

Disher, Maurice. *Blood and Thunder; Mid-Victorian Melodrama and Its Origins*. London: Muller, 1949.

———. *Melodrama; Plots that Thrilled*. New York: The Macmillan Company, 1954.

Downer, Alan S. "Players and the Painted Stage: Nineteenth Century Acting," *PMLA*, LXI (1946), 522–76.

Felheim, Marvin. *The Theater of Augustin Daly: An Account of the Late Nineteenth Century American Stage.* Cambridge, Mass.: Harvard University Press, 1956.

George, A. J. *The Development of French Romanticism.* Syracuse, N.Y.: Syracuse University Press, 1955.

Hewitt, Barnard. *Theatre USA, 1668–1957.* New York: McGraw-Hill Book Co., Inc., 1959.

Hughes, Glenn. *A History of the American Theatre, 1700–1950.* New York: Samuel French, Inc., 1951.

Kaufmann, F. W. *German Dramatists of the Nineteenth Century.* Los Angeles: Lymanhouse, 1940.

Lacey, Alexander. *Pixérécourt and the French Romantic Drama.* Toronto: University of Toronto Press, 1928.

Lucas, F. L. *The Decline and Fall of the Romantic Ideal.* New York: The Macmillan Company, 1936.

Mammen, Edward W. *The Old Stock Company School of Acting.* Boston: The Public Library, 1945.

Matthews, Brander. *French Dramatists of the Nineteenth Century.* 5th ed. New York: Charles Scribner's Sons, 1914.

———— and Hutton, Laurence. *Actors and Actresses of Great Britain and the United States, from the Days of David Garrick to the Present Time.* 5 vols. New York: Cassell, 1886.

Melcher, Edith. *Stage Realism in France from Diderot to Antoine.* Bryn Mawr, Pa.: Bryn Mawr College, 1928.

Moody, Richard. *America Takes the Stage; Romanticism in American Drama and Theatre, 1750–1900.* Bloomington: Indiana University Press, 1955.

Moses, Montrose J. and Brown, John M. *The American Theatre as Seen by Its Critics, 1752–1934.* New York: W. W. Norton, 1934.

Nicoll, Allardyce. See Chapter 10.

Odell, G. C. D. *Annals of the New York Stage.* 15 vols. New York: Columbia University Press, 1927–49.

————. See Chapter 10.

Peacock, Ronald. *Goethe's Major Plays; An Essay.* New York: Hill and Wang, 1959.

Quinn, Arthur H. *A History of the American Drama from the Beginning to the Civil War.* 2d ed. New York: Appleton-Century-Crofts, 1943.

————. *A History of the American Drama from the Civil War to the Present Day.* 2d ed. New York: Appleton-Century-Crofts, 1949.

Robertson, J. G. *The Life and Work of Goethe, 1749–1832.* London: Routledge & Kegan Paul, Ltd., 1932.

"The Romantic Movement; A Current Selective and Critical Bibliography," *English Literary History* (1937–49), *Philological Quarterly* (1950–present). An annual list of publications.

Rowell, George. *The Victorian Theatre.* London: Oxford University Press, 1956.

Sachs, Edwin O. and Woodrow, E. A. E. *Modern Opera Houses and Theatres.* 3 vols. London: Batsford, 1897–98.

Scholz, Janos. *Baroque and Romantic Stage Design.* New York: Beechhurst Press, 1955.

Southern, Richard. See Chapter 10.

Vardac, A. N. *Stage to Screen; Theatrical Method from Garrick to Griffith.* Cambridge, Mass.: Harvard University Press, 1949.

Varneke, B. V. *History of the Russian Theatre; Seventeenth through Nineteenth Century.* Tr. by Boris Brasol. New York: The Macmillan Company, 1951.

Walzel, Oskar F. *German Romanticism.* New York: G. P. Putnam's Sons, 1932.

Watson, Ernest B. *Sheridan to Robertson: A Study of the Nineteenth Century London Stage.* Cambridge, Mass.: Harvard University Press, 1926.

Wellek, René. *A History of Modern Literary Criticism.* 2 vols. New Haven, Conn.: Yale University Press, 1955.

Willoughby, Leonard A. *The Romantic Movement in Germany.* New York: Oxford University Press, 1930.

Part Three

Works Applicable to Part Three

Bentley, Eric. *The Playwright as Thinker; A Study of Drama in Modern Times.* New York: Reynal & Company, Inc., 1946.

Cheney, Sheldon. *The New Movement in the Theatre.* New York: Mitchell Kennerley, 1914.

Clark, Barrett H. and Freedley, George. *A History of Modern Drama.* New York: Appleton-Century-Crofts, 1947.

Cole, Toby (ed.). *Playwrights on Playwriting; The Meaning and Making of Modern Drama from Ibsen to Ionesco.* New York: Hill and Wang, 1961.

Downer, Alan S. *Fifty Years of American Drama, 1900–1950.* Chicago: Henry Regnery Co., 1951.

Fuerst, Walter R. and Hume, Samuel J. *Twentieth Century Stage Decoration.* 2 vols. London: Alfred A. Knopf, Inc., 1928.

Garten, H. F. *Modern German Drama.* New York: Essential Books, 1959.

Gassner, John. *Form and Idea in the Modern Theatre.* New York: Holt, Rinehart and Winston, Inc., 1956.

———. *The Theatre in Our Times: A Survey of the Men, Materials and Movements in the Modern Theatre.* New York: Crown Publishers, 1954.

Gorchakov, Nikolai A. *The Theater in Soviet Russia.* Tr. by Edgar Lehman. New York: Columbia University Press, 1957.

Gorelik, Mordecai. *New Theatres for Old.* New York: Samuel French, 1940.

Houghton, Norris. *Moscow Rehearsals; An Account of Methods of Production in the Soviet Theatre.* New York: Harcourt, Brace & World, Inc., 1936.

Krutch, Joseph W. *The American Drama since 1918.* Rev. ed. New York: G. Braziller, 1957.

Lumley, Frederick. *Trends in Twentieth Century Drama; A Survey Since Ibsen and Shaw.* 2d ed. London: Barrie and Rockliff, 1960.

Macgowan, Kenneth and Jones, Robert E. *Continental Stagecraft.* New York: Harcourt, Brace & World, Inc., 1922.

Mackay, Constance D. *The Little Theatre in the United States.* New York: Holt, Rinehart and Winston, Inc., 1917.

Melchinger, Siegfried. *The Concise Encyclopedia of Modern Drama.* New York: Horizon Press, 1962.

Miller, Anna Irene. *The Independent Theatre in Europe, 1887 to the Present.* New York: Ray Long and Richard R. Smith, 1931.

Moderwell, Hiram K. *The Theatre of To-day.* New York: Dodd, Mead & Co., 1925.

Moussinac, Leon. *The New Movement in the Theatre; A Survey of Recent Developments in Europe and America.* London: Batsford, 1931.

Simonson, Lee. *The Stage is Set.* New York: Dover Publications, Inc., 1932.

Slonim, Marc. *Russian Theatre from the Empire to the Soviets.* New York: The World Publishing Company, 1961.

Williams, Raymond. *Drama from Ibsen to Eliot.* London: Chatto & Windus, Ltd., 1952.

Chapter 12: *REALISM AND NATURALISM*

Becker, George J. *Documents of Modern Literary Realism.* Princeton, N.J.: Princeton University Press, 1963.

Bradbrook, M. C. *Ibsen, the Norwegian.* London: Chatto & Windus, Ltd., 1946.

Clurman, Harold. *The Fervent Years; The Story of the Group Theatre in the Thirties.* New York: Hill and Wang, 1957.

Northam, John. *Ibsen's Dramatic Method; A Study of the Prose Dramas.* London: Faber & Faber, Ltd., 1953.

Sayler, Oliver M. (ed.) *Max Reinhardt and His Theatre.* New York: Brentano's, 1926.

Sondel, Bess S. *Zola's Naturalistic Theory with Particular Reference to the Drama.* Chicago: University of Chicago Libraries, 1939.

Stone, Edward. *What Was Naturalism? Materials for an Answer.* New York: Appleton-Century-Crofts, 1959.

Waxman, S. M. *Antoine and the Théâtre Libre.* Cambridge, Mass.: Harvard University Press, 1926.

Zucker, A. E. *Ibsen, the Master Builder.* New York: Holt, Rinehart and Winston, Inc., 1929.

Chapter 13: *REVOLTS AGAINST REALISM*

Appia, Adolphe. *The Work of Living Art and Man Is the Measure of All Things.* Coral Gables, Fla.: University of Miami Press, 1960.

Balakian, Anna E. *Surrealism.* New York: Farrar, Straus & Co., 1959.

Breton, André. *What Is Surrealism?* London: Faber & Faber, Ltd., 1936.

Cornell, Kenneth. *The Symbolist Movement.* New Haven, Conn.: Yale University Press, 1951.

Craig, Edward Gordon. *On the Art of the Theatre.* 2d ed. Boston: Small, Maynard, 1924.

Dahlstrom, C. E. W. L. *Strindberg's Dramatic Expressionism.* Vol. VII of *University of Michigan Publications. Language and Literature.* Ann Arbor: University of Michigan Press, 1930.

Esslin, Martin. *Brecht; The Man and His Work.* Garden City, N.Y.: Doubleday & Company, Inc., 1960.

Fowlie, Wallace. *Age of Surrealism.* Bloomington: Indiana University Press, 1960.

Lehmann, Andrew G. *The Symbolist Aesthetic in France, 1885–1895.* Oxford: Blackwell & Mott, Ltd., 1950.

Samuel, Richard and Thomas, R. H. *Expressionism in German Life, Literature and the Theatre (1910–1924).* Cambridge: Heffer & Sons, Ltd., 1939.

Sokel, Walter H. *The Writer in Extremis; Expressionism in Twentieth-Century German Literature.* Stanford, Calif.: Stanford University Press, 1959.

Stein, Jack M. *Richard Wagner and the Synthesis of the Arts.* Detroit: Wayne State University Press, 1960.

Wagner, Richard. *Opera and Drama*. Tr. by Edwin Evans. London: W. Reeves, 1913.

Willett, John. *The Theatre of Bertolt Brecht*. New York: New Directions, 1959.

Chapter 14: *THE THEATRE SINCE WORLD WAR II*

Artaud, Antonin. *The Theatre and Its Double*. Tr. by Mary C. Richards. New York: Grove Press, 1958.

Bentley, Eric. *In Search of Theatre*. New York: Alfred A. Knopf, Inc., 1953.

Bowers, Faubion. *Broadway, USSR; Theatre, Ballet and Entertainment in Russia Today*. New York: Thomas Nelson & Sons, 1959.

Chiari, Joseph. *The Contemporary French Theatre; the Flight from Naturalism*. London: Barrie and Rockliff, 1958.

Donoghue, Denis. *The Third Voice: Modern British and American Verse Drama*. Princeton, N.J.: Princeton University Press, 1959.

Esslin, Martin. *The Theatre of the Absurd*. Garden City, N.Y.: Doubleday & Company, Inc., 1961.

Fowlie, Wallace. *Dionysus in Paris: A Guide to Contemporary French Theater*. New York: Meridian Books, 1960.

Gassner, John. *Theatre at the Crossroads; Plays and Playwrights of the Mid-Century American Stage*. New York: Holt, Rinehart and Winston, Inc., 1960.

Grossvogel, David I. *The Self-Conscious Stage in Modern French Drama*. New York: Columbia University Press, 1958.

Guicharnaud, Jacques. *Modern French Theatre from Giraudoux to Beckett*. New Haven, Conn.: Yale University Press, 1961.

Hainaux, René (ed.). *Stage Design throughout the World since 1935*. New York: Theatre Arts Books, 1956.

Houghton, Norris. *Return Engagement: A Postscript to "Moscow Rehearsals."* New York: Holt, Rinehart and Winston, Inc., 1962.

Magriel, Paul. *Chronicles of the American Dance*. New York: Holt, Rinehart and Winston, Inc., 1948.

Richman, Robert (ed.). *The Arts at Mid-Century*. New York: Horizon Press, Inc., 1954. Contains separate chapters on the theatre in each of the following countries: France, Italy, Germany, England and U.S.

Smith, Cecil. *Musical Comedy in America*. New York: Theatre Arts Books, 1950.

Styan, J. L. *The Dark Comedy; The Development of Modern Comic Tragedy*. Cambridge: Cambridge University Press, 1962.

Taylor, John R. *Anger and After; A Guide to the New British Drama*. London: Methuen & Co., Ltd., 1962.

Part Four

General Works

Albright, H. D., Halstead, W. P., and Mitchell, Lee. *Principles of Theatre Art*. Boston: Houghton Mifflin Company, 1955.

Dolman, John Jr. *The Art of Play Production*. Rev. ed. New York: Harper & Row, Publishers, 1948.

Gassner, John. *Producing the Play*. Rev. ed. New York: Holt, Rinehart and Winston, Inc., 1953.

Heffner, Hubert, Selden, Samuel, and Sellman, H. D. *Modern Theatre Practice.* 4th ed. New York: Appleton-Century-Crofts, 1959.

Chapter 15: *THE PLAYWRIGHT AND THE PRODUCER*
Gibson, William. *The Seesaw Log: A Chronicle of the Stage Production with the Text of "Two for the Seesaw."* New York: Alfred A. Knopf, Inc., 1959.
Plummer, Gail. *The Business of Show Business.* New York: Harper & Row, Publishers, 1961.
Savan, Bruce. *Your Career in the Theatre.* Garden City, N.Y.: Doubleday & Company, Inc., 1961.
See also those works listed under Chapter 3.

Chapter 16: *THE DIRECTOR*
Canfield, Curtis. *The Craft of Play Directing.* Holt, Rinehart and Winston, Inc., 1963.
Cole, Toby and Chinoy, Helen K. (eds.) *Directing the Play; A Source Book of Stagecraft.* Indianapolis: Bobbs-Merrill, 1953.
Dean, Alexander. *Fundamentals of Play Directing.* New York: Holt, Rinehart and Winston, Inc., 1941.
Dietrich, John. *Play Direction.* Englewood Cliffs, N.J.: Prentice-Hall, 1953.
Gorchakov, Nikolai. *Stanislavski Directs.* Tr. by Miriam Goldina. New York: Funk & Wagnalls Co., Inc., 1954.
Gruver, Elbert. *The Stage Manager's Handbook.* New York: Harper & Row, Publishers, 1953.
Hunt, Hugh. *The Director in the Theatre.* London: Routledge & Kegan Paul, Ltd., 1954.
Shaw, George Bernard. *The Art of Rehearsal.* New York: Samuel French, 1928.
Sievers, W. David. *Directing for the Theatre.* Dubuque, Iowa: William C. Brown Company, Publishers, 1961.

Chapter 17: *THE ACTOR*
Albright, H. D. *Working Up a Part.* 2d ed. Boston: Houghton Mifflin Company, 1959.
Boleslavsky, Richard. *Acting; The First Six Lessons.* New York: Theatre Arts Books, 1933.
Chekhov, Michael. *To the Actor on the Technique of Acting.* New York: Harper & Row, Publishers, 1953.
Cole, Toby and Chinoy, Helen K. (eds.) *Actors on Acting; The Theories, Techniques, and Practices of the Great Actors of All Times as Told in Their Own Words.* New York: Crown Publishers, Inc., 1949.
Diderot, Denis. *The Paradox of Acting.* Archer, William. *Masks or Faces?* New York: Hill and Wang, 1957.
Funke, Lewis and Booth, John E. *Actors Talk about Acting; Fourteen Interviews with Stars of the Theatre.* New York: Random House, Inc., 1961.
Joseph, Bertram. *The Tragic Actor.* New York: Theatre Arts Books, 1959.
Lewes, George. *On Actors and the Art of Acting.* New York: Grove Press, 1957.
McGaw, Charles J. *Acting Is Believing.* New York: Holt, Rinehart and Winston, Inc., 1955.
Matthews, Brander (ed.). *Papers on Acting.* New York: Hill and Wang, 1958.
Oxenford, Lyn. *Design for Movement; A Textbook on Stage Management.* New York: Theatre Arts Books, 1952.
———. *Playing Period Plays.* London: Miller, Ltd., 1958.

Stanislavski, Constantin. *An Actor Prepares.* Tr. by Elizabeth Reynolds Hapgood. New York: Theatre Arts Books, 1936.

————. *Building a Character.* Tr. by Elizabeth Reynolds Hapgood. New York: Theatre Arts Books, 1949.

————. *Creating a Role.* Tr. by Elizabeth Reynolds Hapgood. New York: Theatre Arts Books, 1961.

Strickland, F. Cowles. *The Technique of Acting.* New York: McGraw-Hill Book Co., Inc., 1956.

Young, Stark. *Theatre Practice.* New York: Charles Scribner's Sons, 1926.

Chapter 18: *THE SCENE DESIGNER*

Anderson, Donald M. *Elements of Design.* New York: Holt, Rinehart and Winston, Inc., 1961.

Boyle, Walden P. *Central and Flexible Staging.* Berkeley: University of California Press, 1956.

Burris-Meyer, Harold and Cole, Edward C. *Scenery for the Theatre.* Boston: Little, Brown and Company, 1947.

————. *Theatres and Auditoriums.* New York: Reinhold Publishing Corp., 1949.

Cogswell, Margaret (ed.). *The Ideal Theater: Eight Concepts.* New York: The American Federation of Arts, 1962.

Conway, Heather. *Stage Properties.* London: Jenkins, Ltd., 1959.

Friederich, Willard J. and Fraser, John H. *Scenery Design for the Amateur Stage.* New York: The Macmillan Company, 1950.

Gamble, William B. *The Development of Scenic Art and Stage Machinery.* Rev. ed. New York: New York Public Library, 1928.

Gillette, A. S. *Stage Scenery; Its Construction and Rigging.* New York: Harper & Row, Publishers, 1959.

Graves, Maitland. *The Art of Color and Design.* 2d ed. New York: McGraw-Hill Book Co., Inc., 1951.

Jones, Margo. *Theatre-in-the-Round.* New York: Holt, Rinehart and Winston, Inc., 1951.

Jones, Robert E. *The Dramatic Imagination.* New York: Meredith Publishing Co., 1941.

Larson, Orville K. (ed.) *Stage Design for Stage and Screen: Readings on the Aesthetics and Methodology of Scene Design for Drama, Opera, Musical Comedy, Ballet, Motion Pictures, Television and Arena Theatre.* East Lansing: Michigan State University Press, 1961.

Oenslager, Donald. *Scenery Then and Now.* New York: W. W. Norton & Company, Inc., 1936.

Parker, W. Oren and Smith, Harvey K. *Scene Design and Stage Lighting.* New York: Holt, Rinehart and Winston, Inc., 1963.

Philippi, Herbert. *Stagecraft and Scene Design.* Boston: Houghton Mifflin Company, 1953.

Selden, Samuel and Sellman, H. D. *Stage Scenery and Lighting.* 3d ed. New York: Appleton-Century-Crofts, 1959.

Simonson, Lee. *The Art of Scenic Design.* New York: Harper & Row, Publishers, 1950.

Southern, Richard. *The Open Stage.* New York: Theatre Arts Books, 1959.

Chapter 19: *THE COSTUMER*
Anderson, Donald M. See Chapter 18.
Barton, Lucy. *Historic Costume for the Stage*. Boston: Baker's Plays, 1935.
Boehn, Max von. *Modes and Manners*. Tr. by Joan Joshua. 4 vols. Philadelphia:
  J. B. Lippincott Co., 1932–36.
Corson, Richard. *Stage Make-up*. 3d ed. New York: Appleton-Century-Crofts.
  1960.
Cunnington, Cecil W. and Cunnington, Phillis. *Handbook of English Costume*
  [Separate volumes devoted to Medieval, 16th Century, 17th Century, 18th
  Century]. London: Faber & Faber, Ltd., 1952–57.
Davenport, Millia. *The Book of Costume*. 2 vols. New York: Crown Publishers,
  Inc., 1948.
Graves, Maitland. See Chapter 18.
Hiler, Hilaire and Hiler, Meyer. *Bibliography of Costume*. New York: H. W.
  Wilson Co., 1939.
Houston, Mary G. *Ancient Greek, Roman and Byzantine Costume and Decora-
  tion*. 2d ed. London: Black, Ltd., 1947.
———. *Medieval Costume in England and France, the 13th, 14th and 15th
  Centuries*. London: Black, Ltd., 1939.
Jones, Robert E. See Chapter 18.
Kohler, Karl. *A History of Costume*. Ed. and augmented by Emma von Sichart.
  Tr. by A. K. Dallas. Philadelphia: McKay, 1928.
Komisarjevsky, Theodore. *The Costume of the Theatre*. New York: Holt,
  Rinehart and Winston, Inc., 1932.
Laver, James. *Costume of the Western World; Early Tudor, 1485–1558*.
  London: Harrap & Co., Ltd., 1951.
Monro, Isabel S. and Cook, Dorothy E. *Costume Index*. New York: H. W.
  Wilson Co., 1937. Supplement, 1957.
Norris, Herbert. *Costume and Fashion* [Separate volumes devoted to Earlier
  Ages; 1485–1603; 19th century]. London: Dent & Sons, Ltd., 1925–38.
Reynolds, Graham. *Costume of the Western World; Elizabethan and Jacobean,
  1558–1625*. London: Harrap & Co., Ltd., 1951.
Strenkovsky, Serge. *The Art of Make-up*. New York: E. P. Dutton & Co., Inc.,
  1937.

Chapter 20: *THE LIGHTING DESIGNER*
Anderson, Donald M. See Chapter 18.
Burris-Meyer, Harold and Mallory, Vincent. *Sound in the Theatre*. Mineola,
  N.Y.: Radio Magazines, Inc., 1959.
Fuchs, Theodore. *Stage Lighting*. Boston: Little, Brown and Company, 1929.
Graves, Maitland. See Chapter 18.
Green, Michael. *Stage Noises and Effects*. London: Jenkins, Ltd., 1958.
Jones, Robert E. See Chapter 18.
McCandless, Stanley R. *A Method of Lighting the Stage*. 4th ed. New York:
  Theatre Arts Books, 1958.
Napier, Frank. *Noises Off; A Handbook of Sound Effects*. London: Muller,
  Ltd., 1936.
Parker, W. Oren, and Smith, Harvey K. See Chapter 18.
Rubin, Joel E. and Watson, Leland. *Theatrical Lighting Practice*. New York:
  Theatre Arts Books, 1954.
Selden, Samuel. See Chapter 18.

Williams, Rollo G. *The Technique of Stage Lighting.* 2d ed. New York: Pitman Publishing Corp., 1958.

Chapter 21: *MUSIC AND DANCE*
Chujoy, Anatole. *The Dance Encyclopedia.* New York: A. S. Barnes & Company, 1949.
Dallin, Leon. *Techniques of Twentieth Century Composition.* Dubuque, Iowa: William C. Brown Company, Publishers, 1957.
Engel, Lehmann. *Planning and Producing the Musical Show.* New York: Crown Publishers, Inc., 1957.
Fleming, William and Veinus, Abraham. *Understanding Music; Style, Structure, and History.* New York: Holt, Rinehart and Winston, Inc., 1958.
Groves' *Dictionary of Music and Musicians.* 9 vols. 5th ed. London: Macmillan & Co., Ltd., 1954.
H'Doubler, Margaret. *Dance; A Creative Art Experience.* 2d ed. Madison: University of Wisconsin Press, 1957.
Horst, Louis and Russell, Carroll. *Modern Dance Forms in Relation to the Other Modern Arts.* San Francisco: Impulse Publications, 1961.
Jacob, Gordon. *The Composer and His Art.* New York: Oxford University Press, 1955.
Leichtentritt, Hugo. *Musical Form.* Cambridge, Mass.: Harvard University Press, 1951.
Lippincott, Gertrude (ed.). *Dance Production: Music, Costumes, Staging, Decor, Lighting, Photography, Make-up, Planning and Rehearsing.* Washington: Published for National Section on Dance by the American Association for Health, Physical Education and Recreation, 1956.
Lockhart, Aileene. *Modern Dance: Building and Teaching Lessons.* 2d ed. Dubuque, Iowa: William C. Brown Company, Publishers, 1957.
Magriel, Paul. *A Bibliography of Dancing.* New York: H. W. Wilson Co., 1936. Supplement, 1941.
Newman, William S. *Understanding Music: An Introduction to Music's Elements, Styles, and Forms.* 2d ed. New York: Harper & Row, Publishers, 1961.

Chapter 22: *THE THEATRE AS A PROFESSION*
Davis, Jed H. and Watkins, Mary J. *Children's Theatre: Play Production for the Child Audience.* New York: Harper & Row, Publishers, 1960.
Fisher, Caroline and Robertson, Hazel. *Children and the Theatre.* Rev. ed. Stanford, Calif.: Stanford University Press, 1950.
Gard, Robert E. and Burley, Gertrude. *Community Theatre, Idea and Achievement.* New York: Meredith Publishing Co., 1959.
Harmon, Charlotte. *How to Break into the Theatre.* New York: The Dial Press, Inc., 1961.
Savan, Bruce. See Chapter 15.
Siks, Geraldine and Dunnington, Hazel. *Children's Theatre and Creative Dramatics.* Seattle: University of Washington Press, 1961.
Vreeland, Frank. *Opportunities in Acting.* New York: Grosset & Dunlap, Inc., 1951.
Ward, Winifred. *Playmaking with Children.* 2d ed. New York: Appleton-Century-Crofts, 1957.
Young, John Wray. *The Community Theatre and How It Works.* New York: Harper & Row, Publishers, 1957.

INDEX

Italic numbers denote pages on which illustrations appear.